I Still Am

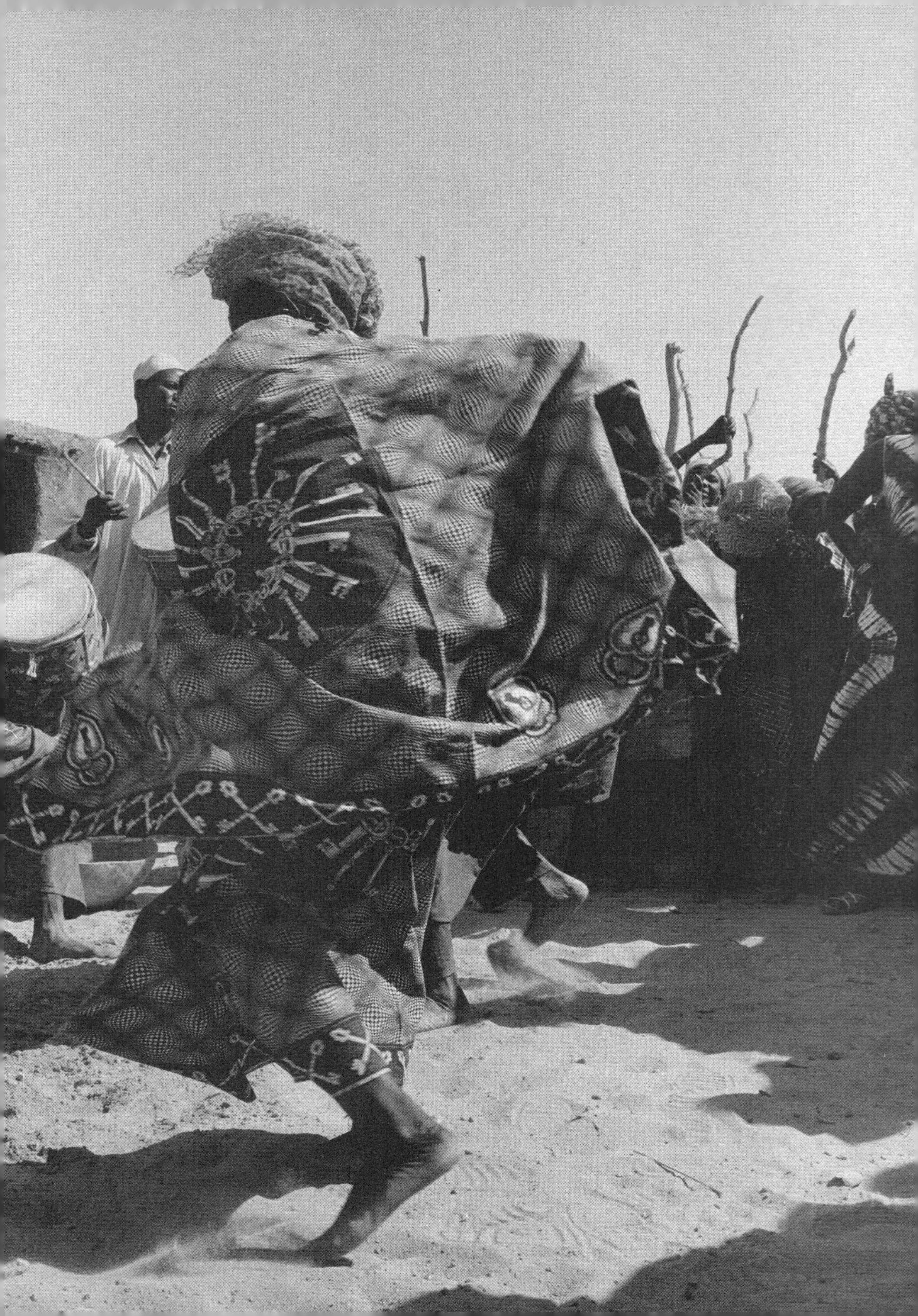

I Still Am

a woman, pissed-off & curious

Su Friedrich

SEVEN STORIES PRESS
New York • Oakland • London

SEVEN STORIES PRESS
140 Watts Street
New York, NY 10013
www.sevenstories.com

LIBRARY OF CONGRESS
CATALOGING-IN-PUBLICATION DATA
is on file.

ISBN: 978-1-64421-500-5 (paperback)
ISBN: 978-1-64421-501-2 (ebook)

College professors and high school and middle
school teachers may order free examination
copies of Seven Stories Press titles.
Visit https://www.sevenstories.com
/pg/resources-academics
or email academic@sevenstories.com.

PRINTED IN
Canada

9 8 7 6 5 4 3 2 1

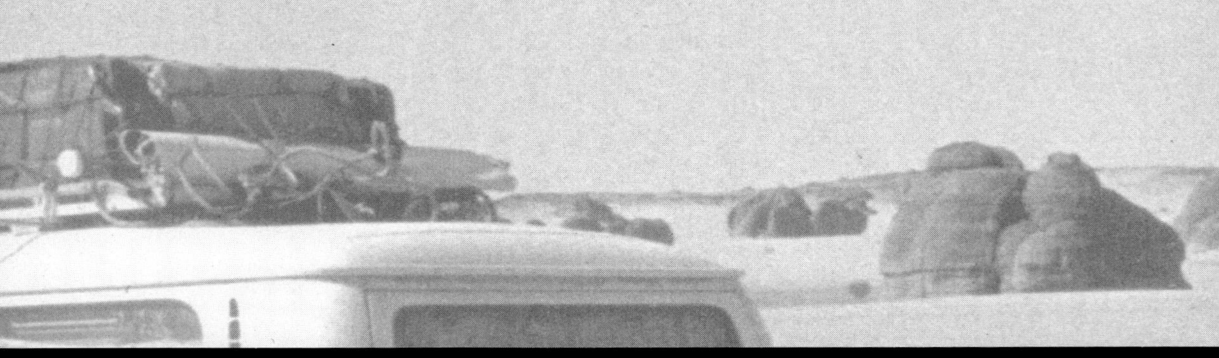

“The general always fractures into the particular as soon as you come close; and the particular, the specific, is persistently diverse.”

—BASIL DAVIDSON

“An adventure is only an inconvenience rightly considered.”

—G. K. CHESTERTON

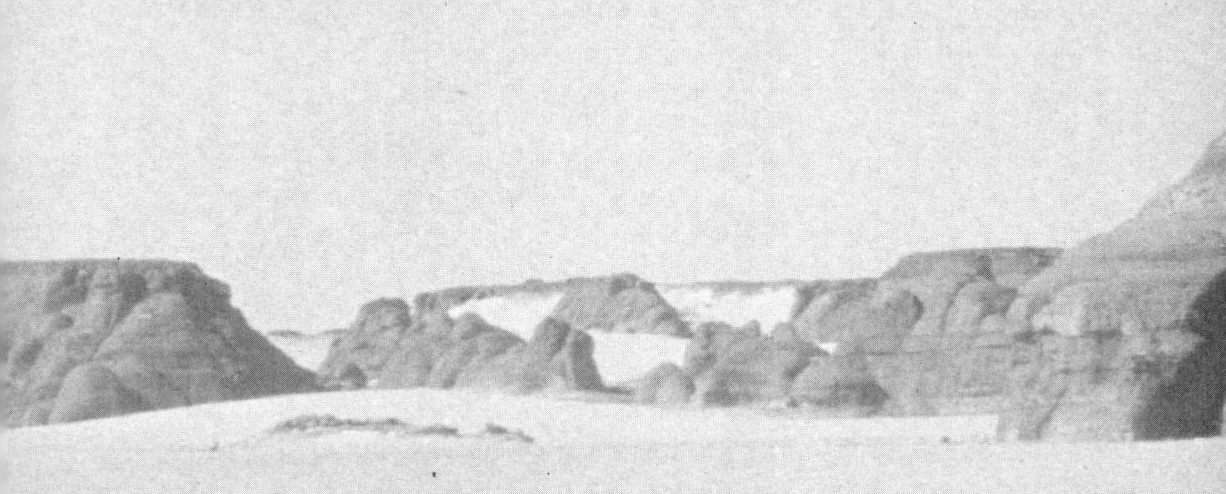

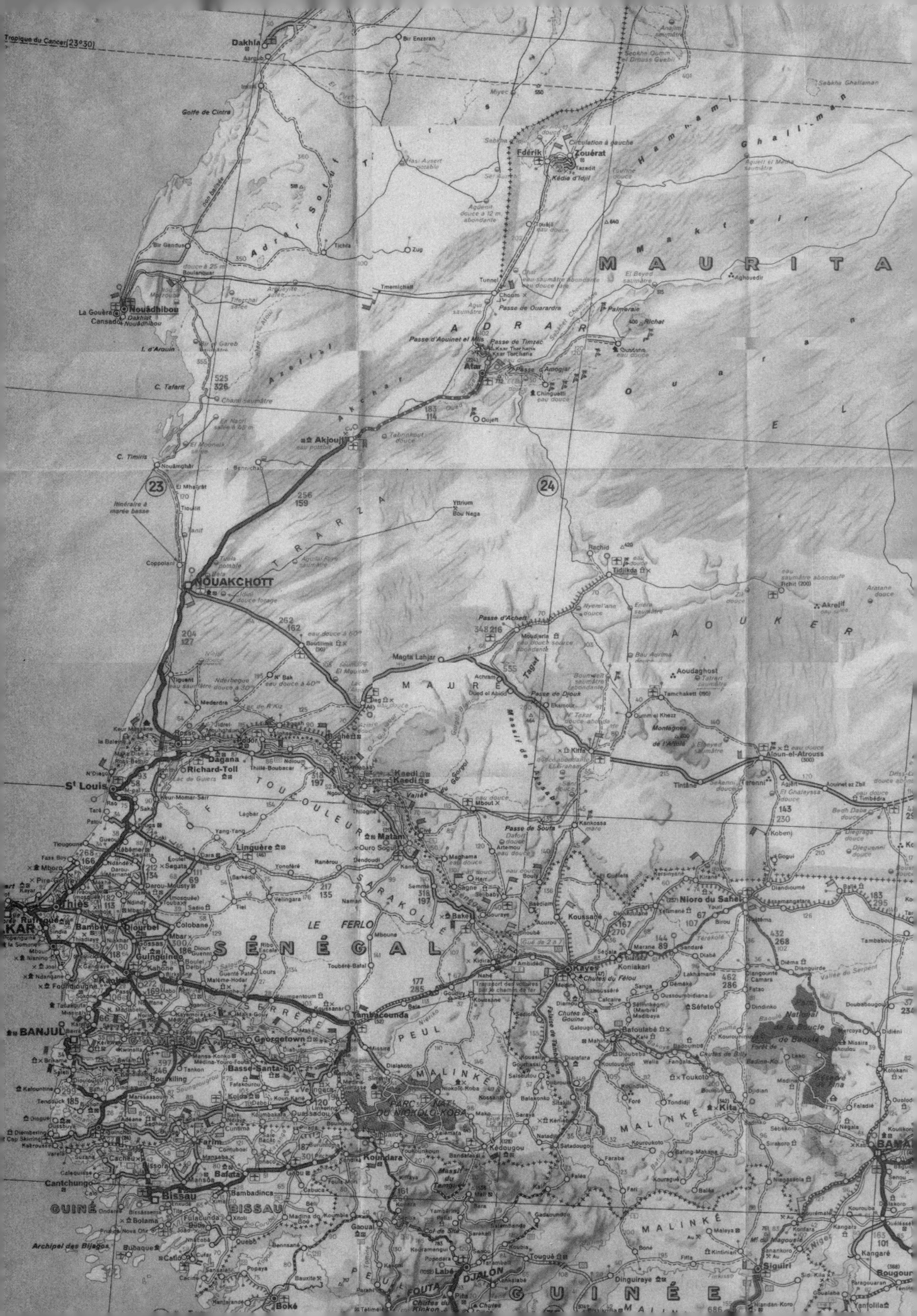

Tropique du Cancer (23°30)
Dakhla
Golfe de Cintra
Bir Gandus
Nouâdhibou
La Guera
Cansado
I. d'Arguin
C. Tafarit
C. Timiris
Nouâmghâr
23
Itinéraire à marée basse
Coppolani
NOUAKCHOTT
Adrar Sotuf
Zug
Tmeimichatt
Fdérik
Zouérat
Kédia d'Idjil
Circulation à gauche
Choum
Passe de Ouarane
Passe d'Aouinet el Mils
Passe de Timzac
Atar
Passe Amogjar
Chinguetti
Oujeft
ADRAR
MAURITA
Aghouedir
Akjoujt
TRARZA
24
Bou Naga
Rachid
Tidjikda
Passe d'Achett
Moudjeria
Boutilimit
Magta Lahjar
AOUKER
Akreijit
Aoudaghost
Tamchakett
Passe de Djouk
MAURE
Tagant
Montagnes de l'Affolé
Kiffa
Aïoun-el-Atrouss
Tintâne
Timbédra
Aleg
Boghé
Rosso
Dagana
Richard-Toll
Lac de Guiers
St Louis
Kaédi
TOUCOULEUR
Mbout
Passe de Soufa
Kankossa
Matam
Linguère
Ouro Sogui
Thiès
Diourbel
Bambey
Kaolack
LE FERLO
SÉNÉGAL
SARAKOLE
Bakel
Sélibaby
Kidira
Kayes
Chutes du Félou
Nioro du Sahel
Koussané
Tambacounda
SERRERE
PEUL
BANJUL
GAMBIA
Georgetown
Basse-Santa-Su
MALINKE
PARC NATL DU NIOKOLO-KOBA
Kolda
Kédougou
Koundara
Bafoulabé
Kita
MALINKÉ
Parc National de la Boucle du Baoulé
BAMAKO
Farim
Bafata
Bissau
GUINÉ
BISSAU
Cacheu
Archipel des Bijagos
Bubaque
Gaoual
Labé
DJALON
FOUTA
Boké
Siguiri
Dinguiraye
Tougué
GUINÉE

Contents

I Still Am

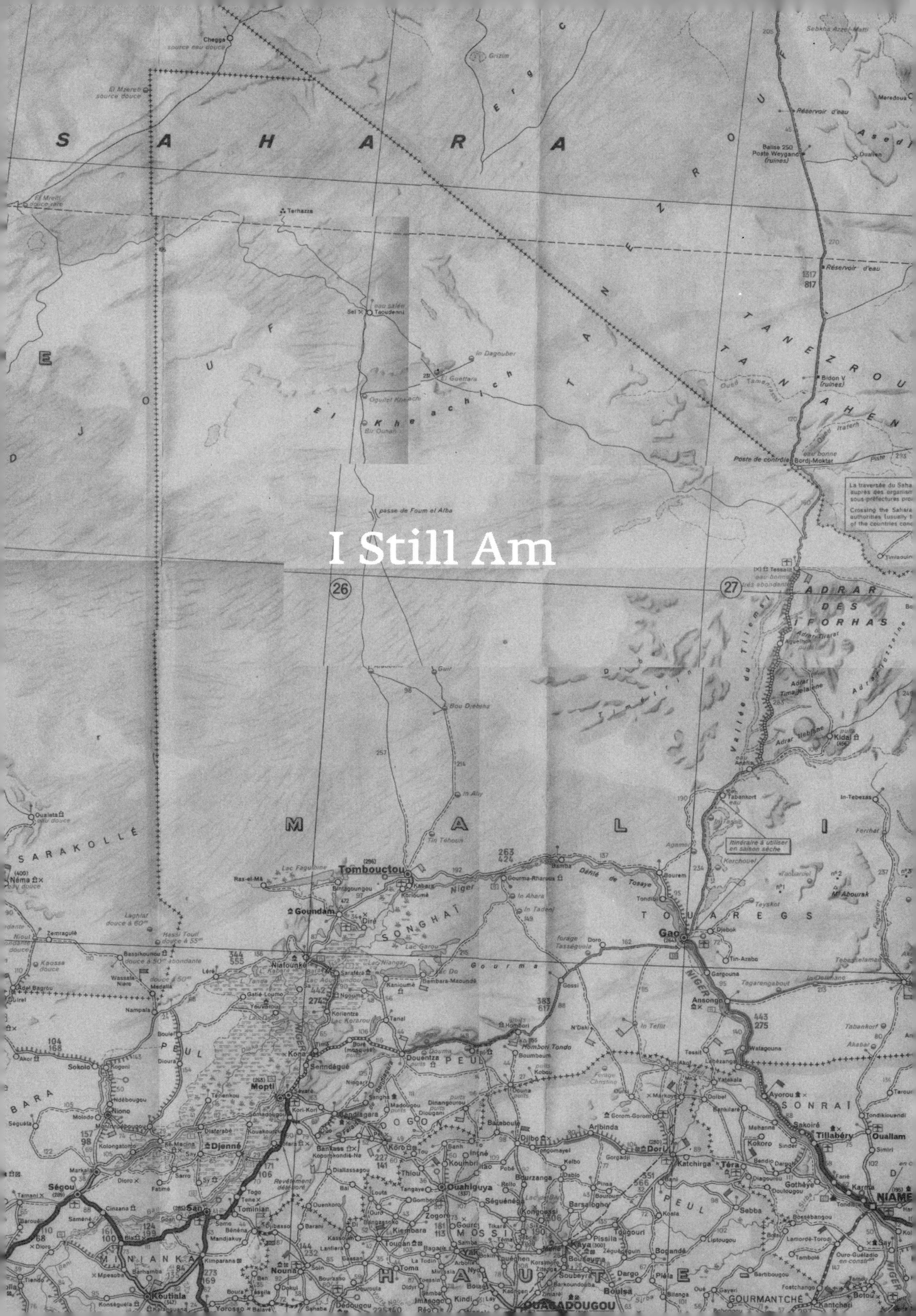

S A H A R A
T A N E Z R O U F T
T A N E Z R O U F T
T A N A H E N
E l K h e a c h i c h
E r g
Chegga
El Mzereb
Taoudenni
Terhazza
Bordj-Moktar
Poste de contrôle
Tessalit
ADRAR DES IFORHAS
Kidal
M A L I
Tombouctou
Gao
Niafounké
Goundam
Mopti
Djenné
Ségou
San
Koutiala
Tillabéry
Ouallam
Dori
Ouahigouya
OUAGADOUGOU
Kaya
Ansongo
Bourem
T O U A R E G S
SONGHAÏ
PEUL
SONRAÏ
MINIANKA
GOURMANTCHÉ
SARAKOLLÉ
Néma
Oualata
Hombori
Douentza
Bandiagara
26
27

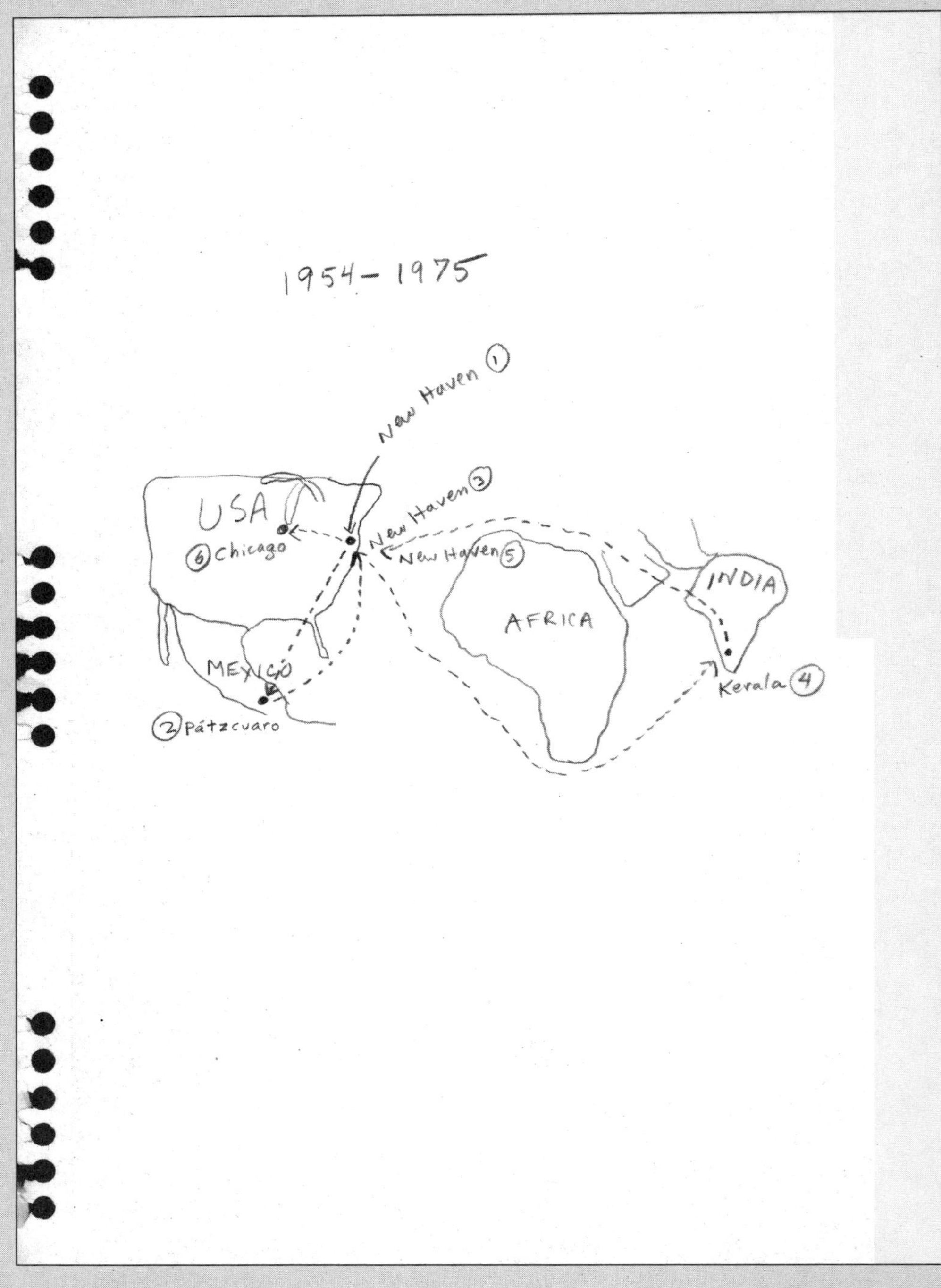

1954–1975
New Haven ①
USA
New Haven ③
⑥ Chicago
New Haven ⑤
INDIA
AFRICA
MEXICO
Kerala ④
② Pátzcuaro

INTRODUCTION

Three Questions and a Few Other Things Worth Mentioning

Why the Title?

This book describes a trip I took through West Africa in 1976 at the age of twenty-one, based on the journals I kept while I was on the road.In a long section at the end of the third journal, as I was traveling back through Europe on my way home, I ranted and raved about the perverseness of Catholicism in Spain and in the world at large.

When I finished transcribing it, I walked into the kitchen and said to my partner Cathy, "God, I was such a pretentious, arrogant, opinionated ass!"

And she said, "Was?"

I grunted and said, "Yeah, I guess I still am."

So there's that side of "still being" but there's also the aspect of righteous anger. Throughout the journals, I was struck by how vehemently I was talking back then about women's experiences in Africa and elsewhere, and my own life as a woman and as a lesbian.

To which I would say, "Back then?"

Forty-seven years later, things are "better" for women, but not by nearly enough, so I'm still talking.

This book is for/about every woman on every continent who still wants, or who still fights, to be free from the bullshit proffered by the patriarchy, and to all the women who have wandered the world to find the world.

Why a Book?

The journals, letters and photographs from my trip had been stowed away for four decades, and I would sometimes wonder, "What was all that?". In the summer of 2016 I finally decided to satisfy my curiosity, which led me to want to do something with "all that."

I'm a filmmaker, but I didn't want to make a Ken Burns'ish film with slo-mo pans of my photographs accompanied by a voiceover of me reading from the journals. Spare me.

So, a book it would be.

Why Africa?

Well, why not Africa? People have had many different reasons for visiting that continent, so here are a few of mine: The primary reason is that I didn't grow up in an all-white world and I've never wanted to live in one, because my white-Brown-Black-white-Black-white-white-white-white-Black-white world started early.

My father was a linguist with wide-ranging interests, which gave us the opportunity to become familiar with other cultures while living outside America. When I was six weeks old, we moved to Pátzcuaro—a town in the state of Michoachán in Mexico—for a year while he was doing research for a book about an agrarian revolt.

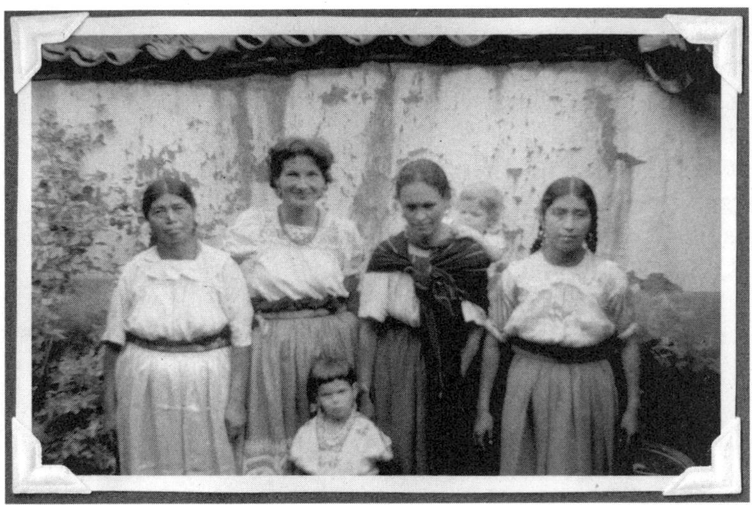

I'm in the *rebozo* worn by Cecilia, the woman who worked for my family and to whom I became very attached. My mother is to the left of her, with my sister Maria in front of her. I no longer know the names of the two other women.

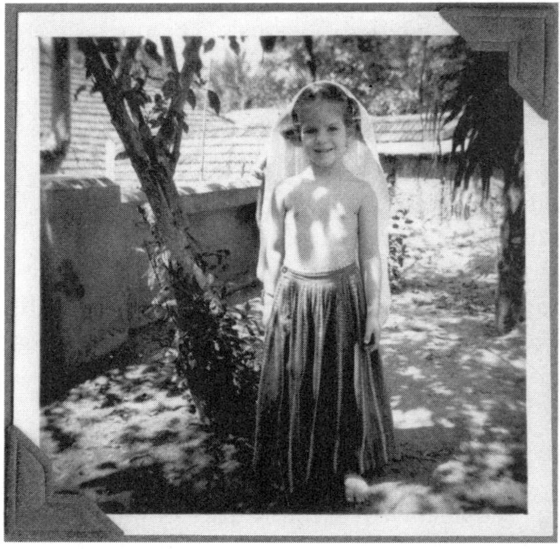

When I was four, we moved to Trivandrum—the capital city of the state of Kerala in India—to live for a year while my father was doing research and studying Sanskrit. And in both Mexico and India, we didn't live in a fancy expat compound, but in typical local housing because my father believed in being as "on the ground" as possible. This was sometimes a hardship for my mother, but for us oblivious, carefree kids, I think it made us more comfortable and familiar with how the locals lived, cooked, ate, etc.

I attended public school in Philadelphia from kindergarten to second grade. I assumed that being in an ethnically diverse group was normal, and that having a Black girl as your best friend was normal.

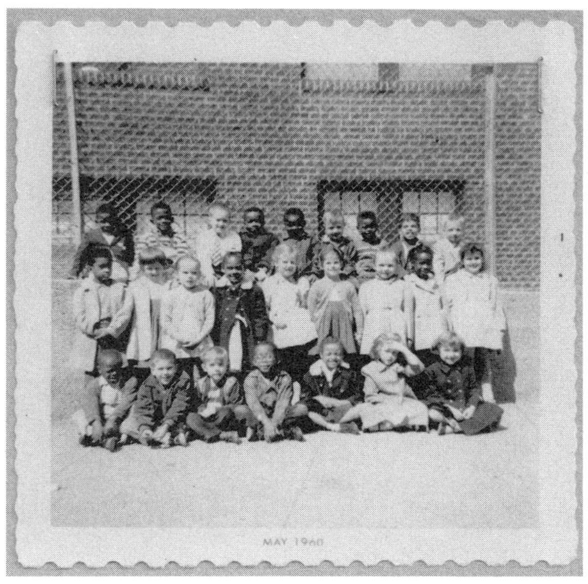

We moved to the South Side of Chicago when I was in third grade. I attended St. Philip Neri, a co-ed Catholic school.
On one of the first days there I asked, "Where are the Black kids?"

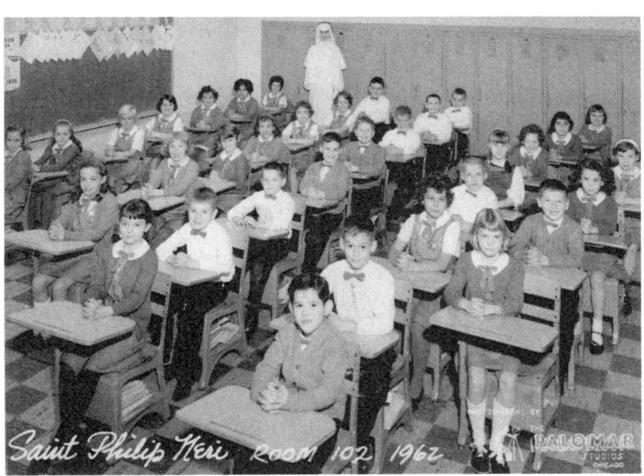

My question was met with incredulity and confusion. By the end of grade school, in a class of sixty-four students, only seven were Black and two were Hispanic.
Meanwhile, white flight had started and the big Irish Catholic families that had dominated the neighborhood and filled the local schools were moving away.

My high school, St. Thomas Aquinas, was also Catholic, but it was all-girls. Aquinas was adjacent to my grade school, so my white friends from Neri whose families hadn't yet "fled" also went there.
The great thing about high school was that girls came from many other neighborhoods, which meant that we had a much more equitable mix of white, Black and Brown girls, which seemed like a great improvement.

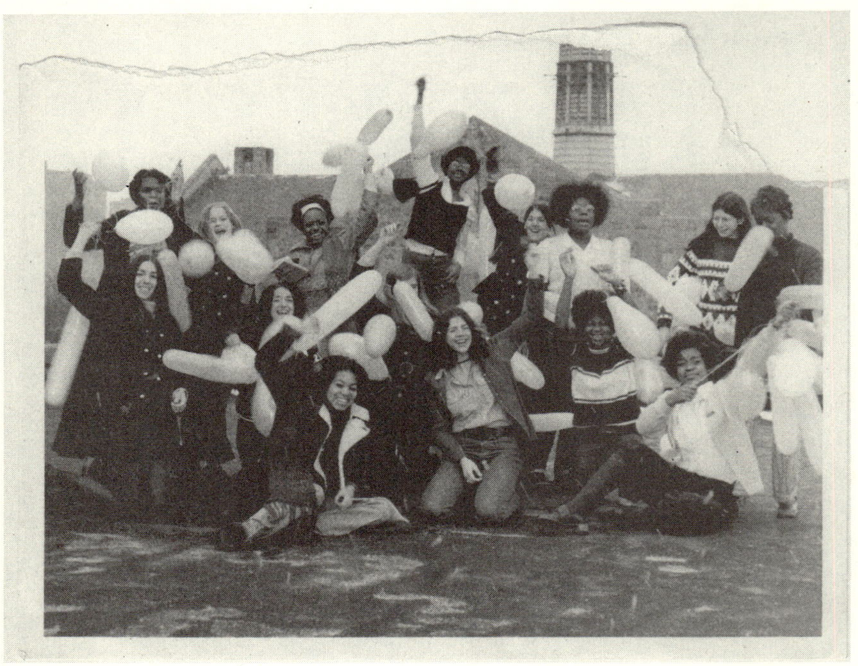

Not to over simplify: there wasn't a lot of mixing socially on the weekends, but we often hung out together after school, especially at Mitchell's Ice Cream and Candies, a "soda shop" on Seventy-first Street, and my friendships with some of the Black (and white) girls have continued to this day.

I don't have college yearbook pictures, but the schools I attended—the University of Chicago and Oberlin College—were primarily white.
At Oberlin I did a combined major in studio art and art history, but also took a course on "Traditional African Cosmology" with Yakubu Saaka [1],[1] a professor from Ghana, and he later became my adviser for an independent study I did about West African art. In addition to being a scholar and professor, he held a ministerial position in the Ghanaian government for four years. I will say more later about his influence on me, but the bottom line is that he made the trip possible by simply saying that I should do

1 Bearing in mind that a reader might not know about some aspect of African history or culture, or a person I mention, I've included chapter notes which are identified by a number in brackets. This isn't meant to be a textbook about Africa, but it can sometimes be useful to have more context than what comes through in the journal entries and the letters.

it, and then he said, "You'll have a great time. Everyone in Africa will treat you like family unless you prove yourself otherwise."

And how right he was.

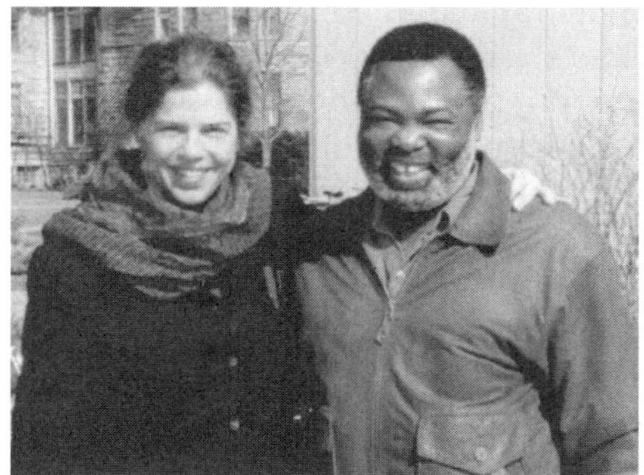

He also advised me to ignore the angry objections of another professor, Kuregiy Hekymara, a Black American who considered it offensive that whites would go to the continent, given the history of slavery and persistent white supremacy.[2] I understood why he said what he did, and his remarks shook my resolve for a while, but I decided to trust Saaka's advice, and I'm glad that I did.

Saaka passed away in 2008; I was fortunate to have a chance to see him in 1994 when I went to Oberlin to screen my films.

Some Musings

I have sometimes lived, studied and worked in places with a relatively integrated community. But those aren't common, so I've also been in places where segregation still operates very powerfully—even in parts of liberal, diverse NYC: for example, in the New York film community and art world.

As a young woman, many of my experiences led me to feel that traveling in Africa would be valuable—that it would teach me things about the people (both white and Black) who I had interacted with up to that point, about myself as a white American, and very importantly, about the Africans I would meet along the way.

In addition, since I was a young girl, I've rejected how women have been defined by men, and I've been aware that my actions are being judged against the prevailing norms.

So maybe I don't act "like a woman" most of the time, and now maybe I'll also be judged for how I've acted "like a white person." So be it.

Who Needs Hotels?

As you'll discover, I had virtually no idea about where I was going, where I would stay, how I would get anywhere, and how any of it would be affordable.

Within the first week on the continent, I found myself being met with utter incredulity and almost immediately after with great generosity. In other words, "What are you doing here??" was promptly followed by "You are welcome to come and stay at my house tonight."

People were certainly familiar with groups of tourists, or with Peace Corps workers and their ilk, but a young white woman climbing out of a truck or a lorry was a rare sight back then, which yielded invitations to stay in many homes along the way. I am eternally grateful to all those families who took me in, fed me, gave me access to a shower, and almost without fail asked me about Al Capone when I said I was from Chicago.

Talking Back to Myself

As soon as I started transcribing the journals, my then sixty-one-year-old self started to contradict, clarify, expand on, and generally talk to, with, and back at my twenty-one-year-old self. Some of those remarks had a defensive "I'm not a racist" air to them. Some were comments about the ideas swirling in that young brain from the vantage point of its much older counterpart. Some compared past and present aspects of American and/or African politics and culture. And some of them provided background about African history which I thought might not be known to the average reader, given the fact that so little is taught in schools or provided by the mainstream media.

They were originally incorporated into the text, but that broke the narrative flow. Rather than delete all of them, some were retained and put in the chapter notes, which you can look at whenever you're curious.

And What About the Money?

With the combination of hitchhiking, taking lorries/mammy wagons, being invited into people's homes instead of paying for hotels, and eating all the basic local food, the five months of travel didn't cost very much.

But first I had to get from New York to somewhere in Europe.

Back then, the cheapest flight was on Icelandic Air to Luxembourg. According to the Nomad Wallet website, a roundtrip flight between New York and London in 1970 retailed for $550, or $3,023 in 2023 dollars. I can't find an exact price for a NYC-Luxembourg flight.

I kept an accounting of the expenses in my journal, which begins after I purchased my round-trip flight.

On December 3, 1975, I had $2,010

$ 2,010.00
$ 470.00 spent in Dec, Jan, Feb
$ 1,540.00
$ 323.00 spent in March
$ 1,217.00
$ 887.00 spent in April
$ 330.00
$ 131.00 for flight from W. to N. Africa (purchased in March)
$ 199.00

That breaks down to a daily expense of $5.22/day for December through February, $6.19/day in March (by excluding the one big expense of the $131 flight from Bamako to Casablanca) and $28.61/day in April (which is so high because that month was spent mainly in Europe, and there was the cost of two very long train rides in West Africa).

That sounds like I was traveling in the cheapest way possible, but $2,010 in January 1975 was the equivalent of $11,051 in July 2023.

Translated into daily costs in 2023, I spent $28.70/day during the first three months, $34.03/day in March and $157.30/day in April.
On the other hand, only spending $28.70/day in 2023 is traveling pretty cheaply.

Anyway, I coudn't imagine how I had saved up $2,010 as a twenty-year-old: I only had poorly paid menial jobs during the summer and fall before my trip. It just didn't make sense.
But I had failed to take my mother into account.
In 2014, at the age of ninty-four, she began losing her short-term memory. We moved her to New York and I was the sibling who dealt with her banking.

After she passed away in 2018, my sister Maria organized all her papers.
Just recently, and long after I'd written the draft about my travel expenses, I was looking through the file folders that Maria gave me and discovered a fat envelope of canceled checks that I had gotten from my mother.
Yes, she had saved every single check that she'd written from the mid-1960s until 2014.

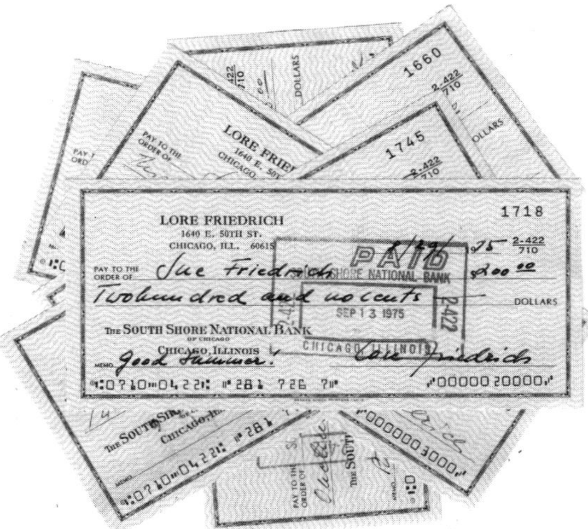

LORE FRIEDRICH
1640 E. 50TH ST.
CHICAGO, ILL. 60615
1718
2-422
710
PAY TO THE ORDER OF Sue Friedrich $200.00
Two hundred and no cents DOLLARS
PAID SOUTH SHORE NATIONAL BANK SEP 1 3 1975 CHICAGO, ILLINOIS
THE SOUTH SHORE NATIONAL BANK OF CHICAGO CHICAGO, ILLINOIS
MEMO Good Summer!

Some had notes on the memo line . . .
for Valentine's Day!
Happy Birthday!
Merry Xmas!
and others were just money she gave to me...why? Because she was nice, or maybe because I worried her with letters complaining about how poor I was.

Between April and October 1975, she wrote me checks that totaled $1,030 (or $5,662 in 2023 dollars!) One was a college graduation present, but one just said *Good summer!*

So now I know that it was her generosity that made me able to jump-start this trip.

As for the rest of this book:
Don't you hate reading a novel set in 1873 and they say that someone inherited X amount of money or someone earned X per annum and you have no idea how much that is in current dollars?
I do.
So whenever I make mention of what something costs, I'll translate that country's currency into its equivalent in US dollars, but then also convert that into the amount it would be in 2024.

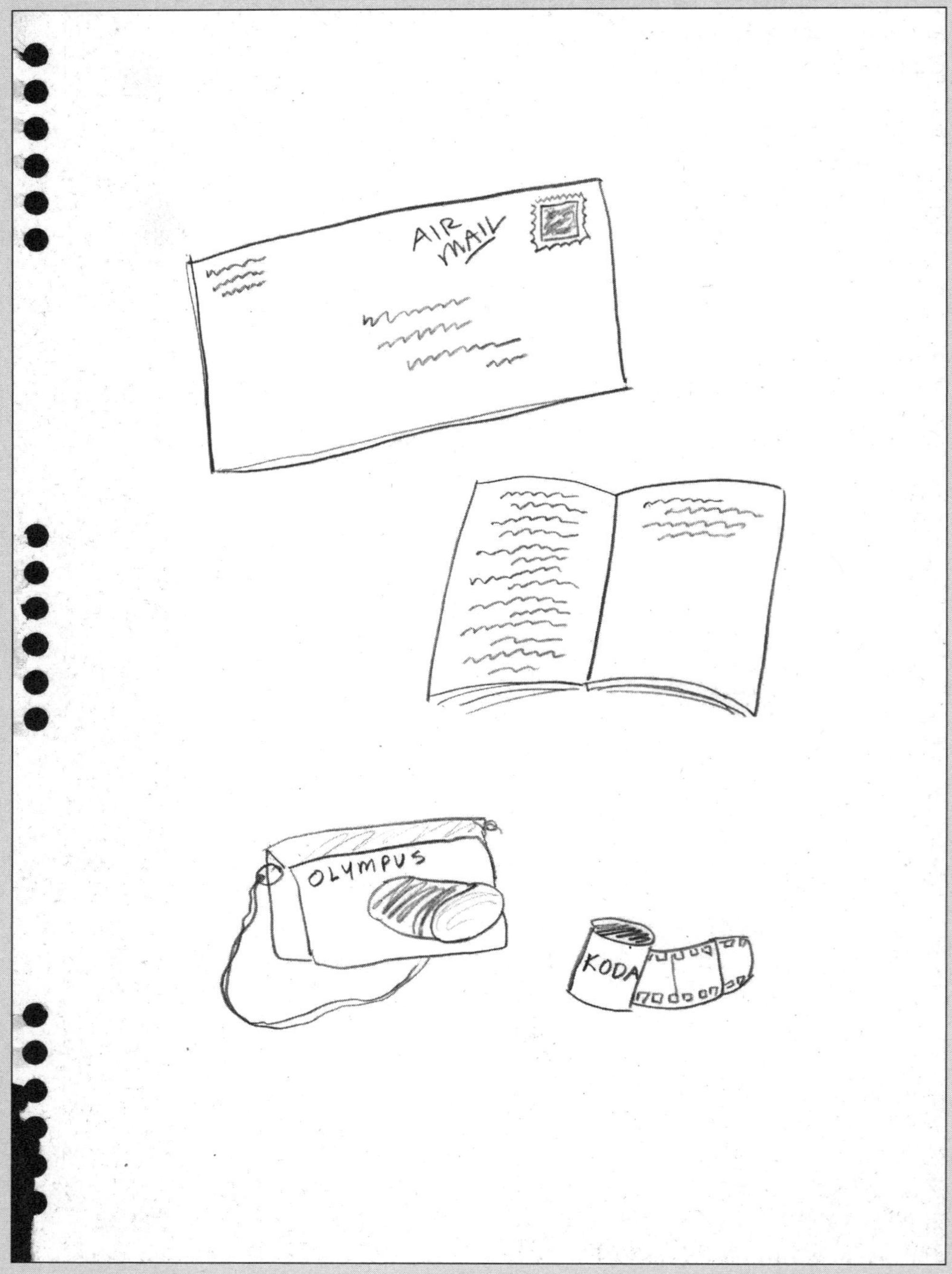
AIR
MAIL
OLYMPUS
KODA

ONE
My Analog Life and How It Turned into this Crazy Book

You've Got Mail

This trip transpired about a decade before we started using email in an ordinary way and a few decades before cell phones and texting. I could only write home with the hope that the letters would arrive, and tell those at home to close their eyes and throw a letter in the general direction of West Africa, addressed to an American embassy in one of six different countries, and hope that I was in that country when or after it arrived.
I corresponded with my mother and brother (who lived together), my father, my friend Cindy, and mainly with Mimi.[2] I assume that I also wrote my sister Maria, but I don't have any letters to or from her. I understand why I still have all the letters I received after my trip from people I met in Africa, but by what miracle do I have all the ones I wrote home while I was on the road?

I'm guessing I retrieved them to use as source material for stories I hoped to write, but aside from having a few photos printed in *Heresies: A Feminist Publication on Art and Politics*, which I was involved with for several years, the journalism plan didn't materialize. It failed in part because I was overwhelmed by the experience and couldn't write about it; in part because soon after I returned they discovered a massive cyst on my spleen, which required surgery and a very long recovery time; and probably because my primary interest was in photography—art photography projects and photo journalism—rather than in writing.

But here's the real oddity: I don't have most of the letters I got from friends and family—only a few from my mother and one each from Cindy and Mimi. Didn't I carry all of them with me and reread them over and over? Without the internet, without ever calling back home, it was my only contact with them. Why don't I have any of the others, to which I refer in the letters I wrote back to them? Good question. No answer.

Throughout the book, passages from the letters that I wrote to, or received from, people at home make an appearance. Whenever a passage isn't germane to the story of this book, you'll see [. . .] to denote a deleted passage. I wrote some very long letters that cover many days of travel and activities, and passages from them are inserted at the appropriate place in the journal, but because the date when a letter was written might not correspond to when a passage from it appears in the book, I've kept the dates out to avoid confusion.

When I got back to New York in late spring, I found letters from people I'd met

2 Mimi is the pseudonym of my first girlfriend, who prefers that I not use her real name.

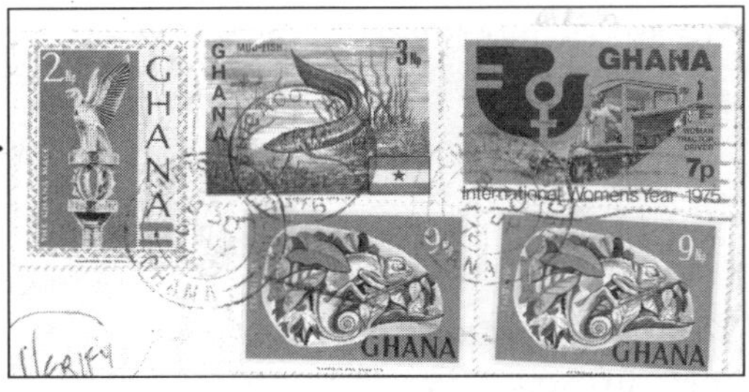

along the way, and I continued getting letters throughout that year. In total, I received nineteen letters from ten people. You'll encounter one letter from each person at the time in the story when I'm with them. A few of the correspondents wrote more than once (and Larry and Sam in particular wrote fairly intense letters) so you'll find all additional letters in Appendix 1.

As for any ongoing correspondence with my African acquaintances: There's a chance that some of the letters never reached the person to whom I replied because I didn't hear back. In other cases, the situation was too fraught to continue corresponding (in the case of Larry and Sam, as you'll see). In others, I was asked to send gifts and I couldn't afford what they wanted so I just (guiltily) never wrote back.

The Written Record

During five months of travel, I filled three journals in a tiny script (to maximize space and minimize my load). I also carried a Michelin map and marked out each place and date, but when I started digging up my materials, it wasn't to be found.

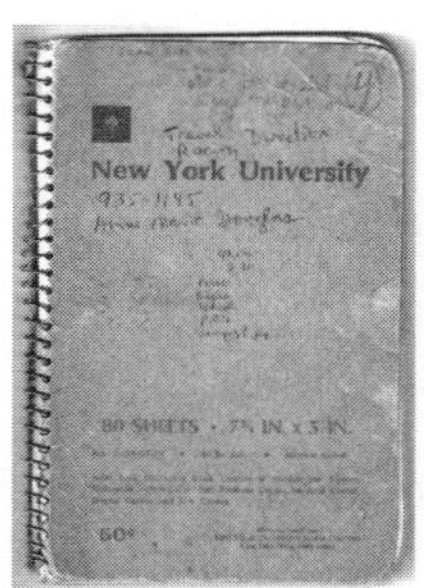

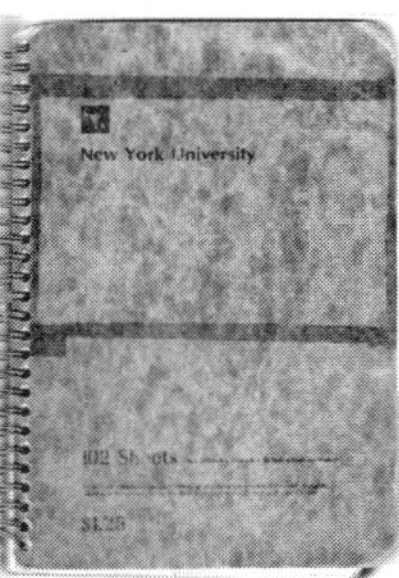

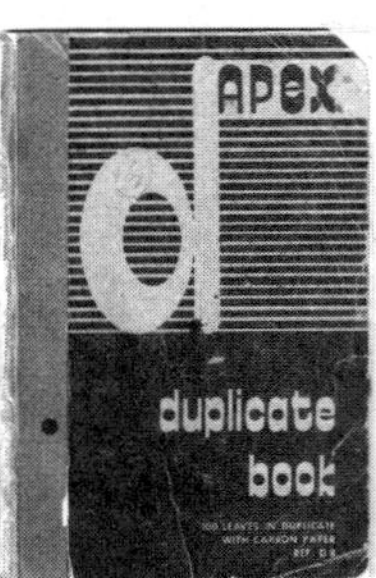

I was distressed because I loved it as a memento but also because the journals are fairly loose: entries aren't always dated, or I would enter a date but then ramble on about things that had happened during the past few days. Luckily, I still have that passport and could use it to determine when I crossed borders, but otherwise it's been a guessing game, which is why you'll sometimes see a single date and at other times see entries like "Jan. 20-22." Despite doing a lot of detective work to establish the chronology of events, I've undoubtedly made some errors.

I was reading a lot of nonfiction books about political issues, and novels by African (and other) writers. In the journals, I sometimes describe the writer's ideas or the plot of the novel, but there are many places with two, three, or more pages filled with what I'd call "college notes" because they remind me of what I did in the library while studying. I guess these were valuable to me at the time, but they would be gibberish for you, so I've left them out.

As a filmmaker, I've learned that two eyes and one brain are never enough. The same was true in putting together this book. I have a writer friend who did a close edit of the book. She sometimes queried me about a point which I remark on in the text, and when that occurs, she will be referred to as "my friend the writer." I then had another friend read it, a filmmaker, and there are also places in which I refer to her remarks, so she will be called "my friend the filmmaker." I thank them both for their labor and their astute observations.

Finally: My handwriting is as bad in the journals as it is in my letters, so the pages won't be shown except in a few places where I've isolated a necessary or interesting detail, like a drawing.

The journal begins in Copenhagen, which isn't an African country, but the experiences there, and the trip south through other European countries, set the stage for some of my thinking as I zig-zagged my way through West Africa.

The Reluctant Photographer

I had a 35mm Olympus camera with various lenses and rolls of black and white film, and a head full of notions about how I wasn't going there as a "tourist" and that I wasn't going to do the usual "tourist photography." The dictionary defines a tourist as "a person who is traveling or visiting a place for pleasure." I imagined that my journalism angle precluded me from being lumped into that category, but of course I also anticipated a lot of pleasure in everything I would encounter. People now use their phones to take fifteen pictures of what they had for dinner, so it might seem surprising to only have 750 images from six months of traveling. Then again, film costs money. And despite my need to economize, my reluctance to take "tourist" images, and the difficulty of photographing people who didn't want to be objectified (by yes . . . me . . . a tourist!), I did manage to take those 750 photographs; I did carefully catalogue all the negatives when I got back home; I did put them in glassine sleeves (which is like wax paper)—and then I did store them in the worst possible way! The sleeves were in a large ring-bound notebook which, due to the weight of the many pages and forty-one years of heat and moisture, made the glassine paper sometimes wrinkle and melt into the negatives, thereby altering the emulsion. Many negatives survived, but some didn't, and they have vertical stripes where the emulsion was dissolved and transformed. Photoshop magic helped to fix many of them, but some that seemed indispensable are included even though their damage is still visible.

Can We Please Go Already?

I think it's time to hit the road.

Back then I might have said . . .

Après tout ce que j'ai dit, là il va falloir prendre la route.

... because I knew enough French to function pretty well in the Francophone countries, and I often dropped French words or sentences into my journals and letters, I didn't want to muck up the pages with footnotes, so I kept the simple phrases in French—the ones that seemed obvious from their context—and sometimes put the English translation afterward [in brackets].

And in some cases, I just translated the longer passages.

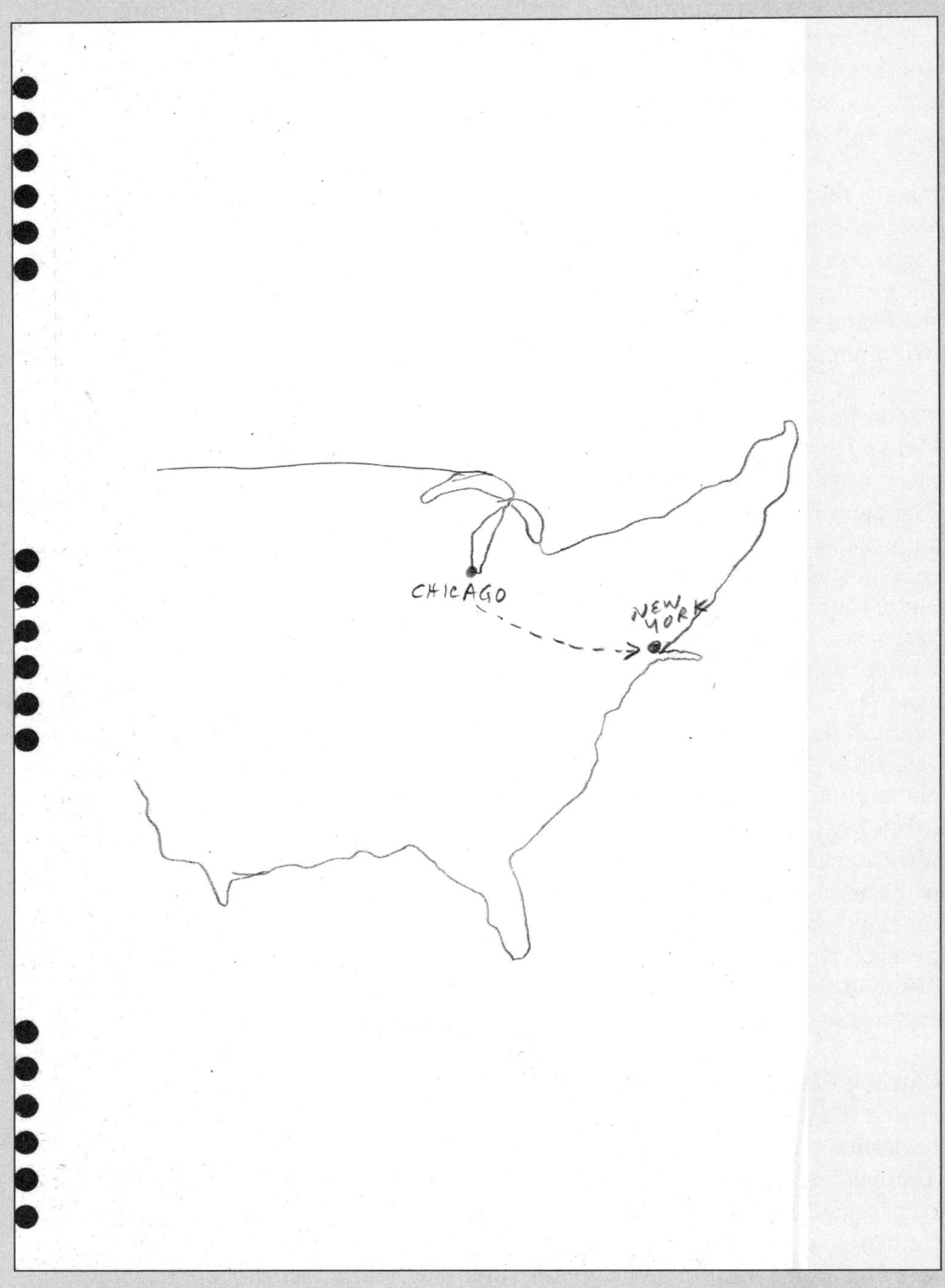
CHICAGO
NEW YORK

CHAPTER TWO

Coming Out and Heading East

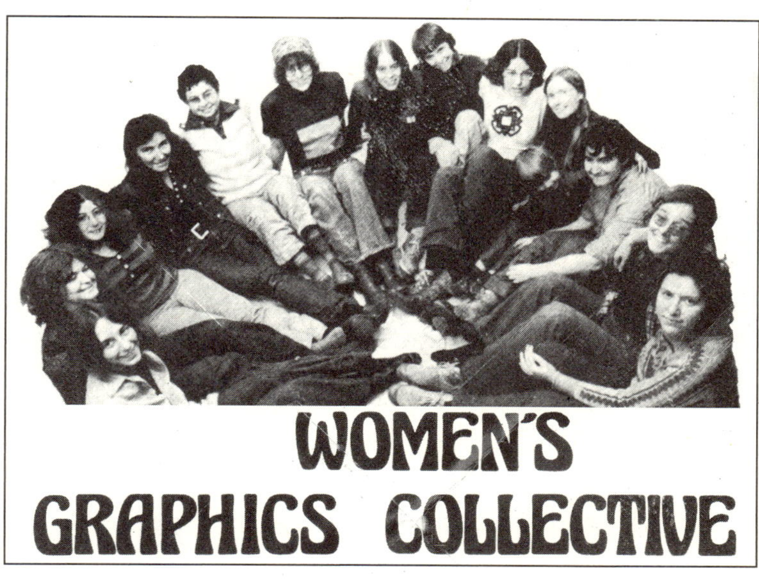

In the spring of 1975, I went back to the University of Chicago for my last semester to complete a few credits. I was a budding photographer/photojournalist but had also studied silkscreen printing at Oberlin and was excited to discover the Women's Graphics Collective (WGC). I spent most of the next ten months designing and making posters with the group and living in a collective house on the north side with a few members of the WGC.

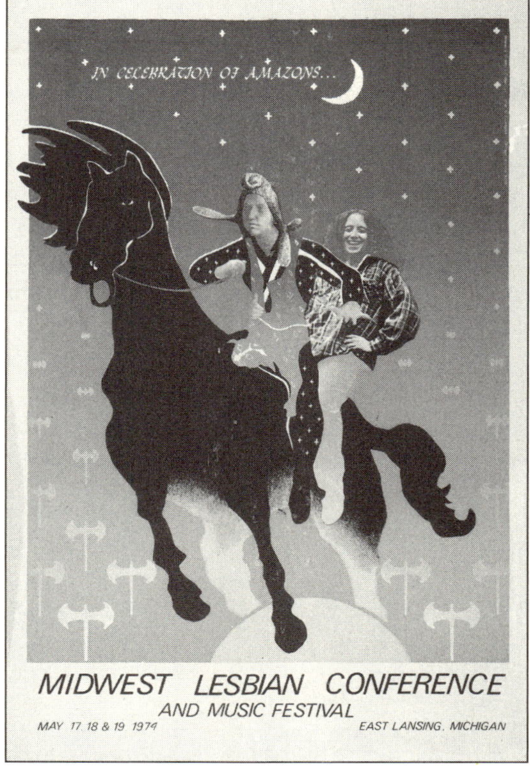

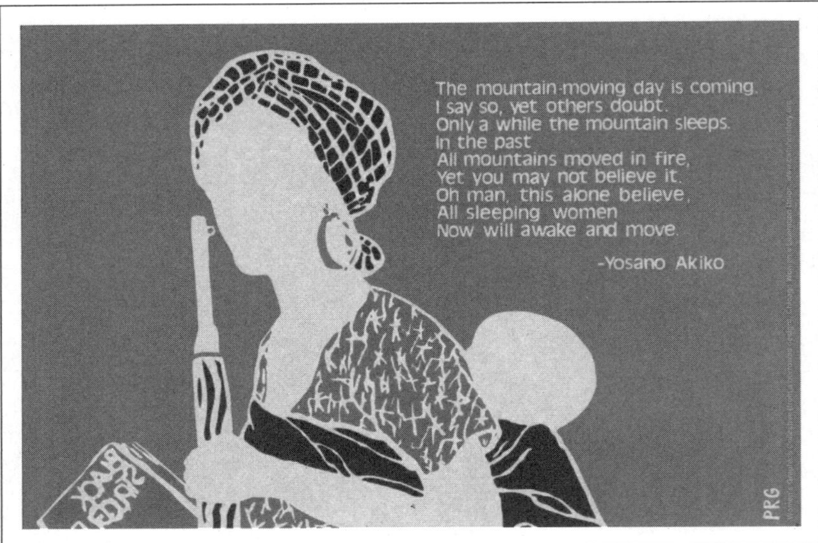

It was great to be part of the WGC and also to work part time at ARC, a women's art gallery in downtown Chicago. I needed to be engaged with other women in making art that would contribute to the debates that were starting to rage about women's role in society.[3] But it also meant hanging out for the first time with "real lesbians." That was a shocker. In 1975, lesbians were barely visible. My cursory knowledge about them was from books—what few existed at the time. For anyone who knows the literature, you might laugh in pity: My first exposure to "the life" was reading Radclyffe Hall's *The Well of Loneliness*.[4] It's a wonder I ever came out.

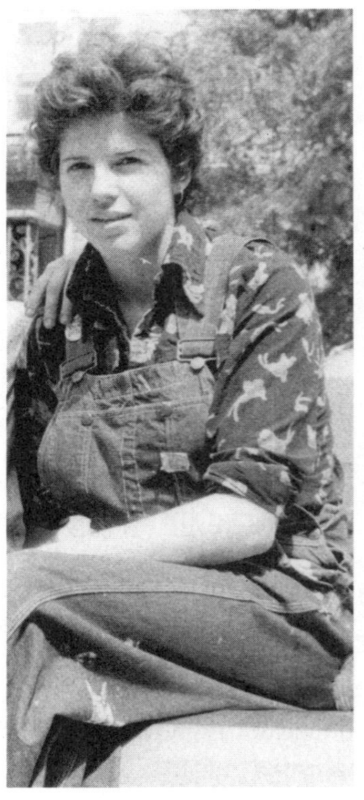

One member of the group was Mimi. After a few months, we became lovers. Yes: I was a '70s dyke who wore overalls. And flannel shirts.

3 *Ms. Magazine* started publishing stand-alone issues in January 1972; during 1971, it existed as an insert in *New York Magazine*.

4 *The Well of Loneliness*, by Radclyffe Hall, was published in 1928 and is considered the first English language novel with explicitly lesbian themes. And yes, it's a total bummer.

That summer, I went to my first gay pride march with Helen and Peggy—two friends from the WGC—and Mimi.
I remember the march being very small. Google says that the first one in Chicago—in 1970—had an estimated 150–200 people in attendance.
In 2019? An estimated million plus.

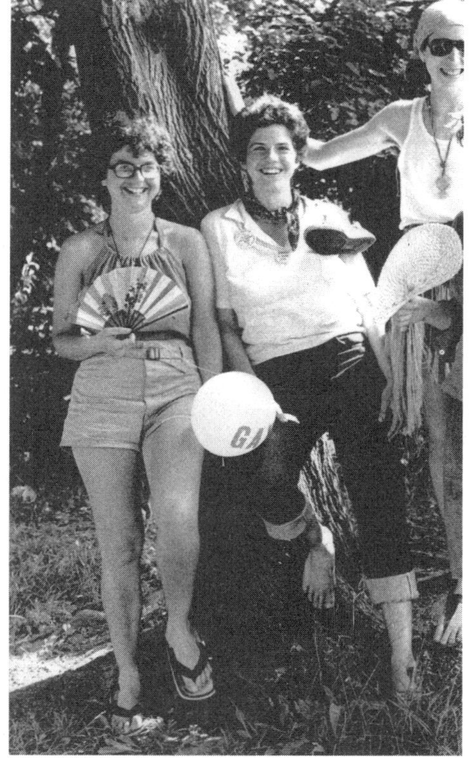

Through the local lesbian scene I also met Cynthia Carr, who wrote short fiction, worked as a journalist, and with some friends produced a monthly newspaper called *Lavender Woman*. Here's Cindy [5] in Chicago in 1975.

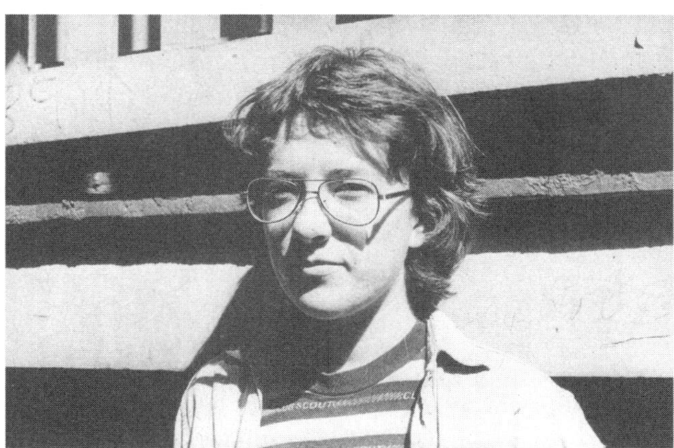

We were young, goofy dykes with time on our hands so, along with our friend Donna Mandel, Cindy and I made little art/comics/collage books and did some photo projects in which each of us was a character.

Mimi moved to New York in the fall of 1975. I didn't want to stay in Chicago without her, and I couldn't afford to live in NYC. What to do? Where to go?

5 Her professional name now as an author and journalist is Cynthia Carr, although earlier in her career her byline was C. Carr, but I always refer to her as Cindy in the book.

I had always yearned to go to Africa and had talked a lot with my father about doing my senior year abroad at the University of Dakar, but that plan hadn't materialized.

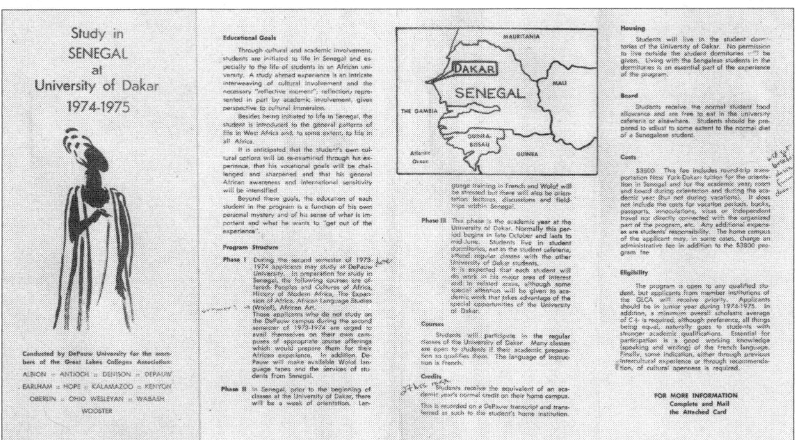

Study in SENEGAL at University of Dakar 1974-1975

Conducted by DePauw University for the members of the Great Lakes Colleges Association:
ALBION ∙ ANTIOCH ∙ DENISON ∙ DEPAUW
EARLHAM ∙ HOPE ∙ KALAMAZOO ∙ KENYON
OBERLIN ∙ OHIO WESLEYAN ∙ WABASH
WOOSTER

Educational Goals

Through cultural and academic involvement, students are initiated to life in Senegal and especially to the life of students in an African university. A study abroad experience is an intricate interweaving of cultural involvement and the necessary "reflective moment"; reflection, represented in part by academic involvement, gives perspective to cultural immersion.

Besides being initiated to life in Senegal, the student is introduced to the general patterns of life in West Africa and, to some extent, to life in all Africa.

It is anticipated that the student's own cultural options will be re-examined through his experience, that his vocational goals will be challenged and sharpened and that his general African awareness and international sensitivity will be intensified.

Beyond these goals, the education of each student in the program is a function of his own personal mystery and of his sense of what is important and what he wants to "get out of the experience".

Program Structure

Phase I During the second semester of 1973-1974 applicants may study at DePauw University. In preparation for study in Senegal, the following courses are offered: Peoples and Cultures of Africa, History of Modern Africa, The Expansion of Africa, African Language Studies (Wolof), African Art.
Those applicants who do not study on the DePauw campus during the second semester of 1973-1974 are urged to avail themselves on their own campuses of appropriate course offerings which would prepare them for their African experience. In addition, DePauw will make available Wolof language tapes and the services of students from Senegal.

Phase II In Senegal, prior to the beginning of classes at the University of Dakar, there will be a week of orientation. Language training in French and Wolof will be stressed but there will also be orientation lectures, discussions and field trips within Senegal.

Phase III This phase is the academic year at the University of Dakar. Normally this period begins in late October and lasts to mid-June. Students live in student dormitories, eat in the student cafeteria, attend regular classes with the other University of Dakar students.
It is expected that each student will do work in his major area of interest and in related areas, although some special attention will be given to academic work that takes advantage of the special opportunities of the University of Dakar.

Courses

Students will participate in the regular classes of the University of Dakar. Many classes are open to students if their academic preparation so qualifies them. The language of instruction is French.

Credits

Students receive the equivalent of an academic year's normal credit on their home campus.

This is recorded on a DePauw transcript and transferred as such to the student's home institution.

Housing

Students will live in the student dormitories of the University of Dakar. No permission to live outside the student dormitories will be given. Living with the Sengalese students in the dormitories is an essential part of the experience of the program.

Board

Students receive the normal student food allowance and are free to eat in the university cafeteria or elsewhere. Students should be prepared to adjust to some extent to the normal diet of a Senegalese student.

Costs

$3800. This fee includes round-trip transportation New York-Dakar; tuition for the orientation in Senegal and for the academic year; room and board during orientation and during the academic year (but not during vacations). It does not include the costs for vacation periods, books, passports, innoculations, visas or independent travel not directly connected with the organized part of the program, etc. Any additional expenses are students' responsibility. The home campus of the applicant may, in some cases, charge an administrative fee in addition to the $3800 program fee.

Eligibility

The program is open to any qualified student, but applicants from member institutions of the GLCA will receive priority. Applicants should be in junior year during 1974-1975. In addition, a minimum overall scholastic average of C+ is required, although preference, all things being equal, naturally goes to students with stronger academic qualifications. Essential for participation is a good working knowledge (speaking and writing) of the French language. Finally, some indication, either through previous intercultural experience or through recommendation, of cultural openness is required.

FOR MORE INFORMATION
Complete and Mail
the Attached Card

However, my conversations with Professor Saaka had been very encouraging, and then after college I learned more about the struggles against apartheid and colonial rule when I designed and printed some posters for an anti-apartheid group in Chicago, so I began to think more seriously about a trip. Meanwhile, the feminist in me wanted to take a lot of photographs and talk with the women I met on my journey, and then come back and write articles, with attendant photographs, about how life was for them.
By a stroke of luck, the WGC got an invitation to participate in a big exhibition of women artists in Copenhagen in December, the *Kvindeudstillingen på Charlottenborg 1975*. This meant I could take all the WGC posters, see lots of art, meet lots of women, and then wend my way, somehow, to Africa. A pretty tall order for a twenty-year-old, but hey.

During the fall I sent Mimi a few letters, clearly written under the influence of the poet e.e. cummings, who shunned capital letters. He was all the rage back then. Before Mimi left for NYC, I had come out to my mother via a phone call; it had been too scary to do that in person.

PART OF A LETTER TO MIMI FROM CHICAGO:
. . . my arms are still aching from the cholera + typhoid + smallpox innoculations. i have to go back twice more. dinner w/ my mother was very civil, she asked once, in a worried tone, whether you'd left yet and i said yes, w/o fanfare. i was looking for signs of her having, at some point after our conversation, freaked out and regretted our "openness," but she seemed really o.k.
i'm certain she's waiting for me to fall in love with a German boy, etc.
w/ love + a hug,
su

PART OF A LETTER TO MIMI FROM CHICAGO:

Dear Mimi,
tomorrow, the beginning of a strange and wonderful and difficult fall
[. . .]
ahh...Last night to the MCA[6] for Mor Thiam and his "drums of fire"—which was 7 (6 Black, one Latino) musicians and M.T. — he burst in during the middle of the 1st song stomping down the aisle hammering on a drum that was hung with clanky bronze things — he was very slight but with boundless energy—he was so absorbed in the music, so exhilarated by it, he would be in the midst of playing a xylophone (of sorts) or his drum and just leap up and shimmy around, shouting things in Wolof to the musicians, banging the tambourine on his hips, his head—his smile was enormous, pure white teeth and lovely dark skin, his eyes were intense, and always joyful. He was wonderful, he would teases the musicians, run up to them and shout something unintelligible or put his thumb on their temple, something curious was always happening, and they played very good jazz, it seemed to be a combination/harmony between western jazz (electric instruments), the rhythms and structure sometimes more like Art Blakey (oh, I don't know the names of who does what here), sometimes pure strains of Senegalese music, sometimes alternating btwn their more "American" arrangements ad his drumming. —Really amazing.
It made me feel very excited about going to Africa.
[. . .]
Reading Isak Dinesen (Karen Blixen) . . . *Shadows on the Grass* and *Out of Africa* . . . aside from the fact that she calls them natives; owns a coffee plantation; loves to hunt (compares it "poetically" to a man's passionate drive for a certain woman); uses quotes like that one; presents examples of cultural oppression (e.g., of Somali women) in a picturesque way to suggest its appropriateness; praises the Somali for being such good servants + how much they like it; and glorifies the Islamic notion of complete surrender (which however does have its good side); AND has many Africans living on her 6,000 acres of land as sharecroppers!—aside from all that, her books are very interesting. I shouldn't begin a comment on her with such criticism, i think, but it's working out my minor disappointment in her elitism and short-sightedness. she is very brave, lived alone there for 10 years after the divorce, + is very sensitive in dealing with "the Natives," and has a lot to say about certain African attitudes, world-views if you will, their resignation or understanding of the material hardships

6 The Museum of Contemporary Art in Chicago; and Wolof is the main language of Senegal.

of life + hence a greater philosophical approach to events, etc.—how true that is i have yet to discover, but she writes well about it.
[. . .]
à bientôt!
w/ the fondest love,
su

PART OF A LETTER TO MIMI FROM CHICAGO:

. . . i'm not as black this eve about my trip as i was on the phone. my moods are rampantly in flux these days, but i'm talking to myself a bit now about the good of going and seeing what i want to see before i'm penniless—but i read a story in *l'express* about a french woman anthropologist who was kidnapped by the chad rebels (chad is west of ethiopia) 1½ years ago for a 6 million franc ransom, & is to be killed if not paid by sep 75.
makes me furious and nervous.

i think the french govt paid it, but of course now the chad govt is pissed at them, blaming them for complicity with the rebels (chad is a french colony)—
enough of imminent doom—
[. . .]
w/ love and a hug,
su

I went to New York later in the fall to get my visas. Being in New York also gave me a chance to spend some final time with Mimi, squeezed into the twin bed in her dorm room.
New York was full of interesting political groups and indie publications, so when I wasn't schlepping uptown to yet another embassy for yet another visa, I started testing out my budding photojournalism skills. Aside from some work I did for the Liberation News Service, I attended a conference about the torture of political prisoners. Cindy asked me to write an article about it for *Lavender Woman* which would include my photographs of the speakers. I worked on it as I traveled and finally mailed it to her in late January from Nigeria.

I was leaving behind my close friends, my first-ever girlfriend, and my family. My brother Pete, a budding cartoonist (and then age fourteen) wrote this to me while I was in NYC.

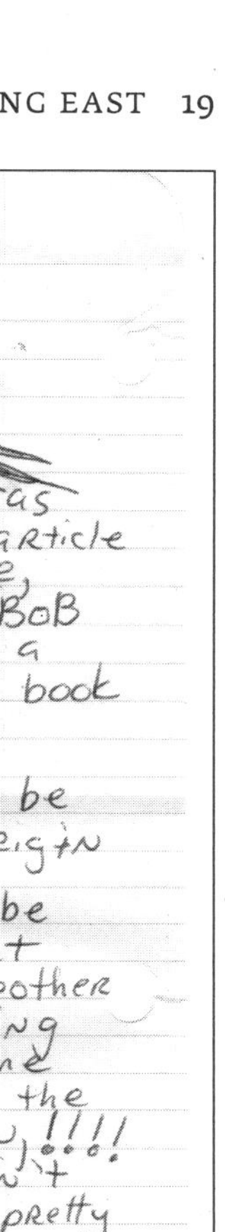
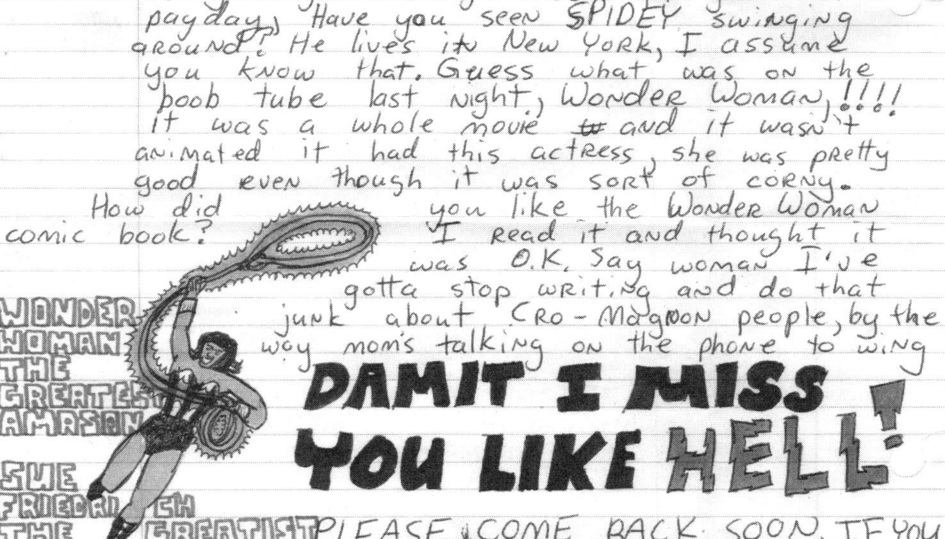

Hello Susie!

How are ya? Is New York as cool as they say? Thanks for the article about those two guys and that store, GUESS WHAT! I'm persuading bob (BoB Katzman, the Newsman) to turning Gullivers, a periodical store on 53rd, into a used comic book store, WooooooooooEEEEEEEEEEEE! HOT DAMN! that would be the greatest thing since the ~~og~~ ORIGIN of comics themselve's. That would be soooooooo baaaaad! Well besides that everythings been goin sewell, I got another payday, Have you seen SPIDEY swinging around? He lives in New York, I assume you know that. Guess what was on the boob tube last night, Wonder Woman!!!! it was a whole movie ~~a~~ and it wasn't animated it had this actress, she was pretty good even though it was sort of corny. How did you like the Wonder Woman comic book? I read it and thought it was O.K. Say woman I've gotta stop writing and do that junk about Cro-Magnon people, by the way mom's talking on the phone to wing

DAMIT I MISS YOU LIKE HELL!

PLEASE COME BACK SOON, IF YOU DON, I LIKE IT

KISS HUG SMACK KISS HUG

BYE, BYE, MUCH LOVE AND ALL THAT CRAP Pete.

WONDER WOMAN THE GREATEST AMASON

SUE FRIEDRICH THE GREATIST SISTER

And he's the greatest brother ever.

SUSIE, DID YOU KNOW TH
ACCORDING TO OVERSTREETS COMIC
BOOK PRICE GUIDE THE 1st ISSUE
OF WONDER-WOMAN IS WORTH
$151.50 IN MINT CONDITION? NOT BAD EH?
ALSO CAUSE I RARELY WRITE, AND JUST LOVE
TO GET LETTERS, WOULD YOU PLEASE, PLEASE
WRITE ME BACK? HUH? PLEASE?
THANKS ALOT. BYE. P.S. HAVE FUN IN AFRICA IF YOU GO.

I answered his request and wrote home somewhat regularly.
I'm not sure I obliged him when it came to the P.S. about having fun.

I also made a pathetic attempt to explain to my mother why I was embarking on such a dangerous and seemingly random trip.

> **A LETTER TO MY MOTHER:**
> mom—words don't seem to work well for me these days. they're too inaccurate or incomplete, and unhappily my "body language" (incl. voice pitch) seems to belie what i'm trying to say/really feeling.
> on the phone today i was so sorry that i reacted as i did but i have to go thru these daily searches and re-evaluations about my trip and i feel so frustrated/raw if someone talks to me about it—it's as if i've worked through (on a deep level) why i want to go (and why i want to leave it "unstructured") but it's hard at this point to convey that to anyone. and being a photographer, the outward achievement plateaus are not as evident/easy to see as in my school work, w/ "graduating," etc.
> [...]
> so I can understand your (and dad's) wariness or confusion or apprehension about this constant "taking off", this avoidance on my part of saying that THING that i'm developing towards—you just have to trust that i'm going to work hard towards that still-unwell-defined aspiration i have. and part of that

understanding is to see why i throw fits when asked why i'm "going"—being done with that cocoon-stage, college, that idyllic protective period (which sometimes i WISH i could crawl back into—it's hard to be "out here"), i feel uncertain. i can't tell you about africa cuz i don't know about it! all i know, esp. from marvin (a friend of mine from malawi in e. africa who I've been talking to a lot lately) is that people are very hospitable, helpful, it is safe, there are good train services between main cities of countries, there is the "Seventh Day Adventist Church" in every large town which is of course white-missionary but which has always welcomed any whites traveling in Africa who need info or a roof for the night—ETC. and i have lots of oberlinian's addresses!

and i won't be hitching in Europe, i'm buying a student-railpass for 2 months so that I can be warm and dry between hostels in winter. that's all i know to say now about my trip. And that i'm working for the Lib'n News Service which i know i've told you about in NY City. a political twice-a-week newsletter, excellent, reliable, widely read, + i'll be sending them photos and stories (although i can't write news well!) all during my trip.

Susie

My poor mother! How must she have felt when she got that rambling, slightly hysterical letter with its most telling comment: "i can't tell you about africa cuz I don't know about it!" ?

And I never got that student rail pass.

But I *did* I know a few things:

1— It made more sense to go to West Africa because several East African countries were in serious turmoil after the end of colonial rule (though I'd often dreamed of seeing the Serengeti).

2— I wanted to start in Senegal.

3— I was keen on visiting the area where the Senufo lived (in northern Ivory Coast and southern Mali), about whose art I had written a major term paper.

4— Professor Saaka had encouraged me to visit Ghana, where I could stay with his relatives.

Given this rock solid "itinerary," I ended up with visas for ten of the seventeen countries that comprise West Africa [1], plus one for Algeria.

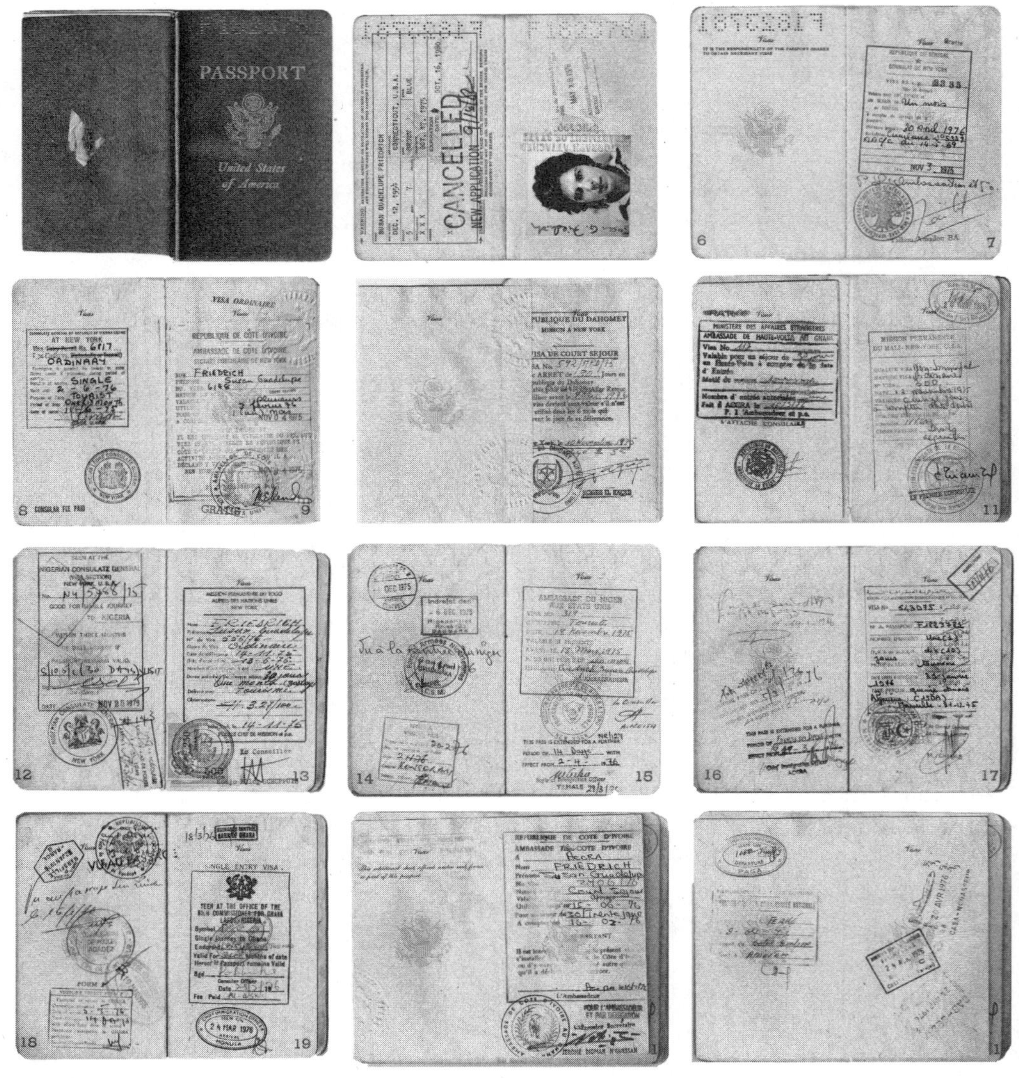

And what was the plan?
I would fly Icelandic Air to Luxembourg because it was the cheapest flight.
After that?
I would travel to Copenhagen by train. I would get to Senegal by catching a ride on a cargo ship from Copenhagen. Failing that, I would fly from Copenhagen to Senegal.

None of which happened except for the initial flight. Details to follow.

I didn't want my mother to worry too much, so on November 28th I wrote her that:

> . . . i'm leaving tomorrow; I got an excellent bk the other day about cheap travel in africa, w routes all mapped out, lots of hostels and cheap hotels. i can't imagine how beautiful the atlantic ocean is going to look down there!
> much love until later,
> su

By the way, I have no evidence or memory of that travel book. I probably ditched it early on because it wasn't very useful. Instead, I had a Michelin map, a few nights accounted for in Ghana, a few other countries in mind, and a "go where things take you" attitude.

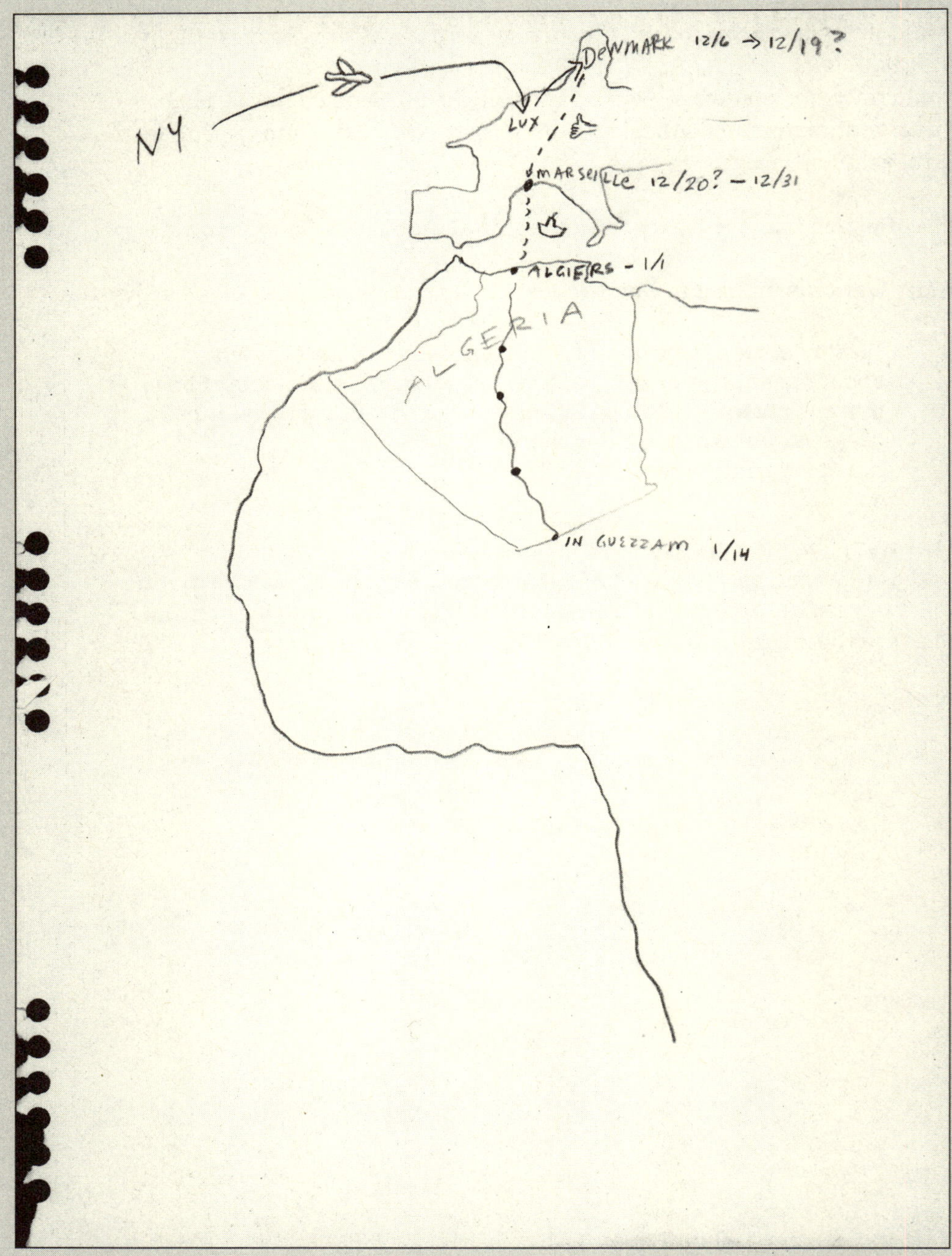
NY
DENMARK 12/6 → 12/19?
LUX
MARSEILLE 12/20? – 12/31
ALGIERS – 1/1
ALGERIA
IN GUEZZAM 1/14

CHAPTER THREE

In the Air, on the Road, over the Sea

On November 29, 1975, I flew from New York to Luxembourg, spent a few days wandering around the city, and then headed north—without that rail pass.

PART OF A LETTER TO MIMI FROM LUXEMBOURG:

. . . today i go out hitching. the train to København is $50, maybe i'll take it back down when it's colder...

[. . .]

met a woman who has a friend—a canadian—who teaches in damongo, a ghanaian village who i'll go visit—she's apparently had every imaginable disease, + the villagers love her—

[. . .]

this first day out—I hope you'll be hearing from me again: it's very foggy and rainy, has been all day, and after being stuck in a hell of a place got a ridefrom a very grandly teutonic trucker who has now asked me about 7 times as the sun sinks into the lascivious west whether i will stay *nach mir* [at my house]. i wish i knew how to say fuck off *auf deutsch*! [in German] he's now eating while i sit in the truck and wonder how i'm going to stay in a hotel tonite when all i have is $4 in luxie money.

after the dark falling the mist deepening + him making further jokes (ha!) about the trucks w/ beds in them (his didn't have one) we got to münster (i'm going to find out tomorrow if the cheese is from here) + i changed my $ at the last moment and ate my can of sardines. my, my, how the trivial necessities of daily life become so imposing when one travels—and i'm only 1/3 of the way to Copenhagen (it'd better be " . . . wonderful, wonderful . . . " when i get there!)

PART OF A LETTER TO MIMI FROM DENMARK:

. . . almost the first thing i saw across the danish border was a sign—

TABAC—KAFFEE—PORNO

and so it goes—
no wonder danish women are so politicized

spent the night in nyborg in a hotel, took the early a.m. ferry to Sjælland, the island that holds Københaven.

I got to Copenhagen on the 8th, the day before the opening of the art exhibition. Among all the photographs I took of the show, I don't have any of the wall on which I hung the WGC posters, but in 2017 Birgit Pontoppidan wrote a book about it, *Det skete på Kvindeudstillingen, Charlottenborg 1975*, and included this image.

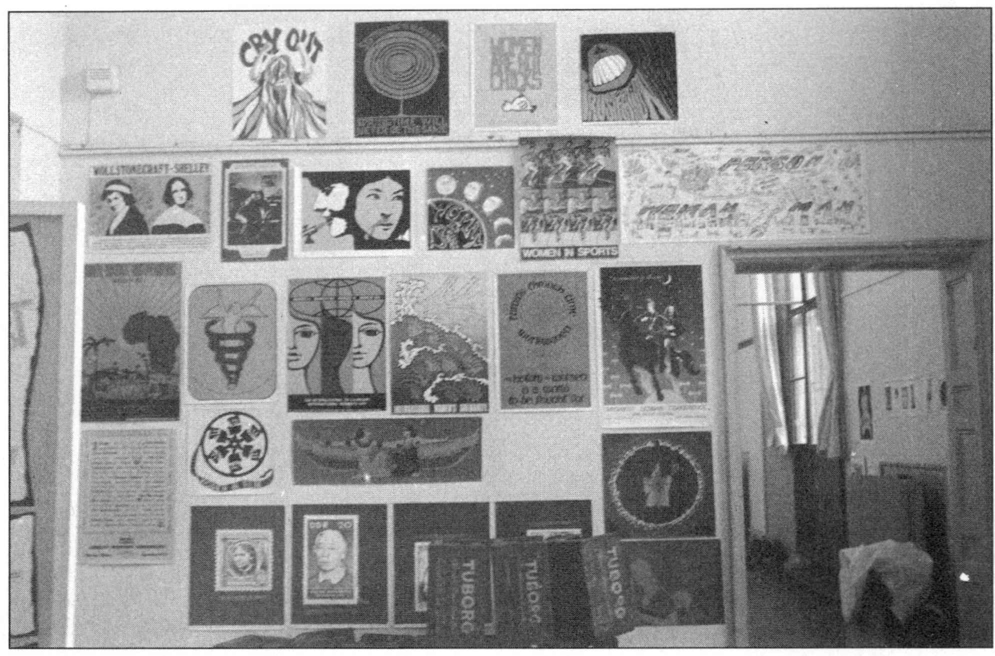

In a recent email she told me: "We were thirty-four women, most of us artists, who worked one and a half years to create the exhibition on the first floor at Charlottenborg. We called the exhibition "XX." A couple of months before the opening, we decided to invite young female artists from abroad to visit us at the exhibition. We dedicated four small rooms for the guests to display their posters, photos, etc. We also invited a few well-known artists to make performances: Marina Abramovic, Valie Export, and Inge Mahn." I already knew about Valie Export, the great Austrian artist and filmmaker, so it was very exciting to see her in person.

> **PART OF A LETTER TO MIMI:**
>
> Oh yes a wonderful performance by Valie Export from Austria (she has a tattoo on her left thigh of the buckle on a garter and the top of a stocking—it's great looking). She tied a bright blue parakeet with about 10 inches of string to a nail in a platform. The bird fluttered and exhausted itself trying to escape. She then asked someone to tie her up, was wound around head to foot—lay down + started to gnaw at the rope on the bird's leg to free it. It took several tense minutes. When the bird was free it didn't fly, just sat and stared at her. After a few more minutes someone came to untie her (she

hadn't asked to be but was clearly waiting for audience response.) then she gave the bird to a woman in the audience. It was very moving + absorbing. Ah yes, also, she wore a yellow top + panty hose w/o underpants, therefore one could see the tattoo.

But there was a PRIMA obnoxious photographer there who sat literally right next to her + kept taking pic after pic + disturbing the concentration of us very much (a lot of people were muttering about it). I think doing that takes a certain gall which should be repressed at all costs (even if one sacrifices a pic.)

Anyway, enough of despising my "colleagues".

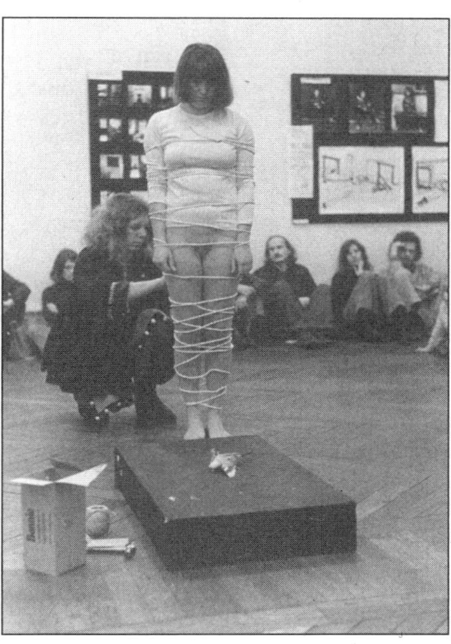

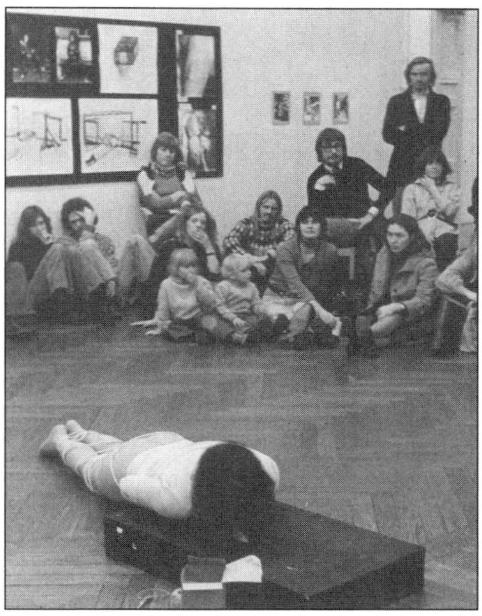

In other letters to home, I'm pretty moderate in my description of the art exhibit, and I had some interesting experiences throughout my time in Copenhagen, but in one letter to Mimi I said what I really thought about the show.

> really most of the art is pretty damn bad, a lot of vaginas, nuns, blood, aprons, writing—an hysterically funny office mock-up w/ paper + carbons strewn everywhere, the phone rings constantly (the phone handle is a penis), all sorts of things are going on. but it's just funny, not brilliant.

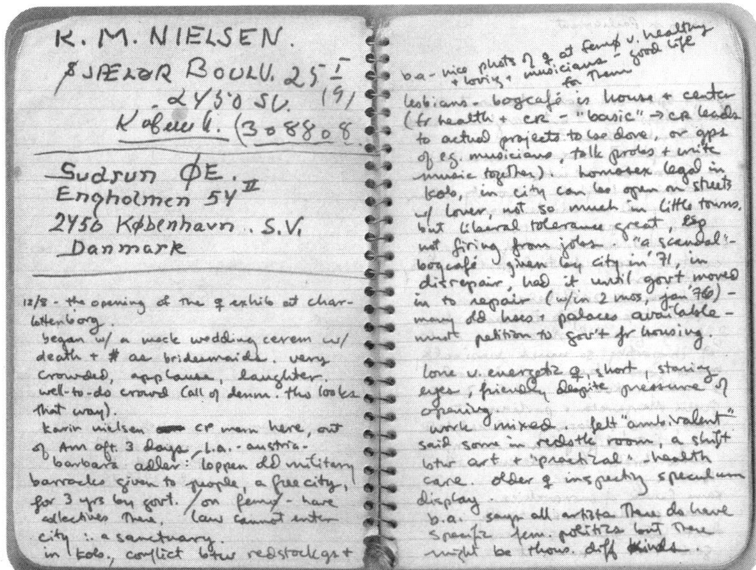
K. M. NIELSEN.
SJÆLØR BOULV. 25 I
2450 SV. (9)
Købh. (308808

Gudrun ØE.
Engholmen 54 II
2450 København S.V.
Danmark

12/8 - the opening of the ♀ exhib at Charlottenborg.
began w/ a mock wedding cerem w/ death + # as bridesmaids. very crowded, applause, laughter. well-to-do crowd (all of denm. tho looks that way).
karin nielsen cr women here, out of Am oft. 3 days, L.A. - austria.
barbara adler: loppen old military barracks given to people, a free city, for 3 yrs by govt. / on femmy - have collectives there, law cannot enter city :. a sanctuary.
in kob., conflict btw redstockgs +

b.a. - nice photo of ♀ at femf v. healthy + loving + musicians - good life for them
lesbians - bogcafé is house + center (for health + cr - "basic" → cr leads to actual projects to be done, or gps of eg. musicians, talk probs + write music together). homosex legal in kob, in city can be open on streets w/ lover, not so much in little towns, but liberal tolerance great, esp not firing from jobs. "a scandal": bogcafé given by city in '71, in disrepair, had it until gov't moved in to repair (w/in 2 mos, jan '76) - many old hses + palaces available - must petition to gov't for housing.
lone v. energetic ♀, short, staring eyes, friendly despite pressure of opening.
work mixed. felt "ambivalent" said some in redstk room, a shift btw art + "practical" - health care. older ♀ inspecting speculum display.
b.a. says all artists there do have specific fem. politics but there might be thous. diff kinds.

The first page of the first journal

My first journal begins with notes about all the artists, the people I visited and what I was hearing about the conflicts between the lesbian groups and the more worker-oriented political activists. No need to tread over that old ground again, but I've included some portions about the time in Copenhagen that have a bearing on my time in Africa. I was set on reading as many novels by Africans as I could find so we begin with my comments about one of them.

But let's pause to get oriented:
Up to now, I've been writing the backstory and the introduction in this font, in Roman. The following entry is the first one from my journal, which will always be in this same font.
But from now on, any factual notes about my travels or contemporary commentary I write in response to the journal entries will be in this font, in italics.

DECEMBER 8, 1975

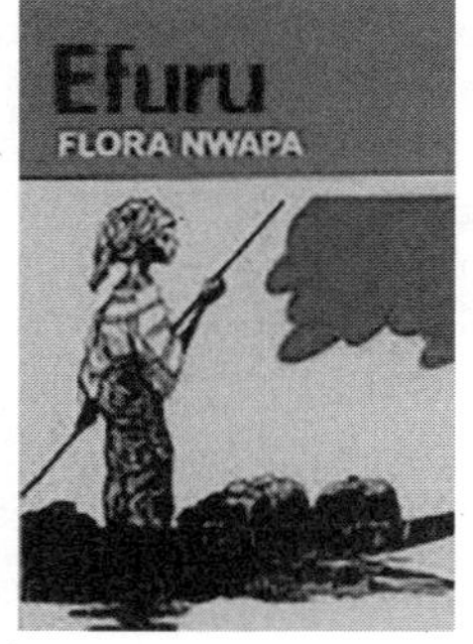

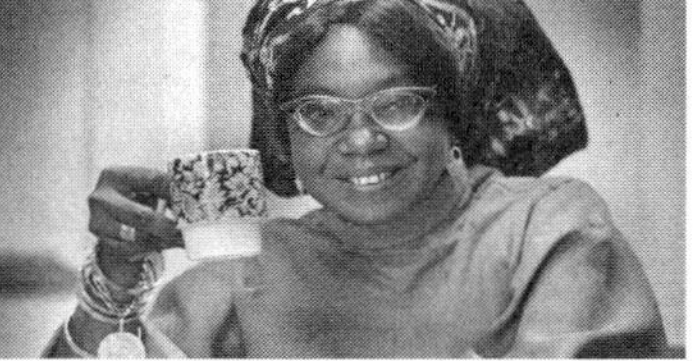

. . . finished *Efuru* by Flora Nwapa [1], a good book all in all. Efuru's actions were always motivated by a basic sense of pride and goodwill; she had the courage to leave her first husband's home when he ran out, and to leave her second husband after years of tolerating his semi-loyalty (having a boy from another woman and not telling

her for two years); when he accused her of adultery she finally left, after consulting her age-group. The prominence of childbirth is central; she has one girl who lives two years, she is a devotee of Uhamiri, the goddess of the lake, who gives women wealth and beauty but no children, and she is greatly adored by the town women.
Efuru's ability to make money is also important, and admired—her skill as a market woman—but conflicts arise, e.g., when she insists on going after a different crop than her husband wants.

There are strong support bonds among the women—her sister-in-law, her mother-in-law and her maid/sister. The social taboos effectively keep women and men apart, e.g., the gossip created when Efuru and her husband swim together, or when women and men friends go out too freely.
Sidelights on, e.g., their attitude to hospitals (i.e., white men) as dangerous and evil places, but when they are fixed up they respect it; and the tone of contempt when referring to the disrespect, ignorance of customs, which the younger generation has because of influence by whites and education. She gives knowledge of customs greater importance than book knowledge.
Also a funny comment re: white women: That they must be bored with their comfortable lives, they aren't as industrious as African women. She expresses a respect for the identity their work has always given them.

I found a comment in a letter when I'm being somewhat more honest with myself.

PART OF A LETTER TO MIMI:
Efuru by Flora Nwapa really speaks for women's experience in Africa in this transitional time, btwn old restrictive/protective traditions, and western influences which can be liberating or destructive (e.g., how she's treated by and treats her husbands.) i love the style, their wry, almost cynical humor which really comes thru in their proverbs, which all seem to be said w/ a sort of symbolic shrug towards the hardships of their lives. but i find that i read some of the African novels more for their (forgive the term) "sociological" value, i.e., rather than being really stupendous literature, i discover in them the habits, priorities, superstitions of a people about whom i am quite ignorant (cf. how i would approach Kafka—a favorite of mine.) in a way they fulfill that "useful" function of novels that we were talking about, + so i feel it's less wasteful/indulgent to read them (at a time when i feel i should be preparing myself in as many ways as possible for such an onslaught of unfamiliarity!)

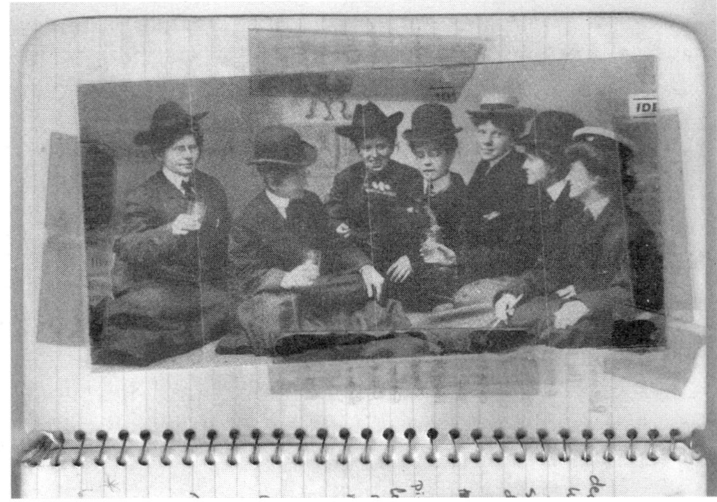

A picture taped into the journal. The women aren't identified.

DECEMBER 9

Why do you wait for the great adventure to begin somewhere out there?

The show in Copenhagen led me to pose some questions which still roil us today in discussions about women's art, feminist art, the woman's eye, etc.

Is it negative or positive? Is the positive too timid?
A retreat.
Yes, we need retreats from insanity, but workable retreats.
How can we incorporate nostalgia, the roots?
Is all this reformist bullshit?
Is it funny to have this in such a contented climate?
Is the contentment only superficial?
(Yes, judging from the number of women with kids, and the activism of the women here.)
Are we looking at this as "another half-assed attempt by the women"?

Is it?
Wouldn't it be better to steal the media?
(to arson the porno-ists?)
Are these only reactions against male traditions or differences within male traditions?
Are new avenues here?
Is painting a housewife radical?
Not if painting is dead—and not if the painting is ugly, therefore unapproached.

Am I convinced by the argument that this only reaches the people who are already aware of the issues?
But am I also susceptible to thinking these ("the influential") are the ones whose minds must be changed—
But what b.s.! As if the folks who come to art shows are the political heavyweights!
These are the constituents who might change their views on a certain referendum.
And anyway, is this about artists, or about women?

A LETTER TO MY FATHER:

Dec. 9—I'm almost 21!

Dear Dad—Hallo from *København*, with the healthiest damn people I've ever seen—
I came here to participate in a women's art show at Charlottenborg, the main museum. In general the show is what I expected of a women's art show—I really am so tired of most contemporary art, except that I find videos very promising & interesting—I've taken a lot of photos & fortunately met a woman who lives in the country in an old Danish farmhouse with a darkroom, so I shall be writing an article about the show for the feminist art journal; but it's hard with this sort of thing to balance art criticism with feminist analysis. *København* is nice, but so very discreet, and too cold—I yearn now for the 112° in the shade, altho when I get south I'll probably wish for snow, and so it goes.
I've discovered that Danes pay 48% tax on their income!
Apparently everyone here is in debt but the social services are so good that one can avoid slumming.
[. . .]
I found a good quote in the paper yesterday from Renoir's *La règle du jeu* [*The Rules of the Game*, a film from 1939]:
"The terrible thing in life is that everyone has his reasons."
Amen.
It feels so funny to me to realize that being in such an orderly, clean, obedient town/country as this almost makes me chafe, & miss the slovenliness & partial anarchy of American cities—
I leave here, sometime soon, altho this cold is a big deterrent from hitching, to go to England to see some political groups which are relevant to my African journey; then probably a boat from Marseille to Senegal or Ghana—I hope there's one soon, altho winter is such a bad time, & the cargo from & to Africa is in a bad economic situation right now.

By the way I don't know whether I said it before but your last letter to me was very dear, & well appreciated.
à bientôt,
Love,
Su
P.S. I'm now reading Bernadette Devlin's "autobio"/political discussion—she has quite a good sense of humor & humanity, & writes readably well—

A LETTER TO MY MOTHER AND BROTHER:

mom + pete—hello from københaven—it's damnably cold here + much too gray in addition to which the cobblestones hurt my feet + the chokolade is too tempting but i'm ok. the women's exhibit opened with a splash, a mock wedding ceremony + a lot of beer (they drink all the time here, Tuborg + Carlsberg, the greats).
[. . .]
met a woman who lives out in the country + has a darkroom which she's letting me use, so i can print out some pics for an article I'm writing on the torture of political prisoners. it's quite depressing to read (1) the papers every day and (2) books about the African liberation movements, etc.—and all the other stuff, the military power struggles, the fact that every day most of the front page is about different struggles that are occurring which have the US + USSR behind them—a holocaust is coming.
it's ok travelling but sort of frustrating bec. i like to read so much but i don't have a house to sit in so I have 10 cups of coffee a day + look for libraries—the museum here is pathetic, and i'm tired (already!) of picturesqueness.
[...]
it's so funny to me to be in such a WHITE country—i always forget that there are few Blacks here, + to see one on the street startles me—although there are a lot at the university.
i'm quite confused right now about my plans, i have to go slowly on decision making.
[...]
pete—i haven't seen any issues of comic books yet, but will keep looking –
love, su

PART OF A LETTER TO MIMI:

i'm at Loppen, a military barracks on the east side of Copenhagen, there's a women's fest here this eve....

I go on to describe the place as being within Christiania, a funky/squatted part of Copenhagen which was being taken over for new developments.

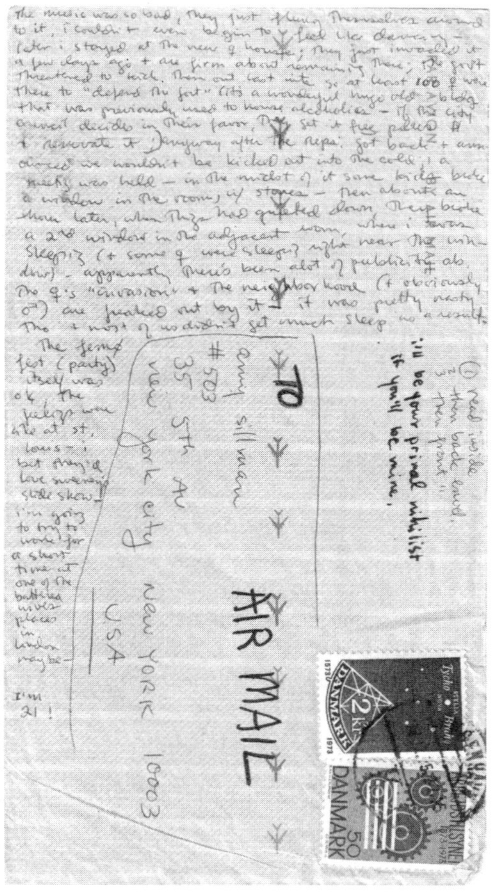

. . . the music was so bad, they just flung themselves around to it, i couldn't even begin to feel like dancing—later i stayed at the new woman house; they just invaded it a few days ago and are firm about remaining there; the gov't threatened to kick them out last night so at least 100 women were there to "defend the fort." it's a wonderful huge old building that was previously used to house alcoholics—if the city council decides in their favor, they get it free plus $ to renovate it. anyway after the representatives got back and announced that we wouldn't be kicked out into the cold, a meeting was held—and in the midst of it some kids broke a window in the room w/ stones—then about an hour later, when things had quieted down, they broke a second window in the adjacent room where i was sleeping (+ some women were sleeping right near the window)—apparently there's been a lot of publicity about the women's "invasion" + the neighborhood (and obviously men) are freaked out by it—it was pretty nasty tho and most of us didn't get much sleep as a result.

I turned twenty-one on December 12th.

PART OF A LETTER TO MIMI:

My birthday was spent as ideally all holidays should be spent: w/o any celebration. (which doesn't mean that I don't love celebrations; just not prescheduled ones.) it came + went + I read about the IRA and petrol bombs. Speaking of which: Devlin's description of being hurtled into stardom (an MP at 21!) is hysterically funny, really, none of the anguish of Kate Millet. She mentions a letter from Vietnam which simply began Hooray! Hooray! Hooray! + the marriage proposals + pics of Bernie with her boiled eggs etc.

PART OF A LETTER TO MIMI:

did you read *women and madness* by chesler? in the lesbian chapter there's a screamingly funny interview by an apparently *very* straight blk woman with a blk lesbian—she's unambivalent in the extreme—sounds like a coherent version of Flo Kennedy. anyway, i was sitting in a discreet (what else?) little bookshop laughing out loud while all these discreet danes stared politely at me. i wish i could've told them what it was all about. they seem to call them negroes here + think they're still waiting for the messiah.

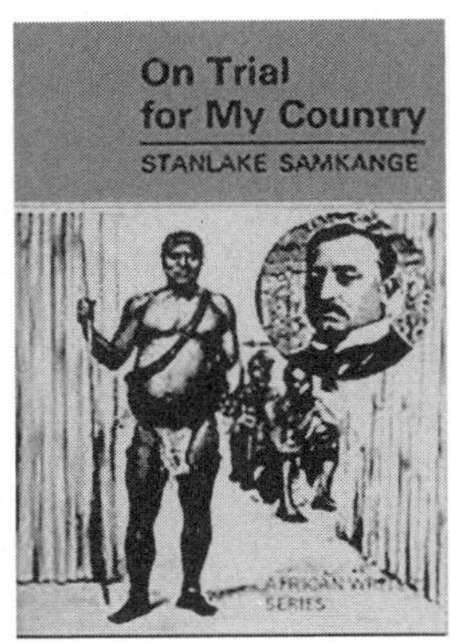

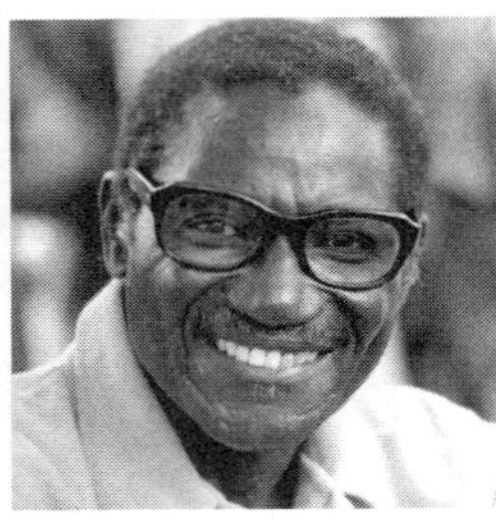

finished *on trial for my country* by samkange [2] about rhodesia's rape by rhodes [3] in the 1880s-90s. he was such a slime. if i hear from anyone anymore about our civilization and what we must do to "maintain" it, i'll get very nasty very...i wonder if he died a happy man? i hope he was stricken with leprosy cholera + river blindness + was slowly burned on a spit + served at the church bazaar.

the black star line office couldn't give me any info re: Africa-bound ships.

A LETTER TO MIMI:

babes—

did I ever tell you the wm. saroyan story, when he cures his obsession with cherries by eating 20 lbs. of them in one day?

My mind has a few extremely annoying memory-idiosyncracies, one being that every morning as I lie in bed half-awake I remind myself of descartes' (or was it pascal's?) comment that all his best ideas were conceived as he lay abed in the a.m.—so I have to have descartes on my brain when I have other things to worry about. does that happen with you? I feel haunted by presences, that often when I'm in the midst of something my thoughts turn towards what someone else tended to do in the same situation (e.g how camus feels when he eats a fried egg).

Of all things, I'm now reading K. Millett's *Sexual Politics*—I decided that she has to prove to me that she has a right to be such a snobby neurotic. Actually I'd only read the Genet section before + have always felt I "should" read it. I'm impressed so far, if only because her language is so unequivocal.

Saw a film yesterday on Femø 75[7]- poorly done film but cer-

---

7 Femø is an island off the coast of Denmark. Since 1971, about 250 women, many of them lesbians, have been creating and running a summer camp.

tainly with attention to "detail": most of it consisted of showing healthy naked smiling women doing dishes doing daycare doing some swimming eating doing dishes. Get my drift, honey chile? At any rate, all I can still think is that they have an awfully good life here, but that goodness reaches only a few, + the situation is no different for the housewives here (except their children are healthy) than elsewhere. They have the same more or less obnoxious husbands who grow up in a beer drinking culture w/ porno everywhere—which is not to insinuate that in their actions the men are more vulgar or brutal here (statistics etc disprove that) but they have because of the porno such a solidly entrenched perception of women.

Had a v. interesting conversation the other day with a Danish woman who's at a stalemate over beginning her 2nd novel because she says the only rational outcome would be the heroine's suicide...& she'd have all of denmark's women down on her! (understandably, & we tussled about the "political need" for not suiciding and she won me over to at least the fact that it's awfully hard to convince someone out of suicide when the only alternative you seem to be offering is what she called, a "mechanically optimistic socialist (communist) line"...i.e., our problems are solved with a new structure. So she's directed herself to "inner politics" (etc.). and despite my reading + talking + thinking about all these political/social "revolutions" or proposed revolutions or failed-but-good-conceptually revolutions, in my private moments I really despair about it all, because of thinking how much further + more difficult the psycho/spiritual "revolution" is. I wish to hell I could get to that laid back stage that most people get into of "well, I know it won't happen in my day"...I almost get embarrassed when I stop and tell myself that no, I'm not the first one to discover all this injustice + stupidity + I should take it in stride + be aware of the efforts that have been made + what the possibilities are now.

But instead I become a basketcase.

[...]

Saw *Modern Times* last night, the Chaplin film, it was <u>brilliant!</u> and very much of the moment. And quite subversive in subtle and obvious ways. Going to a huge Munch exhibit today in N. Denmark with the Englishman. He's nice + quite cynical, + the nervousest person I've probably ever met.

[...]

Reading *Africa*, a fairly good English mag covering politics + economics throughout Africa; discovering different country loyalties; + that Ghana is virtually a police state now; the NRC was replaced last month by the SMC: Supreme Military Council - ! The Englishman knows one of the editors (he was kicked out of Ethiopia for writing an exposé about Catholic killings) so I'd get to meet him when I go there.

I just realized I won't know your forwarding address or new box # if you move. If you can you should send it post haste to that London address—I certainly don't want all my letters to you getting lost!
I'm running out of steam now, will write if/when something happens (here, that's asking a lot).
w/ much love
a hug a kiss
su

(and on the back flap)

I'm so annoyed today with myself, fell into this bad recurring habit I have when depressed to just wander and almost provoke my depression more + eat lots of shit food (i.e. sugar junking) and now I've done it + am fed up with this gray gray gray gray town—so my recourse to sanity is to write you and drink bouillon. I have cured my travel bug I suspect. I so much wanted to work in the darkroom today but things fouled up as usual.
[...]
Anyway, Kate Millet is okay but for god's sake I've already read so many times about Seneca falls, the triangle fire, noteworthy anthropological sexisms, ETC—I suppose I'll finish it, for the literary sections of it.
[...]
You know I really am convinced now of the good old "mass communication" theory that the world has shrunk entirely because of accessibility of almost everything through the media—I really don't feel much specialness about being here—I'm sure it'll be a different case in Africa—at least I HOPE so!
Saw a pic of Caroline Diop (head of the women's union in Senegal) in the paper, she looks very cool—I hope she'll...ah..."give me an audience."
Again, much love, Su

PART OF A LETTER TO MIMI:

sweets—i woke up yesterday with a huge burst blood vessel in my left eye, filled almost the entire inner white area. it has now "leaked" + is on the edge of my iris but look as if it can't penetrate it, or whatever blood does—and now i have such a headache—i think it's from all the consumed rage + disgust generated by reading Millet. i have absolutely unquestionably lost ALL respect that i unconsciously assimilated regarding traditional (male) intellect. they are so full of shit; and what really kills me, but also gives me a certain (however useless) smugness is realizing that all along, whether vis-à-vis nuns/Catholicism, my philosophy prof, the "empiricism" of sociological "research," the wisdom of Art, the impartiality of science, or the venerable status of tradition, i was

RIGHT every time when i criticized mercilessly the fatuousness + self-serving "logic" of the systems—I don't know what it was, holy instinct or a fierce sense of self-preservation, but i was always pouncing on what i saw as a very flimsy + easily exposed rationale for their systems...
[...]
emma goldman was once "complimented" by a man who told her that she, of the few women he knew to do so, thought "like a man." she responded by saying she had never been very impressed w/ men's ways of thinking + would prefer to do it her own way.

. . . and then after going on for 4 more pages . . .

sure enough—now my headache is gone! thanks for listening to "all that"—

A LETTER TO MY MOTHER AND BROTHER:

MOM + PETE
a cold hello from copenhagen—i'm getting ready to leave tomorrow—i can't decide how my itinerary will be—whether to go to london or just go south, relentlessly south—god at this point even if I don't go to africa all I want is WARMTH!
[...]
I read some Stokely Carmichael today of all people! i'm astonished at how BLIND Black male "revolutionaries" can be to sexism, when they spend so much energy exposing racism, which is a perfectly parallel system to sexism, + which, if you ask me, is the 1st + greatest oppression, from which racism is a logical "next step"—anyway, things go along otherwise—oh, i just realized you wouldn't get this til after christmas—was it nice, i hope?
and now i'm 21 + don't feel quite so different but it is nice to know i can rent cars + drink poison + all the other great social amenities we adults receive!
[...]
i'm trying like hell to get out of copenhagen but everything (including of course myself) seems to be stopping me! I've changed my mind about going to london and will just head south, hoping i meet some travelers along the way—but this is a very bitchy cold time of year to travel, i admit!
w/ love + all,
su

I really wonder now why I said "of all people" in reference to Stokely Carmichael.

So I dropped the idea of going to London but, being unable to afford the flight to West Africa, it meant hitching from Copenhagen to the southern coast of France, where I could catch a ferry to Dakar. It's almost 1,100 miles from Copenhagen to Marseille.

A LETTER TO MIMI FROM SWITZERLAND:

Wo ist meine sonne Hoss? [Where is my son Hoss?]
"Bonanza" *auf Deutsch*, of course, in the Karlsruhe Youth Hostel.
Quality living, you must admit.
Today I went 550 miles, just relentlessly south, for some sunshine.
[. . .]
I have a sinking feeling about Christmas; that with the hostels being closed I'm really going to have to spend $$ on pensions and hotels—
I had a happily nostalgic day today in Lausanne, a town which I really fell in love with during my last trip here; I stayed several days.
[. . .]
And today the train to Geneva was full of rosy-cheeked Swiss children w/ skis and ski costumes.
[. . .]
I have to admit/tell myself that I'm scared of cholera + snakes in the near future (cholera shots are 30% effective!). Cholera results in dehydration, which can be discouraged if you get to the hospital *tout de suite!* [right away!] i'm really at heart such a one for bodily comforts—but in fact i hope this voyage "cures" me of an attachment to some of them—notably this chocolate craving which is having a field day here in Switzerland!
it's almost Christmas eve.
Love,
su

PART OF A LETTER TO MIMI FROM FRANCE:

all things considered (and i do), i've had a *très très très gentil* [very nice]Noël!
last afternoon i was so despondent, arriving in a grey Lyons, getting lost + finally arriving in an absolutely <u>hideous</u> hostel, all concrete and formica—but at 9:00 the very sweet family that operates this *auberge* had a *fête pour noël* [this inn had a Christmas dinner]—i was a bit uncomfortable at 1st, trying to be cozy and festy w/ about 10 men, all tunisian + italian + japanese + french—but w/ candles + wine + chocolates + a tape recorder of music + an interesting discussion about relative oppression in the different countries it was really fun + quite a good replacement for any possible feelings of "loneliness" at a time when one is "supposed to be" w/ family et. al.

and, happily, to continue my (short but sweet) history of unorthodox holidays, i had a delicious xmas dinner of couscous in the tunisian slum of lyons. and it's like all the books say, it's all men, the women stay behind in tunisia—very creepy feelings.
tomorrow, marseille and *l'avenir inconnue!* [the unknown future]
BONNE FÊTE DE NOËL!

A POSTCARD TO MY MOTHER AND BROTHER FROM LYONS:

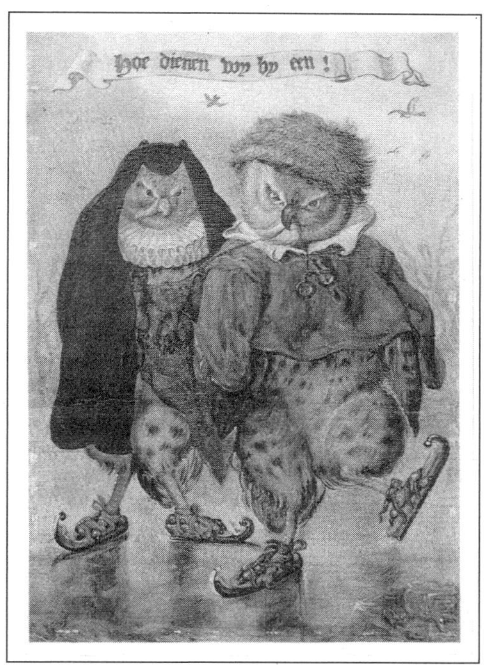

mom & pete—thought you'd like this postcard!
[. . .]
tomorrow i go to Marseille to look for a boat, + i hope it's warmer there! i've been struggling with my french all day and managed to have an interesting discussion this eve with a tunisian law student about zionism + sexism—but i hope my french improves, it's quite bad. i just finished Angela Davis' *An Autobiography*, a fine book although she leaves a few important questions undiscussed and/or unanswered but i do admire her tho i don't understand why she's a communist?! seems pretty absurd to me—anyway, things go along—i wish you both all the peace this crazy world can possibly offer to us now—and much love—su
P.S. a good way if you need to reach me is to write me c/o the american embassies in the african countries (esp. Senegal 1st + Ghana + Nigeria + mark the letter IMPORTANT.)

I arrived in Marseille on the 26th and decamped at the youth hostel.
There were only two land routes to sub-Saharan Africa. One went west across North Africa and then south into Senegal, but the Western Sahara War was raging. The other route went south from Algiers through the Sahara, so I opted for that relatively safer route. I would then be traveling westward across West Africa [4].

A LETTER TO MY FATHER, WITH A POSTCARD OF A VAN GOGH PAINTING ENCLOSED:

Bonsoir mon père—
did I also send you the other Van Gogh postcard? I'm in Marseille—I came here to discover that the boat to Senegal is WAY too expensive, so I go to Algeria, take a bus to Ghardaia, another bus/truck to Tamanrasset, another bus to Agadez *et voilà*, Niger. Hence my trip thru *Afrique* goes east-west, a reversal of plans but o.k. — my visas will cover me most of the way altho some will expire—I'm sure the busses will be safe, & sufficiently uncomfortable (sic). So far things are interesting, my French has major flaws, but I try. At this hostel there are 4 men from Senegal, we've had a few interesting discussions above the din of Latin-American music, of which they're enamored—it's a bit lonely for a woman-identified traveler like me because there are very few women who travel at this time, & so I spend 90% of my conversation time w/ Tunisian-Italian-African-French men, who all seem quite intrigued w/ my theories about POWER—I think about it all the time—and I'm really intrigued by the vulgar face that "western capital" takes in Europe. The absurdly out-of-place americanisations I see everywhere—the visit to the Copenhagen women's art festival was generally worthwhile, I think I got a good feel for the spirit of the women's movement in Denmark, & esp. how it differs from what one sees generally in America—e.g., an important e.g., rape is a very minor problem there (as is racism)—Perhaps in 2 days I leave for Algeria, New Year's Eve will be on the boat (it takes 20 hours!)—
Best of this much-less-than-the-best-of-all-possible worlds to you,
Love
Su

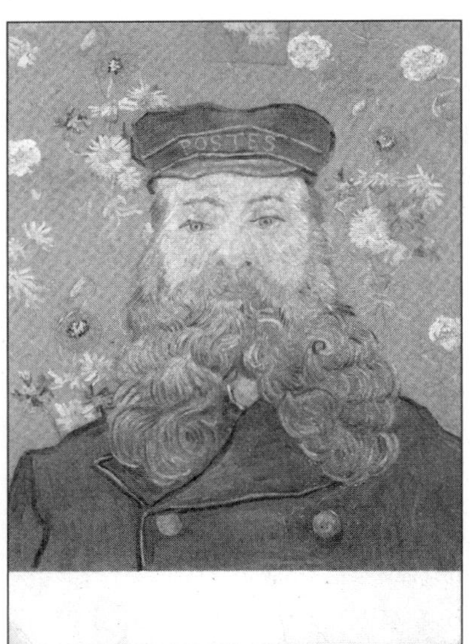

I spent a lot of time in Marseille with these wonderful Senegalese guys. I wish my journal had all their names and some notes about them because they were a great source of fun, companionship, raucous conversation and heated debates during a long, anxious wait for the start of what was now a considerably more mysterious voyage.

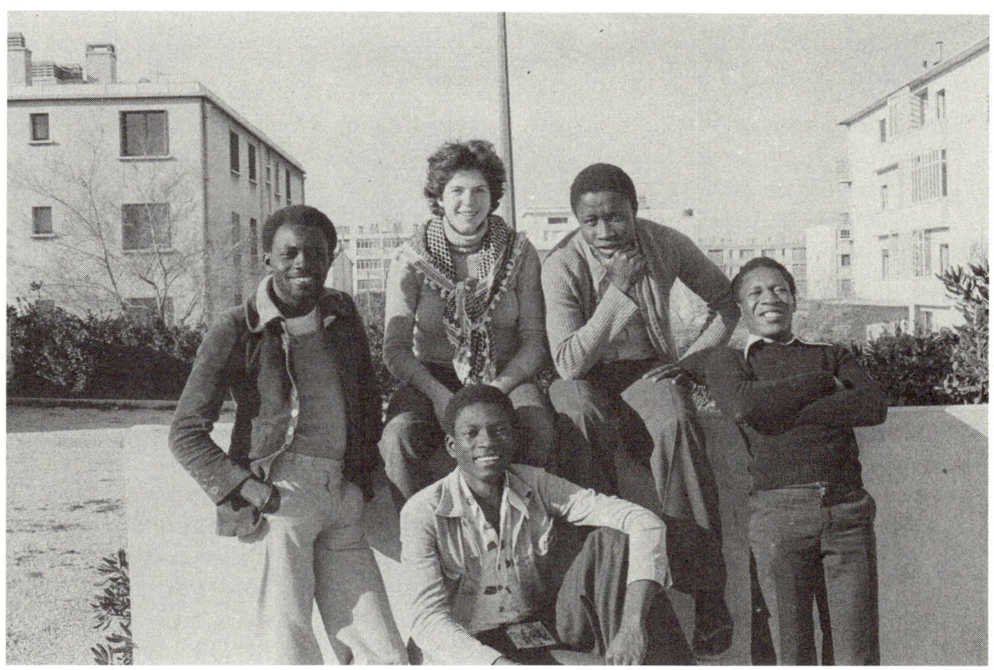

My next letter to Mimi, sent from Marseille on the last day of 1975, included a note written by a Japanese traveler who was also at the hostel:

さいあいなる エミー
わたくしは フランスでたくさんのにほんじんに あいました。
それで あなたは このてがみによって すこしわかるもの
がある。
アフリカまでの ボートは たかいので、マドリッドまで
ゆき ひこうきにのらなければ なりません。
わたくしは あなたが ひとつのノートをかいてくして
しっぽうしなければいいがとのぞみます。
わたくしは こんばん [illegible]では ありません。
ひとうみは わたくしの[illegible]をはればれさせる。

It was recently translated by a friend of mine:

> My Beloved Mimi,
> I met a lot of Japanese in France. And I think you'll understand better from this letter. The boat going to Africa is expense, so I have to fly to Madrid. I hope you aren't disappointed after deciphering my last note. I'm not at my best tonight. The sea of people will clear my cloudy heart.

I have no idea what that reference to Madrid is about . . .

> dear mimi,
> This is the paper French bread comes in—it serves well as light stationery, yes?
> A note on the Japanese—there are 5 in this hostel (all men) & I asked one to translate a note for me—it took him a long time & he said that he wasn't sure it was "accurate" so you might get some curious mishmash of a translation from your friend of a quite uninteresting note—
> I'm *fairing les courses* [shopping] today to buy all the things I need for my desert journey: the boat is $233 (!) one way; I'll probably fly back on that student charter for $133—I think w/ payoffs & bus fare the desert will cost close to $100, but that's ok[8] —
> A new difficulty has entered (this leg of) the journey: the near absence of women travelers—the men I encounter are all very nice, but after a bit I can't help but begin to feel like an oddity (especially when they insist on pointing out to me that I am one!) I really got harassed yesterday by a young boy on a motorbike, he even rode up onto the sidewalk & was edging me towards the wall—I finally shook my fist close to his face & said in a truly FIERCE voice (I didn't have to pretend to be angry!) "*Laisse moi tranquille!*" [Leave me alone!] A look of real fear flickered thru his eyes, then he put on his tough boy face, slapped me on the arm, muttered "*Salaud...*" [You shit...] and sped off. 2 seconds later a car stopped & began honking & whistling—
> And THIS is my fondest memory of southern France—nothing has changed since I was here 3 years ago, nothing.
> A soft blue sky now & pink light covering the stone houses.
> Maybe I'm too much of a cynic to be a photojournalist—instead of taking photos of the folks, I photograph all the crap around them—prettiness, cleanliness, God-in-his-place-&-all's-right-w-the-world (or maybe it's "everyone-in-God's-place" now—), can be dull, yes?
> It's incongruities that I like so much, that's what always makes me laugh under my breath; I'm always seeing/hearing incongruities in others & myself—but that means perhaps that it's all only

8 The translation of these prices into 2024 dollars: $233 = $1,322; $133 = $755; $100 = $567.

funny/incongruous when compared w/ an ideal system which somehow I still retain as a basis of judgment but that in itself is curious because I've certainly never experienced an orderly or congruous world.
I think I laugh to reassure myself that we're really not much more (which has nothing to do w/ our potential; I speak of how we are) than the sophisticated idiots we strive to be—
Have no fear: The next step of my argument is not metaphysics, it's hysteria of the healthy sort—
& so I go, listening, discussing, "studying", being interested & serious, and yet I think I lost my faith somewhere back in the days when Dad gave me *Winnie-the-Pooh* in Latin [5]—
Su

Please try to send a note to an American embassy in Ghana or Togo or Ivory Coast
Dec 29, 1975

I've always loved books with maps in them, especially novels with maps of invented places, like this endpaper from Winnie Ille Pu.

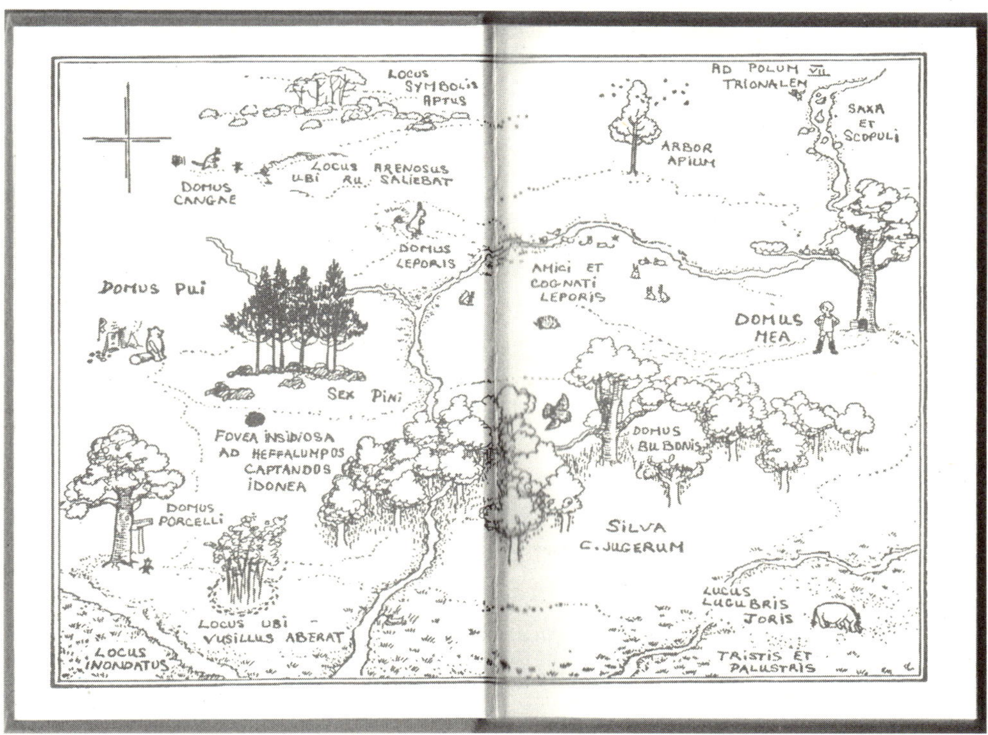

I celebrated New Year's Eve with my friends from Senegal before catching the overnight ferry to Algiers.

The reaction they ended in after each long and heated discussion on changing our natures (and we had several) was *Ça prend longtemps* [That takes a long time]—stressing on me the painfully long and slow time it will take—as if I thought (and I do, every other day) it would happen overnight!
The last thing I heard (and heard and heard) on New Year's was, "Su, it's the end of the Year of the Woman." (1975 had been declared that by the U.N.) [6]
I said, "What a pity."—I should've said, "Not for the women!"

Various African countries honored International Women's Year through stamps, fabrics, etc.

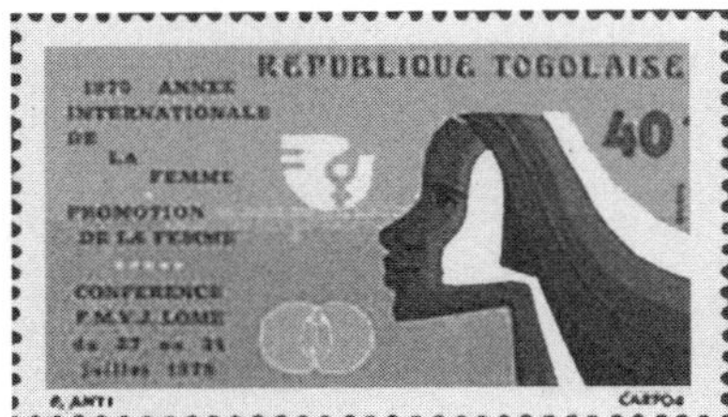

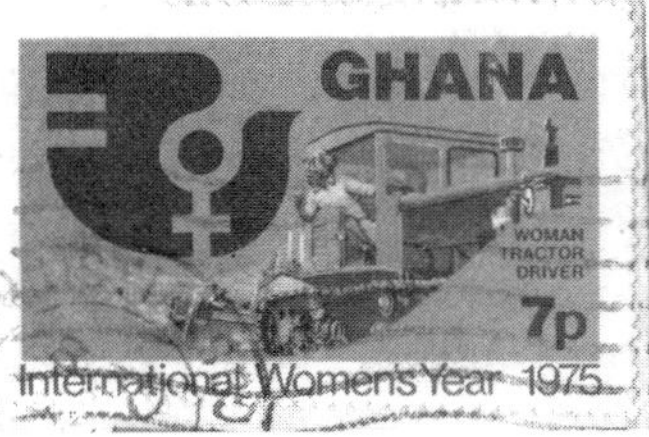

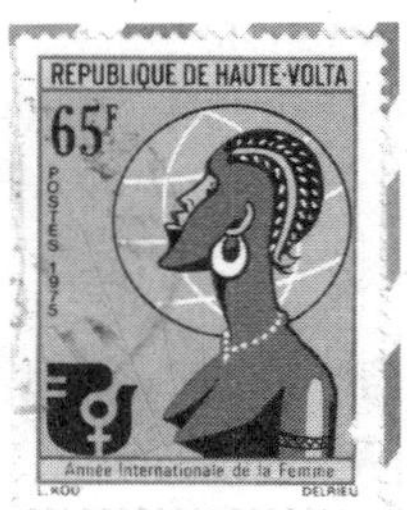

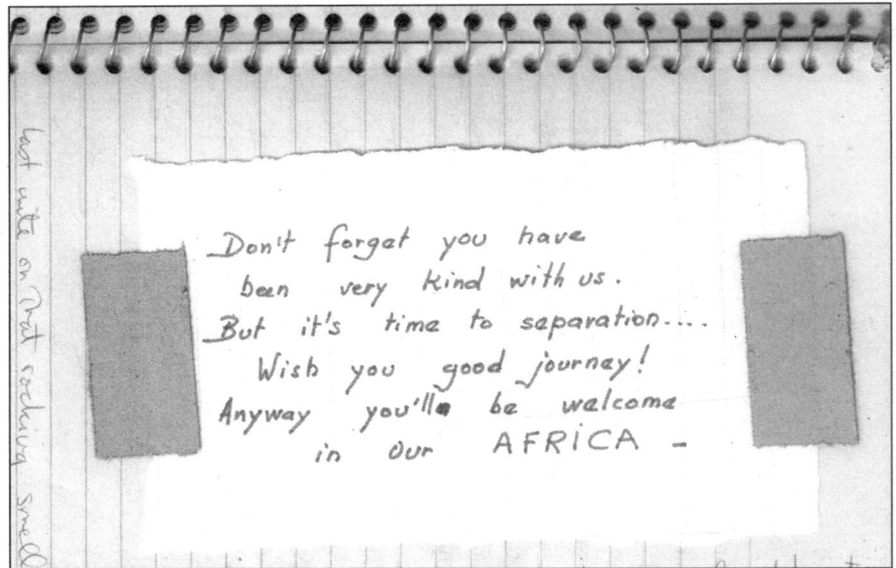
Don't forget you have
been very kind with us.
But it's time to separation....
Wish you good journey!
Anyway you'll be welcome
in our AFRICA -

Below this note from one of my buddies in Marseille, I wrote:

A note from Moussa (Diop), a comrade at heart; I hope it portends equally felicitous meetings during my months in Africa.

The long overnight ferry ride out on the deck was freezing cold and very uncomfortable.

JANUARY 1, 1976

The man at the customs office in Algiers asks for a New Year's kiss and did I want a room for free?
Go to all hell.
Last night on that rocking smelling groaning slumbering boat after days of Marseille men and a few beers I decided that my dream world my aspirations my idealisms just go much too far and are too abstract to be admitted so frequently. I have an old tendency to jump right off the deep end of a subject without slowly plodding thru the preparatory ground, and now it's coming clearer to me, talking to, e.g., people from TW[9] countries, how differently in terms of models and temporal schemes we think, and that my little utopias of 400 years from now (if ever) is like trying to study Ti-Grace[10] before being literate—i.e., I get reactions which tell me that I'm saying things WAY beyond the credibility levels for their terms.

But inadvertently last night the Dutch guy said something quite pleasing: We spoke of childhood readings and their effect on us subconsciously and I offered quite randomly the example of reading *Kidnapped* and playing the pirate's role for weeks afterwards—and he said "Gee, if a girl can play at being a pirate then she really isn't a girl anymore but just someone with a different body."
Right on.
He's lived here 3 years and he told me that the only way he could describe the sex between an Algerian (married) couple is fucking; that sometimes (often?) they might not even speak the same language! (The woman speaks a dialect; the man, Arabic or Berber.)
He described the perception of Algerian women by men as packhorses, not someone to be talked to—and perhaps a difference that has existed between African and Algerian women that has led to what appears to be a greater general repressiveness here is that, in accordance with the Koran, Algerian women have never worked, to the extent that African women have.

Wandering around Algiers:
Little dusty bookstores full of good French lit—Malraux, Hugo, and de Beauvoir, all for very very cheap.
"Solidarity with the Sahara" posters; a Cuban film festival theatre full of good Cuban posters and a spread on the MPLA [Popular Movement for the Liberation of Angola] [7].

---

9 TW=Third World, the accepted term back then for what we now usually call the Global South. The term "Third World" arose during the Cold War and was supposed to define countries that remained non-aligned with either NATO or the Warsaw Pact, but it became more commonly used to refer to "less developed" countries.

10 Ti-Grace Atkinson, a radical feminist, author of *Amazon Odyssey* and other books.

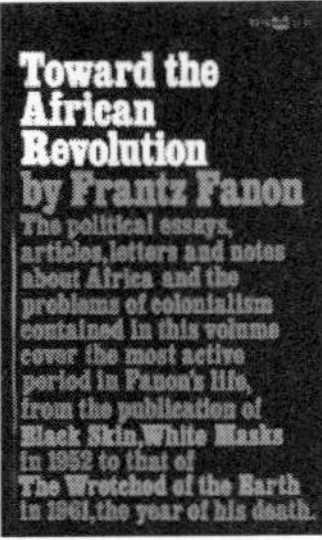

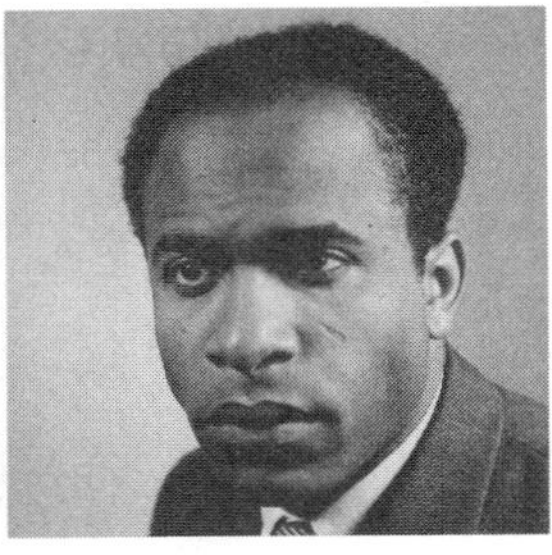

They sell Frantz Fanon's books everywhere. No wonder.
I've only read one, should check out the others.... [8]

A wimpy British couple led me around which was lucky because it gave me the extra oomph to find this hotel ($3.15 a night, toilet, above 2 bars!)[11] but what a wash-out they were; she kept gazing at me with big eyes while he would answer for both: "Are you Australian?" I asked. "No, I'm British." And that apparently satisfied her because she didn't offer any info.
I'll probably run into them in W. Africa.
But the schedule is harassing me—I have to leave Algeria within ten days and god knows it's tough if the trucks don't come along quickly!

I had gotten visas ahead of time without really knowing where I would be or how long I would be there. Algeria was the first test, given their deadline and my mode of travel.
Visas bedeviled me throughout the trip because of the difficulty in getting new ones or updating existing ones and also because of their deadlines, which usually didn't mesh with my wacky plans or with how long it took to get from point A to point B.

DURÉE du SÉJOUR dix (10) jours
MOTIF de SÉJOUR Tourisme
DATE LIMITE D'UTILISATION 31 Janvier 1976
TAXE PERÇUE quinze dinars Algériens (150A)
A Marseille le 31-12-75
Le Consul Général

JANUARY 2-4

The men gape and gape but are easily brushed off.
The women shuffle down the streets, their eyes averted, hands always grabbing to catch the falling veil to make certain they're always covered. It's stranger than I could even imagine, and photos I've seen just don't convey the abysmal feeling one gets seeing them in the street while the men stroll by, eyes roaming, talking, aggressing...I stopped to ask two younger women today for directions and they seemed very startled to be asked advice. Whenever I asked a couple for directions, the woman would fade back and the man would tell me (usually incorrectly!).
Reading *The Best and the Brightest* by Halberstam on the VNM War and American politicians—I felt confused but thoughtful about the roads women have to make into electoral politics—and I think of Bernie Devlin's closing words about the farce of Parliament.
And it all runs in that furious circle.
It's interesting in pointing out the paternalistic attitude that has reigned in America, especially since WWII, about seeing itself as the moral authority of the world—!

11 $3.15 = $17.32

He chose a good term, "muscular Christianity," to describe the particular style and form of "missionary" work that American politicians are indulging in, saving the world for democracy, etc.—

> **PART OF A LETTER TO MY MOTHER AND BROTHER:**
> I'm reading *The Best & the Brightest* by a Pulitzer-prize winning journalist from the NY Times. I'm not altogether convinced either of his skill or of the actual validity of his stories but it's basically a (long) investigation of our involvement in Vietnam, which I find an important thing to understand better, since I was too young at the time to really get things straight—it's ver-r-r-r-y interesting. (He refers to Lein[12] as "that towering but remote figure"—hmmm....)
> It's formidable, the sort of foundations of wealth/brains/connections/family/self-assurance (self-righteousness) those "great" men had as a start—no wonder they "get ahead"—it's a road of roses with just a few challenges to make it seem like a struggle but it's really all been cut out & organized & decreed, and the status quo passes on its laurels to the next generation—and then they say we don't try hard enough to get ahead!
> I'm really interested to get a better insight into all the (necessary-) infighting & back-stabbing & shoe-kissing that goes on in politics—

Every mechanism in the/my human body strains and groans to fend off the undeniable presence here of human misery, vast poverty, illiteracy. A man going thru customs not only needed me to write his police card but he was presumed born in 1909; the French didn't consider it necessary to make birth records for Algerians! The cycle starts of guilt and responsibility towards these people—perhaps one end of it is to channel ourselves out, but perhaps the most deep-cutting act is to work in America to have (1) an open admission of guilt and change for the world-wide problems we've created and (2) a recognition of our problems more than just when something extreme is "exposed."

The question now for a socializing Algeria—to teach the few for high skills or the majority to be literate? There is very little available material and teachers, but they seem to be directing themselves more towards the masses.

Either I hear kisses and "*belle*," or from the older, disapproving men I get hisses or loud grunts as they pass me.
It's so ironic that they would view me as a tourist, as a rich overlord viewing their slums; the picture of America which is sold to them says exactly that—but take a walk thru NY city on a hot day—that's what they should see more of. I feel somewhat upset by the conditions here, but I also feel as if I've seen them already so many times....

12 My paternal grandfather, Carl J. Friedrich, a political scientist.

After being very upset last night by the harassment by men I realized that they feel the same as I feel about the veiled women: Totally astonished and thrown off guard. (I say that because even though they see a lot of American women in pants, etc. I think I show an even more extreme version of that in my 60s styles and my hair as it is now.) Maybe I look so outrageous that I'm scaring them off from even sitting down with me—I'm down by the seaside at a gravely lot with lots of kids playing football.
There are SO MANY KIDS here, three times the amount of adults it seems!
And one third of the women (or more) that I see are pregnant.
If the women look up at all on the street, their brows are in a frown, their eyes often show pain or fatigue.

Strangely enough, I am beginning to cultivate the art of sitting still and mulling.

Had breakfast with one of the sons of the hotel—he talked about the traditional marriage, made without even knowing or talking to the fiancé—he bemoaned the almost total absence of young women on the streets because one cannot meet a potential spouse and because it's unnatural to always be in the company of men.
—he insisted there was no hunger here
—little unemployment
?
At least, he said, it was better than ten years ago, i.e., under the French.
I silently salute every woman who is still veiled.
And every woman brave enough to discard it.
After a few hours, a day, of being a total freak everywhere I go, always eyes on me, it makes me panic, want to hide, be "normal." And what a thrill it just was to see some real solid unashamed women (some rich hippies at this hotel)—like a fresh breath of air.

I yearn to be in a Black country.

The French certainly did a number on Algeria, including not making a decent road between one end and the other—it took the revolution and the Algerians to do it—it's 1/3 finished.[13]

---

13 For more info about the other two-thirds of this road and what it's like to travel on it, see [9].

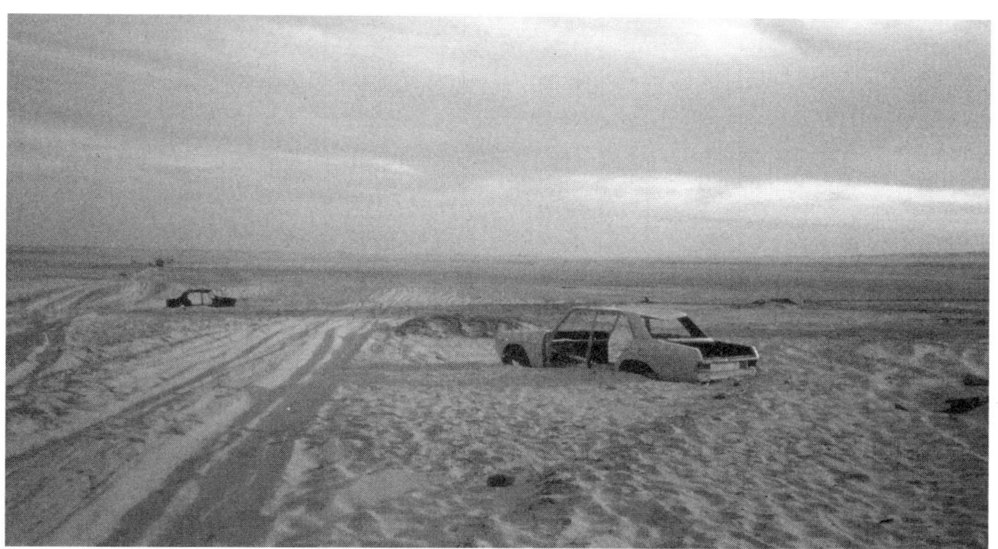

Photo circa 1991

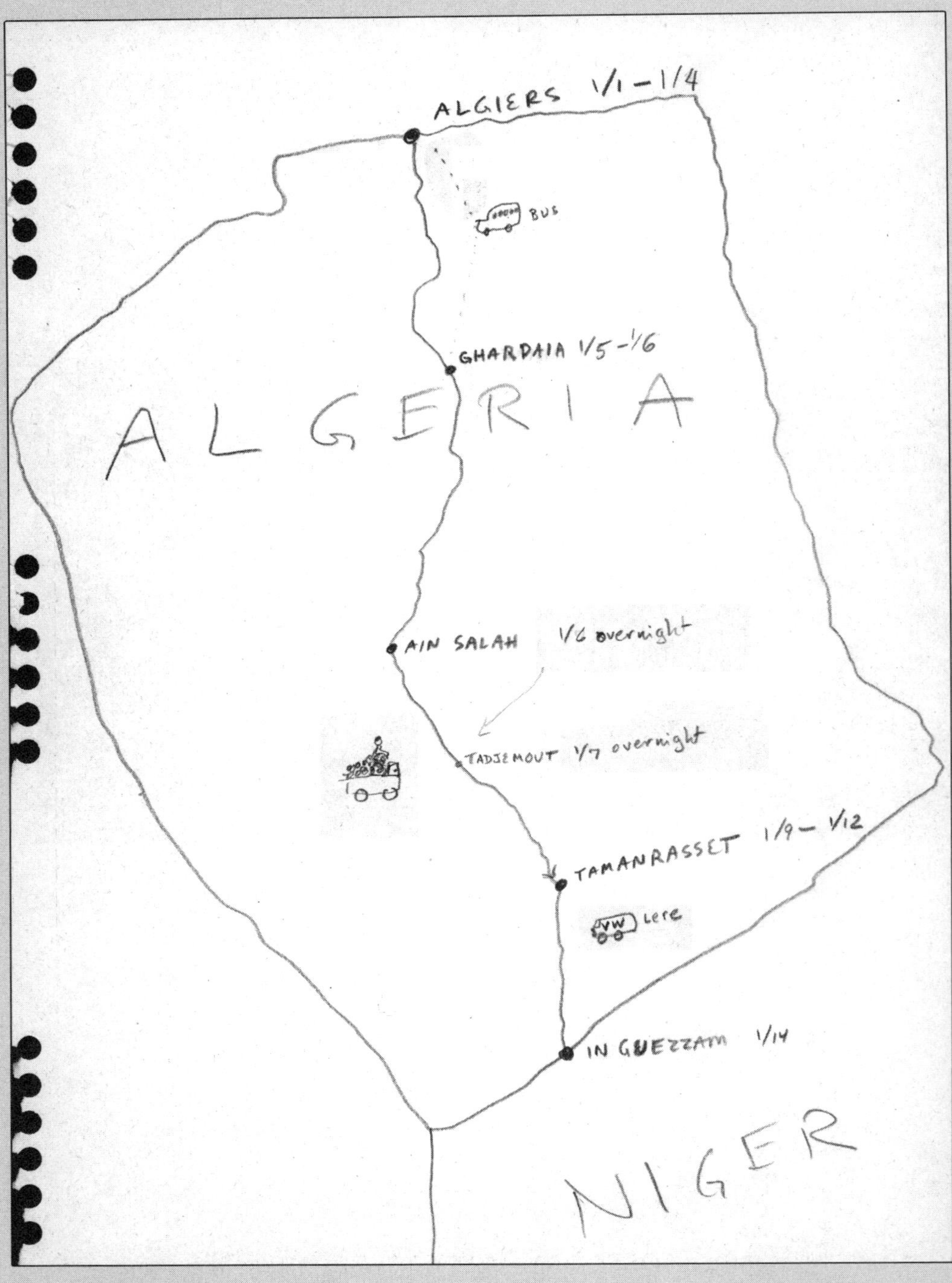
ALGIERS 1/1 – 1/4
BUS
GHARDAIA 1/5 – 1/6
ALGERIA
AIN SALAH 1/6 overnight
TADJEMOUT 1/7 overnight
TAMANRASSET 1/9 – 1/12
VW
Lere
IN GUEZZAM 1/14
NIGER

CHAPTER FOUR

From Algiers to Tamanrasset with Fatma, Alan, and a Million Dates

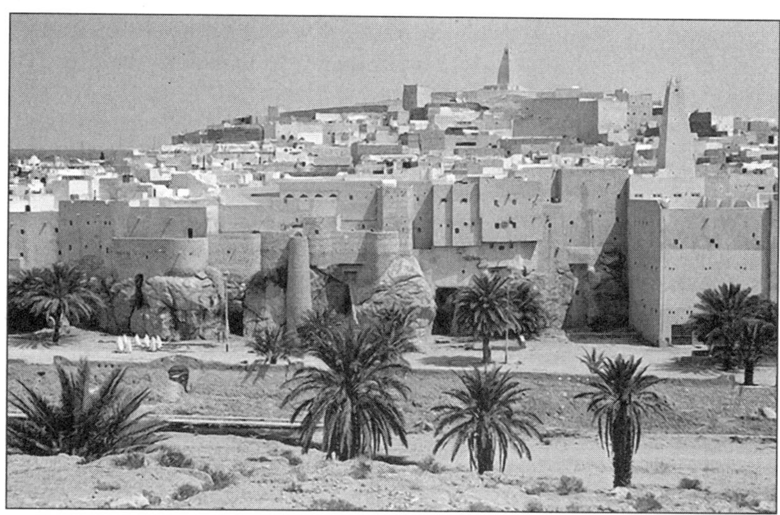

I took a bus from Algiers to Ghardaïa. [1]

PART OF A LETTER TO MY MOTHER AND BROTHER:

Mom & Pete,
Well, if the rest of my trip across the desert is as luxurious as this after a very cold VERY bumpy very long bus ride to Ghardaïa, 600km (360 miles) south of Algiers . . .
I took a long (23 hrs!) boat ride from Marseille to Algiers, found a clean hotel with breakfast for $3.15. I arrived in G. this a.m. at 5:00 cold & stiff & immediately was offered coffee by someone who then showed me to a good hotel—after some hours of rest I awoke & at the bus depot met the proprietor of the hotel, a gnarled gentle old Black man who's lived here
25 years—
He took me on his shopping rounds & gave me their traditional breakfast, called Bennies (sounds like that) which are awful greasy fluffy doughy things & extremely sweet tea. It was nice to go around with him as a breaking-in session for me in this culture—it's really *wonderful* but I certainly feel & must look like a tourist, esp. as a woman with straight-leg pants & short hair in a culture where one is lucky to see 10 women on the street in an

entire day—it's a frightening thing for me to walk past the houses & know that there are women enclosed, never to leave, sometimes on pain of death: If a woman goes out & talks with another man while her husband is at work he can kill her for honor's sake & get only a maximum 3 year prison sentence (if any . . .)—it's really reinforcing all my ideas about male/female roles & how they need changing if we're ever going to be truly humane with one another—but some absolutely lovely & courageous young girls followed me for quite a while this morning giggling every time I would smile at them or ask them a question—I hope they have a more interesting or open life than their mothers—I've been told by a # of people that often the husband & wife don't even speak the same language:
he: Arabic   she: a dialect
I know "it's tradition", but it's so weird nonetheless.
But the desert fascinates me, the architecture is superior for the climate: all the stores are naturally "air-conditioned," & even the dirt doesn't look dirty because one has no concrete or sterility to compare it with.
I either am taking another bus to Ain Salah (another 600 km south, more or less) or getting a lift on a truck with a friend of the proprietor of the hotel, whom I trust. I think I'll be in Niger within a week and then . . .
It's really exciting, so much more interesting than proper old lovely Europe—I must tell you I got very tired of being in Europe, it's getting dangerously close to American detachment from nature & plasticization etc.—but I did more or less enjoy my visit in Copenhagen and my visit in Marseille was quite nice because of those fellows from Senegal, we ate together each eve & shared a few heated opinions about feminism & tradition, and African customs vs American, etc.—

JANUARY 5 & 6

The graveyard in Ghardaïa: pottery shards, unmarked stones, palm leaves faded and dry, narrow paths, a view of the town all cool scintillating turquoise, emerald, cantaloupe, brown, and white.
Very quiet.
Only the sound of animals, distant trucks.
The young girls here all love me, they just smile and stare and say hello.
They tourist me as much as I do them.

The house of Bouarara Fatma—three rooms. A large shimmering woman, gave me cheek kisses in greeting, made coffee, biscuits.
I can never get over the fact (given my background) that something like plain biscuits

are a very generous gesture by families like this—it makes me feel so uncomfortable. As we talked another younger woman awoke, perhaps twenty-five years old, very plump because of children and sitting at home, very beautiful but lost eyes, never spoke much . . .

> **PART OF A LETTER TO MY MOTHER AND BROTHER:**
>
> An incredible afternoon—long walk thru Ghardaïa which culminated in an invitation by about 16 screaming girls to come home with them—I eventually ended up at the house of a very beautiful & generous woman whose daughter, Fatma, my age, was unbelievable—the classic case of a clear, perhaps *very* intelligent mind trapped beneath a world of tradition & repression—at 21 she says she prefers to remain celibate—& I can well understand it, if the alternative is to marry someone totally unknown. She spoke to me in French—I wanted to say it but felt embarrassed to, until she said, "The woman in Algeria is not at all free"—it was a frustrating but very worthwhile & unusual experience for me—
> Tomorrow I go further south.
>
> Love & kisses & a world of anger
> Su
>
> P.S. And after my visit this afternoon in the house it's not just being confined in a house, it's a hellhole or worse, quite reasonably comparable to solitary confinement rooms in prisons—dank, etc.—you know about it I'm sure. Yes, the men get fresh air & conversation & exercise and and and—

With that group of girls today, one of them said, pointing to my skin and then to hers: *ça bon, ça mauvais* [this good, this bad].

A stroll through the dark wet streets of Ghardaïa listening to the tale of the Algerian war of independence. On November 1, 1954, at the casbah, the first shot was fired.

A kitchen scene at the hotel: No wonder I have a stomach ache! The salad dressing looks (in the kitchen) like very rancid stuff although it tasted fine—and the chicken . . . how old?
One day? Three?
I have a feeling at the rate I'm going I'll be (1) too well fed and (2) very sick because I'm not careful (e.g., today I ate cut tomatoes) and (3) babied and tendered all the way thru Africa.

But I'm furious that my knowledge about the intense propriety codes of the women here could make me feel like a prostitute just stepping out the door at night!
But imagine, a man came to my door pretending to be looking for someone else, and I know he was after me because he'd also bothered me in the street—damnably annoying, this.

Some lessons learned at Fatma's: Do not be embarrassed or silly or conversational to cover up the fact of the situation—it is what it is and everyone knows that—do not be fatalistic about women—say how it <u>does</u> change, the generations make their way, media, etc.
Have gifts available—bracelets.
Don't talk down to them—they've been and seen it all—perhaps much more than me in a first-person way compared to my reading.
Try to diplomatically get photos.

غرداية 3 جانفي
رسالة إلى أمي
أتمنى لك سنة سعيدة
وعمرا طويل

Ghardaia. le 3/1/76
Chère Mére
Je vous souhaite
une bonne et heureux
vie.

dear mother: i wish you a good and
happy life –
written by a ♀ i met in Ghardaia, Algeria
in Arabic & of course French.
she gave 2 of these cards to me as a gift,
+ i promised to send her "something American"
i'll have to invest <u>weeks</u> in sending "thank yous"
to all the friends i'll meet during this trip!

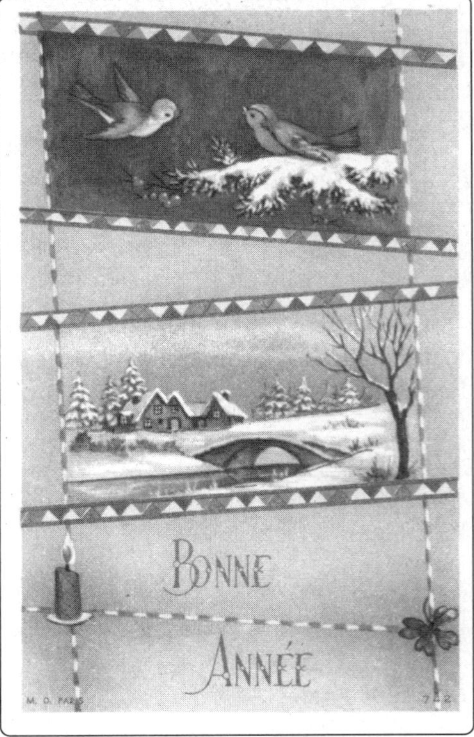

Below the message on her card, I wrote a translation and made a comment:

"Dear Mother, I wish you a good and happy life"
Written by a woman I met in Ghardaïa, in Arabic and of course French.
She gave two of these cards to me as a gift and I promised to send her "something American." I'll have to invest <u>weeks</u> in sending thank-you's to all the friends I'll meet during this trip [2]!

In the ping-pong game I took an offensive (as opposed to a perpetually defensive "female") position. I immediately acquired that security (however false it was: I lost) of being in control, of standing my ground. Needs doing in other realms than ping-pong.

I offer this day to all my sisters who were never able to do this—like all the ones in this town who don't go outside—ever. Literally all the boys with briefcases rush off to afternoon class; the girls play tag with each other.

I don't have any notes about when this happened, but it was most likely in Ghardaïa. I was taken to visit someone in their home. I entered a small, dark living room where a few young women were sitting together; women who for the most part couldn't leave the house. There was a small black & white TV in the corner. They were watching *Bonanza*. I probably expressed surprise or bewilderment that they were watching it. Hopefully I wasn't too rude. But to be in the middle of the Sahara, and to find those young women watching this show? Words failed me then and fail me now.[14]

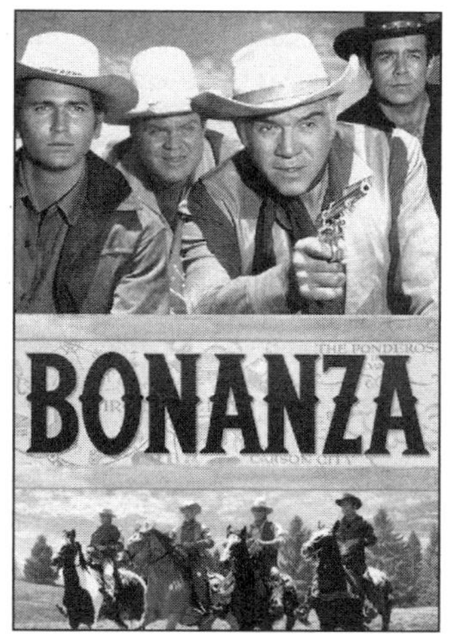

God damn it—how can they have the imperious right to sit back, and with their cool graceful logic and reason WASTE all these lives? These souls of women trampled underfoot, suffocated, always being denied even the slightest human dignity—where the hell is the REAL harmony in this world, not the imposed self-serving harmony of deceitful constructs?
We are not here to be dogs and packhorses and martyrs—we are here to be human, at least somewhat complete—there is absolutely NOTHING of divine motherhood in these women's lives—it stinks outright—

El Moudjahid, the Algerian paper of the Revolution etc. is full of long articles about brotherly camaraderie with VNM (GIAP) and brotherly hatred for imperialists and

14 See [3] for my comments about this situation and my reasons for the following rant.

brotherly cooperative farming and brotherly combat against Saharan occupation and brotherly support for the MPLA.
Get my point? [15]
It's so celibate here, no social contact whatsoever; no wonder the men here are so freaked out to see women/me.
And all the men hang out in the streets "late," until stores close (8:30), I'm sure to avoid the dread of going to a cold house with a disaffected wife and seven kids sleeping around if you did decide to fuck.
What a strange life to impose on oneself for the sake of religion—any god would allow him/herself more pleasure (and it certainly has nothing to do with keeping down a monstrous birthrate).

Men make other men hate (white) women by always giving them preferential treatment and either (1) making the other men wish they were in our/my "comfortable" shoes or (2) making *them* wish to be the one being so gallant.
And the jealous eyes never leave one.

From now on I'm saying that my sister is twenty-four, I'm twenty-three, and that I've been married for two years.

Never trust men.
They never give you any reason to nohow.
Never be so stupid and naïve and assured again as to get yourself in another situation like this eve's.[16]

The issue at hand is this: Since you can never never trust the other/the man to mind his own affair/prick, you must always be vigilant for the old idiot—never assume that he gives a damn. Always expect the worst, and you will probably never be disappointed. Expect good behavior, and you'll be raped. Remember.
And oh their insistence on apology and my forgiveness. La de da. Just a little smile.
If I hadn't gotten very angry and very assertive and not-teasing, the situation could have gone from simply annoying to very nasty.

I could spit on the man sitting next to me (or wherever/whenever) who just by his presence makes it necessary for me to think before I remove a sweater or light a cig. Or or or or or.
And they tell us we're too preoccupied with ourselves! It's their grotesque preoccupation which makes us always prisoners under the lock and key of their constant

15 My point being it's all about revolutions that largely ignored women's revolutionary needs.

16 My friend the writer wrote, "What happened?" alongside that comment, but the specifics don't matter. It was just another night of being intensely harassed by some man—on the street, in a café, breaking into my hotel room, whatever.

observation their lewd eyes their oh shit!
And even the hotel manager oh la de da giving me a purse and conversation and meals and then kissing me good morning and grabbing my breast.
These men will get what they deserve: Nothing in return for the "generosity" which is predicated only on their goddamned Lust.
No *carte postale* or *merci merci*
Creeps
Cochons [*Pigs*]
Salauds [*Shits*]
Men want to be à la mode in every theory, philosophy, etc. except when it has to do with women. Give them anything with which to exercise their nasty high-handed minds and they'll be chipper—but just ask them to once examine their own consciences instead of everyone (race/sex) else's . . . !

My dates and some narratives in the journal and letters conflict, but I probably left Ghardaïa on the 6th and got to Ain Salah that night (about 410 miles, and on a paved road). I got a ride on a truck from a friend of the hotel owner in Ghardaïa, but I have no name for him, and no description, just a few photographs.

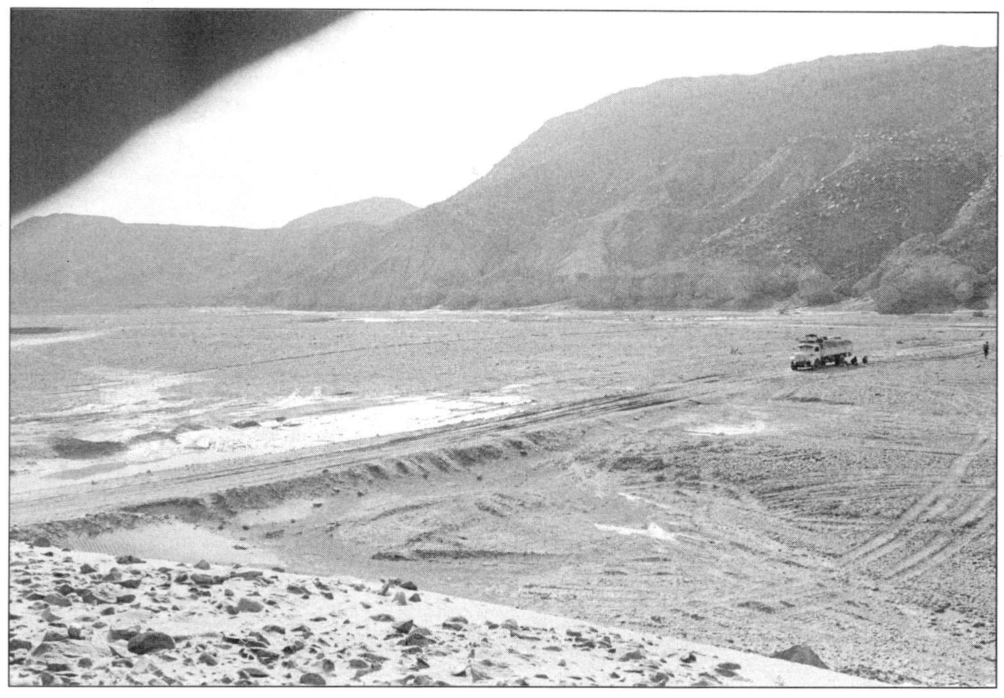

When the truck made a pit stop, I walked away a little distance and scrawled this directive/plea in the sand by the side of the road. It was a Francophone country, so I figured that it wouldn't be understood, or at least it would only be after I was safely gone.

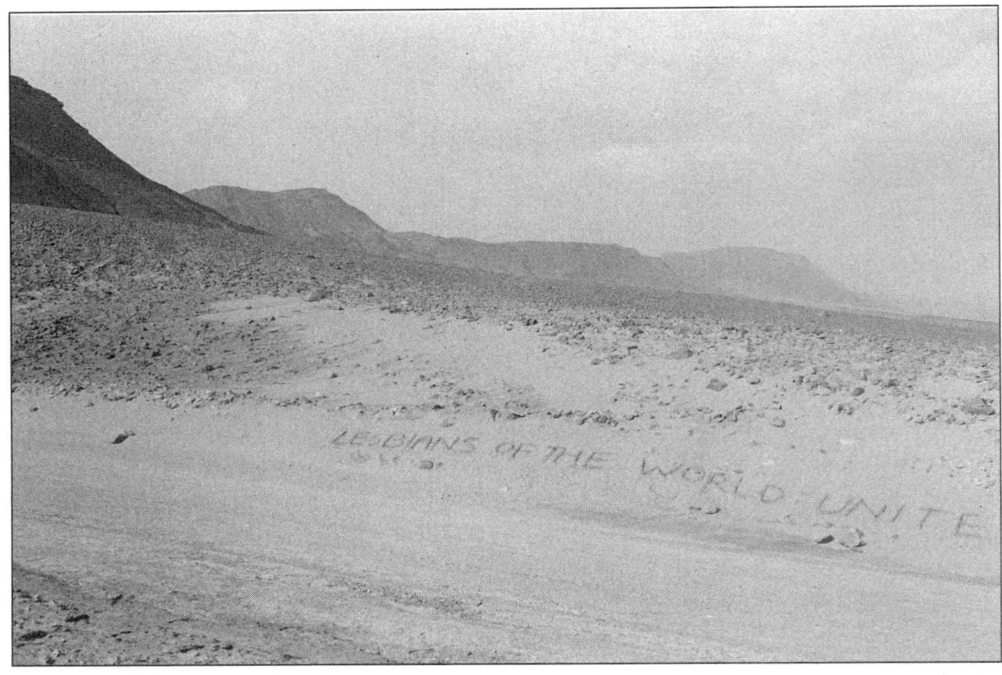

LESBIANS OF THE WORLD UNITE

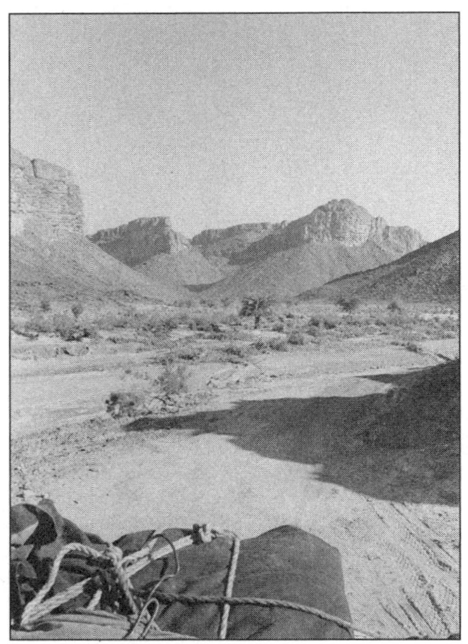

In Ain Salah, I looked around for a truck heading south to Tamanrasset, which is the main stopping point midway through the Sahara. It's another 410 miles, but now it would be slow going on the piste.

I got a ride on a truck filled with dates. Millions and millions of dates. An elderly Algerian couple was also getting a ride. There was only room for them in the cabin with Alan, the driver, so I sat in the open air on top of the date mountain. And ate a lot of them.

The driver (and the other drivers I traveled with later) cooked over an open fire when we stopped for the night and included me in the meals. We slept at night on the sand. This was the first of many nights when I was freezing, despite wearing all my clothes and being inside a duck down sleeping bag. Most people on the trucks usually had nothing more than a thin cotton cloth with which to cover themselves, and I could see them shivering, quite intensely. From day to night, the desert temperature can drop fifty or sixty degrees, so if it's a day-time high of eighty degrees, you're facing a very cold night.

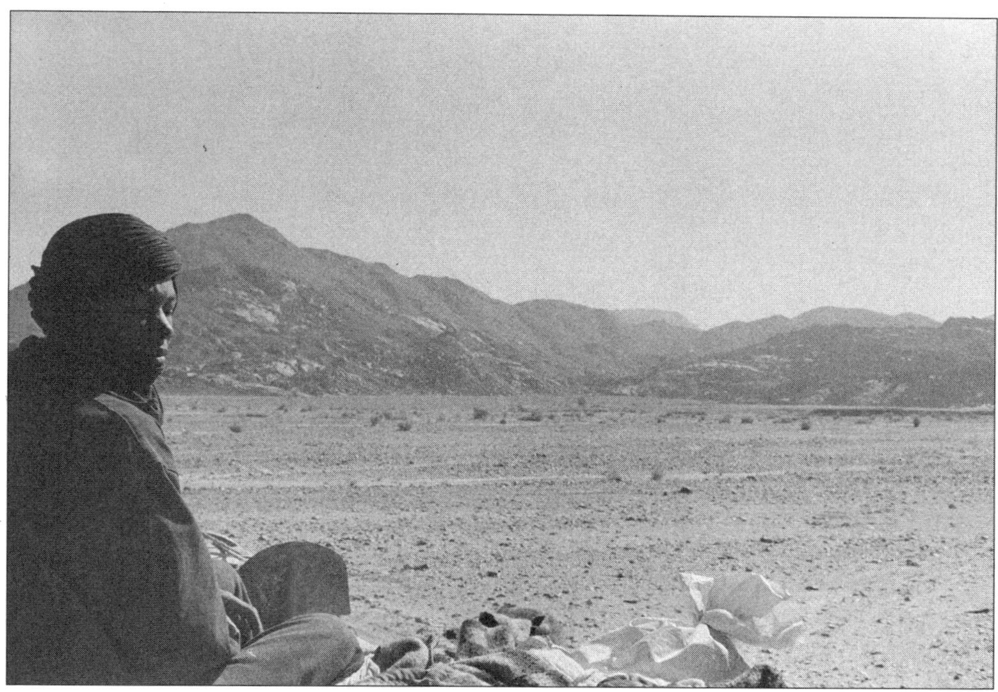

JANUARY 7 & 8

How little is so much when one has to "make do." 27 mph; 37 mph was really a treat.

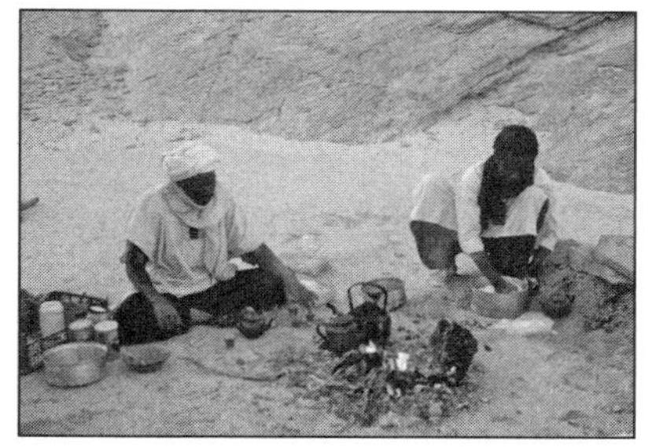

Tea . . . 3x. . . Use one small glass to measure the tea, add a handful of mint and lots of sugar.
We're served 3 glasses in successsion; the first one is the strongest in flavor and not as sweet, but by the last, the taste isn't as strong but it's much sweeter

Date pits are like perfectly formed vulvas.

We passed through Tadjemout—a village with Tuaregs—and the gorge of Arak—24 miles of a gorge with trees.

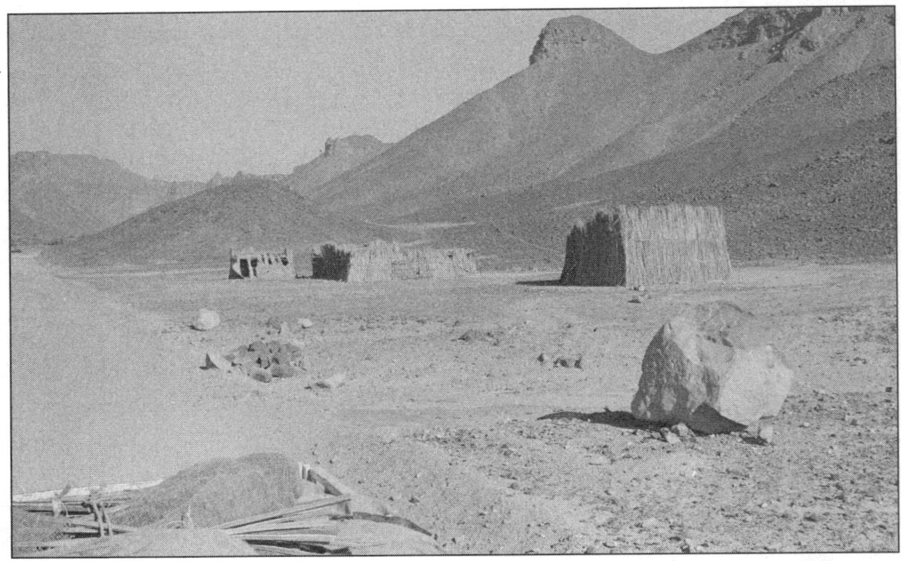

The encampments/shelters of the Tuaregs

Never trust men
Ditto until the day I die, or give up.
The latter, never. The former, a vague possibility.
Beautiful mountains of all rock, softly shaped by the ocean millions of years before man became the prick he has made himself.
The creep wouldn't even eat—he pouted, if you can imagine [4]!
Men are such spoiled brats. They want to make, bake, eat and fuck their cake and then freeze-dry it for posterity.

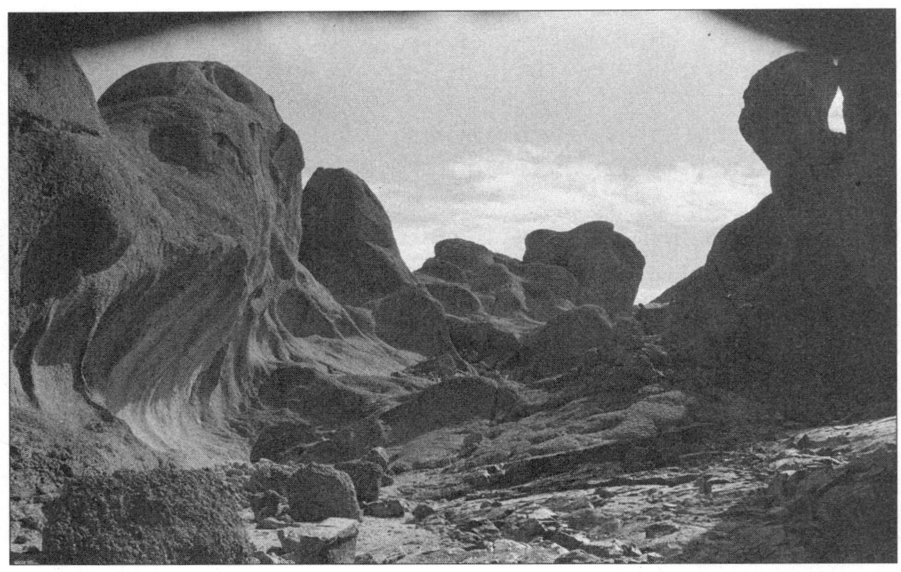

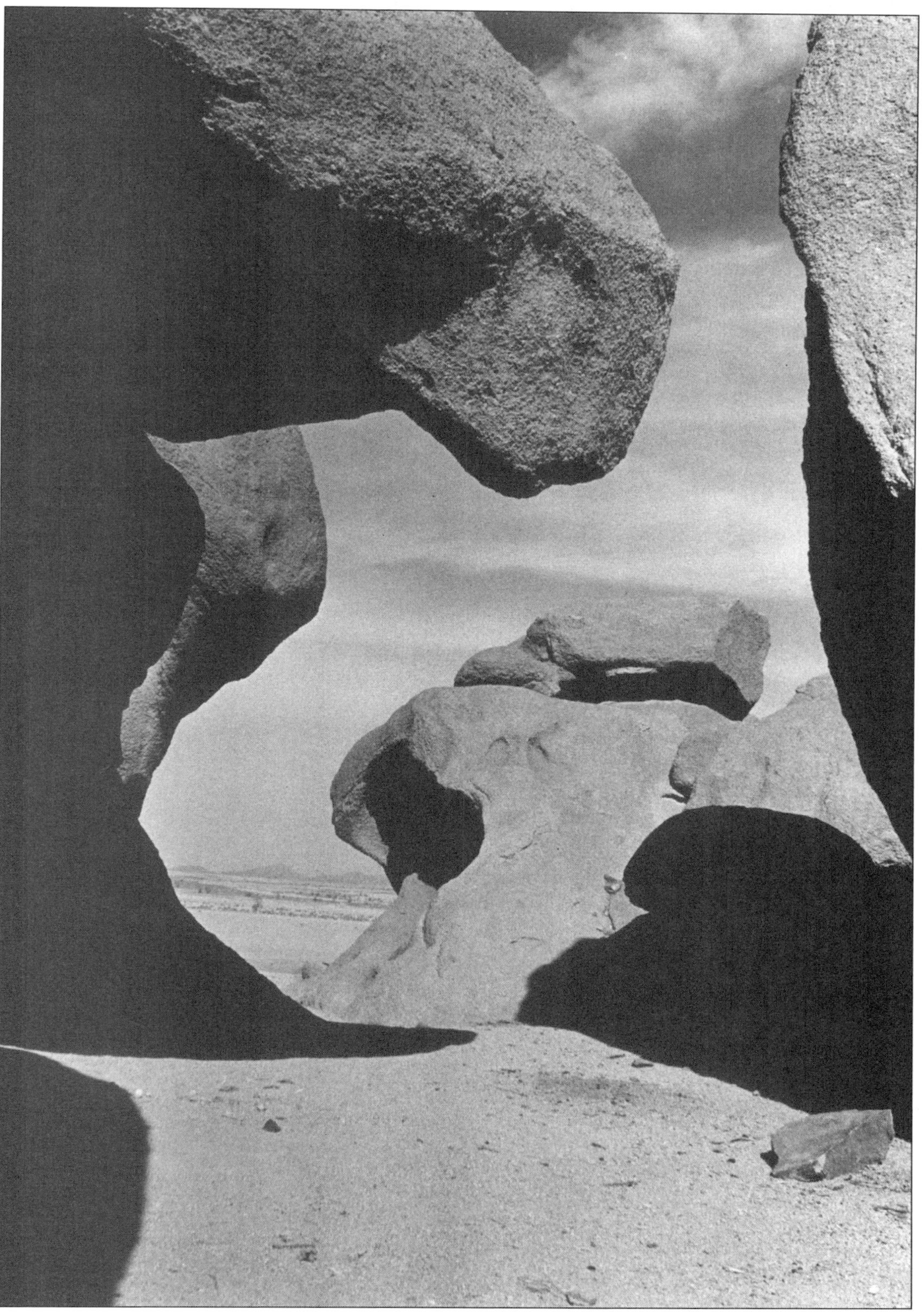

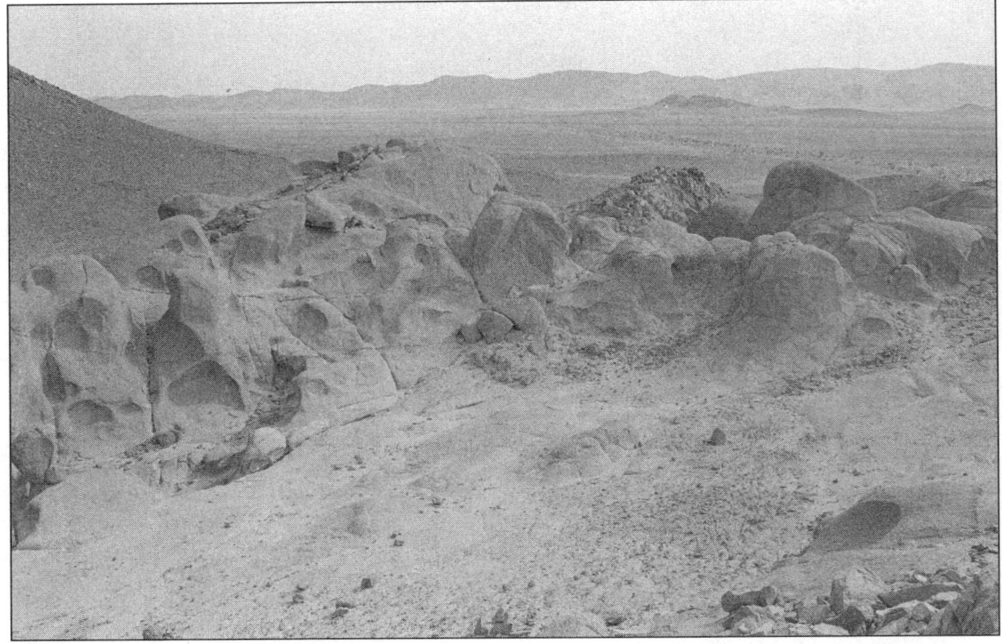

I can't imagine, after being in the Sahara for five days, why anyone would go to the moon to try and make it inhabitable—we have our own moon on earth, and no population explosion could ever fill this up!

And it's really disgusting (thirteen years after independence) to think that the prissy pretentious arrogant civilized French ever presumed to own this land—it is Arab thru and thru, it is inextricably theirs. And Arabic is an exquisite language, tonally—the short round sounds, the clipped ends, and the guttural bubbly quality all sound beautiful in these vast silences and dusty towns.

Crossing the desert makes life seem somewhat ridiculous, very tenuous; we all hang on to whatever's given us as reality—life—culture.

Here's an effort I made at the time to describe this method of travel. . .

Take for example an oven grill. Enlarge the rungs to a three-inch diameter. And make it a conveyor belt.

Put on six-odd layers of dusty clothing, including crusty underpants.

Sit on a backless chair on a pillow on top of a bottle, some cans, bread, and other objects.

Waft some powdery sand through the air, light a cigarette, place a light bulb seven inches from your eyes and a fan blowing a cool strong draft at your lower back.

Continue in this for forty-eight hours, with a parenthesis of a stronger colder wind and some gritty soup.

Call it adventure.

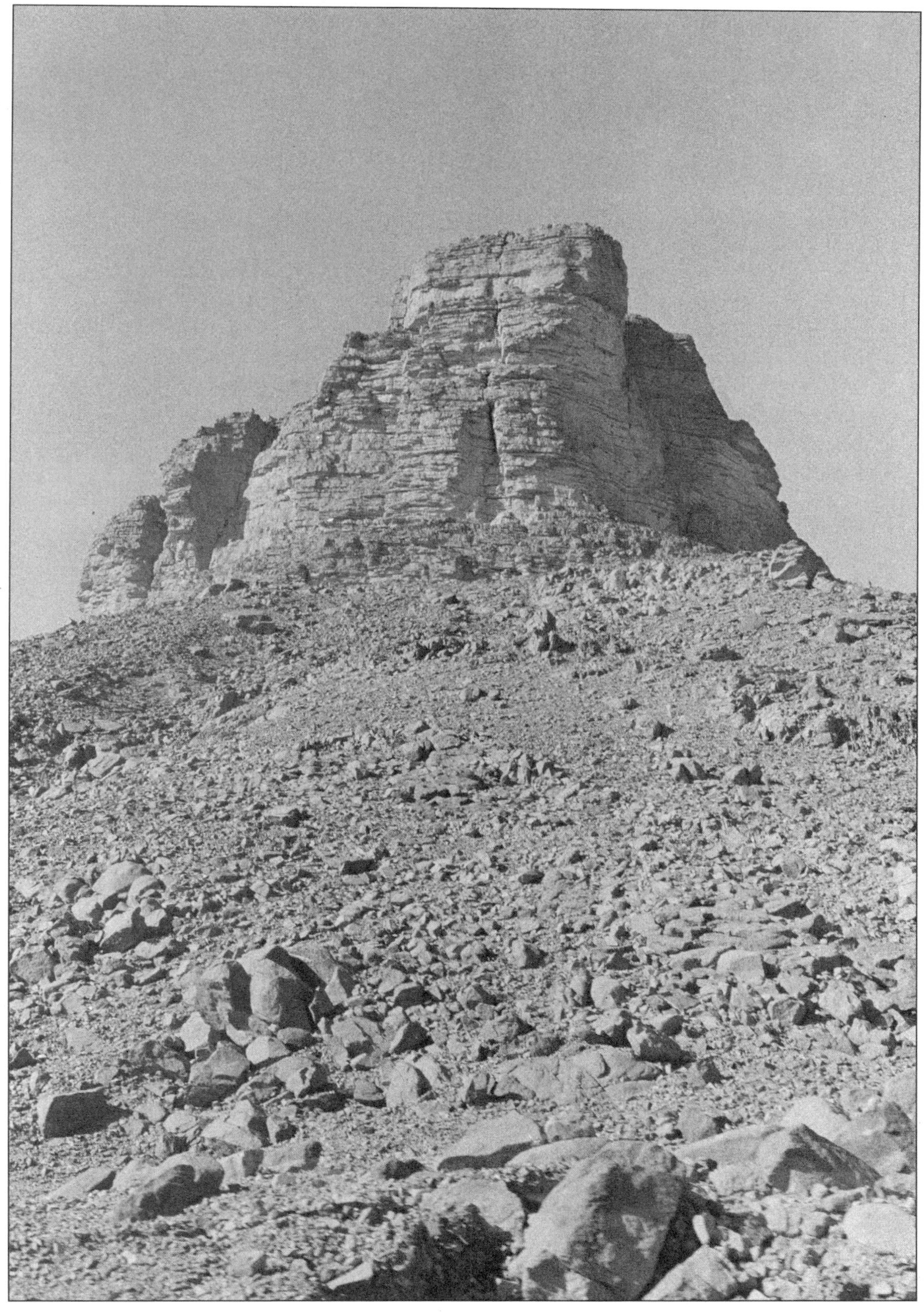

One cannot ingratiate oneself/break the ice with the desert people by smiling; I have yet to see an even remotely substantial grin. Life is hard here, something to be dealt with.

Women at puberty, and men when they grow facial hair, are majors according to the religion, and the religion is what makes THE laws here (as compared to any recently imposed governmental stipulations).

What is it that draws me to these voyages? A woman of purpose, no doubt, but what purpose? Will I ever have (want?) the pragmatism to deal with daily life, full of responsibilities, or am I to continue this? If so, fine—I'm beginning to believe. To clarify the ravine that exists between my spouted ideas and my actions, between my absolute dream world which always keeps me away from much *nourritures terrestres* [fruits of the earth] and my urgency to *faire le bien pour le monde* [to do good for the world].
Aren't I the Christian!

The entire US could be under siege, and I wouldn't know . . . except that the invariable companion of these desert travelers is the radio—and they seem to pick up every known language.
Alan is really a good driver after fifteen years of doing this route—in the pitch dark he maneuvered thru rivers of sand, losing sight of the "road" for long spaces, weaving around—and I understand now how simple it would be to be lost, forever.

I like being dirty and jolted and bread fed.
700kms, two nights, and three days of food: $12.50 [17]

17 In 2024, $12.50 = $71.00

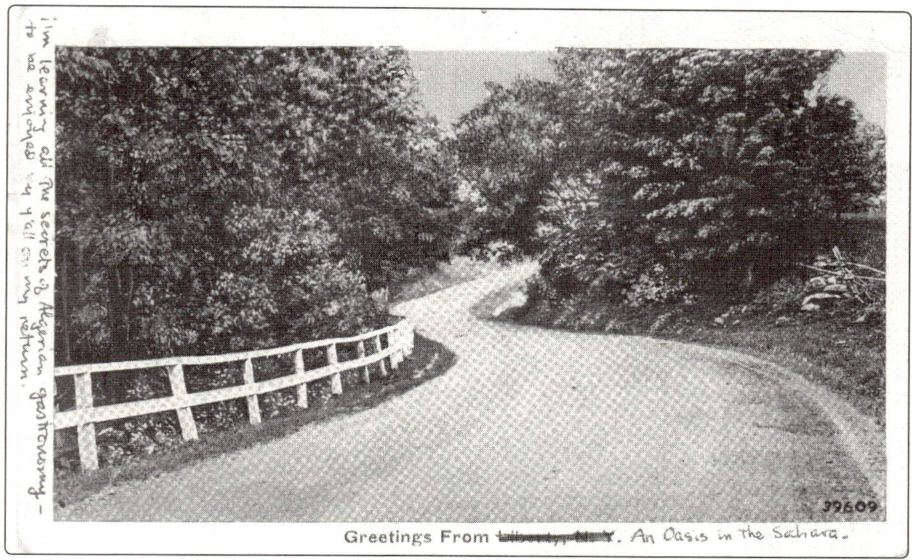

A POSTCARD TO CINDY:

Dear Cindy,
Without the colors, the picket fence, the leaves, and the grass, it's a remarkable likeness; the road is the same.
And I've been absorbing the colors for days *sans cesse* [continually] atop a truck carrying billions of dried dates. My head is wrapped all day in a shawl, dusty inside & out, and cool nights of couscous & tea & the mountains & silence all around. I broke my 35mm lens—bounced & jolted the diaphragm into dysfunction, a very expensive & irreparable damage so early on the trip—a few tears & a lot of anger, also a bit freaked out by being alone with truck drivers & emptiness all around, but a family is with us, so things are as ok as possible. Very effective alienation occurs between me & the women—I'm more or less "one of the boys"— i.e., I sit by the fire, I talk, I smoke, & the woman and child sit apart (and we don't share a common language)—traveling is an obnoxiously endless chain of meeting men!
My lips are sunburnt, my hair is 2 weeks dirty, & our top speed is 26 mph ... I'll write at length later. Salut to all—eat some dates in commemoration of my sore ass. I'm still working on that torture article!
Love,
Su
P.S. I'm learning all the secrets of Algerian gastronomy—to be enjoyed by y'all on my return.

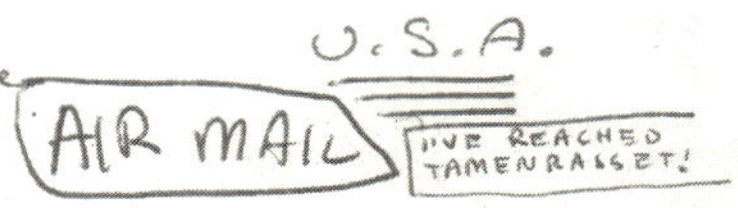

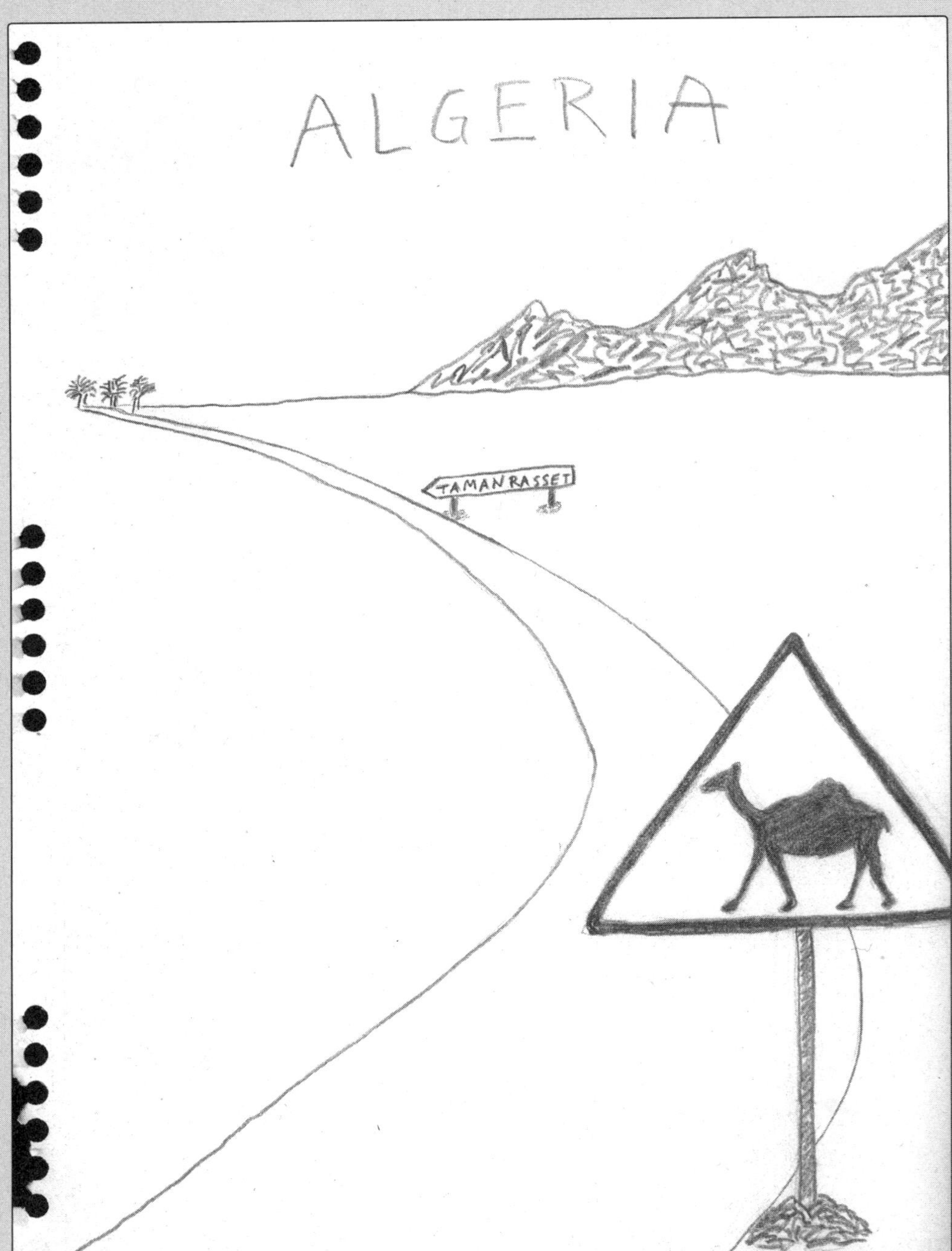
ALGERIA
TAMANRASSET

CHAPTER FIVE

Miriam and Saliha in Tamanrasset

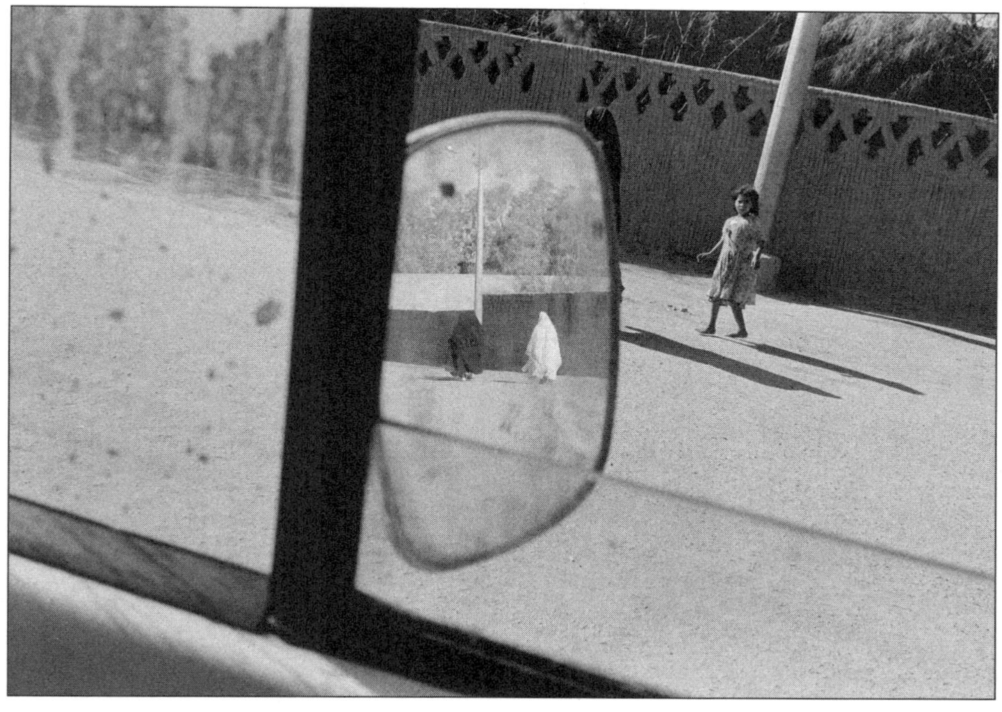

JANUARY 9. TAMANRASSET. HALF WAY. HEARTACHES.

Tamanrasset is an ancient oasis town midway through the Sahara. I stayed there for four days and three nights—the first two nights at the campground, the last one with Saliha.

The tourists! I'm at a campsite and they're a riot. Absolutely loaded down with shit, being so bourgeois and tanned and adventurous.
A very whatever Italiano made conversation with me at the water faucet with the opening phrase (and a laugh), "This is the first time I'm doing this in my life, it's women's work."
He was washing a lousy sweatshirt that had "Property of Playboy Photo Department" on it.

What did I see in the store today but, lo and behold . . . Nestlé's NIDO, that insidious baby food.

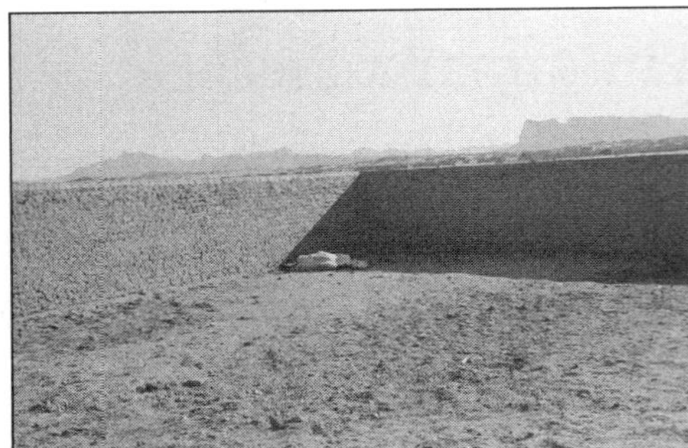

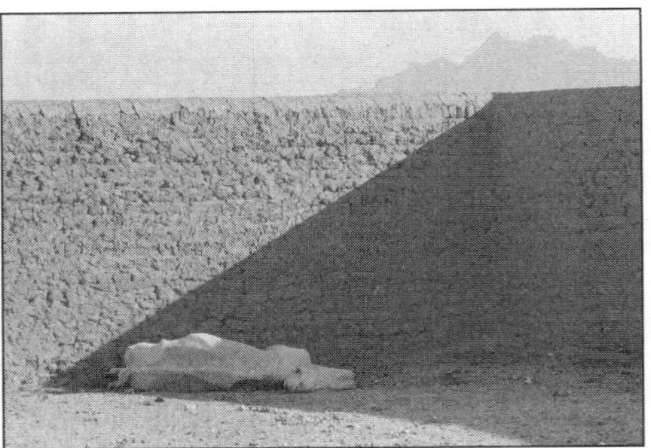

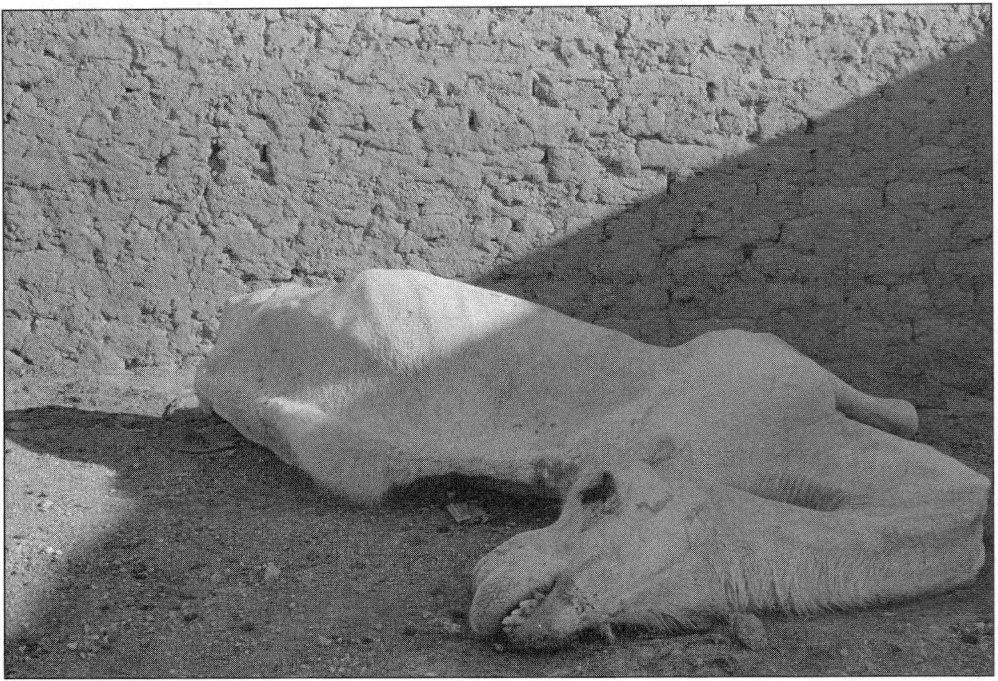

The soldiers here are disgusting (because of their forced celibacy)—I want to spit at their feet when they whistle and gawk—and a French woman in a bathing suit at the campground was constantly being voyeured by "visiting" soldiers. *PIGS.*
Now I know why I found Moussa [at the youth hostel in Marseille] so comradely and easy to feel close to—he was one of those rare men with whom I don't feel a pressing sexuality, a "summing up" of my "capabilities" going on all the time—he seemed to be able to interest himself in me as more than a pretty fuck.

This little dry quiet town is plastered with pro-Spanish-Saharan posters.

The well-dressed, more modern Algerians are generally the light-skinned ones; the Blacks were once the slaves here and are still proportionately the poorer class.

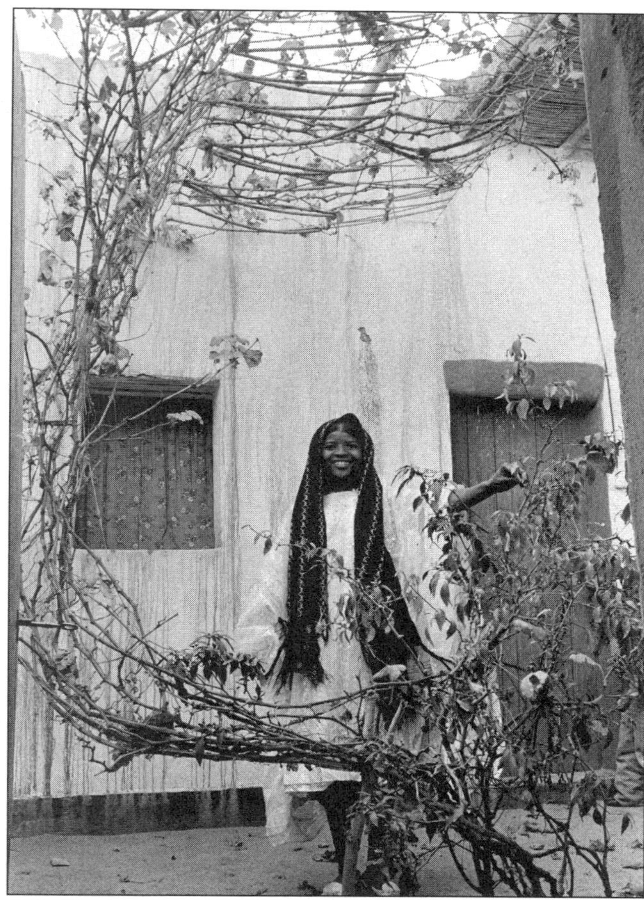

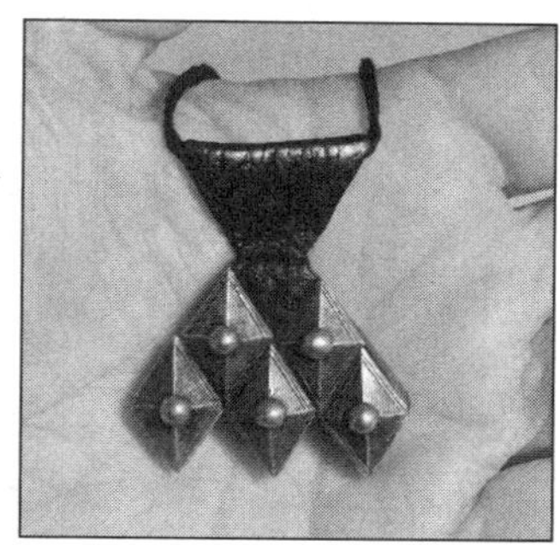

An afternoon surprise invitation to the home of Miriam [Miriam Bint Boudjema], about twenty-one years old with three kids, married since she was twelve years old; her eldest daughter is seven.

She invited me for tea, gave me a Tuareg necklace piece, and I had nothing to give in return—must fix that.

They wore lovely sparkling dresses, she in black and gold, the others in acid green, pinks, gold. She had a gas stove, cool in the noon sun, three rooms, very clean, a soft sand floor. She learned how to knit and sew in a school for girls (now they also learn to write) . . . was in school for seven years . . . The women weave blankets here, lovely bright striped ones, many colors.

No shame in her, or apology, she seemed very pleased with her home, with being able to invite me in for tea.

She was very gentle and friendly, calm, wanted me to photograph her kids.

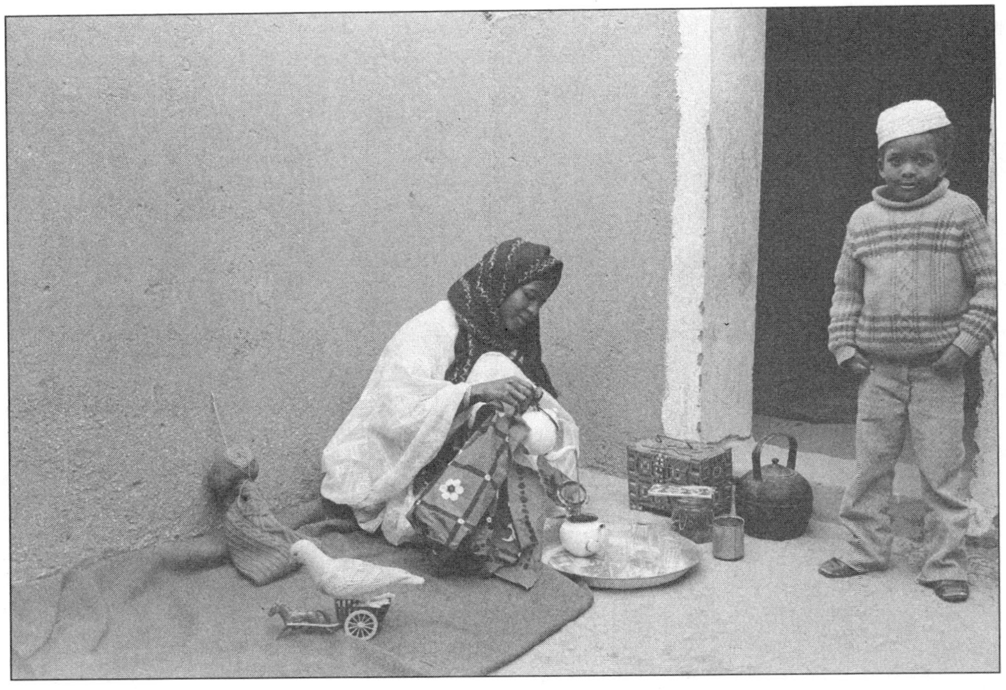

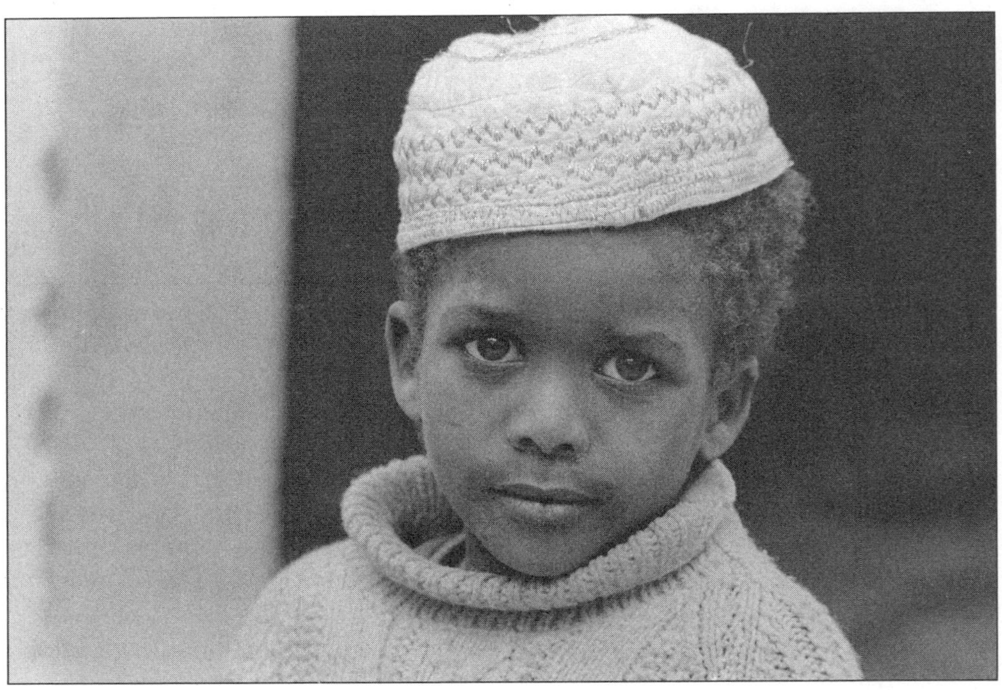

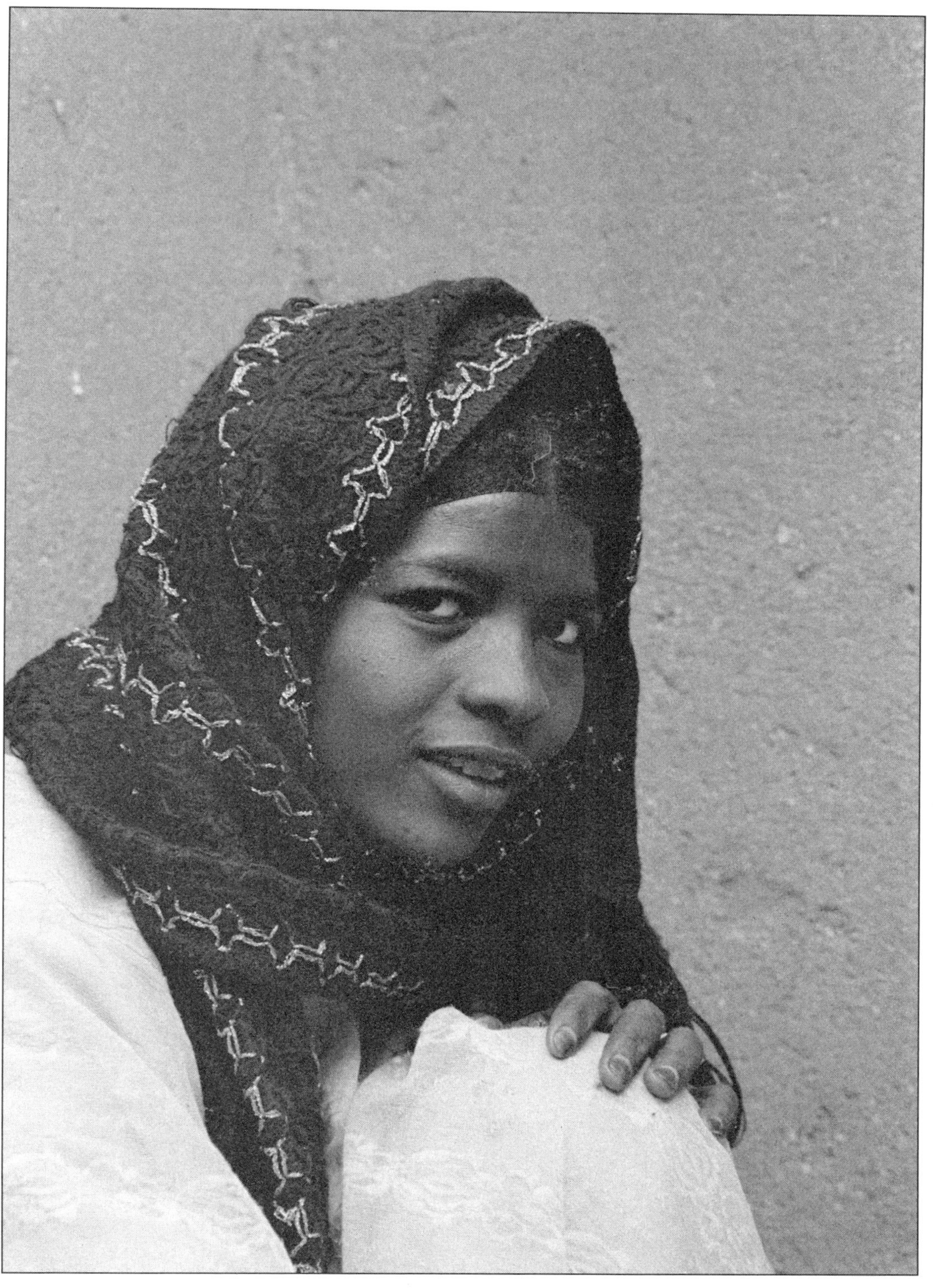

Some Britishers from the campsite invited me with them to a restaurant in order, as one said with a certain undertone, "to taste the local dishes" i.e., couscous *à la* Paris, by way of Algeria.
Two Rhodesians[18] at the dinner wanted to know if Americans were sympathetic to them compared to the Black Rhodesians. When I said no, I felt their minds stiffen into deafness; they didn't want to hear/know hatred. But they'd better learn to listen or they'll find their pants on fire.
Most of the group is headed for South Africa, but the Britishers are going to Rhodesia, to work in Salisbury. Frank is a CPA, Juliette is married to him; she will work as a secretary, doesn't have a profession.
I just can't believe the near-sightedness of those Britishers going there at a time like this—??
The English are so dull.

Su, do not generalize. But it's so hard not to when one finds all their responses so anticipate-able.
I'm so tired of every evening being thrown into contact with another man (men) who are all so eager to invite me to eat, café, take a tour of the town, etc. Makes me wanna oooo hide.
It's like standing in an inescapable circle and being thrown from one person's arms to another's, tossed into . . . what next?
They're playing Lightnin' Hopkins and Jelly Roll Morton at the Tamanrasset Hotel.

On to bigger and less personal issues:
I love this land. I love the space the barren land the rosy mountains at sunset the deepest blue sky the welcome relief of soft green bushes the absoluteness of it the tenuousness the time to think to lose the watchful eyes of crowds—no mirrors no billboards no Musak no speed—a gracious heady lassitude.

Because of the visa restrictions and how far it was to In Guezzam—the border between Algeria and Niger—I had to start looking for a way to get there.

These are times that try a woman's soul.
I really do feel frantic, a thousand miles in either direction from a bus, and no tourists have room in their Jeeps or Land Rovers, and no trucks are safe—
Freak out, quietly, surely.
I can't ask for some string, a cigarette store, a plane fare, listen to good blues, take a stroll, rent a cabin, or ask the time without being surreptitiously or overtly invited to fuck.
The ground is dropping out, I really am alone this time (and no plane).
How could I ever talk about being a political lesbian in these here parts? It's difficult for them to understand even a non-married state (for a woman).

18 Rhodesia was renamed Zimbabwe in April 1980 after a complicated move from colonial rule to independence. See [1] for more info about Cecil Rhodes and his contemptible "Pioneer Column."

And is this what Freud meant by penis envy?: Being in the desert alone, dependent entirely on potential rapists, and <u>wishing to hell I was a man.</u>
God I'm nervous. And at this point I'm going to defy my visa if it means waiting for a safe ride. Fuck national boundaries, I'm <u>not</u> going to be raped.
And me, not being a racist, would never say (or need to say) that Algerian men are distinctively boorish or aggressive. But I credit them with being as piggish as their fellow men the world around.

Should I trust this polite army boy with his friend the truck driver, after he tells me that well, if he's not *très gentil* [very nice] then I should write him (after the fact) and he'd feel bad, it would be worse for him than for me, he says. Christ shit.
Given how many rapists there are in the world, every man I meet seems to have a suspiciously large # of trustworthy "friends."

My sanity on this trip is predicated on me "accepting" myself as a total freak.

Imagine being able to go for hours or sometimes days at a time without seeing a man except for furtive appearances on side streets—and then how weird it would be to see an uncovered unabashed man walking through this woman's environment: That is precisely what I find here—in reverse. I am in a man's world and all the so-called "rhetoric" about woman's historic invisibility is not metaphorical. The world begins to feel every day more like a prison.

JANUARY 10

This a.m. out walking I met Saliha [Aroun-Rachid], dressed *à la mode*. She invited me home, we talked for several hours while she made an Algerian delicacy (I think it's called "brages," made from corn meal and crushed dates, either layered or rolled into a ball and then flattened and fried—really delicious!)

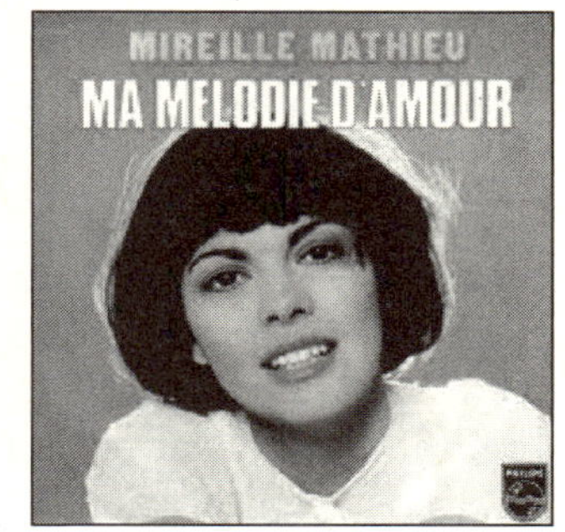

She's an engineer, studied for four years in France, two years in Algiers, has lived in Tamanrasset now for six months with her husband (he also arrived then).
She says fixing machines runs in her family, is in her blood. That women in Algiers were certainly freer than in the south but nevertheless the men can direct their wives even in Algiers; for example, she loves to wear short skirts and showed me many photos of herself in them (and on her Honda motorbike)—now, *le mari* [the husband] decrees they must be below the knees, discreet, etc.
Saliha's father had two wives (one blonde one brown) and together amassed thirteen children. She showed me pics of herself dressed traditionally—quite a change!
When asked about a typically American gift to be sent to her, she requested a wig, like Mireille Mathieu. After we broke the ice for a few hours she opened up to me,

saying for example how many more responsibilities she has daily than *le mari*, who only has to work and rest—she, while at work, thinks of housework, etc. and said men don't really have any idea how much women have to do—there was a blinding moment of contact between us—albeit bitter—in agreeing on that one given. And when her (very handsome, etc.) *mari* arrived for lunch, she spoke less, he spoke towards me (perhaps natural since I was a guest) and then brought out four volumes of a (forbidden) history of the Algerian War—he lost fifteen family members—told me about the OAS [2]—the French who wanted independence for the French only, in Algeria—and the FLN, the guerillas in Algeria. The first attack was made in late October '54 at Arres by six men.
The women were prominent bomb makers (and certainly there were many others less notorious); one was killed living in Algiers.

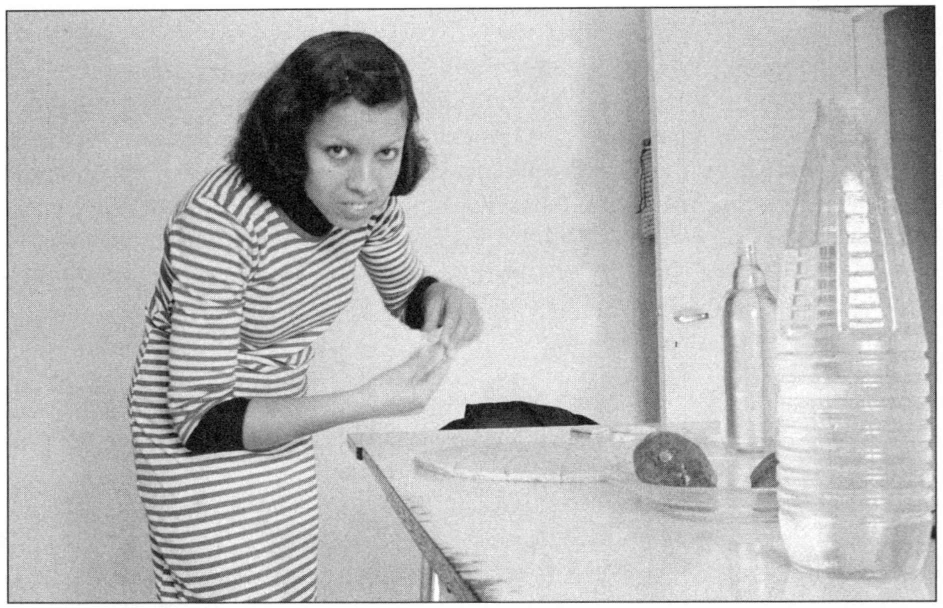

They live in a group of twenty-one homes. They have a huge living room, three couch mattresses, bedroom and kitchen and bath, traditional art décor, quite nice: but there can never be parties here, large gatherings of young friends for the evening . . . Their housing is entirely paid for by the government, plus a good salary; there is such a need for technicians that they are babied and indulged to all extremes. She expressed happiness with life in Tamanrasset, its peacefulness, etc.

There was an absolutely delightful twenty-eight-year-old woman who lived near Saliha. She was forced into marriage at age sixteen to a forty-five-year-old man who left her after one month to go work in France. He will not give her a divorce/release, and hence she lives with her brother and sister-in-law (with their several kids; she has none) and may not leave the house—she can't even go to the market!

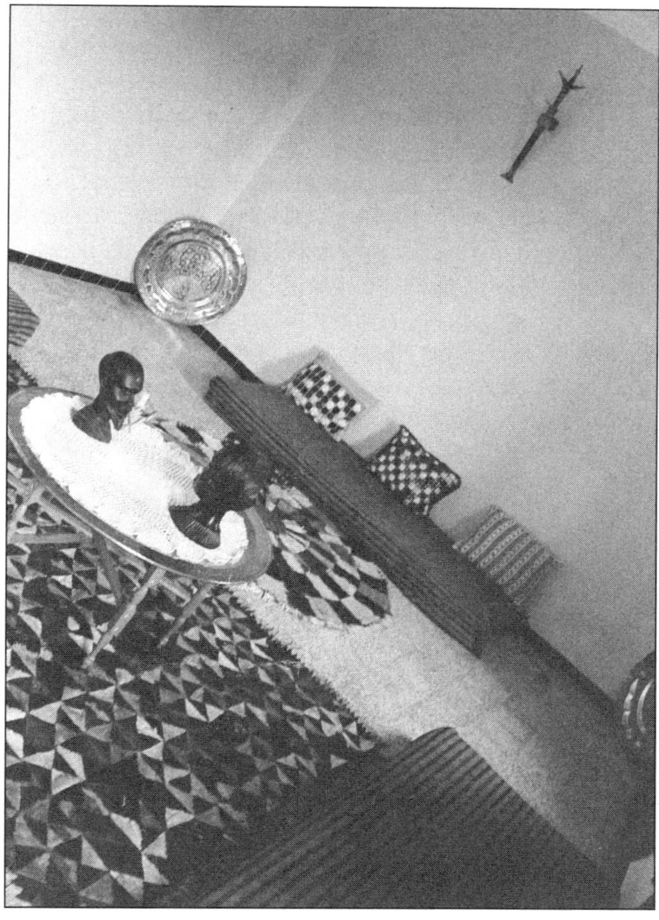

I'm guessing she was able to come over because it was close by and because she was visiting a woman.

She arrived in a bright fuchsia blouse, a blue and white scarf with a live rose tucked in, she was cheerful and very un-shy, none of the retiring quality. Saliha told me that her friend so much wants to be *à la mode*, to work or study or travel, and absolutely cannot.
It almost seemed as if she (the other woman) was free in an ironic way, no children, no hardships with *le mari* like Saliha had told me about, none of the burden and shame or hardness that gets ingrained into women who are exposed daily (or however often) to sex with a dutiful cold husband—as if being celibate she had cried it all out of her and was now somewhere else, mentally. That of course is only from the impression she gave; I didn't have a chance to talk much with her.
Saliha, a professional woman and quite modern, exposed to me much of her own sadness and just plain disgust with the constant regulation of her/their lives.

When I left Saliha that day, she invited me to come back the next day and spend the night at her house.

Rented a bike, it was nice.
Tamanrasset has a string of red-green-white lights on the streets—the colors of Algeria. Ironically, the posters all over town say: *Halte à l'Aggression*. I wish they would extend that beyond the Spanish Saharan issue. (My life is founded on wishful thinking—)
Janis Joplin was right on target—no subtlety, no mincing of words, because this existence is not for the fragile, is not reparable.

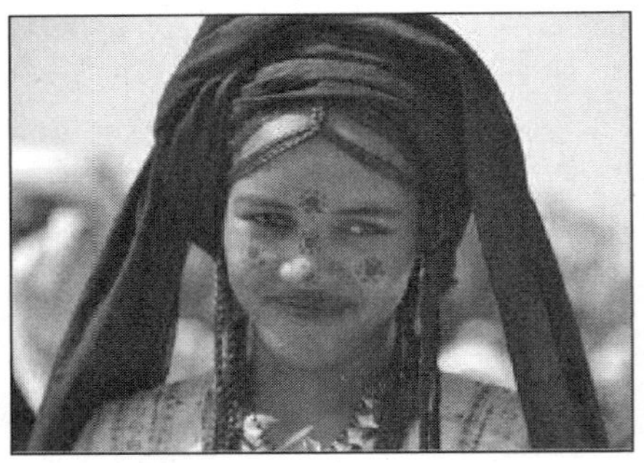

Saw Tuareg women today with blue lips and lovely necklaces and uncovered faces. They apparently are the ones to choose their husbands, and the husband does the cooking. Today at the grand market I saw the first sign of "normal" human contact between an Algerian woman and man since I've been here: Two Tuaregs were walking along with their arms around each other—so simple, yet so hard to imagine here—
Algerian women cannot marry French men, but the reverse, yes.
The Tuareg women are very cheerful on the streets and quite intrigued by tourists.

11 JANUARY

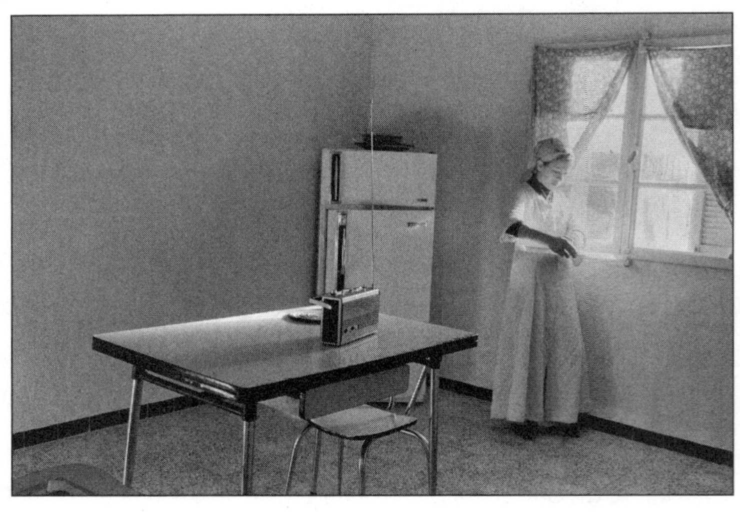

Another Tuareg gift, of tea. Send photos. Saliha and her husband and I went out . . . He admires a certain modernity which however he won't permit his wife—we walk through the back streets to keep from men's eyes—they want a few women to be "free"—i.e., available—but their own, NO.
While he and I sit over an Algerian guide book, she makes bread and cookies and washes dishes and tells me she's been working all day (Sunday). And when at dinner she asks me if I'll marry and I say no, he flinches and grins, and she looks at me with wide eyes and a big smile and says, "That's better."
I've noticed the Algerians are really abashed if I say my parents are separated; it's still a taboo thing here I suspect.
Dinner was couscous with vegetables (onions and hard peas and chickpeas)—very good.

At the other woman's house. Her sister has six kids, each a year apart.
On TV, a puppet American show like *Buck Rogers* (we used to watch it). A show with Giap [3] speaking to his socialist brothers about American imperialism. First time to see such an affair on TV; of course there's nothing like it in the states.
They expressed great pride in him, repeatedly praised the great struggles of Algeria, Vietnam, Cuba, etc.

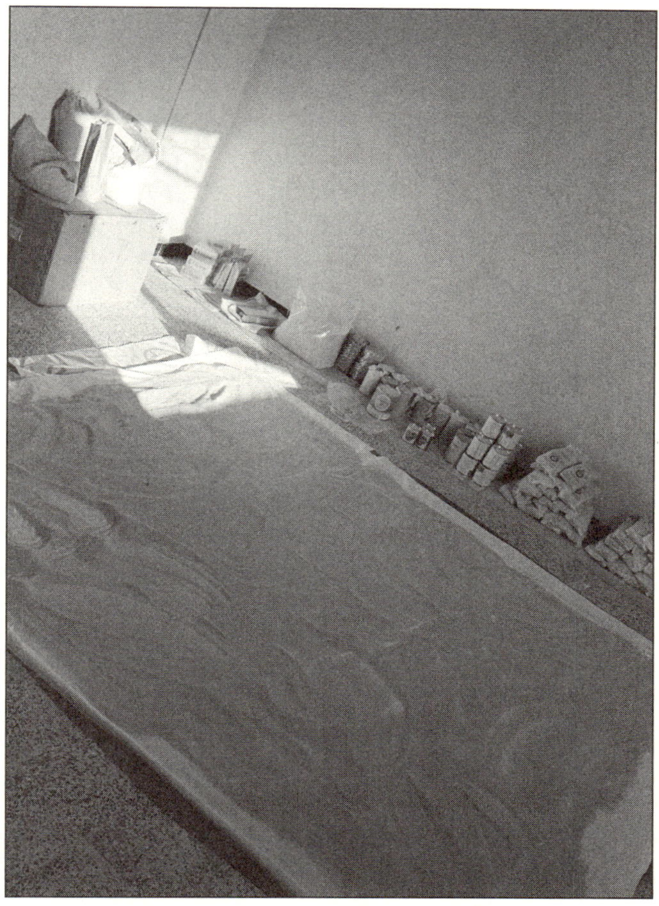
The couscous grain laid out on Saliha's floor to dry

The living room—two mattresses, a TV, a heater, and a lot of empty space. The women chatted together, her husband watched TV. They had purchased a rug and cloth at the fair, it was exhibited proudly. They seemed to be talking about babies and clothes.
Night after night.
A strong handshake from the women.
On the news, wars everywhere.
Vive la militaire, n'est-ce pas?
[Long live the military, right?]

This was an evening when I was smack in the middle of the *most* of a certain life which petrifies me because of its lack of substance beyond the most immediate, and the weirdness of that for me, and the fascination, and the conflict of wanting (needing?) to be exposed to it as well as wishing to (and knowing I can't) "escape" it (psychologically or physically)—
What does it mean for these women to be locked into a furnitureless room with a TV playing fifteen-year-old American children's programs and dreaming of the good life in the West (America)?
I asked Saliha what books she might like. She said he reads but not her, she only wants a wig; at first I was disappointed, but then after watching her do housework from the time we came in until bedtime . . .
Tomorrow, departure. Isis, watch over me[19]—please let camaraderie vanquish any violence from the driver—I think it will.

19 I was referring to the Egyptian goddess Isis, not the jihadist group.

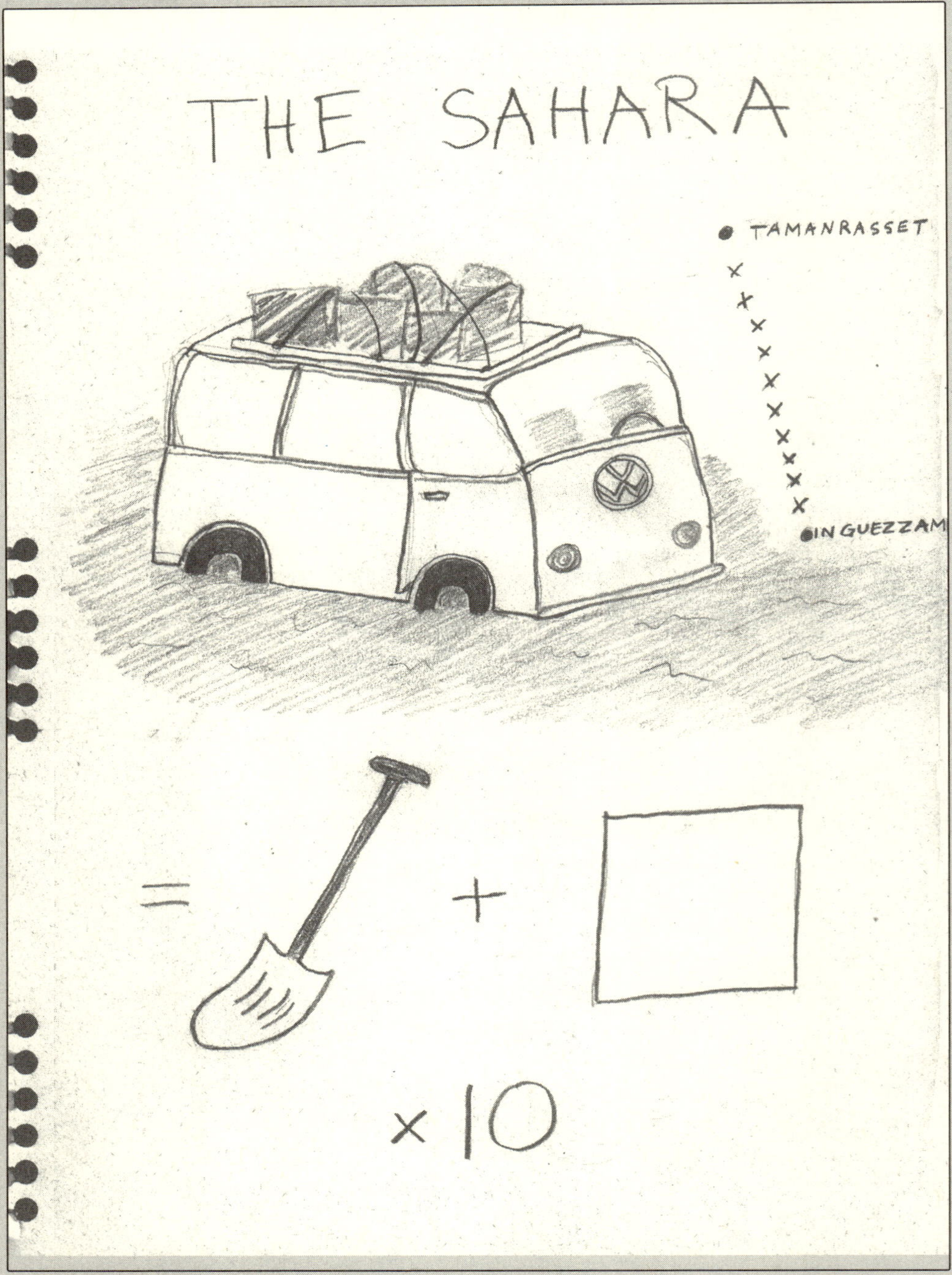

THE SAHARA

TAMANRASSET

IN GUEZZAM

= +

×10

CHAPTER SIX

Goodbye Saliha, Hello Lere! And . . . Good Riddance, Lere, Hello Sanity!

The plan was to travel further with Alan, the driver who had given me a ride to Tamanrasset.

JANUARY 12 & 13

Alan has two houses; the Tamanrasset one has a TV in his bedroom which has a straw mat and tires and crates. A shower. An open-air kitchen with an old stove and the familiar tea and coffee pots from the truck. It's nice for me to be invited in and be able to just sit on the floor in a negligibly "dirty" room and have tea and ignore the environment because (1) he isn't "ashamed" or apologetic for it and (2) it's the human rapport that alleviates the tacky environment [1].

When I asked him about a knife he said, "*Quoi, pour égorger le chauffer?*" ["Why? To stab the driver?"] and laughed. I smiled.

I sure am getting a taste of theory vs. praxis.

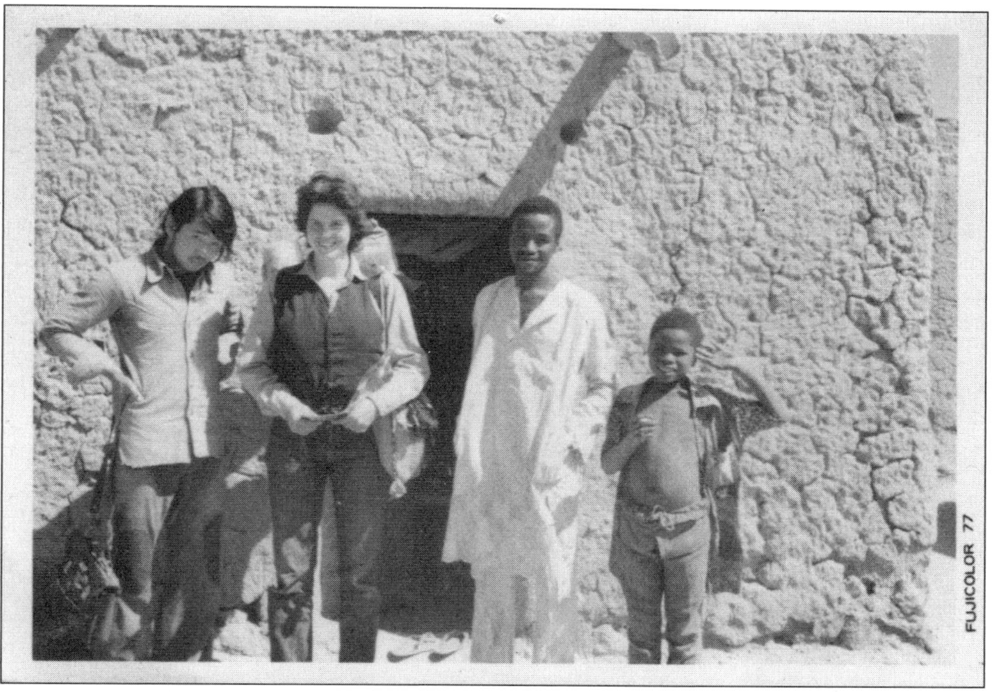

With Alan and a Japanese guy who was also planning to go south with Alan

One waits. It's a pastime and profession here, where little changes and a lot means a lot.
Today in deciding on a ride I was just getting ready (as usual) to put politeness/his "feelings" before my needs, i.e., to not take a different ride because the Japanese guy and I had made a deal with Alan, but I changed plans and then discovered that Alan wouldn't have left anyway, so it was for the best. We're heading off with Lere, who's been living in West Germany.

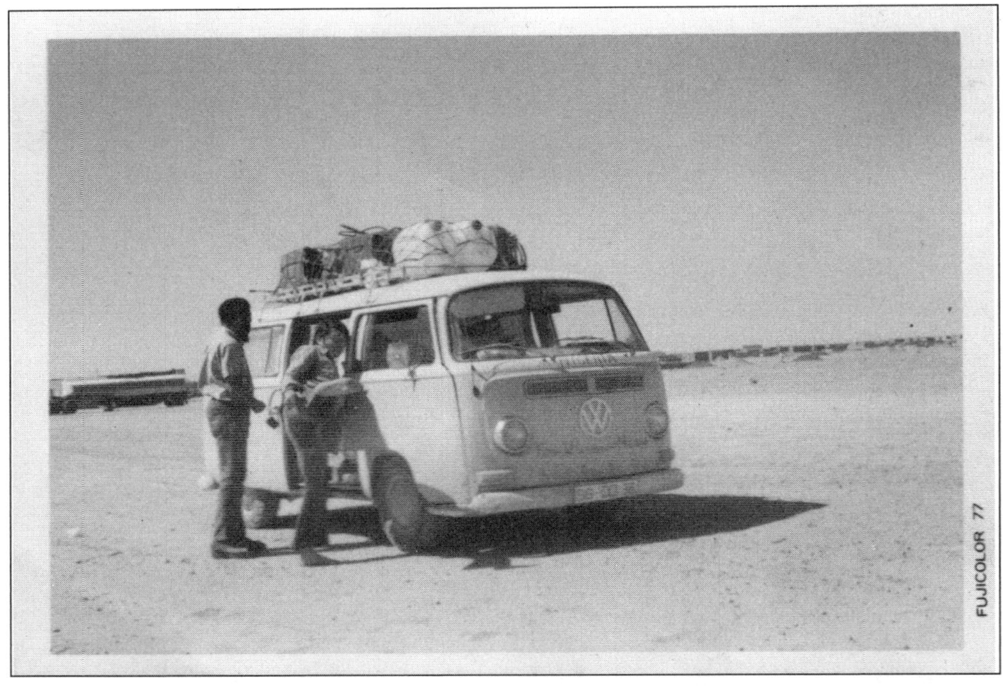

On the front and side of the van, he'd written
"From W Germany to W State Nigeria by road across N + C Africa"

I really admire the itinerants with one little bag and one outfit. "You gotta have nothing if you wanna be free." But me, loaded down with books and papers and enlarging concerns . . .

Saliha muttered my good fortune at being able to travel as we left, with *le mari* in the background.

A LETTER FROM SALIHA AROUN-RACHID

TAMANRASSET August 23 1976

Dear Susan,
I'm sorry for my tardiness in writing you. I came back from holiday almost 10 days ago; I went to Algiers for the holidays.

Thank you for your charming letter and my photo that you also sent to me. I was surprised by your letter. I hope this letter reaches your home and that you're in good health. I would have loved to be in Chicago but unfortunately it's very far. It requires an authorization and a lot of money to go there. I would be very happy to welcome you if you settled in Algeria to work here on your magazine. I would also be able to house you for all the time that you need. In your letter you spoke about sending me some fabric now if you could let me choose, I would really love if you would send me assorted curtains for my living room, preferably in a brown color, actually two (2) curtains because in my living room there are two windows. You would be very kind to do this for me because as you know from our discussion in Tamanrasset, our country doesn't make any curtains. On my part, I will send you some souvenirs but I would prefer to let you choose them. I would love it if you would write me all the time because I get bored sometimes here. I've changed addresses, so here is the address of my husband:
MEKHANCHA AROUN-RACHID
WILAYA de TAMANRASSET
This address is more certain/dependable for my mail especially during the past months because letters can get lost.
My husband would really like it if you could send a checkered shirt size 38 and some blue jeans size 40, if you can.
I think I don't have anything more to say, and send greetings to you and to all your family, without forgetting your friends.
Likewise, my husband also sends his greetings.
Goodbye and see you soon,
Saliha

Ex: Mekhancha Aroun-Rachid
Ex: prefecture) WILAYA de Tamanrasset
Algeria

I have no memory of whether or not I sent her the things she asked for, but I seriously doubt that I could have afforded to do.

Lere's mad because I wouldn't sleep with him; says I lack home training; he absolutely doesn't follow reason, cannot answer questions, tells me not to talk, bosses us, talks about "proper channels" of request; says I insulted him, I say he insulted me, nothing—the most humorless nasty fellow.
He wouldn't admit to being an ass, and having too much of a load (and only ten liters of water for three people!)
And then I was so furious with him that I stalked off into the pitch-black night with my sleeping bag, but as I lay there I started hearing rustling noises. I was

terrified, but too proud and angry to come back. He realized how dangerous it was and begged me to return, so I did.

I'm seeing lots of busted up dead cars along the road . . .

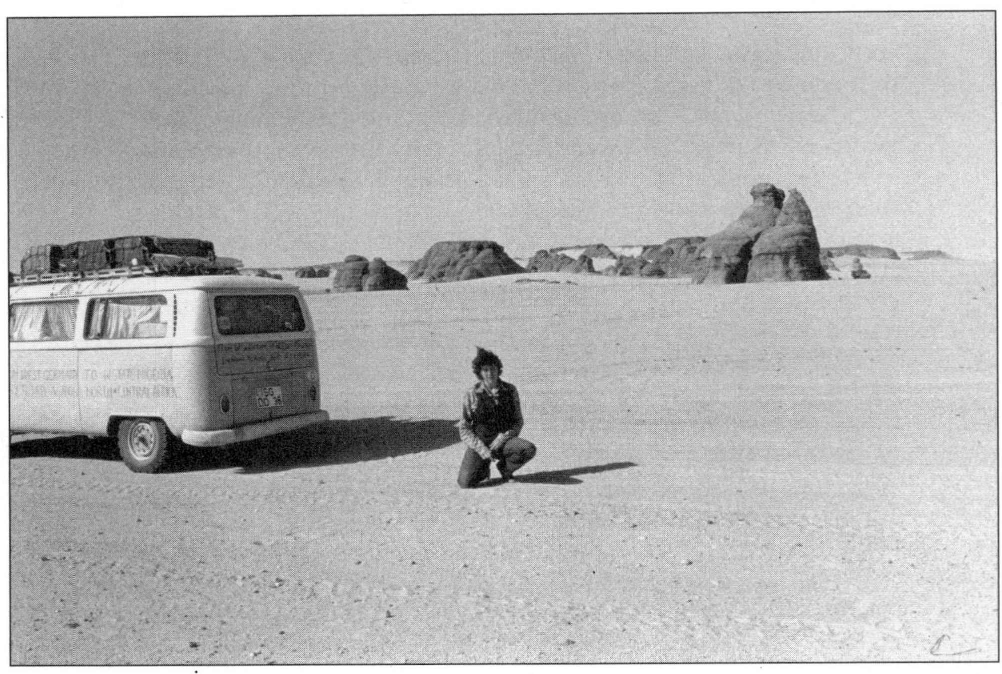

PART OF A LETTER TO MY MOTHER AND BROTHER:

The truck I had planned to take south from Tam (to Agadez) was not ready so I got on board with a Nigerian in a VW bus loaded down with stuff, and a Japanese traveler who was quite dull-witted—it was a mistake which I extricated myself from, in the nick of time, after 2 ½ days on the road & being mired in the sand 10 times; he was compulsive, irresponsible, overly confident, uncooperative, and rash—e.g., he didn't have enough water, only 10 *litres.* each time we were stuck he made us go out and shovel away the sand and put cardboard beneath the wheel to try and drive up and out, or someone would come along to help us out--but in that way we were very lucky: traffic in the desert is not very heavy, but best in January, the winter. I was really fed up with him yelling at us and blaming us for his problems, and he absolutely wouldn't listen to anyone's advice—that his car was too heavy and too low, etc.—so at the border to Niger I left him, to an unknown fate. I am almost afraid they won't arrive, because it gets increasingly worse further south, the sand softer and deeper, and they took the worse of the 2 routes!? I then caught on with

> a truck, a reliable truck, someone who's crossed the route since 1948, and even then they traveled at night with 3 trucks, and camped out together. They were kind and generous with me, and the driver even secured me a sleeping space beside one of the wheels, which somewhat blocked the cold winds.
> One doesn't play around with the desert—excessive caution is much better than too little—it's quite easy to be misled; 2 Americans in a Land Rover are right now lost, and have been so for 3 ½ days with only enough water for 2—It's really an amazing experience tho, and it was quite memorable—

In that letter to my (very worried) mother, I didn't share the details about the last time we got stuck. Lere had driven far off the piste and when we got out of the van and looked around, it was nowhere in sight. For once, he didn't yell at us to start digging; he just looked terrified. We stood there for a while, not knowing what to do, getting more and more scared…and then a large truck came over the ridge and pulled up. It was carrying about twenty workers back from the north. The driver got out, shaking his head, and quickly got all the men off the truck. They surrounded the van and lifted it enough to be carried to a patch of harder sand, and then he led us back to the piste. Needless to say, the driver tried to convince us to go with him instead—which I did after Lere followed him to In Guezzam.

JANUARY 14

Went 140 kilometers [87 miles] more, to In Guezzam, the border between Algeria and Niger, and I gave up with that crazy man. The last things he said were that I should be sure not to take anything that wasn't mine and "to tell them the truth." I certainly did.

Trouble at the border:
A group of Britishers got here—a woman took a piss inside a building (to find some privacy) but it was the mosque; they have to stay here fifteen days.

Two Americans in a jeep are lost.
Thirty-two people in a truck last year went off the road, thirty died.

We left the border and drove the rest of the day south into Niger [2].

Moon bright and high while the sun softly sets.

I learned some important lessons in human behavior while crossing the desert. I have great respect for the Arabs who've done this for tens of years and are calm, cooperative, and of most importance in this undertaking: Cheerful. When they stop to eat, they do it slowly, methodically; when there is a decision, they all talk it out; when it's night they travel in caravans of two or three, a law which some tourists (and people like Lere) ignore and sometimes die for. They leave no synthetic metallic mess behind them, only ashes to mark their place; mother-father-lover-nature can be benevolent if we obey the rigorous demands made.

Each person I spoke to after the incident with Lere agreed how they disliked him, saying, "*Il n'est pas gentil.*" ["He isn't nice."] For example, speaking critically in German about one guy's Arab car-partners so they wouldn't understand, and befriending anyone to get help but being so prideful.

There is no place for arrogance or one-upmanship in the desert—death is never an impossibility, and it's a weird fear, a different fear than, for example, living in a city. This is the feeling that one has put oneself here and nothing one can do could secure or save oneself under the wrong circumstances—a few kilometers before In Guezzam, when we found ourselves on the other side of that large sand dune away from the piste, unable to see it, I was absolutely panic-stricken—that was fear.

I am in retrospect painfully glad (and aware how lucky it was) to have left Lere. As the Britisher said: There are two things you need in the desert—salt and water—and he had neither.

Precisely, and he was dependent on someone else to come along with adequate water to give him some . . . Wow. In the desert, no one is that affluent. Moreover, and more frightening, he said he was going to take the route towards Arlit and I was later told the road was dreadful and even so, one never goes without a guide. Where would I be now with him?

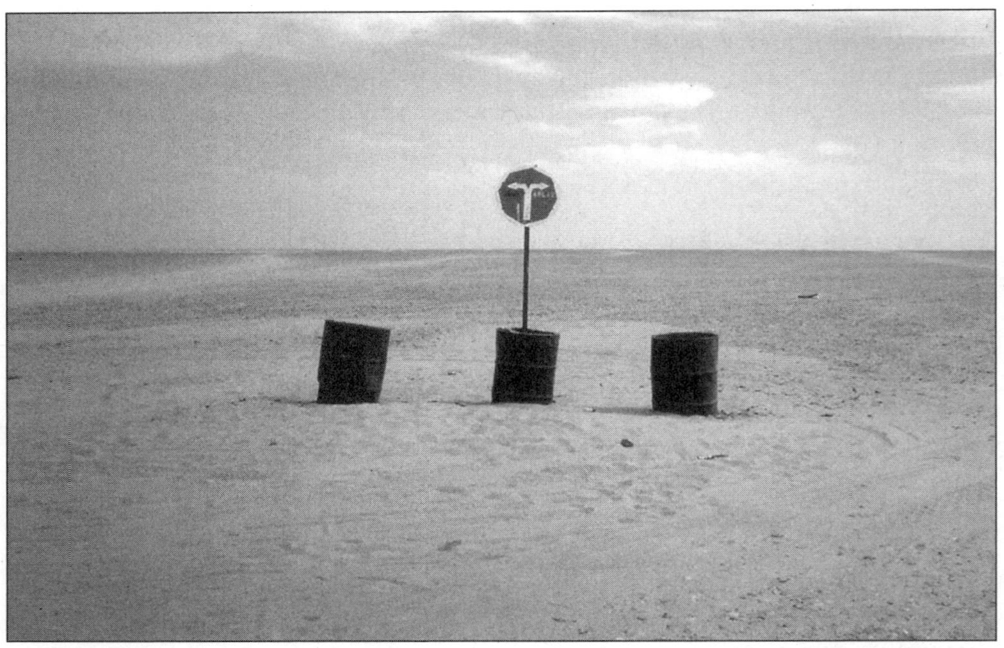

The alternate route taken by Lere and the Japanese guy. It says "Arlit" below the forked arrow.

I think it's my Tuareg women's neckpiece and my ever-keener survival skills that are helping me now.

Hausa [3] or similar music plays on the tape deck—it's really wonderful, lively, rhythmic and optimistic in sound, with many instruments. The modern musicians follow the traditional sounds but it has a good new edge added. It is very befitting this life: it has a negligible beginning and end, and a very long and complex and repetitive middle, a meditative rhythm, something that fills the time without making one conscious of it. I'll look for a cassette perhaps—

JANUARY 15

Last night very late we were stopped, sitting around the fire, and two very dashing and well-dressed Tuaregs appeared, with long swords on shoulder belts, and a few minutes later women came running up, and children.

How different a clean sunrise is, very calm [4].

The chaps who ride on these lorries are really interesting, each individual in his own way: one with a ski cap, one with reflecting shades and Palestinian scarf, one with funny old tortoise-shell glasses and a squeaky voice, a ponderous good-humored old man, etc.
There is a clear and efficient hierarchy which operates here between the driver, the mechanic/cook/underling, the "assistant" and the others.
The cooks are types in themselves—both on Alan's and this lorry—they're a bit off-track somehow but quite proud of their skill—and last night they fed me, gave me a separate bowl with a large amount; I had to give back half but they still managed to slip me four fine pieces of meat—

This morning is the Africa I imagined; low trees and shrubby grass, a long sunrise, cool air, and the Tuareg with his camel coming to say good morning.
And the drive today was tremendous, thru hard dark grey and brown sand with stretches of soft short yellow grass and trees.
I have a certain patient streak in me when it's appropriate—i.e., in NY or Chicago I'm always chasing around and being annoyed for waiting. Here, I sit because there's nothing to chase.

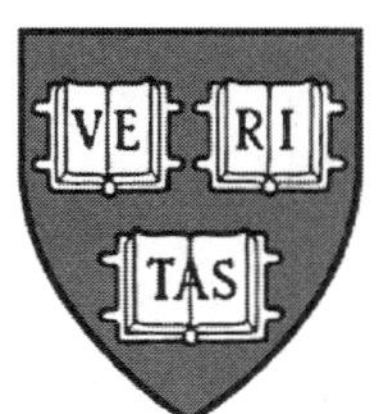

Now we're in In-Gall [5], the last stop before Agadez, for the rest of the day. My reaction to arriving in a clay town of maybe a hundred and fifty people, with camels and sheep, is not the awe I expected but rather admiration and a feeling that they aren't yearning for a chance at big city life—I suspect it's the ones who live halfway between this life and the city, for example in the tourist towns, with TV's, who yearn—ones sees just enough to pique the appetite without satisfying it. But damn, the pleading situation is bad here, every gesture requires a gift of some sort. I already gave away six postcards and four cigarettes <u>and</u> my VERITAS socks [6] to a very admirably persistent boy in green plastic shoes.

It was time again for the tea routine—with the men, as usual—although women appeared off and on. One sat by me nursing and I almost felt voyeuristic, realizing how unattached I am from my "female functions," thinking it's amazing to see a woman's breasts, etc.—Just goes to show . . .
The women here are much more gregarious than Algerian women, one feels right away a looser environment: The couple who sat together and teased during tea, the greetings on the street, the physical contact. But that's only in comparison to Algeria—women work very hard here; they seem to be doing a lot of carrying and pounding and nursing while the men siesta.

Somewhere during my travels, in a conversation, I was told that men are often referred to as "shade experts."

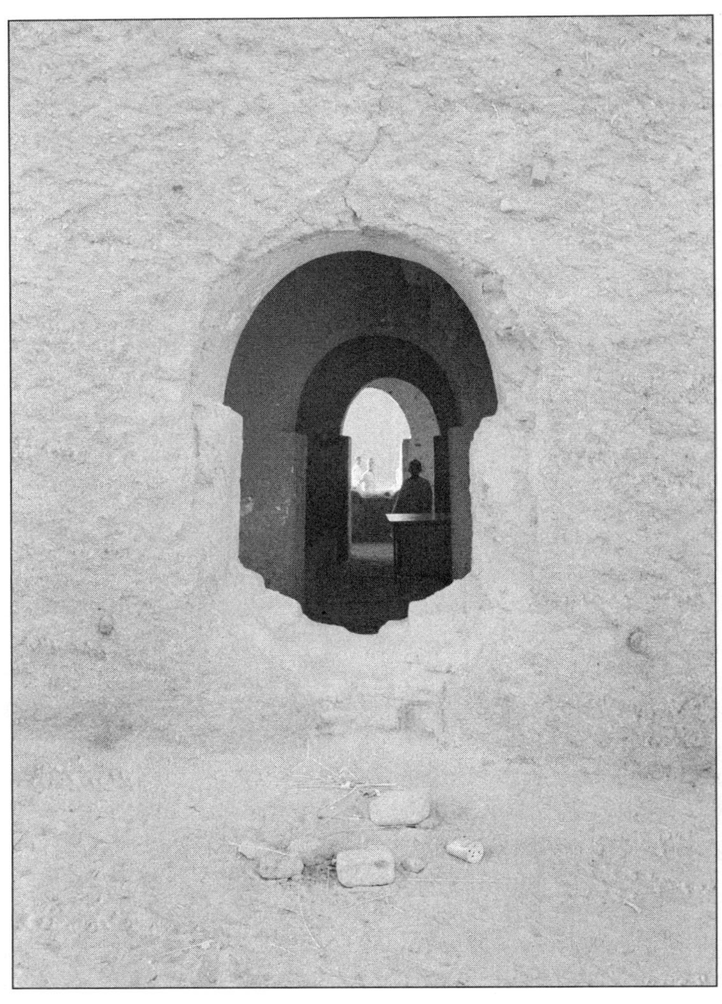

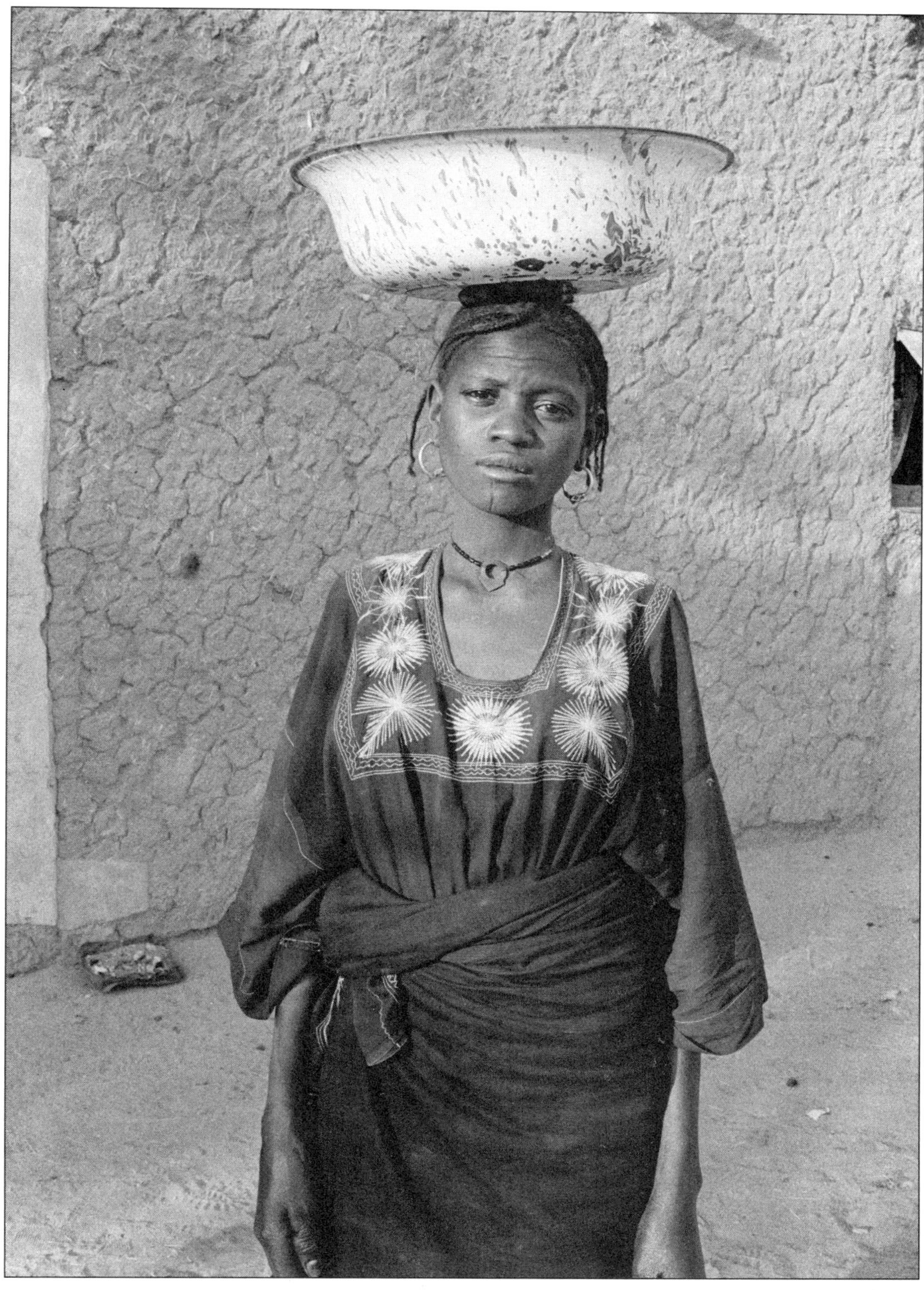

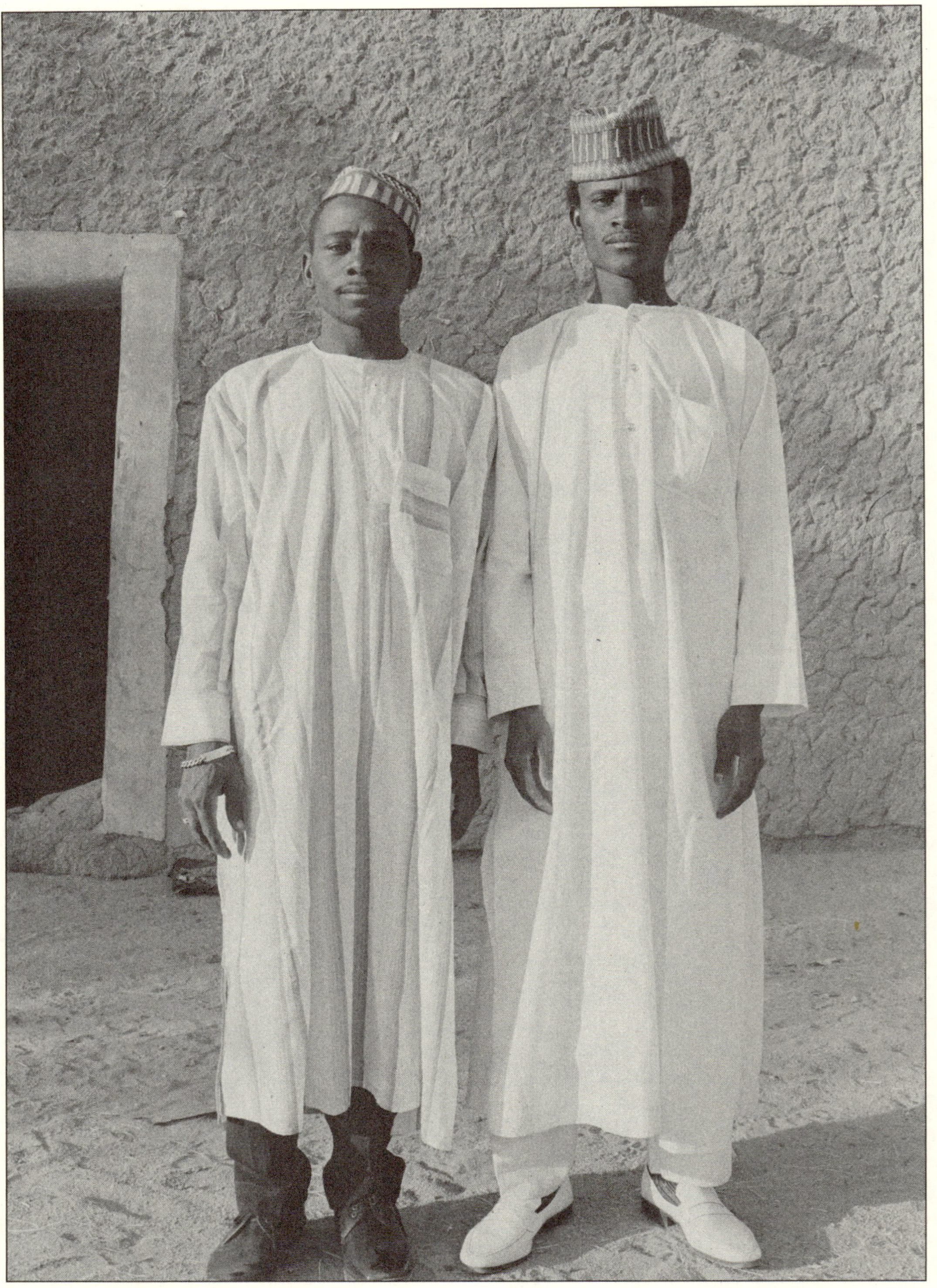

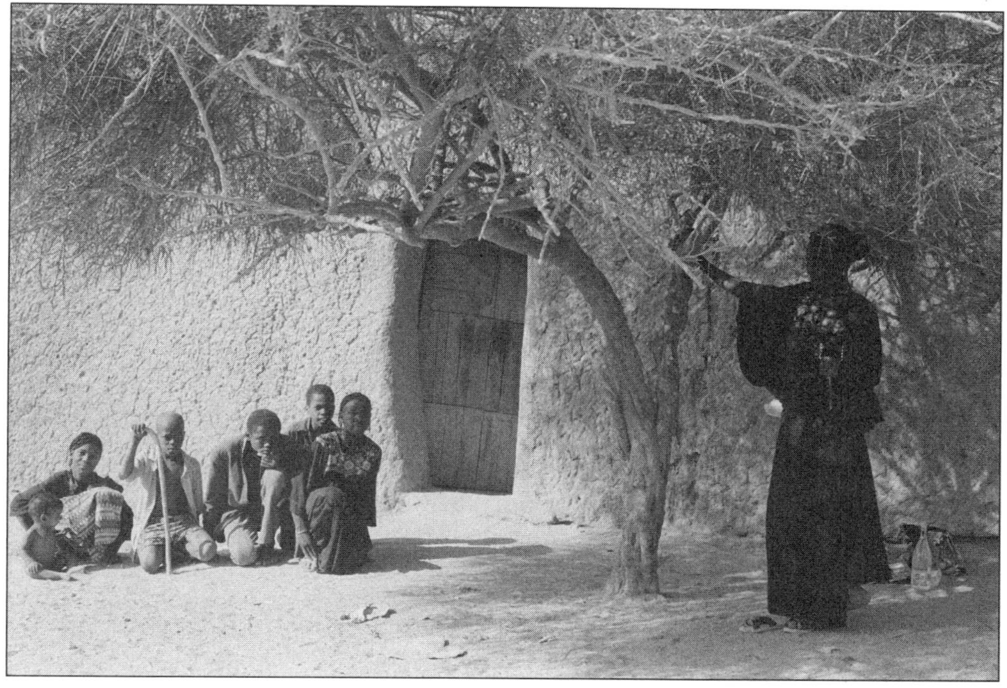

It's weird for me to spend so much time just sitting amidst a group who are speaking in an unknown language (and not knowing what they're saying about me) and just watch their actions and voice tones—the substance of a conversation can be/is very revealing, but sometimes my linguistic ignorance sharpens my other senses.

Dinner again was some sort of meat particles but this time without light so I got a bit squeamish as I was feeling my way thru it—but then on top of that they wanted to give me a huge plate of rice—I deferred.
Even the water with pills[20] is all cloudy and weird—what do I do?

In the evening: women cleaning each other's hair, a laughing crowd, each saying the other is "*fou*" [crazy] and repeating *ça va* [that's okay/how is it going?] and *à demain* [see you tomorrow] over and over.
Ça va is the password here, where the language is Hausa.
Flashlights at night, as they sit and chat and then flash onto the pictures decorating this house, the ads for magazines and underwear and Japanese towels and trucks and tourist attractions in Switzerland and Tricia Nixon and all the other colorful oddities.

20 Water purification tablets. I stopped using them. I also stopped taking my malaria pills because they created weird visions. I then mainly drank beer or Schweppes Quinine/Tonic Water (quinine is an ingredient which allegedly wards off malaria).

It was arranged that I would stay at the home of someone name Ibunu Hriar—maybe he was a friend of the truck driver, or one of the passengers?—and then in the morning I would continue onward in the truck with all the men.

Here I am in a bare room with an oil lamp and a man who's fucking around with his tape recorder (and now staring at me)—fucking goddamn, but it's a free meal and sleep. (Is it worth the psychological hassle? You bet—for a while.)
I'll be able to write a wonderfully thorough guidebook to being a single woman traveler when I'm finished with this trip!

1. Knife
2. Never let your guard down—just once is too much
3. Never underestimate anything, however innocuous

Don't be fooled by "traditional" men, that if they have on a burnoose, etc.—underneath are white shoes and groovy pants and a heavy bracelet and a modern mind—
That was something I learned to watch for early but god the life here is slow—one sits and says hello to the folks who pass, one waits after breakfast for lunch, one waits for the heat to pass, one waits for dinner, one waits in the dark for sleep time—Maybe this slowness is a bit <u>too</u> slow even for my observer status.
They are extremely preoccupied with their tape recorders.

JANUARY 16

Last night's dream was a raunchy Annette Funicello[21] type love story and at the end the boy returned to her in glory and I groaned in my sleep, and then a scene dominated by women, which refers directly to my experience in Algeria—

Some young lovely Tuaregs appeared out of the bush to sell us some goat cheese—[7]

There's a funny wooden painted airplane on the dashboard in the truck—I find that the Africans as often buy "tourist art" as do the tourists—

The road from In-Gall to Agadez: mauve dirt, soft yellow grass, Tuaregs (they're such clean people, so elegant and ordered) and I felt good, felt good about the future in some absurdly remote way, about spending the years traveling, and fuck the "experts," this will be first hand knowledge and with an added twist—my woman vision—it <u>is</u> my sanity—there's no denying it, it feels (however faintly on some bad days) like the one strength in my soul; putting that aside, I realize how intrigued I am by other's lives, even though that requires an incredible amount of time in observing, recording, re-re-re-observing, fine tuning—and I really want

21 Annette Funicello, an actress and singer, was one of the most popular members of the Mickey Mouse Club and later the star of the *Beach Party* movie series (*Muscle Beach Party*, *Beach Blanket Bingo*, etc.) with co-star Frankie Avalon.

to come out with photos which to me are Africa, but it's so difficult when one is harassed to take a photo every time the camera appears—

> **PART OF A LETTER TO MY MOTHER AND BROTHER:**
>
> Did I tell you I broke my 35mm lens? What shit, but I can still use it in the sun here, altho I am running the risk that none of the pictures will come out! The people here love to pose; last nite two fellows got very well dressed, all new clothes and I thought they were going to a party & it turned out they wanted me to take a picture—I'll be printing so many to send as gifts and in return for them letting me take the pic—

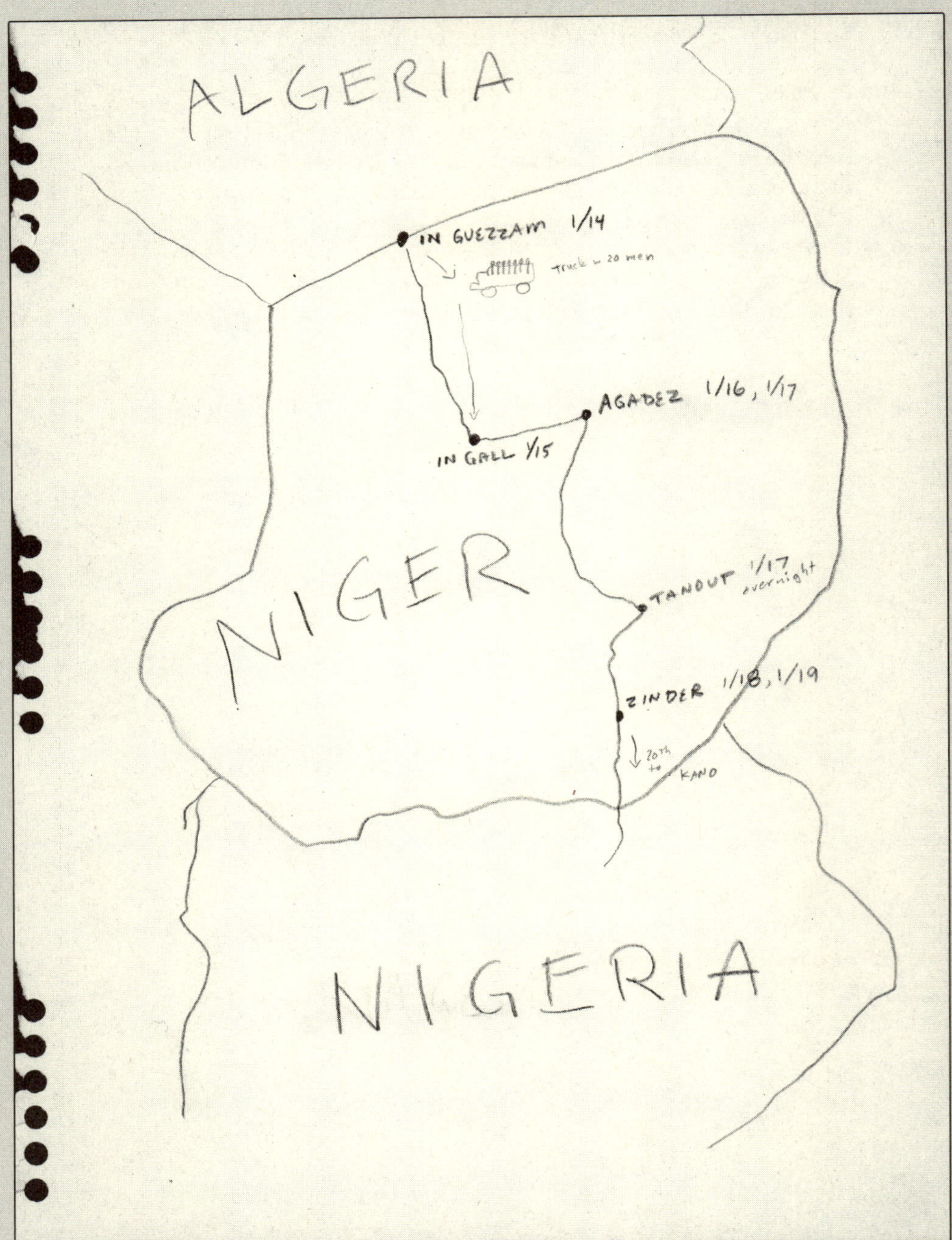
ALGERIA
IN GUEZZAM 1/14
Truck w 20 men
AGADEZ 1/16, 1/17
IN GALL 1/15
NIGER
TANOUT 1/17
overnight
ZINDER 1/18, 1/19
20th
to
KANO
NIGERIA

CHAPTER SEVEN

The Japanese Guy Survived! At a Baptism, and with Hamsatou

When we got to Agadez [formerly spelled Agadès], I bid farewell to the truck with the twenty men. I stayed in the house of a man named Sidi Amadou Bodel. As in the case with Ibunu in In-Gall, I have no clear notes about who he was, so I assume he was probably a friend of the truck driver or someone else on the truck. I would never have agreed to stay alone with a man unless it was someone I'd been around for a while and who had friends whom I'd also met (like the drivers).

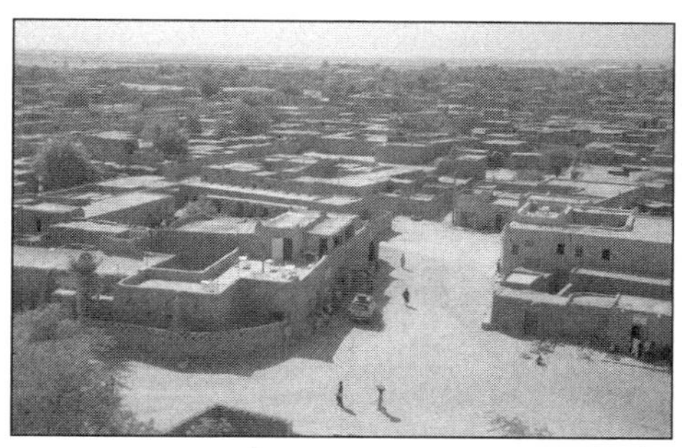

Lost this afternoon, walking for hours to find the house, getting frantic and no one knew the chap and when they might've they didn't budge to help me—this spacy, supposedly calm but largely indifferent attitude reigns, esp. in reference to a frantic foreign woman in a vest—

The begging is formidable—literally every child runs up and says "*ça va, cadeau?*" ["How's everything? Do you have a present for me?"]—It's all they learn of French. A grown man approached me as I drank some orange drink, took the half-full can, and refused to give it back—how annoying—and if you ask for the slightest favor, they want money. The trick here is self-sufficiency or at best an appearance of it. (And if one is cajoled into a gift, they don't show gratitude but rather act as if it was expected.)

PART OF A LETTER TO MY MOTHER AND BROTHER:

I made it across the desert after two weeks of dust and bumps and $$ and a constant search for good water– which I tend to violate if I'm really thirsty, but I haven't gotten sick yet!
[. . .]
—now I'm in a dusty dirty town in Niger; I don't think I'll stay here long, altho it requires waiting for a truck to Zinder or Niamey—everything in Africa requires waiting. I'm half frustrated half amused half indifferent to the system—it depends on the time of day and my hunger (which is always present; one just doesn't find food here in the same way, and I'm always thirsty)—even dates are starting to scare me—it's a curious experience to have to be so conscious of what I eat—
God, I loved the desert, the openness, the constant change of mountains, sandy stretches, areas with trees & shrub, very barren sections, forbidding, sometimes terrifying, sometimes inviting—-the route I took is really the best, they say, the most diverse; the others

pass thru just sandy regions without much change for days & days; I've acquired great respect for the people who live/survive here, 100's of miles from other villages, hanging on the edge of extinction, but very strong and attuned to the life and the requirements of the desert—
Oh I feel dirty at this point despite my attempts at washing—one just doesn't avoid the dust here—
Time to eat, I've written many letters today & must stop now before I blitz out—
Much love etc
Su

16 Janu. 1976
Agadez, Niger, W. Africa

P.S. I'm being treated like a queen, always taken into people's homes, fed, even today someone got a little boy to do my wash! Everything they say about African hospitality is true—

Pete—
The tape deck in the truck had "Kung Fu Fighting" on it, and I was pleasantly reminded of you—I hope you're well, and that the Bull's Eye Mobile is spiffy for the Bicentennial—if you really continue the film-making passion, Africa would be a great place to do one—there've been a lot made already but there's so much going on here, so many different approaches, and especially the desert—it'd be great for a high-drama film, as you seem to prefer—

Beautiful, their dark faces in the soft light of the oil lamp, but haunting eyes, staring, all this visiting—there is for one thing not the privacy one feels so intensely in the states—the houses are open, the streets are the meeting place all day, one isn't cooped up in an office or factory or a thirteenth-floor apartment. But something notably different: Throughout Algeria and now here I've sensed a harmony of the elements in life, a sense that everything is used and done for an efficient reason, whether the elaborate clothes or the food or architecture, even to the smallest manifestations; an indication of the cultural and social environment that is created by the natural requirements (here, of too much sand, a lot of sun, no natural resources)—and to impose our quota of "industriousness" on a place/people where there is little access to anything of industrial possibility is futile and erroneous—they don't have the diverse climate and resources of the USA or Europe, for example,[22] and without that, there is little organic/internal development that can occur (in addition to the enormous problem of being blocked by desert and ocean).

22 How wrong I was!! See [1] for more info.

Here I've seen <u>much</u> blindness as compared to almost none in Algeria—I don't know the reason, but it really appears to be proportionately high—

For someone like me who likes to be inconspicuous (as must befit a photographer) it's hard to always be the center of attention—
And I get so annoyed when fights with "the law" and among men in a group ensue in a foreign language, obviously about me, and I can't understand—

The Japanese I meet are so funny, so freaked out by this culture, they keep saying, "They do nothing, just sit." And, "Ooh, Arab culture very strange . . . "

Some young Tuareg men here told me that American (i.e., white) girls were *jolie* [pretty], Tuareg girls not! It certainly has sunk deep, and is evident in all the white girl pin-ups (adverts from American magazines) in these houses—(but I suspect the women here feel differently)—

I've been sleeping very poorly, trying to adjust my body to a sunset-sunrise schedule in comparison to our artificial time at home—a bedtime chosen rather than imposed by nature.

Here there is a pretty fair balance of women and men on the street, and I think even the fact of the women's bodies being uncovered, breasts, arms, heads, makes the men a bit less crazy—

It's really not one world we live in but many, some of which don't seem to touch at all (they get very little news here of America, mostly advertisements and headlines).

The aspect of America that seduces me the most (I don't mean that other countries lack it, of course) is the level of analysis to find newer forms of human relationship—I don't credit electoral politics or office psychology with that, but us, the less influential and therefore more concerned. If metaphysics is essential to life/sanity, it is the religion of the twentieth century, a religion without a God. I grant some verity to the criticism that it requires a quite affluent standard of living to generate such changes, but that is proving less true as others less affluent and very concerned organize—it's an entire ambience which prevails now (in the world) towards liberation, perhaps more than ever before in history, in self-rule as a basic fact of life—certainly this is being met with the most sophisticated and horrifying opposition, the last vicious battles of a dying régime. (However, these battles might well last for a century or more; and the new problem of a revolutionary government being considerably oppressive in their own special way—for example the rhetoric about how gays are incapable of "revolutionary labor" etc.)

It's again happening. I feel like a whore just because I'm staying at this man's house, although I said, "*Je dorme seule, c'est compris?*" ["I sleep alone, is that understood?"] When his friends come to visit and laugh, I wonder what they must be saying.
Is it better to not accept and have to sleep outside or pay through the nose at a hotel? I'm not sure; time will tell.

Full moon.

That pig the other night told people that I had slept with him!

JANUARY 17

It's so noisy here in the a.m. with the cocks crowing and dogs barking and sheep ba-ahing—

Evaporated milk with coffee [2].

The hospital in Agadez—several buildings, white doctors, much sickness, a listlessness, people just sitting unhappily—seems also a maternity center, many women with babies present.
They have the most annoying habit, for example at the post office, of serving two or three persons at once so that everything takes much longer and is quite confused and inefficient.
I can't escape a certain feeling of hostility and the sense that I am (1) an oddity and (2) a gift-giver—and the listlessness wears on my spirit.

Crazy coincidence! Today I ran into the Japanese guy from the horrible VW van trip, and he's made friends with another Japanese guy somewhere along the way. I can't believe he survived the rest of that trip with Lere. His stories about it were just like I had imagined. We talked about going further south together . . . with a sane driver.

The women here are friendly enough when I pass on the street, but I sense a certain pridefulness, less of a need on their part to draw me in, to invite me in, as I felt in Algeria. It might just be the country—I hear a lot of Nigerians are one sort, Ghanaians something else, some more friendly than others, etc.—
I don't find Nigeriens[23] particularly remarkable (yet) in any way, although every one, man and woman, seems to be a merchant—since nothing grows here (except dates), everything is canned, and there are many stores on each street, and the market is a crowded, noisy, sit-around place. (I think here they see too many tourists and are jaded as a result; it's the great stop-off point across the desert. The camping site has a pool, which indicates something.)

---

23 People of Niger, as distinct from Nigerians from Nigeria.

And the meat section of the market—wow! All sorts of strange slimy parts covered with flies, standing room only—one was even being cleaned and he pulled out the little old balls of shit.
To think that their marketplace is our Field's[24] is a good register of the cultural disparity—
It just wouldn't take much effort, and beyond perhaps three days including organizing to get a huge lorry and a bunch of the "able-bodied men" one sees everywhere (and the women too, although that's asking too much) and shovel up all the garbage, all the piles of old meat and sheep shit and tin cans that collect in certain parts of the town.
The goats here are a riot, they eat anything; one was attacking an old green shirt—it's no wonder the meat is tough.
Reutsch is the big store, a large very empty room with one aisle and dusty old cans and packages, and the listlessness.

I stopped in at a school; I don't know if the guy I was staying with took me there or it was just my curiosity. Mademoiselle Azara Alhadji was the teacher.

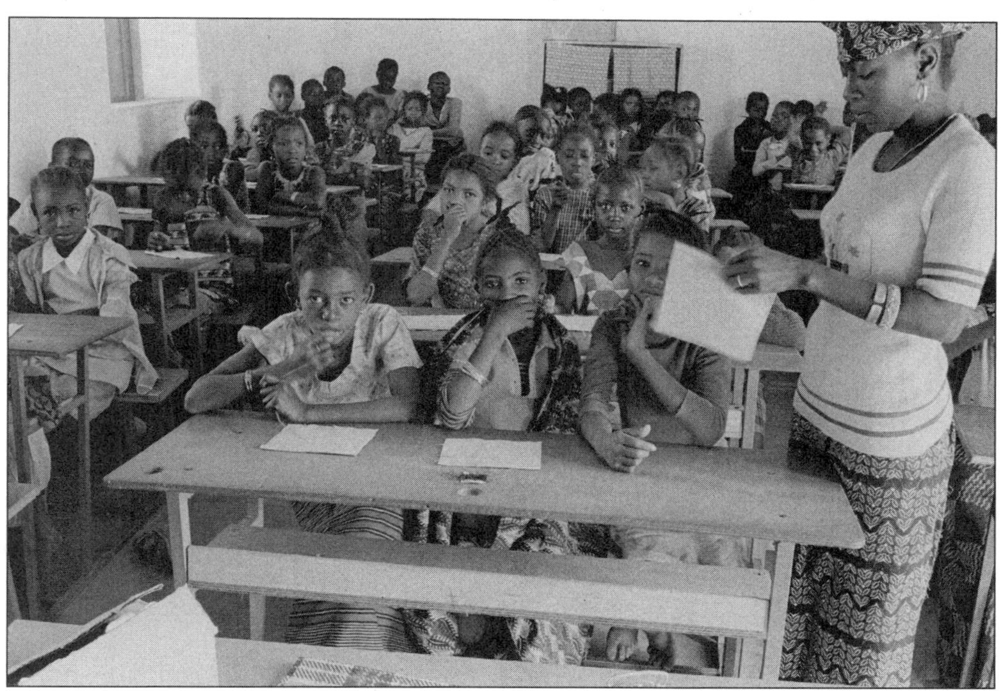

24 Marshall Field & Company, one of Chicago's biggest and oldest department stores, acquired by Macy's in 2005.

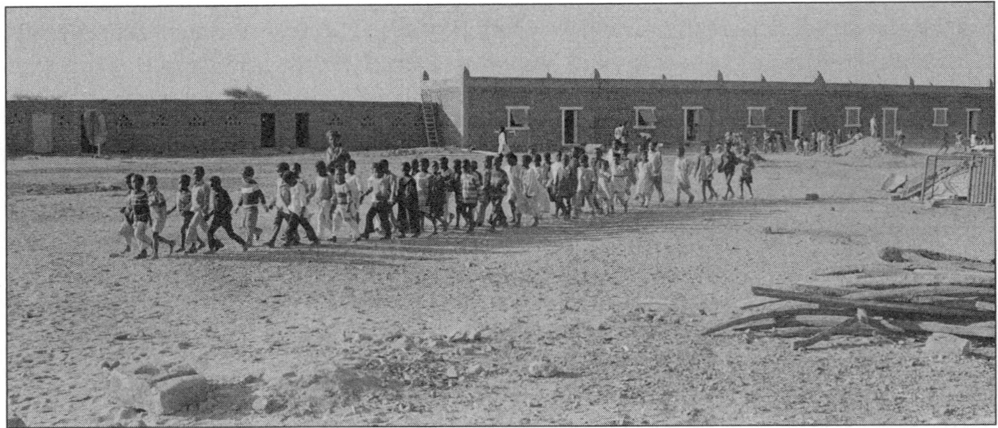

The radio station has about fifteen little boys all saying "Hello Ma," "Hello Sister," etc. before introducing a song. It was a great attraction spot in town.

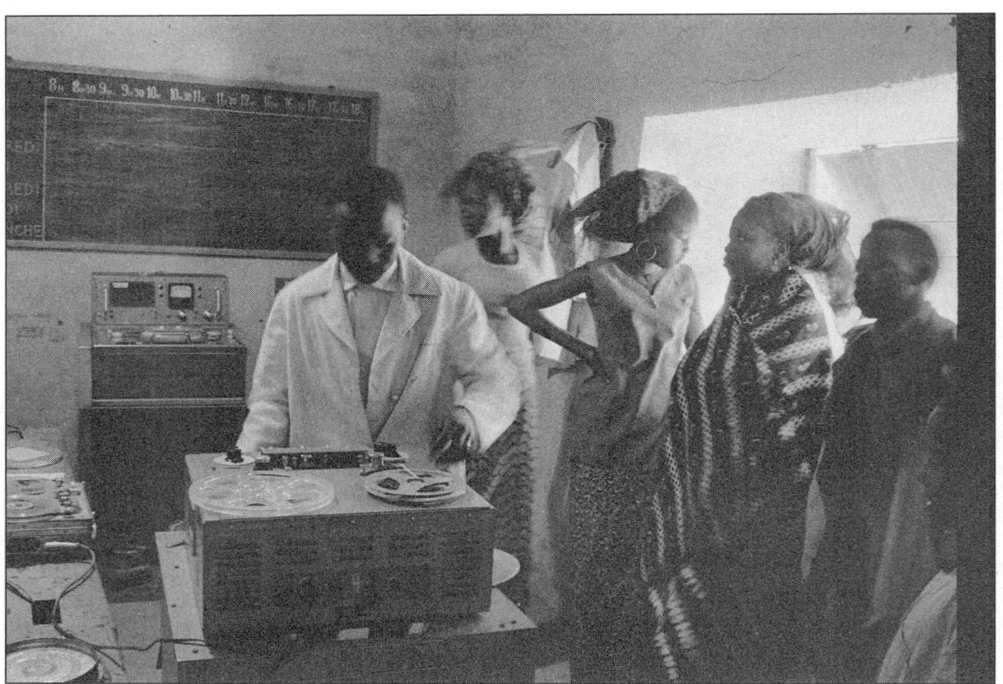

I'm really pissed at that fucker in the other town for saying I slept with him, and here when I say ("admit") that I'm staying at this man's house (Amadou) the eyes roll, the tongues cluck—
I'm sick of male company, god damn it! And I don't want to have to be so grateful for example that he's given me a free lift and will pay for the next truck to Zinder—it's cheating somehow, and I don't like it.

That afternoon, the Japanese guys and I headed off to Zinder in a truck which had some Africans on board, but also a few other foreign travelers. We stopped the night in Tanout and slept out in the open

JANUARY 18

The sunset was very soft yesterday, it slowly pinkened and sank into a grayish horizon, without fanfare. On the road to Zinder, saw sparsely situated thatched huts on stilts often several hundred yards apart, and an occasional village—many women on their way to get water, walking perhaps several miles in the morning sun—stayed in Tanout last night. Forty-four (artesian?) wells are being constructed there on the outskirts; in every village I find much building, the bricks hand-made from the muddy sand by young men; they crumble easily, but without much rain the houses probably last several years.

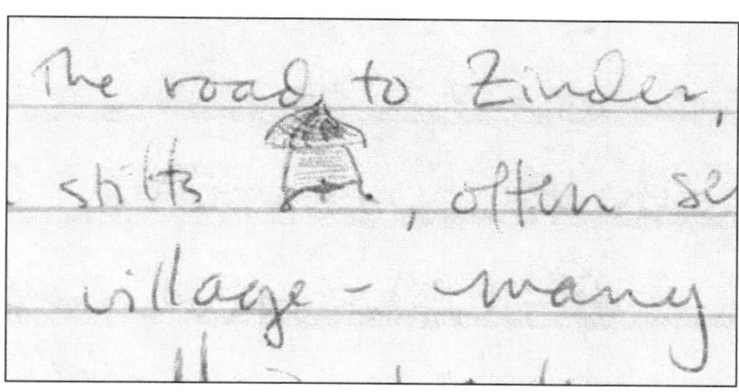
The road to Zinder,
stilts , often se
village - many

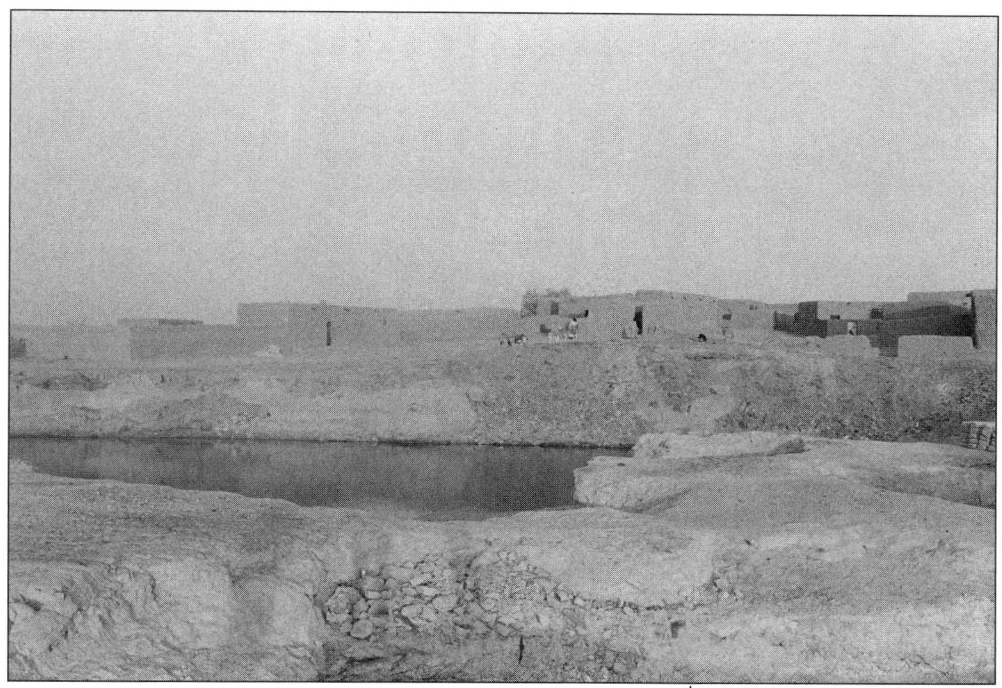

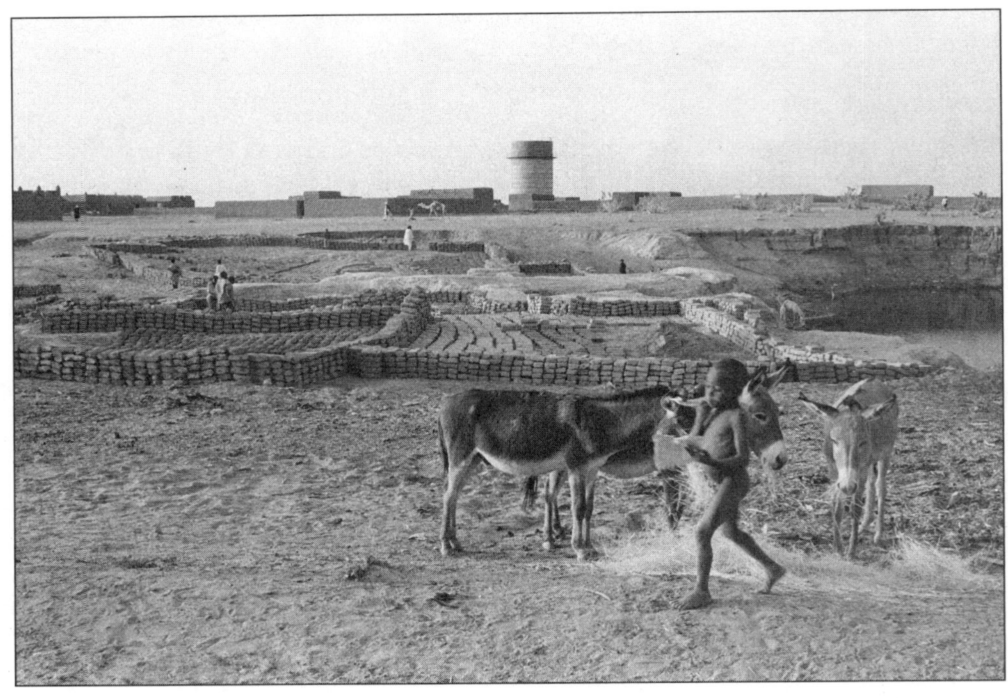

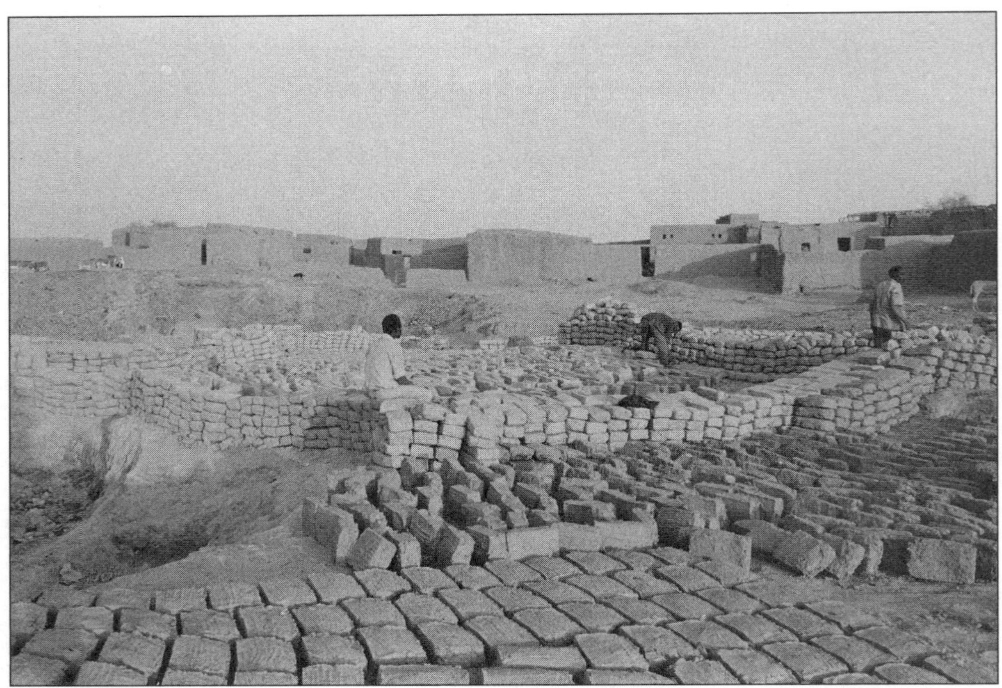

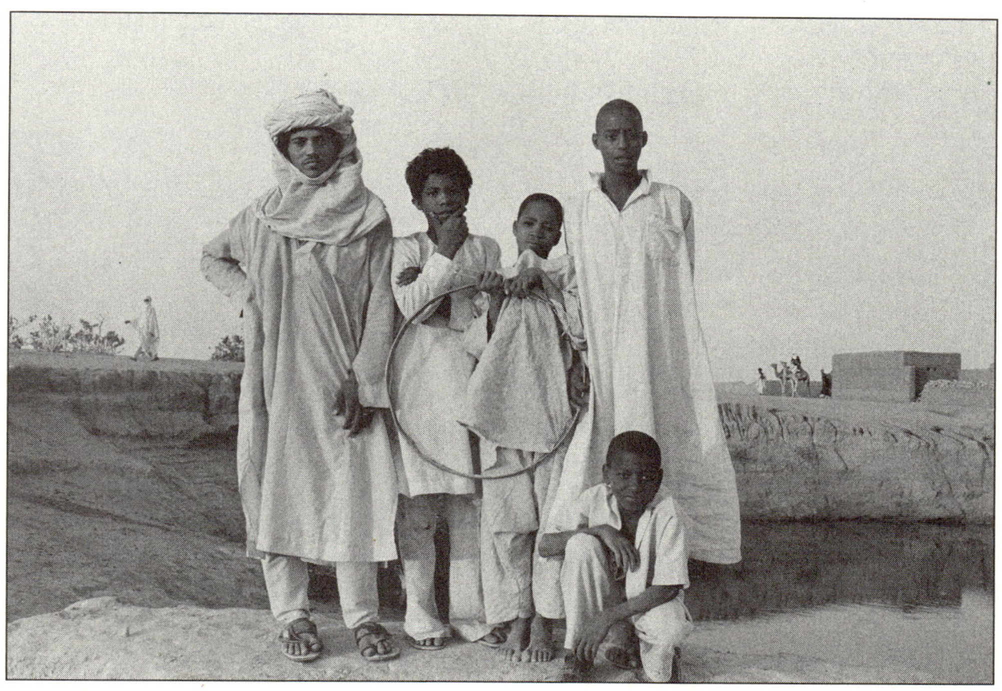

Sitting in this cramped, uncomfortable truck, there are old women and men with literally nothing but a few pieces of cotton to cut off the strong cold wind. A man all last night had one short-sleeved shirt and a thin blanket (which has *je t'aime* [I love you] and hands exchanging rings on it) and he literally shook with cold all night. These Italians tourists are appalling—one of the women bitches and pushes and whines every time someone even slightly invades her space, and in Italian always, which is very disconcerting to them I suppose; even when she gets food she speaks Italian—so incredibly selfish and the Africans just stare at her, amused and pissed off. The girls here learn to be crafty at a very young age, being market women by the time they're eight or nine years old—all along the road to Zinder we stopped at small towns and were swarmed by young and old with their various old and crusty meats. It's a bit annoying that an American/European/Japanese who has relatively much <u>more</u> money will bargain down from five cents to two and a half cents for a huge ripe tomato.

Everything (e.g., the desert) seems (too) difficult before one attempts it—imagination and rumors being what they are—but while in the process the problems get ironed out.

Zinder is a large town with street lights, paved streets, many new buildings, Radio Niger, a lot of traffic.
The men (usually older, more prosperous in appearance) wear lovely pastel

dashikis, especially lavender and yellow, with heavy embroidery at the shoulders in another color.
And there's the one-pant-leg-up thing, and the Italian-style caps on the work men.

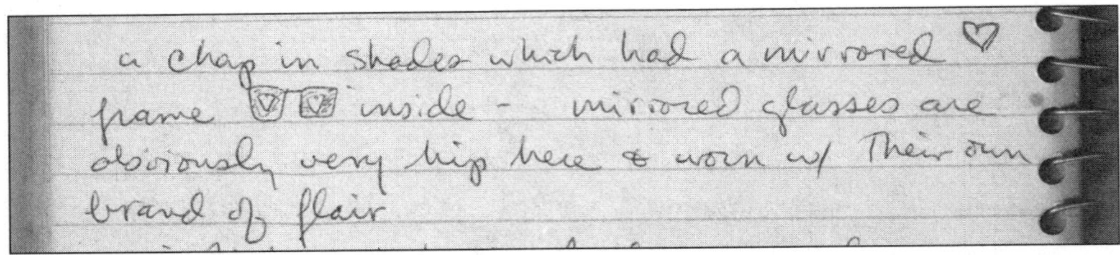
a chap in shades which had a mirrored ♡ frame inside - mirrored glasses are obviously very hip here & worn w/ Their own brand of flair

And a chap in shades which had a mirrored frame inside—mirrored glasses are obviously very hip here and worn with their own brand of flair—
Motorbikes are everywhere here—prized, admired, exhibited, raced in, decorated with old dusty artificial flowers; like the scene that's been repeated in every small midwestern town for years—hang out where it's happening, near the James Brown music and the well-dressed young men who jive around to the music and perhaps think of the big city.

Typical of the incongruity one finds in Africa: A vendor of blue and gold metal canopy beds—a man in a purple dashiki and rust red vest—strolled thru the market calling out and waving and was greeted by all the merchants sitting in the dust. Bought a lovely, well-worked (I hope it holds up) silver bracelet to remember Algeria-Niger, bargained down from $40 to $10—I wouldn't budge my price and they had to sell [3]. I am being careful of two things: not to pay too much for anything and not to exploit their cheap prices. When a skinny raggedy kid wants to sell me a tomato for 4 cents, I'm not going to try to get it down to 2 cents.

These two Japanese are comical; the one with less English, in trying to grasp my words, cranes forward, eyes squinted in effort, like a bird pecking for food. Yesterday he tried to teach Japanese to a cake vender; he was surrounded by twenty or so young, bored boys with his Jap-Eng and Eng-Fr dictionaries.

A marked difference: I can sit and read and young/modern men pass and look with interest but do not harass or plead as do Algerian men.
I think my stay in Agadez was so depressing because (1) I felt somehow nasty/uncomfortable staying in the same room/different bed as Amadou and (2) after aborted conversations I realized it was more or less as futile to expect lavish talk/info from an African truck driver as I might get from his American counterpart.

Reading *The Liberation of Guiné: Aspects of an African Revolution* by Basil Davidson. I like his style, his use of functional, short sentences to describe a mood or place, the good combination of facts/speeches about the land and history and the plain difficulties of guerilla warfare. There's no revolt without revolution, or you are a rebel without a cause. There's no point in destroying the Portuguese colonial structure simply to put bureaucratic Africans in their place.

For example, the policeman who came by yesterday to quell a large boisterous crowd which had gathered at the scene of something—he actually whipped a few people and the crowd scattered like sheep before the sound of a truck—they all laughed and whistled . . . but from my vantage point it wasn't very amusing.

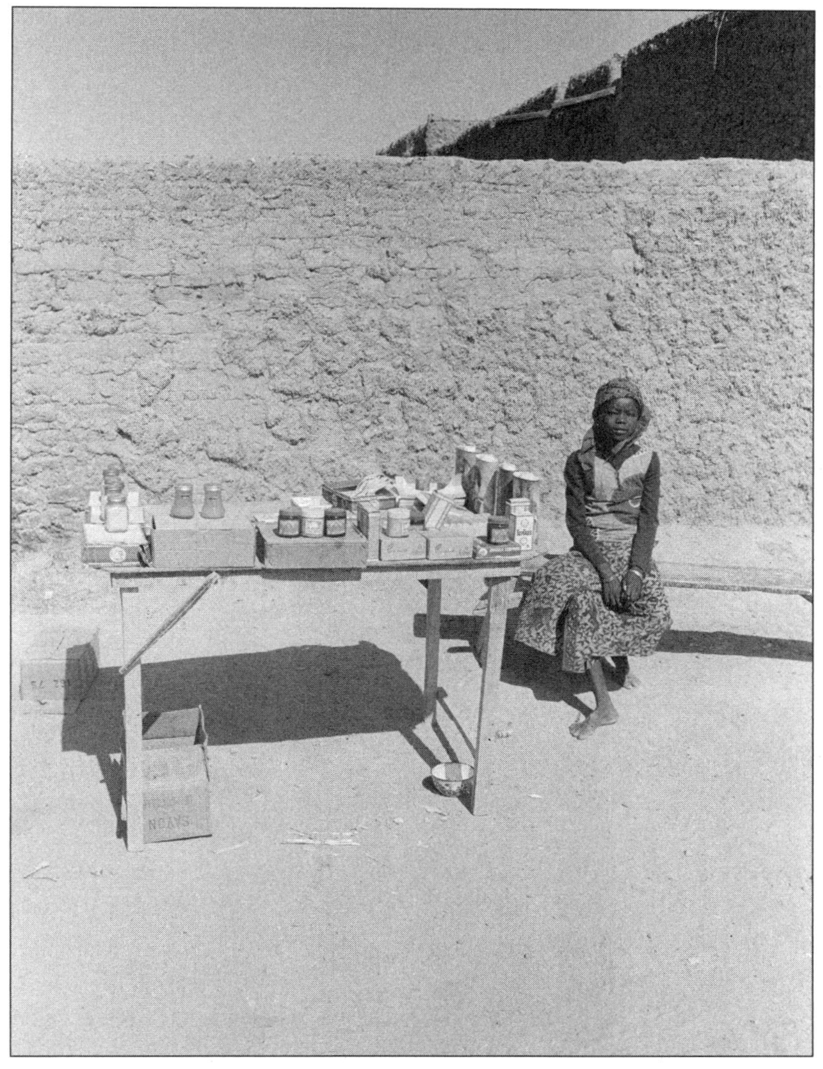

The young girls really do have a lot of responsibilities, and after talking for a while with a few yesterday, I realized one was perhaps fourteen or fifteen, and that she will soon be married. No wonder they age quickly! It's clear that no one can take care of anyone here so it's just as well to pass her off to a husband as to have her in the home until she's twenty or twenty-one.

In a country like Niger one just doesn't get the feeling of a large scale consciousness of "development"—it seems embodied in the self-important officials and profiteers who maneuver through the streets in new cars. In the market, it's the same as ever: Unorganized selling, too much cigarettes and hair oil, too little food, the hungry crowds (especially of children) who gather as the sun sets to buy a bowl (for 25 cents [$1.37], probably what they've earned that day) of a paste (*paté*) made with millet, with some sauce on it; enough to fill the stomach but not more—

I was very wrong about that. See [4].

The U.S. has 7200 nuclear warheads in W. Europe, and 300,000 troops.
I wonder what's happening in America??

The Japanese guys and I had nowhere to sleep, so we ended up in a slightly enclosed area of the main market . . . It was jammed with vendors and shoppers during the day, but during the night it was empty except for a few other sleeping people.

JANUARY 19

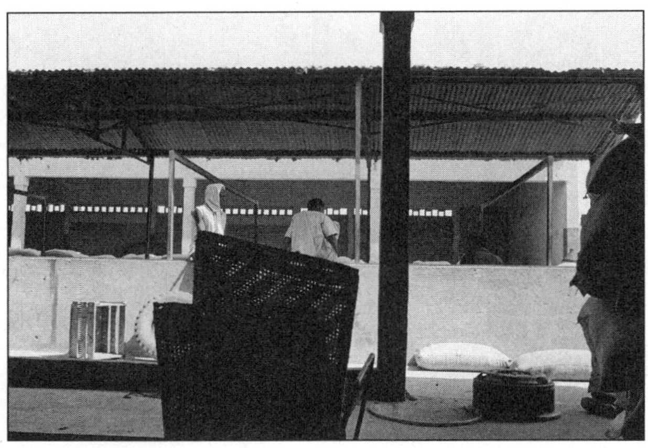

Spent last night in the Zinder storage house at the market place—a lizard disconcerted me, but it was a long and sound sleep. A long dream about Dad and Lauri passing by at U. of C. obviously having come from some work, and he didn't look or say anything to me; then my sister with some dapper middle-aged chap who she discovered had been a lover back in Europe; then some woman whose husband was a work-freak and they lived with a third woman with whom he was talking shop around the clock, she had a baby, some sort of tree house, he wrapped up the baby and covered its head three times to keep it quiet, etc.

I heard *Hijack Your Love* last night coming from Soulissa Moussa, *Vend des Disques* [record shop], and all in a thick vision I was transported to Augie's.[25] Every sight and smell of the place came back to me thru that song.

There were a lot of vultures [the birds] hovering around the meat stalls in the

25 Augie's was a great dyke bar in Chicago—and the first one I ever went to.

marketplace early this morning, and so many people in dusty, thin, partial clothes huddled over small fires. I think they've spent the cold nights crouched in a dirty corner, no comfort, no respite.

I watch the hordes of small shivering unclothed little boys, each with his food pot, swarm after a plate with five pancakes on it, and think of the lives of young men at Exeter, and that they can somehow claim that their success is due to genetics, not their privileged upbringing.
I like that we can sleep in a warehouse and in the a.m. they just come in and go about their business, no big deal—
There's the sound of pounding all morning—men seem to just sit, while women are in the market at eight at night selling dinner, then at six in the morning again selling breakfast, usually a huge bowl of *paté* and sauce—
Paté is <u>miserable</u> food and they eat it every day—I gag on it. But when in Rome . . . .
The woman was working very hard, she panted and grunted as she ground the meal for the *paté*.
And while women work, men have tea, men talk, men never stop telling me I should be married (to them, of course). How annoying.

In a letter to Mimi, I included a note from the Japanese guy. . . .

はいけい．エミー
スウジーとはタマラセッツで会い．それ以来ずっと同じコースを旅行しているみたいです。
タマラセッツからナイジェリア人の車で2日間一緒に旅行したのですが，車が何回も
砂の中に入り込み、そのたびに．スージーと一緒に砂を掘り起し、車を押したものです。
スジーの良く働く事 日本人の男以上のたくましさ……女とは思えない程……
2日目に気ままなナイジェリア人と、口げんか そして，アルジェリアの国境で車を降り
トラックで行った様です。そして又 アガデスでバッタリ会いそれから一緒にゼンダまで来ました。
彼女はこれからナイジェリアへ 行くと言っています，僕はビザを取る為にニアメイに
行かなければなりません．それにしても．アメリカ人の女の子．たくましいですね。
※これをあまり他の日本人に見せないで下さい．下手な日本語で
書いてありますから。それじゃ日本語の勉強，頑張って下さい。さようなら……
スウジーの友人の日本人より

I had no memory of what it said, so I asked my friend to translate it.

Dear Friend,
I met up with Susie in Tamanrasset, and it looks like we'll be traveling together from here. From Tamanrasset, we traveled in a Nigerian's car for two days, but the car kept getting stuck in the sand, and each time Susie and I had to dig up the sand and push the car out. On the second day, Susie got in an argument with the unreasonable Nigerian driver, and got out of the car at the Algerian border. She seems to have gone on by truck. Then we

met up unexpectedly in Agadez and traveled to Zinder from there.
She said she's going on to Nigeria. I have to go to Niamey in order to get my Visa.
In any case, American women certainly are tough!
Please don't show this to other Japanese. It's written so poorly.

Susie's Japanese Friend

Young school children all reaching to touch my arm, my hand, many many times *bonjour*; an albino in a Tibetan-type hat with books and beads; a young man in the shade of a tree reciting the Koran on tablets of wood; the pristine and gracious Librarie de l'Ambassade de France; the bourgeois sector of quite spacious new apartments is quieter; the market is absurd, the meat getting worse every time I see it, absolute garbage being neatly cut and skewered to be baked with tons of spice—such an inefficient system, with anywhere from twenty to fifty women and men each selling very small amounts (a little pile of onions and tomatoes) of things, to be bought by others who take them to the second market to then be sold in smaller quantities. Tomatoes abound.

On top of a hill, the military base: Saw a large supply (several hundred at least) of sacks, probably millet—I wonder how it is distributed, if it goes the way of a lot of food here: rotting.
I dislike the ambience of a country under military rule; one gets the feeling that the general populace is quite ignorant/indifferent to the situation of the country, which is inevitable if they are largely illiterate and little attempt is made to reach them thru other media—

This bracelet is really a beauty.

With the first child, one "doesn't know" the name for several months—they are great teasers, saying a grown man is her son (and she's about sixteen or seventeen).

As I was wandering around the town, I came upon a large group of people having a baptism dance to celebrate the birth of a baby boy to a woman named Aminata Amoukari, who was resting in a nearby room. The next day, I sent a parcel of books back home to my mother and included this note:

A LETTER TO MY MOTHER

Mom – hope you got my letter from Agadès – i meant to send a telegramme so that you wouldn't worry but it was $8 . . .
i've been in Zinder now for 2 days, and yesterday was quite exciting.
i happened upon a large group of women (and watchers) dancing with 3 excellent drummers to celebrate the birth of a baby boy 7 days

prior – it was really beautiful but i ran out of film halfway thru - !
now i'm going south, towards Nigeria –
i've been with 2 japanese for a few days now, & one of them is
frightfully sick & consequently in the hospital here for a few days,
but with meals it's cheaper than the hotel!
love—
the Chesler book is excellent, you might want to read it

At the dance today: Showing money to urge on the drummers; women dance together with sign language, touching face and body, smirking, teasing, telling stories; one woman got very sexual, all the crowd was laughing; very different styles of dance, sometimes subtle, sometimes overt and boisterous, always a sort of counter-tempo to the drummers (done vigorously and for a long time by three men).

They kept urging me to dance. I kept refusing, though I was beside myself with excitement and full of desire to join in. I've regretted ever since that I was too shy to join in.

The *baptême* today was a good look at the solidarity between these women, the comfort and attention the new mother receives in the difficult days after childbirth—but perhaps it's because of her (seeming) privilege; all the women seemed well off.

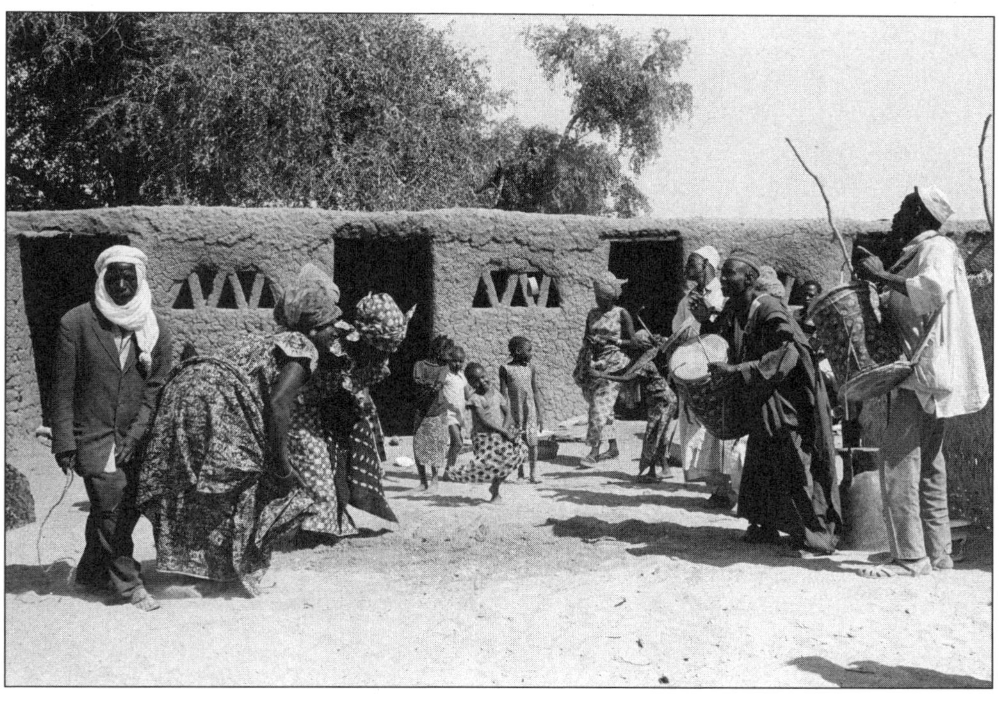

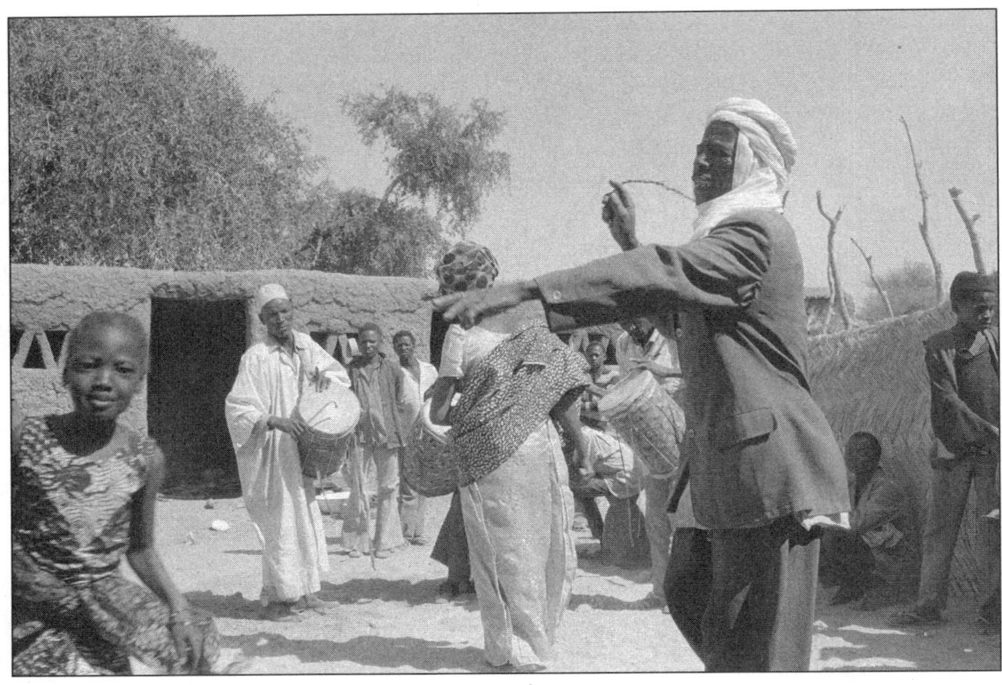

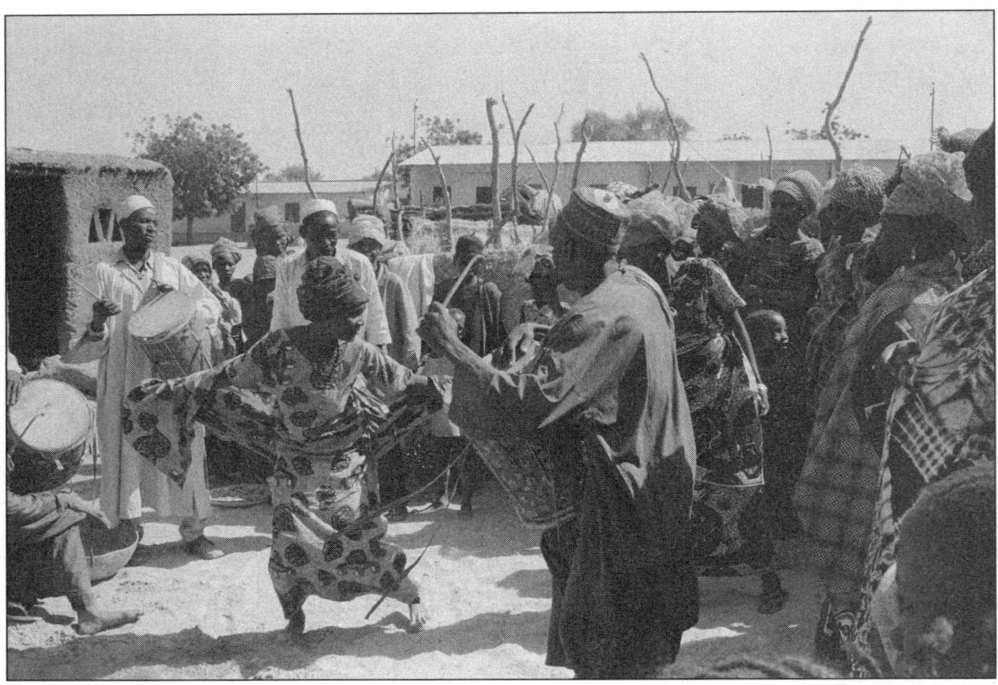

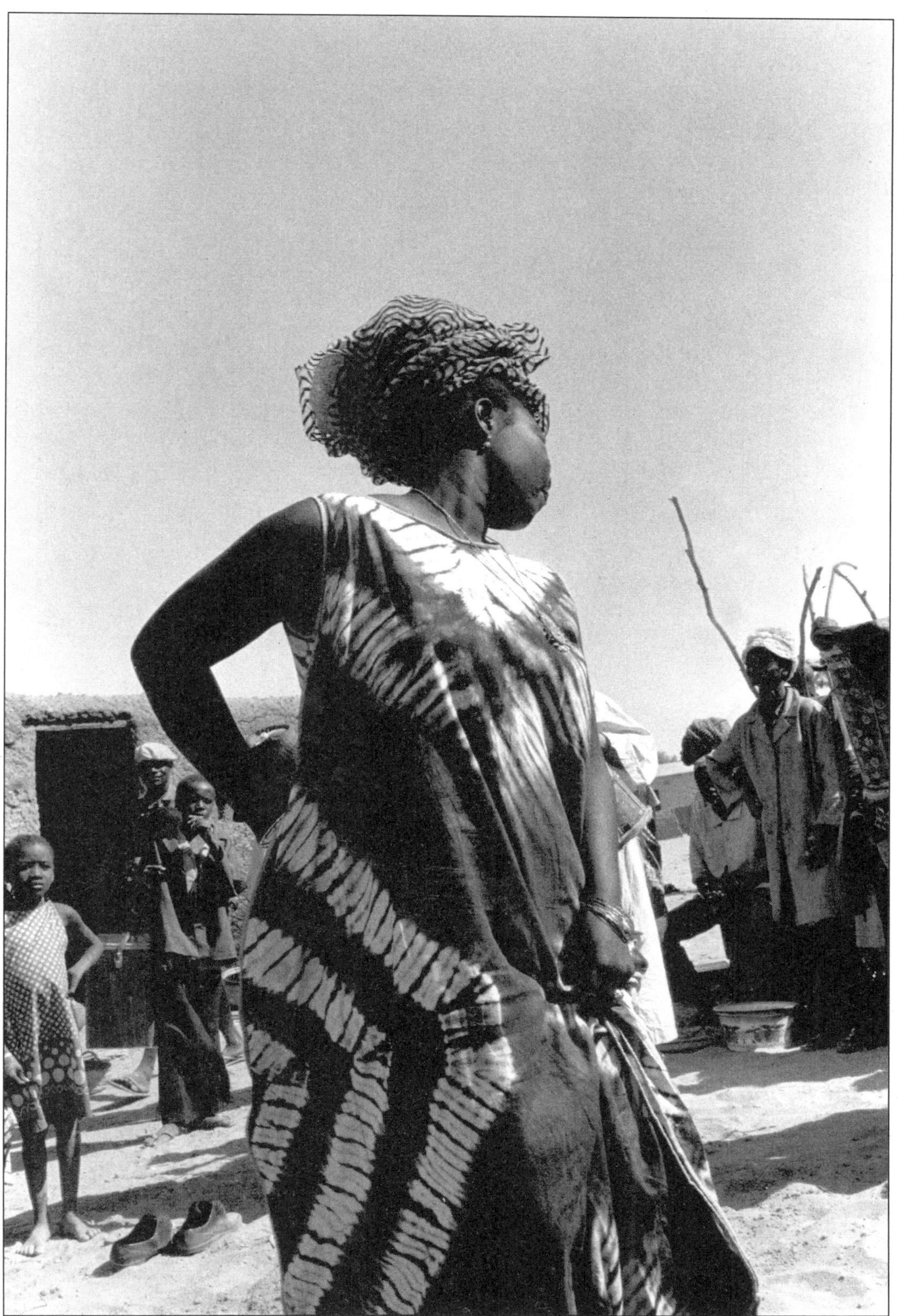

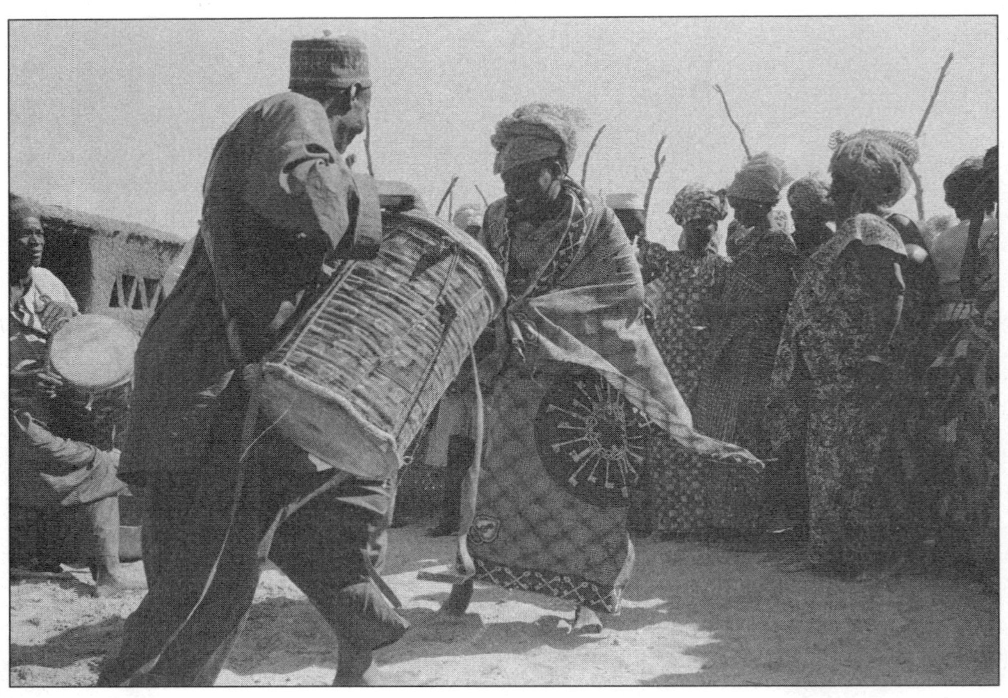

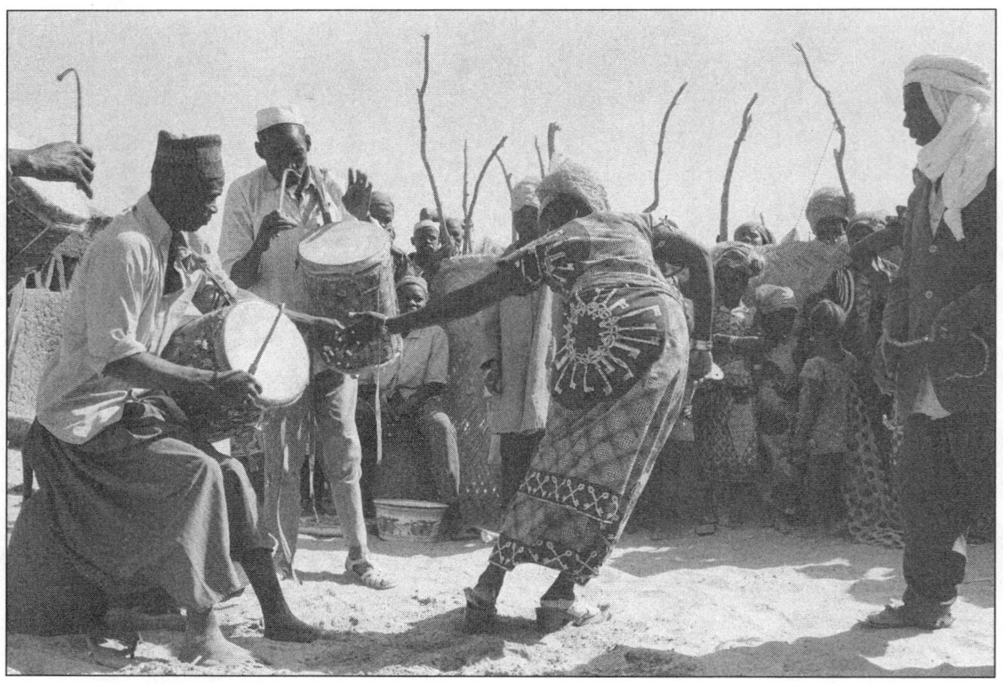

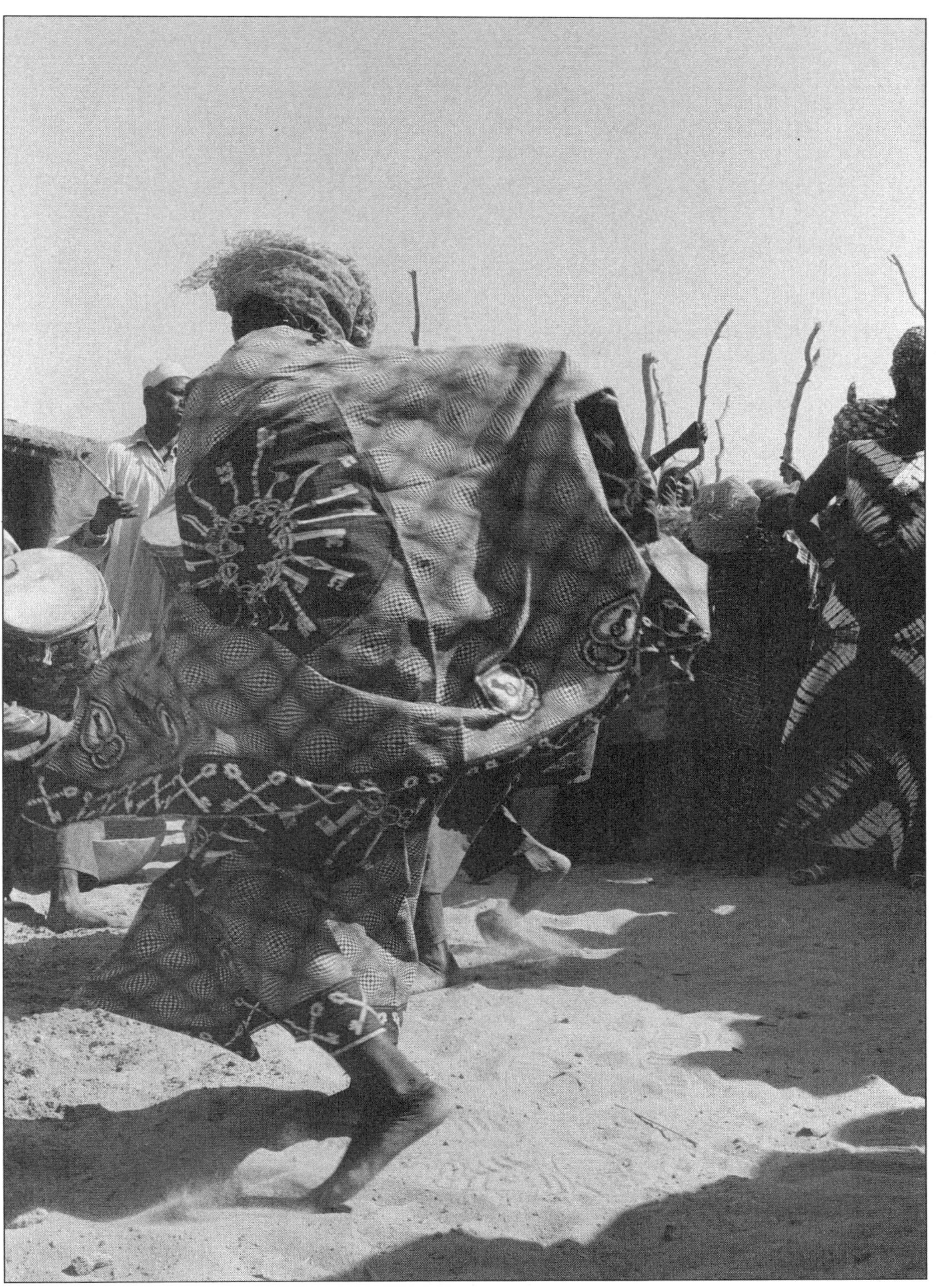

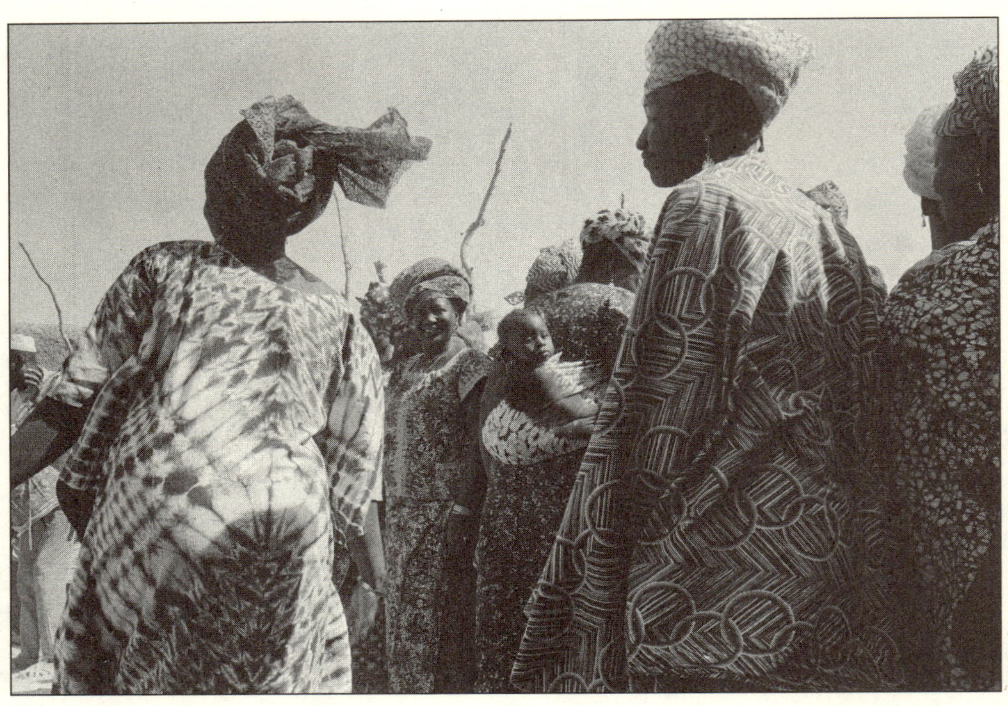

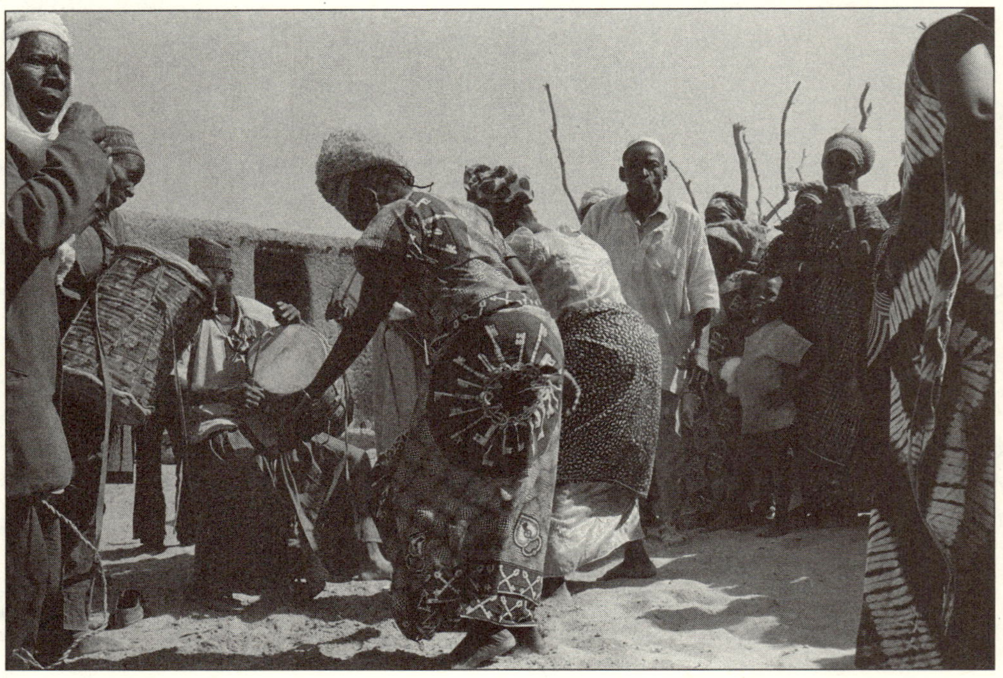

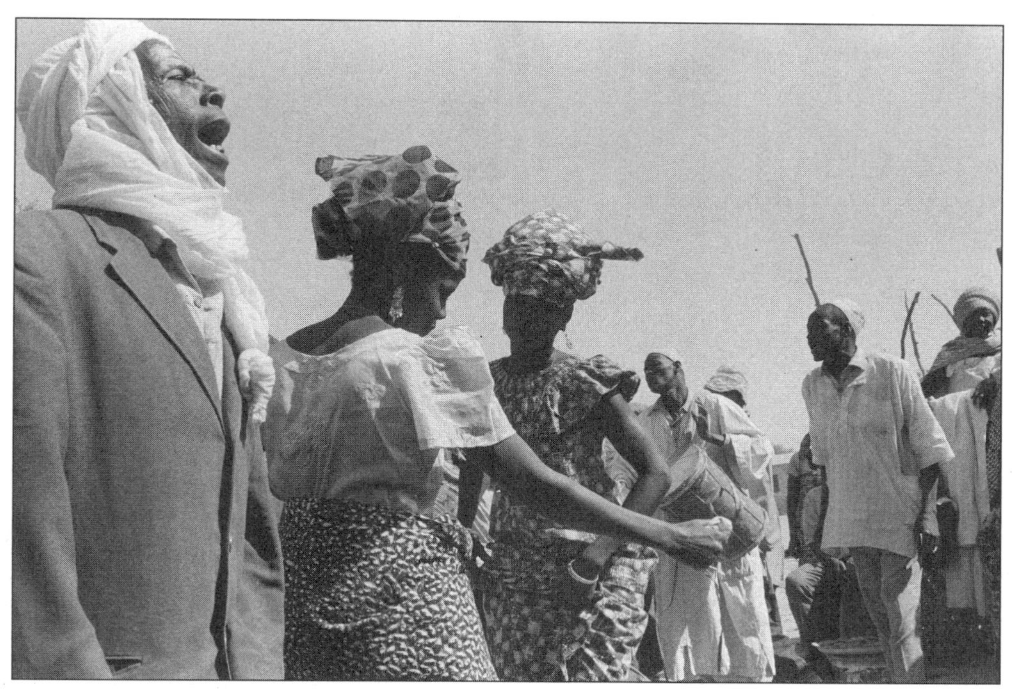

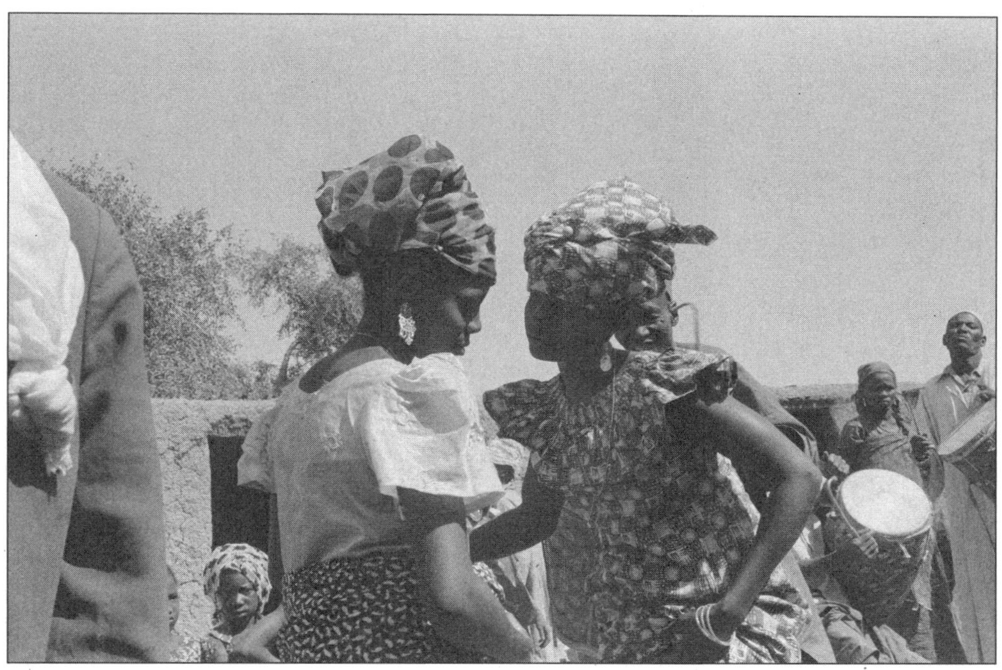

I was invited to spend that night at the home of a woman named Hamsatou Rabo. Maybe I met her at the baptism dance?

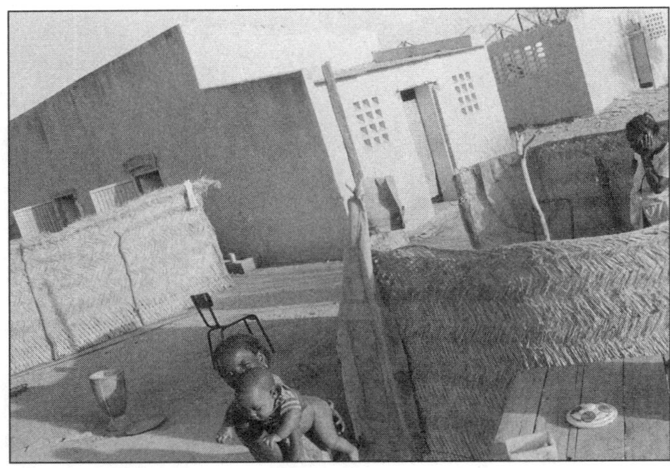

The women (and men) have such intense forms of contact and relation, which shows itself for example in the dance session today, but when the women and men get together, it's the same old shit—for example the husband came home, there was a short bit of conversation, he sat with the army boys while she cooked; after that, nothing. And when I asked what they did in the military they bristled, said "Well, what anyone does in the military?" And they were very into their "profession"; the bourgeois demeanor of the military here is quite indicative of the general situation.

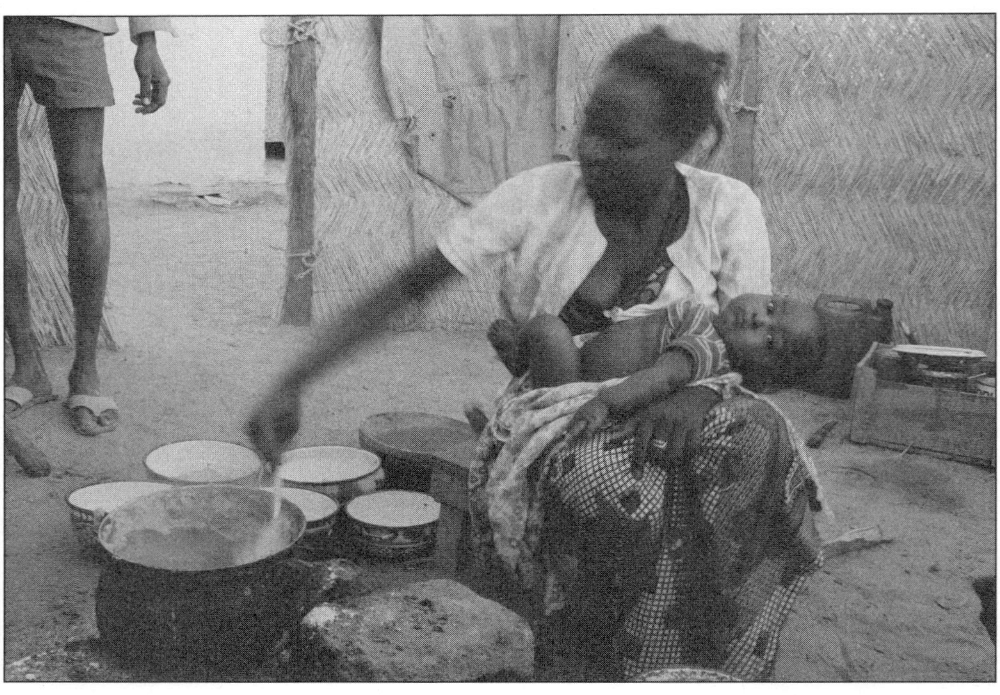

It's such a strange (uncomfortable?) thing to always be sitting with these strangers, not understanding their conversation, saying very little because of my French; it's futile for me to expect them to understand why I won't marry; no matter what excuse/reason I give, it's not natural—do I concede in order not to alienate them, or do I keep trying to have them understand? Marriage is the *raison d'être* [reason for being], which means I am a non-*être*, yes?
The best way into even the slightest confidence with these women is to make talk about material things, for example how she loved to tell me about the *tapis* [tapestries] covering her walls, the cost, etc.
In her house:
The gilt ceramic elephant dishes
The ubiquitous studio photos
"*La Genie de l'eau*" –a painting of a woman with snakes and flying hair [5].

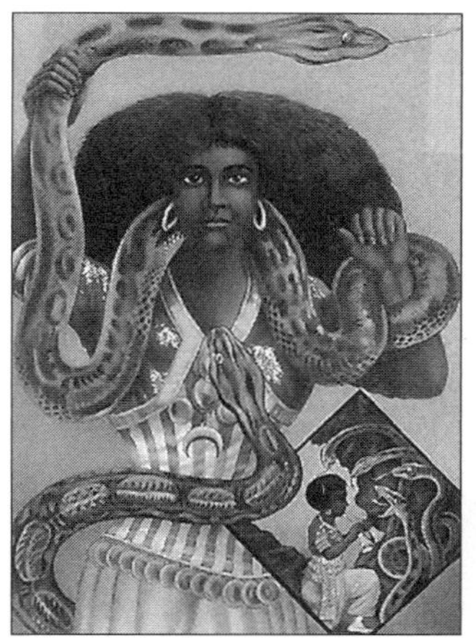

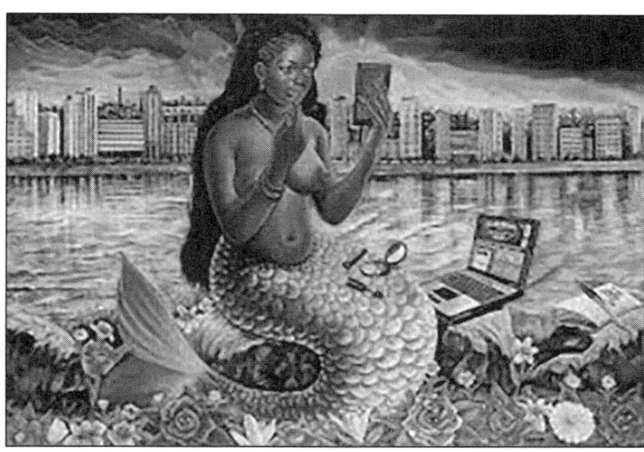

A classic depiction of Mami Wata and a contemporary one.

And so much for my conjecture earlier about that guy I saw in the market: In Hamsatou's house and at her friend's, there were those blue and gold canopy beds—

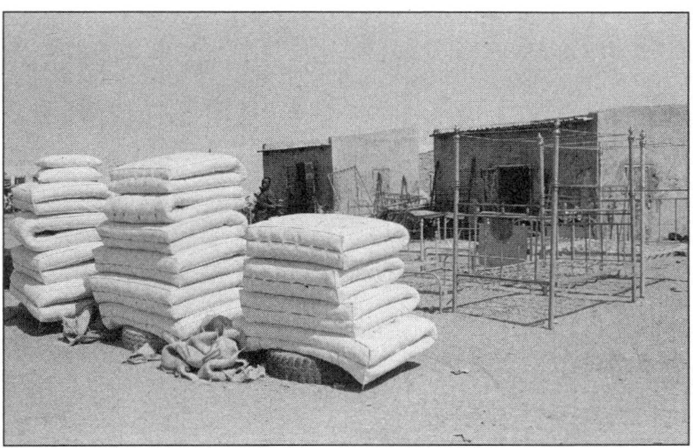

I realize it's becoming a treat to sit at a table, and I haven't seen a lighted room in several weeks. The nights here are dotted with small fires.

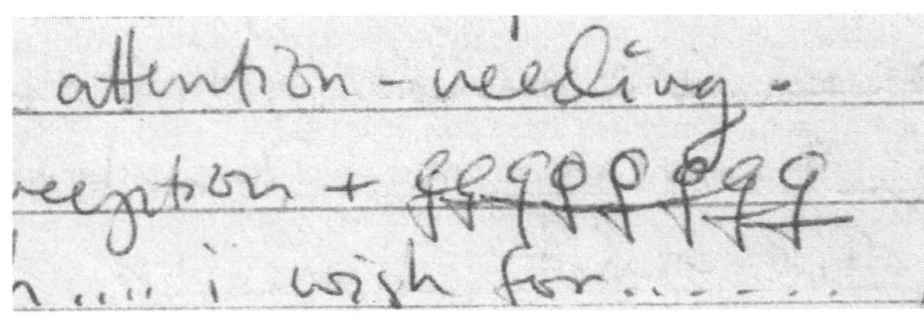

Tonight I had to hold a baby and sure enough, it pissed on me—they're so unwieldy, flimsy, attention-needing—thanks for contraception and [*women's symbols, i.e., lesbianism*] Speaking of which . . . I wish for . . . .

Hamsatou was constantly with the baby, it was on her back or feeding and late at night I could hear it crying to suckle. When I asked her if it felt good to birth a child her face lit up, she explained that, "*Ça augmente la richesse*," ["That increases one's wealth."]—the old tale that when one is old one will have children to work for you, to take care of you, that a woman here means very little if she is childless.

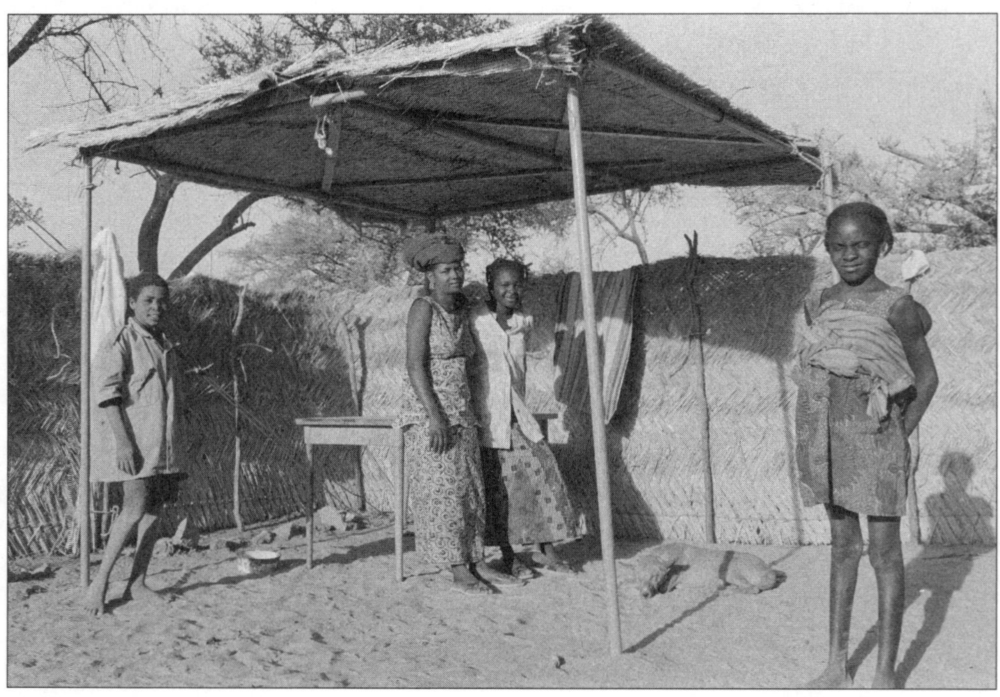

Hamsatou is sixteen. Her first birth took three days, in the nearby hospital. For forty days following, the woman washes with boiled water, consumes no sugar, tea, coffee, and eats a lot "*pour grosser*" ["to fatten up"].

She prefaced most info with "*pour les Africains*," being very conscious of the customs indigenous to her people.
She asked whether, "*. . . chez vous, les hommes frappent les femmes*," [" . . . in your country, the men beat the women"] and she was surprised to hear that they do—her husband doesn't beat her, and though she made polygamy seem a commonplace she was clearly antipathetic to it because of the jealousy and fighting (*la bataille*) that ensues—
Divorce is possible, but I'm sure quite difficult.

Her cousin, eighteen, married to a very dry, shy, anal fellow probably thirty-five years old; she was very gregarious although temperamental. At dinner there was a scene, she being very tired and perhaps not too enamored of him—whenever she expressed affection by sneaking up to him, whispering or giggling, he kept

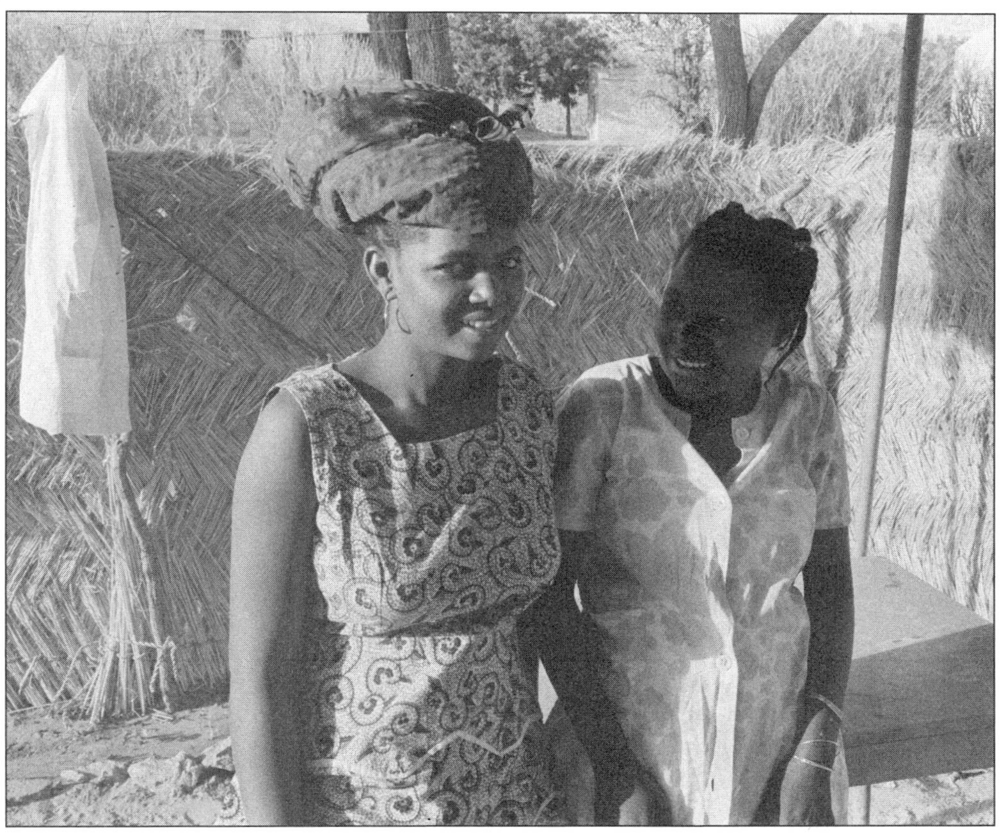

a cool paternal almost tolerant air, did not respond in kind. Once when he said something to her, she put her head down and cried softly, he moronically studied a French-English dictionary, and the other two chatted on—no attempt at reconciliation, he was going to be firm and in the right. She had already (married one year) developed a fairly effective and common defense system: A lot of laughter, running conversation with a woman friend and male visitor, teasing and "light-heartedness" to offset his priggishness.

PART OF A LETTER TO MIMI:

Last nite I slept at Hamsatou's, a Niger woman married (at 15) to a military man, she already has a baby (girl), delivery took 3 days. Dig it. In the eve we played cards w/ the kids who are her cook & lackey & young sister & she told me about polygamy & wife-beating & dowry & why it's so terrific & indispensable to have one baby after another, world without end, amen.(Which I do understand & can intellectually accept the reasons for, but it's an extension of the polygamy tradition, & I think both need reassessment on the local/personal level here.)
I also had to be polite & eat the *paté* she prepared, I absolutely gag on it at the same time—my lips crinkle up from the spice & as inconspicuously as possible I consume a liter or two of water—
(I have such an admirable stomach, I'm not sick yet!)

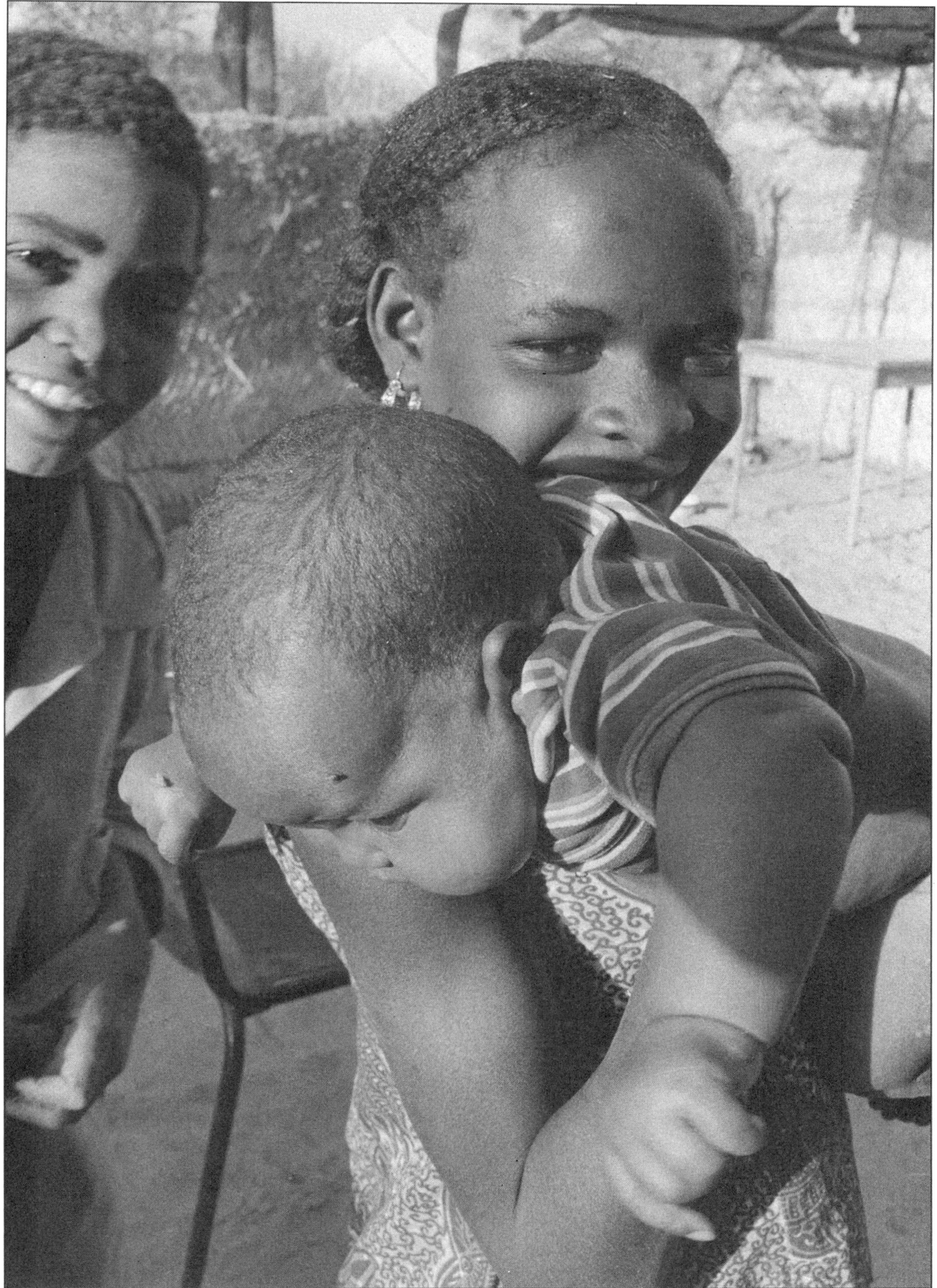

I have no memory of this man and regrettably I no longer have the photos that he enclosed with the letter. He refers to us walking together. Not an uncommon experience, since men were always attaching themselves to me, showing me around, and of course proposing marriage . . .

A LETTER FROM ALI DIALLI:

Zinder, September 1, 1976
Very dear mademoiselle,
This letter is to put you up to date with my news, and in memory of our friendship.
This letter permits me to tell you my news and to receive yours.
In the first place I am in Zinder and in good health, nothing is bad, and I believe that you remember the friend who walked with you. I ask that you pardon me because I was on leave which is the reason that you haven't read my news, I had gone on leave for 3/three months to my home in order to see my family. But now I have come back to Zinder, therefore when I returned to Zinder I found the photo that you sent me, and I am very happy. Therefore here are two photos of my home that I bought for you. I send greetings to your whole family, brothers, mother and father.

By the soldier of the 2nd class Ali Dialli at the 3rd C.P.C of the F.A.N. Zinder

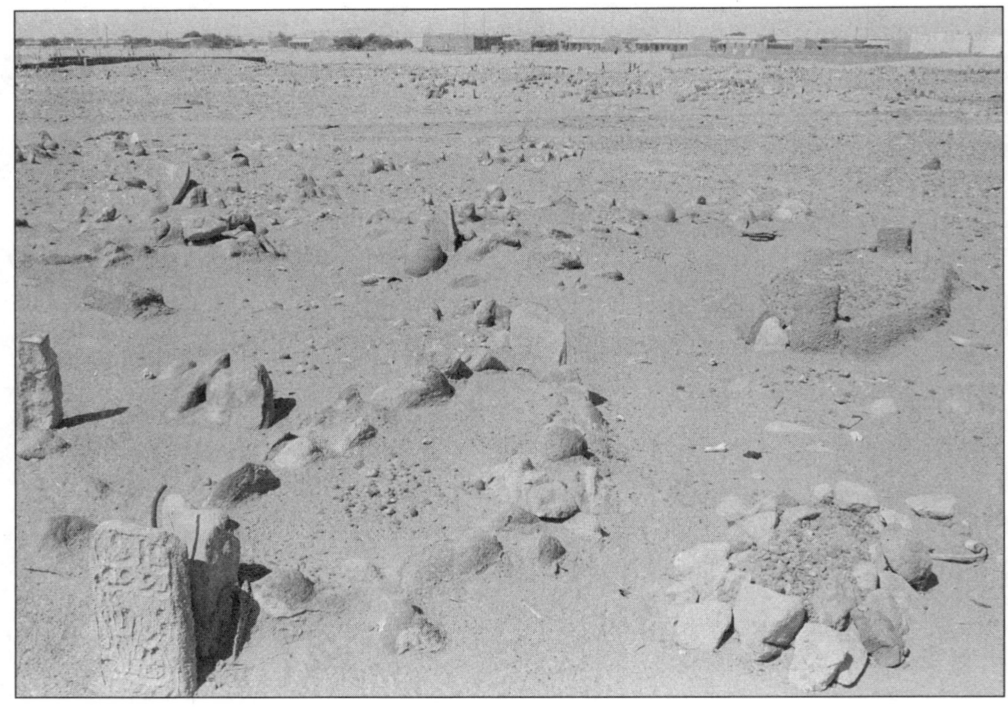

A cemetery in Zinder

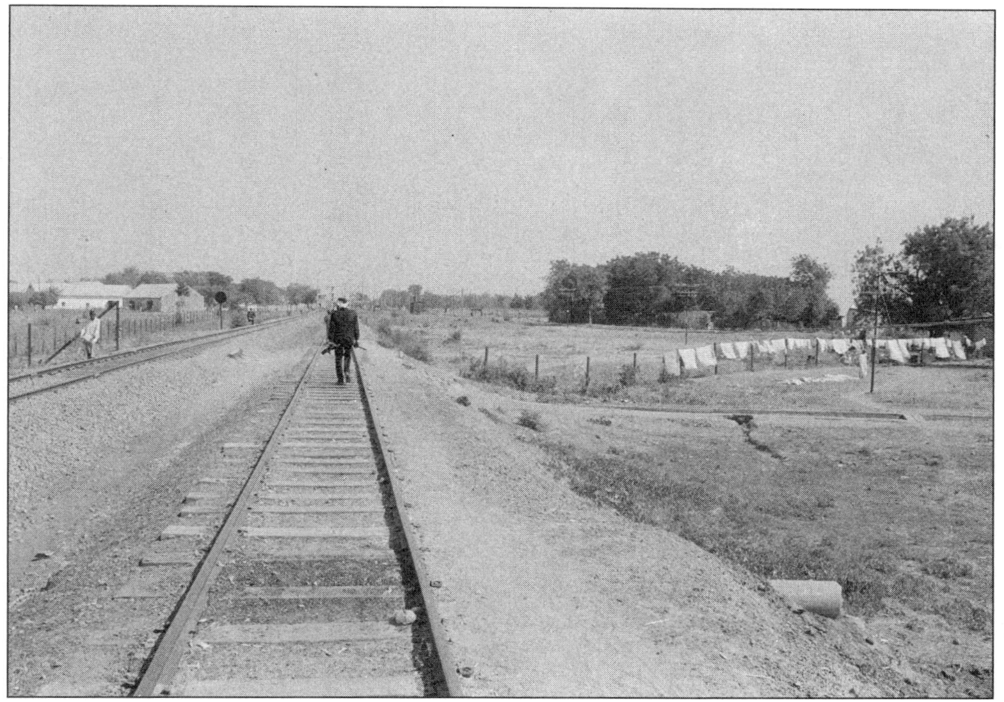

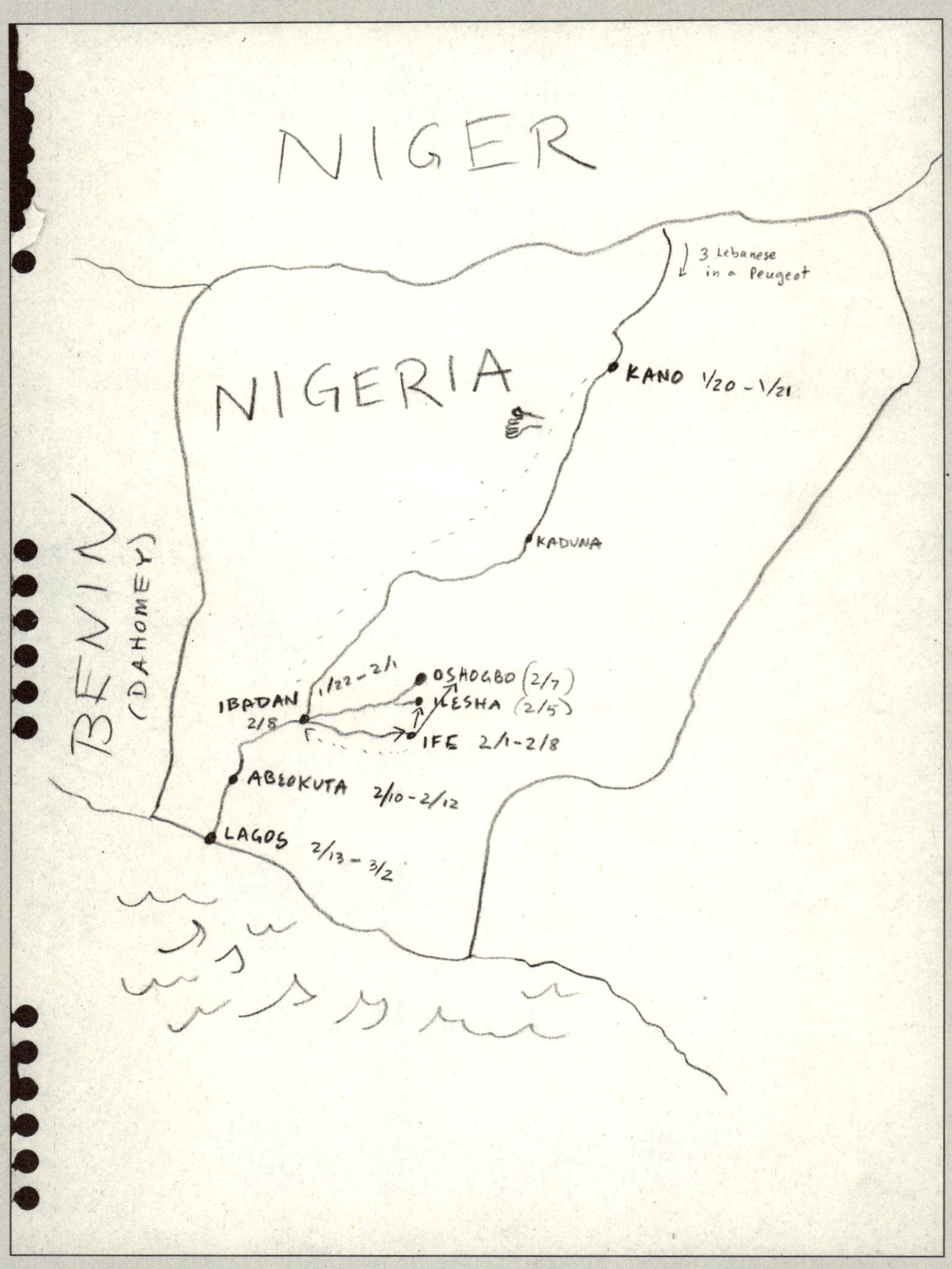

NIGER
NIGERIA
3 Lebanese
in a Peugeot
KANO 1/20 - 1/21
KADUNA
BENIN
(DAHOMEY)
IBADAN
2/8
1/22 - 2/1
OSHOGBO (2/7)
ILESHA (2/5)
IFE 2/1-2/8
ABEOKUTA 2/10 - 2/12
LAGOS 2/13 - 3/2

CHAPTER EIGHT

Crossing into Nigeria: In Ibadan with Godfrey and Grace

I left Zinder early on the 20th. I got a ride across the border into Nigeria with three Lebanese businessmen who were on their way to Kano. Many Lebanese were doing a good business importing African cotton fabrics.

Kano would be my first "big city" since leaving Algiers three weeks prior. I stayed in the campground in Kano for two nights.

JANUARY 20 & 21

Dream about a NY football game in a stadium/auditorium, we first sing "It Takes a Worried Man . . . " Mimi wouldn't sing, all the Neri group [my grade school classmates] came in, the men all dressed in white, Mary Ohlinger had some weird accident with her neck, sat with "the boys." Two fat men and I stand at some fridge (my mother's?) with shelves of large pastries. I kept exclaiming, "Why does she have all of this?

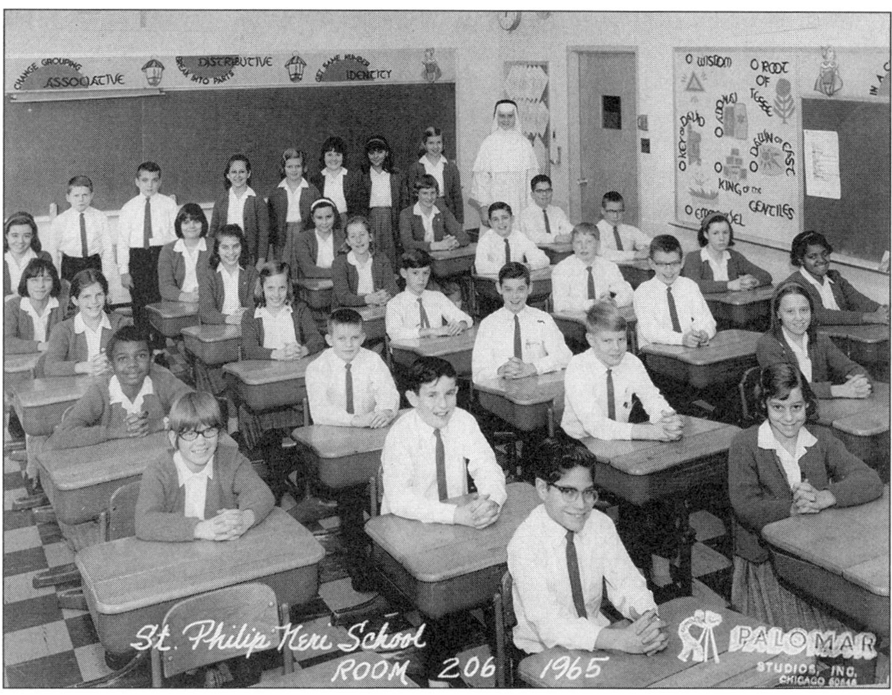

Upset today by the incongruities (in me and here). Whizzing by in a Peugeot with music and clean well-dressed businessmen makes the African woman plodding several miles to market with a calabash of tomatoes even more remote than when

I'm on a lorry surrounded by similar Africans, seeing the land pass at an African pace and level of discomfort—first I spend so much time getting to understand what/how much they are made to withstand on a daily basis, and then all of a sudden I'm reminded of the life on the other side, the "developed" side—
Saw many whites today in Benz' with chauffeurs.
And the corpulent businessmen at the Central Hotel today was a good dose for me of the other side of African life—being a woman certainly has its double insights when traveling, the rich men and local women covering the spectrum.

The following letter tells a story about money, so here's some background:
₦ is the symbol for the naira, the basic monetary unit of Nigeria. 1 ₦ = $1.60 at the official rate (equal to $8.80 in 2023), whereas the black market rate for a naira was 80 cents.
Kobos are the smaller coin currency. The official rate was 1 ₦ = 100 kobos.
At times I had to change at banks because I had traveler's checks, but if I changed a lot in one currency and then went to a different country, I would always change to that currency on the black market.

A LETTER TO MIMI:

Dear Mimi,
Well, if I thought that bribery among Chicago policemen was reprehensible, try to fathom this: I arrived at the campsite in Kano (N. Nigeria). Immediately approached by 5-8 men asking me to change money—(the official rate is 65 kobos=$1)—after some persuasion & attempts by them to cheat me (e.g., give me the same as the bank) I got 80 kobos for 1$, 25% more, from the fellow who runs the "office" here, a typically anonymous office of the sort that proliferate in a bureaucratized country like this. Ten minutes later another fellow came to me w/ a message & led me to the one who had changed my $$—he stood by discreetly while the other gave me back my $20 traveler's check but told me to keep the Nigerian $ he'd sold me—when asked whether he wanted/expected anything in return, he said no, it's just dash.[26] After a short thank you I was led back by his (by now) assistant who explained to me that he had been the one to arrange the $$ return & in consequence I owed him dash in the form of 3₦ (=$2.40)—which I gave him (since it was free $$ by this point). He also "explained" (NEVER BELIEVE A NIGERIAN, LESSON no. 1) that the generous fellow was the treasurer of the office & handled all the (i.e., lots of) $ that came thru & consequently is able to give it away like that—my introduction to dash, the lifeblood of this chaotically & childishly prosperous country: the richest (now) in Black Africa & perverse as a result.
Fortunately I crossed the border w/ 3 Lebanese who make the trip regularly & are on solid terms w/ the border guards as a result of huge doses of dash at opportune moments—they were very hostile

26 "Dash" is Nigerian slang for a payment which is sometimes a gift, but it can also be a bribe payment.

to me & my occupation of "commercial artist" and I probably would've had to wait (& PAY) if I hadn't been w/ those 3. Speaking of whom, upon entering Kano, a large city & dirty & crowded & full of Coca Cola vendors & billboards of Black Beauty Aids & women in wigs, we went to the ritzy hotel for lunch & their whiskeys—it was straight out of a bad movie, the swank poolside lunchers, all elegantly tanned white men chatting profitably w/ suited Nigerians, & all of them the most corpulent people I've seen since Germany—one gets used to seeing, after only 2 ½ weeks here, the skinniest legs & arms poking out from raggedy clothes & old dashikis—a paunch is a remarkable sight & usually accompanied by an ostentatiously expensive dashiki and a Mercedes Benz—

It needs only 10 minutes in such a place to understand the motivation for colonialists; it was reverse culture shock, being re-Americanized but extremely so, in contrast to my recent experience in "the bush." Today however I had a feeling of homesickness due more to a despair & the difficulty of balancing the rapid & extreme incongruities that one lives with here (more pronounced even than NY, which I found difficult enough) than to anything really American that I missed—except of course American people about whom I think quite frequently. After the initial wonder & strangeness of the life-conditions here wore off, I became increasingly depressed w/ how the majority are forced to live and angry w/ the lack of really EFFECTIVE change-of-consciousness being attempted by the governments or people—e.g., in Nigeria & Niger (where I'll grant there are a lot of development programs occurring, irrigation plans & compulsory schooling by 1977 in Nigeria—good luck; no one here really believes it's possible; the population is too uncontrolled uncomputerized, there are all of those who live way out in the bush, etc.) [1]

You can't imagine how obnoxious the military is in these countries—they have the most bourgeois, uppity attitude, makes me wanna speak my mind but I must follow tourist diplomacy if I plan to stay. And altho I'd read so much about the workload of the African woman, it really requires seeing it day after day, letting it sink in, to feel how much it actually is—e.g., that they walk 3-5 miles a day (one way) to get water, 2wce a day pounding the grain for the flour to make the "*paté*" (which is a thick sticky bland paste, like uncooked bread dough, but worse.) Yesterday I tried pounding & was tired after a few minutes—and always they have babies on their backs—lots of them old old women w/ babies; drives me crazy, this.

But anyone (Nigerian) I talk to shows a profound respect & recognition for the status of women here because of her economic independence & amount of work.

[. . .]

I also saw today one manifestation of the "urbanized African woman"—the (quite preposterous) prostitute at the ritzy hotel. I'm interested to see the situation in Lagos, the capital. I heard from an American woman that the brothels here are overflowing, throughout the city, unlimited, cheap. One also never sees bare-breasted women in the cities, a phenomenon I found very pleasant in the towns—it gave back a certain respectability and "normalcy" to something which in our culture is so warped out—
A strange experience today for me at the hotel: I have a terrible phobia/fixation w/ mirrors & seeing ("being reminded of") myself—e.g., in cars I hate sitting in view of the rear view mirror, at night in busses I always avoid sitting where I have to see myself, and wherever I live I keep mirrors at a healthy distance—it has to do w/ my thinking it's (1) "wrong" (2) "too feminine" to be vain: *[the paper is torn and there are words missing here]* puritanism & sexism—but after not seeing my face for 2 weeks I began to forget what I appear like to others & today at the hotel bathroom (electric lights, running water, toilet paper (& a toilet: you can imagine the dregs I've been in to appreciate that?)) so I was quite startled. I look like the prima bourgeois tourist & quite w/o intention—my hair is longer & sort of swept back, a nice tan w/ eyes that look bluer & somehow despite my tacky clothes I look terribly well-to-do. Not to mention the problem that my vest (which I wear every day) does nothing to repel the men. But it was funny, those moments intrigue me, I feel as perhaps a Tasaday [2] does the 1st time she sees a photo of herself.
Ah yes as I started before about the wonder wearing off: I don't mean that I'm accustomed to the life here, because each situation/home/woman is different & newly interesting but, e.g., during the night w/ Hamsatou I began to see thru eyes other than those of a journa-anthrop-tourist-sociolog & saw a very very young woman w/ an equally young & married neighbor spending every day in the same cycle of food preparation, baby-suckling & caring, chatting about husbands and prices, playing cards, a lot of giggling, & being extremely materialistic (i.e., house & body decoration-conscious: she had the tackiest "oriental" & "Moroccan" tapestries covering all 4 walls of the house, she proudly told me the price of each & that they were part of her dowry), knowing minimal writing skills & being at best functionally literate.
And my grandiose plans kneel down in the face of unalleviated reality.
"The general always fractures into the particular as soon as you come close; and the particular, the specific, is persistently diverse."
That keen observation is from Basil Davidson.
Whatever I'm after at this point is somehow terribly elusive, and I

think it will continue to be. The one certainty I have encountered: Africa is very different than I expected, which is little consolation for the problem, yes?

I've managed to learn (after a few aborted attempts) that the best way to the heart/confidence of most of these women is to make small, close-to-home talk, and gradually <u>they</u> indicate when they're willing to move onto more private ground.

I really hope all is well w/ you (& co.)—I get quite anxious not being able to receive news readily here—but if there's ever a problem it's best to mail it to an approx. Am. Emb. & urge them (w/ a little dash) to forward it to me—

Much love, a nice long hug,

Su

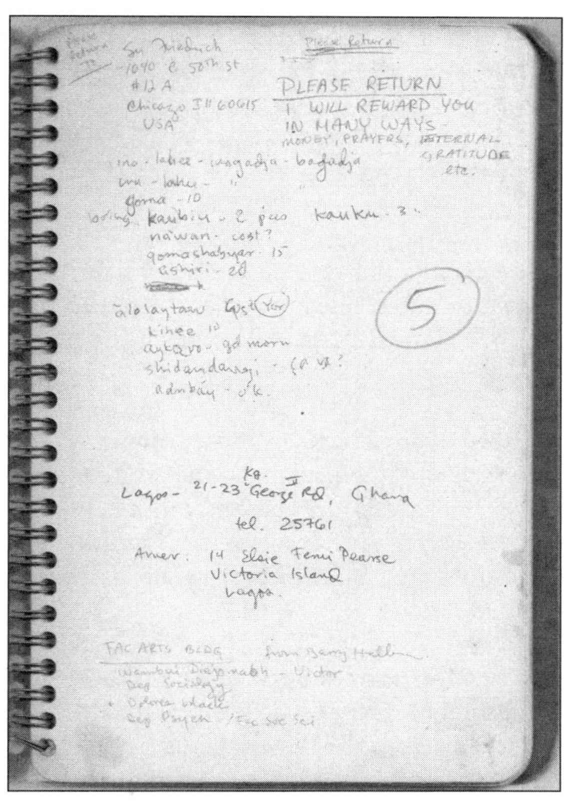

The first page of the second journal.

Spent time with *Africa Woman* and *Africa* magazines —*Woman* is not very well written, and concentrates to a bad degree on successful business/art/political women, and of all things a blurb on world beauty contests and the criteria (white-based) of beauty. In general, however, it is a good albeit bourgeois beginning (an issue on fashion in a culture where the women work harder and for less reward than can be imagined) along the lines of *Ms* magazine.

Nido is being sold by roadside vendors here along with cigs and candy—but I don't know actually how many women here use it—Hamsatou hadn't heard of it.

The wooden carts loaded down with 10–15 large logs being pushed thru the hot noon streets by several raggedy grunting boys—so much for the industrial revolution, it's the *Moyen Age* [Middle Ages], the five minutes of work of a crane occupying a half day of ten men to load a truck with logs or bags or etc.—
A walk thru the old city was predictably discouraging, and again I saw the women very busy always on their way to sell or buy, many men unoccupied. The phenomenon of young bands of beggar boys from five to fifteen years old . . . they even sing chanting rhythmic African melodies to charm us (whites, wealthy Africans, et. al.); but it's notable that the young girls rarely approach me for dash, they appear to be generally first priority of protection by the family (if any is available)—
And they're tremendous, the young girls in scarves and gold and bright skirts and impish smiles and laughter . . . and the attendant worries of learning the merchant skills on which their lives will depend—

In the department store, many of the women wore wigs, the first I've seen [3]. Also saw women in short skirts, the prostitutes.

A Chinese woman in a tennis skirt with a dachshund just came strolling thru the campsite!

At the train station today, seeing about getting a ticket to go further south: The stench of urine disguised by the funkiness of music blaring across the platforms, that element of Africa that I most admire, a certain charm and style in the midst of utter shoddiness and hardship.

Equally so with the resilience and relatively strong spirits of these women, whose lives are immeasurably difficult. I tried to imagine today that the counterpart of the African woman (barefooted, meagre, muscular and tenuously self-sufficient, who is sisterly-cooperative with the other women) is the gartered, hair sprayed, pasta-stuffed and overly maternal American woman crippled in her high heels and tightening wedding band.

Whose privilege do we have more sympathy for? The comforts of women *chez moi* [at home, back home] are clearly and solely external, I begin to realize. The engulfing madness of near-solitary confinement in the fluorescent and Lysol'd kitchens of the affluent world are perhaps a comparable if not more tenuous prison than the struggle for survival here which at least breeds a certain solidarity and companionship—the groups of four or five women going thru the bush for water, the chattering groups selling together in the market, the respect they clearly have from African men (if, however, a respect founded on fear or dominion), or the grudging respect (indicated by his newly-donned overbearingness when in a position of affluence) required when they acknowledge the women as an economic lifeblood of the country, more evident here by their role in the

market AND home than in the US, where the home is dismissed as secondary in absolute economic terms.
Have learned a lesson from Angela Davis, and this trip: Do not romanticize the work of the working class. Respect it/them, yes, for the toil it represents but be realistic; drawing on the romanticized, in-touch-with-the-earth notions of Millet, Ruskin and many other guilty ones only keeps them in their place and looking a bit more bearable to delicate eyes (the hard sculpturesque muscles gleaming in the noonday sun, etc.)—it's paltry intellectualizing.

I learned common words and phrases as I went along. They were from a lot of different languages, and often written phonetically so it's hard for me to determine which is which language. So, probably misspelled . . .
One of the most useful ones?

I am traveling alone—*inata heeah nikadeh*

And my favorite?

Cheap hotel—*wandabiedeechyada*

I hitched rides from Kano to Ibadan [4].

JANUARY 22

What a dream—I had done something in Niger which (1) threw me out of the country and (2) flew me home—a feeling of embarrassment at having ended the voyage so soon, disappointment also in voices of friends, first sensations of driving thru NY near Rockefeller Center in a Rolls-Royce with a corpulent mink-coated older woman; a young boy asked to give aid, came down with pamphlets on horsemanship, he and I were hijacked by some familiar force in a white plane which crash-landed at a beach where lots of middle-aged Blacks were loafing; a huge crowd was gathered awaiting some guru, Mimi was sitting nearby watching me, I pointed up a long dusty African-sort-of road and said quite eloquently (as things appear in dreams) while slapping and whipping myself, "It's the same day after day until the end, for what?"

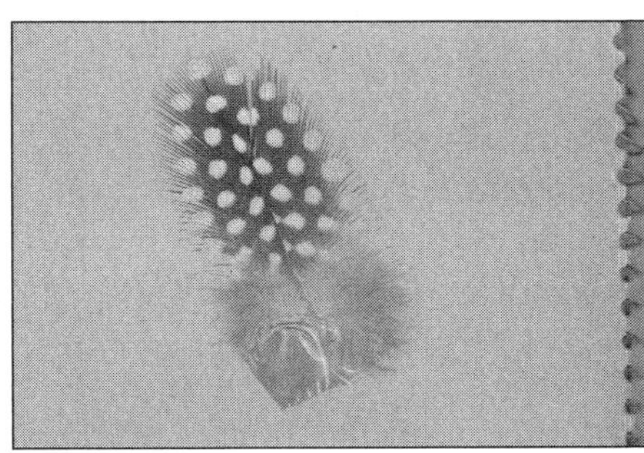

On the first of the rides I hitched, a man showed me the pills he'd bought for a cold: malaria tablets.
He said now with the new government it's easier to find beer. We were accompanied (at my feet in the front seat) by two alive and tied-up guinea fowls, lovely black and white spotted birds.

PART OF A LETTER TO MIMI:

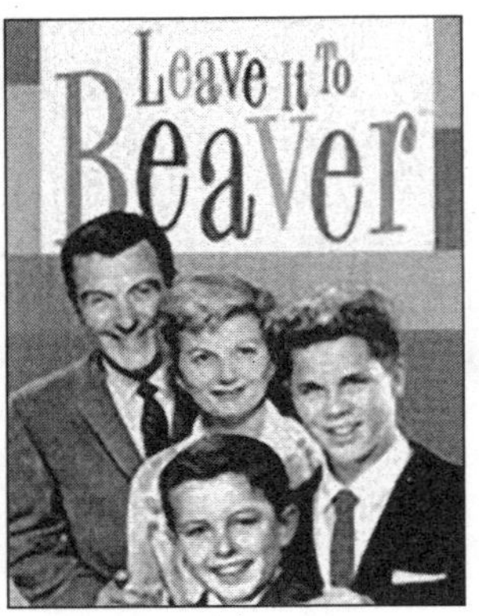

Before this ends I might be a Cleaverite,[27] an American devotee, but no less than the bourgeois Africans who make no effort to suppress their annoyance with many aspects of the life here—they tend to sound more "racist" than the worst tourist. But I've had now 2 long experiences w/ Nigerian men, Yoruba & Ibo, & I find them reprehensible & intolerable (an unfair generalization—sorry)—the first was the desert crossing, the 2nd today a 12 hr. ride from n. Nigeria to Ibadan. They are absolutely childlike in any discussion, they will deliberately say something to prove a point which blatantly contradicts something said a few minutes prior, & there is no chance of finishing a sentence or thought, they burst in with wait wait wait & then there's no chance of being heard above the racket they make—I sat for a long time in the back seat while 2 of them discussed Nigerian politics & celibacy in the Catholic Church. Seriously there was rarely a space when only one voice was heard, it was a constant duologue w/ each telling the other to hold on wait wait while he gave the definitive argument. Hopeless, ridiculous, & enough to dissuade me from wanting to bring up any topic which might be controversial; that only leads to 1) incredible frustration 2) an equally obnoxious debate method on my part. They're just so pissy arrogant, along w/ all the cockiness that's built into the British English which they learn.

Passed an army barracks hazy and sweltering in the midday sun, no trees for shade, row upon row of clay houses with corrugated tin roofs, the women pounding and carrying.
The rows of women trudging single file alongside the highway carrying fully loaded calabashes and babies, their wraps blowing and swaying, slender legs and bare feet, soft dark shoulders, wiry arms.

Bing bread (?)—spicy fried balls, delicious.

As I neared Ibadan and heard talk of Nigerian dramatists and Yoruba culture and the university, it dawned on me that my irritation at Kano, for example, is that it's a mid-city with all the bustle and no content, and that I can only imbibe small doses of "*la vie traditionelle africaine*" [traditional African life] before I chafe and need *la vie contemporaine* [contemporary life].

27 Beaver—one of the sons in the Cleaver family—was the main character in this popular American TV show about a suburban boy and his misadventures.

It's as if enough depression ensued with seeing first hand all the problems and issues that need work, and now I'm interested to see what's in fact being done. Balance.

But I must keep in mind the domesticity and family orientation and desire for small town living of most Africans (and people in general), as long as that is met with the necessary "amenities" of life: like water.

And I am finding that I have to remind myself sternly at each market and roadside stand, when I tend to slide into thinking about the limited availability and outlet for the products, that they are the ones the products are there for. Just because there's an absence of tourists doesn't mean it's a "failed" or empty market. It's as if I have to populate Africa with Africans in mind, so successfully has it been made the domain of/dependent on non-Africans [5].

On second thought it's quite a reasonable and unavoidable perception on my part, as is the mild surprise I'm still trying to conquer in seeing Blacks in good cars, etc.—it's precisely the same with women, even to the trivial extreme of making note when, for example, a woman here smokes or wears pants—
and understanding rich whites
and learning not to criticize comforts

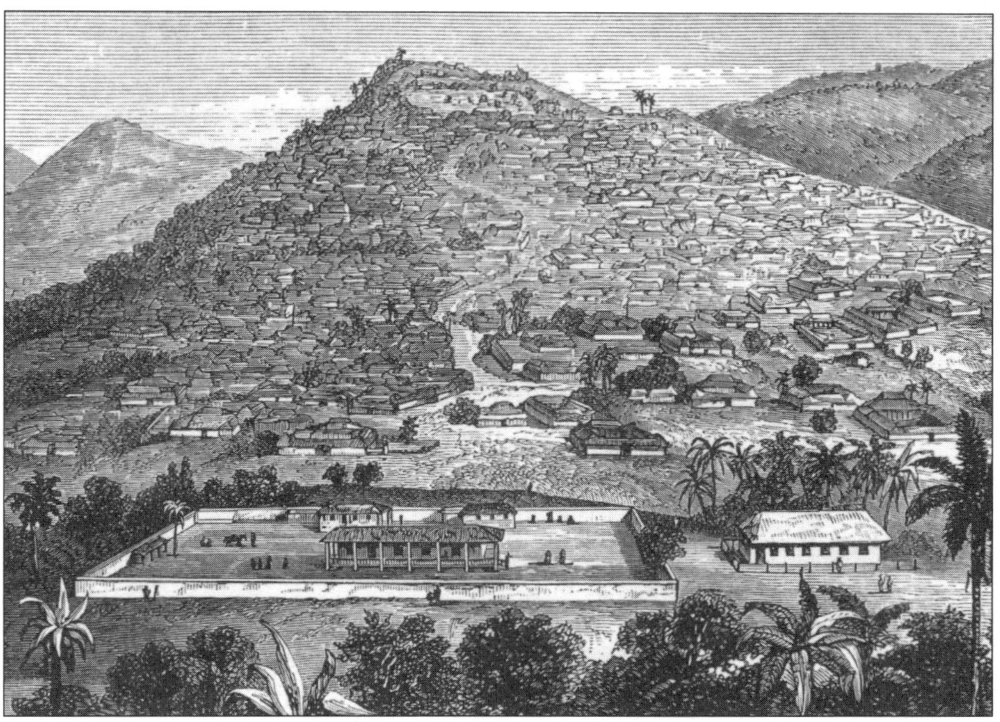

A view of Ibadan in 1854 with the Church Missionary Society compound in the foreground.

When I arrived in Ibadan I stayed at first for a few days with Godfrey Chux Otiri [6], one of the two men who had given me a ride from Kano to Ibadan. He had a Danish wife, but she wasn't there. I also met and took pictures of Grace C. Otiri (who I think was his sister) and some children, presumably hers.

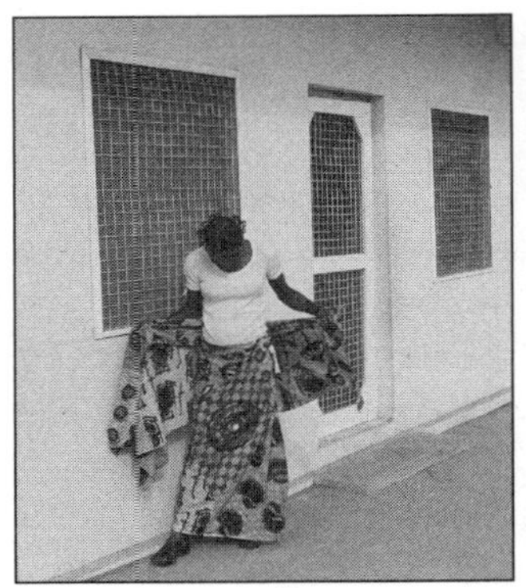

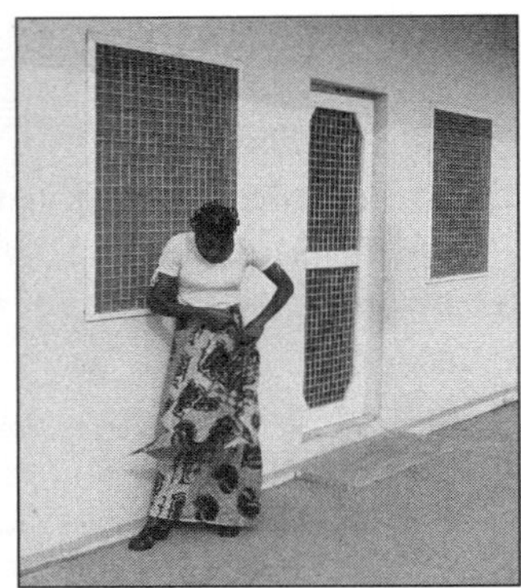

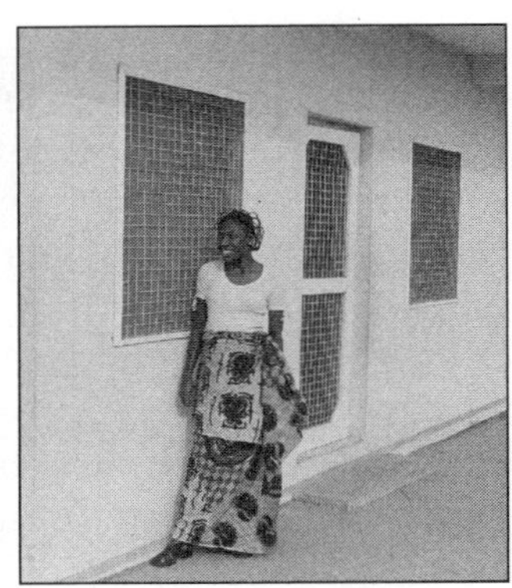

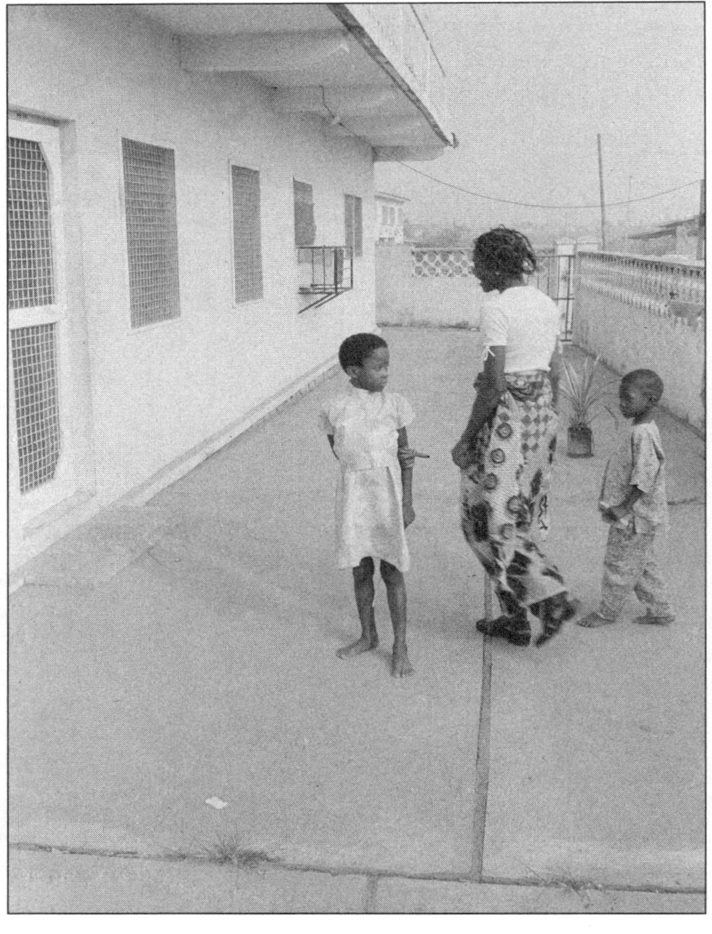

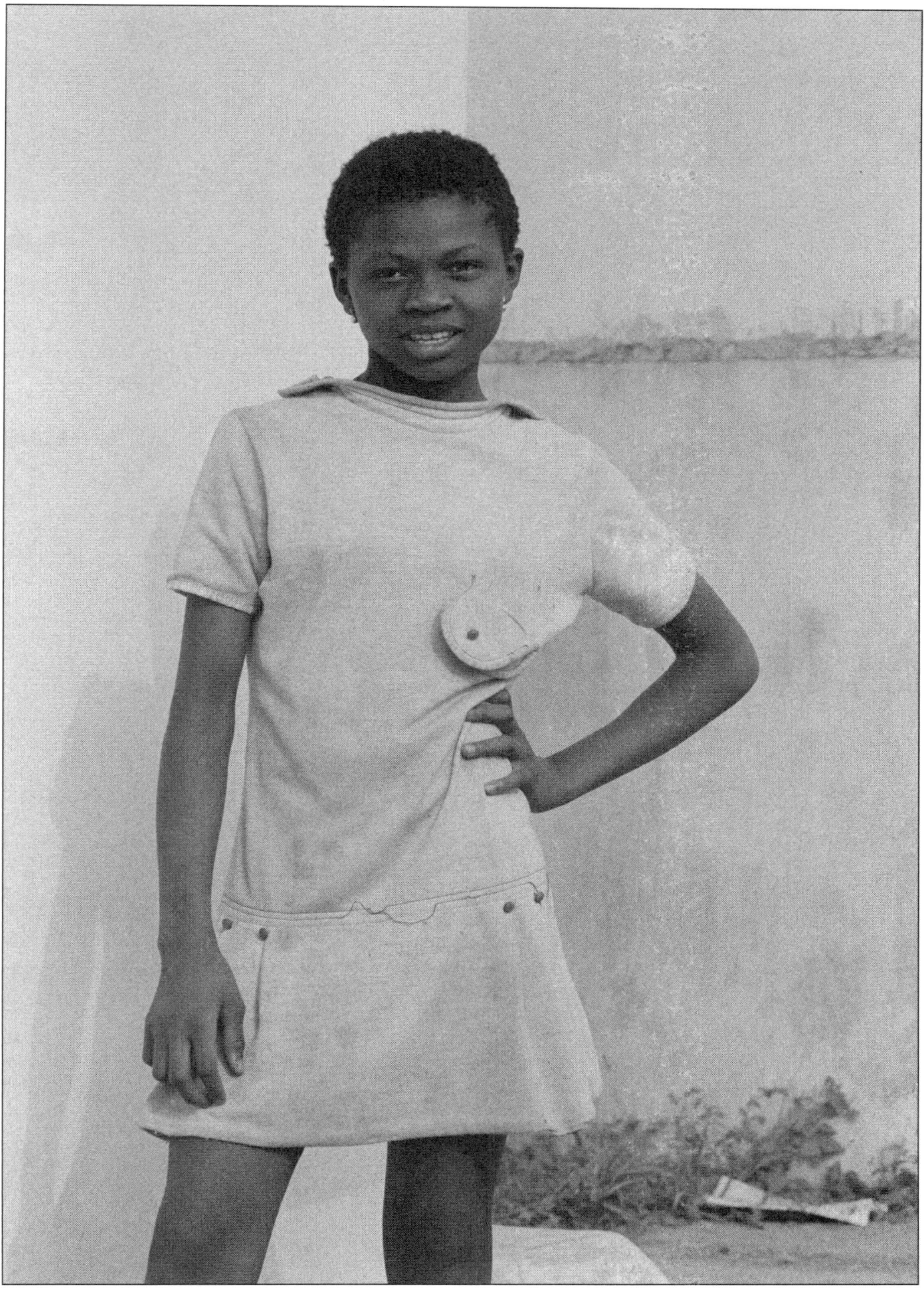

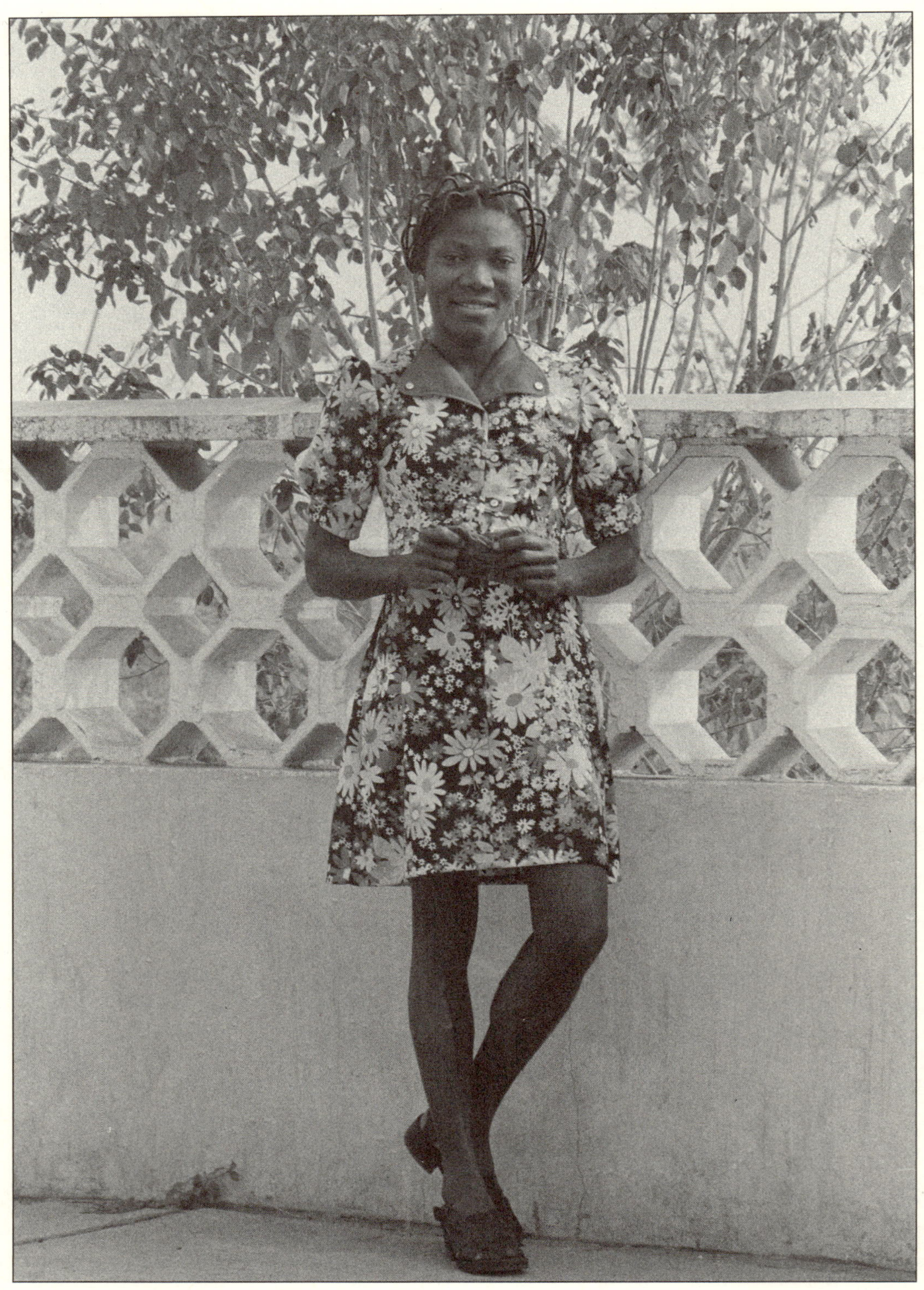

Grace C. Otiri

I'm afraid, getting pangs and flashes of losing my youth through an excessive amount of overly formal, unfamiliar, therefore too serious associations with acquaintances who are also generally older than me. The fact is that I have been very somber lately, walking and reading and making tourist talk and I'm fed up. I need my environment.

The issue/solution: I need *work*, occupation, busyness, filled days, too full; I am not the listless kind, I am not voluntarily someone who enjoys being sedentary, who enjoys just absorbing (which is what traveling essentially is) without spewing out, grinding away—although maybe grinding away at nothing or an evanescent something.

And I hate being taken care of, I hate being shown around, I hate being nurtured and left grateful to people I don't know and don't care about, I hate the *politesse* [politeness] and superficiality and strain of talking with someone who doesn't understand my accent, which necessitates repeating myself at every phrase; right now I'm upset.

Trying to get some insight into the country's women through a man, I hear such things as: "They're great in bed but they just don't know how to take care of house like European women, they take so much longer to do everything."

That, from Godfrey, my "host" here in Ibadan.

JANUARY 23

Ibadan is an impressive town, and I can imagine how proud/refreshed Black Americans are to visit here, to be absolutely surrounded by Blacks (of all classes—nevertheless, the Nigerians are quite stratified, being good students of British social hierarchies).

It's very hilly and lush even in the dry season, the roads towered over by palm trees and haphazard thick vegetation, there's a sense of activity and (relative) well-being and always the good music pouring from roadside record shops; the prosperous slipping kobos to the lame, the young men in very chic American-style clothes, platform shoes being the rage here. The women are a shiny blend of old and new, bare legs and platform sandals with the *geles* [28] or their hair braided up in a vine-like crown perched on their heads, or the handsome corn-rowing which accents the shapeliness of their heads. However, it was also impressed upon me that they are the secretaries and clerks and . . . need I say more?

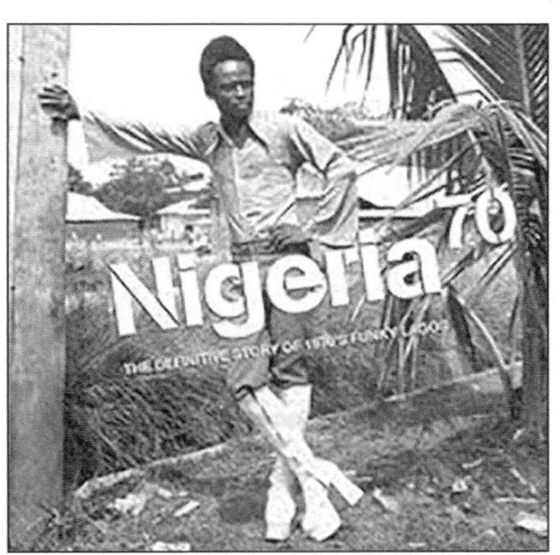

28 Nigerian term for a head wrap.

PART OF A LETTER TO MIMI:

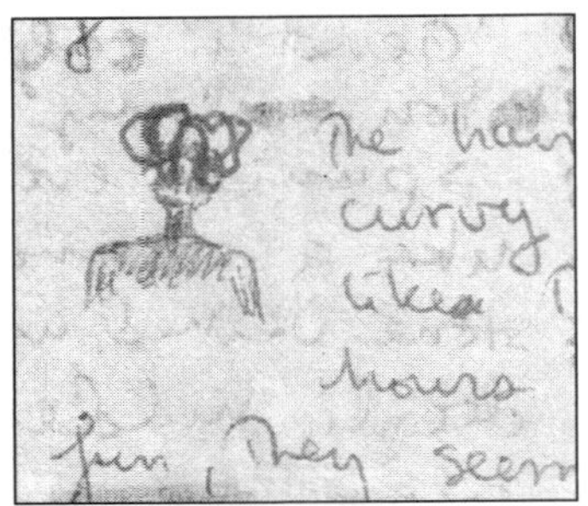

The hair on the women here is either corn-rowed or done like the drawing, wrapped up in little curvy strands by black thread & then clumped at the crown together so it looks like those squat gnarled trees w/ their branches cut off – it takes several hours to be done and lasts 8-10 days.
It's fun, they seem to be generally more full-bodied than American women & are wrapped & wrapped in all different patterns of fabric, sometimes yielding a dazzling effect, or sloppy & "unmatched", but always very colorful & distinctive.

The whites here are really white shorted sunglassed clean clean white.

But the "Ah-hey . . . " and "I think you follow me" and other idiosyncrasies of Nigerian-English make me nervous, as does not being able ever to finish a coherent thought because of unabashed interruptions; aborted ideas build up to make me feel frustrated and unwilling to try again—I don't want to adapt to their style and constantly be in a state of tense debate—and oh god they are good (but not good enough) at talking without knowing what they're talking about.

I'd like a swim now and a few kisses; a swim would suffice.
Saw an exquisite carved door at the USIS by someone I studied, a traditional Yoruba style with scenes adapted to context (for example with a panel of Africans watching a film of the Capitol building.)

PART OF A LETTER TO MIMI:

A woman alone is very very alone, I'm discovering more every day—inextricably, profoundly alone.
In the rare and savored company of women (here) we have at the same time an unspoken but felt affinity but also a gulf between her married childful careworn immobile life and my oddity and celibacy. Nevertheless we sometimes manage to get through, and I can almost feel human.
But my being here necessitates a constant unrelieved unpleasant dealing with men with whom I have little interest and less respect. If I refuse (as much as is practically-physically-temporally possible) to see and experience the country, culture, trip through their (greedy lascivious ulteriorly motivated) eyes, then I am left essentially alone.
Never arrives the moment when a non-domestic mobile woman approaches me for conversation or a meal or an evening seeing the town.
And going out alone is a remote and absurd possibility, sure to

provoke internal hysteria after the first few attempts, with my every gesture being scrutinized & appraised as worthwhile & subsequently solicited. Time after time I am left alone, not defenseless but largely comfortless.
It's difficult.
And further confused by the issue of race, my rejections being met with interrogations re: my ambivalence/distaste for Africans. If it were humanly possible I would explain to each one my real reasons for the NO's; instead I satisfy it with a simple "I'm sick of men & no I'm not married & furthermore no I don't intend to, & . . . "
It rarely suffices but is less expensive to my spirit.
Which is being soaked every day.
I don't think the day will come when I can satisfy or resolve my desire to travel alone with my absolute contempt for & fatigue w/ the men I meet—it makes the world a much less populated and accessible place than is normal—
And interestingly here in Ibadan w/ these (white) university men I at first felt some relief, they kept that distance that lets me relax a bit, until I realized it was just as unsatisfying personally to be in their presence as it had been w/ the Nigerians, but just less harassing—big deal.
Coca Cola does a roaring business here, that & cigarettes & English white bread seeming to be the staples.
The women are tough & wiry & so hard-working & absolutely resplendent in their multicolored wrappings & flashy gold jewelries.
But Nigeria as a mind is really distasteful, every human & social relationship being predicated/based on an economic dealing—there is no chance of a favor being done as such, and one has to be superhumanly self-reliant to avoid the continual doling-out of dash $.
It gets to be almost bestial, the weaselly way they go after a few kobos—I am being very tough & unobliging & at first they are amused but w/ a notable underlying annoyance—
I'm plain pissed off tonite, and haven't had my period for 1 ¾ months & so sick at heart about my camera.
And dreams getting weirder.
And enamored of the tackiness of the products here; everything is funny.
[. . .]
Reading Genet's *Miracle of the Rose* which so far is delightful; a refreshing point of contrast to the quite pedestrian situations I tend to get thrown into when traveling (where are you from & do you want to fuck—not exactly stimulating interchanges).
The land down south is very fertile, dense palm and brush forests, very heavy moist air, a pale peach colored half-moon; the aridness and physical poverty of the northern lands was beginning to unnerve me, one gets such little soul sustenance from the sand & dirt & scrub brush.
Listening to a choir of lepers singing off pitch.

Ibadan, glad to be in a large city, to see some contemporary theater & visit the university students, the other half of African reality, the changing one.
Fried plantains are a breakfast dish here, called dodos. Being lodged at the hot-headed Nigerian's (who has a Danish wife, absent now)—I'm so irritable now, it's getting to the point in traveling where I haven't been going long enough to be adjusted, & not short enough to be immersed; it's the mid and the homesickness point, all I can do is wait until it passes—
But it's exciting to find myself in that part of Nigeria (Ibadan—Ife—Benin City & environs) which is so rich culturally & about which I used to cherish the thought of visiting, back in the dusty Oberlin library w/ my huge volumes on African art & my long paper on "African Art as a Measure of Independence & . . . ."—I've forgotten, but it was quite an admirable attempt & a few years later a book appeared on the same subject & quite inferior to my paper[29]—but theories fall by the wayside the longer I'm here.
I'm thinking about that afternoon at graphics when I had first come, and asked if you (you, Sheila, Elana & someone else I think) had aspirations toward stardom (dig it, he just put on the Beach Boys—?) I remember both admiring & being afraid of your assurance at just being satisfied w/ a life as you wanted w/o the shit of star status. And then my letter after seeing Bourke-White.[30] And my trip. I can sometimes permit my imagination a future "definitive work" or "acclaimed insightful" something-or-other, but then I admit my total discomfort w/ "attention" & my absolutely visceral belief that nothing one can say/describe/categorize ever really touches the truth, that things change too quickly & are inherently evanescent & not to be classified even for the sake of comprehension—
The above doesn't mean I don't do precisely what I think is impossible: For the sake of an A paper or a job I'll collect & process & analyze & adduce & induce & deduce & wash my hands when I'm through. But the question is, can I take myself seriously if I make it a profession? So that leaves 2 alternatives: Do it & always never never never lose sight of the limitations (i.e., who the hell do you think you are to be saying that about something you've only known for a short time? Others have the arrogance/assuredness/need to feel ok about it, not me) or don't do it.[31]
Terrific, eh?
It's the irritation that overcomes me once in a while as I make photos: to/for whom/what am I making the attempt?
And another critical issue at present & in general, I am sick AND tired of being so serious.

---

29 OMG I can't believe I said that!

30 I assume that I had written her about my admiration for Margaret Bourke-White, the great photojournalist of the early-to-mid twentieth century.

31 A question I grappled with all these years later in deciding to do this book. Some things never change. And perhaps shouldn't.

JANUARY 24

Met a nice woman, Olibisi Adewumi, who works at the International Institute of Tropical Agriculture. She agreed to have me do her portrait.

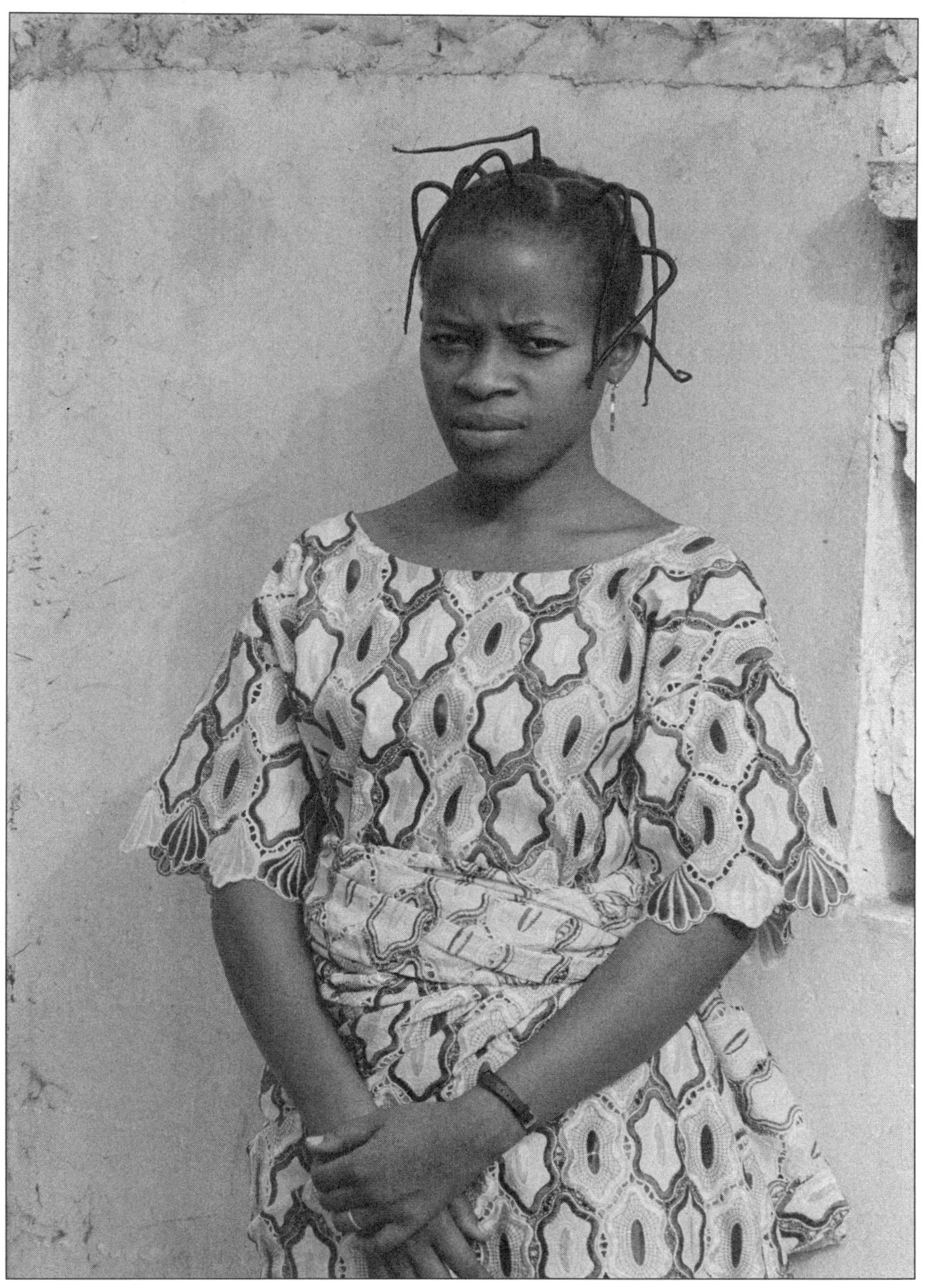

PART OF A LETTER TO MIMI:

I think you understand, as I spoke about it when I was in NY, that I'm always being pestered by a certain formality & puritanism & drive to achieve.

But this life now of spending so much time in the company of people usually older by 5-10 years & men on top of it makes for my never being relaxed. Lovely.

If it seems I bitch incessantly, I don't.[32]

It's just that you get all my complaints at present. It has to do w/ the fact that I trust you & think you'd be interested (if not necessarily pleased or amused) to witness my thrashings-about. And that I feel some glitter-encrusted transatlantic umbilical cord w/ you.

So much for sentiment, however tawdry; I'd like to go dancing w/ you this evening; in its place, I am off to see "Sizwe Bansi is Dead," a probably very "political" play about S. Africa w/ poetry by Dennis Brutus [33] (that S. African exiled poet who was at the MCA) at the Univ. of Ibadan.

[...]

I feel in a terrible fog all the time, a mental & an oppressive physical sluggishness from the heat, the pace here, the sharp sunlight that tires out one's eyes & beats down on a hot head hot shoulders stuffy feet thick throat... it's a lethargy I can't throw off, a heaviness in the bottom of my spine & the back of my head.

I start the day thinking I'll "see the sights & then do some work"—ha! By noon I'm useless, dysfunctional, my energy sweltered & noised & sensated away, you can't believe the racket in this town, absolutely every driver feels compelled to honk at each passing car & person, the chickens & motors & beggars & sellers & radios & preachers & cop whistles all drone on hour after hour encased in dust & heat & light. One doesn't cultivate a delicate spirit here—

I do so much need to be occupied all the time (even perhaps to an annoying or even impractical degree), no matter how nebulous or artificial that occupation is sometimes; when I travel I spend a while being very bustling searching rummaging keening but it peters out after a month or two—it's awfully hard for me to feel that a day like this is noteworthy or worthy: going to the P.O., the bank, the market street, lunching, hearing music, sitting past the afternoon—it just isn't.

Saw *Sizwe Bansi is Dead* by Athol Fugard [7] performed at the U. of Ibadan this evening, began with poems (by Dennis Brutus) read by three people. Then the two characters of the play—the first one (Styles) recounted his life at the South African food factory on visiting day, and his evolution to becoming a studio photographer to "preserve the dreams of his people, and the history of all those who aren't important enough for the big books." It was done entirely thru descriptive dialogue and a great sense of

32 Well, actually, I did and I do.

33 Dennis Vincent Brutus was a South African activist, educator, journalist and poet best known for his campaign to have South Africa banned from the Olympic Games due to its policy of apartheid.

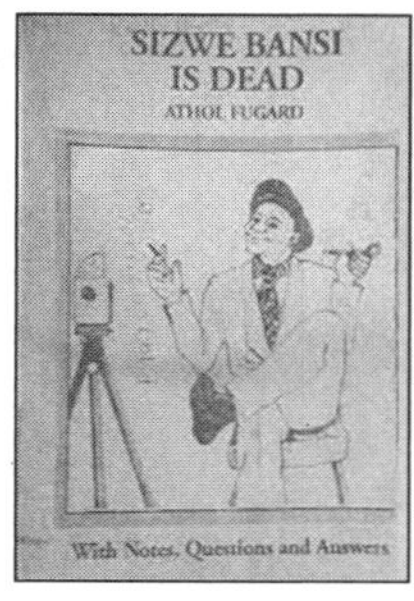

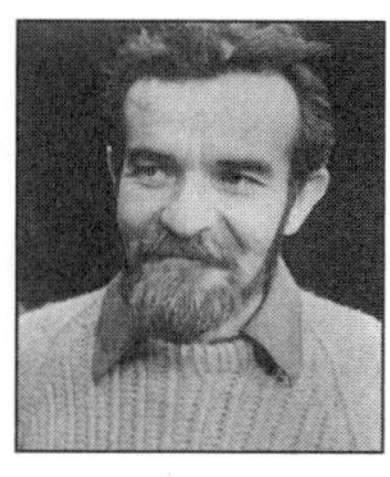

mime; the big White Bass, the translation into Bantu calling him a bastard, the proud (men) who come for a photo to record their attainment of literacy; moved on to a fumbling, lost Sizwe Bansi, a country boy who must learn the ways of being Black in South Africa, always alert, knowing the rules and the ways to get around them, even giving up what little pride he has in order to survive, which he does by taking a passbook from a dead man.
There was a constant stream of laughter by the audience which after a while became annoying because it just simply wasn't funny, but I have heard similar laughter when seeing a performance with dialogue by a "duped" woman—one sees oneself in it too much. The acting by Buntu was superb, lyrical, lively and bittersweet; it was the coming together of a righteously and seriously angry and knowledgeable group (of the academic Blacks here).

Had a fight last night with Godfrey. After a running stream of angry talk from me about the situation for women, he was hopelessly embarrassed and had a continual ridiculous grin on and came up with absolutely priceless arguments: "You've seen the suits the astronauts wear? You couldn't walk from here to the stadium in one." When he said he'd "read an article" (the ultimate validation?) that women like rape I hit the ceiling. Yeah. Another infuriating conversation in which a man tells me women enjoy rape and he's the exception to the rule that men treat women like objects. My god, with all these men telling me that they're the exception I could almost fool myself into thinking it's a safe world . . . until I remind myself that they're all liars.
Now he wants me to leave, which always follows a rejection of sex.

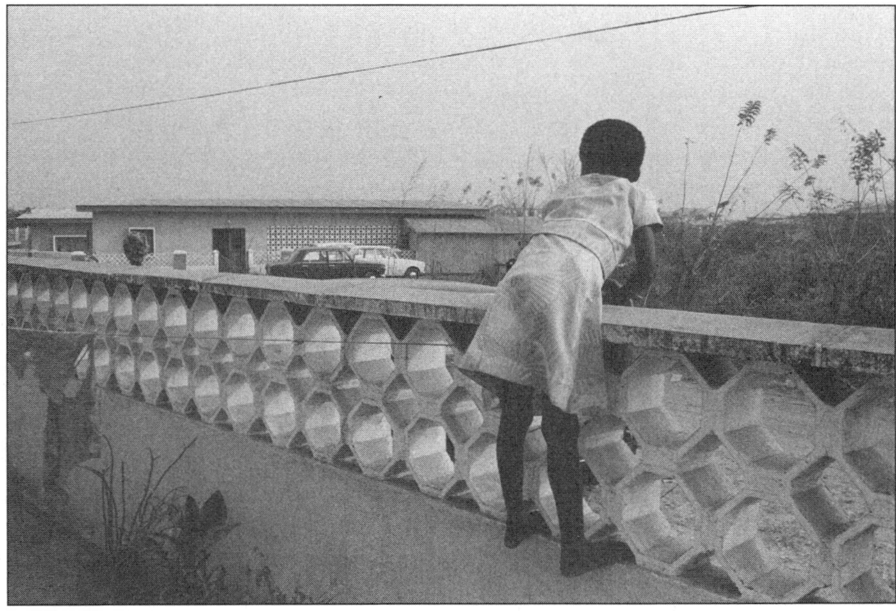

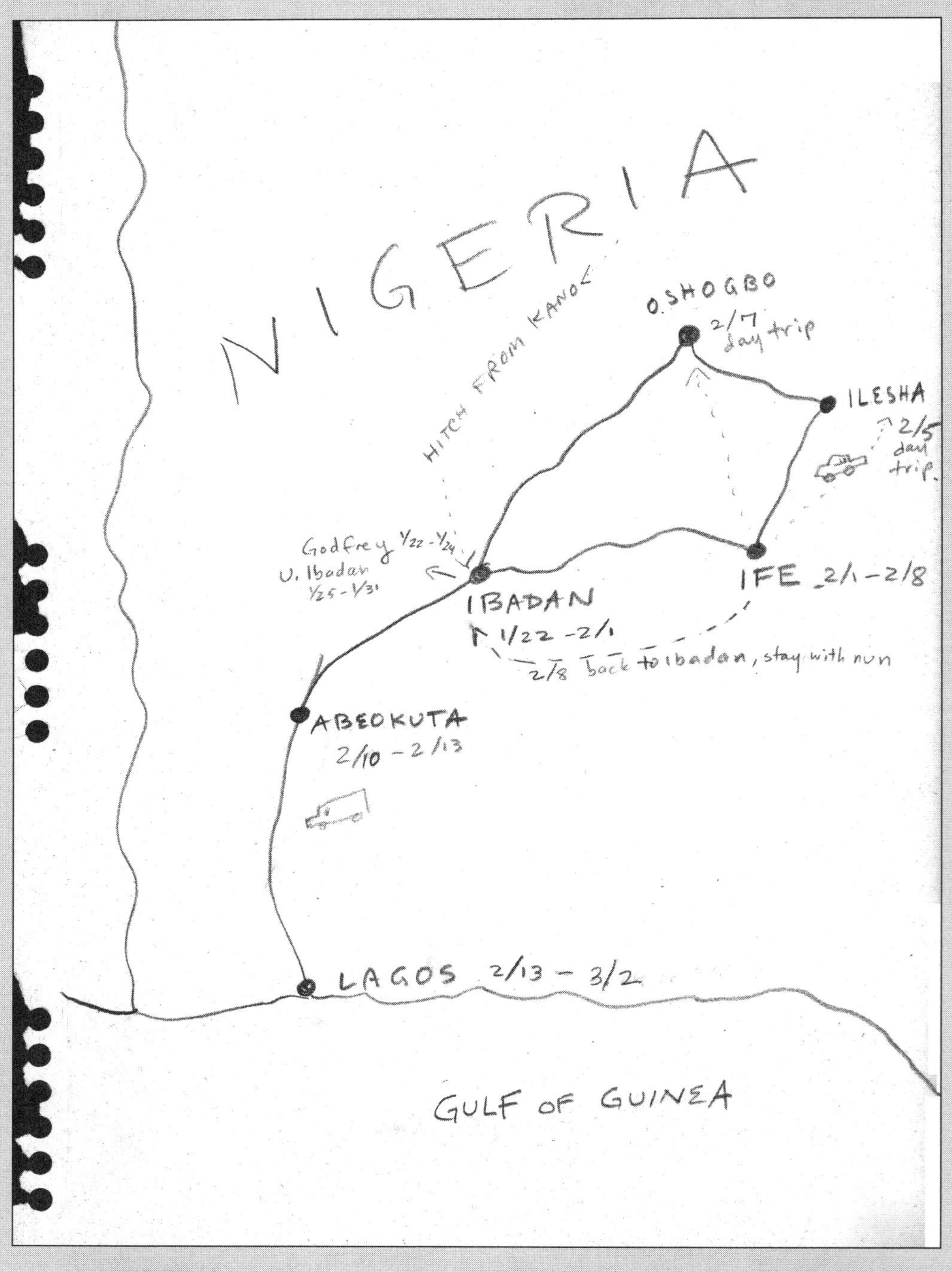
NIGERIA
HITCH FROM KANO
OSHOGBO
2/7 day trip
ILESHA
2/5 day trip.
Godfrey 1/22 - 1/24
U. Ibadan 1/25 - 1/31
IBADAN
1/22 - 2/1
IFE 2/1 - 2/8
2/8 back to ibadan, stay with nun
ABEOKUTA
2/10 - 2/13
LAGOS 2/13 - 3/2
GULF OF GUINEA

CHAPTER NINE

At the University of Ibadan with Nicholas

I packed up and went to the University of Ibadan, where I crashed in the room of a woman named Sue.

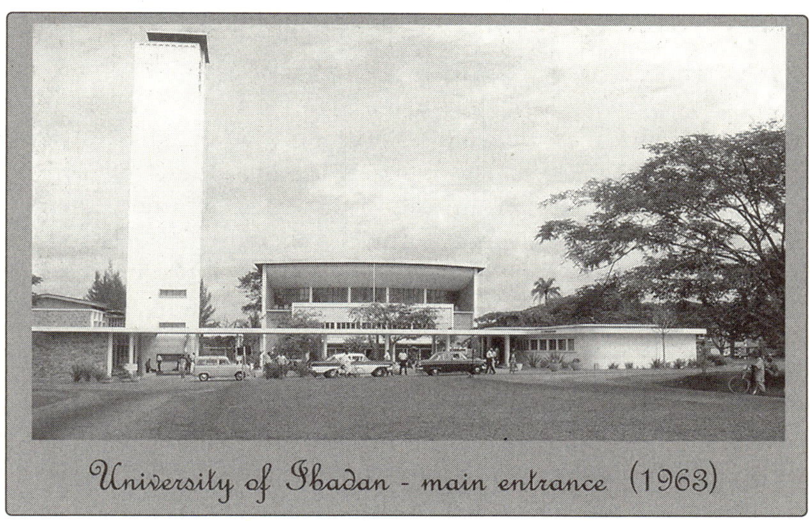
University of Ibadan - main entrance (1963)

JANUARY 25

The face of Sue's roommate is superb, wide and full and glowing—
Stocky thick-chested short bodies of certain men here, or the lanky ones: quite chic.
Plaiting hair on Sunday afternoon in the shade of the front porch, untangling the threads and winding, winding.
In the bush they squat in the dust in raggedy clothes to watch Sunday afternoon pass by. Here, one wears platform shoes and sits in straight-backed chairs.
There's as much religion here as there is overpopulation. Christianity will be the addiction for a long while to come . . . it's so fucking adaptable and saleable.
I'm beginning to feel good again; yesterday was a bitch but I'm thawing out somewhat—the latest hurdle is getting into a dress, a necessity of sanity in this humidity—it'll be like being in drag for me.

JANUARY 26

—Didn't/couldn't do it today, I was embarrassed to go into the dressmaker's shop and look around, as if I was violating some sanctuary, not knowing the rituals, and they would see thru me.
Saw the city's prison today: Grim. But a timidly "high security" place, with one thin rose-colored steel door, people escape now and again; armed robbers are shot by a firing squad IN PUBLIC. Likewise anyone who (unsuccessfully, of course) attempts a *coup d'état* [overthrow of the state].

I spend the days wondering if people will see into my secret life or, if I hold onto it, I leave our encounters with the prevailing thought that they don't know what I really think and was feeling; but it's not anything I want to be cured of, no one's reality is any more or less stable than that, and it's impossible and undesirable and unnecessary to always be in the corrosive/erosive process of adjusting to or emulating other's realities [1].

REMEMBER: use short depth of field for face emphasis.

At UI today, some Americans, and what Americans. The San Francisco boy slow-moving, alert, a one and a half year "veteran" at UI, an archaeology student. They are strange apparitions in this African land, little pockets of Americanism tucked away in a dusty corner of the university campus, collecting artifacts and learning African time (watches with thirty or forty hours); I spent several hours just verry . . . . .casually visiting and chatting, one flows along from one conversation to the next, letting the heat drift by, the sun recede.
I'm spending a lot of time especially now in the company of people with very nebulous sex lives, e.g., the white students here who seem stranded, who don't have Nigerian lovers, all the young unattached, the wistful or aggressive or nervous ones; these fleeting encounters with other rootless beings, displaced, surviving.

Read an obituary in the local paper about an Oba who had thirty-four children.

> **PART OF A LETTER TO MIMI:**
> I get so frustrated: The Americans (& British) here are really a classic brand (the sort Doris Lessing wrote about re: Rhodesia); an eve at the Senior Staff Club at the Univ. drinking European beer & discussing the Cold War and Angola & exchanging prices on African art work—they are so ritualistic & isolated, but I had to admit some feeling of "relief" at talking to them for a while, & it's comparable to the hotel full of corpulent neo-colonialists—it's the other ½ of the still well-entrenched reality here.
> Listened to Minnie Ripperton today but then I tried to stop myself because then I would be thinking of you & that I'm at least 3,500 miles away with nothing much more pressing than to perhaps write another p.c. or have a cold Coke, and wouldn't it just be fine if I was on the D, F or K train now. [34]
> Tomorrow I develop my film to see the havoc that a broken lens has wreaked on my exposures; if those irreplaceable pictures are ruined, I will have to do some serious reassessing—
> At the moment I feel more like serious bathing.
> I'm a perfectionist in an imperfect world. Perhaps it's some comfort that it's a perfectly imperfect world.
> [. . .]

34 Subway lines in NYC. (The K line was discontinued in the 1980s.)

I'm still traipsing somewhere between pessimism & idealism—no solution.
Love you,
Su
P.S.
A good indication of how much I was needing a familiar environment & something more than just touristing: yesterday I worked all day & in the eve on the article.
P.S.S.
I wish it was easier for me to say more directly the things I really want to say, e.g., to cop a lovely phrase from Genet & call you "my Spanish evening"; like a strange stone veined with deeply hidden colors, metallic, or the hues of memory; knowing you & feeling as I do, being a secret I keep close to me, something I have created into my present private reality/life.
Balderdash; what place does Byronic sentiment have in this weird era? We are the main characters in some very amusing, enlightening & crafty daydreams.

A POSTCARD TO CINDY:

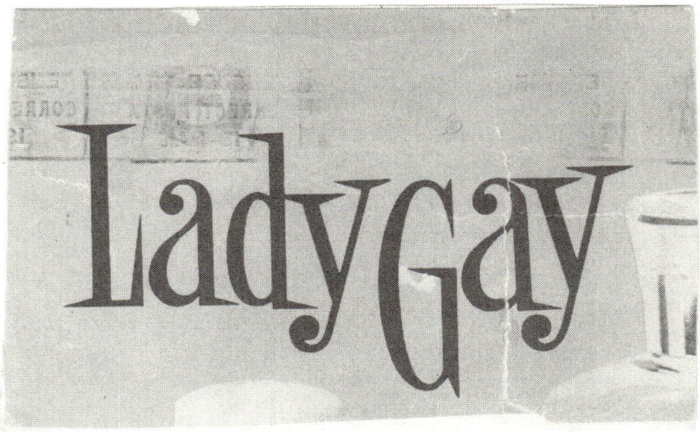

Dear Cindy,
At this point my sense of humor & taste has fallen to a markedly low point, & on that note I designed this postcard. I assume you have a naïve postman. The strain of being a woman is increasing, but I suppose I'll manage—the Nigerian women are great (although only on sight; I haven't yet been in any homes).
[. . .]
I miss our salon(s) & all attendant stimulations, even the breakfasts at Hamburger King—sometimes it's hard to spend days & days w/ the only interesting conversation being w/ myself & my notebooks—my love & shit, and I am bogged down w/ that article amidst the sand & sun & constant changes—
love su—
Ah! It's done and on its way!
P.S. At Univ. of Ibadan—a swimming pool, conversation, a roof.

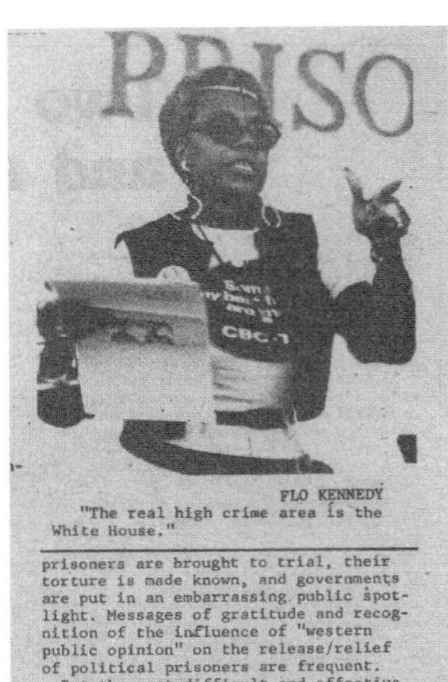

prisoners are brought to trial, their torture is made known, and governments are put in an embarrassing public spotlight. Messages of gratitude and recognition of the influence of "western public opinion" on the release/relief of political prisoners are frequent.

But the most difficult and effective solution has always been to attack the source, to kill it at the root. Regimes dependent on the U.S. can't afford to have their mistakes revealed -- it might affect the flow of "aid" and "advice." This also means that the American government can't afford for long to have its acclaimed foreign development programs linked in public to barbaric regimes. Because these economic and diplomatic factors (in addition to racism and sexism) are responsible for the presence of torture and wide scale imprisonment, we have to concentrate on U.S. home and foreign policy and the God of Power. Flo Kennedy made an appropriate analogy by christening this the "testicular approach" -- to finally get him where it really hurts.

Su Friedrich

The article was published in the final issue of Lavender Woman, *July 1976 [2].*

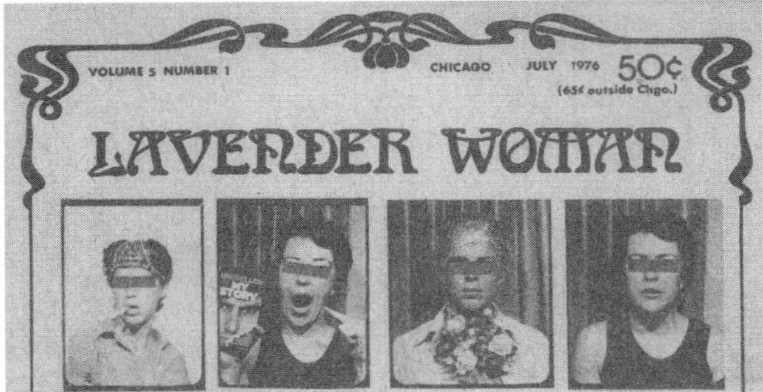

Khong Dan Cho Co

("If they are not guilty, beat them until they are" -- Saigon police force slogan)

"'You don't talk now,' they would say; 'In a few minutes, when our hands will start roaming between your legs, you will be singing like a nightingale."

A presentation by women from thirteen international organizations and defense committees was held in St. Mark's Church in New York City last November. Sponsored by the International Tribunal on Crimes Against Women, it was an attempt to generate publicity (as Flo Kennedy pointed out, no one from the straight media was there) and organize effective

being maimed or murdered, have been used as successfully to control a woman ...as have the savage physical tortures inflicted on her."

Sexism is also evident in the situation for women outside the prison walls: the wives, sisters, and mothers of political prisoners. They are denied basic human needs - the children are harassed or expelled from school, they lose their badly needed jobs and often have no social security to depend on, they are social outcasts and/or sexual targets

few political prisoners are freed each year amidst great fanfare... to avert our attention from the Atticas and Matteawans.

The problem is compounded in countries without a relatively independent judicial system; the few liberal lawyers are usually incarcerated with the people whom they should be defending. Paradoxically, when they do have an opportunity to represent someone in court evidence of torture is generally dismissed as "inadmissable political argument". Gov-

JANUARY 27

Darts at the staff club [3]. What insidious invectives and bad jokes float about in that rarified decaying air.

How boring and maddening the obsession with procedure is here. It's more understandable now, after meeting more Nigerians, that Lere would have chastised me in re: proper channels and home training.

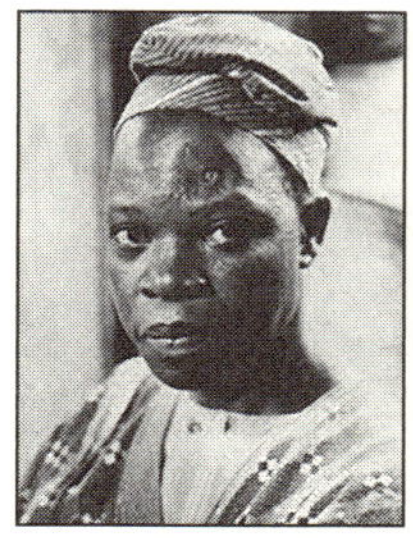

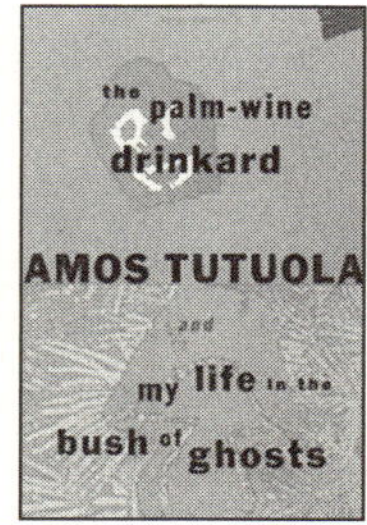

I'd noticed an uncomfortable and unsettling amount of laughter from the audience at Sizwe Bansi; I encountered it again this eve at a lecture by Elechi Amadi and a reading by Amos Tutuola—one aspect, the titillated and self-righteous laughter (and valid; I don't imply criticism but rather I mean to describe the feeling of the laughter) when Amadi derided Christian fetishism or European literary jargonese. The reaction setting in was that they were right just by virtue of having been wronged, etc. (Somehow I'm getting nasty in areas which I'd protect fiercely if I was referring to women—but perhaps not; I am not a drooling patriotic coven-groupie about women's ideas and events, and I don't expect Blacks/Africans to react like that either.) And then there were the ripples of suppressed laughter at Tutuola, the country man seeming a bit put out with those damn microphones and overly theoretical (?) questions; a sort of paternal laughter, a respectful bemused-ness, that he has indeed revived and recorded and extrapolated true Yoruba culture but, "Heavens, let's get on with it and find some more articulate types."—One straddles two worlds.

Tutuola read *Don't Pay Bad for Bad*, about two women friends. The kola nut tree of one makes the other one jealous, she asks to have her clay pot (which sheltered it from bugs) removed, which necessitates cutting down the tree; the village chief decides in favor of it being cut down; later the other woman gives a brass necklace to the friend's new baby but years later (to enact her revenge about losing her tree) says she wants it back, which means the head of the daughter has to be cut off to retrieve it. The village chief agrees, but in the end the woman gives in, says it shouldn't be done because paying for bad with bad never ends the cycle of violence—

He certainly wasn't a dynamic storyteller—

He had all the original manuscripts virtually stolen/absconded by the first publisher (Favor and Favor), and now they're playing a lovely game of evasion with him[35]—

The real irony witnessed this eve was when Amadi spoke about the resuscitation of

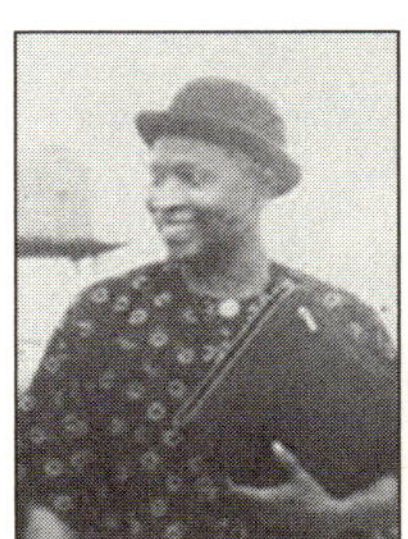

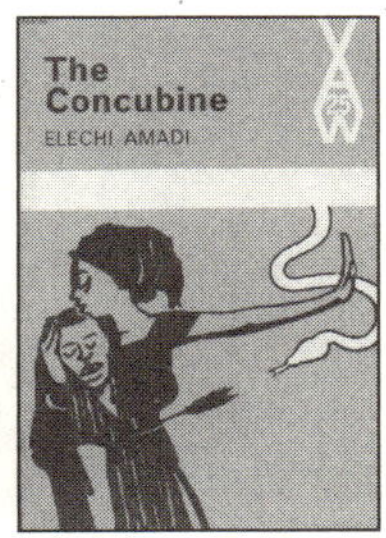

traditional forms and as a point of contrast made several references to the fetishism, animism, and violence of Christian ideology—the students roared in laughter at the foolishness, etc.—which to me indicates an implicit criticism of all religions, not just Christianity, and there they are, groveling in the glory of African traditional religion.

AND he used as an example the confinement of a woman for one month before marriage to learn to be a good domestic, that this "important and beautiful" tradition was being rejected by contemporary women due to western values (which criticized the

35 That's an ironic misnomer—it's actually called Faber and Faber. See [4] for further details about that, and some information about Tutuola and Amadi.

plumpness of the women after a month of sedentary living—)
Beautiful, beautiful, the near-sightedness. I was not impressed, but I was intrigued.

Watch out—dependence on the material kindness of men is leading to that familiar feeling of "gratitude" and security which in turn leads to all sorts of things.

Listening to Dylan—how pretentious his references are.

JANUARY 28

The climate here makes me frantic at midday [5].

Saw women in the market wearing those white cotton spiral sewn bras, like from the '60s. When we used to see a woman wearing one under her stretchy nylon shell, we'd say she had "torpedo tits." Here, they just wear them as their top.

On the news: " . . . the racist South African Minister of Defense, Botha . . . "

I know why I hate/avoid dinner parties with intellectuals: One is supposed to intelligently and cleverly discuss controversial subjects without being too honest—it would upset the smug, aren't-we-aware ambience that is cultivated in every gesture and word. And oh how bored I am by the "filler" conversation—all these things said with an academic accent for the sake of having said them, of a point scored, an obscure reference casually thrown in—it's worse because it's more dishonest than the hour/day-killing small talk of less educated people, who don't pretend to so much importance.
I was horrified (but only mildly, and I've learned to hide my irritation, having heard it all before) by the absolutely callous, unrealistic, artificial way in which the philosopher guy, Graham—British to the anus—could explain away rude doctors or having twelve children to his own detached satisfaction. It's the dangerous game of making one's words the reality and being too afraid of material/physical evidence because it might very well disprove your words.
The British here really live up to their reputation, making references to some Nigerian who has achieved "really good English, without an accent" etc., and making witty and liberal color jokes—oh god.

> **PART OF A LETTER TO MIMI:**
>
> I have the awful sensation that if the country is "being brought into the modern world," it usually means that the wife of the President has a microwave oven & that the facilities for tourists are improving—(even Ibadan, like a village but w/ electricity & too many cars—there are the few here who live well, and the U.I students are quite bourgeois).
> [. . .]
> Right now I don't want to be with Africans, and I don't want to be with whites who don't want to be with Africans, & those are my alternatives.

Had an evening upstairs with some of the students for a French meal, for which we were all (expected to be) duly grateful as a "relief" from the usual plate here. If you really want to know, I prefer my bananas & groundnuts [peanuts] & occasional soup or stew—yes, I realize I've been bitching about the food here—but that's not the point in this case.
We had to sip good wine & savor good-rare pork & consume good whiskey beer cognac & make good intelligent circular witty DULL DULL talk, being as we were white & educated & liberal & such an interesting group: a philosopher, a translator, a vet student, a primary school French teacher, & yours jaded. Electricity in the tweed-scented air when I ignored the rules & followed a controversial topic to its obvious & incriminating conclusion rather than leaving it to be dangled & twitted & licked & admired & explained away—I absolutely despise this sort of evening—they're so fucking SMUG, they can afford to say words which to others have a more pressing (& inescapable) reality & can't be treated so lightly—they can create & alter & prettify & justify theories which have absolutely no relation to the truth of the matter. I really think being around my father, grandfather, & other academics gave me an instinctive insight into their systems & games—it's hard for me to expose or define what exactly it is, but I feel it all through me, I know it—and I'm sure that's had a lot to do w/ my deep-seated skepticism about my own words & theories—I'm always afraid that I'm busy at the same game—"What's a girl to do??"
Ibadan University is a little haven in the midst of a berserk/charming city—Ibadan is lush, built on hills, full of palm trees & brilliant/fragrant flowering bushes & beautiful women—none of whom I dare approach, not even for statistics or current opinion.

JANUARY 29

Such lip service men pay us when we're talking about women's issues. Dinner with two British boys and Anne, a Bryn Mawr woman here studying literature. Underneath their comments and "well, I suppose's" I sense a distinct boredom and intolerance—not to mention the comment about women's nasty temperaments, etc.

But Nicholas [the chemistry and physics student] and I spent a very pleasant and interesting hour or two talking about the comparative lives of Nigerian and American women.
He described the attitude towards women students here—that generally men students don't marry them, there's fear of earning less than women, they don't want a professional wife. That the women students tend to assimilate western values, take on notions about their "delicate bearings" and consequently demand that men treat them preferentially, etc. Perhaps true; they dress like southern belles (and the boys, like southern gents . . .) and are in a ratio of 1:6 here which makes

them quite hunted down I'm sure—

Not too many here in the sciences, but a good beginning.

Nicholas says that the university students have an upper-class status here; there's an assumption (and therefore distrust) on the part of the public that these young university folk will be the power quotient of the next generation, and the students take on a lot of the self-assured arrogance of an élite.

He constantly returned to the aspect of strength in African women, their status due to economic independence in the market and amount of work in the bush.

That awareness is definitely at the forefront of everyone's experience here; he derided the "chivalry" tradition in American, says here the women would feel foolish/insulted if treated in such a way.

Except for students.

Funny—he asked me whether we always have a good water and electricity supply in Chicago; it's an issue quite central to Ibadan, with very frequent blackouts.

Also he admitted men just don't/can't take as much as women, they complain much more, etc.

Nicholas also talked about the difficulty/indifference among Nigerians when they mix with Europeans; the cultures are too different and it's uncomfortable when they're together; claims it's better with Americans, they aren't as concerned about keeping a distance, they'll, e.g., go out for a drink in a local pub, etc.

JANUARY 30

Aufniewiedersehen, the Sahara journey month.[36]

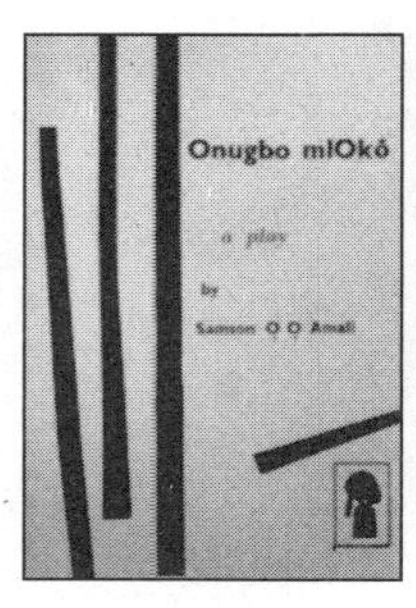

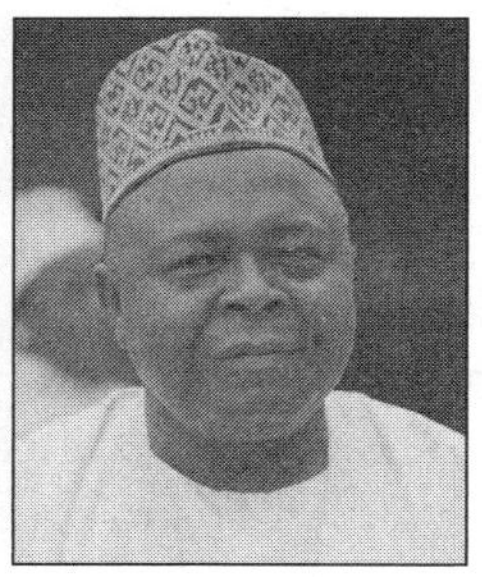

Went to see a performance of *Onugbo mlOko*—a play in Idoma by Samson O.O. Amali [6], translated into English, presented by the African Studies Dept.

A brother kills his younger brother out of jealousy over his hunting skills; there was stuff about age privileges and responsibilities; the judgment of elders; accusations of the work of evil spirits (the white horse).

And great dance sequences by women in cloths, bells at ankle, muscles and soft brown strong shoulders, lithe bodies; men compact, energetic, sweaty, leaping, stamping; and animal masqueraders, the aloof bird, comical elephant, aggressive bush pig, the lion standing guard over the kill—and the stilt dancers, two of them, wearing Igbo maiden and death masks, acrobatic, amazing, looming above us, squatting and striding and jumping and dancing without faltering.

There was a dull scene of village elders. It's a fine line between wisdom and senility. The audience was visibly bored.

---

36 My silly invented "German" word to say that I would never see the Sahara again. And I haven't.

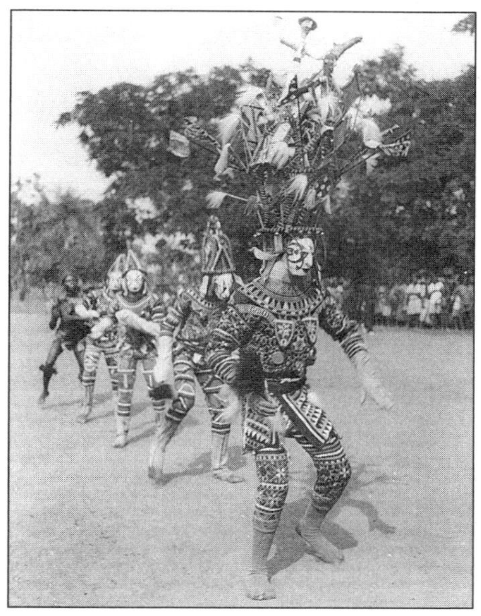

Agbogho Mmuo, Igbo maiden spirit maskers near Akwa, north-central Igbo area, Nigeria, 1935. Photo: G. I. Jones.

And they do get quite incredulous or impatient with some of the traditional "wisdoms" and jujus, this "sophisticated" college crowd.
The soft night wind, stars above, palm trees and grass walls around us—flute and drums, chanting.
It's like their Shakespeare and Bolshoi Ballet—very impressive (not necessarily this play, but generally).
All colonialism, color, and continents aside, I really love African traditional dance/theater and music.
It was an interesting contrast to *Sizwe Bansi*, both student productions.
Curious: No one except a scattered few applauded at the end—

PART OF A LETTER TO MIMI:

Things are getting exciting.
You can't imagine how difficult it has actually been to realize that I am in Africa. For example, last evening a performance of a traditional Idoma play & there were stilt dancers (marvelous) & I observed, "Hmm, Ibo dance masks" (having been a good student) & then I had to tell myself that this wasn't the MCA or a film, but Iboland, I am here, at the source. [7]
A momentary thrill.
Like seeing all these exquisite people dressed in dashikis & wraps, & realizing they're not Afro-Americans in search of their history, but that this is their way of life. It comes from my built-in association of "Black" w/ "American" & always having felt that Africa was so far away & a bit unreal.
No, I must mail this letter before it gets too heavy for an envelope—

I'm still trying to get it to sink into me that that I'm in Africa and these are the original people, not Blacks who are trying to revive a foreign culture. My association of "American" with any Black person makes it confusing/disorienting sometimes, to realize that despite the same physique, color, even sometimes gestures, there's also a great difference, the disparity that's natural between the indigenous and the transplanted. Although I've been feeling that a certain mood in the markets and neighborhoods here is very close to that in Black areas of Chicago: the rhythm and pace and sounds and just certain indescribable ways of being and doing.

It also gives me a deeper respect for American Blacks. Despite the complexes that exist here as a result of colonial rule, there's an overriding naturalness to the fact of their existence, which has been undermined in America, with its atmosphere (until now, and still) of always needing to apologize for one's existence (as Black, lesbian, etc.) [8]

Someone here is very à la mode; they're playing all the good bar songs—"The Hustle," "Fly, Robin, Fly," etc.

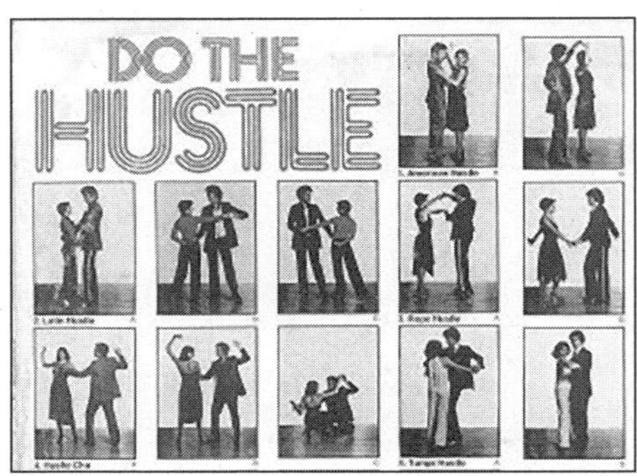

JANUARY 31

I decided today I'm going to be a bit more decorous (but not overly) with my body; one can't be here too long without feeling the influence—it's such a natural, simple and beautiful thing; the body decoration/elegance/colorfulness is in its most basic and therefore most attractive form, nothing artificial. Makes me want the same [9].

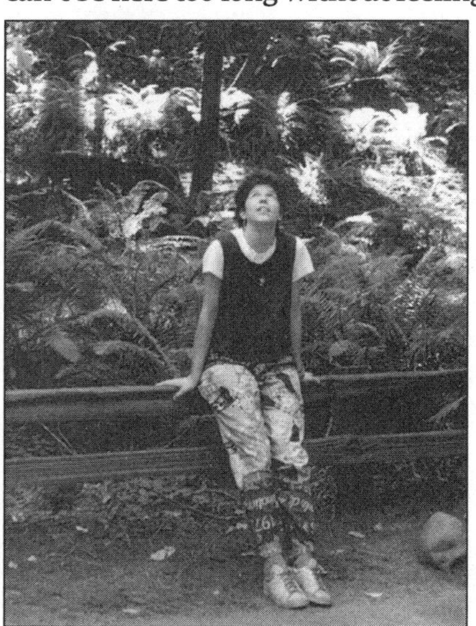

I'm really getting attached to the lizards here, so much like our squirrels, flitting about, harmless, scared to death of any sounds, especially the little ones that hop after their mother, and the larger black red white striped ones.

I have to get more organized about the "research" part of this trip; I'm missing things everywhere (e.g., the great dye-works at Kano, renowned . . . I didn't even know about them!) and must get up the gumption to visit "officials" to find out more about women, e.g., as commissioners and businesswomen.

"It seems that American Blacks are more white than the whites."
"Is it true that they're very violent?"
—comments from a Nigerian history student

Had another conversation with Nicholas. We fell so much into our prescribed roles by getting into a more-oppressed-than-thou battle, he telling me how much more basic racism in Africa was, and me trying to compare rape and apartheid—and fittingly, we were listened to by Graham the whole time.
Nick made me really angry by insisting that ("for me and among all my friends") the only hope to end apartheid was to blow up Africa—what a bourgeois attitude! He said it's gotten so bad that they literally have nothing to lose, so blow it up and start over. Political theory, Level 1: Fatalism.
When I suggested that perhaps they did have an important something to lose—all their people—he said it was better for them than living like they do now under apartheid. (But I'm sure the people in SWAPO and ZANU feel a bit more committed!) [10]

—We talked about Leninism, the recognition of need and the positive function of bureaucracy in a revolutionary situation.
—The assumption of Marx about the inherently reactionary classes, e.g., students.
—That changed attitudes are predicated on changed classes, not vice versa, i.e., if bureaucrats are a power class, they can't diverge from that within their job; the nature of the job must change first.
I feel disturbed by our conversation; I don't get very far here trying to convince people of the shittiness of America. It's one of those paradoxes—they believe that America is EVIL but it seems they'd like to hear something racist from me/whites to give them the satisfaction of answering back in anger (instead of being relieved by hearing me share their feelings). (Same thing I feel sometimes with overly sy/em/pathetic men; a certain insincerity—I'm sure Nick thought I was overdoing my hatred of America.)
The issue for me seems a great divergence of immediate concerns, albeit the same sympathies. He and I are both aware/concerned about African development and racism and American imperialism—but he's at one end of the activity and I want to get at it from the other. It's a question of commitment to the same struggle but towards different aspects of the enemy, which is "only natural" (what a curious term) because of our

That sentence stops short, but then I add the following comment:

And how can he talk about the decimation of Africa and be studying physics here in order to land a job at a petrol refinery development in Nigeria? One implies fatalism, the other a look ahead at self- sufficiency.
We've all been so goddamn colonized.
When he said that Africans tend to see all whites the same I should have asked him how he felt about all men being considered the same, if that seemed a "fair" political theory to him.
But then we'd be back to semantics and this is more a question of the most deeply felt suspicions (toward whites and men).

THE SECOND OF TWO LETTERS FROM NICHOLAS UNAZOI:

University of Ibadan
21K Hall
Ibadan
22/10/76

Hello Su,
Yes just received your letter after a long delay in Nigeria. So you are now in New York, what a sharp contrast from the biggest city we have in Nigeria I guess.
Yes the petroleum industry in Nigeria is still in its infancy state and the main oil companies are Gulf, Shell B.P., Texaco, Mobil, and a host of others struggle to take part in the daily activities. The Petroleum Industry is divided into several parts (1) Exploration (2) Drilling (3) Production and (4) Refining (5) Marketing. So what you have near your house[37] deals only with the refining of the crude oil before it's separated into different components. From elementary chemistry and physics crude oil is a mixture of many components having different boiling points. Remember at boiling point a liquid can evaporate and then be passed through a condenser where it can be cooled to recovery. So in a refinery evaporation and condensation is always taking place and as the crude oil is heated up and at the various temperatures evaporation takes place. Depending on the kind of liquid you want to recover condensation takes place. There is more to this but this is the elementary explanation of what takes place in a refinery.
Happy to hear of your work for somebody in the Pan African Congress.[38]
In your reply explain what photography entails? Yes I have the ambition of coming over to the states for my Masters and intend to specialize in any of Electronics, Nuclear Engineering, or Geophysics. Please can you get me some address of good universities over there. Greet your friends, and mine wish you well. End so far and expecting the picture.
Okay So Far So Good
It's me Nicky

Graham's comment made me feel more sharply the disparity; when I said that there were some people so poor in America that they were lucky to get a plate of potatoes once a day, he said, yes, but that's the daily diet here.
This is like a blind person trying to teach a cripple to jump hurdles—we both need so much help that we have precious little to give each other (but perhaps more than would be expected)—but it's so hard to get it from the really affluent that we have to resort to picking at each other's scabs.

37 Maybe I told him about the big steel refining plants on the south side of Chicago? But that has nothing to do with oil...

38 I designed some anti-Apartheid posters.

"We have no godfather, no protector."
The fatalistic attitude: Precisely what is most beneficial to the South African regime—something too big and too old to fight becomes "natural," unchangeable—like sexism, so pervasive it boggles the mind.
Giving up now would be suicidal.
Is modernism an implicit prerequisite of feminism?
When he was laying claim to the primacy of racism (in an abstract way) I should've told him a bit about what Black women have to put up with—

The men here dress in loose pajama-style outfits, or at most new pants and tight shirts—but it's not unusual to see a man in a light pink or yellow lace-patterned outfit, or something in a flowered print. Today for the first time in a month I saw someone fully decked out in business suit and hat—he was more apparition than reality, it had such a feeling of costume about it—and the general attire here, lacking shoes and heavy clothes and things like our style of hats, is much freer, less like something to put onto one's body (as our culture seems to do it) and more natural, functional, unpretentious (especially the bare feet).
When I saw all the platform shoes at the university, my heart sank.

A major requirement to involvement/understanding: To lay aside (temporarily; as much as possible) my own values and practices, indulge for the given time in the unfamiliar environment, think whatever I think without needing to verbalize/show it, and later do the reassessing and rebecoming. But only if I'm willing to pick up/consider all the aspects of a foreign culture/situation will I begin to learn about it.

Had a talk with Gabi Balogun, a chemist who'd studied in England; he was depressed about Africa, bemoaned the amount of work that has to be done, the rampant attitude that if one has money all problems are solved, especially in rich Nigeria, where one can buy up any required technology or food, etc.—which is an immediate solution with no long-range effectiveness.
He said the women fritter away their $$ on trinkets and clothes.
He said he wants to live in America for a while "in the future, instead of here where we are always living in the past." Whenever I hear things like that I tend to agree, in my heart, and then immediately say to myself in some perverse sort of penance, "He said it, not I," as if me/white/America isn't permitted those observations because of the potential havoc it wreaks (and the implied racism).
He talked about a consolidation of resources, e.g., a good farming project in one fertile and populous area compared to less serviceable programs scattered about the country, especially in naturally unconducive places.

Strange habit here, after you have talked to someone, to say thank you. For example, if someone asks me about my travels and we exchange words for a few minutes, instead of saying goodbye they say thank you.

SHOWTIME IN IFE

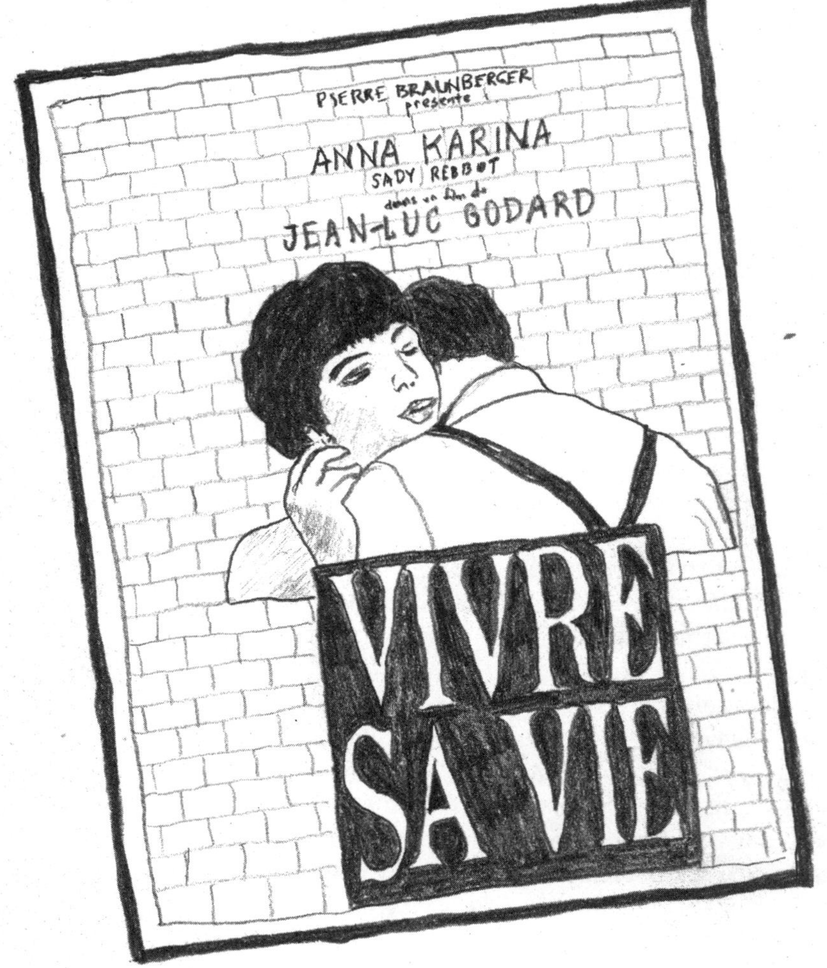

CHAPTER TEN

A Darkroom, A Godard Film, and Sunny Ade

FEBRUARY 1

Gabi the chemist gave me a ride to Ife, very nice of him. Found a place to crash with someone at Unife.[39]

Men walking arm in arm, or arm around the waist, here.

Shit, I want to read everything all at once and don't get anything finished—too much to know. Do I concentrate on culture, on political transition, on women, on economic development, on photography, on on on . . . ?

Dennis Brutus, *I Am the Exile*

I <u>am</u> the exile
am the wanderer
the troubadour
(whatever they say)

gentle I am, and calm
and with abstracted pace
absorbed in planning,
courteous to servility

but wailings fill the chambers of my heart
and in my head
behind my quiet eyes
I hear the cries and sirens.

FEBRUARY 2

Visited Ori Olokun.[40]
The renowned and excessively promising Ife attempt at African-art nationalism is now a dusty and uninhabited place, which however puts on theatre at least once a month. I shouldn't be quite so critical, but the astonishing gap between my expectations (based on those glowing articles I was always reading in the *African Arts* magazine) and the place was a bit disturbing.

---

39 The University of Ife. I have no record of who it was.

40 An art center named after the Yoruba deity Olokun. For more info about the art center and the Ori Olokun sculuture, see [1].

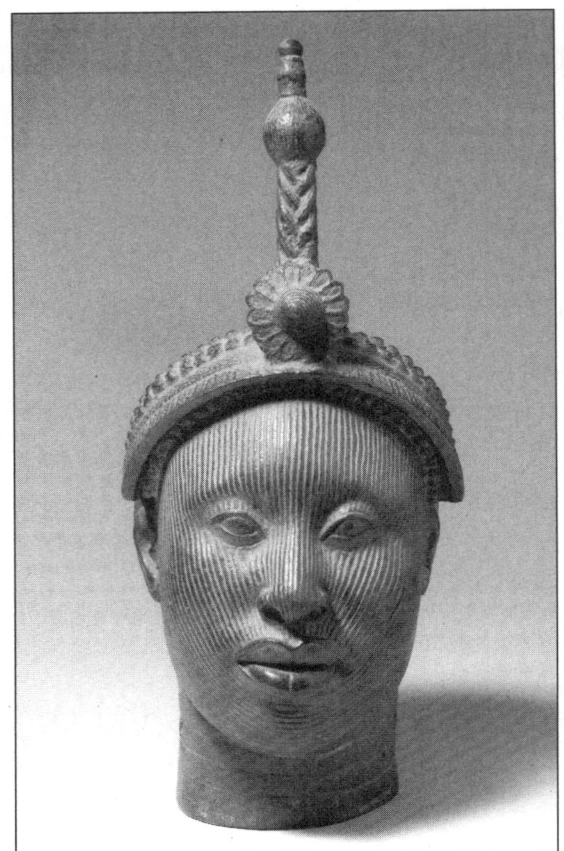

The original bronze Ori Olokun sculpture, which is life-sized [1].

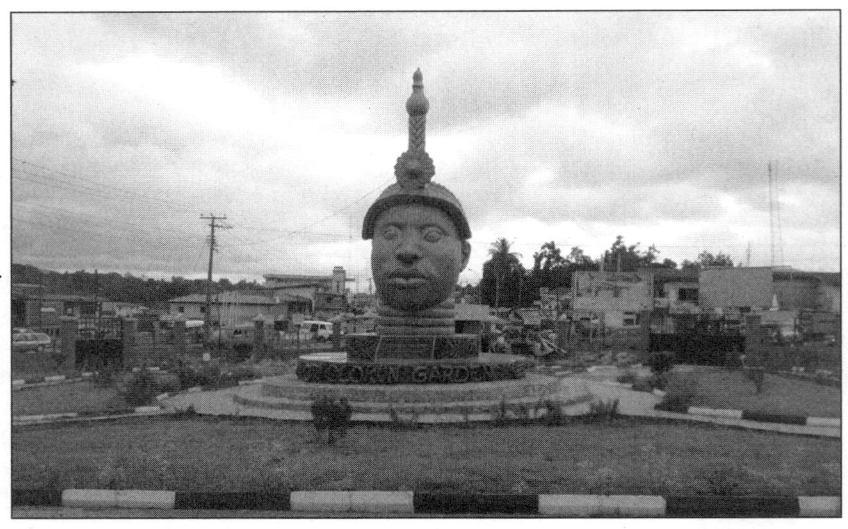

An outsized replica of it installed in 2013 at the renamed Ori-Olokun Roundabout in Ile-Ife, formerly the Mayfair Roundabout.

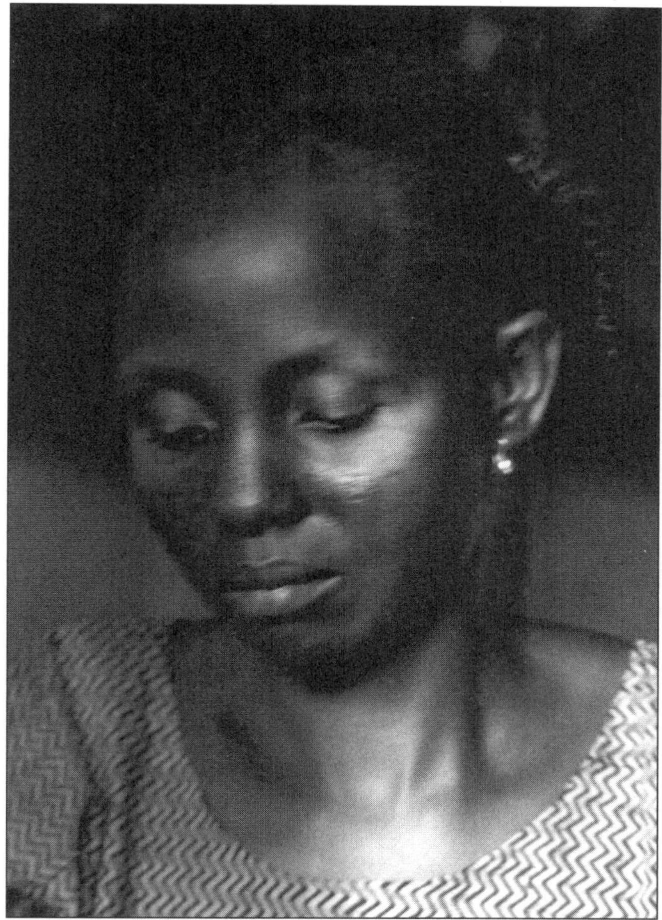

Bought some nice yellow patterned fabric and went to a seamstress, Mrs. J. A. Odewale to have a blouse made. Tried to take some pictures of her but the shop was very dark. [This is what I managed to get of her.]

Have been noticing an absence of mirrors; seems it's traditionally considered an ill-omen.

There's a looseness of physical contact here, touching isn't unusual. I have to drop my defenses. I read somewhere about the belief in "disciplining the face so that pleasure does not reveal itself." And the use of coolness as a force, as a control of one's reality, a domain; in dancing, the gestural conversations which are so specifically and privately understood among the women; the function of children and what occurs in the event of not having children; the composure of the women dancers at Zinder, sometimes broken by a funny or "lewd" sequence which brought laughter and a more heated dancing [2].

In northern Ivory Coast and southern Mali there's the Women's Sandogo divine society. Oh god, I'm entranced by all this cultural/spiritual traditional stuff, and I'm so teeth-gnashingly atheistic—

FEBRUARY 3

Managed to finish developing all my film rolls today at the university darkroom, thanks to access given to me by Olu Elufowoju, but then I was assisted/deterred by three fellows who tried and tried to make me use D76 at 94°, and then told me they liked my spunk when I refused.

PART OF A LETTER TO CINDY:

Cindy—people keep asking me why I don't want to stay in Africa & work for a newspaper here . . . Well, it would be simple: I wouldn't have to bother with grammar, or with pictures which even vaguely resemble the subject, since they all print in a range of 2-3 medium grays. Developed all my negs so far, 10 rolls, very exciting—Univ of Ife has luxurious darkrooms. Nigeria operates thusly: If it can be purchased, buy it; we'll worry about how and if we can operate it later. No qualms w/ having 3 expensive enlargers & no functioning photo department, or 3 electron microscopes which have been untouched since installation last year, or about $14 million for a (2nd) theater at Univ Ife & no adequate hospital—and it goes on . . . There's really no one person or ideology to blame it on, it's all a confused & perverse chain of attitudes & policies & colonial hangovers. Back to the negs: Ones from Copenhagen very thin but adequate & some delightfully tough ones of the women musicians & theater. I'm tempted to set aside the still art that happened there & concentrate just on the events, the music, etc.—the still art wasn't worth much mention save for a few works. Have some good shots from the baptism dance in Niger, & apparently my destroyed 35mm lens is still reading & shooting correctly, albeit w/ large dirt hunks wedged inside the lens—will do some prints next week.
Hope you received my article. After mailing it I regretted not ending it differently, realized I'd left the issue of women hanging a bit, but at that point was so burnt out that . . .

Notes from conversations . . . Dispersal of wealth from oil refineries to the army (with very high salaries), the intensive consumers in this society, in this way it gets passed down to the local merchants and subsistence farmers, but then almost no recycling of the $$ occurs, it dribbles off in 10K pieces spent on a bit of yam or a bar of soap, no investment in collective farming projects, etc. (and taxes are never paid because of no workable income rate for the majority of the population). Soybean—an easily grown protein source but it's not accepted into the diet because of its bad taste (understandable but regrettable, and Nigeria is, with all its $$, becoming a great meat-consuming nation, which means that grain-consuming beef are proliferating).

These staff clubs and the endless beer consumption and conversations about Nigeria's inefficiency are really making an impression. As are the foreign-educated Nigerians who all seem to bitch ferociously about living conditions here, unabashedly.

I'm becoming quite a sociable sort, sitting down for a beer and staying a few hours, and all that—it's essential to African *politesse* and the rhythm of time here.

Saw Godard's film *Vivre sa vie*—about a prostitute. It was met with a hell of a lot of laughter, the laughter directed at her as a fool/nitwit; there was absolutely no empathy for her, which was apropos, she being the object even to the extent of audience reaction; it ended in her being shot straight through by the pimps who were selling and buying her and had been cheated—some interesting passages (but labored), like the conversation with the "*philosophe*" who kept dropping names and rambling on terribly about the necessity of wisdom as a death within life, about having a strong sense of detachment from daily realities, and she quite simply says that detachment is impossible for her. *Touché*. How does one escape a body/the pedestrian elements of life while being a prostitute?

A terrible rundown of the pimp explaining how it works: You take any man, do it 5-50 times a day, sheets won't be changed between customers, learn to dress so that you're immediately recognized, pay off the cops and ministry and get health exams. A scene with her first trick as she desperately tries to avoid being kissed on the mouth; with another man being paid to just sit by and watch him fuck another woman; her speech about being responsible oneself for everything in one's life (well-brainwashed), and the tale of the friend with deserted hubby and two kids . . . and she's responsible?
Passage from "The Oval Portrait" by Poe about a woman being the perfect subject for a painter, whose face-essence he can recreate to breathtaking superperfection, step back, admire as his own creation, say Ah, this is Life and Beauty, and then find his subject dead, nowhere near as desirable as the artifice he has created.

Congress voted 322–100 against Angolan aid, overriding Ford's pro-military stand.

In an article by Vorster[41] on South Africa, he says that people in SW Africa and Rhodesia are "some of the happiest in the world"—Yep, he said that.

US aid to Chile went from £50mil to £315mil <u>this year</u> [3].

Now Nigeria has nineteen states, the better to distribute the programs and wealth (and ease some tribal tensions).
The military in E. state[42] were disrespectful at a ceremony which precipitated a riot which killed 20–200 civilians (depending on whose story one reads). The soldiers simply opened fire on them—they're quite *verrückt* [crazy]) here; so juvenile; there's a burlesque quality, even as traffic cops.

FEBRUARY 4

Amazed, moved to one of those very noisy silences, full of messages, when I saw the ten or so bronze heads at the Ife Museum [4]. The queen mother and king were flawless. The variation in poise, structure, mood of each head was well marked; they had such a dignified, intense presence.

---

41 B.J. (John) Vorster was the Prime Minister of South Africa from 1966–1978.

42 I don't know if this was in Ekiti, Ebonyi or Ebo state. There had been seven states but the president, Murtala Muhammed, had just raised the number to nineteen. There are currently thirty-six states.

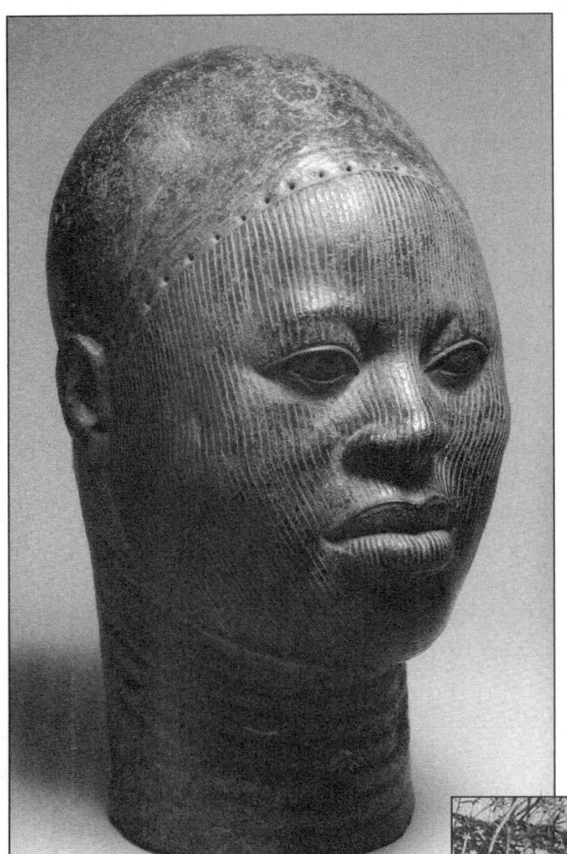

There were many more beautiful works in the Nigerian National Museum in Lagos, which I saw a month later and write about at length in Chapter 14.

Oba Sir Titus Martins Adesoji Tadeniawo Aderemi (Atobatele I) with some of the artworks from Ile-Ife. Aderemi was a Nigerian political figure and Yoruba traditional ruler, the Ooni (King) of Ile-Ife from 1930 until 1980. He also served as the governor of Western Region, Nigeria between 1960 and 1962.

The funk art-street crap here has its own charm and humor, although I can't collect all that I would like or I'd soon look like a tinker with posters and buckets and tin cans dangling from my pack.

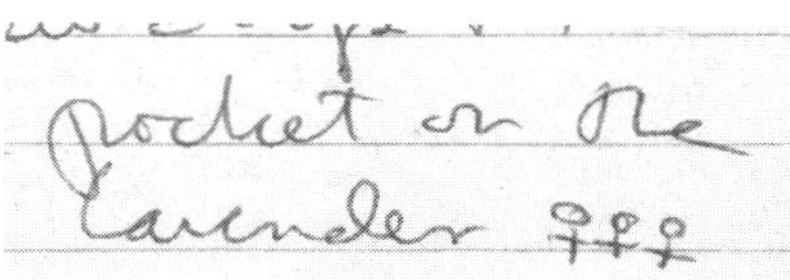

I've been in a skirt now and new Yoruba blouse for a few days and I feel good—and the back pocket on the skirt has a reassuring lavender (*lesbian symbol*) embroidered on it—

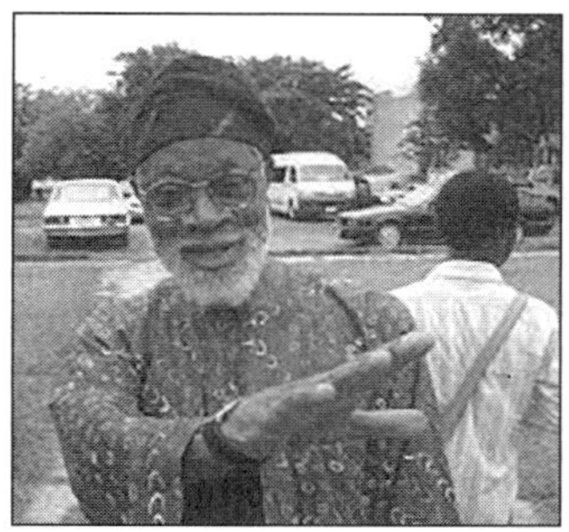

Went to see a play in Yoruba "written in 1973 and prophetic of current events"— *Kòseégbé* by Akinwumi Isola [5]. A businessman dressed to the T like an American baby-faced executive, his assistant in bow tie and Alabama summer straw hat, and a chic secretary with straightened hair. He wanted to clean up and speed up his corporation, cut out the dolts. A worker's coup; his seduction by/of a "beautiful Lady" (here in Nigeria they use Lady rather than woman, consider it more polite); the treason of his assistant. The audience was in an uproar continuously; in the seduction scene they were really jumping and screaming—but noticeably the men more than the women—the jeering being "any man who's hip would grab the chance to get his hands on a woman like that"—she was large-breasted and in a very obnoxious low-cut, backless American dress.
The women all had minor and/or insulting roles. And so it goes. The audience was really in an uproar; they never really stopped chattering and leaning to the person behind them with a comment or joke.

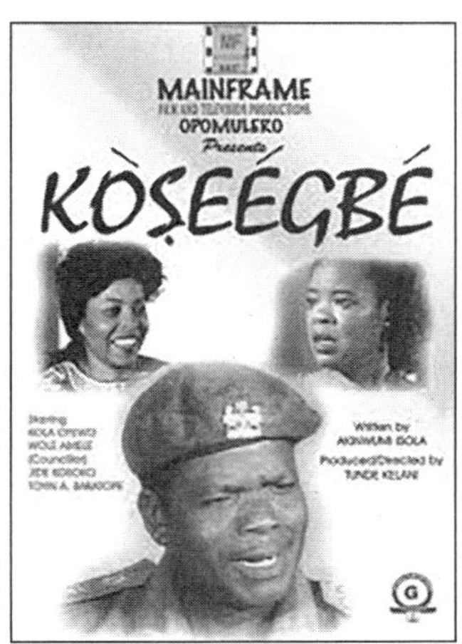

Film adaptation directed by Tunde Kelani (1995)

Later I heard a corrective from Alice [a student] about the play: The corporate executive was attempting reform and was blackmailed by real crooks, and in the end it came down to a question of whether he would go along with their blackmail and take them back into the company, or expose them and risk being himself exposed . . . He took them back . . . The evildoers were "too strong a force to combat" etc., that being the moral of the tale and of present Nigeria, with Gowon [43] being part of this whole corrupt government.

A week later, the play would be proved prophetic

43 Yakubu Gowon, head of state for nine years, was overthrown in a coup in 1975. See Chapter 13 for many other details about him.

Moynihan resigned at the UN.
"Dr. Kissinger" thinks that foreign, compared to domestic, policy should predominate. And that our foreign policy, "despite some problems, has been remarkably effective in the last thirty years"—
Oh yeah—

FEBRUARY 5

The unnamed student who let me crash in her dorm room (thank you, mysterious friend!) was nice enough to let me use her car.

I'm so sick of being full it makes me lethargic, and after a few days of being isolated on this campus I determined today to get out somewhere. Driving to Ilesha, alone in the car, afternoon sun whitening the heaps of rain clouds, clumped and straggly and sky-reaching and clogged tropics around me, red clay road, traders walking home, funky Yoruba towns, cyclists with their dark glasses and platform shoes—"Su, you're in the African bush, you are here," like the afternoon along the Allegheny, me and my bike and my strength (and my privilege, never forget) [6].

When I arrived in Ilesha, on impulse I stopped at the Olubukola Maternity Center, did lots of pics, asked as politely, quickly, and seemingly unpryingly as possible, all the questions—and it felt very good afterwards. It's a deceptive but satisfying thing, to catch a few photos.

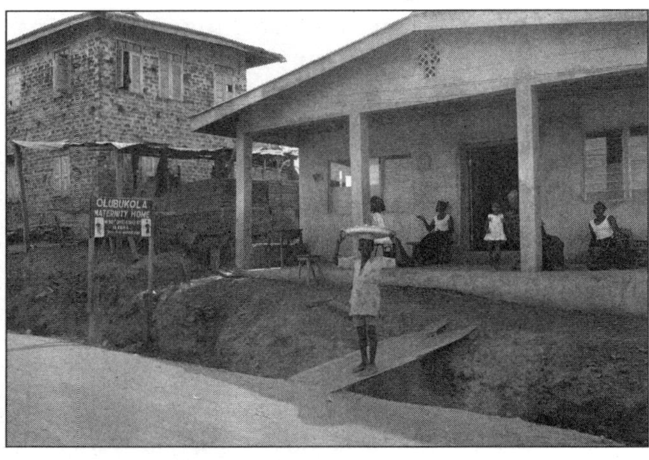

The proprietress, Mrs. B. O. Akinbolagbe, has been a midwife for fifteen years; was educated in London. No patients yet, it just opened. Had three sparse cots, a dusty basinet, bare delivery room, linoleum'd waiting room, crusty old bottles for medicine—she hopes to have five to six women a week. She's training young women who finished primary six (probably equivalent to high school) to be ward mates, assistants to her. She named it after her first son. Worked with the Save the Children Fund, now taken over by the Nigerian government. Will keep women in three days after birth; plans to have educational classes but it's difficult to plan now.
On the way back to Ife, I gave a ride to a woman with two kids and a load of wood and tobacco—she had the most stupendous and hard-earned arm muscles I've yet

seen. She had a load in a burlap bag that I couldn't budge out of the trunk, but she managed to get it out.

PART OF A LETTER TO CINDY:

Visited a maternity clinic in Ilesha. The proprietress responded to my request for a portrait of her by lying down on her bed Odalisque-fashion.

I'm getting the knack about how to approach w/o rushing, to ask rapid-fire questions w/o seeming overly inquisitive, to take 5 pictures in the space of an expected 1, to make my interest seem only of the purest motive, etc.

It's not a question of learning to be deceptive, but—in this corner of the world—to be mutually exploitative—everyone here wants something for even the slightest gesture, & one learns to respond in kind; like when I go driving out in the bush (the character I'm staying w/ in Ife gives me free rein w/ the car) & see a woman w/ a heavy load I give her a ride—she should according to the system here give me 5-10 kobo as a taxi fare, but I've been able to see her & she thinks she's been able to soak an "Oyibo" (honky)[44] for a ride, so we say goodbye & thank you, mutually satisfied.

It takes getting used to, but it's the only way to keep above the system here.

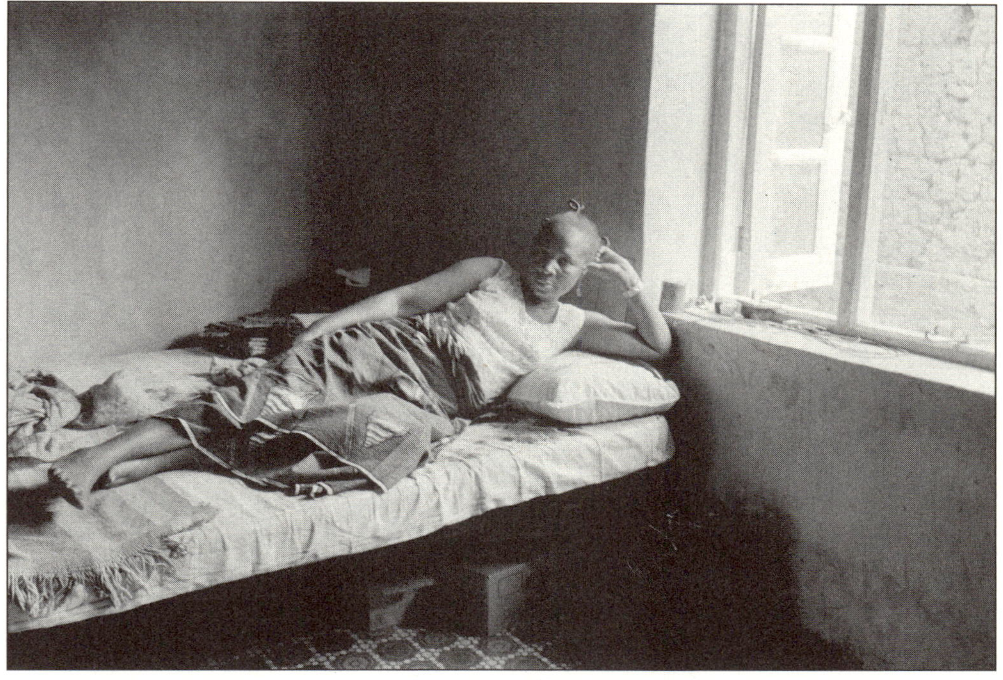

44 See [7] for info about the American origin & usage of "honky" versus the meaning of *oyibo* in Nigeria.

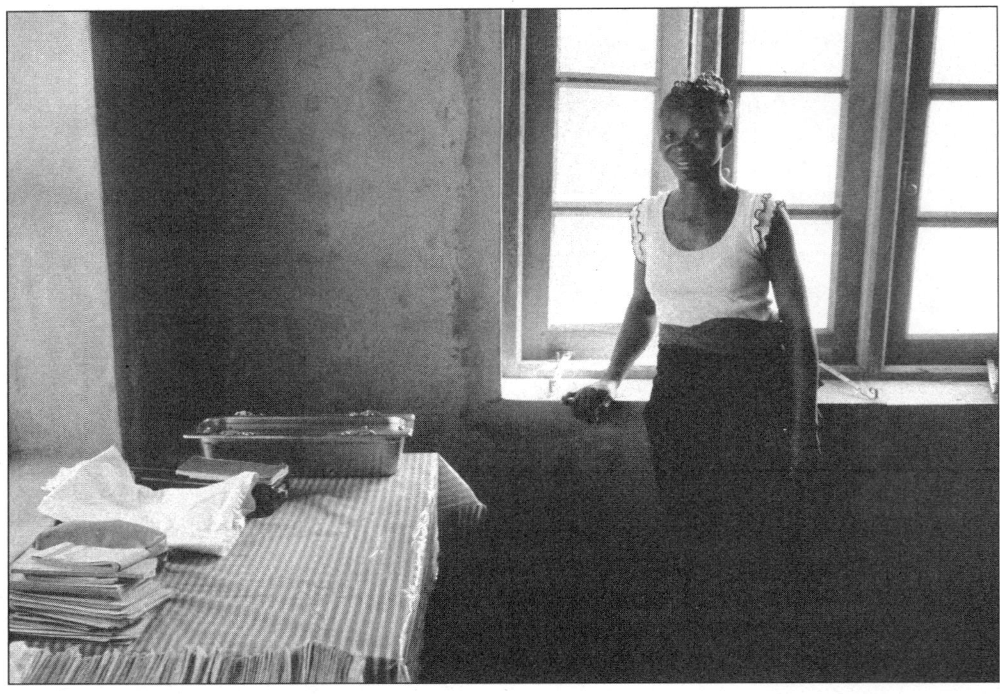

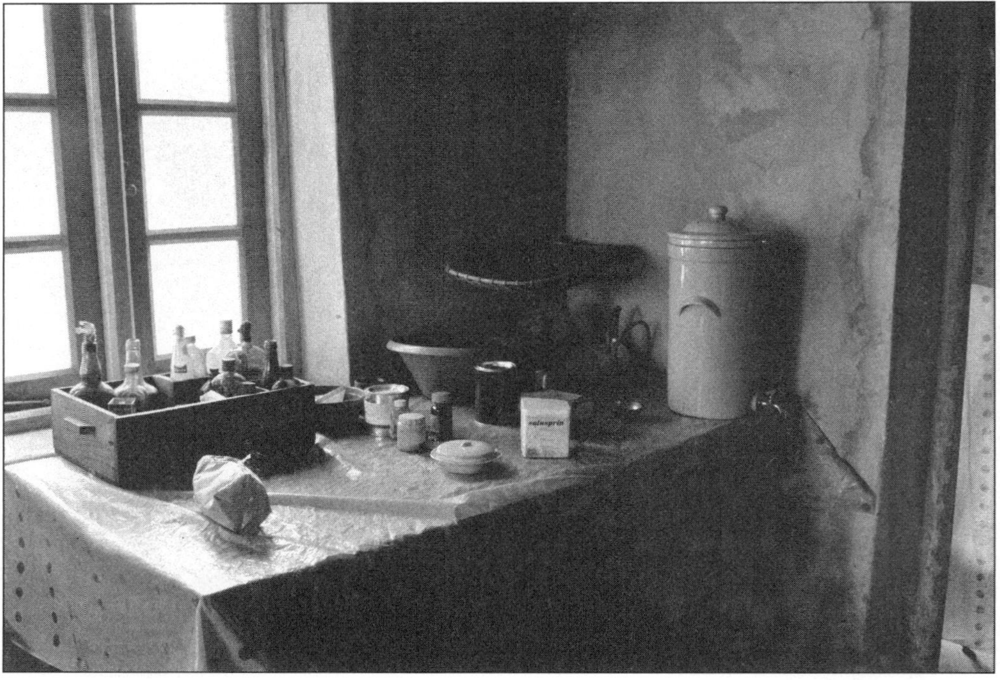

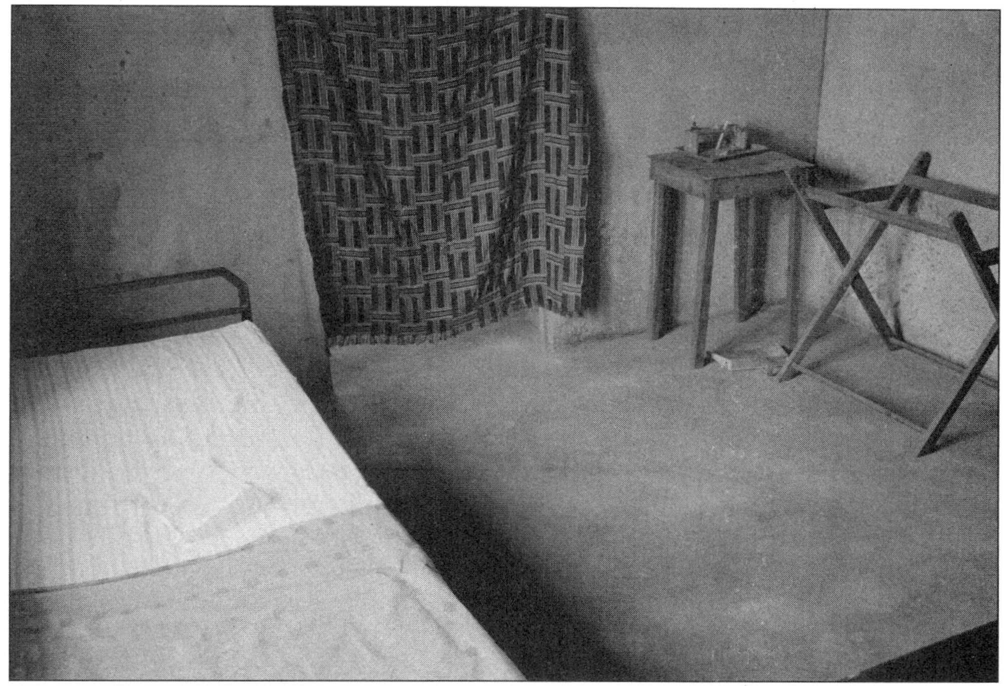

Funny—after a few months on the road I'm getting into the habit of doing things/ being as I wish—smoking, having my hair a certain way, wearing a skirt and the African blouse, etc.—as if I'm permitting all sorts of shoved-away things to resurface as they will.

Same with food; I realize I'm in a terrible pattern of assuming that because my behavior has been so food-obsessed, that it should continue to be, although that goes against my wishes/feelings, which are that I don't feel hungry, or I'm not interested in food and yet I take it anyway because I think to myself—Yes, Susie, you're such a glutton you know you can never say no. Although I'd bet that if I just simply said no and believed myself, I'd be easier at mind about the whole stupid issue. It's some anachronistic punishment cycle I've been on, self-derision, etc.

The pro African-traditional-life, do-or-die, uncritical ideology is just to no avail. As much as I truly love, as much as is possible, the musical/artistic/(some) social traditions here, their "philosophy of life" and other fine terms, I cannot see only that and decry modernism.

The realization, as one is on the road, of the breathtaking natural beauty and wonder of Africa is diminished drastically with entrance to a town. Hard to witness the abject conditions of health and knowledge—a functional knowledge, I speak of, not an alienating otherworldly knowledge.

It's little surprise (although perhaps depressing) that the students here can be so bourgeois AND Africanistic at the same time—it's like us women who hold men in such contempt while living off their "good" systems.

Started to read the Dolores Klaich book today, *Woman + Woman: Attitudes Towards Lesbianism*, published in '74-75. Turned to the dust jacket expecting a "dyke;" saw instead a woman with long hair—and oh god, all the things I enumerate about her will show how badly warped out my thinking is, how deeply my fears about lesbians run; despite surface words *au contraire* [to the contrary] I still expect a certain "sort" and was ashamedly run amuck today.
My thoughts (as compared to my emotional responses, which go beyond it) still fall into patterning of m-f/butch-femme; I assume that if baby acts tough or unsmiling, i.e., fits all those butch labels, then it's appropriate/complementary in the war of opposites that I be/see myself as "sentimental," a sucker, etc. I don't think we actually operate (to use such a term!) like that but I fall into trying to understand it along those lines—the slave mentality, the psychological structures of the oppressor.
Anyway, good book. Took me home. Made me feel the different levels I'm living on now travelling in this other world—

Colette:
"Look for a long time at what pleases you, and longer still at what pains you."
and
"Orgasm is the proof of mutual trust."

PART OF A LETTER TO CINDY:

Hard to talk to the women here, the students; I'm in fact intimidated by them, their apparent "airs", they're all quite chic & usually in groups of 2-3 or w/ a man—so I sit back & admire & observe—went to a party last weekend here, a bunch of students, took me back to sweaty bump-and-grinding beer sodden high school days, women short skirts bored looks trapped eyes, men being aggressive, thrusting their pelvises as we danced, & they were hanging all over me—if I hadn't been perversely justifying it as "research" I would've screamed & run—I survived unpenetrated, I'm happy to announce.
It sucks here for women.
Period.
All that glory of African womanhood strength and economic independence ballyhoo aside, it sucks.

Picture it: every day now I wear a (jean) skirt + loose brightly printed blouses + jewelry! one can't resist it here.
The barefoot + pregnant complaint is carried to a higher + more treacherous

Picture it: Every day now I wear a (jean) skirt & loose brightly printed blouses & jewelry! One can't resist it here.
The barefoot & pregnant complaint is carried to a higher & more treacherous plateau: How does she pull herself up by her bootstraps if she's barefoot, pregnant, a baby on her back, a 50 lb. load of yams on her head, two kids trailing behind, and still 10 miles to walk before she gets home to fix dinner?
Amen. A men.
I can't go into Dahomey (now Benin) because the Benin-Togo border is closed so if I go to Benin I'll have to go up & through Upper Volta & back down into Ghana & then back into Togo which is bullshit so I'll go to Lagos & get a boat (?) to Lomé in Togo & pass up Benin—I've heard it's in quite a fascist state right now—
Things are going slower, I don't rush from place to place, I check out the best options, I've passed the stage of hating traveling (hits me at the 2nd month) & now feel quite comfortable being here—maybe it'll be hard to leave, but after some months maybe not—I wish I could let you know how absolutely weirdly different it is here (despite the presence of so much western crap); I'll have a good bit of adjusting to do back in the states, I think. So, things are as well as they can be; I hope they are for you—have you had a coup at Gestalt? Please pass on my greetings to Linda.
Love
Su
& to Donna, all the best

P.S.
Let's have an ad hoc program on "Famous Women of the American Revolution" on July 4th—how about "Jane Addams and her favorite student nurse"?

P.S.S.
Tell your friend at the Gestalt Institute that I have my eyes open for an African goddess figure for her—I've seen a few bronze pieces but none were "just right" . . . but there are goddesses everywhere so I'll be sure to find one eventually—I'm keeping my eye out for a glimpse of an Amazon dashing thru the bush but all I see are muscular sweating child-burdened strong women striding down the roads . . . a reasonable facsimile if one scrapes the gilt off the Amazons—

These are some clippings that were enclosed with the letter.

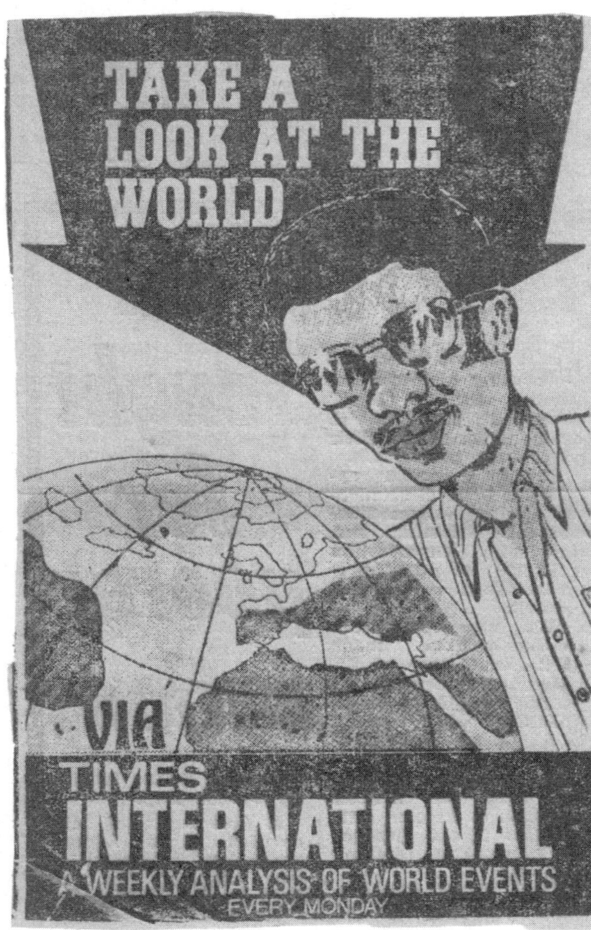

His mission was to cause witch-hunting in the ranks of African leaders and consequently to break the OAU. Africa rejected his bait. Africa has grown.

Last week he was a wrecked man after confessing that he was a tool to a bank that went bust after milking millions of pounds from the public.

He is also now a social wreck. He was named as a homosexual by a former male model, his lover.

How could Jeremy prove innocence by his statement: "It is well over 12 years since I last saw or spoke to Mr. Scott. There is no truth in Mr. Scott's wild allegations." Tell that to the marines.

Which itself was a disservice to a public that gave him the privilege to sit in the House of Commons and to lead a party. What a moral degeneracy! This Jeremy!

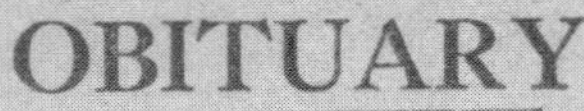

OBITUARY

We regret to announce the sudden and untimely death of our dear sister

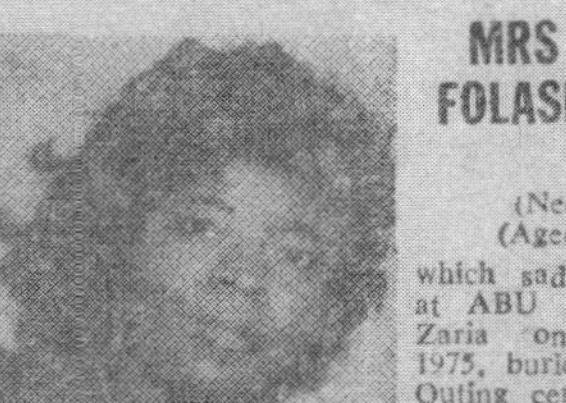

MRS FLORENCE FOLASHADE ABIKE ALABI

(Nee TAYLOR)

(Aged 46 years)

which sad event took place at ABU Teaching Hospital Zaria on 24th December 1975, buried 26th Dec. 1975. Outing ceremony takes place at St. George's Anglican Church, Zaria, on Sunday, 8th February, 1976.

S. I. OGUNBUNMI &
BIMPE TAYLOR
for the family.

IN MEMORIAM

In loving memory of our dearly beloved friend

Adetokunboh

Oluyemisi Bologun

Senior Prefect Ansar-Ud-Deen Girls High School, Surulere

Died 6/2/75

Simple, charming and brilliant Toks. We could not believe you are no more. Why and how your life is so short thou. We praise Allah that is well spent. A promising child, who propose to be a good leader of tomorrow Allah knows best. We just cannot take the blow off our hearts. R.I.P. Love Toks.

Fondly remembered by

Molade, Sidi, Kehinde, Kudi, Dolapo Sheri, Moji, Moni, Risi, Yanju, Bisi, Danmola, Ottun and Mulnat.

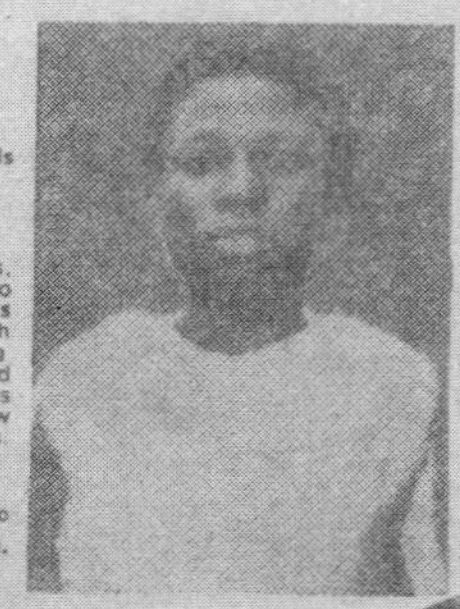

Alongside the ad for **Julie** *I wrote:*
This from an <u>*African*</u> *paper. When I enter the cities I see a noticeable number of women with pressed hair and WIGS.*

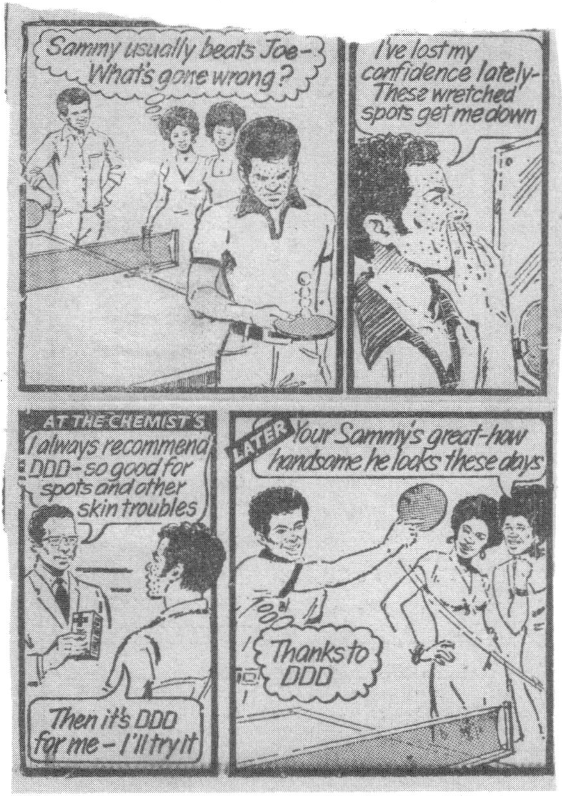

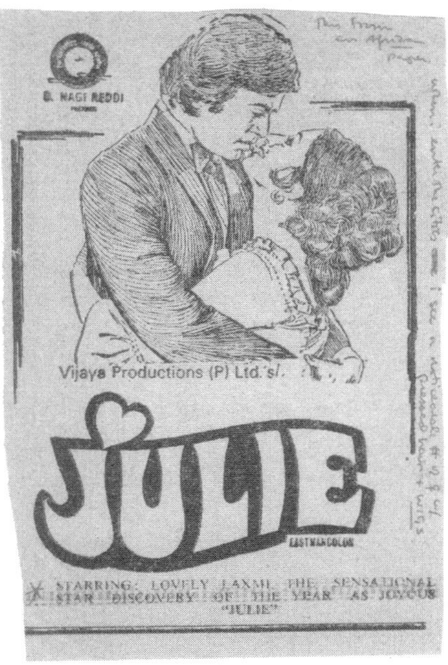

THE 1976 Times Motor Show, the third in the series, is scheduled for Sunday, February 22 to Saturday 28, at the National Stadium, Surulere, Lagos.

The Federal Commissioner for Industries, Col. M. I. Wushishi, will be in the chair at the opening ceremonies.

Highlights of the seven-day event include a motor rally, a motor-cycle rally and a Miss Motor Show.

The motor show will take at the exhibition

FEBRUARY 6

First there are several pages of notes about a book I was reading:
Can Africa Survive? Arguments Against Growth Without Development *by Basil Davidson*.

What a test it becomes of one's patience, humor, sense of irony, and persistence, to think, "Oh I'll just go to town and buy some . . . ."
In this case, some developer so I can make prints in the Unife darkroom.
Dusty, crumbling Liberty Photos had some. 3 ₦ [$2.40 on the black market].
Looked antiquated.

The next stop, one pitiful old dusty bag of Agfa developer, a 1950s model. At so-and-so's "Photo Stop," portraits hand-colored and dazzled to please. She gave me her two assistants as field guides—we submerged ourselves into the twisting backroads in search of a curious someone who "has developer": No one home. A chair materializes on which I must perch (it's on the verge of crashing into several splintered fragments) and wait for this certain someone, on whose door is chalked: "Think and Thank."
By now the whole neighborhood is involved in the search, each advising where he will be found, each pointing in a different direction. Their performance is sprinkled with *oyibo*, this apparition willing to go so far for an extravagant item.
An old woman, pulling her wrap up modestly over her previously exposed—lovely—breasts, opens the fellow's window. A jam-packed, pack-rat sort of room, clothes, books and papers stuffed everywhere and two green badly corked dusty bottles, which she indicates to me are the reward of my journey. She, in Yoruba.
I, in English, politely protest that no, they don't seem to be quite right. Ah, then this?...a small opened packet of powder. *Looks* like developer. Also looks like fixer.
Ah, no thanks, not the stuff. Thanks, thanks . . . and five *kobos* to each assistant.
Back in the car, back to Liberty Photos, pay a soaking 3 ₦ for the dusty D163. No fixer? No, come back tomorrow. 7 a.m.
Oh, I see. Seven in the morning? Yes.
As the Yoruba say . . . .Ah-hey.

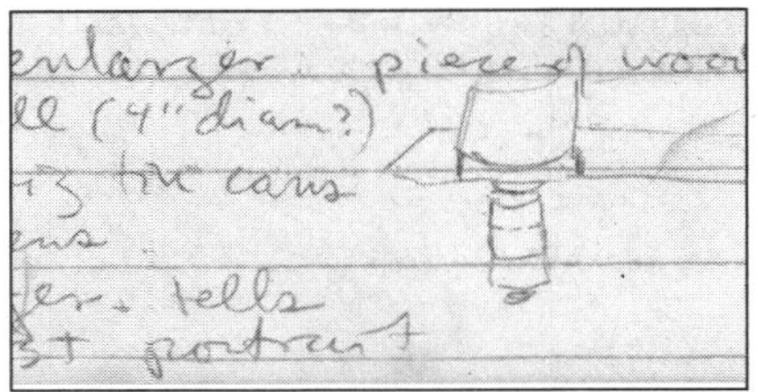

Willem the food researcher described to me what one needs to make an enlarger: A piece of wood, a large tin can as the condenser, a small (4" diam?) condenser lens, two tightly fitting tin cans as bellows, a fairly nice Agfa lens.
He tells me that with the cost of a real one, most portrait photographers here in these funky studios use such sorts of "machines." I'm newly impressed and amused.

Assessment of the staff clubbers of Unife:
They are the mediocre the small who need those smaller than them to make themselves feel big. It's quite aggrandizing to be an "expat" on these campuses, to have the leisure to sit and bitch about African ineptitude and African this and that non-European non-academic non-quality and call them all sycophants and naïve bureaucrats, but the quality—if any (my arms are a rich honey brown)—of their own work hasn't overwhelmed me, it's mostly "in the planning stages" and the alleged "heavy work hours" seem to be more than compensated for every evening at the staff club.
For example, Chris telling me he spent four hours preparing for an exam, when I ate lunch with him until past 2:00 and saw him (without him seeing me) at the club at 5:00 with a beer or two down already.
Agnes has a Nigerian sweetheart and lives in town (albeit on the school compound) and generally is very unimpressed with these expats—she, as I, finds them

the least interesting of what Nigeria has to offer (and rightly so, although they tend to think quite the opposite).

Chris was a desperate self-listener. In talking for a few days with some difficulty to the clubbers (men) and then to Agnes, I immediately felt the difference, the willingness to listen that women cultivate (are forced to cultivate)—of course it's to their detriment in general because one can't get anywhere talking to (being talked at by) men if one only listens. But when with someone who listens and talks, it's a sudden relief from the nervous anxiety that develops while wondering if he's listening, or when I'll be able to sneak a thought in edgewise.

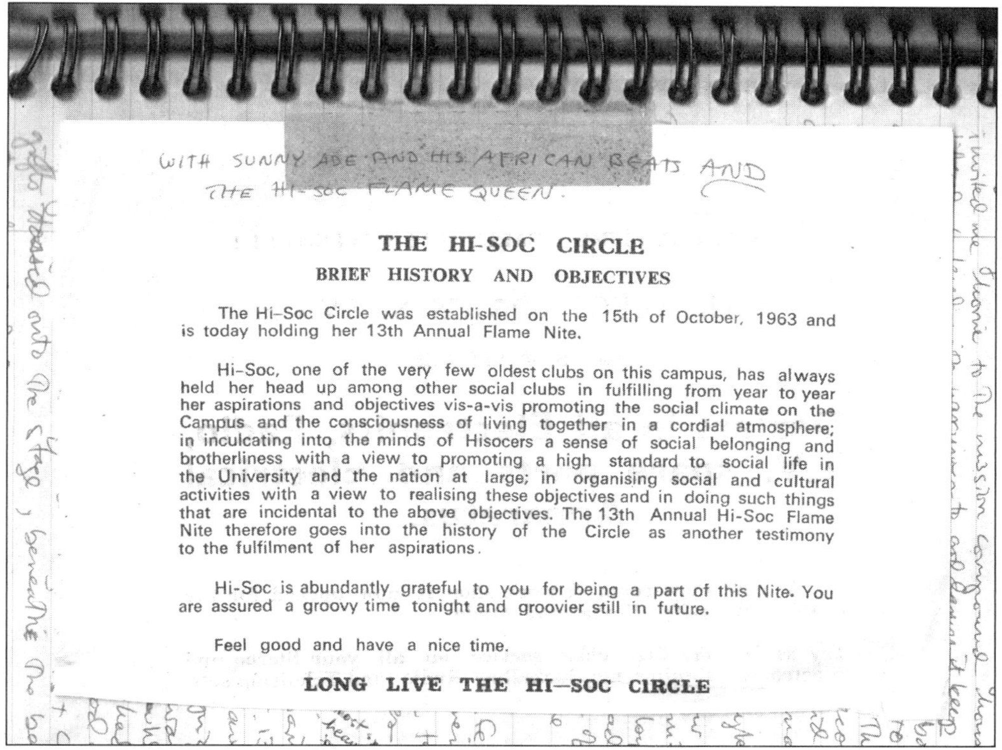
WITH SUNNY ADE AND HIS AFRICAN BEATS AND THE HI-SOC FLAME QUEEN.

THE HI-SOC CIRCLE

BRIEF HISTORY AND OBJECTIVES

The Hi-Soc Circle was established on the 15th of October, 1963 and is today holding her 13th Annual Flame Nite.

Hi-Soc, one of the very few oldest clubs on this campus, has always held her head up among other social clubs in fulfilling from year to year her aspirations and objectives vis-a-vis promoting the social climate on the Campus and the consciousness of living together in a cordial atmosphere; in inculcating into the minds of Hisocers a sense of social belonging and brotherliness with a view to promoting a high standard to social life in the University and the nation at large; in organising social and cultural activities with a view to realising these objectives and in doing such things that are incidental to the above objectives. The 13th Annual Hi-Soc Flame Nite therefore goes into the history of the Circle as another testimony to the fulfilment of her aspirations.

Hi-Soc is abundantly grateful to you for being a part of this Nite. You are assured a groovy time tonight and groovier still in future.

Feel good and have a nice time.

LONG LIVE THE HI—SOC CIRCLE

Saw Sunny Ade and his African Beats at the Unife "Hi-Soc" dance [8]. Women dressed like Cosmo, men like Viva and/or royalty—heavy brocade tuxedos, red suit, white tie, seven-inch-high platform shoes, eyeshadow and prom-gowned "ladies"—*le haut bourgeois* [the upper class]—

We sat and gazed and chuckled and bemoaned. [45]

Sunny Ade was tough; the band members wore velvet vests and pants patterned with cowrie shells, each different. Thirteen musicians and Ade, and the crowd just boogeyed away. They start by jutting out their asses and dropping their shoulders

45 I don't know who I was bemoaning with. Undoubtedly with an expat student, not an African.

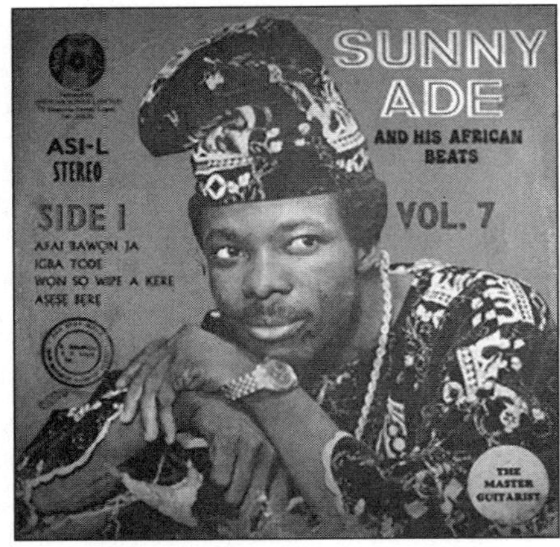

and then they shimmy and sway and ripple to the continuous beat—hard to tell what function some of the "musicians" had, who didn't really play anything, but their good dancing precipitated a lot of admiring cheers and cash gifts tossed onto the stage beneath the benevolent cool gaze of Ade.
A most spontaneous heave and splash into joy; a breathless sigh of "Ah, that's good . . . "
And, unavoidable: An all-women's band from Lagos was paid half of what Sunny Ade got, and consequently didn't show up.
He sings proverbs rather than love songs, e.g., of a father and son and horse; each change of the situation (who's on the horse) displeases another neighbor; one must live according to one's own feelings, can't satisfy all the others, etc.

A LETTER TO MIMI:

Baby,
To the strains of Art Blakey I've written this valentine's smudge to you. It's a sultry night, somewhere between Shanghai Express & East Harlem.
An anecdote from Dolores Klaich, chapter on Sappho:
Niobe was the proud mother of seven beautiful sons & seven beautiful daughters. Leto, the mother of Apollo & Artemis, was getting fed up with her friend's boastful maternalism. She had A & A kill the fourteen beauties. Niobe, freaking out, turned to stone.
Sappho comments:
Before they were mothers
Leto and Niobe
Had been the most
Devoted of friends.

Thinking of you, and loving the memory.
Sappho, again:
 . . . ; but I say
That whatever one loves, is.
Susan Guadelupe[46]

P.S. I've been unexpectedly & thoroughly seduced by this life
P.S.S. Ah; I developed all my film, 10 rolls, and it's fine despite my broken lens! Some tough faces lovely dancers funky poseurs elegant dykes.

46 I was baptized in Mexico and my birthdate is the feast day of Our Lady of Guadelupe, so they gave me that as my middle name.

On the back of the aerogram:

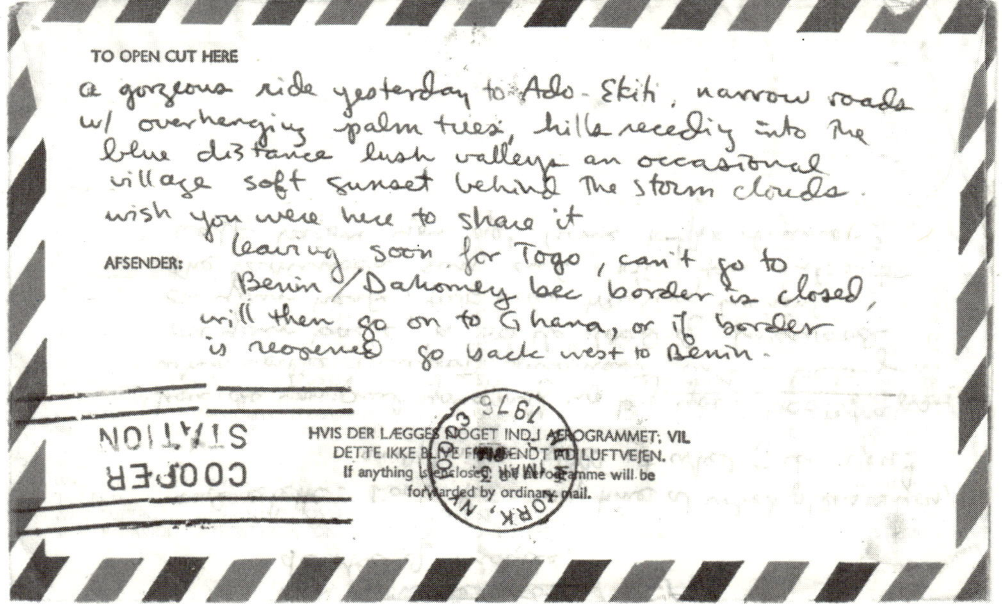

TO OPEN CUT HERE

a gorgeous ride yesterday to Ado-Ekiti, narrow roads
w/ overhanging palm trees, hills receding into the
blue distance lush valleys an occasional
village soft sunset behind the storm clouds.
wish you were here to share it

AFSENDER:

leaving soon for Togo, can't go to
Benin/Dahomey bec border is closed,
will then go on to Ghana, or if border
is reopened go back west to Benin.

HVIS DER LÆGGES NOGET INDI AEROGRAMMET, VIL
DETTE IKKE BLIVE FREMSENDT AD LUFTVEJEN.
If anything is enclosed, this aerogramme will be
forwarded by ordinary mail.

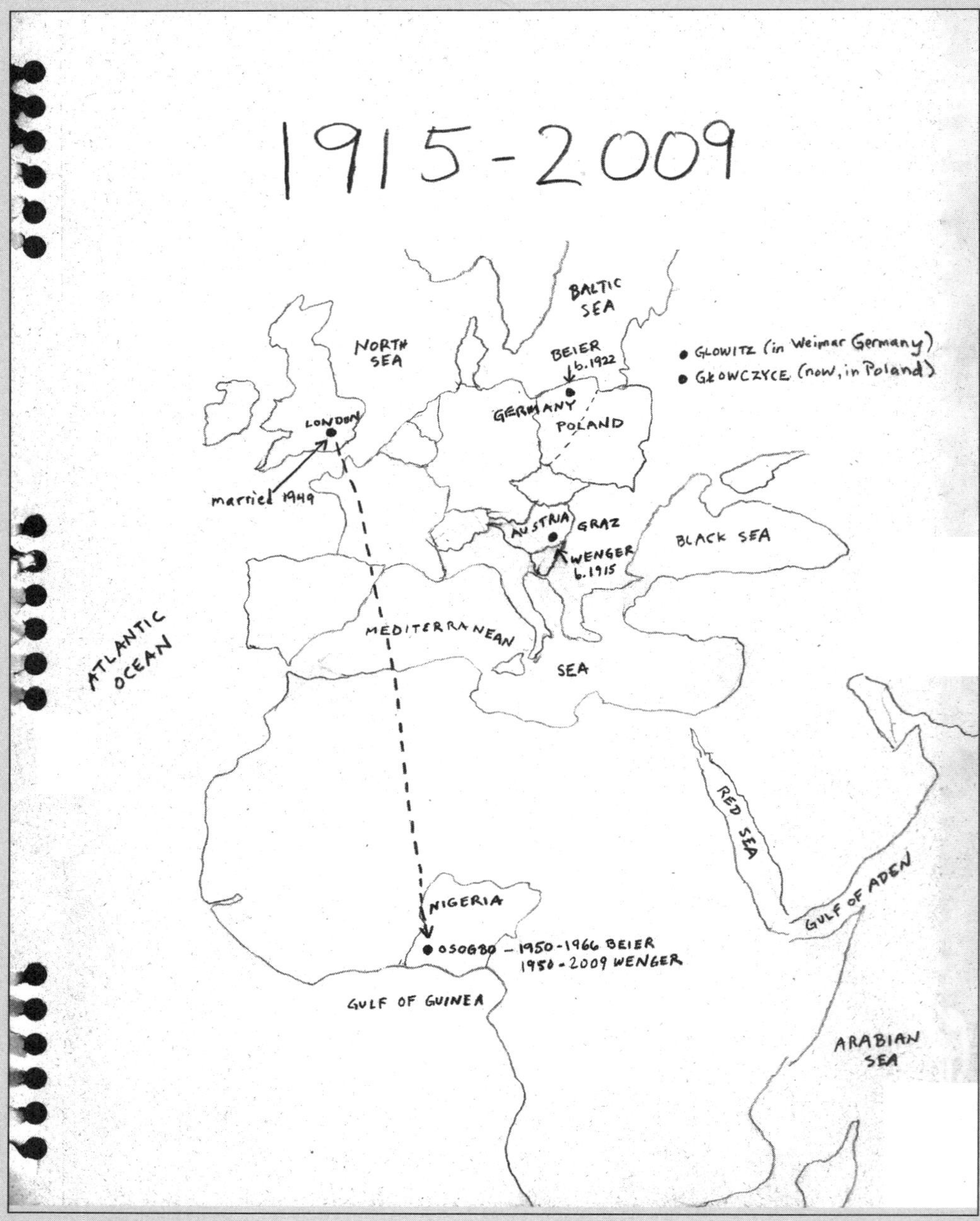
1915-2009
BALTIC SEA
NORTH SEA
BEIER b.1922
• GLOWITZ (in Weimar Germany)
• GŁOWCZYCE (now, in Poland)
LONDON
GERMANY
POLAND
married 1949
AUSTRIA
GRAZ
WENGER b.1915
BLACK SEA
ATLANTIC OCEAN
MEDITERRANEAN SEA
RED SEA
GULF OF ADEN
NIGERIA
OSOGBO – 1950-1966 BEIER
1950-2009 WENGER
GULF OF GUINEA
ARABIAN SEA

CHAPTER ELEVEN

Mbari Mbayo in Osogbo

FEBRUARY 7

I took another day trip from Ife to visit Osogbo, the site of a famous shrine dedicated to Osun, the river goddess. For a student of African art, it was like a student of French art going to the Louvre for the first time.

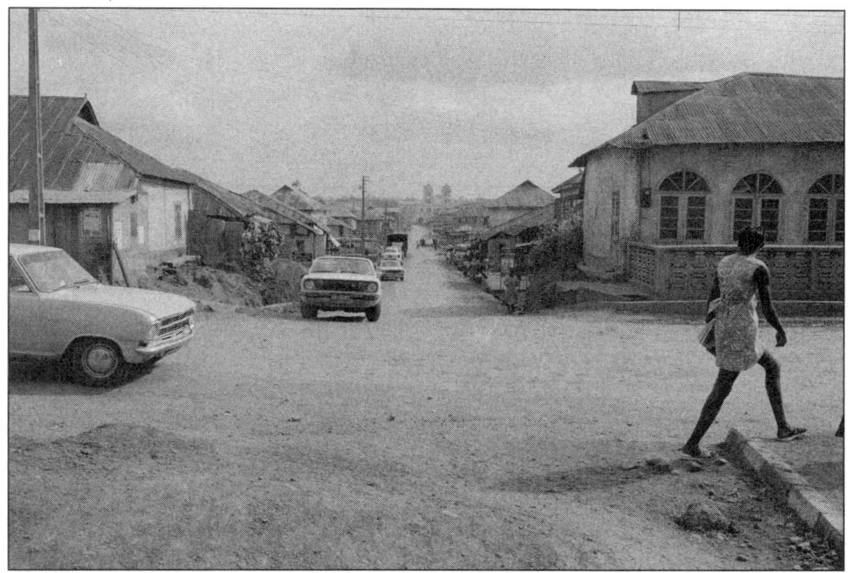

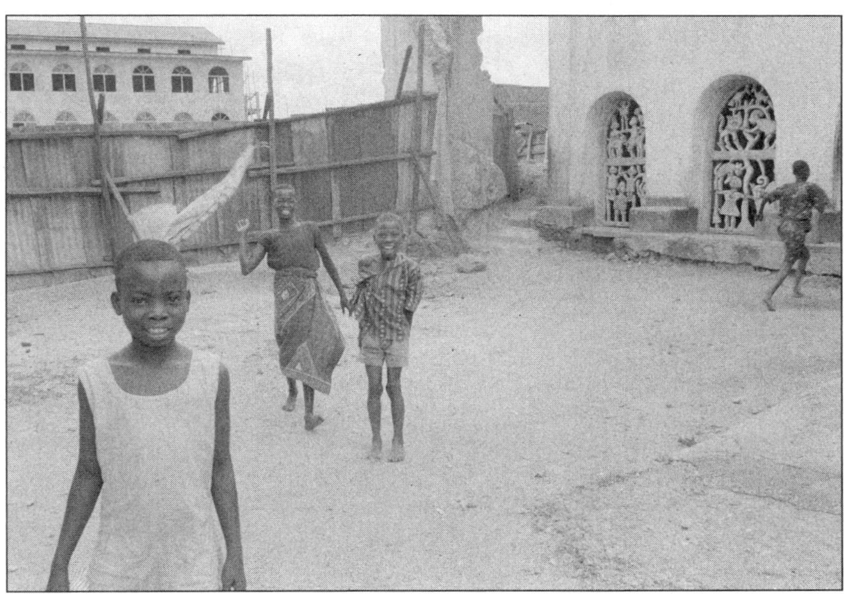

The Ife-Oluwa Grammar School was adjacent to the shrine. I asked some of the students if I could photograph them.

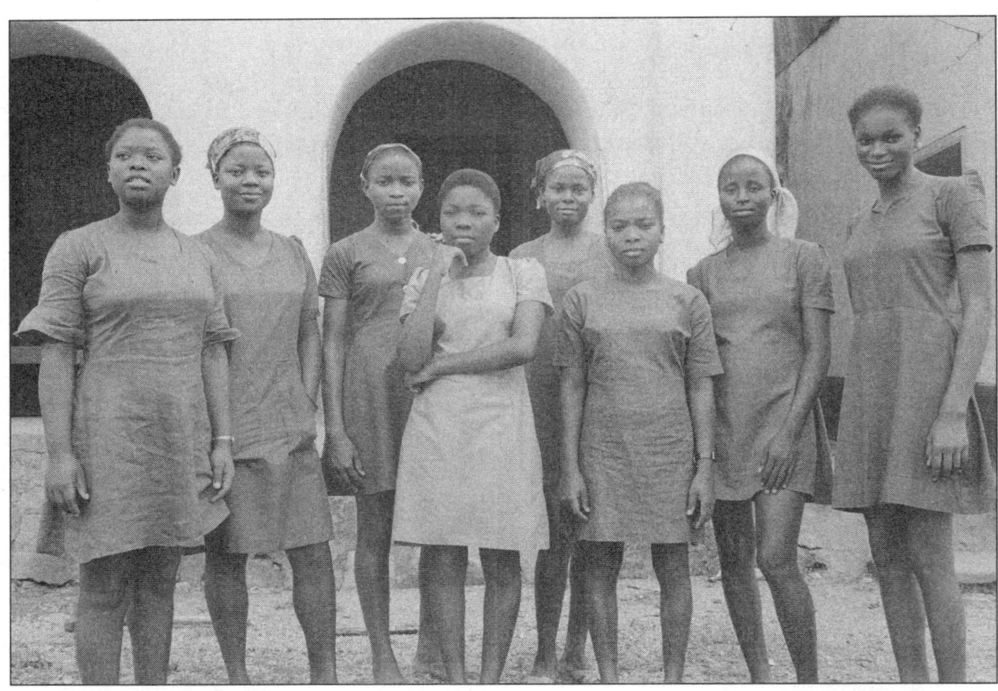

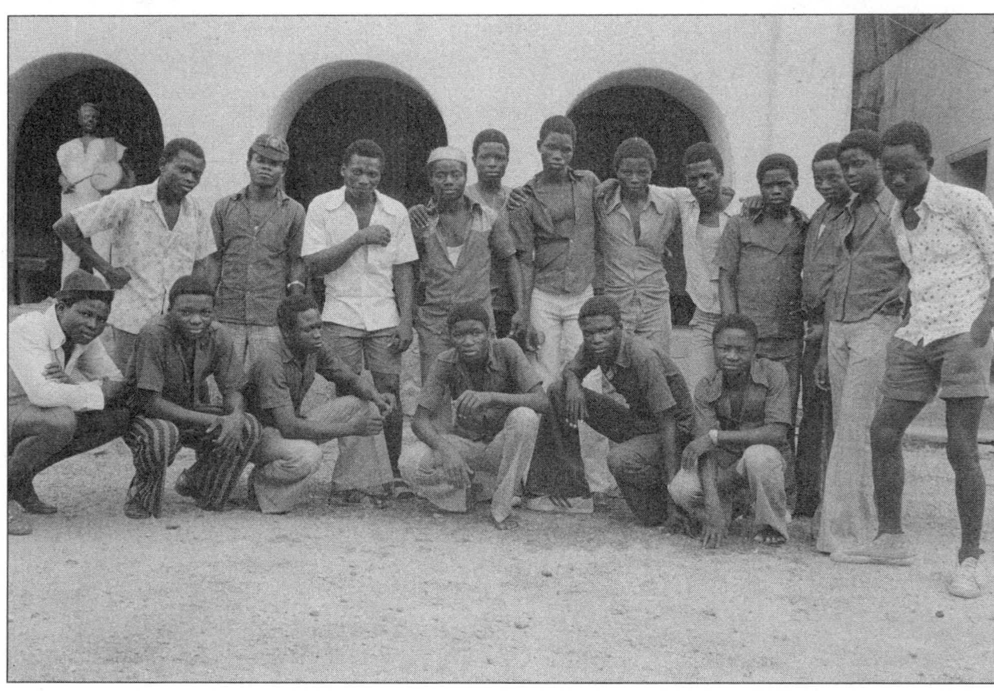

In the land of Ulli Beier, the great Yoruba homeland center-of-the-world, Mbari Mbayo, and all these artificial contemporary artists doing sufficiently attractive but obviously uninspired work.

Ori Olokun was the first stop a few days ago—the chipped, crumbling, once acclaimed murals, the deserted theatre, the infrequent although extant productions.
Then the Ife shrine—a stone pole; oh yes, big story behind it, son of Oduduwa came from Mecca, etc. Fine. But just a stone pole.
But again the feeling that it's the life-meaning-history that overshadows/energizes a (to us, an unkempt) thing.
And now Osogbo, pulsing center of feverish artistic activity and growth, the healthy products of a vibrant dialectic between history and change, all of this duly hurrahed by *African Arts* and Beier.
And of course Susanne Wenger's shrines: I couldn't begin to dream up the terms they've used to describe her and justify her shrines.
And the African Arts Festival postponed year after year.
Mbari Mbayo—When I saw this I was supposed to have been happy, as the translation advises.[47]

But it's also kind of amazing to be here after all the hours I spent with his books in the art library at Oberlin. A disappointing dose of reality, yet still pretty cool.

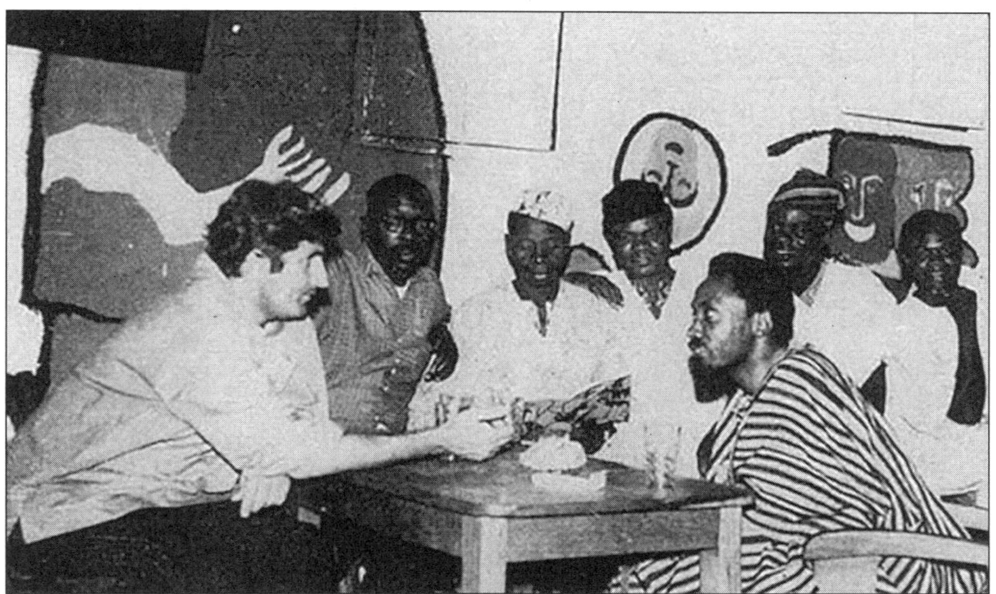

Ulli Beier with members of the Mbari-Mbayo group
(who aren't identified in the source for this photo).

---

47 There's a lot of history behind Beier, Wenger and Mbari Mbayo, and a lot to unpack about my responses to it. See [1] for all the details.

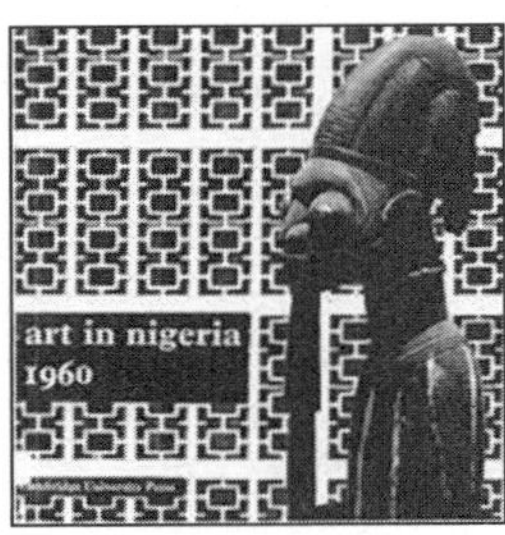

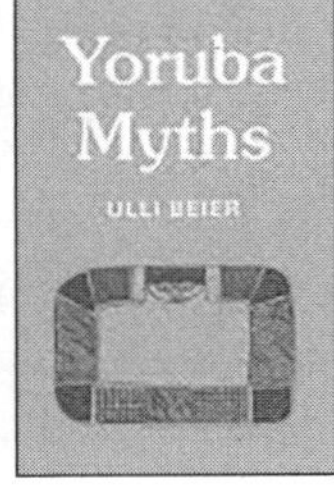

I purposely avoided going to the "Buraimoh Art Studios" and the "social development office" had holes in the floors, vague long-past chalked invocations to "pass well through this door" and "keep jesus in your heart." Lots of cobwebs on the sculpted windows, red dust in the Olatunde panels...

And the Osogbo museum—placards explaining rooms "The pottery room is unfinished. We're busy at work . . . many more objects . . . hope to be completed by early 1973 . . . "
One learns to ignore such things.
Some fine some corroding some nice things in the museum. A metal crown, little JC and VM[48] medals stuck on for good charm. An Igbo mask with a rainbow painted above a scowling face, done in silver and assorted colors.

But outside, a vulgar statue of a nude woman looking somewhere between Chinese and American Indian but not an African priestess, with her gilt necklace and small pert breasts. The oba [*king*] —who might be named Chief Fashina Agboola, Maiyegun of Osogbo based on what's printed on his clothing—asked me for a photo, pointed to her breasts, cupped his hands at imaginary breasts, and then tweaked one of mine! How do you slap a king and survive to explain?

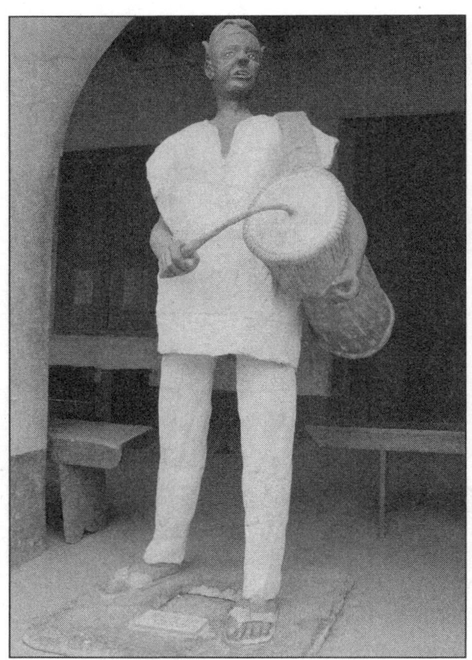

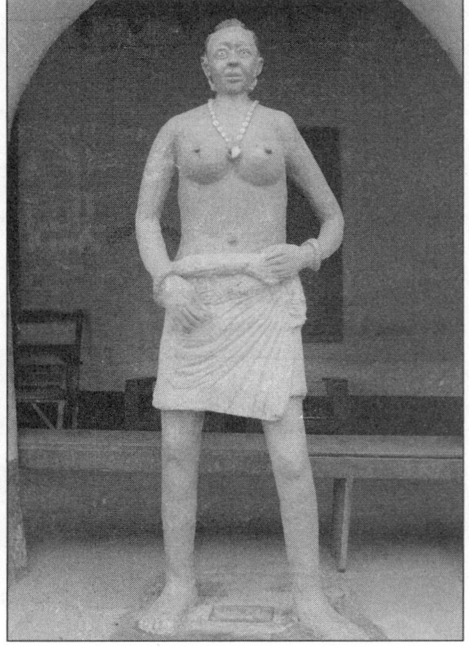

48 Jesus Christ and the Virgin Mary.

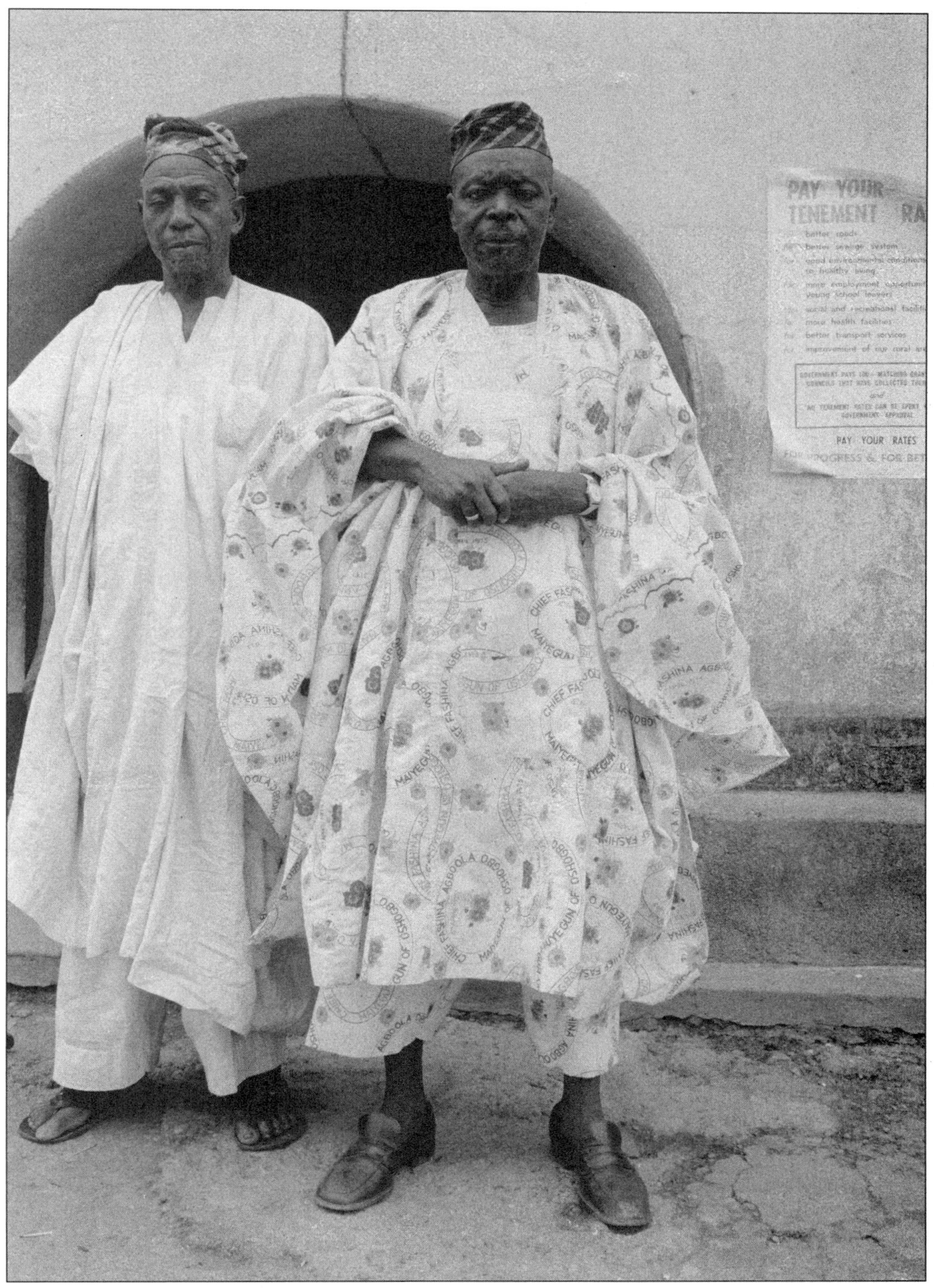

(maybe) Chief Fashina Agboola, Maiyegun of Osogbo

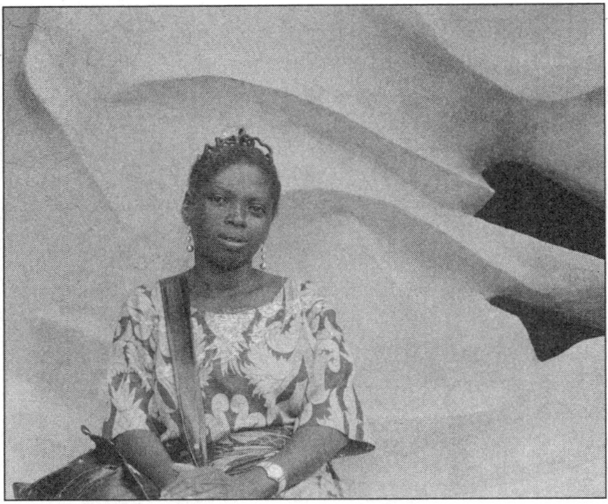

Miss P. T. Ogunbodede was my guide at the shrine. She teaches nutrition to women and nursing mothers, who then teach their friends. She's been at it for seven years. Studied at Ibadan, and now she works in the Social Development Office at the Ministry of Social Welfare (or something like that).

There were various public buildings around the shrine. I happened to be there on the day that they launched the "Keep the Western State Clean" campaign there.
My reference to the "market women" is only a way of describing local women as distinct from the functionaries and special guests.

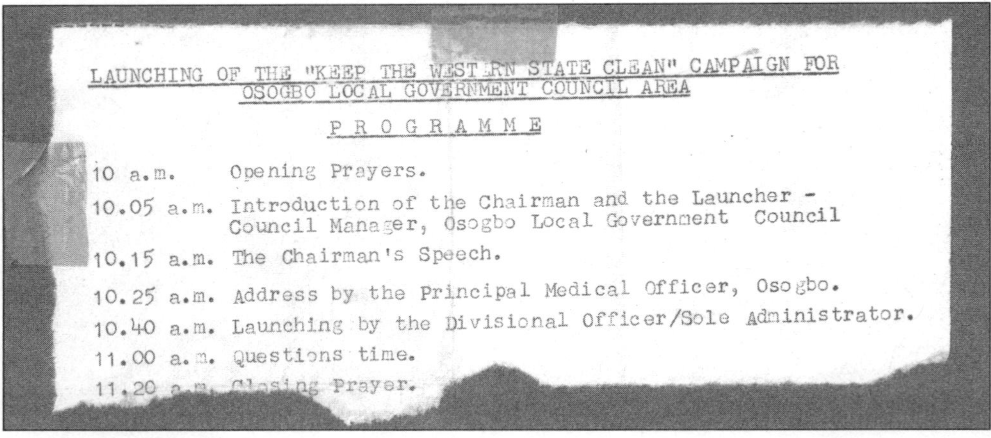

LAUNCHING OF THE "KEEP THE WESTERN STATE CLEAN" CAMPAIGN FOR OSOGBO LOCAL GOVERNMENT COUNCIL AREA

PROGRAMME

10 a.m.	Opening Prayers.
10.05 a.m.	Introduction of the Chairman and the Launcher - Council Manager, Osogbo Local Government Council
10.15 a.m.	The Chairman's Speech.
10.25 a.m.	Address by the Principal Medical Officer, Osogbo.
10.40 a.m.	Launching by the Divisional Officer/Sole Administrator.
11.00 a.m.	Questions time.
11.20 a.m.	Closing Prayer.

There were many big gregarious dignified old women chiefs, strolling about with the Obas who'd come for the Keep Clean campaign, a farce of jolly proportions. I had to sweep along with the rest of the hot and uncomfortable bureaucrats while the market women looked on in cynical bewilderment.
And a fat short police general, shaped a bit like von Stroheim[49], with cracked patent leather shoes and a really starched uniform with all sorts of buttons and pins of a nondescript but flashy nature. He even had a dusty old telephone on the desk. Trouble being that they never work and it's a major achievement to get through to Ife. He had a big pinky ring, a black gold-tipped walking stick and a very comical body.

49 Erich von Stroheim (1885–1957), the Austrian-American director, actor and producer.

I'm getting the hang of this bowing and scraping—was down on my knees today before one of the women chiefs—then of course I had to give her 1 ₦ to let me into the Osun shrine—which I <u>think</u> was bullshit but unavoidable.
She was a real toughie, big and barefooted and braceleted in heavy gold. She wouldn't let me in the first time, I had to come back with Miss O.

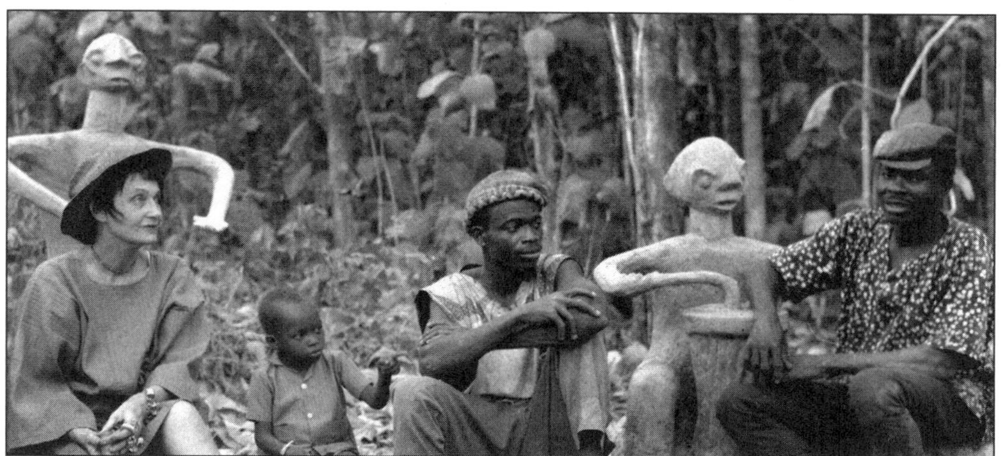

Susanne Wenger in the 1970s with Adebisi Akanji and Rabiu Abesu, two local artists who worked on the shrine (the third was Kasali Akangbe-Ogun) [2].

Wenger's shrines → The reason they're so "impressive" is that they're so ostentatious and bizarre.

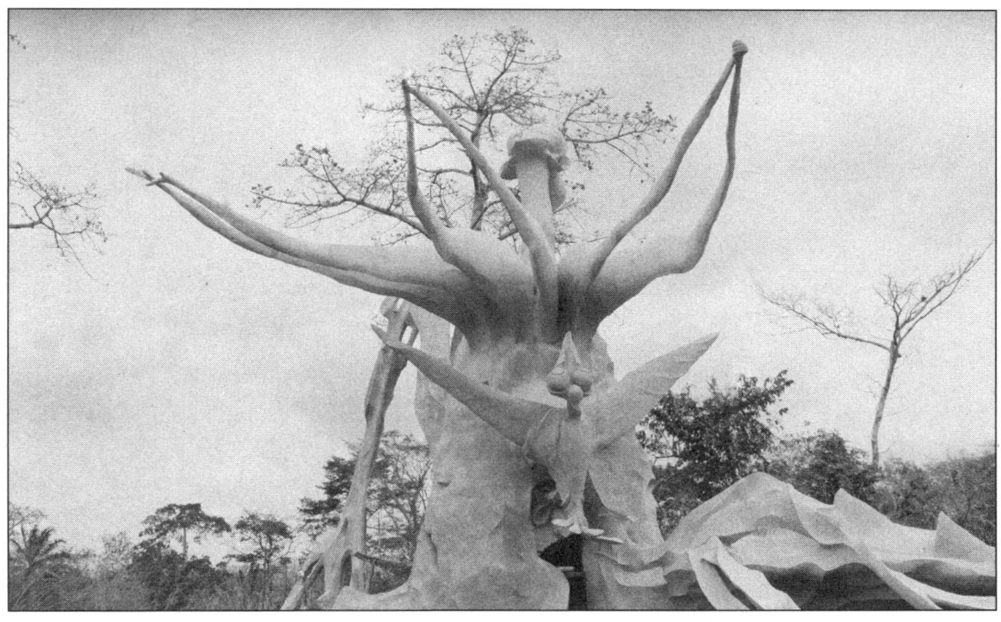

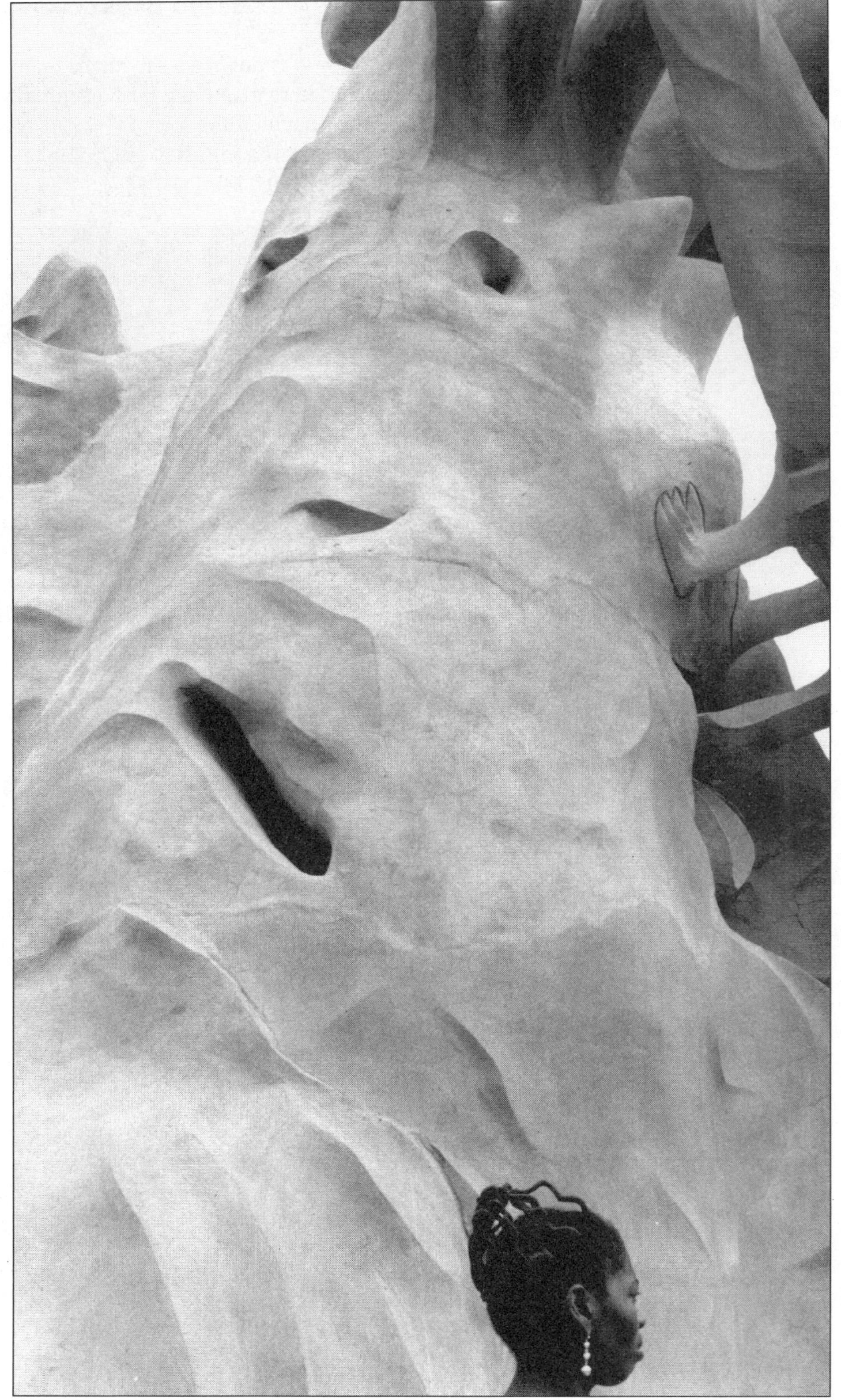

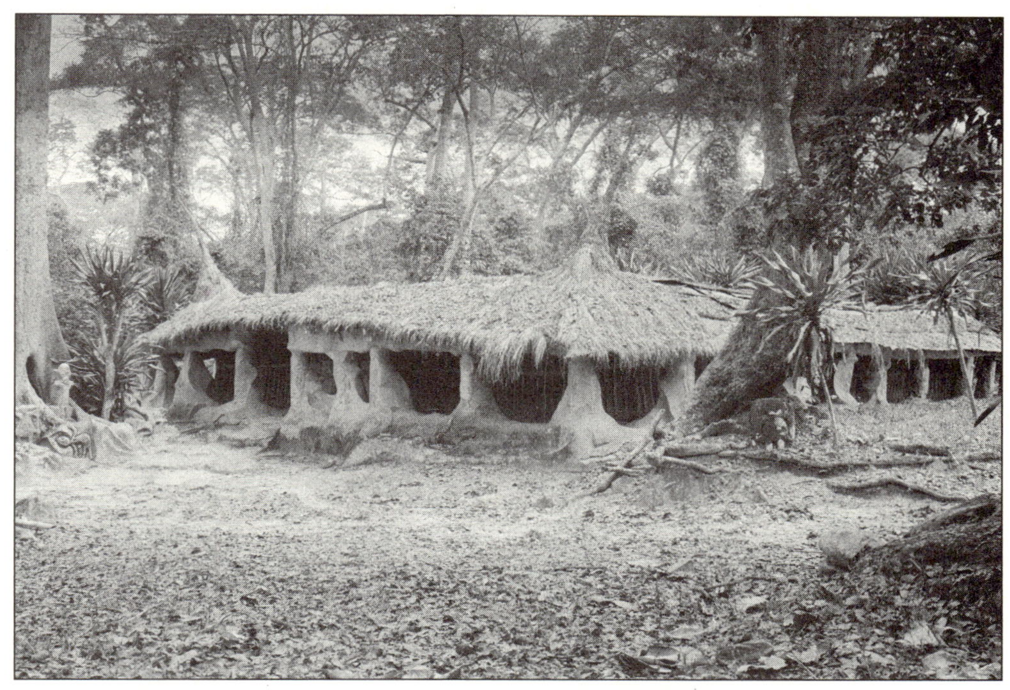

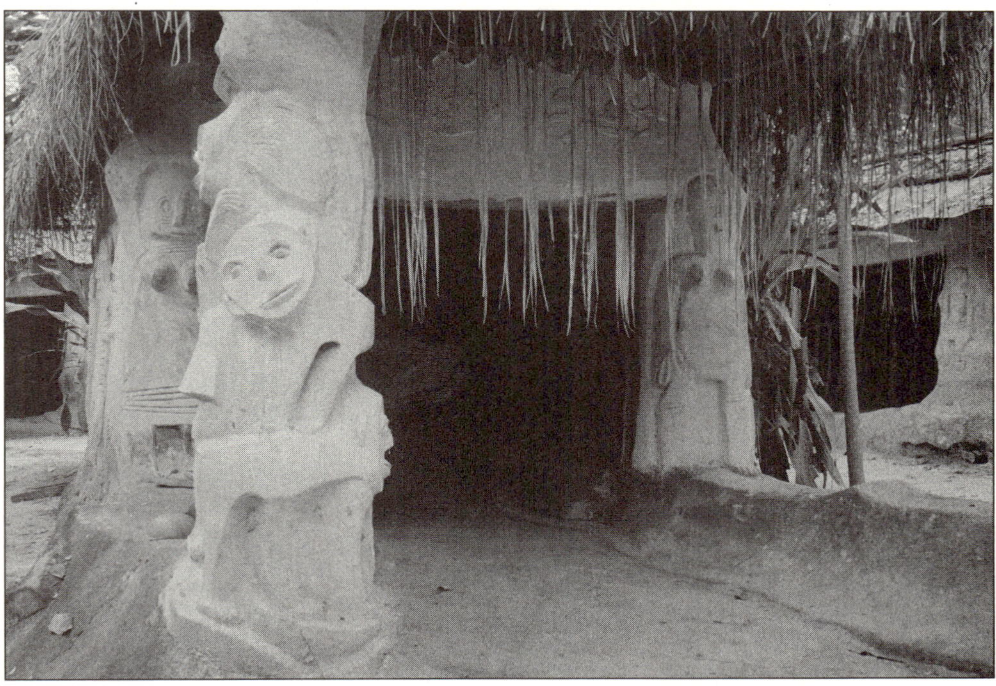

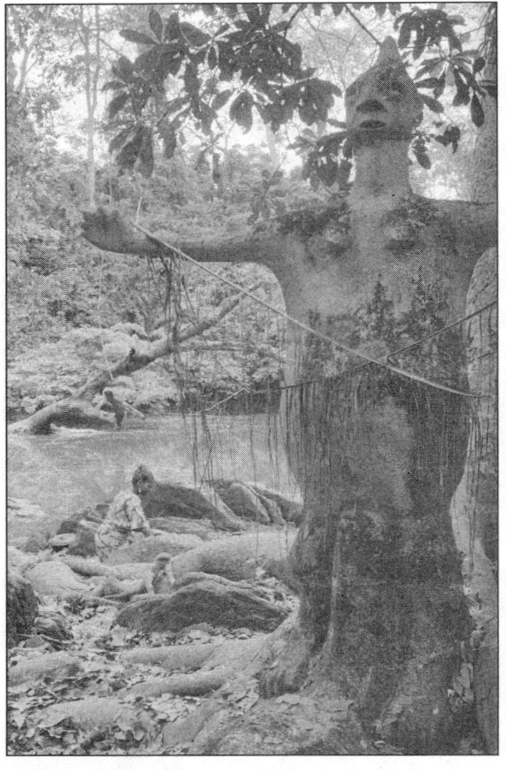

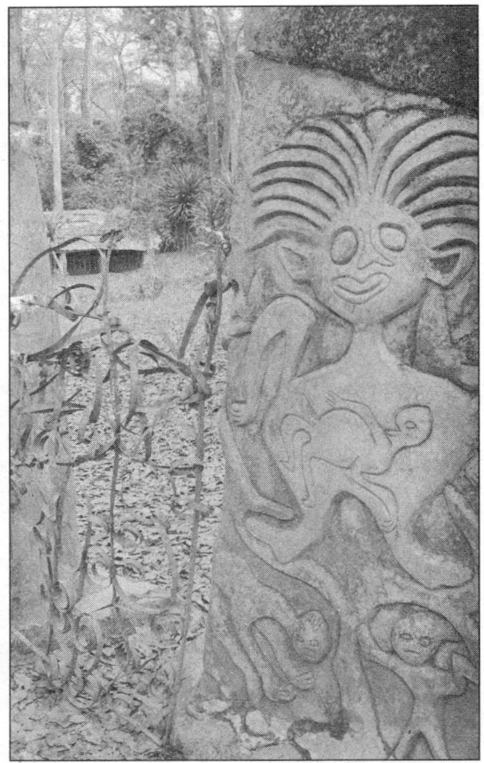

Miss P. T. Ogunbodede at the river paying homage to Osun.

Osun—the goddess of the Osun River, a sluggish brown river behind the shrine.
Barren women drink her for fertility—"It works" says Miss O.
There's a festival once a year. Old toughie is chief chief.
Nine days of merrymaking.
Young girl wears huge basket of food—all dance around, it's offered to Osun. She stays with chief until marriage.
If you pray to Osun the wish is granted BLAH BLAH.
I'm every day re-relieved that I got out of African art/history—I'd have to listen sincerely and continuously to these traditional beliefs, and the pretense wouldn't last very long—
I really feel nothing about all this except in the gray matter. Little heart. Just a *wee* bit of women—etc. not much.
Despite that ancient history class and my vain but fervent efforts to rekindle some sort of "spiritualism"—I just can't be a part of it [3].

On the way back to Ife today, I saw this sign: "Accidents don't happen, they are caused." A logical fry from start to finish.

This university life, somehow separate from daily Africa, can be fertile ground for developing alienation from the problems here; one sees it in the response of students, that they want to get away from it, the grubbiness, etc.

So much for Africa's unlimited respect for women—who exactly has POWER is always the most telling question: Women here have only a token representation in government, just like anywhere else.
And the women here never cease to freak me out—they trudge down the roads with literally ten to fifteen large tree limbs on their head and a baby on their back—it must weigh at least seventy-five pounds.
Muscles like a man, they are relentless workers.
Constantly occupied. And those large beautiful dark eyes that keep a firm and open gaze into mine until we pass, never averted never nervous.

I had so much fun today bargaining for a gorgeous strip of glittery cloth—but she was very firm on a price of ₦1.
I'm getting into being an *oyibo*, we play such games with each other.
But I'm getting a bit loose with my finances; also bought some *adire* cloth. It's very fine because it's not the usual block pattern (I tend not to like things done in a usual way even if it is a "traditional" design) but a full scale design with a funny king and queen and a non-real alphabet. ₦3. She wouldn't go down.

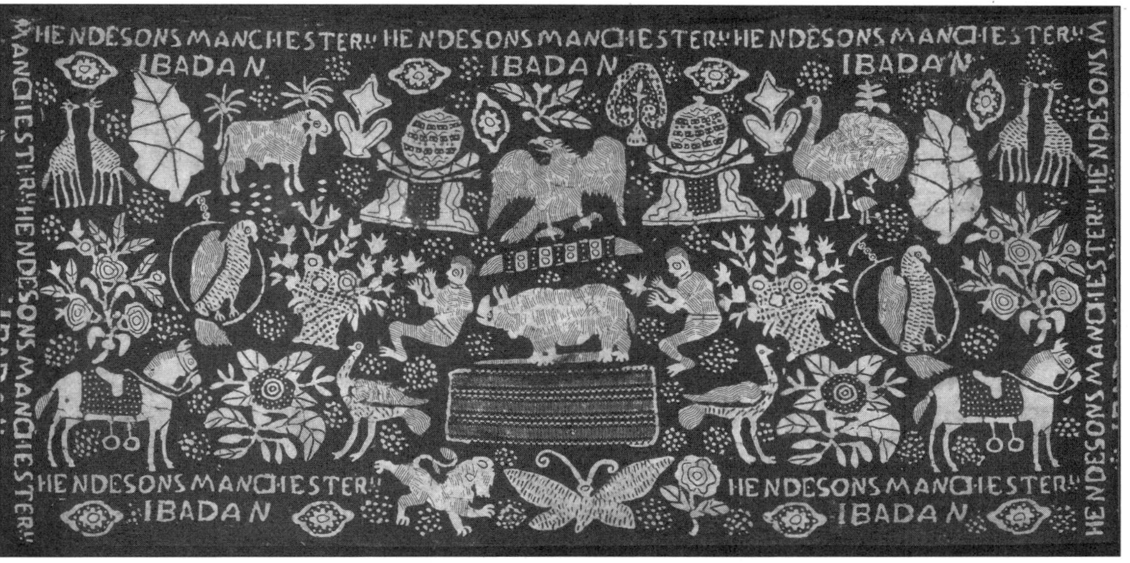

Stencilled *adire* cloth, Nigeria, ca. 1900–1924.

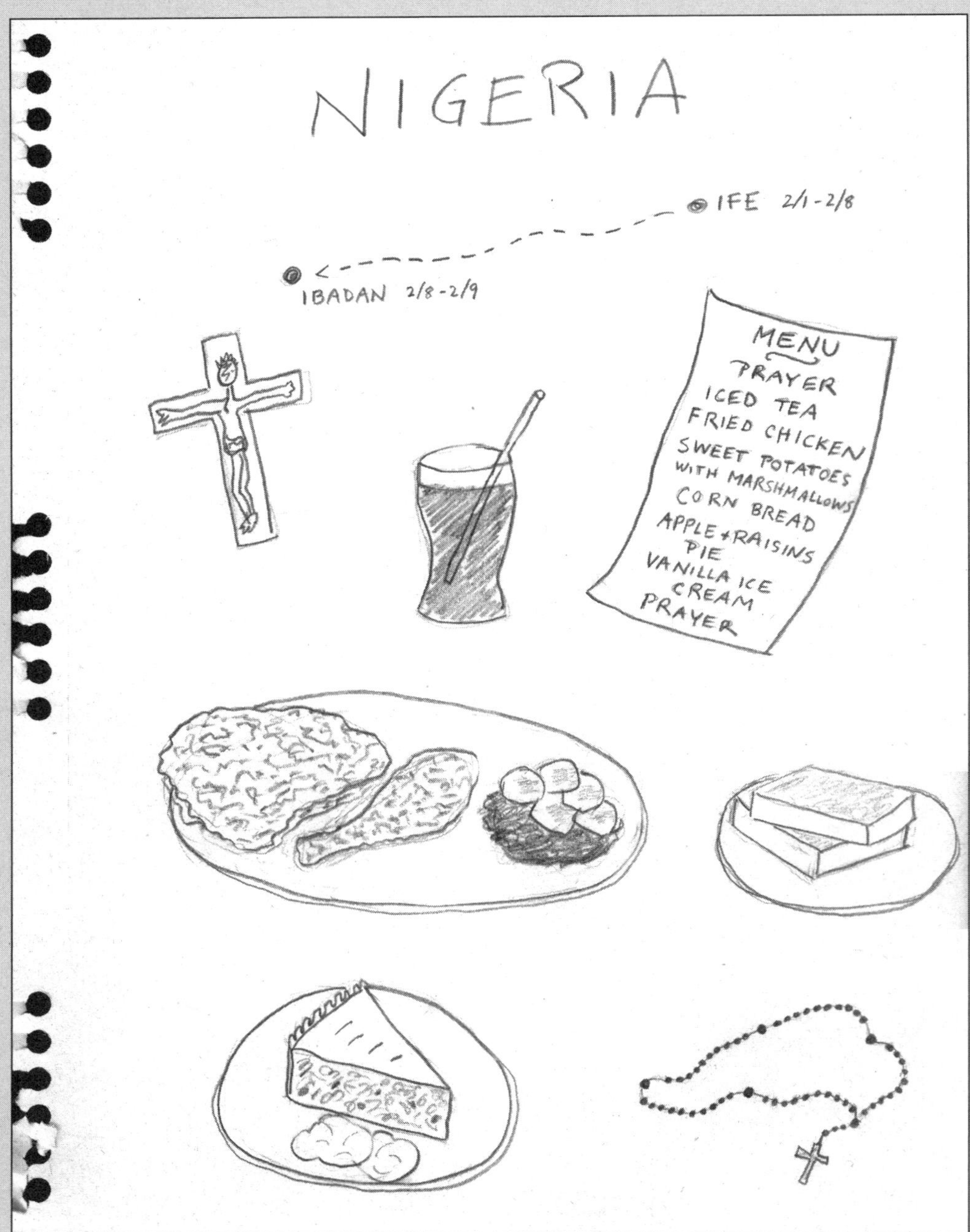
NIGERIA
IFE 2/1-2/8
IBADAN 2/8-2/9
MENU
PRAYER
ICED TEA
FRIED CHICKEN
SWEET POTATOES
WITH MARSHMALLOWS
CORN BREAD
APPLE + RAISINS
PIE
VANILLA ICE
CREAM
PRAYER

CHAPTER TWELVE

Back to Ibadan for Some Southern Fried Chicken and in Abeokuta with Twins and Janet

FEBRUARY 8 & 9

I returned to Ibadan but for whatever reason didn't stay on the campus. I stayed with a nun who I might have met in the Baptist bookstore. Regular bookstores were hard to find so I often went to the missionary bookshops, which had things besides religious tracts.

Three and a half hours to go fifty-two miles, mammy wagon fashion.
Stunning women
Sculpted faces
Carved large lips

Ah'm stayin' weith Mary Frances Kirkpatrick, a Baptist missionary. She's lived in Ibadan for more or less twenty years. She's concerned with the spiritual development of students, brehgen' jaysus chraast intuh their haarts, etc.

I had to say I was Catholic but not a mass-goer (she invited me home to stay at the mission compound house plastered with warnings to god damn it keep Jesus in your heart, or else . . . and little cutsie proverb booklets and African Virgins) (yeah, I'll hold them close to my heart, if only I had the chance!!) and a well-thumbed Montgomery Ward catalogue and olive green décor (a dead giveaway), blankets on the beds, Kool-Aid and marshmallows. A tall Mississippi woman, single and middle-aged.
I think she sees thru me, this irreverent dyke.

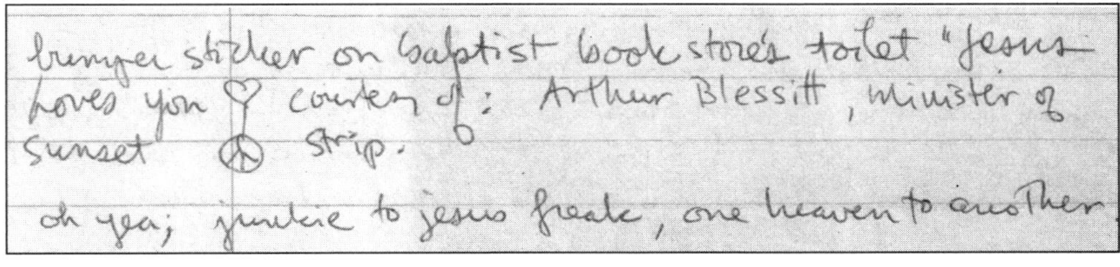
bumper sticker on baptist book store's toilet "Jesus Loves you ♡ courtesy of: Arthur Blessitt, minister of Sunset ☮ Strip.
oh yea; junkie to jesus freak, one heaven to another.

Bumper sticker on the Baptist bookstore's toilet door: "Jesus Loves You. Courtesy of Arthur Blessitt, minister of Sunset Strip."

—More on Arthur Blessitt[50]: He's thirty. Has seven kids. A wife, dutiful. Carries a ninety-pound cross with a little tire on the end of it. He walked across the

50 Now he's eighty-three and still at it. See [1] for more info.

US, Europe, and Africa raising eyebrows and Christian consciousness. Walked, sweating, exhorting, with that lousy cross on his calloused shoulder. His wife was in a Land Rover a few miles ahead. Mama Kirkpatrick met him at the Nigerian border with two busloads of students—Baptist Student Union students. Christians. Holy rollers.

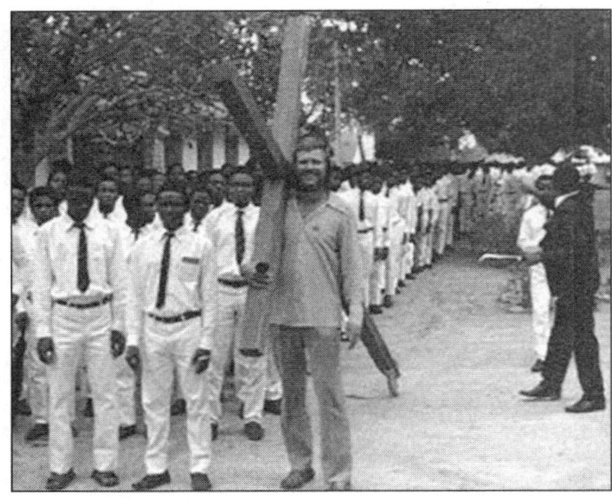

Visited the kids in the Baptist school. They started up a chorus of "We have come to you, dear Jesus" as I was leaving, in their African-accented English and white shorts and socks and sandals. Squeaky clean brains.

Mary Frances served me fried chicken, sweet potatoes with marshmallows. Apple and raisin pie (hot) with vanilla ice cream (her mom's recipe). Cornbread. Iced tea. And Jesus.
She told me she was called here by Gawd. After Texas, Louisiana, and Mississippi. Came by boat, quite adventurous twenty years ago. And did you know, there are so many young people here now who call themselves Christian but don't really know what it means to have Jesus in their hawrtz?
Jist lahk winn a Muslim child is made Muslim bah hiz payrents, or a child of pagans who worships some heathen idol. Verbatim.
Yep, that's what she sayz. Imagine it. She sayz they duhn't know abaout the seen in their lahves. The sin. The sin in which they live. Sin.
Sounds dismally like a religious Cold War mentality. It is.
She's baking' cookies fer th'American wimmin's cluhb tomarra. They run a school for the deaf and dumb, and fer motherless chillen'.
Am I being a bitch?
I think not.

I told her at nerve-wracking length about Oberlin's missionary zeal. She seemed to appreciate my efforts [2].
And I said amen after the invocation to let this here wunnerful food give us th'energy to continue our werk fer Gawd.
May it give me the sinew and gristle to continue my gleeful subversion.
This is another situation like the staff club initiation. A mythical African phenomenon (the Christian missionary) that I'd "always read so much about"—and still wanted to wish out of existence.
Flesh and bloody. Too alive. The relentless search for a harbor and an audience.

Preferably an admiring one. Enraptured. Thirsty and hungry! Avid. NEEDY.
We are indispensable, therefore . . .
The "therefore" is what I'm discovering now, or rather witnessing. Someone once called it a charming debacle.
We all insist on our separate realities.

I get very heated anti-white anti-privileged-American's reaction when I try my best to shed a little light by trying to get them to see the distinction between white male privilege and ours/mine as a woman.
Be grateful to the Lawhd Jaysuss Chrast—now I know why I have such an aversion to dependence, to admitting that anyone is taking care of me. She had Bible reading. I could've choked to hear Monday (her "man-boy," their term for a servant) reading about the Pharisees and Jaysuss in his broken Nigerian English, and she reading the interpretation "by Moussa X, from the north, a Hausa man, who was probably brought up a Muslim and had to struggle with many things to see the light of Jaysuss." This Moussa traitor actually said, "There are some traditions which could never be a part of the Christian practices, for example the ritual dances of an ugly nature . . . "
What was Monday thinking, I wonder? Walking a tightrope.

—That way the Yoruba have of sucking in their breath and uplifting their head and eyebrows, a quick gesture of comprehension, their long drawn out "Ah-hey . . . " when something's really been said.
—The cackling barking sound when someone's been pushed too far or gotten a bad deal.
—On the street of the cloth vendors today: Dark black women in wine and midnight blue velvet laced with gold, surrounded by bolts of the same cloth—splendor, elegance, richesse in the midst of the Ibadan dust and sewage.
It's inconceivable, being here, that in America's downtowns the women are all occupied with wandering about aimlessly or frantically simply buying and consuming. No one here does/dare do that.

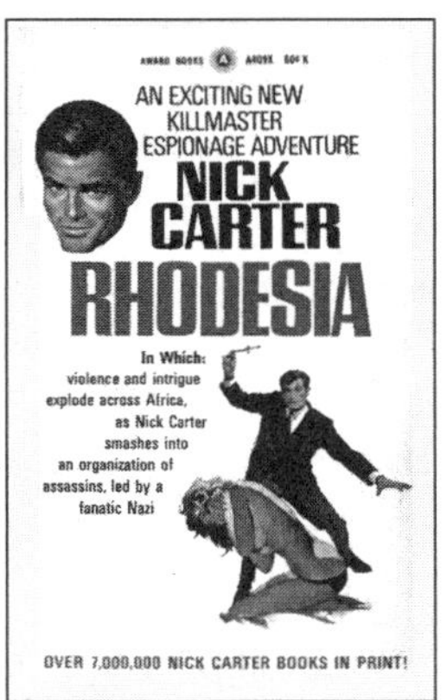

It never ceases to amaze me: First I found the Dolores Klaich book, and now in the Ibadan department store amid Victoria Holt, Denise Robins and Nick Carter (Nigeria's #1 bestsellers by far) I found an Ivy Compton-Burnett novel, *More Women Than Men*. Looks bad but I bought it on principle. It started with a description of a short, strong-featured, low-voiced woman telling a friend she "couldn't" marry him. Not a bit of dykedom to be found. It sucks.

"In Which: violence and intrigue explode across Africa, as Nick Carter smashes into an organization of assassins, led by a fanatic Nazi!"

A LETTER TO CINDY, ENCLOSED IN THE PACKAGE WITH THE COMPTON-BURNETT BOOK:

dearest c.c.—
An unsolicited & perhaps unexpectedly disappointing package:
I discovered this book in the department store in Ibadan of all places—I'm sure they didn't know about her—but in fact right nearby was the notorious "The Other Faces of Love—A History of Homosexuality"—I tried to look at it but there were 2 nuns also browsing the same bookrack, and you know the rancid waters of youth run deep . . . .
I skim-read it after a concerted but annoyed attempt at reading every word—she doesn't in my estimation know much about the art of writing—
So here's for your perusal & archives.

No mail in Ibadan!

Hurts me (and it hurt me then, but I wouldn't show it) to see and understand how the manifestations of my hostilities towards men infect my reactions to women. Thinking of New York. Hard to keep from returning to that tumbled and profane month before I left on my trip. Mimi. Always thinking she wanted to be left alone, that I was being a drag, or that I would put on a face because I felt gloomy or confused and then wouldn't kiss her good day, even asking permission (in the form of giving a functional reason: too cramped) for putting an arm around her in bed. One night she responded with a tired/irritated plea—"You don't have to ask, Susie." Of course I don't, but do I realize that? Oh no, just turn dizzy and claustrophobic circles around my childhood paranoias.
The retreat before a good time—fear of losing cool which in the presence of men is always exploited somehow (not necessarily sexually). The whole bargain-barter scheme-usurp system has frightened me away from even being able to feel loose with someone like Mimi.
A damn shame.
We could've had so much (more) fun that month, gotten closer gradually rather than those last too short too riveting too revealing moments on the way to the airport when I realized how good I felt with her.

Iya oja = mother (in the) market = the woman head of the market. There's one for each market in all Yoruba towns; she's an advisor for all market activities.

I took a lorry south to Abeokuta and somehow ended up in the home of a generous and friendly extended family—Janet Sola Buyide, Twins Adeniji, E. Witty Adeniji, Grace Adeyemo, and Albert (no last name for him).

FEBRUARY 10

A bizarre dream last night of some gay actors and actresses doing a street play here and being met with confused and bewildered stares.

In Abeokuta—staying in town, with Janet.
Room, olive green and peach. JC with blazing golden halo dragging the cross.
Studio photos. Dusty jar full of trinket jewels. How Albert held it in his hands.
Vision of young married couple learning secrets. Persistent and incisive questioning. Inconceivable to them (and unrealistic) that I travel without eventual financial recompense.
A table full of yellow and white hunks, seeds, roots, leaves, all to be ground and mixed to cure malaria.
This large apartment-type house seems to be mostly one family all crammed into small rooms.
Jehovah's Witnesses only permit one wife, which at least cuts out polygamy among a certain small percentage of African families—but brings an attendant hyper-religiosity.

Twins stroked my leg and said, "Oh, I like your color. Me, I'm Black and it's not so good, I would like to be white."
—Now how do I protest without sounding like an insincere fool? Because in her eyes I am somehow privileged for this white skin and I tried to explain to her how beautiful Black women were—hah!
She said (aged 17), "By the grace of God I wish to marry an English man."
Had lots of photos of women with straightened hair and wigs that look like they're made from mattress stuffing.

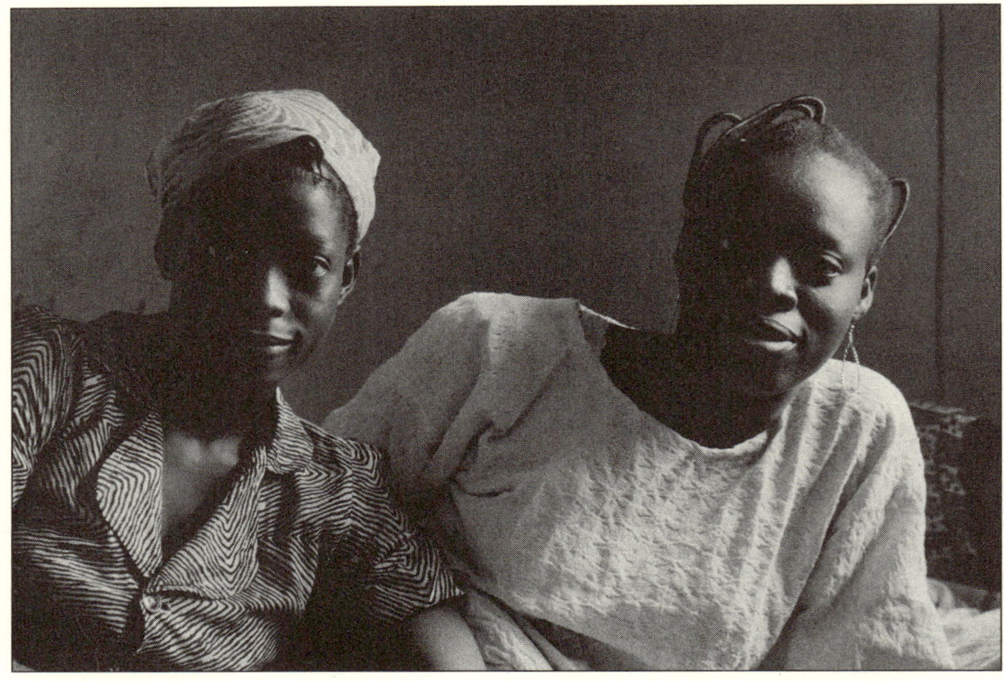

Janet Sola Buyide and Twins Adeniji

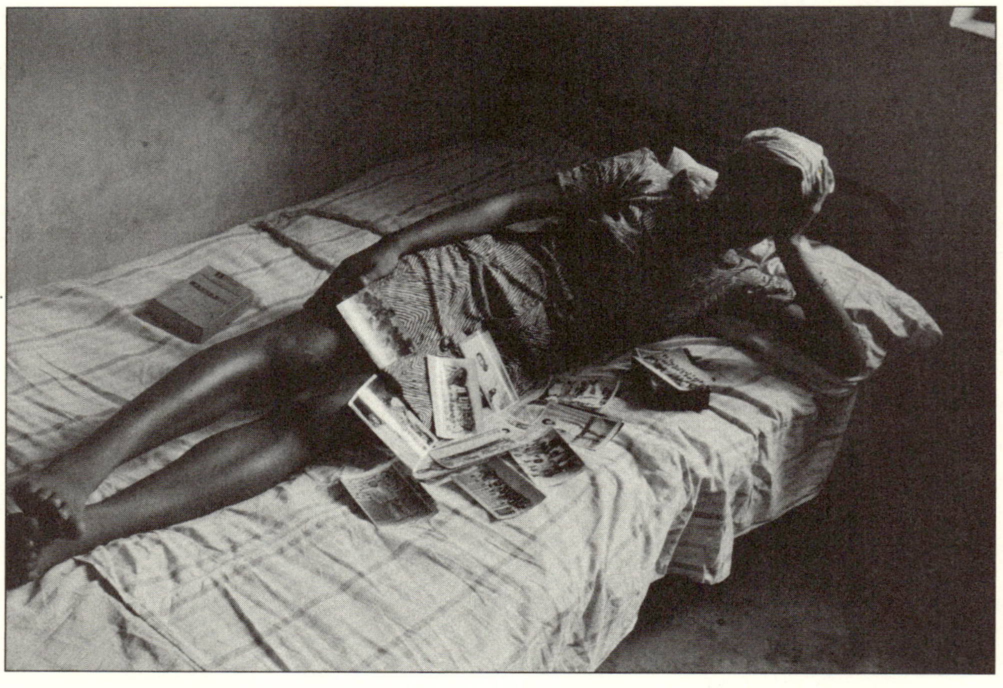

Janet and her collection of studio portraits of her friends and family

FEBRUARY 11

First full-scale attack today as I photographed yam pounders. Two men came to tell me I was ridiculing Africa—that they'd seen *oyibos* like me before in the market, that I was going to go home and say how primitive they were, etc.
There was no hope of convincing them otherwise, although I tried.

He: Where are you from?
America.
He (*squinting his eyes*): Are you in the CIA?
And then as we walked away a truck sideswiped me and came awfully close to breaking my elbow.
Sweat.
All eyes on me.
Both contrite and pissed off.

> **PART OF A LETTER TO CINDY:**
>
> Also haven't been photo'ing as much this week, got very bitched at by someone in Abeokuta, that I was ridiculing Africans by my pictures (I was ironically taking some pics of 2 muscular handsome women pounding yams—as an example of the strength, etc. of them—not the "primitiveness" or whatever he may have thought) and I just couldn't talk him/them out of their anger—and naturally they ended by suggesting that I was "CIA", a scapegoat-all-inclusive term for us honkies.
> Real cheerful, real encouraging—but if I expected anything different, I'd be deluding myself, yes?
> Love,
> Su

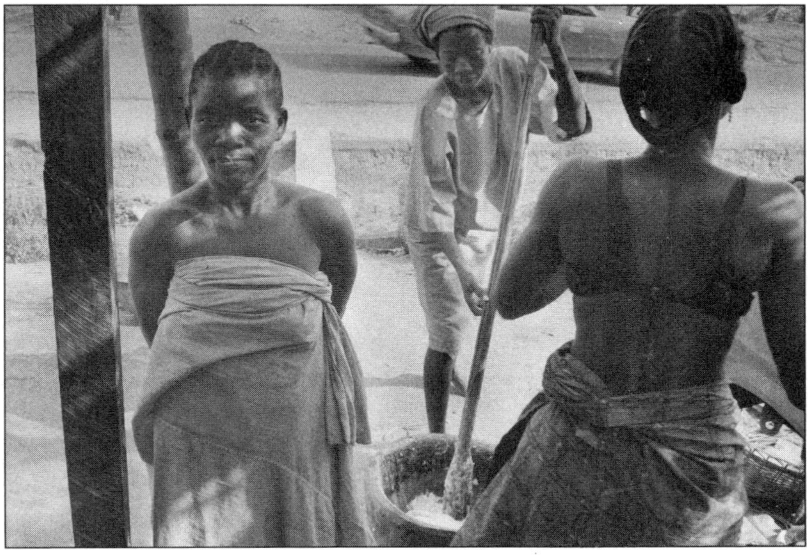

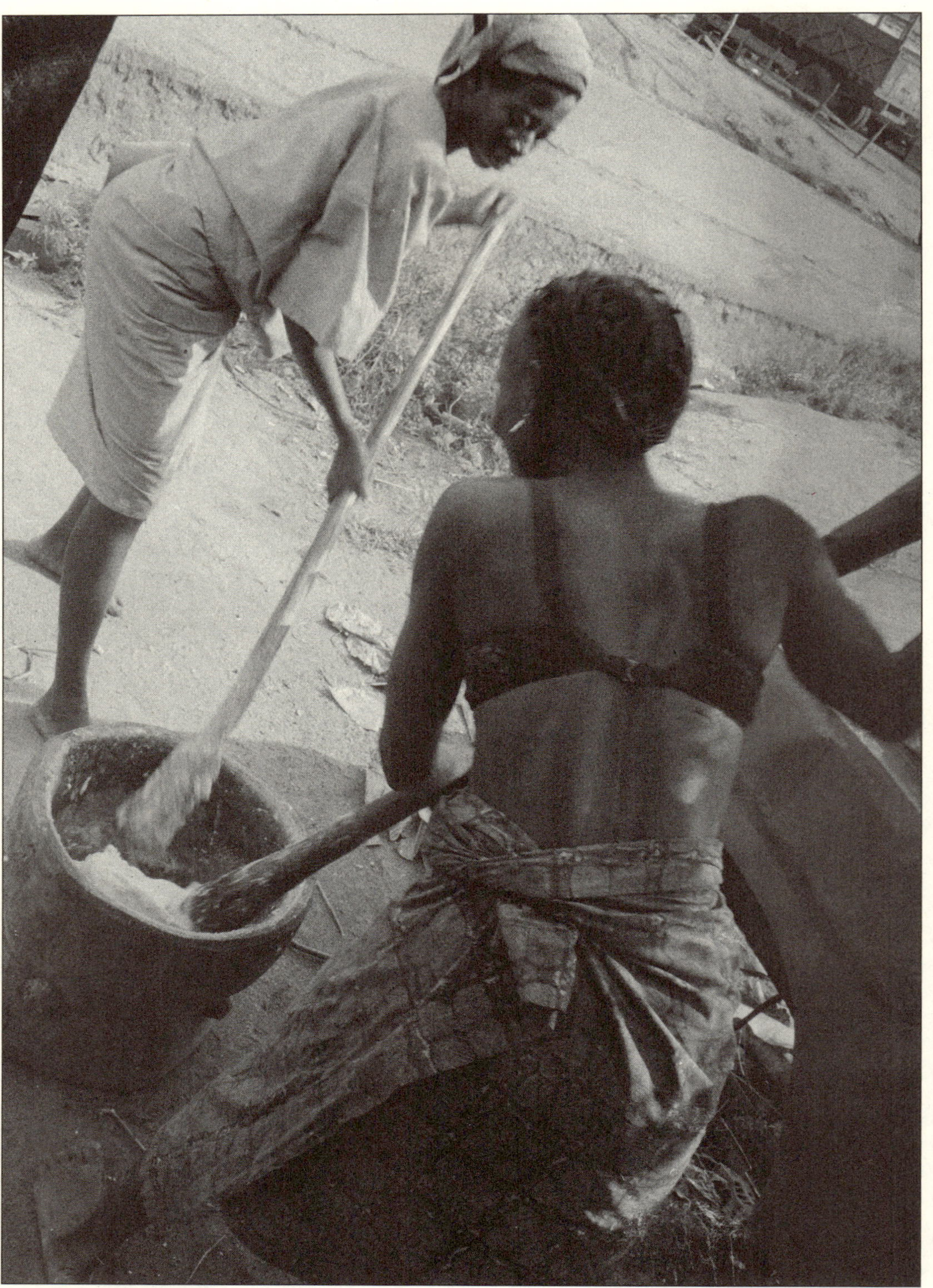

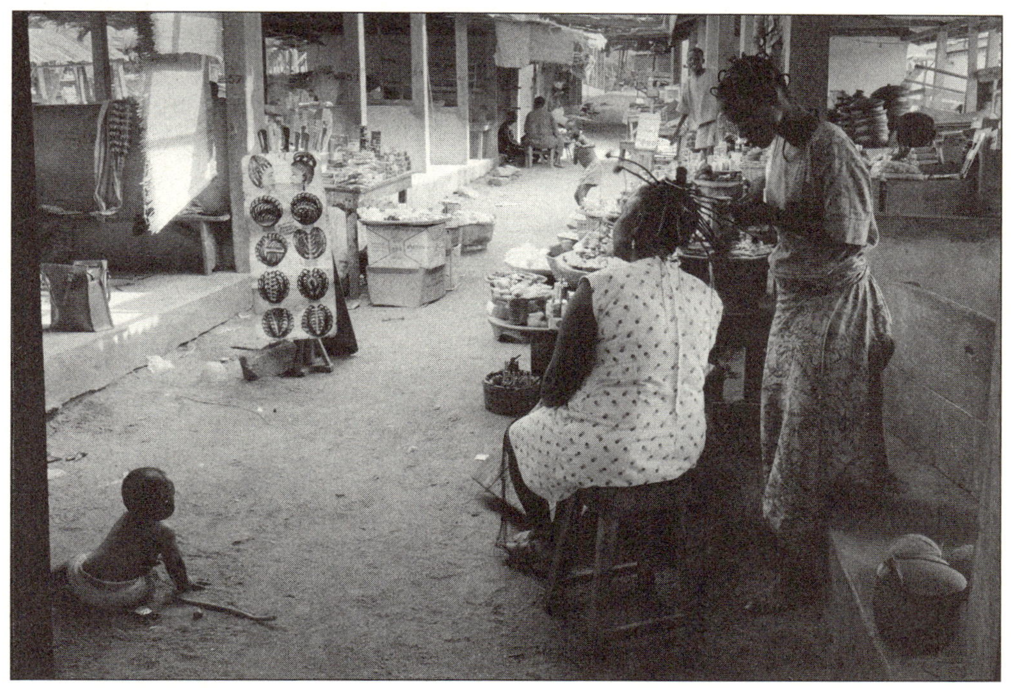

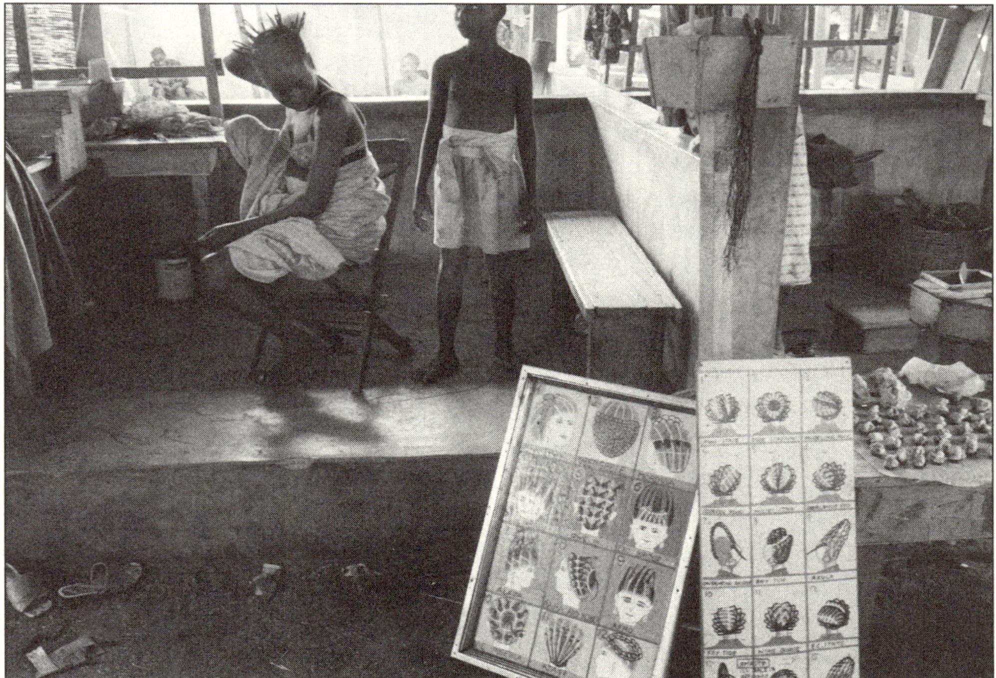

Some of the hairdo names: Eko Bridge, Lagos State, Naira and Kobo, Key Side, One Nigeria.

A fight today between lorry drivers—they tend to yell and jump around and flail their arms more than they actually fight—no solid punches to be seen. Just ten people all shouting and gesticulating at the same time [3].

At the market with Twins. Saw those masqueraders who pressed the embarrassed *oyibo* for a few *kobo*, their faces in white masks, in a thin crocheted top and pants with false breasts, sticks and noisemakers and laughter.
Lots and lots of "native medicine," tumbled crammed stalls full of wood chips and roots and greens and gray-haired, wiry saleswomen.

Twins, as we sat at her senior sister's shop, leaned over almost with her head in my lap, stroking my legs, said with her pretty accent "I love your body" with such a plaintive voice.

When Twins and I were returning from the market we saw a procession, but she made me leave so as not to incur their wrath. I asked her who they were, these elegant and somber women chanting softly to themselves, the leader in a white cloth holding a horsetail switch, the next one with a baby who was carrying a red painted Yoruba female figure with huge strong breasts and a baby on its back, then a thin line of followers, older women, a few erect and serious young girls. No joyous response from the crowd. She asked a friend for a translation into English of *olamali* (or something like that): Idol worshippers.
If cultural anthropologists spend so much time writing about the negative ideas that Europeans have about African artistic and religious traditions, they should take a closer look at Africans' ideas. Again, to test their response, I asked Albert and Witty about the procession today and they both responded, "Idol worshippers; they believe in those sorts of gods and spirits that are supposed to help them with all their wishes." This was during our dinner. It had begun with our heads bowed and Albert muttering "We thank you our God and Father for all the good things you have done for us in this day; help us to live in strength tomorrow from this food, and carry us along the right road." AMEN.
If one more person asks me my religion . . . ! (I might get honest and tell them I have none!)

A POSTCARD TO MY MOTHER AND BROTHER:

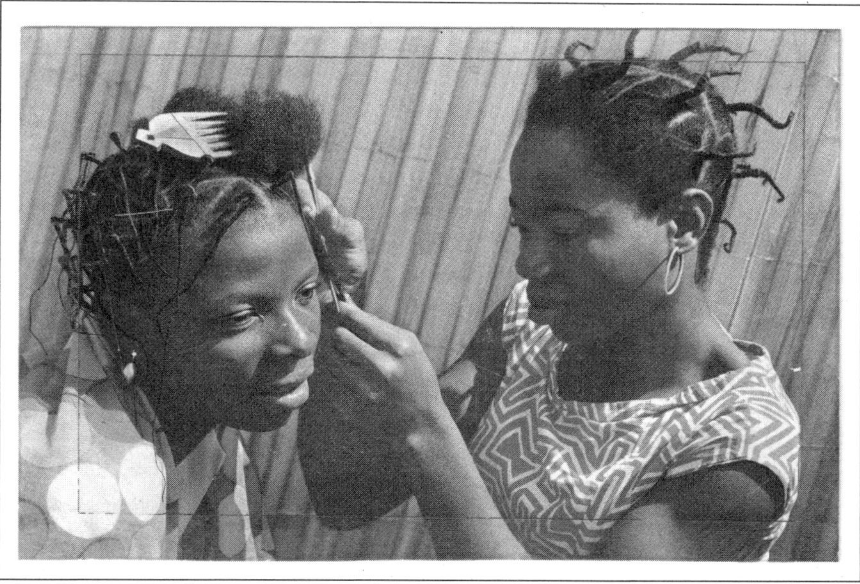

Dear Mom & Pete—
In Abeokuta, the home of *adire* cloth, an exquisite blue died stenciled cloth (or tie-dyed), & the new capital of a new Nigerian state (there are now 19)—here for 2 days staying in a woman's home. She lives in a room of a large house w/ other relatives (hotels are very costly). Then on to Lagos, where I fervently hope I find some mail!!. Ife was pleasant, went to a lot of nearby towns on day trips, got some gorgeous cloth woven w/ gold strands & black/red/blue strips—hard to describe. Looks a bit Indian. Got some good photos today of women plaiting hair (like this postcard). They have some very elaborate & handsome styles. I'm surviving the heat, having made myself a skirt & gotten 2 Yoruba-style cotton blouses made, which are comfortable & pretty—the cloth here is endless, I've almost bought a yard a day! A steady stream of packages will be arriving, I hope they don't burden you too much. Did you hear, Kissinger might be coming to Lagos! What a joke. Broken camera doesn't seem to be affecting my film . . .
After Lagos going to Togo because Benin-Togo border is closed & so will just go Togo-Ghana & west (probably fly from Lagos to Togo over Benin.)

The other day I overheard a man-boy performing a perfectly, wittily satiric mimic of his Madame's voice giving an order, to the glee of another man-boy standing in the yard below.

Bathing in the courtyard—dark, moonlit—with Janet, buckets of cool water streaming over her dark lithe body, each of us darting curious glances at the other. All these visceral, sensuous aspects of life here, e.g., the market's narrow tunnels and crossing paths and congestion, as if clambering thru the veins of some great organism, the skin, the glistening dark muscular smooth skin, the openness of their bodies, nothing "contained" as is our fashion.

And their dresses—first time last night I wore one, a feeling of protective softness at the waist, all loose and light and flexible. I think that if they think of a woman it seems most right to think of her in this dress, and so if I wear it I'm greeted with interested, not derisive, smiles—

But nevertheless these days have not been good, I feel somehow unnerved and can't reconcile it.

Moi-moi—pepper, beans, palm oil, salt.
Amala—yams, pepper soup and meat, shit. Like paste up north.
Eba made with cassava, same stuff, argh . . .
A heavy wave of a certain sort of desperation comes over me—my feet twitch frantically, I have trouble swallowing, I cram my mind with all sorts of trivia when I eat (most) local food, the varieties of "glop with spice"—it's always really hot, and either bland or too hot to savor, greasy, it just gets me nervous, the fated quality of it, the inescapable routine. The small children with heaping bowls of spiced rice rice rice.

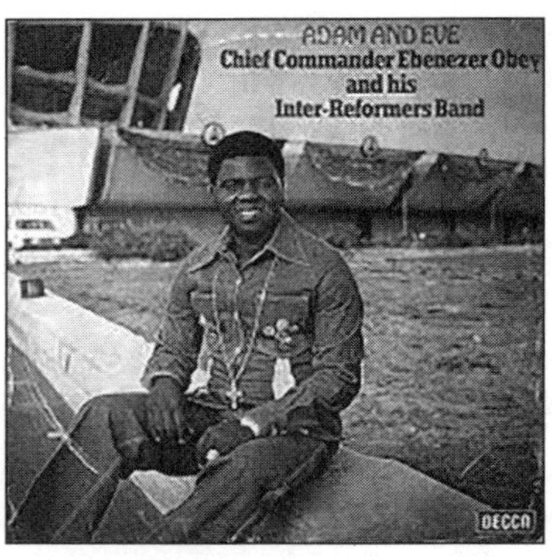

Shared a bottle of "Dubonnet, the Tonic Wine" with an administrator and Albert and Witty—Ebenezer Obey filling the narrow hallway. Crying babies, two pregnant wives, four kids. One wife, towering in her pregnancy, at least 6' tall, large features, black encircled almond-shaped eyes, subtle gestures. Very regal. Taught me to tie a head scarf. I looked a fool but put on a good show. The junior wife, wraithlike (although pregnant), staring eyes, very young, sitting and sitting and sitting.

Again my status—foreign woman—made me "one of the boys"—a recurring and inevitable problem—I learn of these women by second-hand observation—I want to know how they really feel about that stout punky typical administrator.

On a cool cool night such as last, we slept in this cement room, the windows held shut. I woke up at 2 a.m. with a thick layer of sweat at my neck— ?

There is no privacy here
(but do they desire it, is that need part of their psyche?)

FEBRUARY 12

Last night was one of those unrepeatable, remarkable, anachronistic moments one can still experience in Africa—"the photographer's studio"—the "Elegance Photo Shop." Backdrop painted in yellow, black & pink, with images of a TV, radio, fan, and clock. Witty and Albert wore clothes of the same cloth as me. We sat on a thin couch, I was perched between them, knees together, with a firm and freaked out stare. He set up two bulbs and got out his simulated Rolleiflex. "Smile". Poof, lights, that's it— [51]

He showed me his album:

A proud Hausa and his finest white ram

A Nigerian hippy guitarist, his shoulder-length hair parted in the center and brushed back like wings or appendages

A guy with a '65 look, including tough stance, pulled-in stomach, dark shades, backdrop of an airplane embarking for London

And all the stiff proud well-dressed families and associates and businessmen and marriages.

Today, Albert and Grace took me to see Olumo Rock[52], dressed in the same outfit that I wore for the photo.

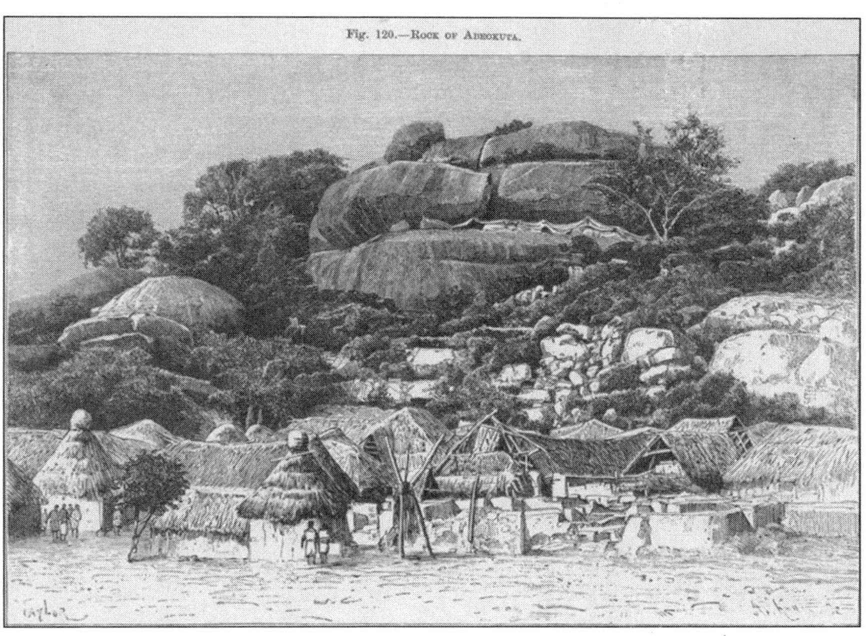
Fig. 120.—Rock of Abeokuta.

51 They probably mailed it to me, but unfortunately I never got the picture.

52 Olumo Rock served as a natural fortress and refuge for the Egba during intertribal wars in the nineteenth century. It's now a popular tourist site which offers commanding views of the town and the Ogun River. Abeokuta means "under the rock," and it is.

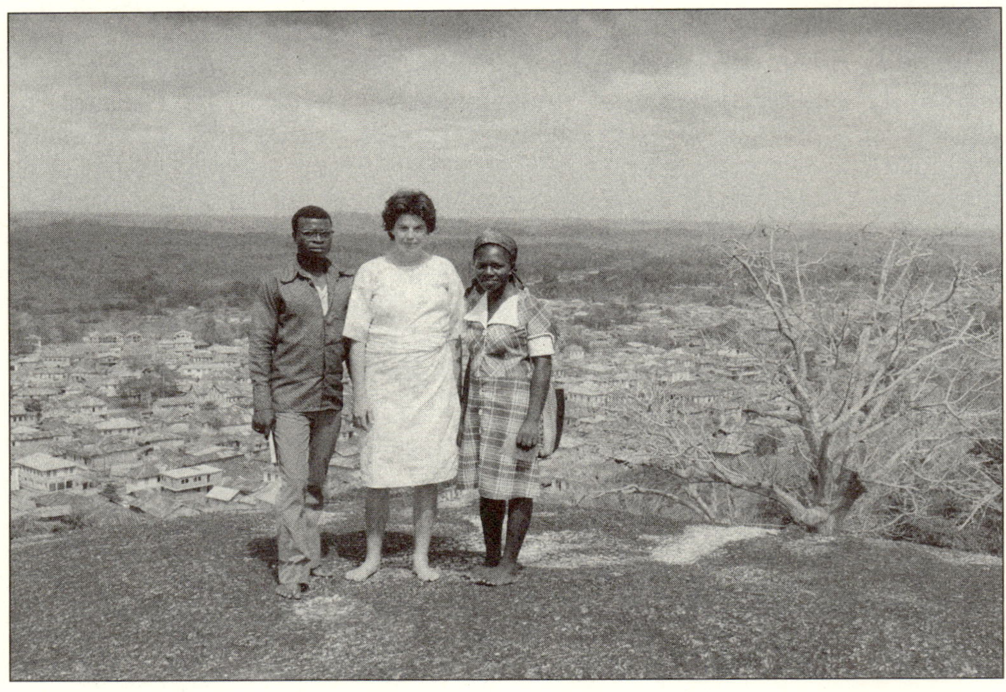

With Albert and Grace at Olumo Rock

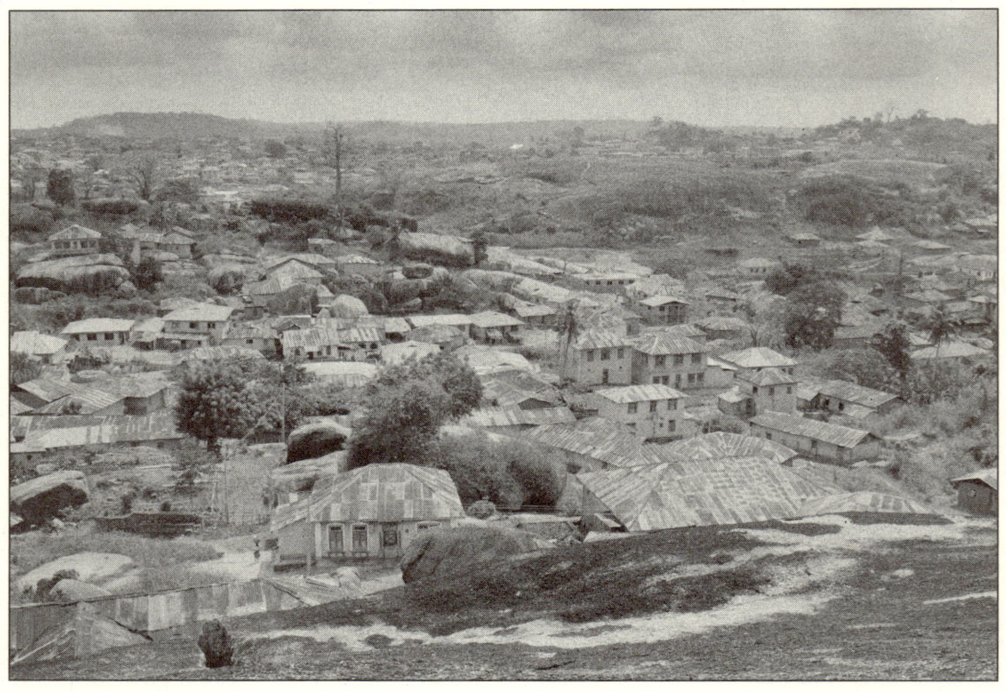

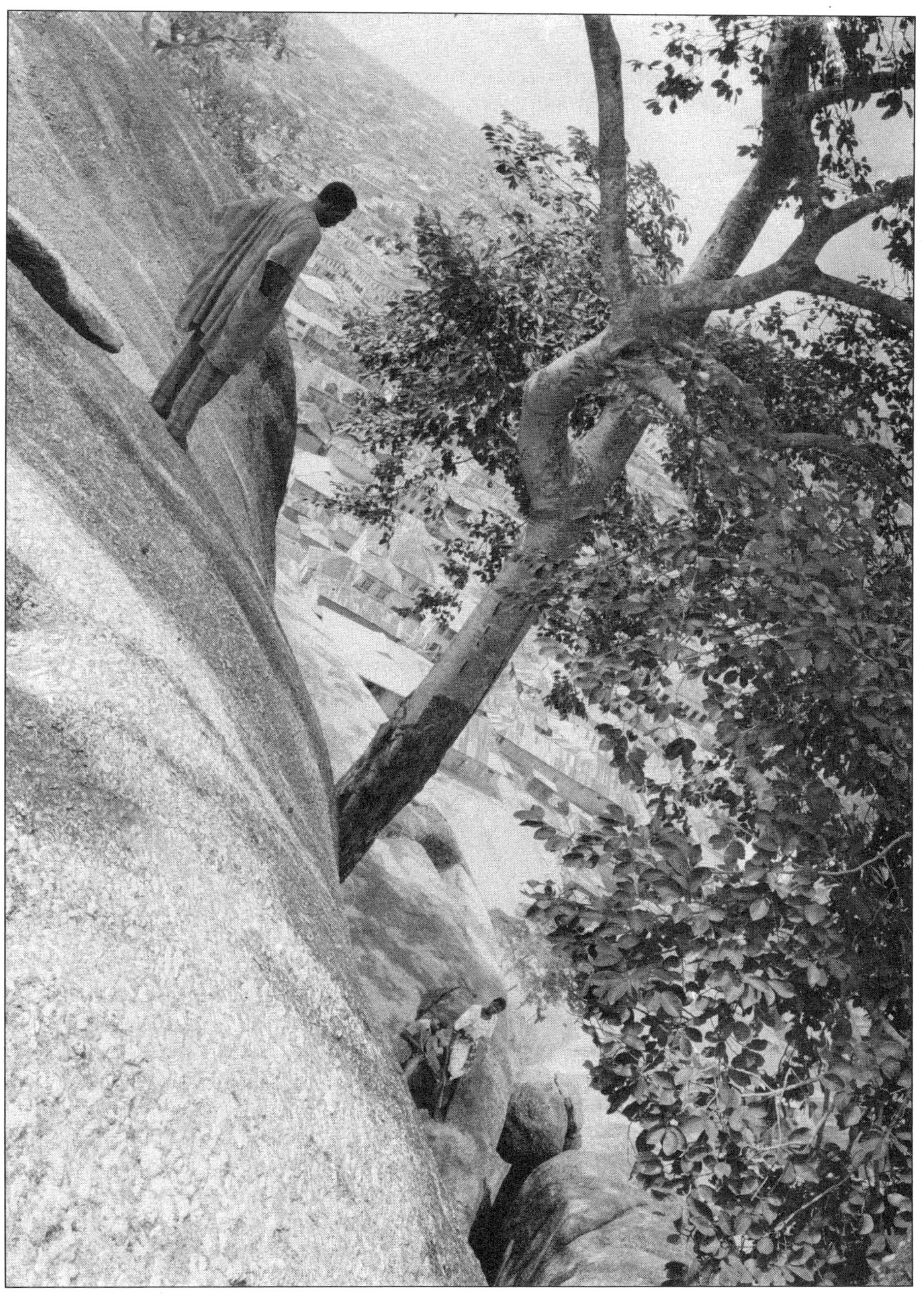

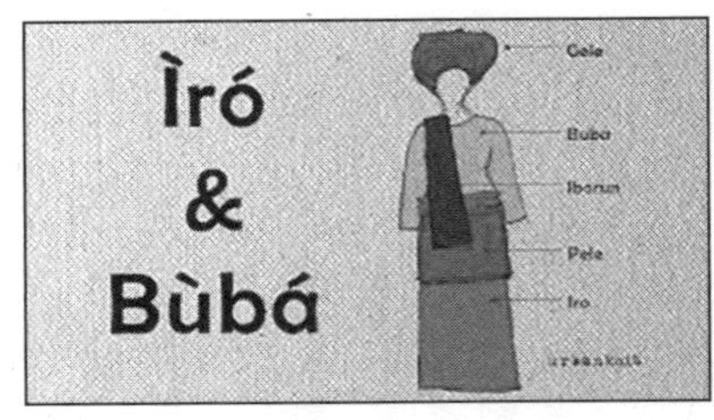

The village women/market women <u>love</u> me in this wrap and booba (*yalo* and *buba*); they comment on an "*oyibo* who knows how to wrap it correctly" and I was offered a lovely comb from a hairdresser because of my "doing like the Yoruba."
And a yellow-white-gold plastic bracelet which they said "suited me."
They said how they're afraid to take you in, but when they know you or think you're a friend of their friends . . .

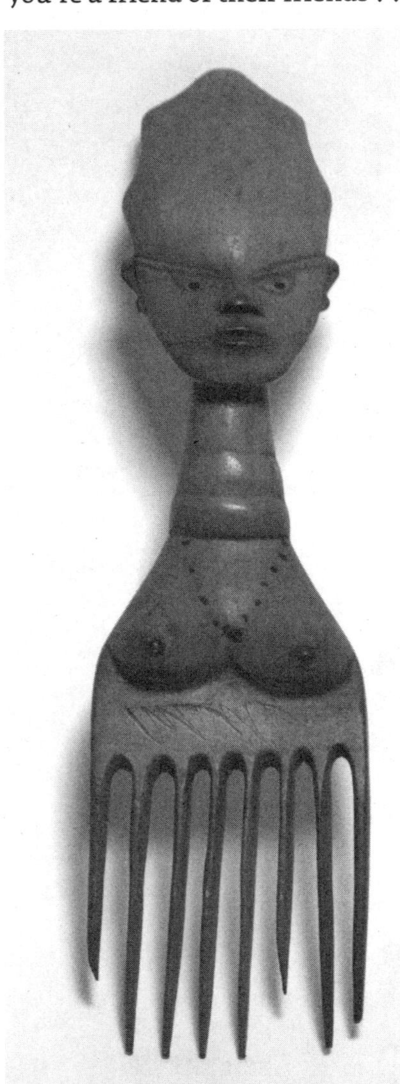

I really have trouble stepping outside myself and believing/seeing that it's me trudging thru the marketplaces in Yoruba dress greeted by shouts of *Oyibo*, *ikabo*! (Greetings, honky!)
It seems like a hokey movie about race relations or Peace Corps workers.

But ah this heat is so oppressive, all one can really do best is sit and talk and make a lot of time-passing heat-forgetting noise. The markets here are superb, the women
 the women
they really are coming alive to me. They are flesh and action and fire and command and response, far from our anemic models. They have a very very very visible role in life; in fact it's almost the reverse visibility of our culture—here the presence of the women on the streets far outweighs the men.

A newly married woman came thru the streets, head covered in a red and gold cloth (with a wrap of same and white embroidered cloth blouse)—for five days she never shows her face, until the fifth day when she's officially a married woman. She was accompanied by seven or eight companion women.
When traditions like that are explained to me they always come with " . . . but of course the literate don't follow these customs anymore"— A<u>hey</u>.

When Grace's husband's family fed me/us lunch, the mother was very pleased; I was told countless times and in many ways how pleased they are to have visitors (Nigerian or foreign) and will go to any length to make us happy. After thanking her profusely with a frozen grin for the meal, she said, "Ah, you have shown your love by eating with us today," and further and more elaborate gratitudes passed back and forth. They really do abide by the most courteous and communal traditions, and usually the sentiment is voiced thru a proverb or stylized phrase—
Had more *amala* at lunch, but with fish and much better. In fact, it was enjoyable and edible.

I had to hold and admire and cuddle and grin at Grace's baby Gideon for about twenty hot and sweaty minutes—they're such little lumps of quivering nerves and dribbling spit—I couldn't couldn't ever have one, ever.

Someone in exasperation the other day said, "Yes, the Yoruba are great talkers."—They sure are.
Our day consisted of waiting until 9:30 a.m. to go out (eat and then rest for an obligatory 45 minutes to an hour) to a house to wait (with Coke and carrots and baby) until 10:30 for a friend, go clamber up Olumo Rock, then rest in breezy shade for an hour, talk talk not small small, then to a house to eat and rest, then trudge thru the market and to the pig farm and back to the market and visit and trudge and snack and Coke and *odabo odabo*[53] and taxi and rest and wait til X comes "soon" out again to meet more friends trudge rest Coke rest rest talk talk visit talk hot loud sleep.

There's nothing more exhausting-debilitating than absorbing so much energy (sensory overload) in the form of activities and sights and new friends and loud talk without being able to recycle and redirect it outwards in the form of talk or work—I get absolutely sound-bloated.
After a few more days of "African life" I would be a nervous wreck (or will I be; it doesn't seem as if it will cease very soon—perhaps it's just the Yoruba?) [4]

A bright eager smiling piercingly attentive boy last night during a visit: "I wish to come to America with you."

Finished reading Friedan's *The Feminine Mystique* and I understand something now more clearly: My father has never been able to reconcile/balance a career and a home, a life of academics and a personal-immediate life with another human being. Which helps to explain my retreat to home/bedroom/books in that crucial time around sixth grade[54], and my still abiding shyness.

53 *Odabo* = goodbye. Interesting: An estimated thirty-eight million people speak Yoruba, but Google Translate does a crap job of translating it, even though they have it as a pulldown option. Like they think *odabo* means "alphabet."

54 When my parents were getting divorced.

I remember now reading Margaret Sanger's biography in high school[55] and having to hide it from the hawkish eyes of Sister So-and-so—this heretical, anarchistic topic of selective maternity.

Also another interesting book, *Women of Tropical Africa*. Nice to read something that really focuses on the experiences of *women*.

People of all ages refer to each other here as sister and brother and auntie, and when in Abeokuta much of the time has been spent walking hand in hand with the women, whether Twins or Grace or Janet, no self-consciousness, a gentle camaraderie.
And when first trying out the *yalo* and *buba*, Albert just stayed in the room while I changed, no embarrassment or question about it, just stood there advising me how to wrap it. I couldn't put on my private western face, so I just gritted my teeth and undressed.
There are all these what-I-feel-are grungy or dispiriting rooms-homes, the tiring blood-thinning diet, the heat—and what emerges from these homes are attractively dressed, vivacious people. By contrast, we have so much that the slightest discomfort or obstruction provokes all shades of bitchiness. Here, paying the long and graceful—artful—visits from one finger-scuffed-walls dusty-floored unmade-bedded dim room to another as the day passes slowly, one ignores the surroundings and becomes involved in the face and figure and style of speech of the companions.

Albert again, the last day, squeezing in a few strong questions about "our life," he described his first day in NY: "Everyone looked as if they were attached to some electric rods. Whenever I said hello or wanted to talk no one would answer. People there don't know how to enjoy themselves—when do they go visiting, talk, stop working? Here, if we see a friend during the day we rest, we visit, that is what is important. And I think there is a lot of hatred between white and Black there, so that when I got close to a woman there and wanted to have sex she would say no, and I think it's because she felt hate."
When I tried to explain the hate as being actually fear—of the unknown, of something they've never thought of as a human being—he was only grudgingly in agreement.
But he clearly didn't admire the "CAN-DO" ethic.

55 In 1916, Sanger opened the first birth control clinic in the U.S; she spent her life championing a woman's right to reproductive care.

A LETTER FROM ADEBOLA OYADOKA, A YOUNG GIRL I MET THROUGH WITTY:

Abeokuta Grammar School
P.M.B. 3006
Abeokuta
7/1/77

Dear, Su Friedrich,
Happy to write you this few line. Hope everything is going on systematically. How are all your family, hope they are all well both Spiritually and Physically.
Since the end of June 1976 I was afraid, when we don't see your letter we thought that may be you have an accident or you are ill. But we saw the letter that you wrote to SIR WITTY with the Photograph.
If you don't know me again, you can search for the Photograph of I and my Junior sister. My name is Bola.
You know you have promised to send us some gift when you gave my sister Taiwo a cardigan sweater. So now what I want is transistor-radio, watch and get camera with some film, cloth and some money.

I'am your's in love,
Bola Oyadoke

N.B. Please don't forget to send all those things to me for I would be happy if I saw your letter with the things

So now this is my address:
Adebola-Oyadoke Abeokuta Grammar School,
P.M.B. 3006
Abeokuta
Ogun State

Maybe it goes without saying, but I was scraping by in NYC with part-time work, trying to be a photographer, ergo not in the position to send huge care packages with items like the things she requested. So, I guiltily ignored the letter—or maybe wrote an apologetic letter explaining why I couldn't do it?? I have no record, no memory. All I know is that I sent some people pictures, perhaps ones I had taken of them, or a picture of myself. Beyond that, I doubt I sent anything.

LAGOS

February 13, 1976

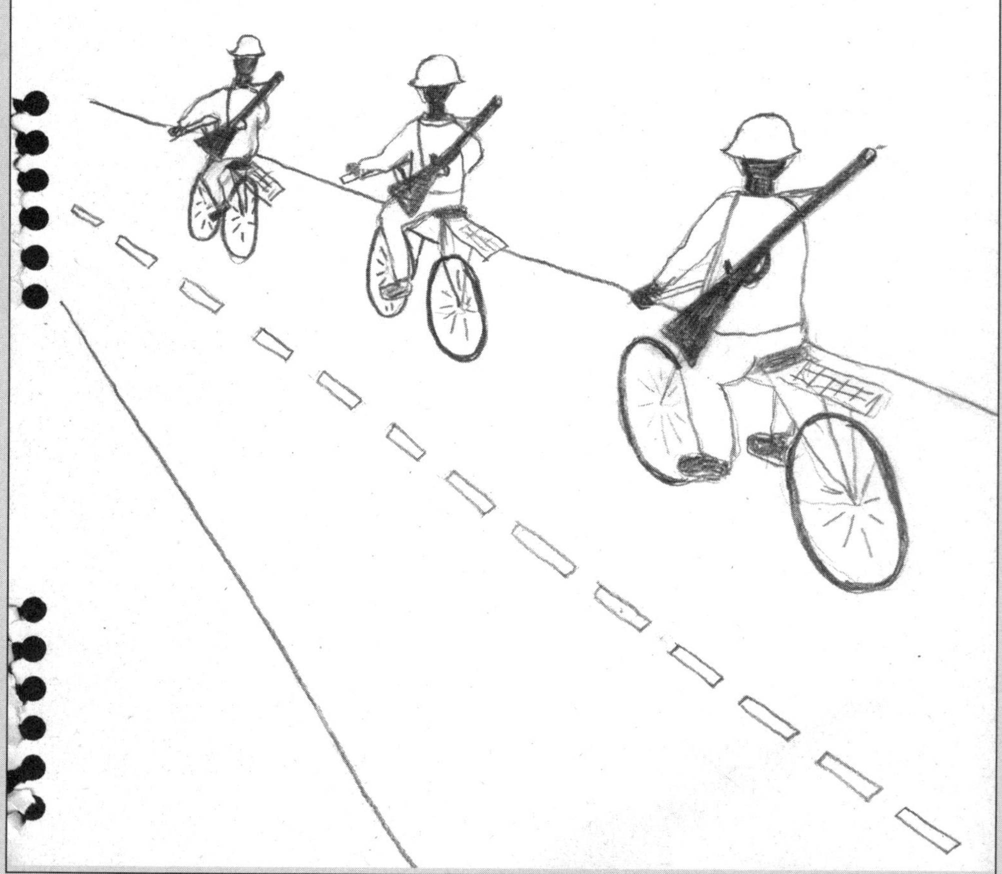

CHAPTER THIRTEEN

Not Turning Back, Eh? Well, Try This on for Size

On February 13th I left Abeokuta on a lorry bound for Lagos, the biggest city in Nigeria. Unbeknownst to me, a crisis was unfolding. To understand more about the causes and the players, see [1].

PART OF A LETTER TO MIMI:

Dearest Mimi,

With the timing that's becoming a matter of course for me, I left Abeokuta on the morning of the by-now well-publicized & quite confused "attempted counter coup." Two hours in a jam-packed, yell-filled lorry which turned back ½ way to Lagos because of "fighting reported." I shrugged & went on, the ever confident one, little realizing what had happened that morning, even after arriving in Lagos after many hot & tiring hours and feeling a certain distinct & by now familiar fear at seeing military men with guns on their backs. I pursued my course to the university.[56] Put up w/ an American woman w/ an extra bed. By 6:30 the news broke that Muhammed had been killed w/ 3 companions in the car on his way to the office, the car a shattered mess, covered w/ bullet holes, & today further news that Taiwo [57] was done in, in Ilorin, about 150 miles N. of Lagos. The idiot Dimka was the "mind" behind the coup, which failed in an overall way but miserably undermined the present tenuous stability here—there had been so much general trust & hope invested in this new regime—Gowon had been such a scoundrel, & Muhammed (despite his military background & present rule, which I can't reconcile although everyone says they're "necessary" now, and evidence almost proves it) was—however fragile it might have been—making an effort to strengthen the present state in Nigeria which had reached such a dismal low under Gowon. At any rate, in this twisted world where no one's loyalties or decisions can be correctly assessed before there's another upheaval or shift of focus, he seemed to be investing some direction into the country (but I don't withdraw my earlier feelings that things were, with Muhammed, still being more or less directed from the top down rather than preferably from the bottom/people up.)

---

56 I couldn't afford an expensive hotel, and being in one of the cheap ones would make me vulnerable to whatever happened in the public spaces of the city. I went to the University of Lagos (UNILAG) campus and was taken in by an expat, an American student named Mary Evenson.

57 All the people I refer to are described/explained in [1], as is the history leading to this most recent coup.

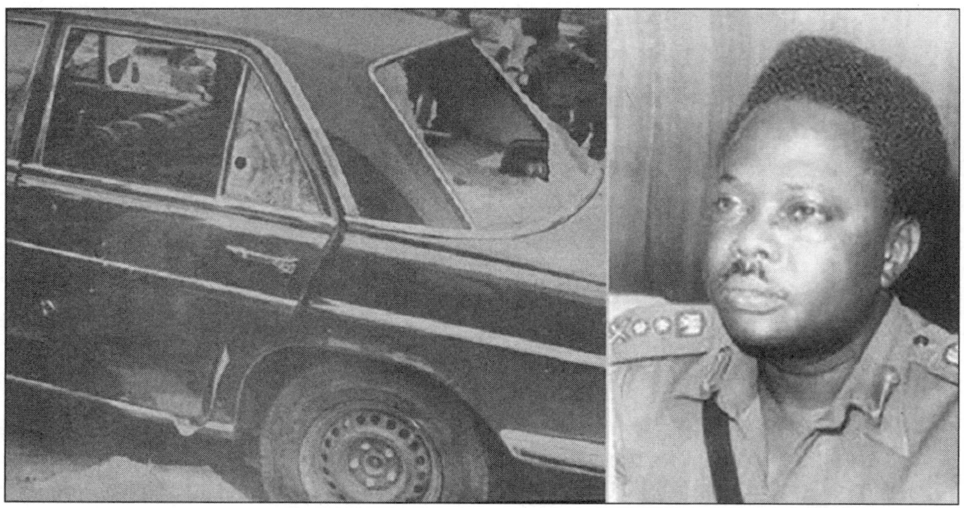

The car in which Murtala Ramat Muhammed, his aide-de-camp and his driver were gunned down on his way to work.

PART OF A LETTER TO MIMI:

The reaction here was deep and sorrowful—all day people have been listless, mournful, muttering "what's to become of us . . . ?", showing all the desperation that's come to be a part of all these countries: that there's no escaping the wrath of power . . . and the very possible hand of the CIA. I was greeted several times on my arrival w/ "CIA, go home!" With Nigeria standing up first for the MPLA & throwing out a recognized CIA operation up north in Kaduna just a few weeks ago, it wouldn't at all surprise me if they played a part in this. I have a feeling I've been cut loose from whatever feeble moorings I ever had—as if there's no going home because home is all that I hate & there's no home anywhere else if you're a white American & aren't willing to be "arrogant" to a point of self-preservation—i.e., if I really believe here all the things about America that I talk about at home, I have nothing to turn to, there's nothing to be proud of—and it makes it all the worse because this America that I & they talk about, the all-consuming & rapacious America is some abstract, disembodied monster, the mythical machine which runs down & shits on everything, indiscriminately, but America to me is also humans, is the only country I can call home & refer to in my heart, but that really means only so few people & special landscapes & foods & books & moments, all of which somehow has to be for the sake of sanity separate in my mind from the monster—but here there is no separating it, and I am a representative of it despite all my protestations of sympathy w/ their own angry & hateful feelings about that ugly Amerika—I at once want to show

& feel my solidarity against the tyrant, but I then grope around desperately for some other foothold, or threshold, and there is none. I'm not really welcome here, or there, or where. I'm not being melodramatic, it's a very real fear—and made more pronounced here than I ever could have imagined and empathized with while at home. All the reading & haranguing & crying about "third world tragedies" from our aware-as-possible position in the states does little compared with 10 minutes in the midst of students who burst into tears at the news of his (M's) death & ask, pleadingly, what is happening to our Nigeria? They have nowhere to turn.

There's no respite. It makes my head race in circles, my feet slow down, my nervous laugh more frequent, my cigarette consumption . . . well, that's another letter.

I'm SO PISSED about all this! I'm so sick & tired of never having a day's peace—

Mary, this American, is a certain breath of fresh air; she has a marked interest in women's situation & when I showed her the catalogue [from the WGC] she responded to the lesbian posters & somehow she showed her colors [2] but the conversation was cut short by the arrival of a friend—we commiserated together today about the mess here (and our fear) & she put it very simply by, after a long & tense day, saying, "I feel ashamed." There's no way (even if I could know or think that America didn't have direct responsibility for this or other things) of escaping the feeling that America is at the top the guilty party.

Dispiritedly yours,

Su

P.S.

In the thick of this week, I needed something to make me smile, and I remembered Diane DiPrima's oreo winter (or was it year?) and the mauve walls [3]

At the beginning I was very limited in my movements: there was a curfew, whites were anathema, etc., and then all routes by land or air were closed.

FEBRUARY 14–17

Had to pull into myself today to get a better grip. At 10 a.m. a bus or two of students set off for the city center for "condolence and sympathy" and a nervous and excited male student demanded Mary's and my I.D. and told us, "At this time, we just don't want to see any white faces, please go back to your dorms."

Anger I felt, at being a scapegoat, frustration at being seen as something which I don't feel (or as best as I intellectually can): That I am a part of US interventionist terrorism. Despair at all our worldwide confusion, no one really knowing who the Enemy is except that it's too big and too abstract and too rich.

But the CIA and all it represents is the nearest we/they can come to the source. This evening, hidden away in our expat lodgings, puffing furiously on cigarettes, listening nervously to the shouts and pounding coming from the men's hall, we heard about the students' invasion and partial destruction of the American and British Embassies in Lagos. So much for getting my mail!

News—from Tony, who was at the embassy riot—
The US flag was at half mast
They only broke windows
At British embassy, they went in and fucked up all the files; he claims he saw employees also throwing out papers and books
Dispersed with tear gas by police after damage was done
The Nigerian gov't refused Britain's compensation

I am damage done.

Nigerians Storm British and U.S. Offices

By JOHN DARNTON
Special to The New York Times

LAGOS, Nigeria, Feb. 17—Several hundred students stormed the British High Commission and the United States Embassy here today, smashing windows, wrecking cars and causing thousands of dollars in damage.

The demonstrators, from Lagos University, charged foreign complicity in the attempted coup Friday that led to the slaying of Gen. Murtala Ramat Muhammed, the head of state.

Chanting "C.I.A. must go," and waving branches of palm leaves in the air, the protesters

Lagos Students Charge Foreign Complicity in Coup Attempt

New York Times, that the British High Commissioner met for 15 minutes on Friday with Lieut. Col. B. S. Dimka, the leader of the abortive coup, who is still at large.

Account Printed in Lagos

The rebel leader, introducing himself as the new head of state, demanded to place a telephone call to Gen. Yakubu Gowon, the former head of state

In another development, the Reuters correspondent, Colin Fox, was deported last night. His family, placed under armed guard, was driven to neighboring Benin, formerly Dahomey. The Reuters office was closed and two Nigerian assistants were arrested.

The Nigerian radio said Mr. Fox had been expelled for reporting what was contrary to the "communal interest." One of his dispatches cited unconfirmed reports of unrest in the northern state of Kano, the home of General Muhammed, who was buried on the outskirts of the city of Kano on Saturday.

The battle now in me is the tendency to sit inside, subtly panic-stricken, telling myself I'm just biding time when in fact I'm working myself into fantasies of being spat upon and jumped upon if I show my *oyibo* face on the campus/in the city—but when I-we do go out, the paranoia subsides, I realize that it isn't as hostile towards *oyibos* as I think, but rather it's a general unease and fear and anger (like our feelings after hearing of yet another rape-murder).
But I am afraid.
And I am ashamed and sick about the US. I've never experienced such a physical awareness of their "reputation" and their GUILT as now, having been thru this coup situation.[58]

58 "Their" instead of "our": Growing up during the Vietnam War and then with the ensuing situations in Chile, Central America, etc., it was hard to identify as an American—in America, not just when I was outside the country.

From the first I've been both willing and resistant to believe that there was American involvement, on a few grounds:

1) It's very hard to admit that I am from a country that is so amoral as to get involved in an action that is both so ineffectual, unwanted and unwarranted by the overall climate and situation here (it's the last thing Nigeria needed or expected at this point)—and it's been a lot easier to accuse America of vicious dealings in other countries when I've been seeing it from my home, but when I am surrounded by the emotions and sorrow and anger and despair of the people it is that much more incredulous and makes me more anxious to wish the reality away, to hope that just maybe, this once, America wasn't responsible (but I fear the worst).
2) I don't like to see such an immediate/unfounded accusation arise, especially among the students here (and I do believe I'd think the same if they were shouting KGB or anyone else) in looking to the outside for blame. Of course we all know how much blame can be rightfully laid on the Americans for the general situation here, but this particular incident is so confused, and stems from so many internal and long-term conflicts, that I just shy away from such a reaction (but if I step aside from such a rational pattern and respond to it emotionally, I feel solidarity for their outburst).
3) Feel a bit angry or pissed off at what looks to me like hypocrisy in this sudden "politicization" of students who generally carry all the adornments and prejudice of the new and even stronger African ELITE.

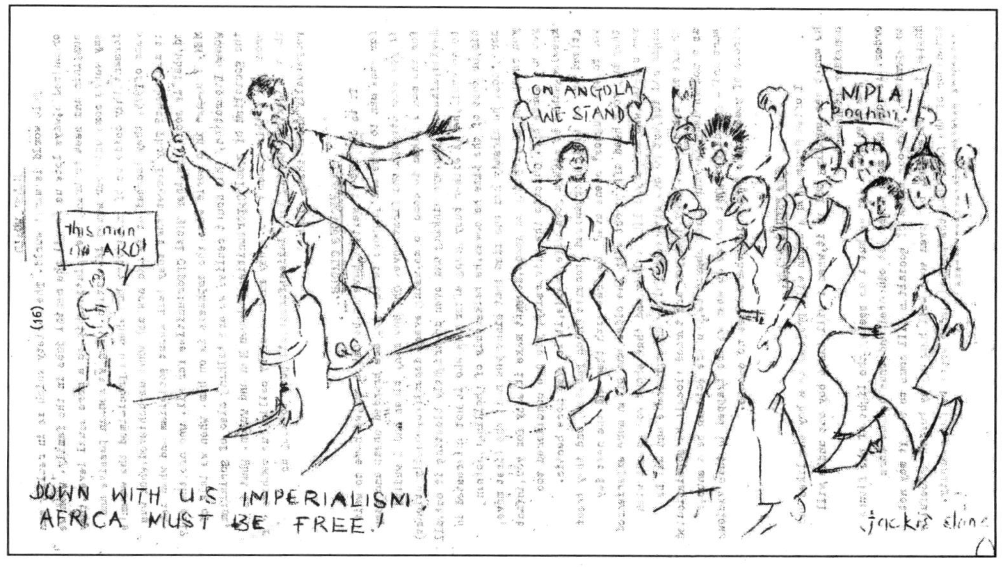

A page from a UNILAG student newsletter called *The Eye*.

There's talk that the promoted soldiers from the civil war were supposed to have been replaced by up-and-coming Sandhurst [59] officers, as promised by Murtala after the coup, and these young officers were angry that he hadn't done as promised and therefore coup'ed him.
All sorts of other rumors float by.

But whatever the final analysis, or evidence, it certainly wasn't done for the good and the stability of this country.
Such timing: The eviction of the CIA base in Kaduna and Kissinger's speech about "not permitting another Angola in Africa." What cheek to say that as an American representative at such a time.

A mournful wail from one of the women here when the first news came about Murtala being killed, and in the hopes that Taiwo wasn't dead she insisted, "But he'll have juju to protect him." [60]

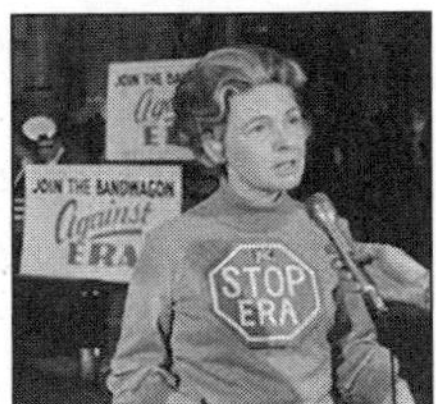

I am reminded of Angela Davis' warning: "As long as we see all white men as the enemy we'll never be able to develop a workable political theory."
Perhaps they have to admit that Dimka is a damn traitor—uncoerced, unsponsored—like our very own Phyllis Schlafly [61], suffocating women for her own self-righteousness.

Murtala's government was even described here as "radical;" he was admired for his humility and religiousness.

When Dimka made his memorable "speech of acceptance," people shrieked in insult. Ha! He tells us all of Nigeria is behind him and any action to the contrary will be met with death. Fine sentiments of solidarity!
And in my trapped and confused and hurt moments I yearn to get back to the US—not to feel secure, but at least to know that I have my own fight to wage, a clearer idea of the plot and players, and a working group—here I cannot express or work out my solidarity because they have no reason (?) or desire to trust me or to care even where my sympathies lie.
Remembering Phyllis Chesler's point about not "curing the world," but curing ourselves (women).
I'm always eager to see more evidence of America's rapidly deteriorating image in the outside world—but my personal nerves get in the way here.

---

59 The Royal Military Academy Sandhurst, thirty-four miles outside of London, is the premier military training academy for British army officers.

60 Ibrahim Taiwo had played a central role in the prior coup that ousted Gowon and brought Muhammed to power. The juju didn't work; he was killed on the day of the coup.

61 In the 1970s, Phyllis Schlafly (1924–2016) led a successful campaign against the ratification of the Equal Rights Amendment. She was an influential figure in conservative American politics, arguing against feminism, abortion, gay rights, and for what she termed "family values." Schlafly's influence on the Republican Party reverberates strongly to this day (Trump spoke at her funeral).

But I won't let my fear overcome me.
And I won't let the limits close in on me. This life is such a monolith of mutually excluding and suffocating structures that I can't bend to all of them, but rather have to keep sight of my bearings—however tenuous they may be/are.
In re: developing capitalism in Nigeria, and Davidson's warnings about the tortuous history of capitalist development in Europe:
Who wants to rent a house in a burning building?
I wish they'd see.
(Which is not to suggest that some don't, but that the majority doesn't—comparable to reformist feminism—we're all victims of it to more or less degrees.)

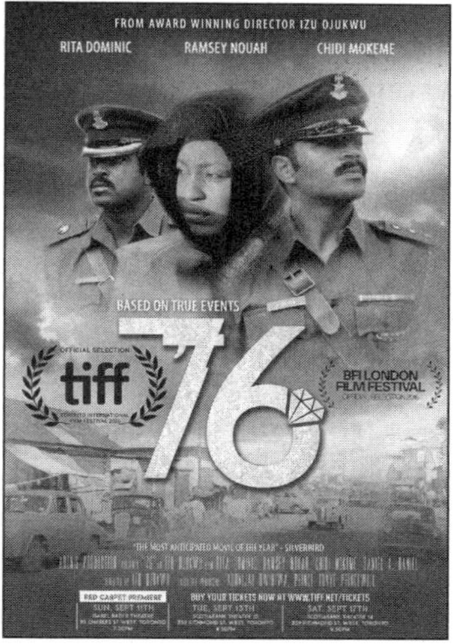

76 directed by Izu Ojukwu (2016)

Carry away (when appropriate) one's impressions and responses, and take time to think them through.

One day I hear: "We try to keep a hatred for official America separate from our feelings towards, for example, you as an individual"
And: "*Oyibos* are wonderful" or "I love your body (white skin)"
And: "Go home CIA"
And my mind reels, races.
When news broke on Friday evening that "the attempted coup has been crushed," the women's dorm rang loud with cries of "We have peace, we have peace!" but the next few days, with news of Dimka's escape and the tension about America and Britain, things settled in for a psychological siege.

I am treated with an unfamiliar chivalry which is not offered to their own women—it would be an insult to these self-sufficient women, but they assume that as an *oyibo* I expect it, and so they play by the rules.
I can't get rid of my feelings and cannot decipher whether it's simply a human feeling/need or a post Whitey assumption of expecting to be welcomed and desired (in a non-sexual sense) and I'm somehow disappointed if I sense a rejection or cool welcome.

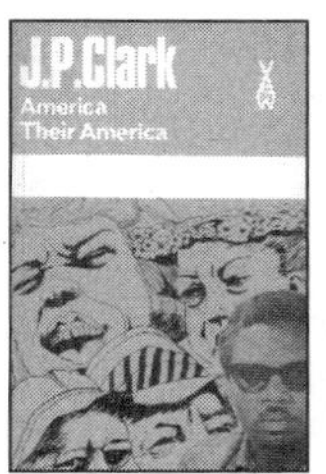

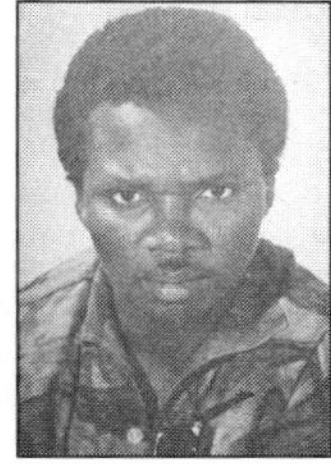

Read Nigerian poet John Pepper Clark's *America, Their America*. It started not surprisingly with a scene of his seduction, on the first night of his arrival in NY, of a sexy blonde sort.
His year at Princeton [62] was punctuated by trips to every imaginable Amerikan [sic] monolith of a political or industrial or cultural nature and he exposes the

62 I taught film production at Princeton from 1998 to 2023. His (quite critical) description of life on the campus was fascinating to read again so many years later, and there's a lot of truth in it. See [4] for more info about Clark.

shoddy quality of our "democracy" circa 1961. He isn't too sensitive to the childbirth pains of the Black movement, criticizes them on once-valid but now fourteen-years-late invalid grounds (hypersensitivity to Blackness, accepting all that's Black as good to overcompensate), sometimes gets very bogged down in his desires to see a predetermined something, but is very quick-witted, never backs out of a confrontation, and gets an absolute thrill from embarrassing paunchy fleshy cocktailed bureaucrats.
Interesting discussion on relative merits of sending Africans to America with African $ for schooling versus developing the educational system here; and defends polygamy in a rationally quite adequate manner, though is somewhat naïve to some of the less glorious aspects of the system. He comments on the typical American inability to visit in the artful way practiced here due to our TVs and telephones and fortressed homes; and on our style of conversation, where things are often said just to score a point or prove one's debating skills, not to contribute to a final consensus for the group.

"But as de Tocqueville well stated in his testimonial, America is one vast house of chance and contradiction, with a structure unwieldy beyond understanding."

"If New York is some overgrown, gross, ugly hostess, stalking on stilts, retiring to bed with her wig on, and with more than her bosom lifted and powdered freely, if she throws garden parties in and out of season while thousands hunger at the gates . . . "

Our conversations (Mary's and mine) compared to those between women in the dorm here—a totally different genre of human communication, reveals much of the cultural/personality differences, in the tone, the pace, the level of emotion (not right term) or "aggressiveness"—same as I used to feel between for example me and Rita being with Denise and Toni at Mitchell's—wavelengths which only temporarily coincide. [63]

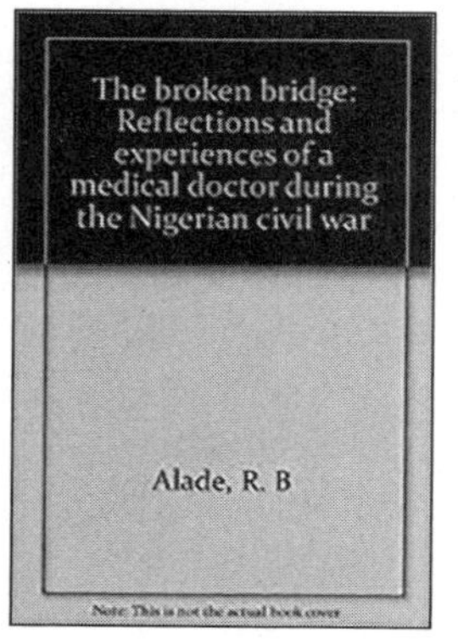

Read *The Broken Bridge*—Raphael B. Alade—about the Nigerian Civil War, July '67—Jan '70

Dull book, but informative.

63 Me and Rita: white. Denise and Toni: Black.

Read *Wedlock of the Gods* by Zulu Sofola [5]—an *African Romeo and Juliet*—
Will we ever learn freedom?
How I despise tradition, and the notion that your actions are so responsible to and engineered by your family's "name" or "face."

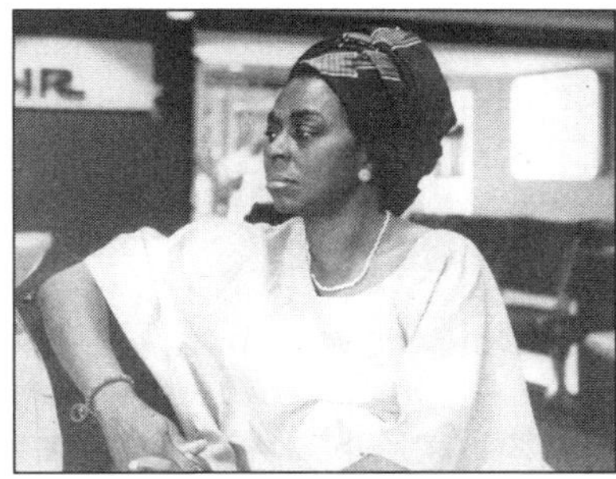

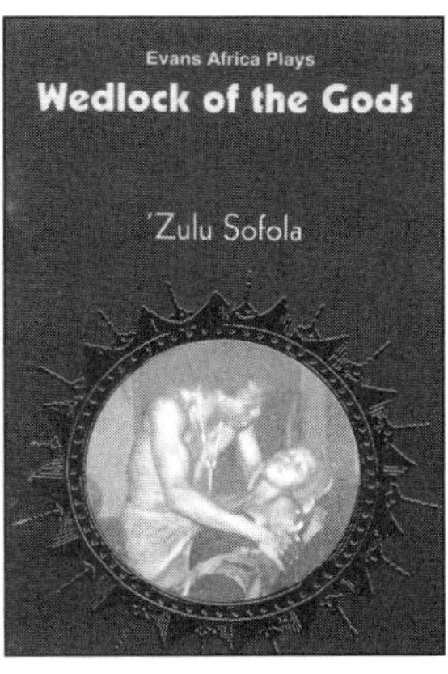

A LETTER TO MY FATHER:

Hello father, from the land of outrage and dry heaves. I have been in Lagos since the afternoon of the coup last Friday the 13th—don't believe anything you read in American papers.
It's been quite an enlightening experience for me, seeing first-hand the rage & frustration & sorrow of a people who have to live through yet another period of chaos and fear. After the last 15 years of upheaval and constant, unalleviated changes, they had just settled into a period which everyone considered to be one of development, relative stability, sureness of direction.
[. . .]
At this point, I'm a bit tired of the Yoruba & of Nigeria in general—not because of the coup (I had come to Lagos to get my mail & go west) but because I feel as if my personality & "style" clashes w/ the Yoruba spirit, which is quite distinct—gregarious, highly charged, etc. (I could explain it best in words & by showing you their most typical gestures during conversation)—just as the Algerians are quite different, I expect to see & feel differently in Ghana or Ivory Coast & know right now that I need a change.
I've been reading more & more (w/ this dusk-dawn curfew & my disinclination to go out in the city during this week of mourning) about the Biafran war, Rhodesia, a good "African Romeo & Juliet" set in 19th C. Nigeria by Zulu Sofola (a woman, significant when considering the character portrayed in the play), Shirley MacLaine's book about travels—it was curious in respect to my experiences here (i.e. the growing realization that as much as I might (I'm not sure I even do) wish to set my sights on the village-traditional life of Africa I am in inextricably thrown into contemporary problems) because she was granted a trip to Bhutan, the holiest of all holy Buddhist lands in the mountains of NE India, in order to learn more about mysticism, etc.—and during her short stay she became an accomplice in the escape of one of the prince's accomplices who was under suspicion following a coup which killed the king (or premier)—there's no getting away from

> it all, the confusion & terrorism on which this life seems to thrive.
> Your toughie daughter is now bedecked in a skirt & brightly colored & patterned "bubas" (loose blouses worn by all the women here except the bourgeois Europeanized students who dress like Fifth Avenue) & beads, silver, tan—and sandals. I feel as if I'm reclaiming my body, the warmth makes it impossible to enclose oneself in the sort of clothes I wear at home—it's the same comfort as when I was younger & 99% of the time barefoot.
> There are others, but the major frustration now is not being ever in a darkroom—my concentration span only permits me to read for a certain # of days or pages & then I need to be "at (what I consider) work"—so I wait. Hopefully I'll find one in Ghana at the university.
> For the time being I gaze around in amazement & consternation.
> Love
> Su

I couldn't believe it—Last night we were beering with the local neo-colonialist couple and she said, in her most guttural mournful British drawl, "I do wish they could clean up the trouble in Rhodesia. It's really the only country in all of Africa where Black and white have lived peacefully side by side, and it's been self-governing since 1924."
(In fact it's a white autocracy "independent" of Britain.)
Shades of Vorster calling "his" Blacks some of the happiest people in the world.
And he said it would be a shame if trouble broke out because you know they always kill the educated, the liberal intellectuals (i.e. the Cambridge-bred ruling class).

I simply can't (and am not wanted to) do any "good" while I'm here, and with this coup atmosphere all I can try to do is give as honest an account of things when I get back home, very carefully weed and sift through my confusions and patterns of response.

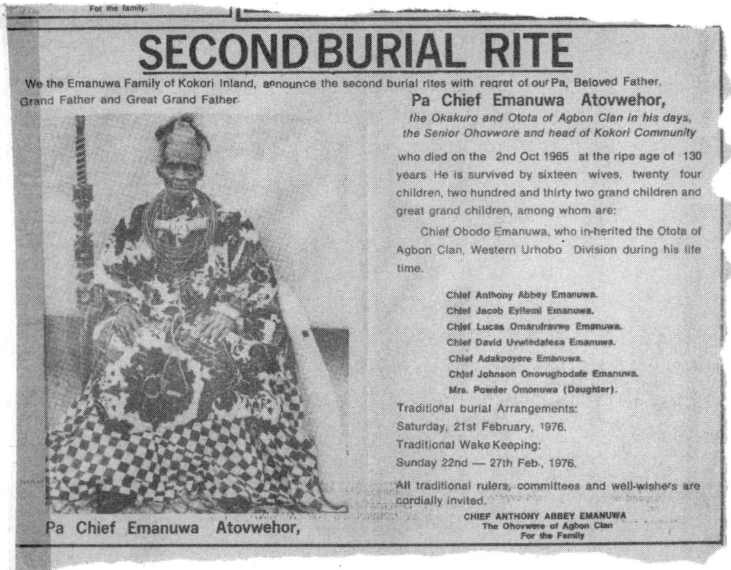

For the family.

SECOND BURIAL RITE

We the Emanuwa Family of Kokori Inland, announce the second burial rites with regret of our Pa, Beloved Father, Grand Father and Great Grand Father.

Pa Chief Emanuwa Atovwehor,

the Okakuro and Otota of Agbon Clan in his days, the Senior Ohovwore and head of Kokori Community

who died on the 2nd Oct 1965 at the ripe age of 130 years. He is survived by sixteen wives, twenty four children, two hundred and thirty two grand children and great grand children, among whom are:

Chief Obodo Emanuwa, who in-herited the Otota of Agbon Clan, Western Urhobo Division during his life time.

Chief Anthony Abbey Emanuwa.
Chief Jacob Eyitemi Emanuwa.
Chief Lucas Omaruirawe Emanuwa.
Chief David Uvwiedafesa Emanuwa.
Chief Adakpoyere Emanuwa.
Chief Johnson Onovughodafe Emanuwa.
Mrs. Powder Omonuwa (Daughter).

Traditional burial Arrangements:
Saturday, 21st February, 1976.
Traditional Wake Keeping:
Sunday 22nd — 27th Feb., 1976.

All traditional rulers, committees and well-wishers are cordially invited.

CHIEF ANTHONY ABBEY EMANUWA
The Ohovwere of Agbon Clan
For the Family

Pa Chief Emanuwa Atovwehor,

130 years old?

The sunset is very soft and inconspicuous here, not like the blood red metallic agony we have at home, thanks to all that metallic dust from the steel mills.

Narrow roads, avenues of palm—towering taut slender hard gray palm trunks—and chaotic elegant under-brush, the tropical sort, lots of arching leaves, aggressive vines.
I'm intrigued by incongruity, or the impossibility of it—because seeing it implies a preconceived notion of order and a natural harmony of things and I don't believe in natural law or the workability of a world that's ever consistent or on schedule. So I roam the streets laughing and laughing to myself at these same (and really sublime) "incongruities" while reminding myself that they're not new or unusual, given the intrusion of some displacing element (a comment a person an object a thought) into every and any situation I've ever known.

NY, that cyclops, is almost innocuous compared with the streets of Lagos on a busy day.

Oh god . . . .just finished Dee Brown . . . *Bury My Heart at Wounded Knee* . . . What an infuriating and heartbreaking history.

FEBRUARY 18

More news:
Dimka did go to the British High Commission at 9am on the morning of the coup. Three hours later the BBC reported the text: A cable to Gowon, a list of who was to be assassinated (Muhammed, Obasanjo, Taiwo, Danjuma, Yar' Adua et. al.).
It was given as:
To clear out the "growing communist influence" (because of their Angola policy).
In revenge for non-promotion of some and wronged promotion of others (esp. Danjuma).
To restore Gowon and all previous governors to power.

Gowon allegedly had full prior knowledge of the coup, and gave consent, had army contacts come to U.K. with plans.
(I wonder how much truck Gowon had with the US during his nine year regime?)
A suspect Afro-American snuck onto Danjuma's plane returning from Angola, he was pulled in for interrogation, no info yet.
Some/all of the old governors were apparently involved in the coup plans, it was to have been that day and that's why it was botched—when news broke, those in Ilorin responded by killing Taiwo, but others were unprepared.

One of my few consolations here is that the architecture of the dorm at the top (white with slanted juts) reminds me in spirit of the Algerian villages, which I sorely miss.

The first issue of *African Woman—Women in Politics*— had a long and angry article by the editor in reference to the IWY [International Women's Year] conference and the pushiness/theo-centrism of the American women. We have to be very very careful not to promote American brand feminism with our (albeit "well-intentioned") missionary zeal—it's the primary characteristic of Americans that makes us least respected, and we as American women in a very particular historical and psychological era cannot risk the presumption that others' liberation must follow on our lines—we are not the model for the world—it's a continued (even if unconscious, therefore worse) disrespect for the vision and wisdom of others who best understand the idiosyncratic needs of their situation.
The article talked about their mutual aid ideology—efforts between women and men against outside forces, the history of cooperative life which was altered but not destroyed in the colonial era. She said that we have something/a lot to learn from Africa about family systems, etc. (not vice versa).
"Changes must be sought for the rural woman in terms of her needs and interests, rather than in terms of abstract idealism."
Seventy percent of agricultural tasks are done by women.
Either enhance women's agricultural role, or take an even more radical approach: Integrate rural women into the national effort to diversify the economy.
I'm sure the whole of this trip will help me to accept how little we (American women) understand about the nature of African women's lives and African social patterns, and to believe that its programs, ideologies, philosophy can really and truly only be developed indigenously (but with a continuing and hopefully fertile contact with western and eastern ideas).
And one good example of the complexity of problems just within Africa is between Muslim and traditional/Christian groups, whose foundations are so diametrically different, the psyche here being tuned to a position of mobility, the women having "bargaining power" in terms of the structural security of the culture, and them being so depended on for services beyond the biological, compared to the position of relative weakness from which Muslim women have to work. We've all been brainwashed.

Camus: He who despairs over an event is a coward, but he who holds hopes for the human condition is a fool.

I am less convinced now of "foreign backing" (1) on a large scale (2) as instigator—there is and will be sufficient wealth (and uncontrollable sources) in Nigeria to inspire these sorts of coups, particularly when it was organized specifically to reinstall Gowon and his rich corrupt governors. They alone with their embezzled millions of naira are an obvious source of backing.

Two more pages from *The Eye*.

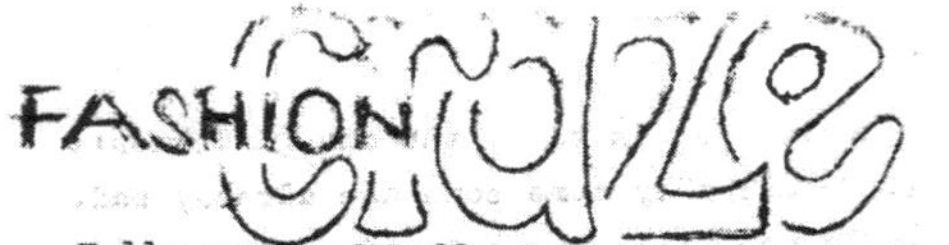

(10)

Hello Guys and Dolls, i am back again on that column that blows your mind real hy. It has always been my belief that, the way and manner you dress portrays your personality, hence this you favourite column.

For this fashion season, Guys fashion seems to be on a stand still, with Jeans taking the lead in both DISCO and CASUAL WEARS.

Dolls on the other hand, have a handfull. Their's the always the moving thing.

HAIR DO?- Talking about this, i prefer the short andcute Afro-cut but the IN VOGUE things include parmed hair.

SCARFS - When first i saw it, me thought it was Arabian coz it sorta looks like what Arafat puts on, but i later discovered it is refered to as 'CLEOPATRA JONES'. A special sort of scarf it really is, just like Cleopatra Jones herself, different, cute and cool.

DRESS: - Mini used to be IN VOGUE, last year it was the knee length but now, it is longer. But wait a minute coz there's a clash here in that some dresses and skirts if below the knee look awful when while some other look just graceful when they are well below the knee espercially when accompanied by the Big Belt for Dolls with big waist, and also accompanied by the 'CLEOPATRA JONES'.

SHOES : - The in thing is the STELETO. There is also the low heeled ones running vis - a - vis the really flat SANELETTE. These are for the Dolls who want

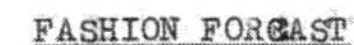

real comfort.

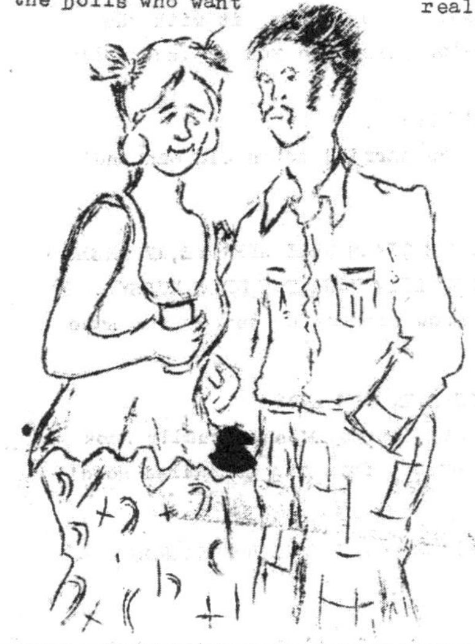

FASHION FORCAST.

DENIM SUITS I.E. THE JEANS JACKET, BIKINI WEARS, SKIRTS AND DRESSES HAVE COME TO STAY AT LEAST FOR THIS FASHION SEASON.

THE DENIM DRESS COULD GO OUT OF FASHION IN THE NEAR FUTURE, BUT NOT THE JEANS PANTS AND IT'S JACKET.

THE DENIM KNICKER - BUCKERS ARE JUST WAY OUT. THE MONKEY JACKET TYPE IS MORE FOR GUYS AND WHEN WORN BY A SLIM, TALL BROAD SHOULDERED, HANDSOME GUY, THE MINDS OF THE DOLLS ARE USUALLY BLOWN REAL SWELL.

SO GUYS AND DOLLS WHO CARE HOW THEY LOOK, OVER TO YOU.

GINATO
Your Fashion Correspondent.

****

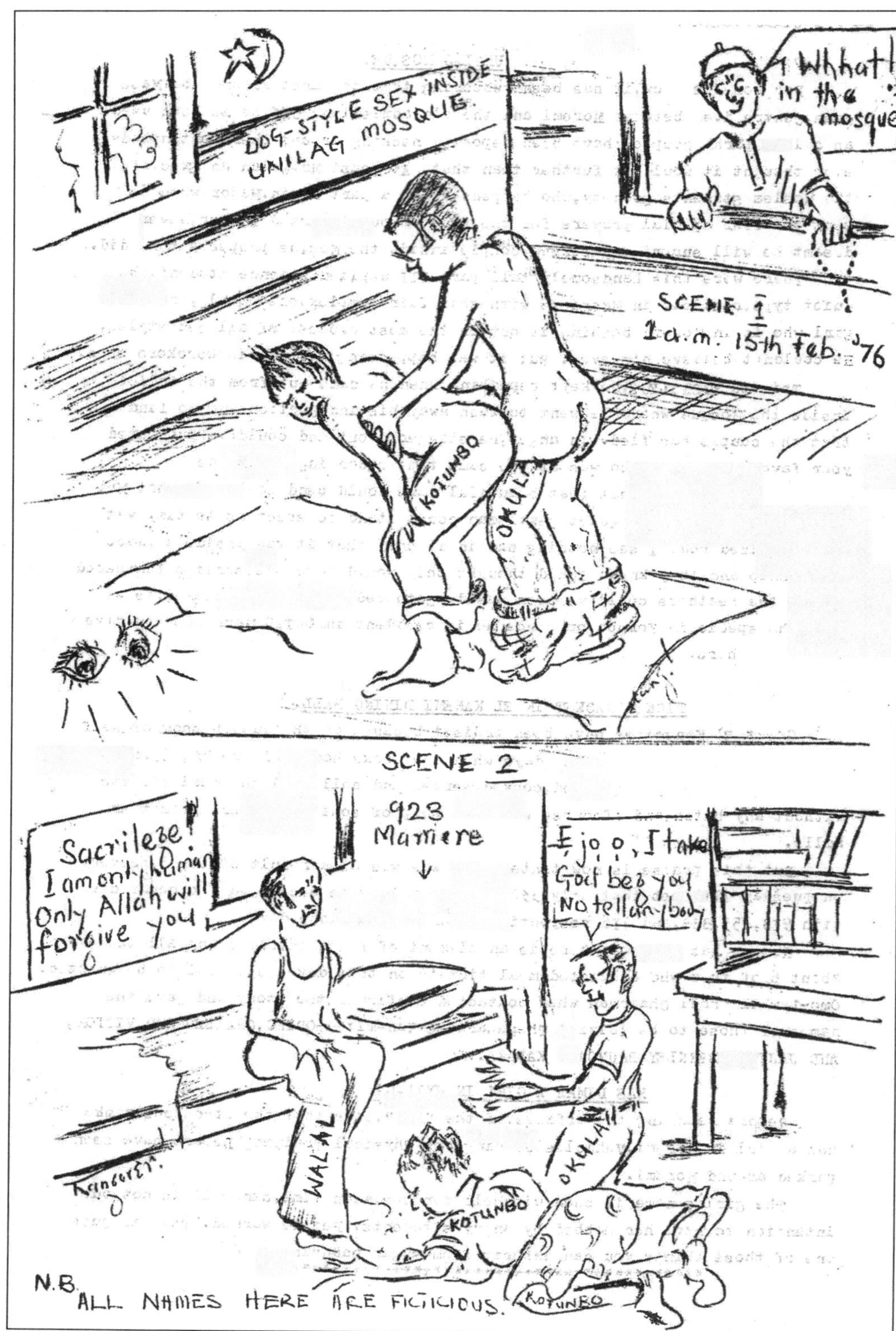

DOG-STYLE SEX INSIDE UNILAG MOSQUE
Whhat! in the mosque
SCENE 1
1 a.m. 15th Feb. '76
KOTUNBO
OKULA
SCENE 2
923 Marriere
Sacrileze! I am only human Only Allah will forgive you
Ejo o, I take God beg you No tell anybody
WALAL
OKULA
KOTUNBO
N.B. ALL NAMES HERE ARE FICTICIOUS.
KOTUNBO

"One of the drearier legacies of colonialism was the belief that education means schooling and that the pre-colonial Africans had been re-educated . . . It is in part the prestige that the colonial system of schooling acquired that makes it hard to change."

FEBRUARY 21 AND 22

I wish I could do more photographing but this week of mornings and nights has discouraged me from being a brazen hussy of a journalist—if only to protect my camera—and at this point it is literally an insult to be on the scene, taking it all down for a posterity whom I'm sure they think will be contemptuous. Also I don't just want to work with images of the traditional woman, these lovely portraits and work scenes I've been recording.

I'd like something more "impressionistic," but it's impossible to be left alone here to photograph in peace (or do <u>anything</u> unobserved).

I don't want height, I yearn for depth.

With my photographs, which tend to concentrate on individual women, I would much rather put out a series on each woman, with two or three photos and excerpts from her conversation. Of course they couldn't speak for the entire trip or the unfathomable diversity here but each (so far) to me represents a certain space and time between tradition and modernity—the gentle face of Miriam, house-bound and strong, or Saliha, who's tasted the seemingly free life of Europe and has returned to a husband who doesn't find it quite so irresistible, Hamsatou the child bride and child mother, and Janet, who "admits" with both trepidation and nonchalance that she isn't married yet, at 22. They become points of reference in a sea of unfamiliarity.

I would like to make inextricable from the photos my awareness that photographing is a sublime artifice.

"Militant" as a term of alienation, to set apart those who speak truthfully by calling them "extremists."

Most middle-class are the ones who are "militant" (Toni Cade Bambara)—it's no different than the accusation leveled at the left or women's movement.

Whether or not it seems trivial that a well-fed and underworked suburban housewife needs liberation compared with her slave-level Black sister, the primary and most far-reaching effect of women's/Black liberation <u>BOTH</u> is to undermine and castrate the justification for power hierarchies.

They say the problem is racism and that they've always had economic responsibility compared to the white women—

But true also in Africa and look at what's happening (and being immediately fought against, of course) here with the balance of education and positions of influence.

What am I <u>doing</u> here?!!

Reading *War Crimes in Vietnam* by Bertrand Russell. I feel as if I'm finally waking up, as if my real education (the factual, hard core one, to confirm and activate my childhood awareness of war's suffering thru my mother) [64] is just beginning, and I had a glimpse of how hard it might be to peel away the layers of laziness and wrong associations so that I can see more clearly. It feels like the third eye but not the one we usually mean—this isn't a vision of harmony, it's insight into the man-built structures and lies that disturb that harmony. Halberstam's book [*The Best and the Brightest*] was good, but because of the length and repetitions he diminished the impact, which it appeared he was trying to build by making it so detailed. Russell's managed to put it in a nutshell.
But Halberstam did what he stated was his intention: To expose the American psyche that could lead us into such a death spree: the belief in power and the commitment to our self-deceptions. I feel as if I'm learning my history for the first time, learning to understand how and why others see us and how we've been seeing ourselves—I'm ashamed at how ignorant I've been but now I have to be on guard to know, to be prepared, to have a clear idea before they start running their media and policy machines.
And if it's true that one can only effectively bargain from a position of power, then it's even truer in the case of criticizing—which means each of us has to know who the enemy is so that we can collectively reject reject reject all those lies—because just one or two brave dissenters up in the Senate or House aren't enough—not anywhere up high, because it's easy to shut one or two or ten mouths.

We Americans—and I feel okay speaking on such terms—have to learn that the rest of the world doesn't need us to do their thinking and creating and sustaining. To see a Black face (or any other non-Caucasian) and believe, without even having to be conscious of it, that there is a reliable mind and history behind it—and to not PITY them. To treat them equally is what they'd prefer to being pitied.
I.e., to see the humanness in them, and to see what connects us rather than always what sets us apart, distinct, we have X and Y and they have only Z, etc.
To see that they eat and bathe and watch their children and cry and booze and pray and dream and that these acts are what makes each of us alive and proud of ourselves and our people [6].

Last night we were discussing Yoruba names and I discovered I would be named: [65]
Born-on-a-Sunday born-on-the-way born-by-the-legs a-girl-is-good-also born-near-Christmas Friedrich
They study the conditions at birth ("look at the back of the house") and give an appropriate name so you know something of a person's history when you first hear their name.

---

64 She grew up in Germany (as a Christian) during the Second World War.

65 See [7] for all the errors here, as corrected by a student of mine from Abeokuta.

Bose-de . . . . .born on Sunday
Abiona (o) . . . . .born during a journey
Aritetsoma . . . .anyone is a child (i.e. girls are okay too)
Abiodun . . . . .born during a festival

Detail. Clues thru minutiae.

I'm really attached to the sturdiness and welcome of the American (eastern) countryside.

To hear Arab music now evokes all the mystery and strange joy of the desert, and those people who watch the world with those large dark silent eyes framed by windings of a long scarf; the yearning tone in it, the suggestion of more life than the tangible; it carries the night air and the sway of the walk beneath swaying robes, the activity amid the silence, and this whether from a deserted and dimly lit café or at a ceremony or blaring from a tape deck as one hurtles and shifts across the desert night sands and sky, breaking the everlasting silence with its yearning contentment. And sometimes it sounds like sheer noise being made to rend the vast silence.

Nice change of pace, the performance tonight!
"For contributing to our music and dance, women have much to be proud of. Men would have great trouble proving themselves superior to them. Here are women from . . . "

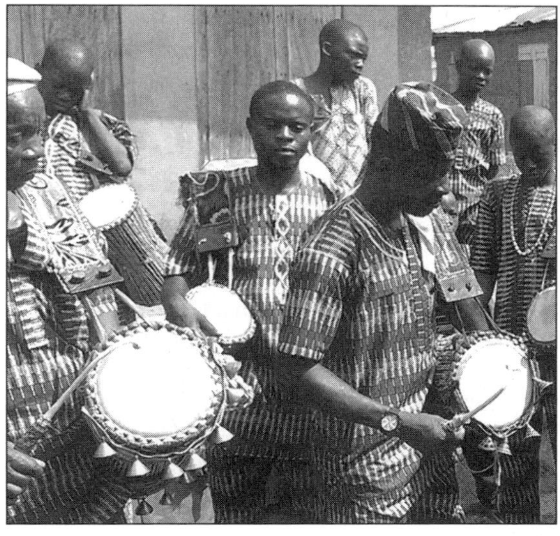

And a long joyous raucous piece followed: a leading voice and chorus answering, outdoing each other in agility of voice and speed, the various drums underlining her words, each absolutely on tip toe, alert for the rhythm and flawlessness—
One learns to hear the nuances, the complexity.
No great finale; an abrupt end and always, it seems, at just the right time.
Even news is announced with drumbeat.

The holding power, the tenacity and energy in the juju [8] music is so much like the concentration and expense in personal relations and visits, the willingness to absorb oneself entirely and at whatever length into a good time; the strength and energy to enjoy oneself after the hard work of the day.

The Yoruba tell me that they're lazier than the Ibo, that what concerns them is having a good time, enjoying life; that the Ibo students are always in their books. As if out of the confusion of the country and the need to feel more secure grows an obsession with "great leaders," a desire to grab at all their good while it's available, and with this comes a resistance to valid and helpful criticism—it's like grabbing for an overinflated life raft—that bursts—but it <u>seemed</u> good, and having been undertrodden for so very long makes one overcompensate now, and reify someone like Murtala.

Pidgin English for some objects:

Saw: The knife that comes back
Sun: Big light by Master Jesus
Moon: Small light
Bike: Chair go ahead

I walked around the area of the coup, past Dodan Barracks and NBC [66]—a tank and too many lazy submachine-gun-armed soldiers sitting about, red-eyed (beer or tears?) and suspicious, the one fellow in mid-road with his gun resting on a saw horse, pointed at oncoming traffic—
And as usual I was escorted to and fro by a friendly Nigerian fellow—I've never seen such people who will go to such lengths to insure a visitor's security.

Got a happily tearfully welcomed letter from Mom—written more than a month ago!—and again as at Oberlin or in Europe when she was the only one to "come through" with a letter, I said to myself, yep, do or die, spit or kiss, parents are always the most loyal of friends.

> **A LETTER FROM MY MOTHER:**
>
> Dear Su,
> Postcards, letters, packages from Denmark, plus latest aerogram from Algeria are all here, but where and when will this reach you if ever?
> I let off a sigh of relief knowing that you are now, as you said yourself, in warmer climes. It makes no sense to go over the why's of your pro-winter departure again. You had reasons, I shan't know all of them. But I often felt near tears thinking of you in your flimsy pieces of assorted clothing and reading at the same time of the violent winter storms howling across the European continent with unprecedented force – at least that is what we read about here.
> Again – there is, aside from the tears, another feeling to be tackled with: that of envy: that you are young, ambitious, adventurous, industrious – and that you can leave and go as you wish. This personal freedom from the bondage of a life of duty, imposed on so many

66 Dodan Barracks was the residence for Nigerian heads of state from 1966 to 1991. NBC was the Nigerian National Broadcasting Commission, not the American network.

millions, is something to be considered. I am glad you "got away," I am envious, but also truly happy for you. It will be very strenuous at times – dangerous perhaps – frustrating which you also experienced, but as long as you keep in fairly good physical shape and remain open-eared and open-eyed you should be able to make it.

That you are open-minded you have demonstrated clearly by choosing to put a distance between that which began to oppress you and the unknown of new cultures and new worlds. Your letter from Algeria is but the beginning of what I hope is a series of "unforgettable" experiences jotted down on paper. I assume you keep a journal as it would be a cinch to get such a "travelog" published. Just think of my simple Angelito story [67]—-

It must have been known to you from our many tales of India (also Mexico!) how many women are still "in captivity," and it will take many a decade to change these long-established patterns, i.e. male-female roles. I am not sure if we shall get as far as you personally think we will or should. I tend to think that still a vast majority of women will always remain what they have been for centuries: the wives of men, the mothers of children because this is what they wish to be, just as much as you want to be a liberated woman pursuing equal footing with man.

The Arab world seems very mysterious to me – I know very little about it except what we saw in Port Said and Cairo, Egypt, which was relatively little. I am sure there are vast differences between the cultural patterns of the Algerians and Egyptians, but there must also be many similarities especially pertaining to women and their role in society. But you are heading towards the Africans and I tried to figure out which route you might take, which is, of course, impossible. I can't even find Airi Sadah [68] on the map. Neither do I know yet where to send this letter, i.e., I have to call for the address of the Embassy. But maybe in between another note will arrive from you . . .

[. . .]

A strong winter storm had blown in a couple of days ago, but today is clear and Pete has gone skating with dad. I am "suffering" from a nasty allergy, which leaves my eyes red, my lids puffy, swollen and itchy. I will have to call Dr. Fish tomorrow and get something for it. It's not only uncomfortable, but I look ugly as hell . . .

I would give a lot could I just have a chat on the phone with you now . . . .

With much love and a long, motherly-sisterly hug and kisses
And keep writing, writing, writing . . . .
Mom & Pete

---

67 When we were living in Mexico, she wrote a short story about the funeral of a small boy which she witnessed. "Wake for an Angelito: An Incident in Mexico was published in *The Humanist* in 1958.

68 I guess she means Ain Salah. My handwriting was terrible.

A LETTER TO MIMI:

I feel as if the only way I can get a grasp of myself these days is to "write home," where my reactions & attitudes don't have to first run through the grinder of diplomacy and cultural maladjustments. This week hasn't been such a happy one, and only quantitatively productive, i.e. I've read 8 books, being stranded on campus, afraid of the anger I might easily provoke as an *oyibo* (honky) on the streets during a week of mourning, but I've had my fill of African universities for a while, having spent the most of 3 weeks on Nigerian campuses—

I don't retract my dismay & flailing spirit re: America in the 1st letter but I've come to see that I have to do some close reading into our history & get a more solid picture. If one can only bargain from a position of power, it's even more true that one can only effectively criticize/understand from a position of power (i.e. knowledge). Intuition is fine but not enough. And as much as I'm afraid of this point in history I also find it terribly exciting. Am reading an account of contemporary Russia by Laurens van der Post, *Journey Into Russia*, which made me come to a disturbing (but not surprising) realization: that I haven't been able to think of Russians as individual humans with appetites & dreams & summer vacations & idiosyncrasies; they had been transformed into that corporate soviet worker-patriot or lone dissident. But in his account, based on contact w/ an incredible variety of people, I begin to understand the vastness of Russia, with as many ethnic & racial types as Africa, so many distinct (& often conflicting) cultural traditions which go back thousands of years, such a deep religious strain running thru all of them, and this rich diversity is being not-so-gently compressed into the muscular hug of the soviet bureaucrat. IF, as in the equally idealistic case of an economically unified socialist Africa, there could thrive all the welfare plans (irrigation, housing, blah blah) without squeezing the blood & soul out of the cultural diversity, wonderful. But.

I'm really beginning to understand the fierce pride & fight for self which motivate Africans to maintain their ethnic identities despite (or maybe to spite!) the chaos it creates in the face of an officiating modern world.

Nigeria alone has 200+ languages & dialects, & it's been re-divided, from 12 to 19 states, to better deal w/ the different major groups. I wonder more & more how America holds together with such a mish-mash for a beginning.

I miss the desert so very much. I've only been out of it for a few weeks, but the 2 ½ wks I spent in the crossing was not enough. If the weather permitted, I'd go back as I came but the summers are relentless. In the Russia book he says: "As the sea moves us by its sameness so did the desert behind me by the constant reiteration of its single truth which was like a solitary phrase of illumination repeated endlessly in Buddhist prayer."

It opened up a corner in my heart to a deep respect for nature, so imperious, unassailable, dignified.

Esp. because now I've been hustled from one big town to the next, each more rowdy & tangled & dusty than the last. The Yoruba are traditionally city-town dwellers, and even the smallest size names on the map turn out to be bustling, vigorous, & exhausting places. They are the most artful & tenacious people when it comes to visiting & social intercoursing of all sorts. I've spent entire days going from one warm reception (always w/ food & beer; one feels quite ill after a few days of this) to another; long after I've been satiated with the laughter & noise and rituals of welcome they're still going strong, ready for another friend another beer another long-winded and funny story, usually told w/ the maximum # of appropriate proverbs.

And baby, if you & I thought that they can dance holes in the floors of N.Y. bars . . . .These people will go on and on and <u>on</u> without relaxing the incredible tempo & complexity of the dancing. Esp. the "highlife" dances of the east & midwest regions, where one piece lasts ½ hour at the least & a new one starts up promptly after. It's virtually a test of one's social fitness to last out until the end. And this gracefulness & verve is carried over into even the most ordinary moments, in the style w/ which they communicate, the gestures of their hands, the facial expressiveness, the sinuous & flexible bodies, and the harmony between physical type & style of dress.

It has always amazed & intrigued me, how perfect each culture's traditional dress is for them, their physique & spirit & landscape.

Shit I'm full of mosquito bites & find myself, when I awake in the middle of the night, with my hands frantically & persistently clawing at my calves & feet, where they seem the worst. In the rainy season now they'll get even more bold & bloodthirsty.

I made myself a very nice sleeveless blouse yesterday out of boredom—I try to brighten up the top ½ of me to make people overlook my ratty jean skirt, hairy legs & desert boots w/o socks. But there's no competing w/ the univ. women here who all do their damndest to be "Cosmo girls". Quite disconcerting to my cowgirl ways.

Really anxious to do some photographing but it would've been the most undiplomatic gesture this week, with the newspapers carrying daily exhortations to clean foreign espionage out of Nigeria, etc.

But I get so restless w/ just reading & smoking & talking & strolling & really need to keep up a regular (well, more or less) relationship w/ my camera.

There's one predominating image I have had so far of (Black)

Africa that I want somehow to express in photos—the particular sensuousness here, the open & vigorous quality of the human body; seeing such a large portion of the body uncovered is more remarkable to me from a culture where we so much contain & shape our bodies thru clothes. Here one is so aware of skin & motion & muscle & sweat, and yet if I try to get close shots of people in certain parts or poses they don't let me. The minute they see my camera they leap into a standard pose, smile, and then ask me to send them a copy. Somehow I have to outwit them. But it's tough—they're old hands with us travelers.

Hope your *joie d'étudier* is continuing, and that you are happy.

Love,

Su

Thirty-two men implicated in the coup were rounded up, and on March 11 they were executed by firing squad.

Dimka escaped at first but was apprehended later, and on May 15 he was executed.

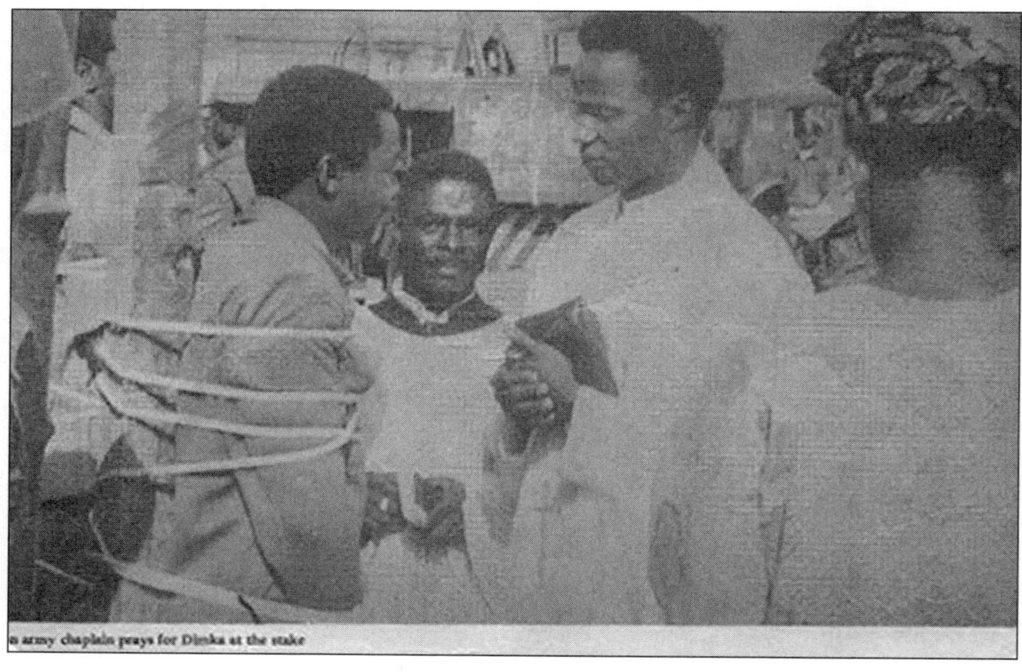

n army chaplain prays for Dimka at the stake

The caption reads "An army chaplain prays for Dimka at the stake."

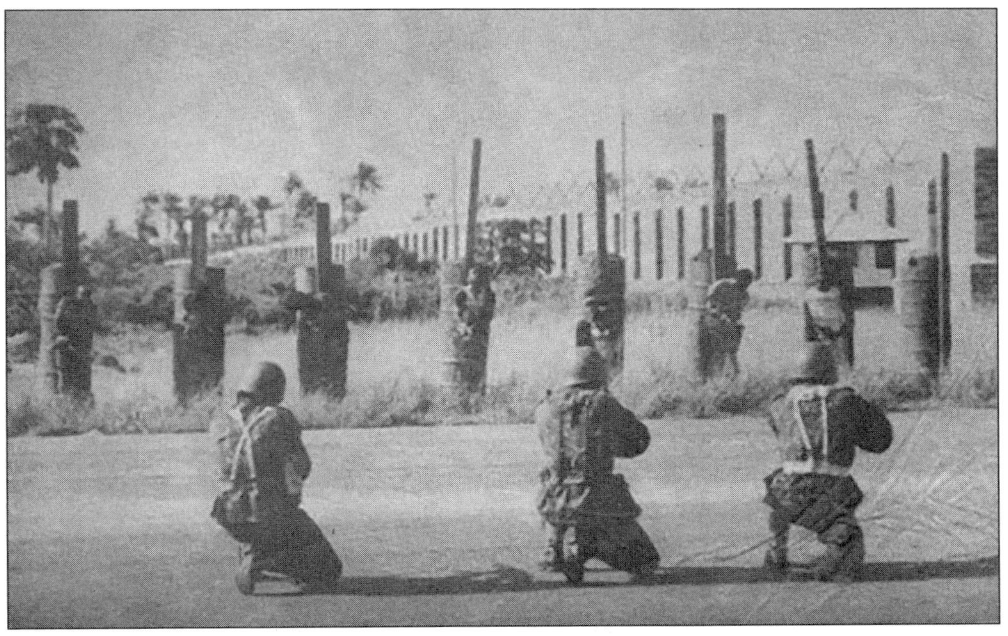

"All to the same end. They are lined up at the stake ready to be shot."

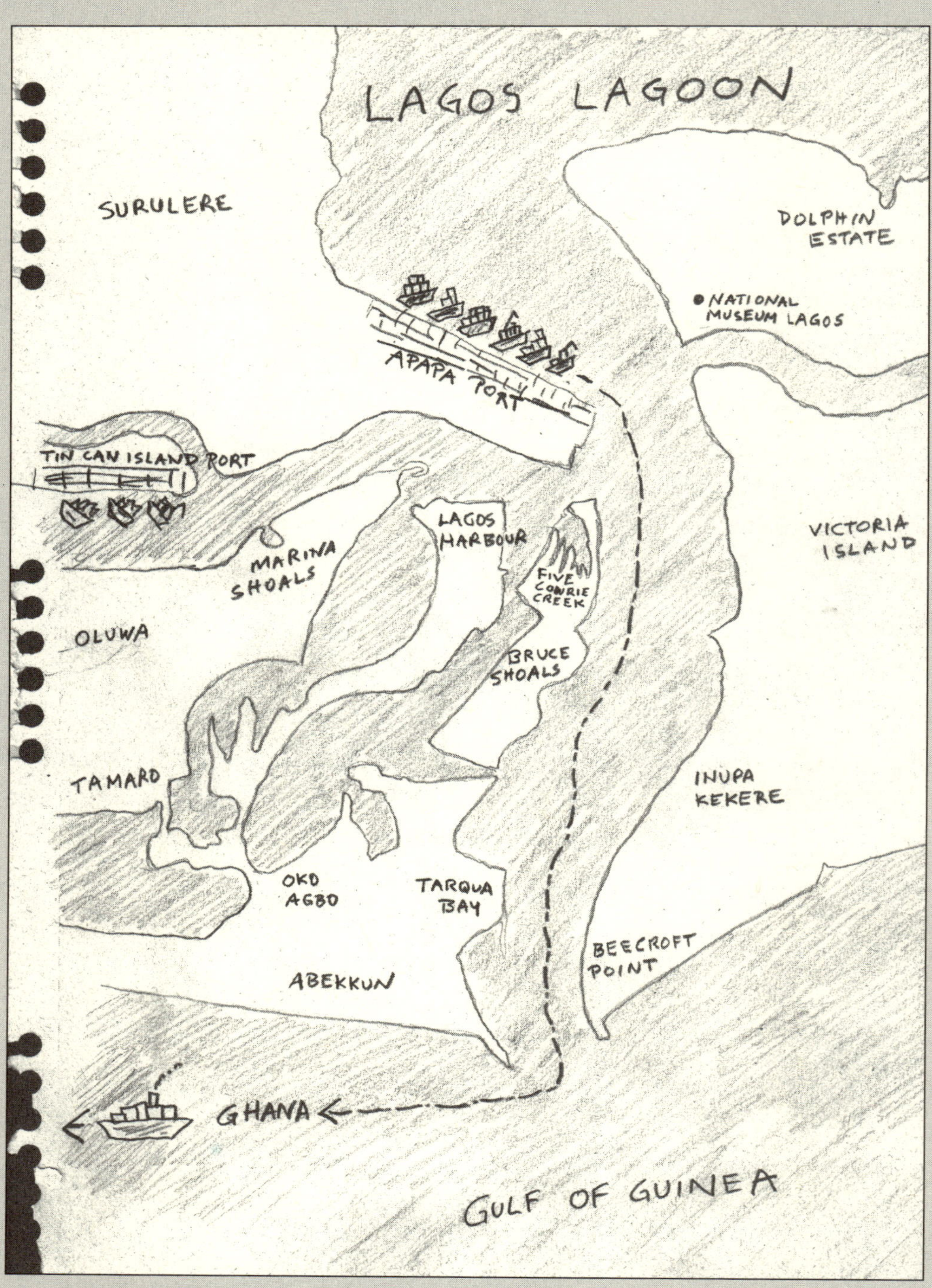
LAGOS LAGOON
SURULERE
DOLPHIN ESTATE
NATIONAL MUSEUM LAGOS
APAPA PORT
TIN CAN ISLAND PORT
LAGOS HARBOUR
MARINA SHOALS
FIVE COWRIE CREEK
VICTORIA ISLAND
OLUWA
BRUCE SHOALS
TAMARD
INUPA KEKERE
OKO AGBO
TARQUA BAY
BEECROFT POINT
ABEKKUN
GHANA
GULF OF GUINEA

CHAPTER FOURTEEN

The Escape, Thanks to Larry

All the borders had been closed after the coup. Maybe planes were flying but I couldn't afford that, so the only way to get out of the country was by hitching a ride on a cargo ship.

FEBRUARY 23

I had quite a new day going about the Lagos docks, getting a glimpse of the seaman's life. First stop, the Danish ship—Carlsberg lemon, gin and tonics, a raucous sit down with three corpulent officers and two others, all in shorts with paunches and pink pink cheeks from too much boozing out of boredom. They had a storehouse full of derogatory African jokes (for example, "dry them out and use them as wetsuits") which they apologized indirectly for by saying they were applied as well to Germans and Belgians!

On the German ship, the blond haired blue eyed sharp mouth couldn't believe that my mother was German. When I pressed him for a reason he shrugged and said, "Well, I suppose children have to do the opposite of their parents."—Meaning how could anyone of even the thinnest German spotless-and-in-order extraction come to such a dirty dirty country? I smiled to myself.

Ah but what a <u>lunch!</u> Brown bread, herring in mustard sauce, a new plate for each serving, smelly cheese, Carlsberg beer, pickled cukes, a white tablecloth.

And sailor lore. Such a world they inhabit. Just one more brotherhood. Women wireless operators are the one intrusion (and maids of course). When the conversation turned to children I could see most clearly what a life on the sea for months at a stretch means: Their young boys who don't want to really be with them when they come home on leave, all the Daddy tricks they use to get back into their children's good graces.

Such an edge of resignation as they spoke of it. And the look of pride, the wide happy eyes of the younger one who said he had his fifteen-year-old boy on a whole voyage once and how much fun they had.

But then the bitchiness about Africa started again and I even heard "nigger" once or twice which was <u>too</u> much, but just like yesterday when Henry [one of the American students at UNILAG] said that the folks in the remote villages on the Niger River (which he floated down with friends in leaking canoes, sick as all hell and freaked out) were the "bloody <u>stupidest</u> people he'd ever seen, but the happiest."—I click and grind and record and if it's necessary and/or useful I interject a, "Now, <u>really</u> . . . " but usually I sit and chew on it, the careless and unfounded words that spew from mouths (perhaps not so much from Henry but, e.g., these captains.) Gerd (one of the officers) did concede to the viability of the "witchdoctors" here as in Egypt 1,000 years ago or the Incas doing brain surgery in B.C. (which the Christians spent so much energy and blood destroying).

Oh . . . The dock workers unloading cement, endless awful broken bags of cement, the air heavy with its dust, a dense sweetish smell from it, the men stripped to shorts covered in a thick layer of gray powder, their dark lips and rings about the eyes giving them an unreal quality, remotely human—the dregs, really.

And then the American ship. . .with their Miller beer and Coke and eastern twang.

On the French ship, the Frenchman teaching himself bookbinding and looking glassy-eyed at the imitation Corots in his office, insisting that my trip was an empty dream, a delusion to think I could ever break through the surface and know the country. He also laughed when I said I studied African art—this is not art (Art) because it was done for a reason beyond Art—i.e. religion. Also got a visible thrill on arguing that all the shit in the British Museum was faked.
My my.

And then AH . . . .
Really AHHH . . . .An "I know I'm going to like this" ahh . . .
I met the cap'n of the Offin River ship from Ghana, and he was the same open gentle funny sort that Saaka is, and his friends, the two women who were in the office. And I was immediately reassured and relieved to think that I would be soon in a country with such people and get my distance from these wear and tear Yoruba.
And god how those women bitched about Lagos, how dirty it is, how clean Accra is. It's true when I see this city—to see the residences in Ikoyi for the moneyed (and formerly the British) and then the abject slums of the city proper; a mess, a damn mess, and the reason that I don't harp on the slovenly environment is that if I did I would depress myself too much and feel a desperate wish to escape it. So I just sit back and watch it and say, "don't ever forget this" and "wishing it away won't do a damn thing" and "you are not in Europe and cannot expect it to be like that."

So it's really a two-sided issue because (1) perhaps I do (I do) prefer the living conditions in America so I should admit that but (2) that doesn't mean that I have to use my system to color my observations of Africa. Because if I did I just couldn't survive here. One has to face these conditions as the present reality of Africa, not just a fluke or an aberration.
One of the women in the office was a riot. Her short (or as they would say here, small small) Afro, tiger print blouse, and her talk full of "right on's" and "shit, man" and how much she "digs American life." But very tough and I liked her style. I hope I get passage on the ship. Yaiee—I'm really excited now to be heading for Ghana.
So much for Murtala who so assiduously and heroically cleared the shameful ports . . . so that the papers report that there are only seventy ships . . . From four captains today who do know if anyone does, I heard that there are between 350–400 boats off shore. A-hey.

The government controls the press here, yes, but such a distortion is really out of hand.

FEBRUARY 24

And again today at the docks, stories of soldiers beating up "thieves" (layabouts) with belts and gun butts, and to see them strolling about in groups with the ubiquitous guns. The literally inescapable military presence is frightening, oppressive, annoying, ugly, provocative.

Saw a dayglo poster of "I am I and You are You" etc. with two blissed-out Blacks in bell bottoms reaching towards each other against a fuchsia sky.

The *oyibos* in downtown Lagos really make me understand why the Africans are so derisive and ambivalent about them/us—every blessed one of them was corpulent, pale, sweaty, their white hairy legs poking out of Bermuda shorts—but the paunch is really the telltale sign, like a neon Thanksgiving feast [1].

I'm worried. Today I ate a dirty carrot in the market. Teasing cholera is not funny.

(Written alongside that later . . .)

Nothing happened.

I've been meeting so many Nigerians who have a very nasty opinion of American "Negros": that they're violent and/or lazy, hostile, shiftless, etc.—I've heard it all before, from the same mythmakers who brought us the rhythmic Bushmen and a chicken in every pot.

Students here are held in such contempt by the outside, the city people. They're considered "opportunist," completely (and voluntarily) cut off from conditions beyond the campus. But then to hear the students talk of the manifold and mounting economic pressures on them, e.g., to educate their junior brothers and sisters, perhaps to build a house for the family, pay for a cousin's operation, another cousin's funeral *ad infinitum*, since they will be the one bright light of affluence in a huge extended family which is quite probably poor. They have a long-understood responsibility to their family first and foremost. Consequently, it's suicidal here to drop out—or even go traveling. It just isn't done; you'd have to go live in another country to escape the wrath!

What you hear as an *oyibo*:
In a singsong chanting child's voice: Hello funny looking stranger!
In a taunting perfumed voice: How d'y do my fine white Lady?
In the laugh and cackle of an old woman: Welcome daughter sister who dresses like us, marry my son.
With a spit and hiss: Go home, spy, with your money.

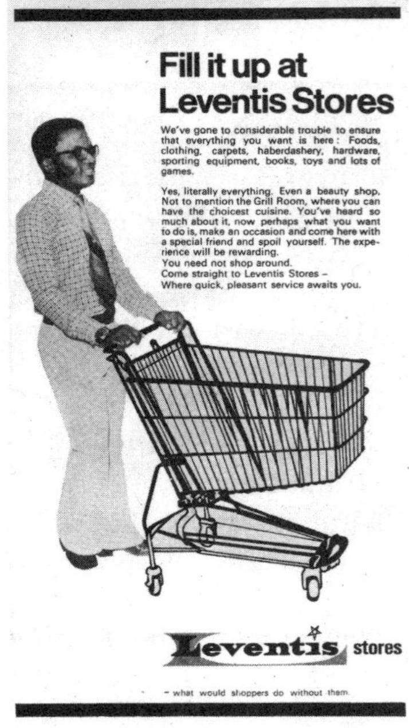

This is typical of the relative affluence here: Each time I go into a Leventis department store I mutter bitter nothings to myself about, "Oh these *oyibos* . . . they always want things like at home . . . air conditioning, pastries, imported everythings." But Leventis is the equivalent of less than a Woolworth's [69] at home. And here it's the house of dreams, of fluorescent light and plastic gadgets and new clothes and canned exotica.

It's difficult to imagine anyone here, any lifelong inhabitant of Lagos, cultivating a delicate spirit. Maybe a high-strung one, or a hyper-sensitive one, but not a calm spirit. The clamor and crash and shouts and dirt are everywhere: It isn't a city with a soul really—yes, it has a lot of character, but no grace. Just evidence of money, and of those without money. There's very little feel of it as an "African" city (whatever that may be), just of aspiring to European models, e.g., in the architecture.

The stadium is really a sight! The gateways are topped with twelve eagles stiff and haughty and sharp-featured but painted a silly red, and six monstrous bulky muscled horses, a flat silver, their balls jutting out, rearing up with their heads cocked at an uncomfortable and ungraceful angle. And the tree-shaded road facing the water lined with palatial spreads—pink stucco of course or light grey and white. As I walked along a long, striped fence marked by "Lagos House. Justice and Progress" I spotted three bald, stoned-out men (workers on the grounds) sitting amid some trees, one giving a fix to another.

A curious occurrence twice today in the busses as we were stuck in a go-slow. [70] People would call out derisive things to men they saw alongside the road taking a piss or a shit. The poor fellows would mask their shame and continue, but the crowd didn't let them off lightly.

FEBRUARY 25–29

I saw a reflective glass window today in Lagos and realized with a start that here one really never sees expanses of reflecting material, which in the states both makes me self-conscious but more importantly gives the street and crowds a double dimension, an added commotion and visual dialogue. It was fun watching people surreptitiously or quite proudly sneaking glances at themselves as they passed.

---

69 A classic "five-and-dime" store, ubiquitous back then, which closed its remaining stores in 1997.

70 Nigerian slang for a traffic jam. In a 2019 article about this problem, they said that a driver in LA spends an average of 128 hours per year in a car as compared to 1,516 hours for a driver in Lagos.

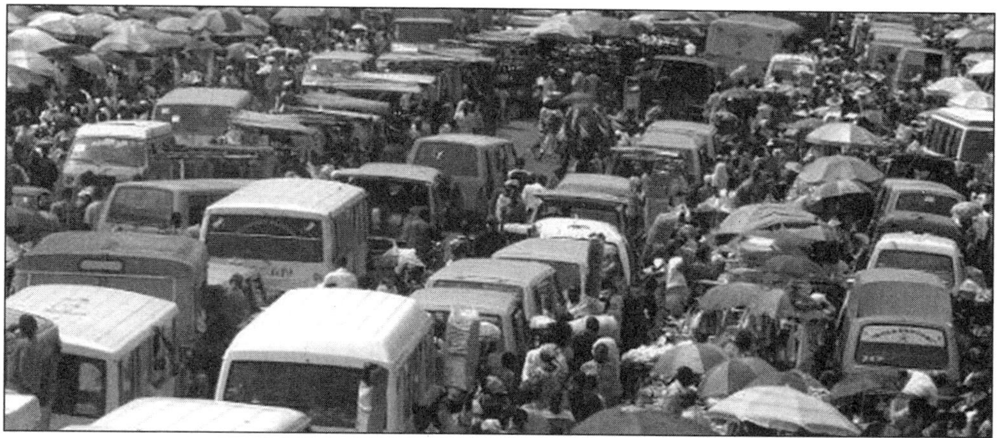

Only a vague chance of getting on the boat to Ghana, dammit, after two days of rushing about (well, at least rushing from one go-slow to the next!). I'm glad I'm only a visitor here, this city would set me off the edge in a short time, it's too brutal and blunt.

Saw three most amazing and disquieting girls yesterday sitting by the road with morning coffee and white bread, identical dresses all blackened from the waist down, filthy feet and hands, had a row of unidentifiable small bottles (shoe shine?)—but they, at probably fourteen or fifteen, had the eyes and voices of old women, even old men, and solid slender bodies, curveless, their mannerisms so clearly showing the hardship of their lives, the absence of comfort or protection or peace.

Billboards are really a blight in Nigeria, from the Salem-typed cigarette ads to Nivaquine with a gray and shriveled family suffering from malaria being revived to their yellowish-brown selves. The Venus de Milo pseudo-Black beauty, the Woman's Own iron tablets, Mr. Vigoron yellow and muscular, all those working milk-filled mothers who are advised to use Nido, those beauties who should bleach and cream and lose weight and gain weight. You may think you're beautiful but you're not until you've tried . . . .

Stuck on this campus, so I figured I might as well check out some classes, but was so infuriated at one of Mary's the other night. A really idiotic lecturer who couldn't keep the attention of the students. Upon our entering the class, a giggling boy hissed "CIA" and everyone took up the call, whistling and laughing and hissing at us. Throughout the 45 minutes they threw paper airplanes, spitballs, and then

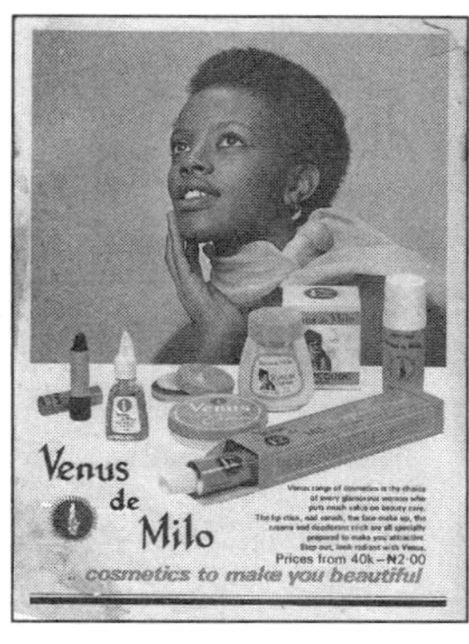

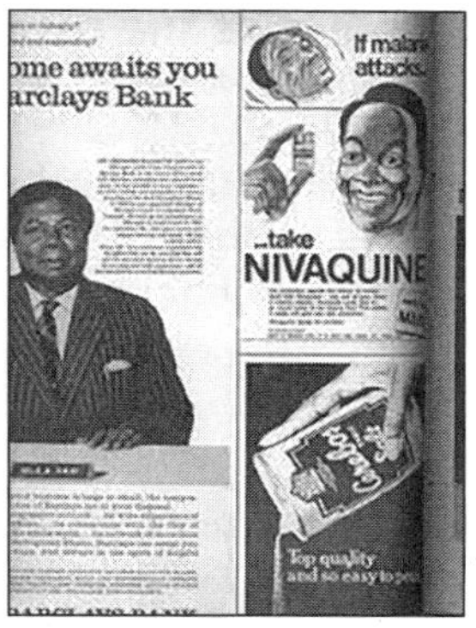

some of them conspicuously left the class while others kept on making a hissing noise. But amidst these politicos who are so keen on the CIA they sat reading "Lagos Weekend," which is nothing more than a schlocky magazine with pin-up style photos of white women who they inspected and compared and drooled over. If they think they're on the right road because they can muster hostility towards such an obvious target (the CIA) without cleansing themselves of what I consider the more insidious disease, namely the "Weekend" stuff and the whole money-trip they're into here, they'll never get out of the grip of this thing which they claim to hate.

In addition to which this lousy lecturer was trying to make a case that divisiveness and chaos in Nigeria/Africa was not the result of tribalism but of international intrigue. He didn't speak with an ounce of conviction and kept insisting that they substantiate their exam essays with facts, which he clearly wasn't doing in his own lecture.

I'm all for exposing the machinations of international capitalism, but for Christ's sake, a place like Nigeria has been in the competition for long enough that some of the present inequality and grossly inadequate distribution of wealth has to be criticized as coming from inside.

Last night there were four women from the dorm standing in a tight group in animated talk interspersed with harsh laughter, and shimmying to some love song, and a lot of heads nodding in wry agreement with a story that one woman was telling—after a good ten minutes of it, getting more heated and apparently vexing (in Yoruba), they burst out, "God, men are dangerous. They're so *deceitful*. Why do they have to lie so much and give a sweet mouth with sugar words?"

The hilarity and furor were broken up due to the lateness of the hour: They all went their separate ways to get painted jeweled pressed sleeked artificed-up to go to a party and deceive those deceitful boys.

I'm really coming to dislike the insincerity here in regard to visits, the sweet gracious voice which says, "Oh I'll be sure to drop by tomorrow and see you..." (flashy smile warm handshake twinkle in the eye) and then I never see them again.

Started to read *Inside the Third Reich*: His mania with monumental architecture, gross proportions; the obsequious adulation by his followers; even an educated man like Albert Speer chose to ignore the sick, tyrannical side of Hitler in order to further his architectural career. The young being brought up in an atmosphere of the conservative monarchy of the Weimar Republic, taught to accept rather than question the political situation, turned to Hitler out of desperation. Germany in the early 30s was in a terrible plight.

Yesterday I was followed to the library by the same strange man who nudged me in the store; he raced up to me on the stairs, but when I asked him why he was

Another page from the UNILAG student paper *The Eye*

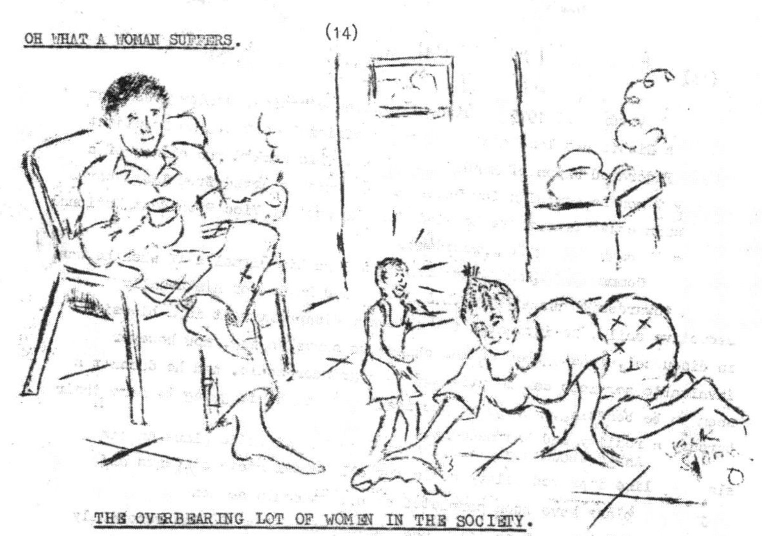

THE OVERBEARING LOT OF WOMEN IN THE SOCIETY.

Being a member of any sex has it's own problems and worries,so don't think i am lamenting coz i have burden to bear,but by being born a woman you automatically inherit a more than proportonate share of the overall problem of mankind. I

Nature has so made it that,from the sexual union of both sexes emergies a child. But it is the woman that bears most of the problems. She has the child inside her 9 months and after the horrors that usually accompany childbearing,feeds and takes care of the young child until it is independent,all the time bossy man will be lording it over her,feeling unconcerned,and ever ready to rod any stray female The woman is not even compenseted,rather the child is taken away from her, for it must bear the surname of his father. Yes, it belongs to man who knows nothing of the horrors child delivering other than just pouring and pouring with his ever ready rod.

THE BIBLE EVEN LENDS A HAND.

The Bible even lends a hand in this seemingly universal conspiracy against womanhood. Woman is said to have been created from one rib off man,(though i am yet to see a man with one rib short). She is reputed to have been the cause of his downfall, accepting the forbidden fruit from the Devil and given it in turn to man. The sins of man had thus been attributed in the first cause to woman. Even our very appellation bears this curse. Woman is said to have been coined from the words WOE - TO - MAN, that is ever woman was given to man by God, she had been a curse to him. Also, the word FEMALE, IS said to have been coined from the words INFERIOR - TO - MAN.

CONTINUED ON PAGE (15)

following me he protested and went on ahead of me. A few minutes later he found me in the stacks and with a hunted, apologetic look in his eyes and a trembling mouth he said, "I'm sorry if I caused you any trouble but . . . " "Then why are you following me?" "Because you're so beautiful." Then he left as quietly as he came.

I think I can't stand the noise and dirt much longer.

THE FIRST OF TWO LETTERS FROM MARY EVENSON:

24/7/76
Sue,
How are you doing? I've been meaning to write for some time but you know how it goes, you keep saying I'll do it tomorrow until you realize that tomorrow was a month ago. I went to Ghana in April and took some of your suggestions though I had a place to stay. I met some people who came through Lagos, a married couple both clinical psychologists who now have a job at Accra's Legon University.
I want to visit them in August or September. Have plans to stay in Lagos for 1 more semester (until December). I'm staying with Lynn and Onuora the couple Carol stayed with. They are excellent people and really make me feel at home here. Onuora will be leaving for the U.S. (Madison) then on to S.E. Asia, he will be gone 3 months so Lynn and I will be "bach'ing it".
I traveled to the north for 2 weeks, stayed in Zaria and Jos and saw Kano and Kaduna for a day. I've been invited back to Jos and hope to fly there at the end of August. Went by road last time but found that return flight is about the same as by road (with stop offs). I went with a classmate and we went to his village in Benue State for 3 days. Couldn't believe how much difference there was between Tony's (Ibo) village and Adem's (Idoma) village. It's a whole different world and they are only about 8–10 hrs. from each other. The personalities, lifestyle, eating habits & food and child raising practices differed especially. Idoma women ran their own farms and seemed much more independent than the Ibo women. Saw a traditional market which was very different also. Many more crafts, etc. After a long search in Lagos I located 2 yds. of the Adire material you requested. Visited about 20–25 market stalls before I got it . . . but I got it. Will be sending to Madison with Onuora or bringing it in January, so will get it to you then. Will be at school in Madison 2nd semester and will surely visit my brother in Chicago at some point. If you want I can send it but at the cost and risk of loss I would rather wait. Write and let me know what you are into these days.
A friend always,
Mary
M. Evenson
c/o Lynn Nwuneli
Dept. of English, University of Lagos, Akoka, Nigeria

MARCH 1

I am in a state of bliss—at least as much as is possible this side of the ocean. After a wretched weekend with a cold cough, continuous headache, too many visitors, nightmares about Mom and go-slows and baby and Pete and constant worries about getting the hell out of this stinking depressing city, I spent two hours in a go-slow to the port and am now safely and irretrievably ensconced on the Offin River ship with my own cabin [2]. However, it means doing some amount of work, and being tits and ass: It means typing, which I don't do very well. But considering that it's two nights and two days and about 250 miles, not bad!

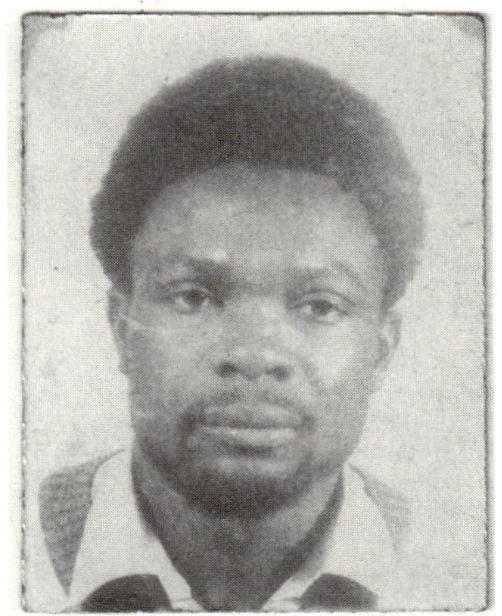

I was indeed lucky to get passage, and it was mainly due to the persuasive skill of the second captain, Larry Dzameh, pictured here.

An occurrence this bleak morning on my way to the ship struck me as typifying my experience here and the certain twist of the Nigerian mind: I arrived at Yaba [71] coughing, a slick layer of sweat over my face and back, the usual a.m. hordes and busses all shouting and spitting smoke. I asked a briefcased fellow the way to the bus that went to the port. After a moment's pause he directed me to walk one mile down a certain road to a big

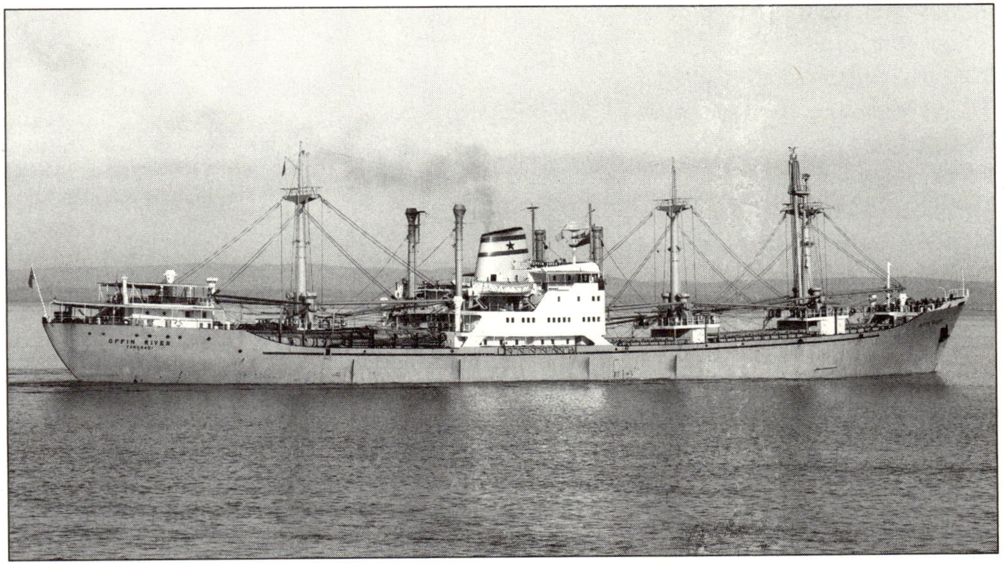

The *Offin River* arriving at Avonmouth, England on March 2, 1974 [3].

71 A suburban area of Lagos.

junction which I did grudgingly, suspiciously, hotly. Then another directive later from someone else to go a further third of a mile. At hot-dust-sweat-sag last, a bus careened in shouting, “Wharf!” I crashed on, shoving aside pregnant and old indiscriminately and sure enough . . . He grinned up at me sheepishly and slyly, and muttered something about, “Ah good, you found the stop.” I asked him in a stupor whether he’d gotten the bus at Yaba. Of course he did. Why ask? Why try to understand?
Patience pays. Now I’m really beginning to understand or experience what people mean when they say that if you travel in Africa sometimes you have to sit in the most hellish place for weeks before moving out. Two weeks plus in Lagos, a city I didn’t even want to stop in. My stay with Mary and Ivan was nice, and I got a good look at the students here (who don’t command much respect, I’m afraid) and I did a hell of a lot of reading, but it’s been such a nebulous, flat period. Feeling listless, in synthetic rooms, harsh music, slow conversation, slower walking, tossing and scratching and sweating nights, fitful dreams.
I’ve been eating less, took in my skirt, with my hair shorter, and the back of my neck and shoulders is a deep brown; I’ll be all patchwork when I get home!

They aren’t leaving for a few days, so when some of the guys go into Lagos they take me along. Don’t want to just sit and wait on this ship all day, and I wonder about that typing they said I would have to do as barter, there doesn’t seem much work. . . .

This morning I saw a medicine man with a wonderful sign, numbered from 56–82 with such things as (*all direct as printed*)
To cure pensular
To get luck of moon
To make wife conceive
To get lorry to collect passenger
To hunter from head of baby
To get see your star
To sweet woman
To preven germs from eating
To make wife obedience

And saw a funny place today: “Afro Ringo Star Photo Studio,” hand-painted signs of Black hip cats and chicks with shades and bells and snapping fingers and platforms and groovy words and bold colors.
Been spending too much. $200 month is average. $6.60/day is not necessary—first, all this treat food and secondly, books and sending packages. Since I live in houses for nothing I shouldn’t be having such a high average (especially since I don’t buy many gifts).
This month, $150 or <u>less</u>. No more five Cokes a day bullshit. [72]

72 In 2024, $200=$1,135, $6.60=$37.50, $150=$851

Down at the port, those two funny Americans, pa and son, are still here pacing the docks looking for their saving vessel to South Africa; the boy is really spaced out but also funny, alert, like young boys are, as if it's all a game just tripping around the world, he's been at it probably (to guess his age) since he was twelve or thirteen.

A LETTER FROM MY MOTHER:

Dear su,
Enclosed Xerox of policy. I wonder if this will get to you. I have been sending letters to Niger c/o Embassy wherever that might be, and also Nigeria, hoping something will get through. The State Dept. mailed a list with addresses, some full, some only showing the country—it's maddening that there is no way to get in touch. Letters, postcards from Denmark, Algeria and Niger and packages with books, postcards – posters, etc. all arrived, all immensely appreciated, and very interesting to say the least. I admire you for your stamina, your guts, I have written about it in my other letter. I envy you your youth [73] and your strength and I know that you are also as filled with anxieties as any other human being.

You are constantly on my mind and that is not an exaggeration. That is true of Pete, who misses you and who tore open the package from Nigeria wondering if it contained some of the "promised" comics. He is working on a comic book together with a friend of his. His drawings are remarkable and I told him that we should go one of these days to the Art Inst. to find out about their new school. Wing [74] and I keep in touch about you—she calls me and I call her when we get something from you and Omi [75] too called the other day and also wrote with great admiration. God, stay well and don't let anything happen to you.

It was reassuring how sensible you are in reading your account of the VW truck w/ Jap and Tuna[76]—and there is no reason to think that you will act any other way in the future. Why does one not think of sending you off with two cameras? Or two lenses? What can one do? It is plain madness to think that you might end up not being able to take any pics.

The days pass here, white with snow, blinding bright sun, or bitter cold and windy—which left me with raw and sometimes swollen eyes just walking to 55th. The concerts are there, also the ballets now, so are the exhibits—wrote about one, now comes the French. And the books. Otto's *Going Crazy* is out with excellent reviews.

73 She was fifty-six at the time.

74 The nickname for my sister Maria.

75 The nickname for Lenore Pelham Friedrich, my paternal grandmother.

76 She calls him Tuna; I call him Lere. I no longer know if he had two names or not.

> Tilli [77] got a complimentary copy, this time I got none, so I am going to spend some money and buy it myself.
> I might discover myself in it. As I do feel that there is often a strange madness in me, caused by frustrations which I don't seem to be able to control. Or get over with - conquer, whichever. But we are living in a mad world and reading the paper today about the possibilities of a war between Algeria and Morocco, the hellish situation in Lebanon, the other pure hell of Ireland—the constant bickering of the Middle East countries—who could be called sane? And no matter how much we read, how much we talk and fight against it, the corruption is everywhere and yet, maybe in another 50 or 100 years the constant, even stream of attention by only a fragment of our society might bring eventually a change for the better.
> [. . .]
> And so I wonder where you are now and what has happened since you last wrote—and whether you will be in Lagos waiting for this letter. Do write as soon as you get it and also where I can send my next letter and if you need anything (money?) any possibility to mail c/o American Express?
> Maria has three more lectures to go. So far all went well, but she is very tired. She wondered if you were going to be home for her graduation and I said, that I thought you were going to stay much longer abroad. Am I mistaken? Weren't you thinking of a year or so? Although I can't imagine you could remain that long with the little money you have.
> I doubt I will move in May from here.
> [. . .]
> At any rate, I would always leave information for you "on time" or just remember that your father is a permanent resident in Chicago, that I have friends whom you know and who would know where you could reach me. Your things will be with me, so don't worry. Take care, keep ears, eyes open and steady and think of your health. We love you and we miss you and we admire you.
> Mom
> Pete's at a hockey game w/ friends

God I miss my brother, I think of his nice young face and the day I saw him selling papers at the newsstand in a red and blue shirt with white collar looking so Lab School-y and teenaged and realizing he was growing and creating his life and I just come and go through it infrequently. Mom writes that he misses me too. I'll have to find him some good gift, but what he seems to want most are comix! And when I see him be so nervous and high-strung I see Mom in him and I see us in him, and realize the raging energy that's always underneath my mother, like she's sitting on a powder keg of dreams and ideas. I shook when I read her letter and she said

77 Tilli is one of my father's sisters. Otto was her brother.

she was going to read Otto's book about craziness and "maybe find myself in it"—of course she can swim 2 ½ miles a day and bike to work and clean clean and etc. galore because there's so much that's probably not being channeled to her satisfaction—but I need her to be real to me, I need to feel her a part of me more than before, I can't keep doing what I used to do for the sake of my "freedom," to pretend that she didn't have any hold over me, trying to forget her or diminish her. I think if I let myself see her more clearly I'll learn to see others more readily also.

Sensually, Nigeria is beans, *dodo* and *pepe*[78], Sunny Ade's sweet boy voice, bus fumes, lethargy, dirt, skin, money.

MARCH 2

I think my "work" on the ship is a put-on. In this air-conditioned cabin, just given a sumptuous lunch, now I'm headed back to Lagos, the man says it's "no problem"—hmm.

Yesterday a curious shy smiling fellow was on a boat with me across the bay. He followed me into Leventis and after a few moments took me aside and asked me for 20 *kobo*, then reappeared a few minutes later with a photo of himself on which he wrote his address, writing Lagos three times (?); today he came to see me, asking if I could give him a job as a steward. I had to tell him to his dismay that I was only a passenger and didn't have any pull in the shipping agencies. Giving up that line of attack he asked me for my shirt. I declined and tried not to laugh; then I realized how I must appear to some people here: this white madame traveling by sea along the coast of Africa—

Apparently the Nigerian crews are very lazy, sometimes it takes weeks to load a ship, while the Jap and Danish do it in three to six days. Muscles here, the sweat glistening, down in the smelly hatch with tons of cocoa and salt. Some of the men with leather *gris-gris*[79] and armbands, the massive steel beams dangerously suspended midair above a group of workers—sometimes the cables break. They tell me about the immensity of it all, the impersonal scurrying around, shifting weight, displacing and replacing tonnage. The hoarse shouts and the bodies, the bodies so lean, so underfed, and their overworked nights in the dust, washing up from the lagoon water, filthy. The continual stream of activity—or appearance of activity: There's as much sitting about and bullshitting as there is actual work done—the industrial side of life, the stuff that makes our stomachs and our cities big.

But shit I am now going thru white face withdrawal again, the damnably inevitable human reaction to minority status—when someone today said, "Oh, you're the only white girl on board?" I just could think, why must I be always reminded of my aloneness? Yet it's hard to feel I've been away from Chicago for four months already.

---

78 Dodo are (delicious!) fried plantains; pepe is pepper stew.

79 A talisman, voodoo charm, spell, or incantation believed capable of warding off evil and bringing good luck to oneself.

I swear, a boy who passed me at the wharf today had a head like a Benin bronze—flawless.

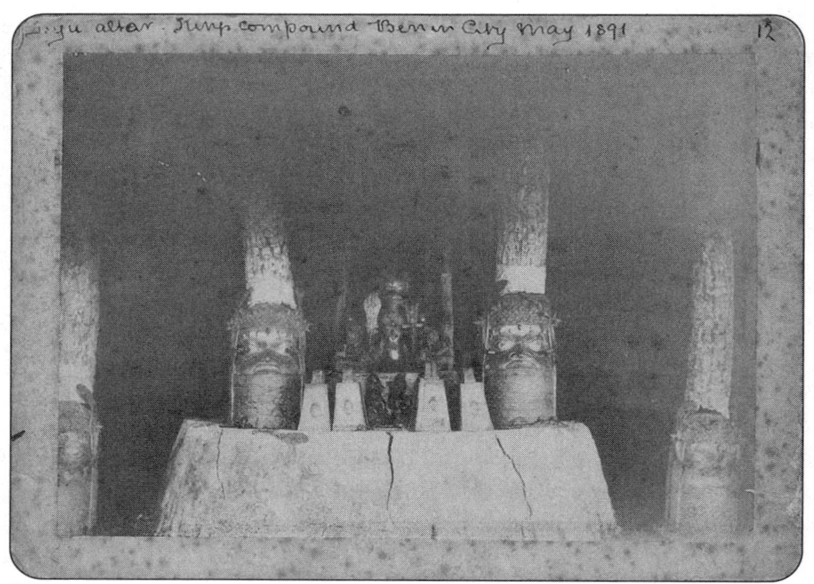

Earliest known photograph of the oba's compound in Benin City, May 1891.

Today to the Nigerian Museum, [80] a proud Akwanshi stone figure in front, open airy rooms, lots of funny mistakes on the cards, and both a thrill at finally seeing the pieces I'd read about in college, and a restoring calm at not having pursued my African art studies—e.g., the brass cup with the cast twisted rope handle that I so clearly remember admiring, really admiring, when I first read the article about its discovery at Ekpu (?), along with the encrusted bronze sea shell with the miniature leopard on top. Now, to see them so small so oxidized so much less significant and handsome than I made them up to be, I see how I couldn't have been entirely sincere or devoted to such studies (despite my one-time fantasies about doing art historical digs here in my khakis, etc.). But the real kick was the Benin amazon sister, arm outstretched. Described as "not done in the style of the region"—her eyes were even *more* fierce and protruding, that tough belly, brazen breasts with almost aggressive nipples, but she wasn't on the stand with the bow and arrow as pictured in the art history book. And the Ogboni witch, the horned oh *so* fierce and unequivocating madame, sitting more than upright, knees out, clitoris prominent, bulging eyes, about two feet tall, head at least half of it. And a no-joking mouth. She had religious, political and judicial power, was a mediator between king and council, earth worshippers.

80 The Nigerian National Museum, also known as the National Museum of Lagos, was founded in 1957 by K.C. Murray, who was referenced in Chapter 10 as the founder of the Ife Museum. See [4] for many more details about the British pillaging of Nigerian artworks and their later fate.

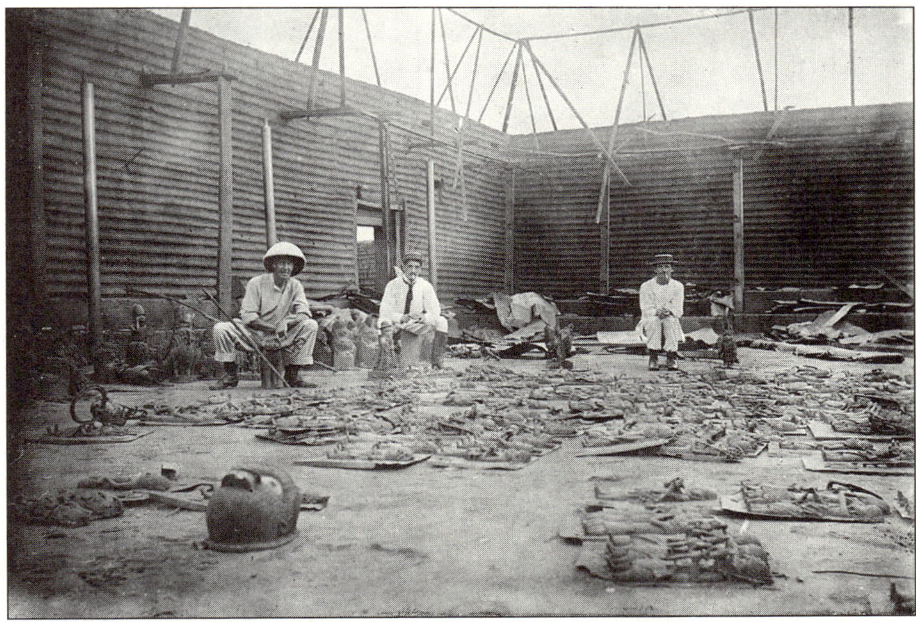

Interior of the oba's compound burned during siege of Benin City, with bronze plaques in the foreground and three British soldiers of the Benin Punitive Expedition. Photograph by Reginald Granville.

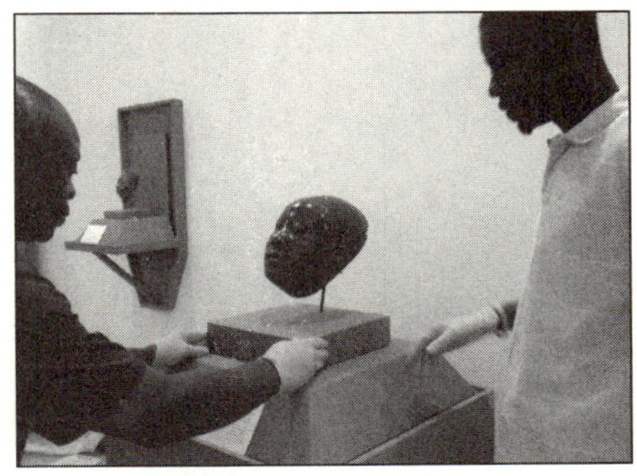

In one display of "Stone Age axes" I saw examples which looked familiar . . . Ah yes, I'd seen a boy chopping wood with one the other day.

The leopard jars were quite handsome, elegant, well-crafted, but I am tiring of the Benin chief chief always chief plaques except one curious ring piece with a chief with obviously female breasts and female musicians behind, and a cool cruddy ivory lady with a big pancake mouth, well-worn pubis, stout breasts.

The time spent watching Nigerian faces so sculpted and (with what we consider) "exaggerated" features gives me a greater feeling for these masks and figures, and e.g., the massive Yoruba Egba (?) mask,[81] massive with the mother triumphal, severe, absolutely alive, her two children perched on each knee, one hand on her breast staring out just as the babies do in busses and lorries from their mother's back sling, and her breasts, it was like live flesh, soft, full, large—after the women I've seen these few months, it all makes a lot of sense and joy.

81 It's Epa, not Egba, and the one pictured on the next page is in the Toledo Museum of Art.

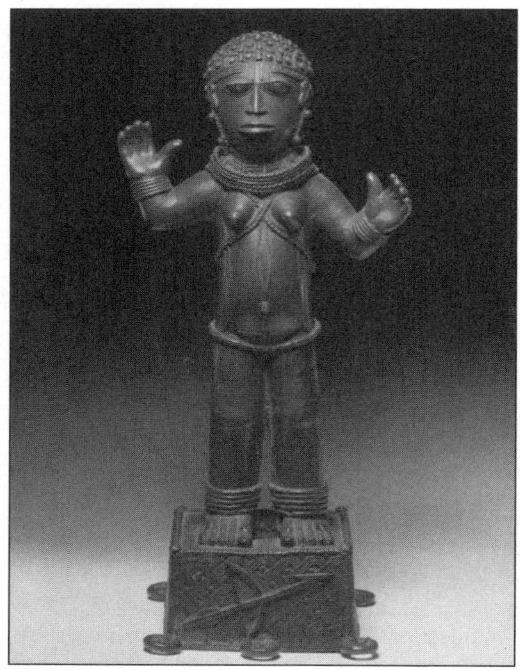

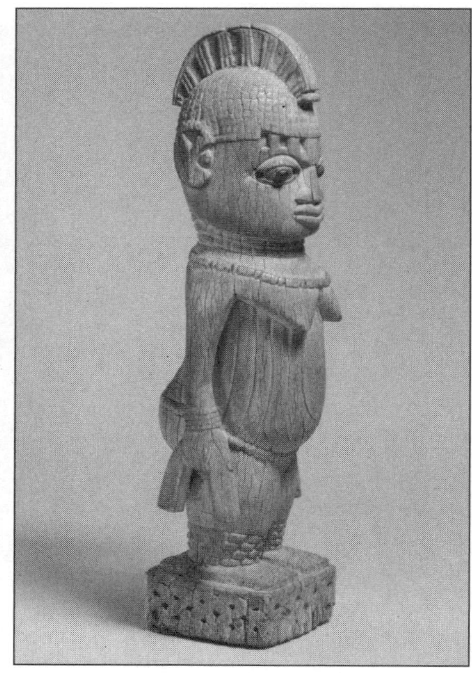

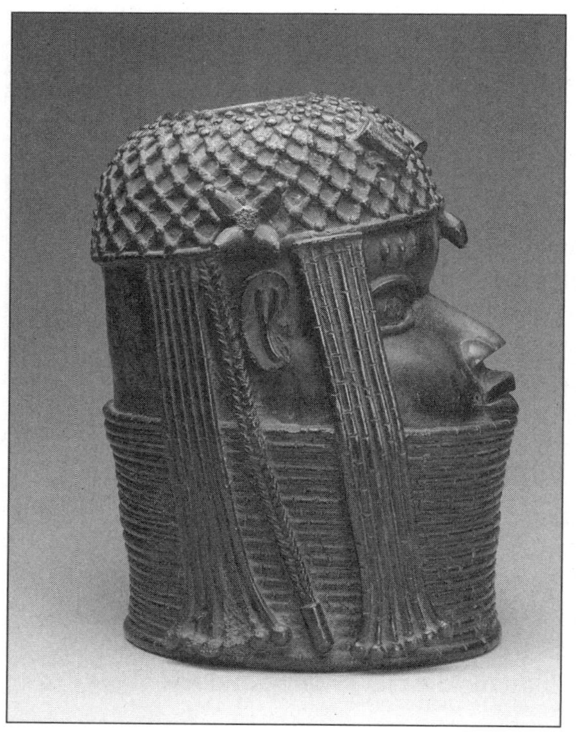

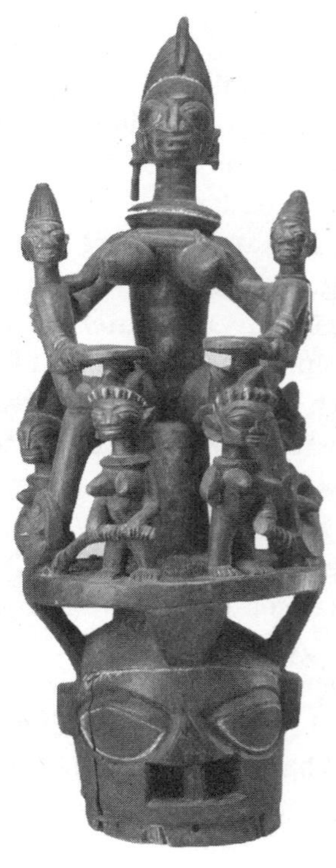

This head of an oba has been stolen twice [5].

Bought *Claudine Married* today. Shows how hard up I am, right? The back reads (of course), "What happens when a young wife falls passionately and hopelessly in love with another woman? *The Well of Loneliness* looks reassuringly English by comparison."—I swore after *The Pure and the Impure* that I was through with Colette insofar as gay lit went, but shit, it's better than the others on offer: a Nick Carter or *Teach Yourself Mechanics*.

So it seems the francophone countries still hum the Marseillaise . . . and French officers run the Ivory Coast military.

It's a classic shit being a white woman here; most of the time I'm either treated with uncalled-for contempt/fear or with an excess of sweetness, neither of which makes me in the least bit interested in talking to the person. But it's the inescapable condition of travel like this that 89% of my contacts are with single men. I keep my private world to myself and carry on with talk of agriculture and the condition of the roads and the quality of Nigerian beer; sometimes we dance. Not often. Their hips have a lot of elastic and they snap always in the general area of my thighs . . . but the music is the sort to send young blood cruising and your legs twitching.

Ooh I'm <u>stuffed</u> after two full good meals on this ship!

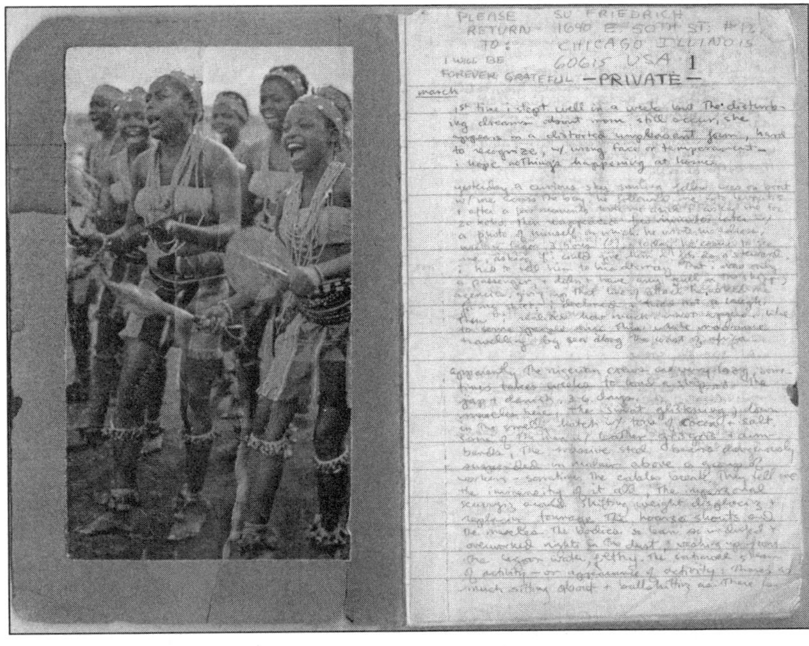

PLEASE RETURN TO: SU FRIEDRICH
1640 E 50TH ST #12
CHICAGO ILLINOIS
60615 USA
I WILL BE FOREVER GRATEFUL
1
—PRIVATE—

The beginning of the third journal.

MARCH 3–5

First time I slept well in a week but the disturbing dreams about Mom still occur, she appears in a distorted unpleasant form, hard to recognize, with wrong face or temperament—I hope nothing's happening at home.

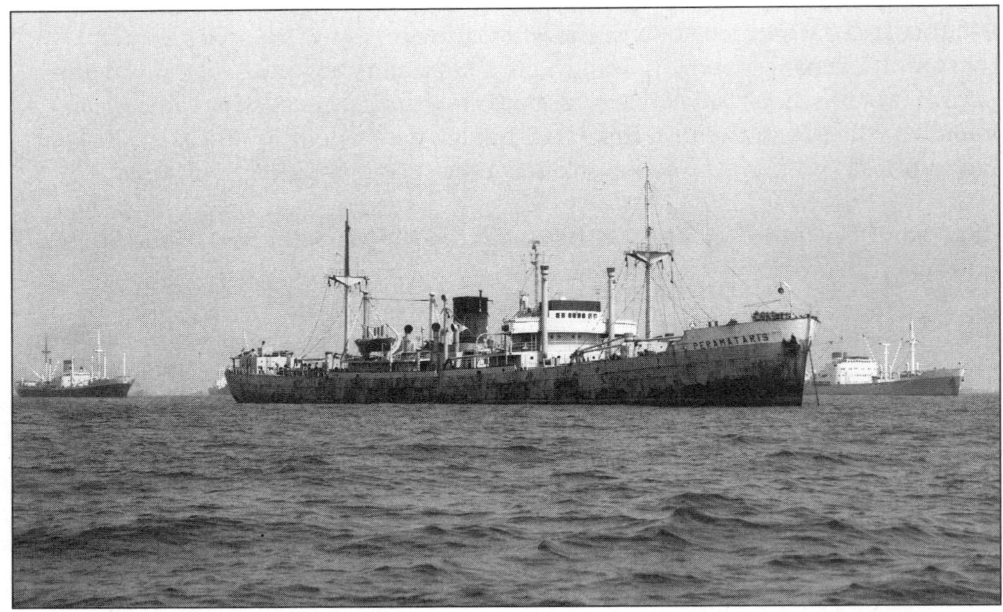

Photo by Malcolm Cranfield taken on January 1, 1976 showing several of the hundreds of ships anchored outside the port of Lagos.

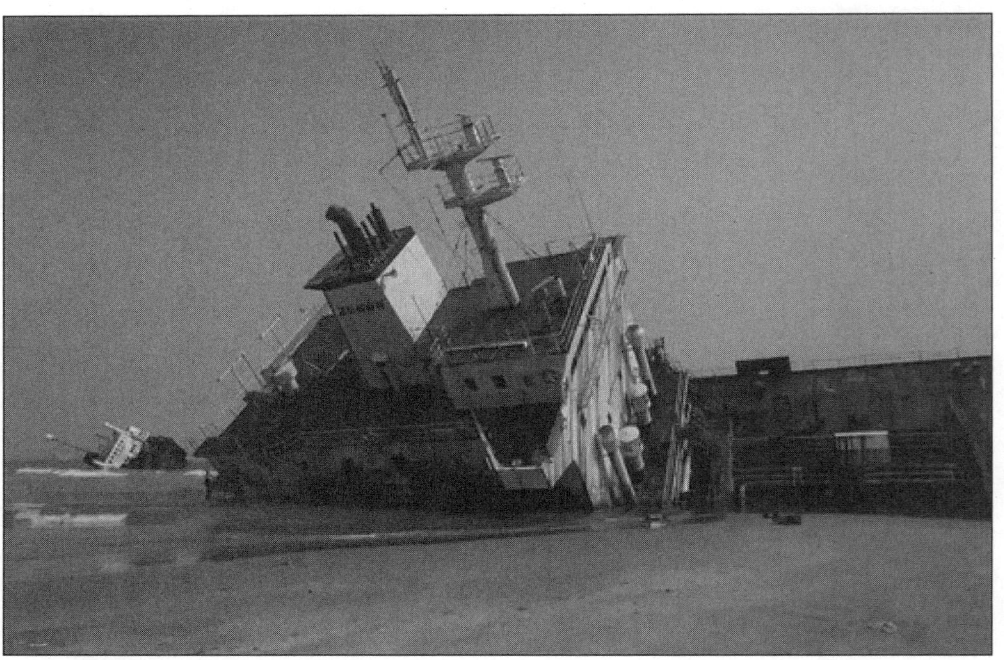

A recent picture showing two of the many ships that have washed up since then.

The ocean is reviving the feelings I had in the desert—it's bliss to be far from the madding crowd.
This boat is 460' long, goes 13 mph, and serves good meals.
If Ghanaians wanted to prove their hospitality they couldn't have surpassed this gesture, a free boat trip with meals and friendly crew.

But wow! Now I can see what those other captains were telling me about all the ships anchored out at sea! It's unbelievable, and all due to corruption... [6]

Oh god the specter of go-slows is beginning to haunt me . . . I'm in a water-bound one now, dazzled dangling outside the port of Tema counting minutes counting waves counting blazes of sunlight and beads of sweat.
I've sent this letter off to Mimi and there's no turning back—it satisfied me to write it, to see my feelings for and impressions of her really laid out straight and clean, but every day brings reconsiderations of "my nature."

> **PART OF A LETTER TO MIMI:**
>
> If all that these seamen have to say of Ghana is true, it promises to be as tidy as a Buddhist monastery. They wrinkle their noses at the "dirty Nigerians."
> The night is coming over the sea, we rock gently, waiting now one day, two days, to enter the port of Ghana. It has given me time to be silent.
> And be damned here I sit thinking of your carefully-tended box collection, funky rhumba with the glazed eyes, sleeping bag always slumming off your bed, some hot saxophone player (whose name I never remember . . .) edging your nerves, those flat finger-tips, and some rapid-fire conversation purely for the pleasure of conversing . . .
> It's what comes from being far away but never too far.
> To sign "with love" would be a bit redundant.
> Su

Well, my boat trip was indeed memorable, but not so much for the passage as for the waiting in Tema. After the first rush of furtive hellos and soft glances from so many of the crew, I got to talking with and made good friends with a few of them: The sweet-eyed, leopard-eyed John, remotely like John Flynn. And Larry, so nervous and self-effacing and over-eager to please, laughing too much, peeping in or around at odd moments to check on me; and Otis [Domkor], with the sweetest eyes, sort of witchy eyes, he could be soft and almost childlike and then get tight and witty and cool, and had a fine face, a nicely organized small body and was a real rascal—sired four babies—all with young girls. First time when he was seventeen, he's now twenty-five with a seventeen-year-old girlfriend who he claims he's going to force to have an abortion (?). At first he played up to me and then just

treated me as a friend, no nookie no tension. And Manny the engineer reading *The Pickwick Papers* and a teetotaler (he drinks a lot of tea) with his tape of *How Long Has This Been Goin' On?* which made my palms sweat and head (or heart?) spin.
Otis, when proudly recounting his captivations and impregnations of virgin sweets said, "See, Black girls can't stay away like white girls can. It's really easy to convince Black girls to be a lover. We Blacks don't stay separate so much like you do." He told me a white prostitute in Accra is "very expensive. $6." [82]
And from Larry, "See, these Americans, they're very very clever, they come to Tema (referring to the Kaiser Aluminum plant there) and build a big aluminum plant and tell us our bauxite is flawed and they bring their American-mined bauxite here to be processed with cheap labor. Now others tell us we have the finest grade bauxite in probably the whole world, so we're forcing the Americans to use ours."

THE FIRST OF FOUR LETTERS FROM LARRY DZAMEH: [83]

If you'll reply before 1st week in July then use this address
M.V Offin River B.N.L.
c/o Bahr Behrend & Co. Ltd
32–35 Duke's Place
London ECSA 7LR
Avonmouth-Bristol
U.K.
14th June 1976

Hi Su,
Hope you are back home and trying to put things in place. Also I guess you haven't missed your bicentennial celebration. It would have been a great miss, if you did, for we might not live to celebrate the tricentennial.
How was your sister's graduation; you remember we talked about it. You had a nice celebration, ain't it? Would you mind telling me about your bicycle. Is it still in good condition? Hope your brother took your advice and never used it in the winter.
I have been long wishing to write, but I feared you've not returned home yet. When did you arrive home? A happy reunion with your mom and dad. Hope your mom ain't talking or complaining about you smoking, which developed while you were in Africa.

Su, can you guess who is writing this letter? Let me lead you a little. You could remember when you made your trip from Lagos to Tema-Ghana on our ship. I took to you just on seeing you for the first time but could not see you to Accra because of the nature of my work. On arrival in Tema I gave you something which you rejected, but I talked you into taking it. You promised

82 In 2024, $6 = $34.

83 Larry Dzameh is a complicated part of my story. See [7] for more details.

visiting Kpandu (where I come from) when cruising on the Volta Lake, which you did. I directed you to see my sister at Kpandu Secondary School for assistance and guidance. My brother Moore wrote to me, that you were there, and hope you never complained to me.
How was your stay in Kpandu? [84] You never encountered any trouble, I think so. Su, you know I was in love the moment you came on the ship? Maybe you didn't realize it. I was a bit scared because of the Captain, who was jealous and even warned me. When you were leaving in Tema I had wanted to come and see you off, but he intentionally gave me a job to do—and when you were gone he was teasing me. I felt bad in a way, and only gave a [illegible].
Su, I'll be very glad to meet you again but it seems my ship will not be calling in to States this year. In my case, if we do call, I'll try and give you a call. I promised sending you some Ghanaian records—I'll do as soon as I get your reply.
How's the summer back home? Will you go out camping? For you've had enough travel and need a little rest at home.
Su, would you mind sending me a picture, for I've been thinking of you. I know not what's happening and just can't overcome it. I may go on transfer and if that happens I'll have the chance of meeting you soon. In any case keep writing so I know the trend of things, and that I don't lose contact with you. I'll also send you my picture if you are prepared to keep it. Su, yeah, I think you'll reply early to let me hear you on paper. A lovely girl you were.
Take all mistakes for love and kisses.
Yours in love
Larry

Larry Dzameh, M.V. Offin River
Black Star Line
Q.O. Box 259
Takoradi
Ghana West Africa

My note on the envelope: "wrote back 9/29/76."

84 This visit with his sister is described in Chapter 17.

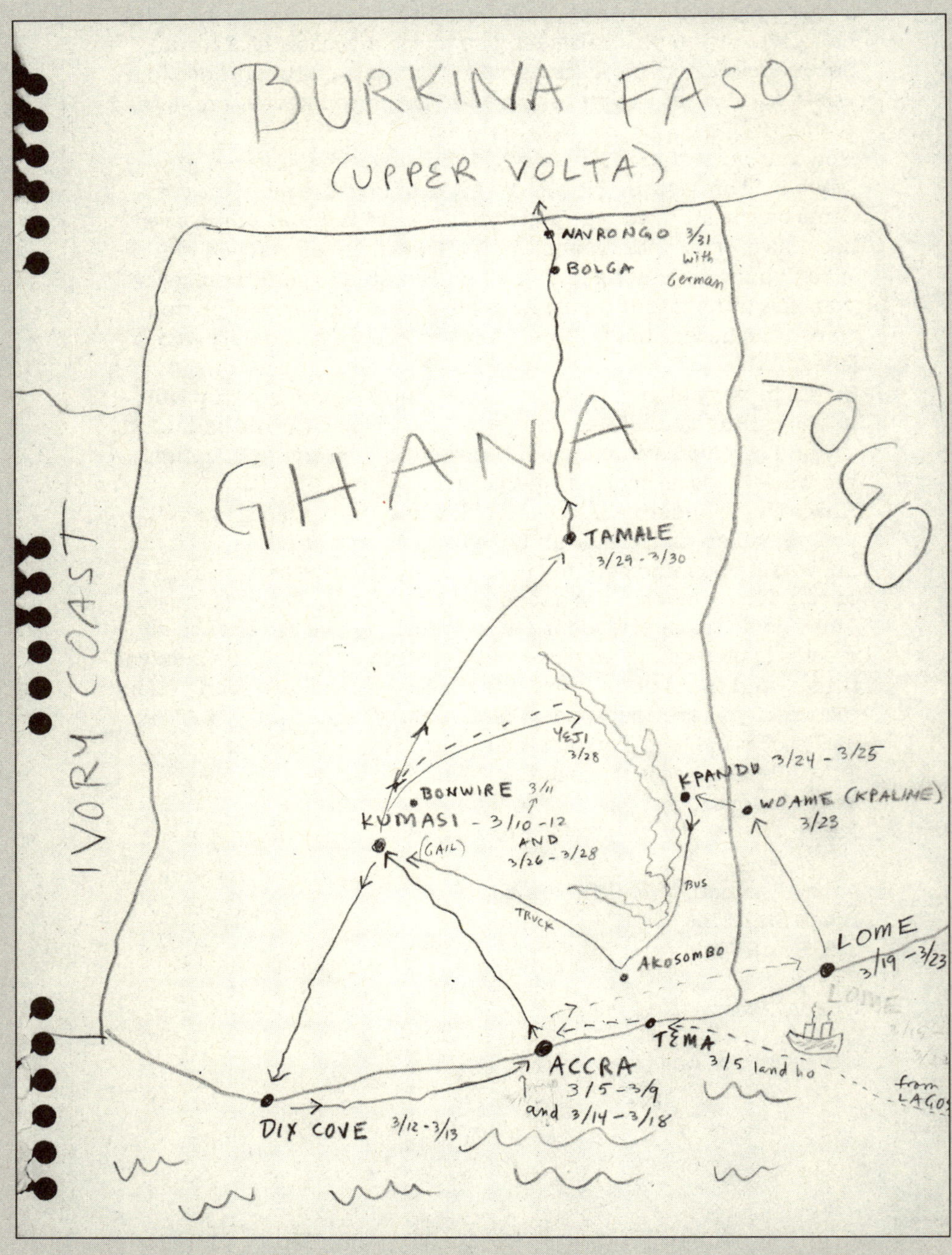

BURKINA FASO
(UPPER VOLTA)
NAVRONGO 3/31 with German
BOLGA
GHANA
TOGO
IVORY COAST
TAMALE 3/29 - 3/30
YEJI 3/28
KPANDU 3/24 - 3/25
WOAME (KPALIME) 3/23
BONWIRE 3/11
KUMASI - 3/10 -12 AND 3/26 - 3/28
(GAIL)
BUS
TRUCK
AKOSOMBO
LOME 3/19 - 3/23
TEMA
3/5 land ho
from LAGOS
ACCRA 3/5 - 3/9 and 3/14 - 3/18
DIX COVE 3/12 - 3/13

CHAPTER FIFTEEN

Sam and More Sam

We docked at the port of Tema, a small city sixteen miles east of Accra. It is one of the two deep seaports along the Ghanaian coast.

After much hustle and push and squeeze and great sad frustration I found a cheap taxi to Accra and as we rounded the bend and I looked out over the sea, the palm tree groves, the fishermen cutting thru the glare of late afternoon sun silvering the sea, the tape deck came on with "Highjack Your Love" and there I was being tossed and battered and soothed between elation and utter resignation. A more-and-more-despite-the-sorrows travelling.

MARCH 6

An absolutely American of all imaginable Americanas evening: the Friday night drunk at the Marines' bar [1].
Yes, the American Marines, those boys in brown and black who live like hogs and cut their hair and guard the embassy. I got absolutely plastered. Like I haven't been in years but I was still talking coherently and walking. But there we sat in all our whiteness and tanness and no one danced and the women sat and the men stood. We all drank like elephants or Oba and that was it. Absolutely, remarkably uneventful.

MARCH 7

I am very carefully and patiently fending off a case of raving depression. I understand now that it comes from thinking about and wanting to do too many (i.e. any-) thing here. Today after my friend the diplomatic alcoholic Peace Corps guy left [85], I again felt a glare of ALONE standing knee deep in the gulf of Guinea, all around me laughter and kerplash and family scenes, and I had to come back to this dingy room—actually it isn't such a bad room but to be alone in it is, there's no distraction of good conversation or a face to stare into. So I move very slowly back this way, burnt a nasty red on my thighs and nose, strolling the broad peaceful streets of Accra's "better section," the billboards proclaiming "Exports Gain! Imports Drain!" and "One Nation One People One Destiny," down Cabral Avenue and Guinea-Bissau Street and Lumumba Drive and Independence Boulevard and National Redemption Circle. I chanced to hear some good drumming and went inside a nice white stucco open-air building decorated on the front with Ashanti Akua-ba dolls [3]—observed some

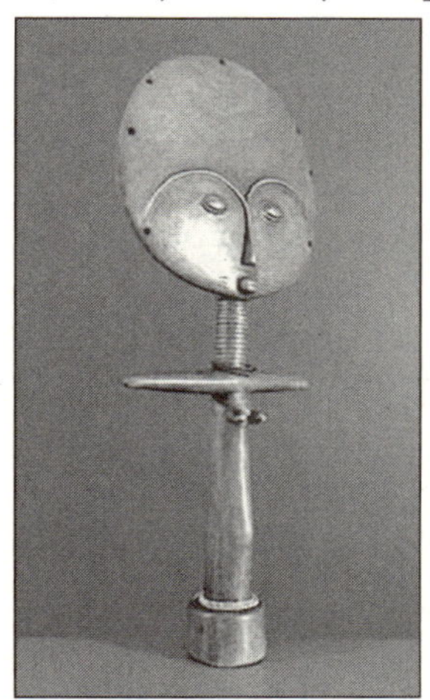

85 From now on, referred to as PCV's—Peace Corps Volunteers. For more info, see [2].

young and adult dancers and drummers. I am always moved to jealousy and awe to see them move to drumbeat—it goes beyond the possible, that totally fluid, serpentine, "off beat" movement; it has so much character; so many human quirks and moods come through the shimmy of their shoulders and jerk of the hips. I was told they were Ni Shin Shro Shin Buddhists, of all things, and they were studying their people's culture in order to bring them a sense of unity. Unity and of course brotherhood are the passwords here, despite the disquieting fact that Colonel Acheampong [4] is <u>not</u> loved by his people as much as he would wish or need to be, and his wife is in the car business; calling that for Africa a "lucrative" venture would be a gross inaccuracy, it's a goldmine.
I suppose these days it would be more apropos to say an oilfield.
The other evening on the ship Larry in the dim light of my cabin tried to kiss me; we flailed arms and I cried out "No" but in that brief encounter I was flooded with a feeling of need for sensual/sexual contact with someone. Also just being in this culture has opened up my eyes and nerves to bodies, to physical energy and smooth muscular skin and a casual hug and a total involvement of the body in social situations, the dancing movement when they laugh, the histrionics indulged in during a heated conversation, the grace of their hands, the sensuousness of their faces; today at the beach I was appalled to see the flabby bodies and pinched faces and muscleless arms of the *oyibos*—the throngs of young Ghanaian kids out romping and cartwheeling in the waves, the young girls in sleeveless white t-shirts, their firm small breasts and muscular arms and long strong legs and the young boys often naked, arched spine, child's biceps, leaping and crashing in the surf, all so active and laughing, always laughing and shouting and teasing.
A gentle sight, four boys strolling on the sand, the first with his arm about the second's waist, who had his arm around the third's shoulder who was holding hands with the fourth.

MARCH 8

Used a phone yesterday for the first time in four months; thought it sounded awfully peculiar and unpleasant, that scratchy disembodied voice.
I had burnt cashews on the beach today. Met a young guy who's planted a cashew farm—three acres but it won't produce for another seven years. We crushed the charred, bulbous shells beneath a sharp stone and picked out the tender roasted nut.
Everyone here is mortally afraid of the US cities. They describe them as if one is lucky not to be mowed down by a trigger-happy idiot in broad daylight. They say "Aw, New York. That's a <u>fast</u> city, too0000 fast."
Here at first I would cringe away from "comforts" which are equated here with "rich Europeans" and vaguely discomforting in my mind in general. But I had a conversation with Steve [86] this morning about American standards of living, and the way he said, "All Americans are rich" made me see it clear thru—Yes we are. Even if we say someone has little, for example just a car and a shitty flat and usual food, that's still

86 I met so many people in passing and didn't always make note of who they were or where they were from.

far and above the norm and it is a physically comfortable life. I realize how much I've come to see class here thru African eyes, and whereas at first I responded in the usual indifferent way to professors and businessmen, I've come to understand just how privileged they are here—now I treat them as the awesome anomaly. I think this trip has cranked open and glued my eyes into position an extra five inches. And my heart.

I had *fufu* [87] and snails and ice cream and cakes and pictures of the whole family from Madame Regina Allotey, mother of ten (five boys, five girls) and thirty-four grandchildren, most of whom apparently live with her—e.g., her son's kids, after his wife split and he went off to Monrovia. She was an enormous woman and quite the businesswoman, one of the best bakers around and always with her eye to opening an African bakery in America. Our land of sweet and corpulent dreams is still that for Ghanaians—they are very quick and proud to tell you how much they love America and one day will go there.

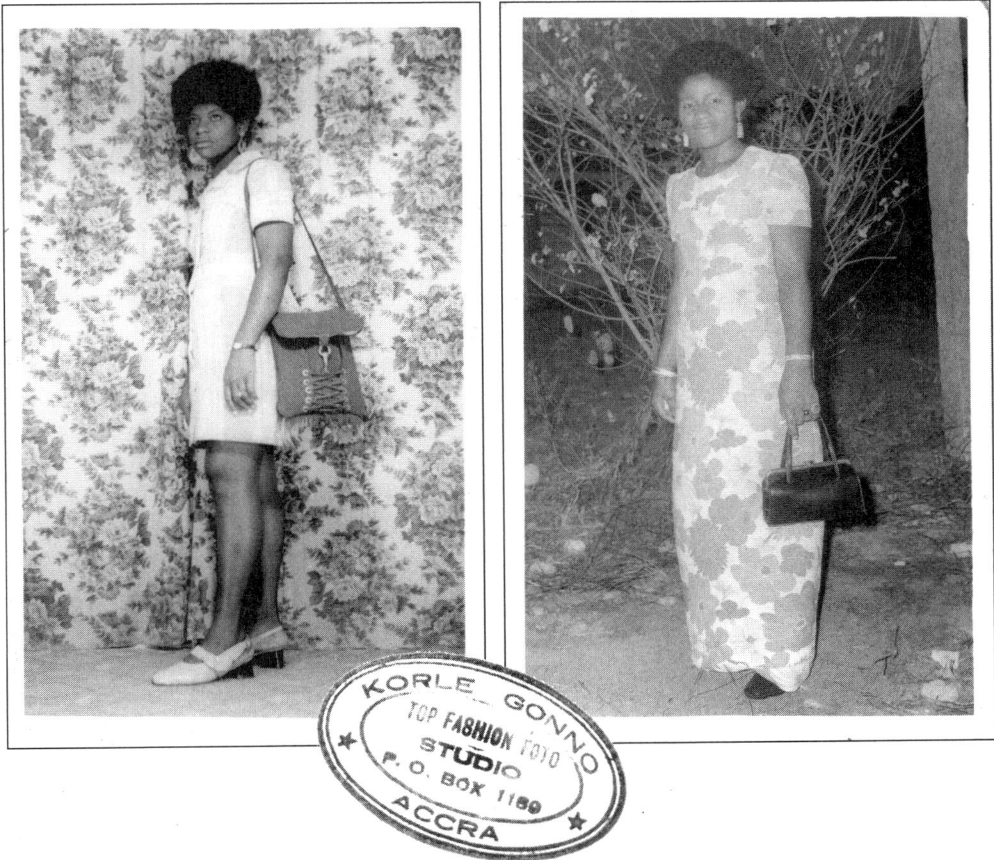

Two of Madame Allotey's relatives, Margaret Okutah and Esther Okutah.

87 The Ghanaian name for the paté that I wrote about in chapter 7.

The snails were big gray rubbery suspicious tasting things that they all exclaimed were "sweet and makes your blood strong." I ate, grinning all the while and wishing it weren't so hard to chew and so big to get through . . .

Sam Lawson—her nephew, a seaman—within one hour of meeting me expressed, "the great love I feel for you, and hope you will let me enjoy you tonight," all in ever the smoothest voice and puppy dog eyes and I just wanted to slug him. But here the frankness of sexual contact between men and women is very different than in America, and I have to approach it with that understanding (ha!); in other/their words, "don't be afraid to say no because no here is quite casual."

After dinner we went to the Playboy Disco and over loud music, Coke and too many cigarettes he told me that we should live according to Socrates who said we must love our fellow man, and Buddha . . . and proceeded to tell me the whole damn tale of the Bodhi Tree and just kept reiterating how much we should love each other and give as much as we can because tomorrow we die.

And when I said I agree and that it's good to have money so you can share good luck with others he said "Susi, you're truly American." It was so uncomfortable to sit with him and devise money schemes to get him to America, for me to sell African goods, etc., and for him to tell me he'll come and get rich in NY and pay for me to visit Ghana, etc.
There's no hope of convincing them that America is not the place to get rich quick these days, because we all look so rich.

> **PART OF A LETTER TO MIMI:**
> Ghana is pure pleasure after Nigeria, the people are fine, the sea, the sea revives my spirit I frolic in the surf and do my best to forget about careers and money and schedules (which hang heavy at the thought of returning home.) I'm getting back into the travelling groove (rut? no, w/ the right spirit) after being so bogged down the past few weeks. I eat fish in the market & pineapple for breakfast & go on the daily hunt for a cold coke & just am amazed at the beautiful cloth & leatherwork & faces here. The evening falls so gently, and then it's time for highlife & the discos, full of dayglow posters & sleek Ghanaians.
> I envy your survival of winter and anticipation of spring. The seasons are so important to me and here it's just a constant light and heat.
> <u>Please</u> please send me a note AIR MAIL even registered to the American Embassy in Abidjan, Ivory Coast about your summer

schedule, when you'll be in/not in NY, how to reach you to tell you when my plane arrives, etc—
Amer. Embassy Visitor's Mail
Rue Crosson Duplessis at Blvd. Reliue
Abidjan, Côte d'Ivoire,
W. Africa

MARCH 9

The beach was a renewal, resting beneath the palm trees, the silvery crisp light on the waves, and the fisherman and sea lovers literally frolicking in the waves. I've never witnessed such a recreational, joyful response to the sea—the harmony and suppleness of their bodies made them burst into cartwheels, flips, somersaults, sprint high speed and then crash into the waves, or simply stand arms upstretched face to the sun breathing deeply and fully.

As we sat on the beach talking of American dream schemes Sam said, with a wistful look in his eyes, "I was born in the wrong place. I should be living in America, I am the sort of person to be there because, you see, I much prefer to mix with whites." How bittersweet, obnoxious, and fun, Sam only willing to cease his exclamations of "love and desire" for me when I "admitted" to him that, "No, I can't, my heart is with someone at home." When he pressed me for details (as these incredibly (and understandably) inquisitive people do) I told him that <u>he</u> was twenty, studying in NY, maybe we'd marry . . . ? Double identity can really bring the tenuousness of words and of life into sharp focus. Sam was absolutely obsessed with the American dream. Thru him, I experienced or learned how the frontier mania can get hold of someone's waking and sleeping mind, run close and dizzy circles about endless schemes. Each sentence, always spoken in a breathless, urgent staccato with those wide, over-trusting eyes was prefaced with, "When you get to the states, I'll send you . . . " or "I hope I get to NY and make a lot of money to . . . " I shudder to think how much he'd lose in one week in NY after seeing his recklessness here, where he should know prices.

At one point in a taxi I glanced over to see him, unaware of my scrutiny, gazing at the passport photo I'd given him with the most blissful dreamy smile I think I've ever seen. I've become another in his retinue of white friends, of whom he's so proud and so deluded—it makes me feel tremendously uncomfortable and deceitful to be encouraging his schemes, promising to send money if I can sell all the "many many beautiful African goods" he wants to send; it's not possible to gently dissuade someone from their dreams if they've been projecting their entire future on them, but how can I sit and promise to find his sister a secretarial job and his brother a plumbing job (??) and not feel like laughing or weeping?

THE FOURTH OF FIVE LETTERS FROM SAM LAWSON [88]:

Make sure you write to me anywhere you hear I am.
PEACE OF GOD BE WITH YOU NOW AND THE COMING YEAR.
MAY LONG LIFE AND LOVE FOLLOW YOU IN THIS LATEST 1977 COMING AND ALL YOUR LIFE TIME WITH ALL THAT YOUR HEART DESIRES.
LOVE AND PRAYER
Sam Lawson

Dec 16th 1976

Dear Susi,
I am very sorry that you have not been hearing from me regularly, it is not that I have not been writing to you. I have been doing it at all times but I don't know whether you have been receiving my letters or not. I suppose to post you something for Christmas but I am afraid that it will not get to you, that is why I wanted to hear from you before, I say it is unfair that I might tell you saying I will send you this or that but because of your address and how I have not been hearing from you when you posted me a birthday greetings of love and future goodness. I am coming to Monrovia now and I carry on me all that is good for you for the XMAS. So please reply my letter now to Accra and they will write me and send me your address to enable me posted to you, they have been bought already only waiting and willing to hear from you then I say my good friend here is something that is good for your soul. I am not suppose to go to Monrovia but because I can no more hear from my sister and as well as you Susi.
Susi you knew me and all where I live in Ghana, I can pay my fare (ticket) and come to you with all genuine paper to sail with either Palm Ships or Delta Lines Ship. I have work with them too. Susi I will write to you immediately I arrive at the airport in Monrovia and do your best to write if you receive my letters. If there is any help you can give me sometime to ask can you pay your fare to Chicago to live in your house for 1 week or two to make things not to be expensive for me. Because many people have fraud or dupe me many things but only God enjoy on his name. Susi I expect to receive your letter immediately I write you from Monrovia above and I will receive it early too that is your letter before I go away. I will not spend Christmas. I have posted to you some Christmas card which shows the RIGHT LIGHT THAT MEN AND WOMEN ALL CREATION MUST FOLLOW. He lies in a manger and eat nails?? hails????? [illegible] food of animals but he was filled with HOLY SPIRIT.

88 See [5] for some more info about his letters and our interaction.

The letter came inside this card:

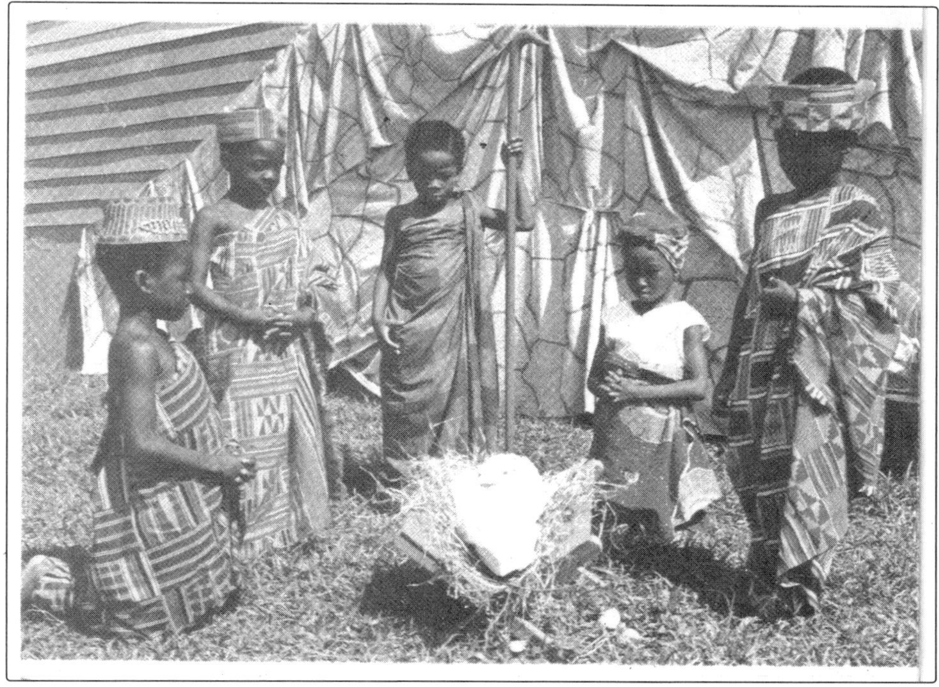

From Sam
To Susi

The peace and joy
of Holy Night
Stay through the year
as guiding light.

Sam's aunt (as he said, "You remember, the big woman, the tough woman"), the matriarch with the economic and psychological burden of scores of dependents and about 300 lbs. on her frame, spoke proudly of her sons and daughters, three of whom had finished college and were heading into lucrative careers and "lived like Europeans" but then she spoke in a hushed, cautious voice about the mortal danger to any Ghanaian who aspired to and succeeded in such a life. Her son Mr. Daniel McCarthy had to flee to Monrovia to escape the voodoo of jealous neighbors who could try to poison him, kill him off.

A LETTER FROM DANIEL MACARTHY:

Daniel A. Macarthy
15-2-1977

Dear to be,
I am very happy to write to you and to inform you of my interest to become your friend.
It might interest you to know all about the writer of this letter; but I shall do that after I have received a reply to this letter. But in order not to keep you in suspense, I will give you a small account of myself.
I am an accountant. A Ghanaian by birth and now residing in Liberia and working with the W.V.S Tubman High School, a instructor of Economics, Accounting & Business Maths. My mother by name Madam Aku Alloty give me your address from Ghana; and asked me to get in touch with you.
Could you remember meeting a woman in Chorkor? She is a baker and I was made to know Odantery [I'm guessing; the name is hard to read] send you there. In fact I have received your picture and is very nice. Kindly write to me with the address inset here. I just vacationing here in Ghana.

Daniel A. Macarthy
W.V.S. Tubman High School
Box 1545
Monrovia Liberia

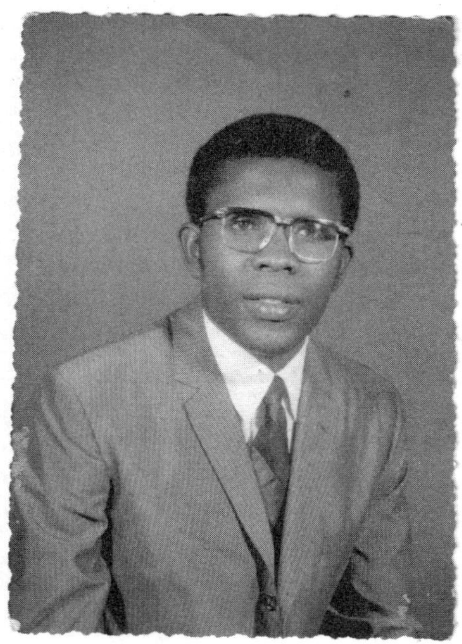

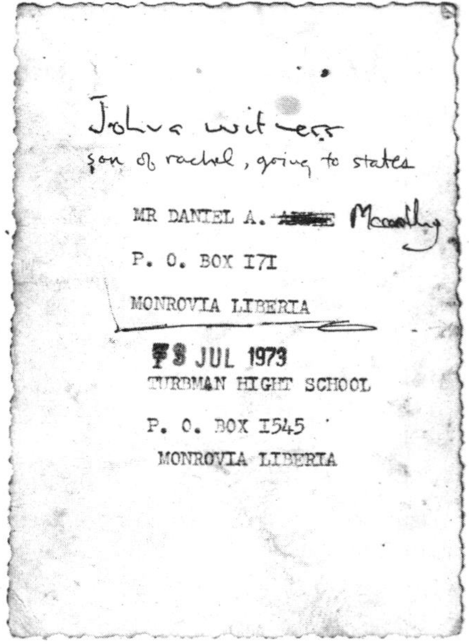

She prayed to God as a staunch Jehovah's Witness that we would meet again. It's really moving to meet these people who are so sincere in their sisterly love for me, they just care for and about me in that absolute, trusting way which we seem to have lost hold of; it's a form of innocence and faith in the goodness/importance of human beings to feel or empathize totally with them. It pulls one into their lives, thru a whirlwind of affection and concern, and once I've touched it and been a part of their lives I'll never forget it. In the states we have a tendency or even preference to subdue or withhold our expressions of camaraderie until the "testing period" is over; it doesn't usually come bubbling forth in the immediate way that I find it here.

And I am being taught perhaps for the first time (and it's long overdue) that regardless of progress and the life of the mind [89], people are the backbone and the guts of life and that one of the finest human capacities is to be able to express love and concern for another human being. As Sam's bro said, "Here our houses our doors and our hearts are always open to anyone. We never can or want to shut ourselves off from other people because then we would truly have nothing."

I'm back into the real Africa (after affluent Nigeria), where one goes to five bars looking for one with beer, and I hear that there's no Coke to be found outside of Accra—and the economy is getting thoroughly screwed by the black market exchange because it's 300% of the official rate, so with no one changing in the bank they have no foreign capital to invest, for example, in American equipment. And so it goes.

There seems to be a lot of divorce and/or desertion around here but people think thrice before doing it—they run a great financial loss (the men lose dowry or women lose bride price). Sam wanted to give me a watch that was with his girlfriend who "lives like a harlot but she's very beautiful"—they cost about five to seven dollars here and he told me that all the women (young, sharp dressers, good dancers, beer drinkers and smokers) at the disco were harlots.

Cliff, a PCV living in a small village, told me of the prostituting system there. If a young girl doesn't want to get married, she takes on maybe six or seven steady lovers who are all compelled to give her a certain (lucrative) sum each month for her favors. If one wants to marry her, fine, but he has to be able and willing to pay the equivalent of all those suitors. It's accepted and recognized in the town and condoned by the parents . . . who get a good cut of the profit.

Among the Ewe a wife isn't too expensive; it just takes three rounds:
1st round: Four bottles of beer, two bottles of minerals (4.20 cedis) [$4.83] [90]
2nd round: A bible and lovely clothes
3rd: Declaration of marriage

---

89 I first heard the phrase "the life of the mind" when I was a freshman at the University of Chicago, which prided itself on being a place where one lived that life. How right they were. There was no social life to speak of.

90 Cedis are the basic monetary unit of Ghana. In 2024, $4.83=$27.50

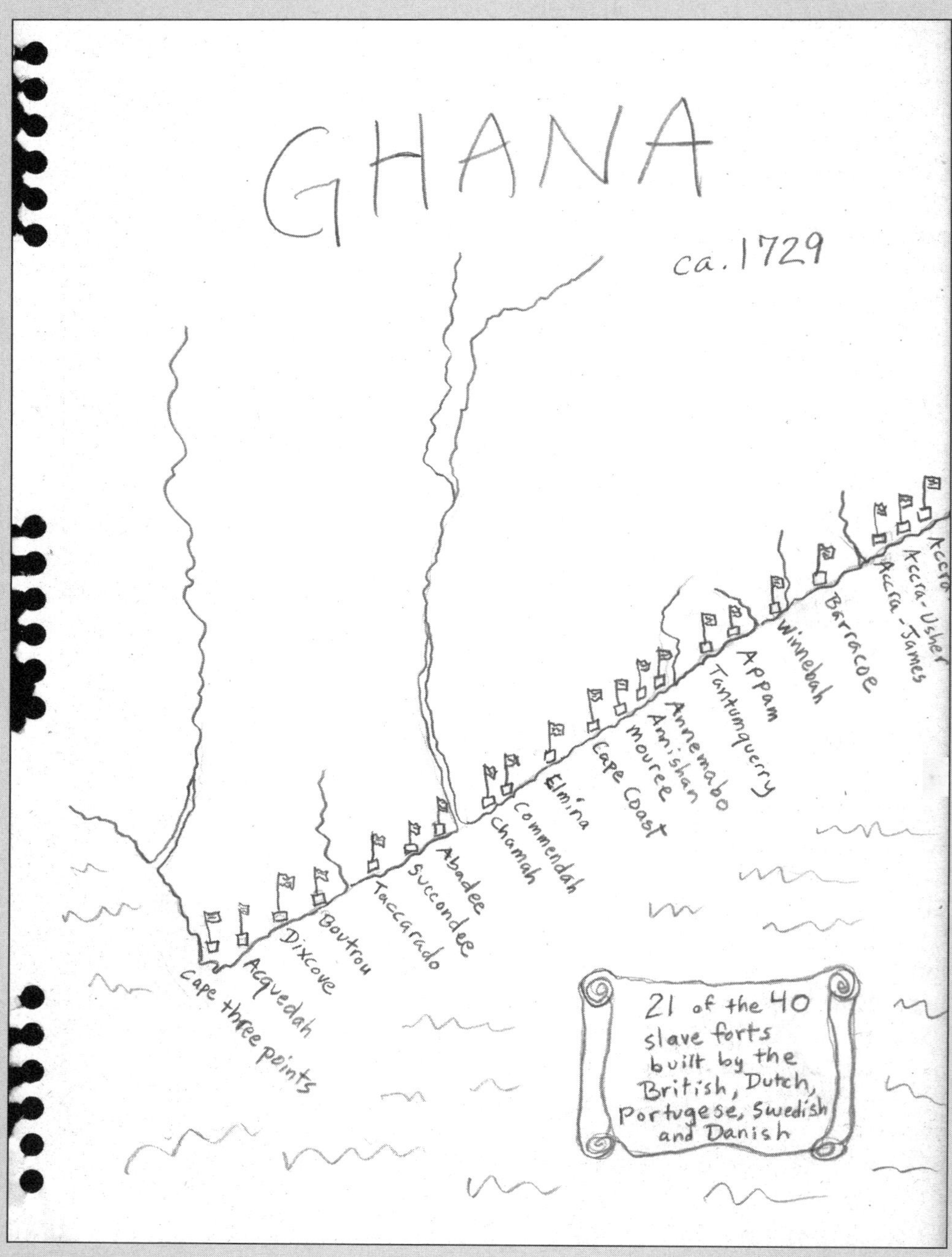
GHANA
ca. 1729
Accra
Accra-Usher
Accra-James
Barracoe
Winnebah
Appam
Tantumquerry
Annemabo
Amishan
mouree
Cape Coast
Elmina
Commendah
Chamah
Abadee
Succondee
Taccarado
Boutrou
Dixcove
Acquedah
Cape three points
21 of the 40 slave forts built by the British, Dutch, Portugese, Swedish and Danish

CHAPTER SIXTEEN

From Kente Cloth to Slave Forts

Last night at a point of utter depression I met Gail, the first American white woman travelling around here alone; we'll go to Kumasi together. She hails from Kansas City, and we've shared all our nightmare experiences with men.

I sense now how limited visual/still art is as a means of expressing or conveying African life—the heat, the tempo and color of life comes naturally thru music and dance. I can feel the rhythms in the street, the music in voices and sway of hips as the men weave down the busy streets under a one-hundred-and-fifty-pound load and the sculpted sensuous breasts and backs of the women. I would really like to see an African *Roma*,[91] without any political diatribe—just the pulse and energy of an African city.

MARCH 10

Kumasi. The Menka Memorial Hotel: strings of colored lights and traffic and beer drinkers in the patio below and a thoroughly enjoyable Ghana. Took a dusty trip with Gail to Bonwire, the epicenter of kente cloth production—around every corner was another weaver hunched over his loom, thirty feet of thread stretched taut before him, working rapidly, accurately. I bought two gorgeous pieces, with gritted teeth, scraping the miser off my mind.

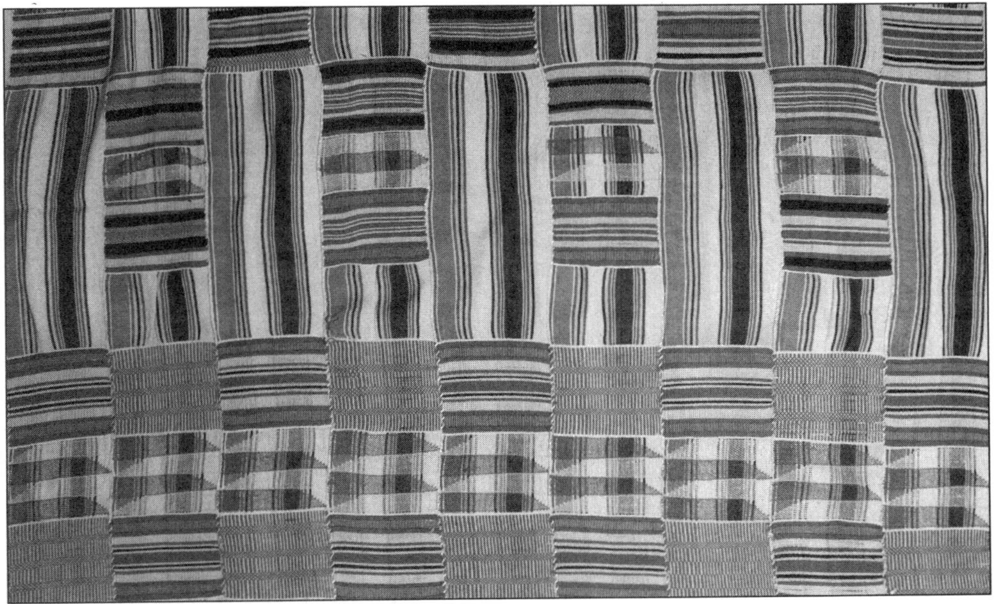

91 I'm referring to the first *Roma* (1972) directed by Federico Fellini. My comment was made before the great Senegalese filmmaker Ousmane Sembene was more widely known by the American public. He made *Black Girl* in 1966, the first feature film by a Black African in sub-Saharan Africa, which first screened at MoMA in 1978.

And the economics lecturer at the local technical school told Gail he wanted to marry her but was afraid somehow of white women: "Blacks don't have such pointed noses, and maybe if we were in bed, I wouldn't know how to be with you because I know the ways with African women but perhaps you kiss differently and if I saw you all white in your underwear I'd think you were a ghost."

!

It's a soothing reprieve to have a travelling companion.

The calm in the lorry today clearly due to the subdued color scheme: almost all black—the silk and dyed black patterned scarves on the women, the deep red or rust orange and black sleek bald heads of the old men in their Adinkra wraps, quite a visual and psychological change from the blaze and funk of Nigerian dress. [92]

Kumasi is a sweet little town.

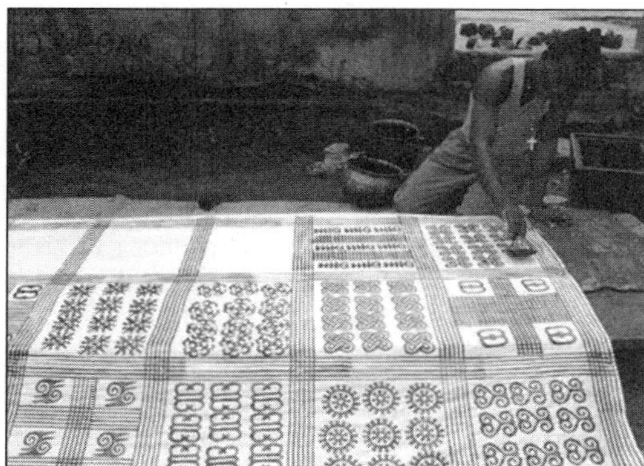

Anthony Boakye prints an *adinkra* cloth with a calabash stamp in Ntonso, Ghana.

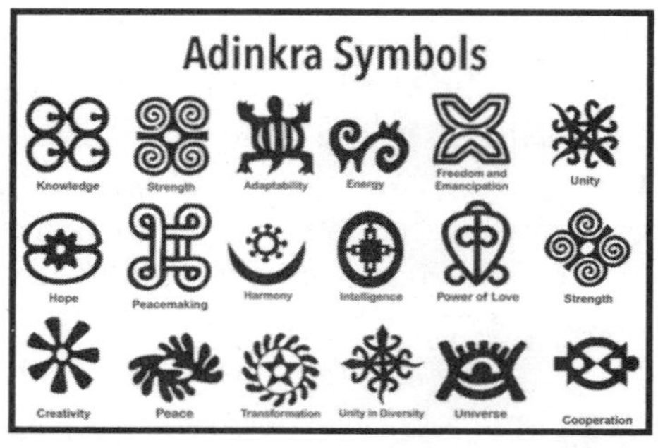

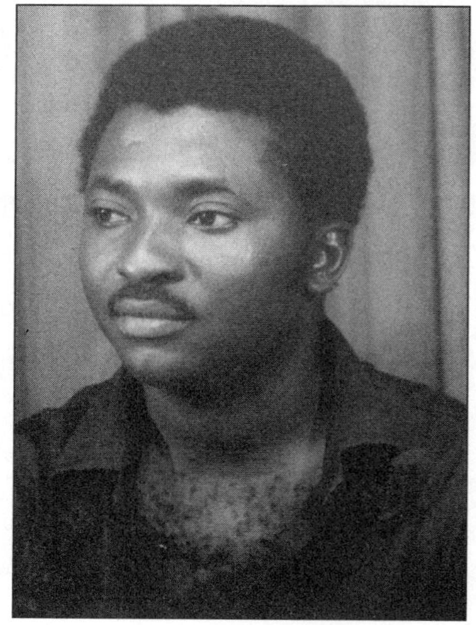

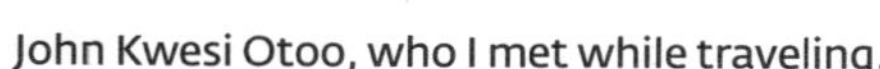

John Kwesi Otoo, who I met while traveling.

92 The word "adinkra" means "good-bye." The cloth was originally worn when guests were departing, or by people attending a funeral, and then it was white, not orange.

Gail and I traveled southwest, down to the coast.

MARCH 12

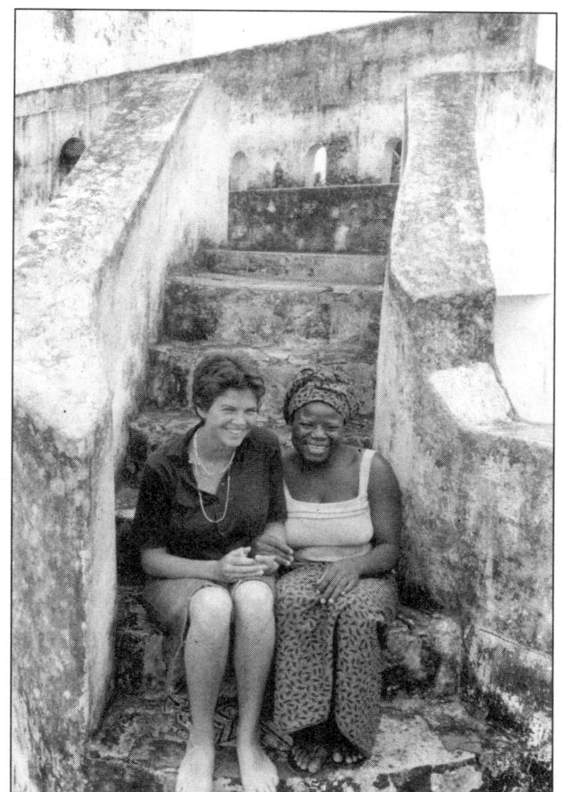

I am thoroughly burned and pleasured out, this luxus day of surf and lobster and swimming naked next to the palm trees and sky. We're at Dixcove, slave castle turned hostel: how strange, refurbished for the comfort of us hard luck travelers [93].

These PCVs are just what I expected, full of talk about their illnesses and the little work they have to do—it's basically the boredom which makes it sometimes a job under duress.

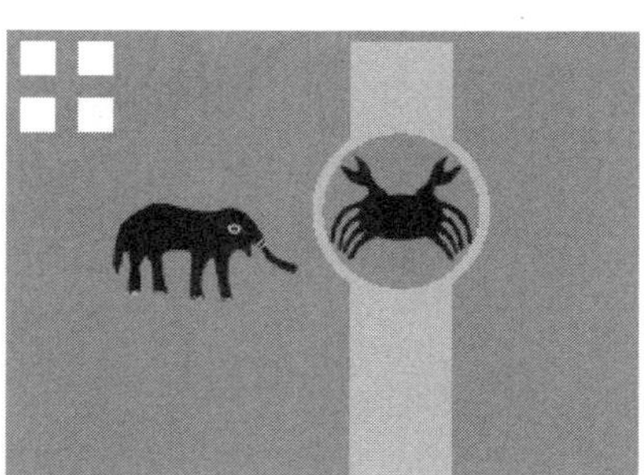

The official flag of the Central Region, where we were.

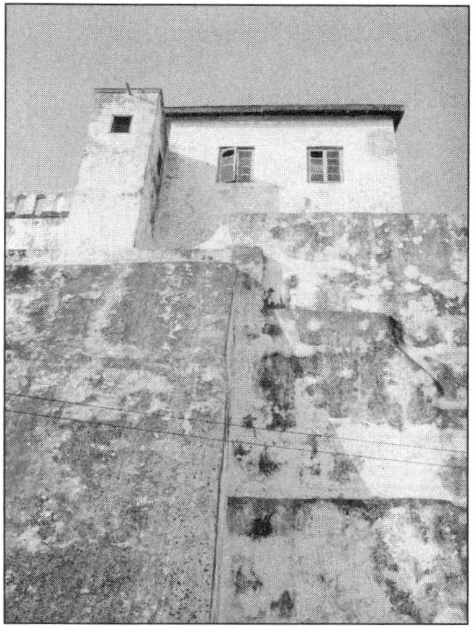

93 For some history about the slave trade and the many slave forts in Ghana, see [1].

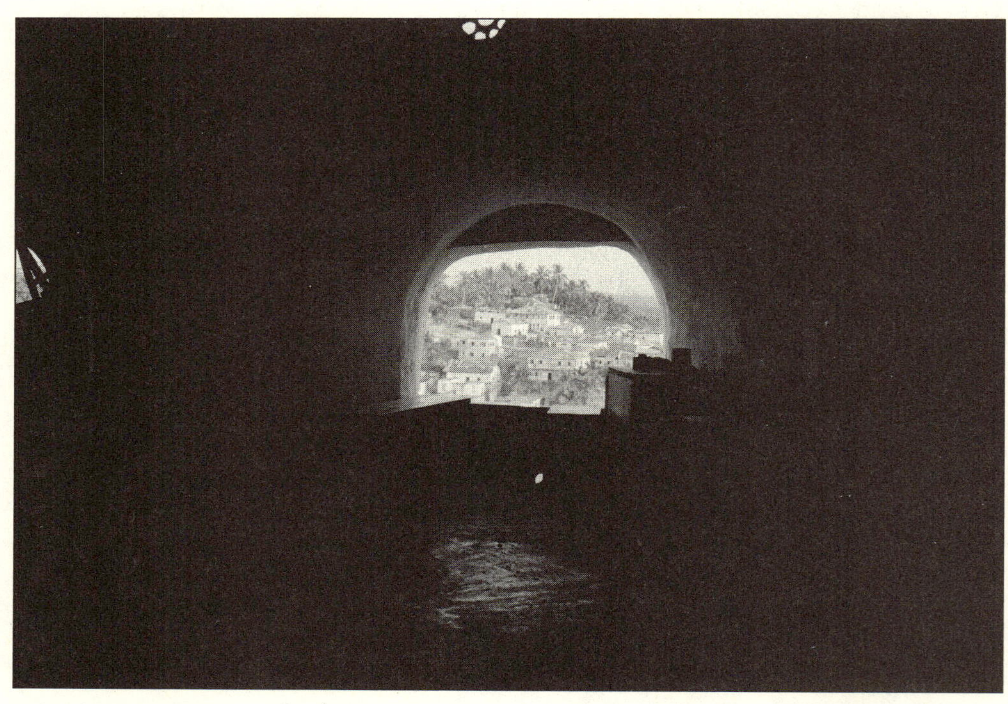

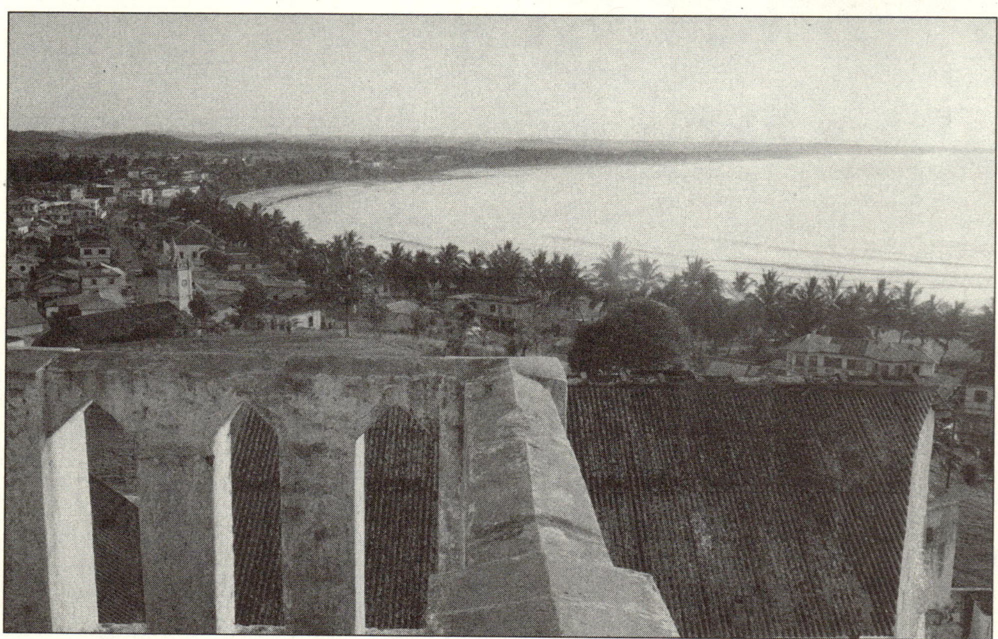

After a few days of feeling increasingly oppressed by the stunted conversations with Gail she told me of her former fiancé at UC law and her intimidation with academics. "I'm basically a simple person and see things in a simple way, etc." That, and the talk of Barry this and Barry that, makes me glad there's other company around.

But last night Paul [94] and I got into a heated controversy about Blacks (he was maintaining, in the most whiny smug voice, the "up by their bootstraps" bullshit) and the others started muttering in exasperation, "Blacks and women, God let's change the subject," and on came a Dylan tape and out came the reefer and we sank into oblivion.

The men here don't say, "I want to marry you.," They approach, smile, and insist, "You're my wife."—"Oh," I say, "Sorry, but I have five husbands at home." They are so shocked by that, it almost makes them retire—but no, an excited discussion follows about how can I sleep with all my husbands and have so many children and be their master, and I insist until they burst into incredulous laughter and harrumph and reassure themselves of their separate reality.

Gail hooked up with a guy named Soren in Dixcove, who we then saw again in Accra.

MARCH 14–18

Back to Accra. I feel almost as if it's a homecoming. Gail infuriated me at Dixcove. After three days of trying her moody, spoiled routine on an unsympathetic Susi she outdid herself in the company of the lone French and American admirers at the beach. Wide eyes, smiles timed perfectly to make her eyes twinkle and their chests swell, that obnoxious whiny plaintive tone, the daily complaints about the *pepe*—she, the only one of about fifteen at the table who had been in Africa for months and had not yet accepted the dietary conditions and was just hogging down the lobster and even begging it off others. I despise (but damn it also can't help but empathize with) women who are so taciturn (i.e. HONEST) in the company of women, who are less eager to please us, and who then just flood the boys with charm and ignore the women. And the Danish guy Soren, at Mama's Chop Bar, in the midst of an anxious, jostling crowd of probably very hungry young kids, bitched about how long he had to wait and whether it would be substantial and then, to Mama, sweating and imperious, he even managed to ask, "Do you have a spoon?"

You see, eating with hands is primitive . . . oh yeah.

Met in contrast a hardy Australian woman named Kay (deciding to travel within Africa needs a sinewy sort of person) on her own, five months already, full of the openness and variety and good cheer required for understanding these countries which I haven't found in many other whites. I'll be meeting her again in

---

94 Paul was some white guy either traveling, or working as a PCV, who was staying at the same hotel where Gail and I were. The "others" were likewise; the usual gaggle of travelers, expats, students, drifters, etc.

Lomé—have decided to change my course again because I regret not having gone through Togo and getting the famous sandal maker's wares.

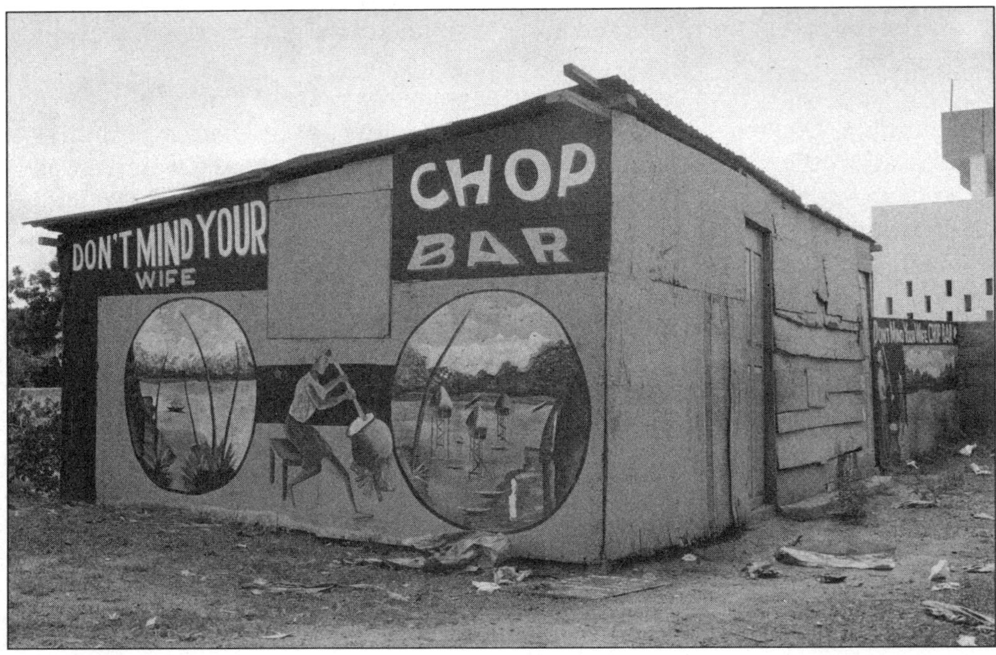

I was told repeatedly and gravely before I came that feminism here was not, could not be, should not be the same as our Western-American style. Even *African Woman* had a heated diatribe about the virtual incompatibility of the two cultures' women's movements. That position, after my experience and newspaper reading and bureaucracy-observing of the past three months, is as shortsighted as that of an idealist who insists that African nations at this point in development only need highly trained farmers because that category of laborer covers "the masses." The real dearth in these countries is the lack of honest leaders and/or capable leaders (and an even more painful absence of self-government by individuals . . . .which is not to suggest that there aren't a lot of men capable of making others follow them to the tune of a marching band and Hail to the Chief), but in the practical modern business and political areas, the women are being channeled clearly along our paths of secretary and clerk and assistant minister of a small government branch. And if the attention here doesn't cover both ends of a woman's "role," in the future there'll be a lot of women with birth control and boredom [2].

In the exhausted grim office-laden halls of Ghana House stood a blackboard:
One Nation
One People
One Problem

Instead of One Destiny. And their destiny is a problem; they'll never get anywhere with their cedi at $1.15.

The scene here is closest to a *Dreigroschenoper* [95] as any on earth—the ragged and hungry trudging thru the streets, "We want our rights and we want them NOW!" and the usurpers and sharks smiling beneficently at the conclusion.
Giving, kindly, to beggars is a much more straightforward process here than the embarrassing, sidling-up-with-averted-eyes gesture we manage at home. Beggars might be something to be ashamed of here as well as anywhere else, but they're also a fact of life and of need and not wished out of existence by raised eyebrows and a quickened pace.
Have been privy to the most repulsive display of sexual politics and romantic love as a counterrevolutionary force between Gail and Soren. He and I had been together for a day before G showed up—we got along ok but I didn't play up to him, and found him at times to be force without substance. So "on the scene," seduction supreme in the form of watery blue eyes and a whine of "gimme shelter," and they were fucking within a day. And so commenced the "sweetheart, do you have . . . ?" etc. and his talk of "my woman" and all her goddamned GAMES and he ate it up like a glutton in a Swiss bakery. And to my credit, I think I didn't feel any pangs of resentment or "failure"—I was glad to see myself uncompromised. And sick to see her so voluntarily compromised . . . and without apparent need. She had Barry and Jean Pierre and every other imaginable male with an uncontrollably chivalrous impulse.
VACHE, they say. [96]

Lovely letters from Cindy and Mimi, full of grimy news (the Chicago arsonist, divorce, Joan Dixon, another suicide, Donna's ankle) and love. Mimi's letter almost scares me—it's all positive excesses of love and admiration that I've needed to hear and receive for so long now and it means the most coming from her and yet it was so strong that I almost can't fathom it. I hope she gets my letter from the ship.
A few days later, and I think of little else; wish she was here so I could "kiss those sweet lips again."

Aside from the letters from my mother and the one from Mimi (which is too personal to include here), I only had this one letter from Cindy, though I think she might have written others that were lost. Its history gives some idea of how disjointed communication was in that pre-digital age.
In a postcard to her in late January, I described my overnight stay with Hamsatou, and now in Ghana a month later I found her mail at the embassy. One letter was dated February 5 & 6, and the second one, dated February 28, was written on the back of it.

---

95 *Thee Threepenny Opera* by Bertolt Brecht, Elisabeth Hauptmann and Kurt Weill, based on John Gay's eighteenth-century play, *The Beggar's Opera*, is a critique of the condition of the London poor.

96 COW.

A LETTER FROM CINDY:

Feb. 5
Dear Su – Have thought of you often on your date-filled desert & hope this finds you well if slightly sun-streaked. In fact, I hope this finds you. I'm sending copies to both Togo & Ghana & will send another letter to Ghana towards the end of the month. That's terrible about your wide-angle. I assume you still have the telephoto & can take pictures of anything you stand far enough away from. THE NEWS: the city feels like a war zone – maybe the planets are lined up in some weird aspect if you believe in astrology. We've had 16 fires in the neighborhood in 3 weeks, all of them set by a still-at-large arsonist. One of them was in Donna's building – one person dead. No damage to her place, but she's still without gas & has limited electricity.

[. . .]

Feb. 6 – Got your postcard today from Nigeria. How did you end up spending the night with a wife + mother in Niger? This is all going to work up into a terrific article which you'll sell to *MS. Magazine*, OK? Are you finding places to develop film, or will that wait?

[. . .]

Love,
Cindy

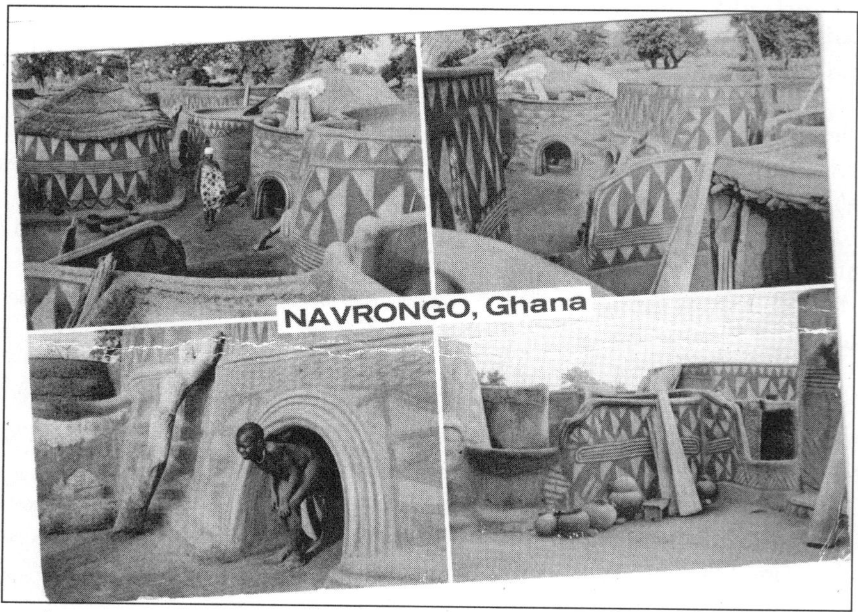

The front of the same postcard sent to both Cindy and Mimi.

A POSTCARD TO CINDY:

Dear Cindy,
BLESSINGS for your letter. I sat for a good 10 minutes sweating & giggling in the American Embassy over the arsonists.
[. . .]
A German-trained camera technician has made me a working photographer once again! Ghana is sweet-talking its way into my soul, I'll be sorry to leave it—lovely beaches, highlife in the discos, fresh fish, and a population (falsely?) enamored of Americans—I am well-fed & in good cheer.
[. . .].
Hope you got my article, altho regret not finishing it off better. Yes, will beat on the hallowed doors of *Ms.*; thinking of short stories on a variety of women w/ whom I've stayed, & photos accompanying—a lot of darkroom work when I return; is the enlarger still in limbo?
Off to meet a friend. Give my love to Donna & speedy recovery; don't get roasted by those crazy arsonists before I have a chance to cook you some African chop (prepare your buds by gargling w/ a tbsp. of tabasco before each meal). Again many thanks for the letter; the luck of a full moon.
Susi

A POSTCARD TO MIMI:

Sweets—I also think Patty Heart is an asshole, and as for the rest of the letter, "thanks" isn't enough for how good it makes me feel. I got it at a point when I had despaired of ever hearing from you & now my "mammy wagon" trips over dusty country roads will be filled w/ daydreams of that gen'l direction we can travel together on. I hope you understand how inadequately these words serve my feelings.
More important is a letter I just posted last week to your old dorm address, where I've mailed many letters in the past 2 months. Please go there & dig them up; I expected them to be forwarded but suppose they haven't been. Also got a wonderful letter from Cindy, all about arsonists & suicide & heartbreak (which is not to suggest it wasn't hysterically funny.)
[. . .]
Traveling is settling in me, a vague contentment, even anticipation at conquering the next border hassle or search for a cold beer.
Glad to be in Ghana, an amiable & inexpensive country w/ lovely beaches & woven cloth. Going north, back to the desert towns of white clay & silence. My love to you & I hope you find those letters!
Susi

> Got a sweet letter from my mother re: her wayward & maladjusted daughter—the 1st time she really spoke of it.

And here is that part of the letter from my mother:

> Yes, there were many things unsaid before you left, Su, and I have, as you might surmise, done a lot of reading and thinking and crying, even.
> A soft crying, silently, as a mother would and I keep wondering if this is a transitional stage in your life and just how much the divorce has played a part in this. I deeply regret now having shown so openly and disturbingly my extreme anger, desperation, deep hurt, humiliation before and after the divorce proceedings and which might have contributed to you being turned off by man, away from man, and also, in a sense, away from a "normal" life. [97] The one thing I would have avoided, could I have, was a divorce from a man of whom I have children. Because of the children. But maybe you think this is all rubbish—
> [...]
> I kept thinking about that strange affair [98] and how much it may have contributed to your turning to woman more than to man. Not ever having experienced this kind of feeling I am at a loss to comprehend it, i.e., anything beyond a deep and good spiritual friendship with women friends as I have with mine.
> I am glad you told me, and I am sure you felt relieved afterwards and I am further sure that you will allow me time to try to understand. And I want you also to feel assured of my love.

I witnessed a grand protest yesterday in Accra. Hundreds of market women in red scarves and red armbands surging down the main streets of town, the entire complex of market stalls deserted, protesting a plan to move some of the stalls out of the main market into outlying neighborhoods. A shouting and laughing and teasing match erupted between an offended male merchant and the women; he hurled sand and stones as they rushed forward, cussing, and then dashed back laughing and grabbing each other. Continuing on to the city council building, they massed in groups across the street and against the fence but were locked out by disapproving officials. A select committee represented them to confront the police, who were trying to remove them from the central city to their home locales, which would result in a large loss of business and much-needed income. I chatted with a few and was given "permission" to take some photos, but as I stood feebly aiming my camera at the heated crowd, through the lens I saw to my horror several very angry women, with muscles and curses, rushing towards me. They threatened to break my camera and said, "We aren't just pigs sitting on the

---

97 I am so impressed that she put "normal" in quotes.

98 With a guy I'd met after high school. I don't recall anything "strange" about it; he was a nice guy.

street!" There you have it, their notion of the interests that motivate any corrupted *oyibo* photographer. There was no convincing them of my solidarity. When they started pushing, nudging, and slapping my breasts and ass I sensed that I'd better clear out. I did. Without any pictures, but with a vivid memory [3].

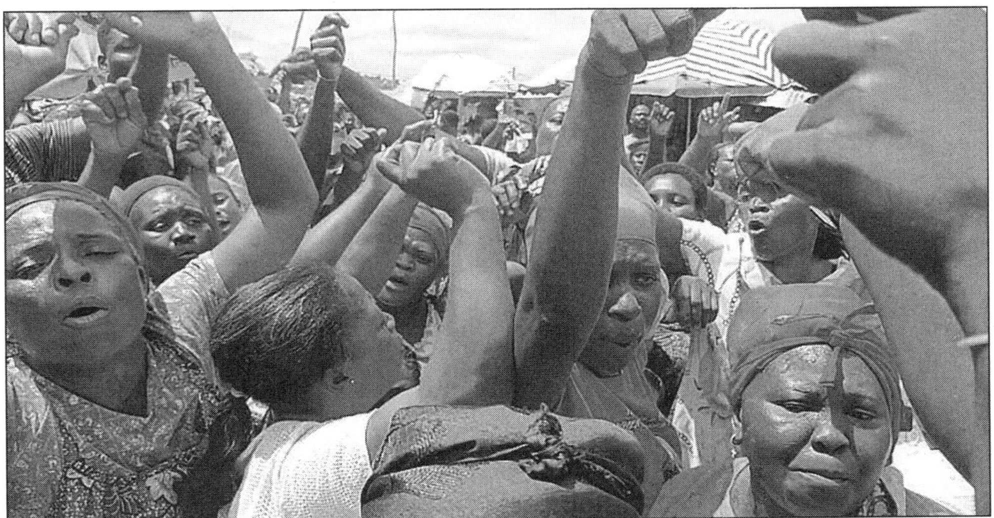

Women protesting in Ghana in 2015 about the same issue.

Had a beauty of a dress made for mom—I hope she's pleased.

God I get so angry at the Westerners at moments.
Had a conversation with Gail and Soren about a Ghanaian who Soren met who showed him around and told him of his plight of being unemployed for two years now with no prospect of a job in the near future. We haggled about the relative "happiness" of unemployment in Africa and America and they concluded to their easy consciences that it's oh so much better to be out of work here, one can still survive and yes, even be happy, imagine that. A juju feat to surpass even the hardiest poverty case in America. I'm sure they weren't meaning to sound like foremen on a southern migrant farm, but Jesus: Africans are such soulful people they can just dance their way through lifelong hardship? Indeed. They should read A.K. Armah's *Beautyful Ones . . .* to know the other/true half of the sad story [4].

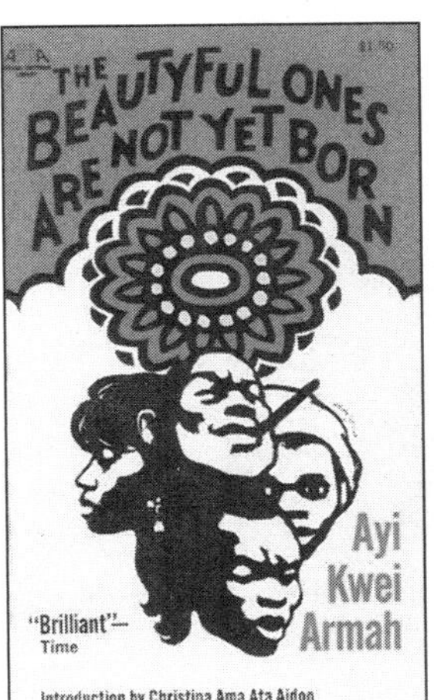

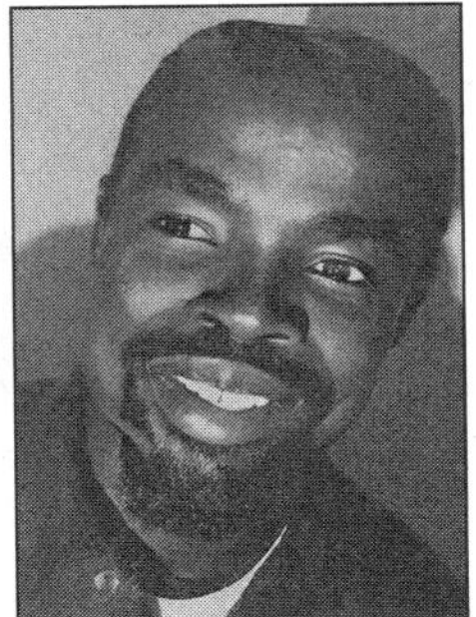

Soren was another good lesson in my tentative attraction to men with me assuming that they might even be attracted to my independent mind until I see them totally gripped by their primary need for ass-kissing—which he got from Gail and clearly resented not finding in me, like in his comment, "No matter what we talk about you have an opinion" (referring to the African mask he bought that I insisted was a fake).

I wouldn't be so disappointed in men if they didn't so consistently prove themselves disappointing; it's a deadening cycle which I'm quite happy to ignore and step away from.

Dropped in on a course about family planning at the Labour College; spoke with two very nice women (Charity Sakyi and Comfort Larbu) who were heading off to the villages afterward to enlighten and ease the pain of the women. They usually give them Lippes Loops, it's more reliable than the pill, which they'd invariably forget to take. They're aiming at three or four children, well-spaced—they said a lot of Ghanaians are already on the pill (which costs about 30 cents a month.) [99] I feel a small measure of relief when I hear things like this.

At the Accra National Museum there was a display of engravings of the "courageous" British massacre of the Ashanti which "succeeded" in destroying the town of Kumasi in 1890s but they didn't succeed in pilfering the Golden Stool of the Ashanti. [100] The British troops were uniformly mustachioed, trim and busy, and then there were the hordes of packhorse women carrying supplies to the hardy troops and the patriotic, traitorous Ghanaian slaves fighting their brothers and sisters.

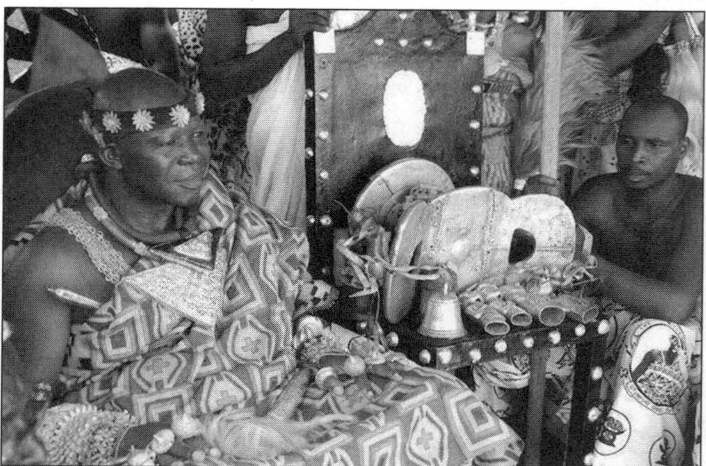

The current Asantahene, His Majesty Otumfuo Nana Osei Tutu II, seen with the Golden Stool.

99 In 2024, 30 cents = $1.70.

100 Ashanti or Ashantee was the more common way of spelling it back then, but Asante is the other, and now the common usage. See [5] for a history of the British rampages in Ghana.

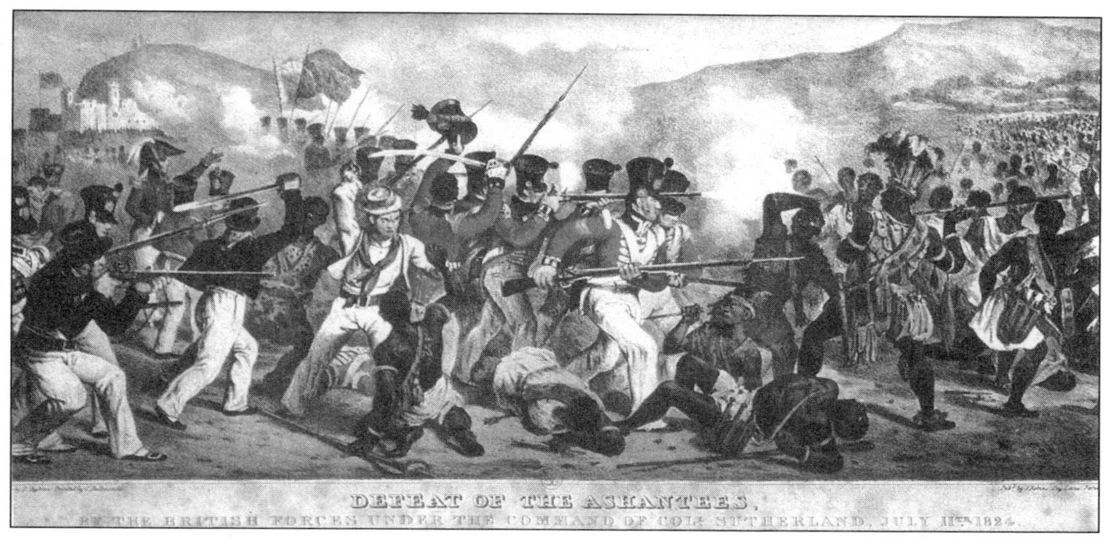

Defeat of the Ashantees by the British Forces
Under the Command of Col. Sutherland, July 11, 1824.

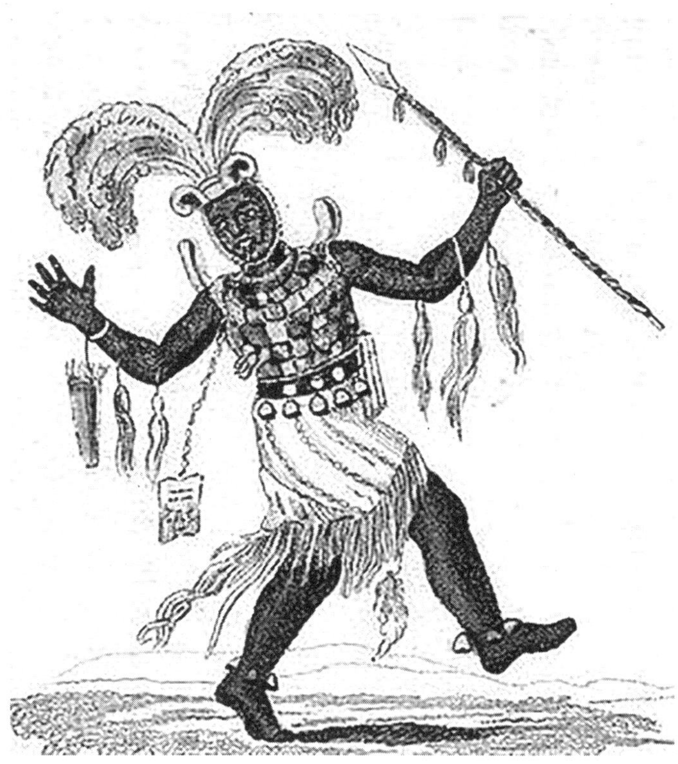

Ashantee captain in war dress, c. 1834.

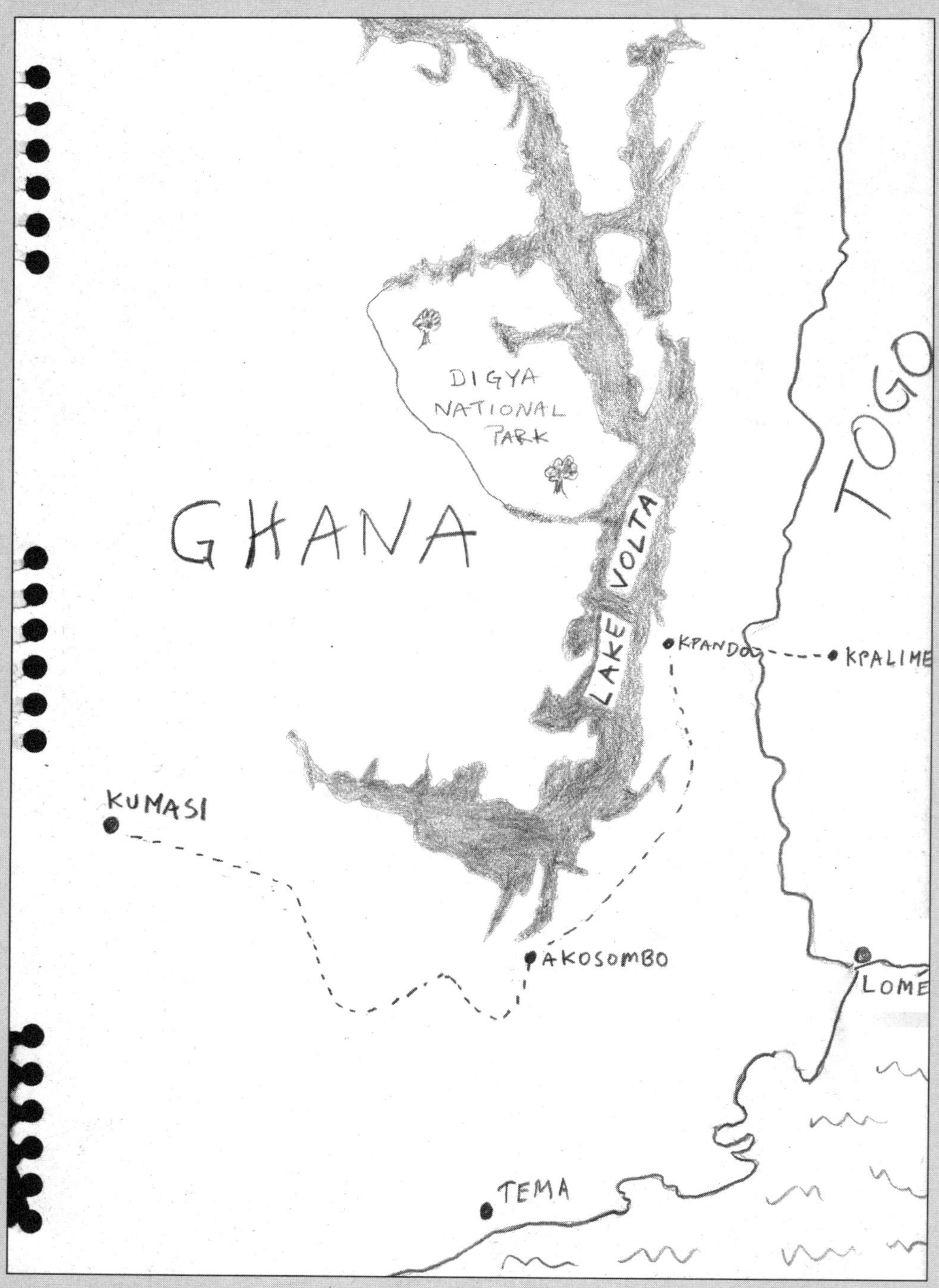

DIGYA
NATIONAL
PARK
GHANA
TOGO
VOLTA
LAKE
KPANDO
KPALIME
KUMASI
AKOSOMBO
LOMÉ
TEMA

CHAPTER SEVENTEEN

In Togo and Back into Ghana

I took a lorry east to Lomé, the capital city of Togo, and met up with Kay, the Australian.

MARCH 19–23

Kay and I were strolling absentmindedly across the city square in Lomé engrossed in a discussion about corruption and French pastry . . . In a calm monotone I said, "Be careful Kay not to step on that six-foot black and silver snake crawling your way."
It was a juju man with his enticements, and I'd bet they were venomous and anti-American. We fled.

The rich rich chocolate cake today made me glad I wasn't eating it so much these days. My taste buds right now prefer smoking a Gauloise.

A quite lucid local crazy man was berating some layabout young men near the French pastry shop. He was fixated on his "force" —which included military threats—but castigated them with, "How do you think you can live in a world of such technological advancement without being able to read and write? I have power because I'm educated (claims to be a doctor) but they are afraid of what I know and won't give me the power I need," and other similar and often painfully perceptive rhetoric about the impotence of a certain African type, the Cassandras.

"He could have asked if anything had changed after all, from the days of chiefs selling their people for the trinkets of Europe."
—*The Beautyful Ones Are Not Yet Born* by Ayi Kwei Armah

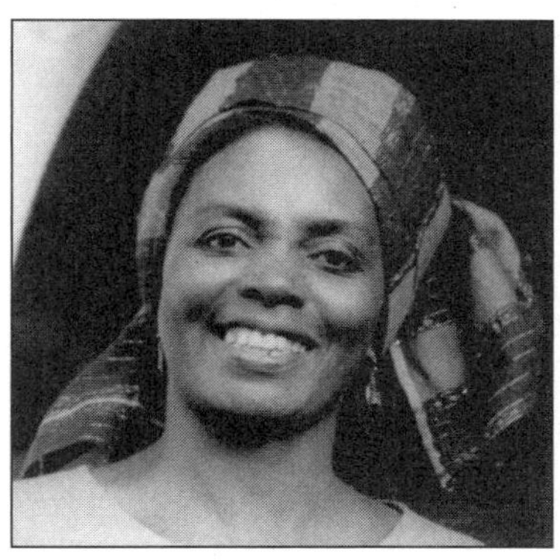

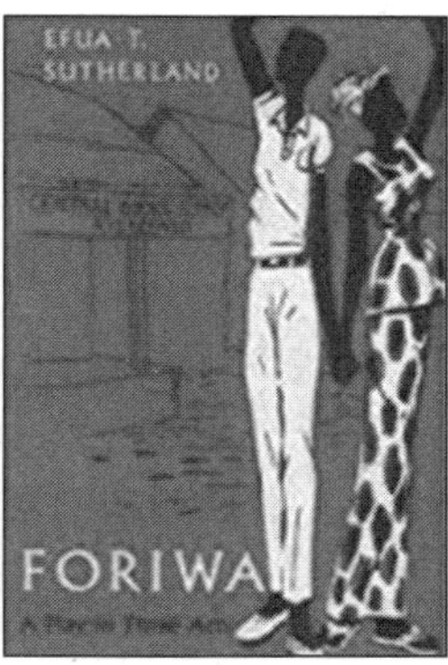

"They say that if you wonder how to do a job, do it, and wonder how you did it."
—*Foriwa* by Efua T. Sutherland [1]

I had a funny encounter with a Togolese student of English. He invited me chez lui [to his house] to practice his grammar and I discovered that he was engrossed in and struggling thru preparation for a debate on "women's lib" at the university. He was assigned the "pro" position, and asked me to write up a few arguments, which I did, haltingly, but ending with a flourish about the antagonistic relationship between husband and wife today—

A LETTER FROM THE STUDENT, KOMLA MARTIN BANSAH:

Martin spoke French—Togo's official language—and was not fluent in English.

BANSAH Komla Martin
Etudiant en lettres
Université du Bénin
B.P. 1516
Lomé - Togo
Lomé 05th June 76

My dear Friedrich,
Such a name could be unknown to you in your first view. It's true though you have known many people by going through all over Africa. I think you have done better research and I believe that before you left Togo, you have been given sufficient documents about women here in Togo, and how women are fighting for their liberation. In my next letter we shall discuss about it.
Excuse me for delaying some minutes before coming to our rendezvous last. This because a friend came to me and in our custom here if a visitor come to you at anytime you have to give him a full reception. But after all I tried to be at the hotel 8:30 but you have gone already.
How did you spend the following trip? How do you find Africa? Excuse me to end my letter in this way because we are in Exam period and the moment is very hard. Hoping to read from you soon. I stop here with greetings.
Yours sincerely,
Martin

PART OF A LETTER TO MIMI:

Baby. Such an interesting walk I had tonight in Lomé, capital of frenchified Togo. Here for 3 days to get renowned sandals & visit a friend, an Australian woman traveling alone for 9 months. Sturdy & good-natured. Anyway the walk . . . .streets here immensely wide, 2 lanes plus no paving, soft cushions of sand, quiet pitch dark streets punctuated by kerosene lamplit peanut vendors & fufu w/ pepper stew outdoor dinners, the cement houses alternate between spare noisy populated but clean Togolese and austere invariably newly whitewashed fenced discreet Frenchies' homes . . . by which I don't exclude frenchified Togolese. But a very sensuous walk—the tender ground, star-laden sky, babies' voices, pounding of fufu, mothers suckling their 9th or 10th baby . . . a sight to bring a searing pain to my crotch when I remind myself she's probably, at most, 28.

Witnessing a spontaneous dance at the moment sitting on the balcony of the hotel facing the beach, a crowd of women after market day pass all loaded high w/ pots & sacks & babies, they stop, unload themselves & begin teasing each other into silly dance steps, each braving a few seconds' worth & collapsing in laughter, repeated by the others. A strolling man comes along, they accept the impulse & begin to follow him, single file, making monkey hands & mimicking his waddle, and off they go to another late nite of pounding yam & stoking fires & counting the day's money.

[. . .]

Got a fantastic thick old yellowed ivory bracelet yesterday, & tomorrow will get some funny stiff little fetish figures.

[. . .]

I don't think I mentioned it in my last letter: Got plane ticket, in Accra, after an exasperating bureaucratic runaround, in cedis (Ghana $), i.e. at 300% the official rate (3 c. to 1$ compared to 1.5 c to 1$ at bank)—i.e. making ticket from $350 to $131. It's Bamako (Mali) to Casablanca. Figured that was an uncommon route to end a curious trip. Changed plans again, will be back to Ghana, up to Upper Volta, down by famously comfortable & cheap train to Ivory Coast, over to Liberia, back up to Mali.

My route now has become this:

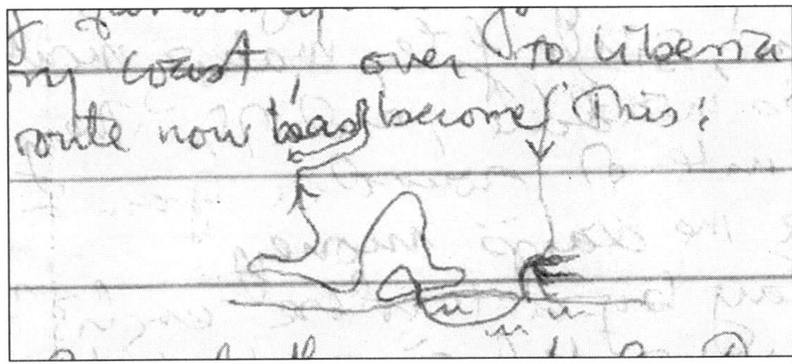

Went to the UNFT (The Union Nationale de Femmes Togolaises) in an air-conditioned empty office in the RPT building [101] with its copper reflecting windows. As with all unions and movements here it is under the benevolent wing of the Eyadéma [102] government.

101 A major convention center and the home of The Rally of the Togolese People (*Rassemblement du Peuple Togolais*, RPT), which was the ruling party in Togo from 1969 to 2012.

102 Gnassingbé Eyadéma was the President of Togo for thirty-eight years. See [2] for more information about the comic book and his crazy reign.

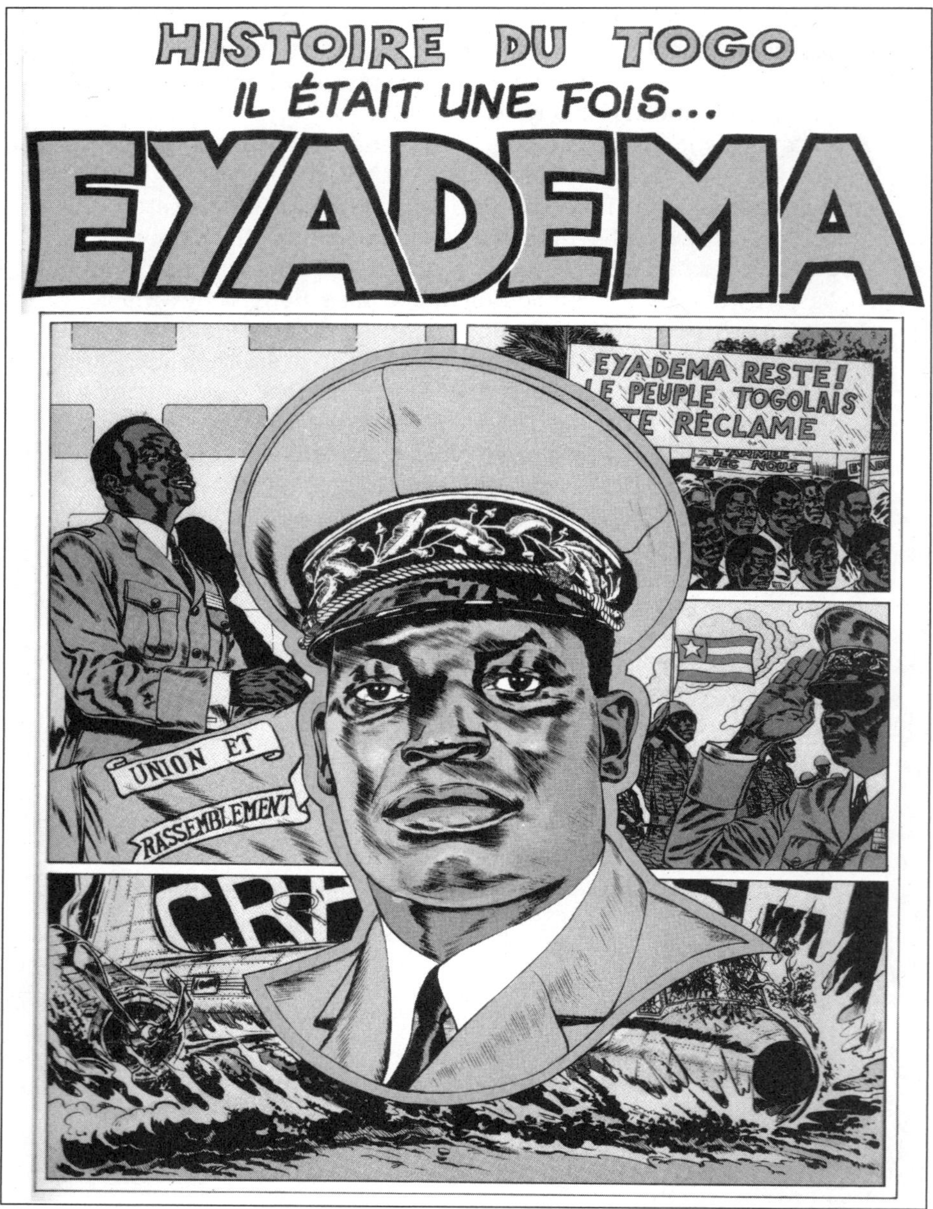

Once upon a time . . . Eyadema by Serge Saint-Michel

Eyadéma always claimed that he was the lone survivor of a plane crash on January 24, 1974. He wasn't.

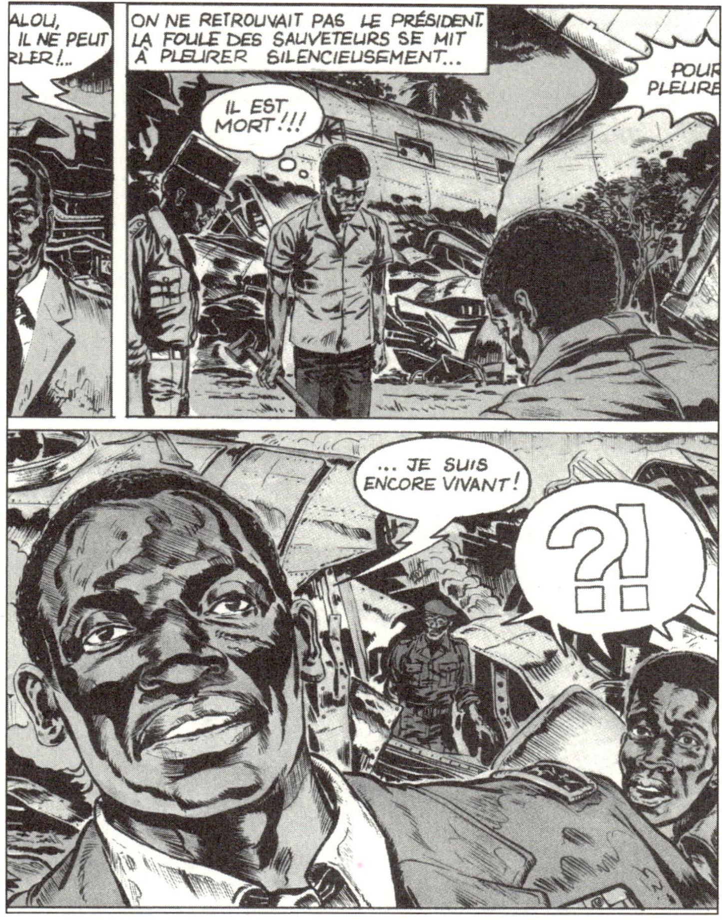

On ne retrouvait pas le Président. La foule des sauveteurs se mit à pleurer silencieusement . . .
[The President could not be found. The crowd of rescuers began to cry silently...]
Il est mort! [He's dead!]
Je suis encore vivant! [I'm still alive!]

PART OF A LETTER TO MIMI:

Oh god, or goddess, give them the strength! the *Union Nationale de Femmes Togolaises* is an air-conditioned sterile thoroughly undynamic office in the sleek government building in Lomé, four women chatting two of them sitting unoccupied & glassy-eyed behind electric typewriters the other two just sitting. I really tried to squeeze something anything out of them. Nothing. Any programs? What do you mean exactly? Well, let's see, how about for the market women, or birth control, or?

No, sorry, the president isn't here today; if you'd like an appointment . . .
Thanks, but no.
At least I got an IWY-Togo poster from them.
Smiley *mercis* of promise to send a graphics poster in exchange. Yea yea.
And a mimeo of their bylaws. Lists, I suppose impressive to the wishful, of officials & regulations & appendices & conditions of membership, etc.
The real *union des femmes* goes on in the markets here—unofficial & immensely subversive to the new systems which are being perpetrated by Mercedes Benz owners w/ yearly promotions. Have ordered the women of Accra to take their stalls to the neighborhoods . . . and clear the way for junior executives. But those women are crafty & fierce & all I can do is grit my teeth & hope they succeed against such a sleazy enemy: price control & efficiency . . . ha!
[. . .]
This letter is being orchestrated by James Brown and *Gitanes, bout filter*. A caress to a throat ravaged by Nigeria's 555 ("For That Special Taste of Success"—a white man big car coat casually tossed over right shoulder.)

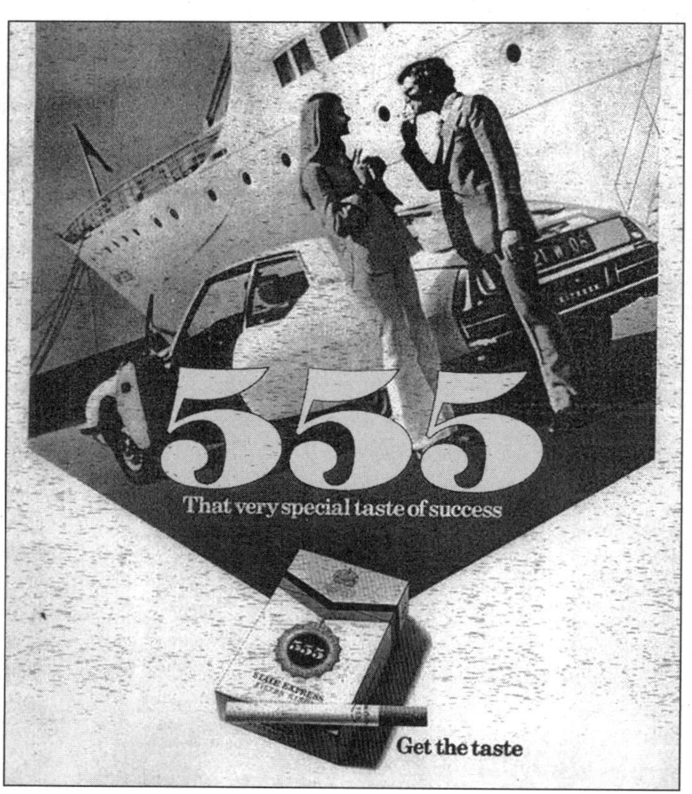

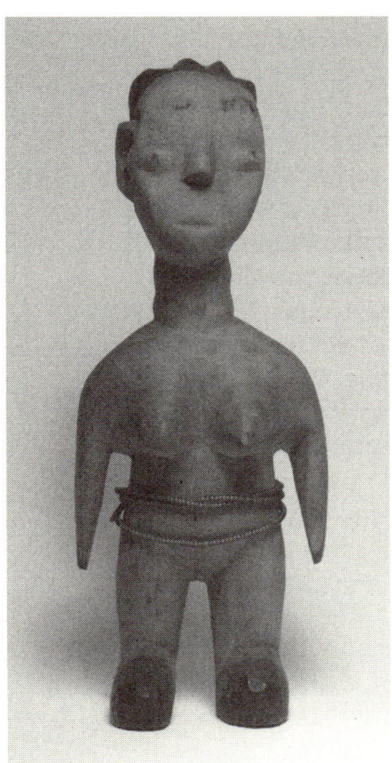

I bought two funny ungraceful American Gothic-faced pointy-assed wooden juju dolls/women to be laden w/ beads & feathers & soft stroking. Not a pseudo-aged tourist one, but a crude unpolished crooked new one, at one of the many weird smelling fascinating juju stalls in every town. And a juju bell! When I picked up the bells & noisemakers the nearby market women began to "ayeee" & click their tongues & stop me w/ hostility (no, fear) in their voices. But a great 8-belled staff in rough iron, & a snake symbol & two-pronged hook at the ends. A bitch to transport around for another 2 months. . . .
(I lost it in Lomé.)

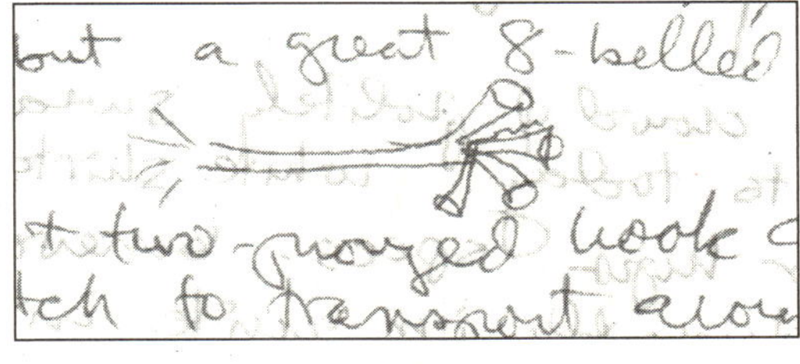

Oh I'm getting so attached to this life this air & noise the bodies the time but I also know it would never be enough because I always will be operating on different premises than is required to live here. Certain assumptions about the type of people I'll be wanting to live with & realizing I would never find them here.
A crab is coming my way & he doesn't seem the least bit disconcerted at my jabbing Bic pen, my "hey, hey!"
I have come to admire insects here for their size and audacity. Rats & bats for sale in the market, cooked or fresh, to your liking. And Bazooka bubble gum. How can I even miss B&C's [103] if I have a big juicy wad of sugary American stuck between my teeth? Excuse me, it's the reefer from a small fishing village 40kms out of Lomé (worth remembering).
Damnable things, these women walking 5 miles a.m. & p.m. to market, 30–60 lbs on their heads, baby hanging on, their husbands on motor scooters to a day as an anonymous negligible file clerk of equally negligible "Ministry of . . . " This place is a combination of Kafka & The Threepenny Opera with a daily overdose of social realism.
[. . .]

103 Bonnie & Clyde's was a great dyke bar at 82 West Third Street in NYC which ran from the early 1970s to the mid-1980s.

Lomé was by far the finest African city I've visited. I think Abidjan will be a kick in the ass, being infamous as the most European of W. African (or African) cities, full of "modern school" architecture & expensive restaurants (& grocery stores that have food on the shelves) (no small accomplishment here).
The most obvious, & my major, regret is that I don't speak the language(s); as much as I sit around & watch & make Pidgin English talk w/ the people I miss so many of the subtleties; the glimpses I get of, e.g., the way they speak in proverbs makes me wish I could share that part of them (I get some of it from African novels). But at best & as hard as I try, I only skim the surface. Visually/sensually I'm very involved, but I can feel a big gap in my understanding (which doesn't necessarily lessen my experience).
In your letter you said something about both of us being thru a time of growth but mine being a "more extreme one"—I don't really feel that it's extreme, just a lot of completely unfamiliar and therefore unclassified information bombarding me. It doesn't feel extreme, just excessive at times.

On the 23rd I headed for Kpandu[104], a town on the edge of Lake Volta on the eastern side of Ghana. Miss Teresa Aymah, the sister of Larry Dzameh from the Offin River ship, lived there and Larry said that I would be able to stay with her.
Seemingly, the most sensible route was to head north in Togo as far as Woamé (near Kpalime) and then cross the border back into Ghana.

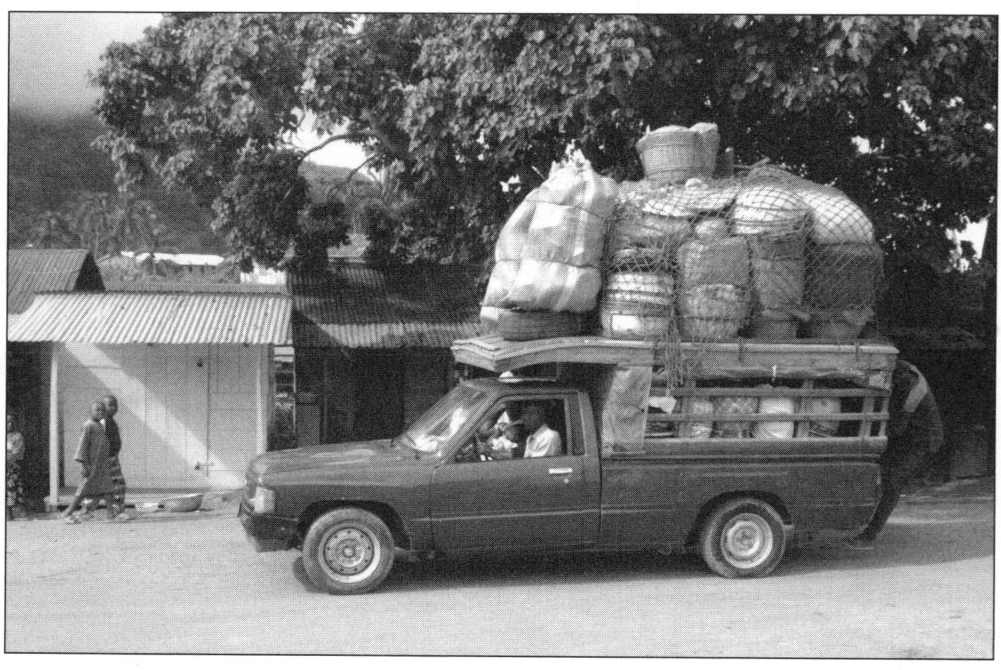

104 I spelled it with a "u" but online now most sources spell it as Kpando, with an "o".

PART OF A LETTER TO CINDY:

Jesus Christ if I have to grin a sweet international accord grin to one more bright African child I think I'll scream (it's the afternoon sun and tenth cigarette.)
Sending you these books after reconsidering my mother's reception of them. You'll understand why when you peer within. The 2 African novels[105], worth the reading, speak some bald truths about this Africa.
[. . .]
A sleepy town, Woamé, center of Togo. I expected housing w/ the Peace Corper I met in Ghana; he of course wasn't here & I was lodged fed bathed at the house of the bar owner, David Kojo Anthony, who has 3 wives, 23 children ("*pour faire un monde*" he says [106]). Funny funny murals painted ages ago on his walls, a sleazy woman in western dress being sweet-talked by a man w/ alligator eyes, above is written in French "if possible I will sell my car"; a highlife-type female vocalist in the toilet. A naked white serpent lady in the courtyard, green hair, pink eyes.
[. . .]

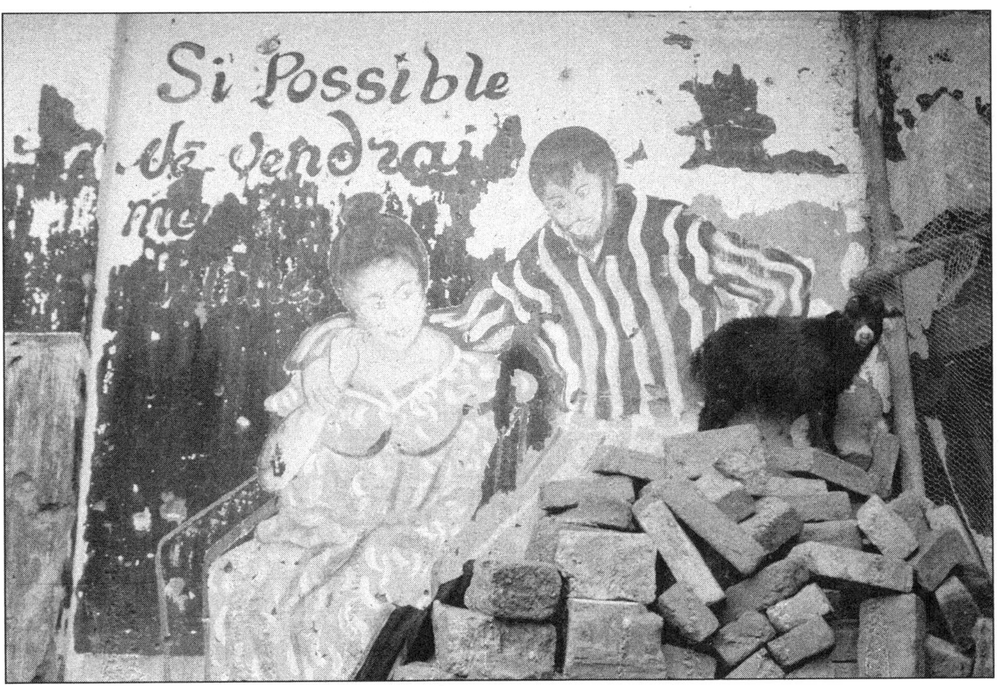

105 Cindy and I can't remember what they were. The ones that I didn't want to send to my mother were undoubtedly the lesbian-themed books.

106 "To make a world"

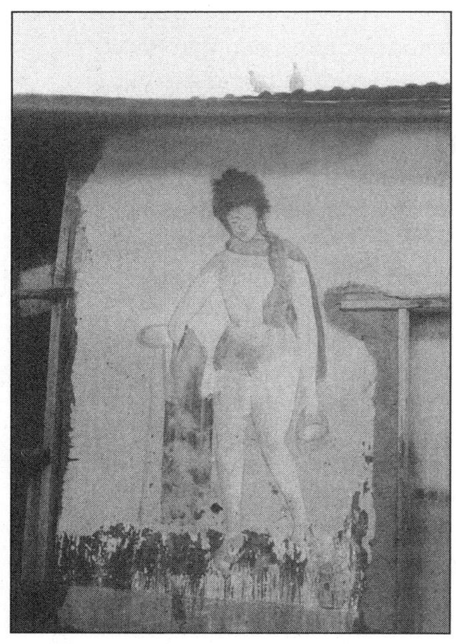

I fluctuate wildly between fascination & boredom in these villages; fortunately the barman speaks good French & we got into a very funny conversation last night about *gris-gris* (voodoo)—his contribution to the demolition of African traditional belief was to repeat at each protestation by us that, "*Gris-gris, c'est zero!*" [Voodoo, it's nothing!] very emphatically, w/ an edge of contempt.
Like the woman in Nigeria who told me that a lovely procession of women w/ sculptures on their heads, chanting, were "idol worshippers."

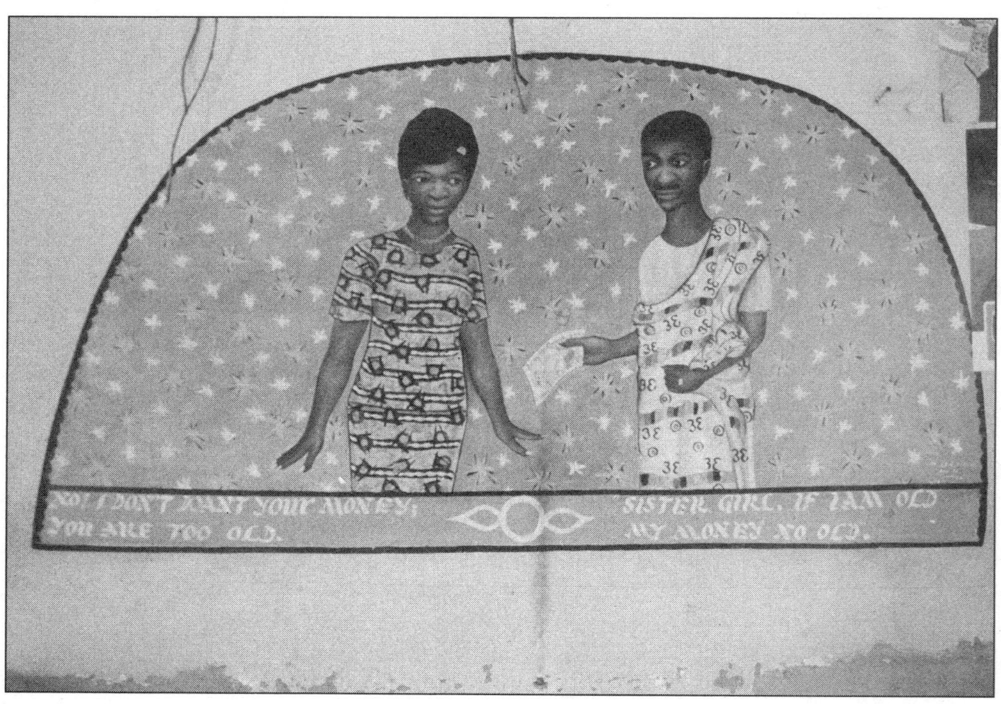

NO! I DON'T WANT YOUR MONEY;
YOU ARE TOO OLD.

SISTER GIRL, IF I AM OLD
MY MONEY NO OLD.

PART OF A LETTER TO MIMI:

So many dim-witted blissed-out French men here in Togo w/ two of whom I went strolling along a mountain stream today to alleviate my boredom; returned to the village to be immediately surrounded by wide-eyed children scrutinizing me as I ate, every gesture provoking laughter or murmurs . . . esp. when I licked my left hand, a thoroughly impolite thing to do here. All this sitting about tends to dislodge the critical senses, one watches and watches & imperceptibly begins to accept it all, as it is, without reference to preconceptions or previous misconceptions. And yet I can't quite believe that right now I'm hearing Rita Coolidge on a Togolese radio station in a town of at most 200 up in the bush and a guy just walked by w/ a bicycle-style pack w/ the "Keep on Truckin'" guy on it. I once would have disapproved . . .

[. . .]

Spent the night w/ the town barkeeper, in the wives' quarters, was well fed, rice, duck meat, beer, wine, even Marlboros and another of those memorable outdoor showers beneath a clear moonless sky—I now

really appreciate rooms which I used to be uncomfortable in, the cement-walled small-windowed rooms, the only decoration a government calendar & ageless photograph of some anonymous well-dressed elder. And the proud array of sweet sixteen talcum powder & Woolworths-style earrings.

Remember my funny body?[3]

Well, the days w/ whites improved it markedly but once I go back into the hills & stay w/ village people I'm fed & expected to consume huge amounts of starch. Raw starch. And enjoy it & take more. Breakfast lunch dinner. W/ warm beer.

I refuse to refuse it, on any grounds, because when you are offered, proudly, a well-prepared quantity of the one gift they probably can afford to give me, I don't make rude protestations about my waistline or anything else equally inconceivable (the women here are generally about my size & content w/ it). So I spend days eating starch & then days on oranges & cigarettes & it works out to an even zero.

One eventful thing: the French bakery in Lomé enticed me to buy an apple tart which to my dismay did nothing for my spirits. I've gotten quite indifferent to sweets—even a thickly iced piece of chocolate cake, which 2 months ago I was hallucinating about, made me feel more uncomfortable than blissful.

I think it was the luxury of it that made me queasy. A well-prepared western meal, yes, but the ostentatious pleasure of chocolate cake was too much (don't worry, I'm not an ascetic).

The next morning, I continued my effort to get to Kpandu.

PART OF A LETTER TO CINDY:

God damn it, I'm stuck on a dirt road outside Woamé, the lorry is mired in the mud after a heavy night rain, they keep accelerating & getting in deeper and deeper.
And it's going to rain again & I'll miss my boat.
Such are the tribulations of this thrilling adventure. I want to <u>move</u>.
A guy just passed w/ a 2 ft. rat hanging limp in his hand. I exclaimed, & he insisted that it was a small one.
[. . .]
Later, we stopped our lorry when the driver sighted a woman by the roadside selling a <u>bigger</u> rat; he didn't get it because of the price; I swear if he had I would've had to hold it in my lap next to him on the front seat. Ahem . . .
It's absolutely impossible! There are 9 strong grown men here "working" on the road, i.e., standing around watching the bus get stucker & stucker & a bunch of 10 year olds from the nearby school are pushing & digging & NONE of the men have offered to help, after an hour of work. I am beginning to smolder. (Then I remind myself that I've seen it all before.)

During one of the times of waiting, I watched some men play this game, which I had already seen elsewhere. It's variously called Mancala, Oware, and Awalé.

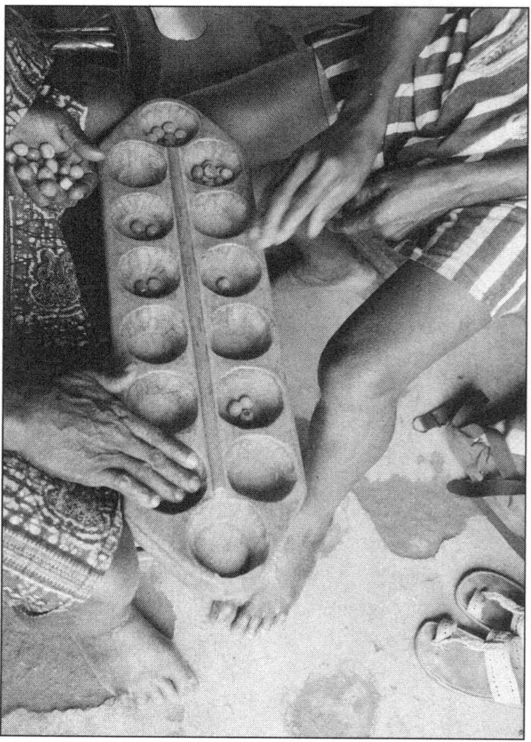

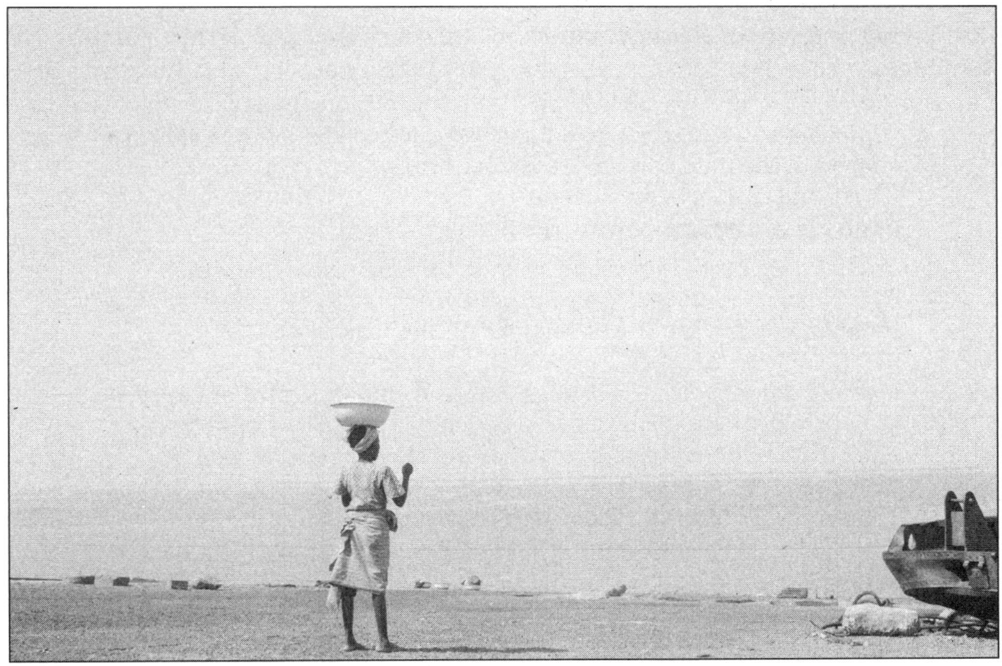

MARCH 24

It took me seven and a half hours to go fifty miles, from Woamé to Kpandu. So much waiting and smoking. But at least it passed thru some beautiful countryside—the scarps [4] of Ghana: tall, forested hills and wide valleys traversed by winding roads, fresh mushrooms, flawless bananas.

At the Bwamé junction a Fulani man with glazed eyes and reddened fingers sat with me muttering in an incomprehensible mixture of Ewe and Pidgin; all I could decipher was that he wanted to marry me and could I buy him an orange. The ladies at the stall were unabashed in their mockery of him, addressing him as "Fulani" with a spirit in their voices and telling me not to get him the orange, everyone with such threat or sagacity in their eyes (that "you know what will happen if you give him one; he'll expect more" type of racism/classism) and there I was, between the burnt-out Fulani who clearly didn't like the insults but had to live with them, and the upright schoolteacher who was concerned that he was bothering me.

I stayed in the uncomfortable limbo that I always find here, not wanting to step on their customs but being drawn to do just that by my own different values (e.g., defense of the underdog/"weirdo"). And it's not just theirs, but a worldwide custom of fear of unpopularity and the need to conform. Witness how good they felt being on the laughing side of the joke, and how they expected me to indulge in the same "relief."

I'm staying with Miss Teresa Aymah, who is the headmistress of the Kpandu Secondary School. Bed and bath and tea. She's such a non-conversationalist. I feel like an interrogator, always asking the questions (which are usually answered in a short sentence followed by a long silence), but it's a recuperative stay after that dreadful trip.

PART OF A LETTER TO CINDY:

I bullshitted my way back across the Ghana border (for which I *didn't* have a re-entry visa) and was proposed to by a slightly mad Fulani. (Fulanis are the Polish joke of Ghana.)

[. . .]

I am comfortably set up at Miss Teresa Aymah's, sister of Larry, the seaman-friend from the trip to Ghana. I used to dislike traveling from one "contact" to another but these roads, & food, & rain-heat . . .

The room is, of course, decorated w/ framed pictures of hippie Jesus, and oddly a book on Tolstoy in Ashanti (a major Ghanaian language).

Got two juju dolls in Lomé; one is for Helen, who asked me, of all things, to get her a doll from Africa & though these would never be used as toys it's the closest I can come. Toys are not a priority here for hungry kids.

Oh god there's also a March 1972 *Reader's Digest* here w/ "It's Time to Speak Up for National Defense" by Margaret Chase Smith.

Looking forward to a dinner at the crêpe place & telling you about all the silly things I've seen here. (I tend to overlook the tragedy these days; they do, and it's pretty damn fruitless to do otherwise. I may still listen & criticize & shake my head in disbelief, but my tendency towards messiah-talk and outrage has diminished.)

Like "they" say, it's always easier to have all-inclusive dreams & plans about a thing that keeps its encompassable distance. But to be wading thru all this tradition & corruption & so very lopsided change really makes me ease down. Maybe I'm just overwhelmed by the proportions of everything. One good example: the number of babies (and all that implies) (and necessitates).

[. . .]

I've met a number of women chiefs & they're all I wanted them to be: imperious, uncompromising, shrewd. (Why the hell can't I get out of admiring those macho characteristics when I meet them in women, damn it!?)

Must go join my hostess now for chop. I hope it's good; I brought her some fresh mushrooms (my first in 5 months, perhaps).

Love love love to you all—sometime soon,

Susi

My Ashanti name is Esi: born on Sunday. I like it.

I reread Mimi's letter and still can't entirely believe the intensity of the words, not because I doubt her sincerity (which is so clear in her words and the simple straight forwardness) but it's too much of that best of good things: to be loved by someone I love. And I do.

PART OF A LETTER TO MIMI:

A boy named Thomas just came to my room, the junior brother of the seaman who gave me the address of his sister w/ whom I'm staying. He asked me to send him a wristwatch from the states. You see, I'm a rich white, we're all rich whites. And as much as I protest that category, that inseparable adjective from white, I have to admit that we are all rich, richer than we can imagine until we come to a country like this. All the givens at home are extravagances here, all of them, even a different meal every day or a few changes of clothes. A coke a day, buying a full pack of cigarettes instead of one or two loosies, having a room of one's own. And to be moderate & tell them we can earn $300/month sends them into tirades of awe & incomprehension.[107]

So I play it very cool.

At least I've gotten somewhat over the guilt of walking down the street w/ food in my mouth/hand.

(I shouldn't complain; West Africa (at least in the southern end) is relatively well-fed & housed. It's the desert that sends me spinning.)

But damn it, all it seems to do, after the commiserating & stupefaction, is make me miss like hell the psychological freedom at home from such a relentless battle for survival. I know we have our problems, but at least we also have diversions from them, a very crucial complement. (I realize I'm speaking for a very limited "we.") I admit it: I miss intellectual (and feminist) stimulation. What I get here is in a different form, and not completely satisfying.

Sorry; a full day of traveling always brings out these nostalgias.

And I miss you, which has a lot to do with it, yes?

I'm off, to "see Kpandu at nite" (and buy some mosquito coils!)

I wish you could share one of these nights w/ me, the air is so fresh, the chorus of animal sounds comfortably far away, the sky so dark & clear, the coolness such a long-anticipated relief from the steamy day (it's rainy season, the thickest & hottest time of year). And always these simple rooms & creaky beds.

I'm getting excited now at the prospect of going to Morocco (altho I'll be there at peak hippie season), one place I never wanted to go until I went to Algeria & grew to love (the non-sex-related aspects of) Muslim culture. And I think I can like it only in small doses; being there continually it would be impossible to overlook/forgive the vulgar sexism.

---

107 My rent then was $150 (in 2024, that's $850). I earned about $500/month but, considering our relative annual incomes, I didn't want to mention larger amounts of money.

I hope New York still holds its charm for you; I remember it quite affectionately.
After this letter not much, because the P.O. service up north is impossible. I'll be safe & sunburnt & thinking of you (at final exams & otherwise).
I embrace you,
Susi

A LETTER FROM THOMAS MOORE DZAMEH:

25 April 1976
Dear Suzi,

It is a great happiness on my part for writing you this missive. How are conditions going in Chicago? I hope and guess everything is alright. I am the boy whom you came to see at Kpandu Secondary School, I am Larry's younger brother. Please I (told) asked you to buy me a wrist watch and you promised me to buy it for me when you reach home. I am therefore begging you to buy it for me. In our school if you don't have any wristwatch, you will find it very difficult to go to school on time and I always go to school late because I have no watch.
Please I will like to have one of your pictures (photograph) for remembrance.
Kindly reply this of my letter, I beg.
I remain with warmest greetings
Yours Ever
Thomas Moore Dzameh

Kpandu Secondary School
PO Box 48
Kpandu – Ghana, West Africa

From Kpandu, I attempted to take a ferry westward across Lake Volta to go northward in Ghana.

MARCH 25

A thoroughly fucked day. A dusty morning with Teresa to the long-awaited boat which I was misinformed would not come until next Tuesday so off I went with Erwin back to Kpandu and then down to Akosombo to go by road north. I almost knew, before I got to the boat, that somehow the trip was foul, unmeant . . . when we approached Kpandu yesterday I felt greasy, drawn away from it, and now I understand why . . .
But I should've listened to my information rather than the officers at the shore... everyone here is more or less full of shit.
And then there's my new acquaintance Erwin, who I met yesterday at Bwamé junction and who at that time told me a preposterous story of his good friend the American astronaut.

Africans Lionize a Pride of Spacemen

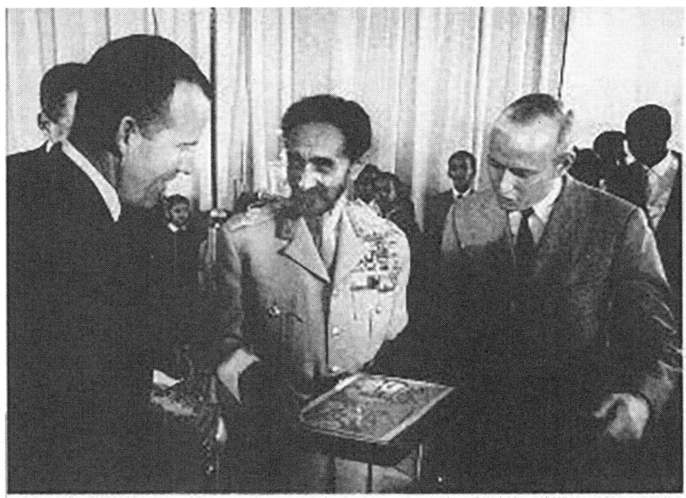

LION IN WAIT. Standing a respectful distance from lion chained to top of steps at left, welcomers await the astronauts at Addis Ababa airport. The lion got fidgety and was taken away, sparing the astronauts the necessity of stepping over him. Above, at the palace, Cooper (*left*) and Conrad give Emperor Selassie an album of photographs they took from space.

MEETING MALAGASQUES. Pete and Jane Conrad swap greetings (*below*) with citizens along the route to a U.S. tracking station in Tananarive, the capital of the Malagasy Republic.

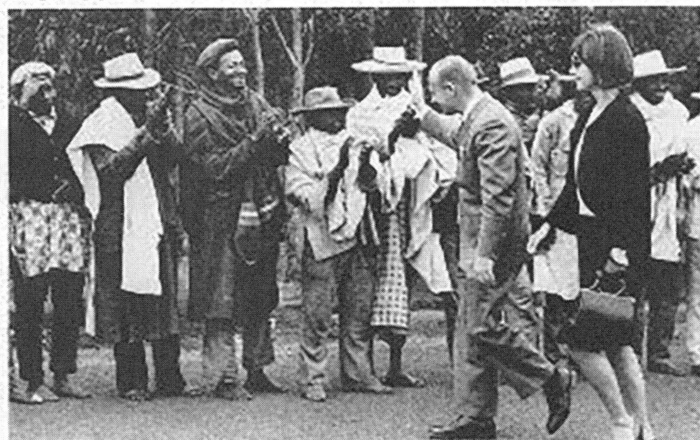

When Africa sets out to lionize visiting celebrities, there is no half-measure about it. Making a good-will tour of Africa, Astronauts Gordon Cooper and Pete Conrad were awaited at Addis Ababa, the capital of Ethiopia, by an airport welcome (*far left*) that might give pause to the most intrepid of space heroes. But before the plane arrived with the astronauts, their wives and Cooper's two teen-age daughters, the big cat got tired of impersonating a red carpet and was led away. There was a leonine encounter anyway, with the Conquering Lion of Judah, Emperor Haile Selassie (*left above*).

In Nigeria and again in the Malagasy Republic (*left*), crowds turned out to cheer the men whom local U.S. tracking stations had helped keep tabs on. In Kenya, Cooper and Conrad described their own fireball re-entry to the man who is known as "The Burning Spear," President Jomo Kenyatta (*left below*). Flying to Kenyatta's version of the LBJ ranch—a game lodge in the bush country—Cooper took over the controls of their small aircraft and promptly got lost. He finally found the landing strip just in time for a war-dancing welcome from Masai tribesmen and the gift of two 6-foot spears from their host. "We've been wanting these for a long time," said Cooper. "They're just the thing to stick in our director of operations."

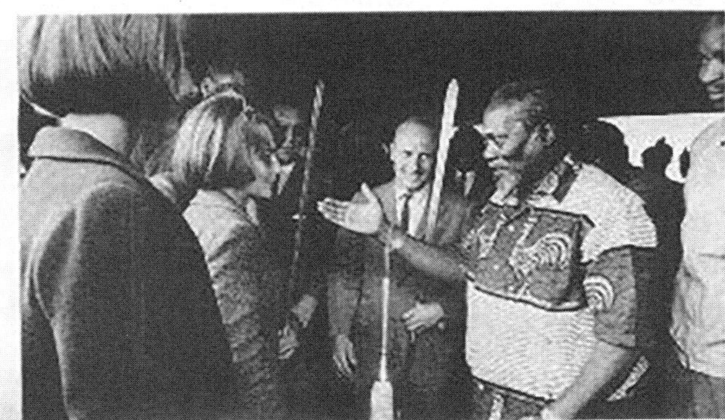

SPEARS FOR SPACEMEN. At his game lodge in Kenya, President Kenyatta tells Trudy Cooper how Masai warriors make spears like the two he has just given to the astronauts.

Today, with his antique double lens camera and battered Agfa pack, he gave me the full story.
Eight years ago Lt. John Cooper II of NASA came on a goodwill propaganda tour of Africa after his moonshot. My companion, then allegedly a security man for Nkrumah, presented a picture of blue-eyed, square-jawed Cooper with two live turkeys at the airport and had his picture done in color. "He brought so many European ladies on his plane, maybe twenty . . . "
His eyes glazed over, a weak smile of memory, bittersweet, played on his lips.
I'll not forget him sitting on the bus, the official photo of Cooper with the inscription "with are (sic) best wishes, to Erwin" dangling, cracked and worn, from his slender hand, and his lost-in-memory gaze out the window as he relived that one moment of glory in his life.
He insisted that if I'd let him accompany me to Accra he'd introduce me to all the important people, and he just couldn't fathom why I didn't want to meet Shirley Temple Black or why I wouldn't drink beer. Or why I couldn't accept (exorbitant to a Ghanaian) the offer of twenty cedis [$23.00][108] for a night with him.

Rumor has it that Shirley Temple will replace Moynihan as US ambassador to the UN. How politic (although she is a raving success with Ghanaians).[109]

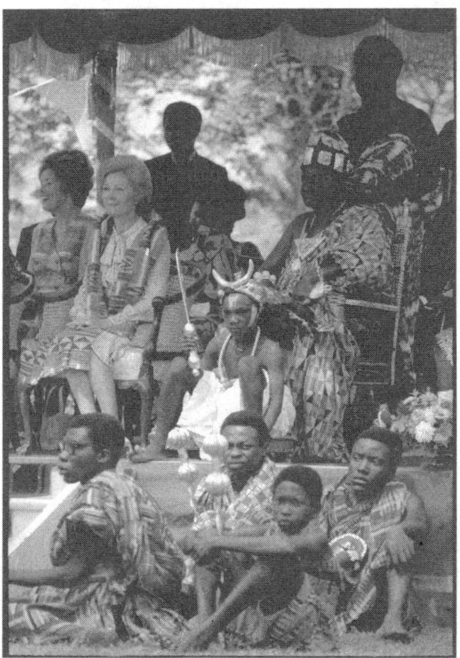

Temple (far left) with First Lady Pat Nixon and Chief Nana Osae Djan II in Ghana, 1972

108 In 2024, that's $130.00.

109 Temple served as the US ambassador to Ghana from 1974 to 1976, and my snarky comment was quite ignorant. See [5] to learn about her impressive career.

No American news for weeks now.

Another seven and a half hours from Akosombo to Kumasi, entirely nerve-wracking, with a drunk, nasty drunk, loud drunk lorry driver and aimless circles.
But I managed to spend most of the ride on *The Egoist*, which just gets better all the time despite Clara's misgivings and the damnable charm of Horace de Craye, her knight to the rescue. An amazing treatise on the arrogance and self-servingness of man and the total coercion of women. His first attacks aimed at "crushing" her to his will, making her suffer for the impudence of rejecting him, HIM, and then a double take to a phony renunciation of need for the world's admiration, and a satisfied pronouncement on the good and evil incompatible halves of the world . . . Guess who the evil one is?
And she, so caught in a battle between duty and honor, her honor for once, her pride in herself, not to supplicate to the demeaning wedding bed. It has all the ponderous and convoluted qualities of any respectable 19th c. English novel but through it a clear light shines—or glares.
But the outcome is yet to be seen . . . will she succeed? Will she be a Victorian with a room of her own making, or will it be made by a less reprehensible man than Willoughby, but still a man? She seeks the love of friendship and for that alone she has my unfailing respect.
Today I saw two women with International Women's Year (African style) fabric on—quite an ironic relief in the midst of my gloom.

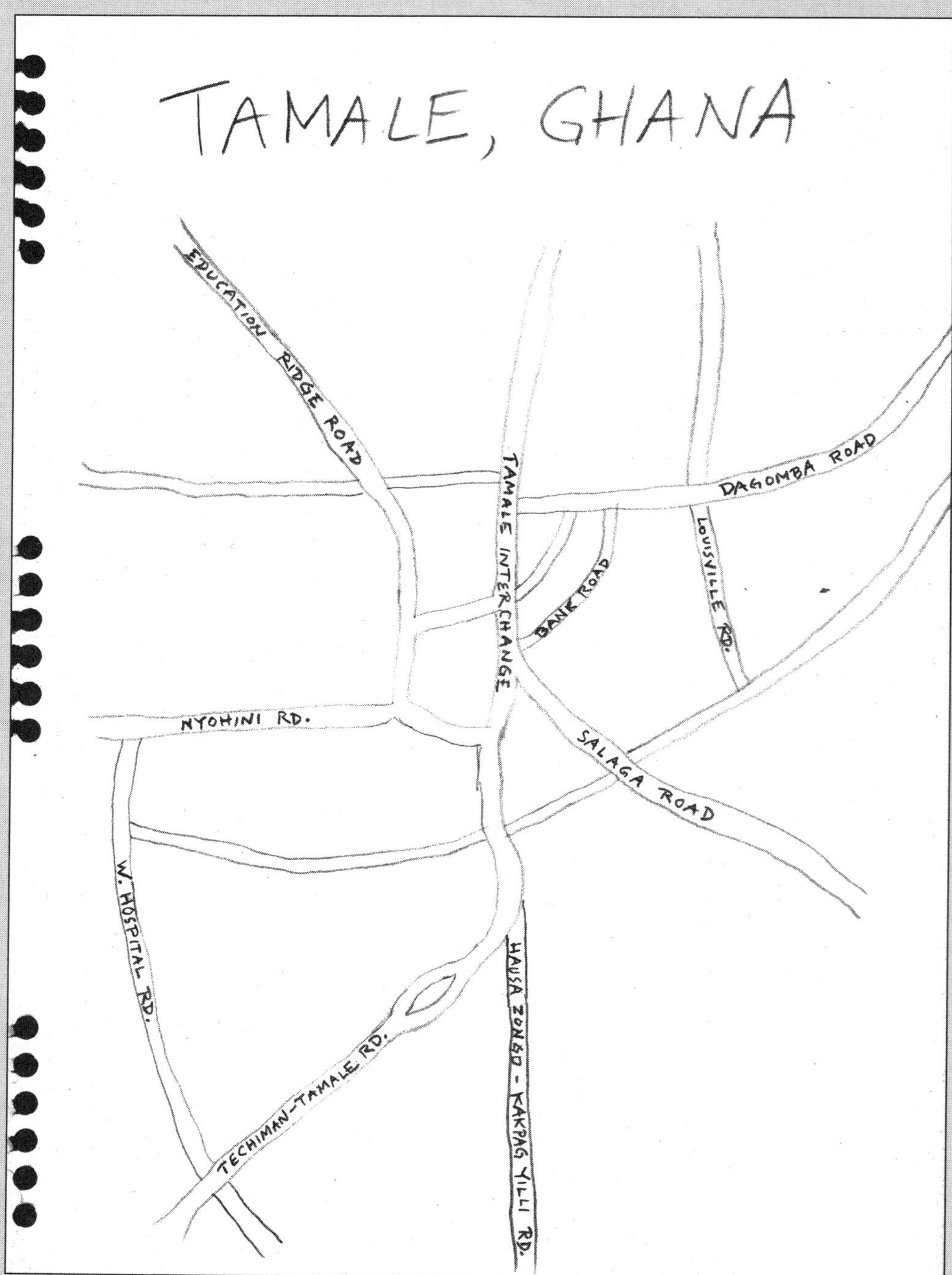

TAMALE, GHANA
EDUCATION RIDGE ROAD
TAMALE INTERCHANGE
DAGOMBA ROAD
LOUISVILLE RD.
BANK ROAD
NYOHINI RD.
SALAGA ROAD
W. HOSPITAL RD.
HAUSA ZONGO - KAKPAG YILLI RD.
TECHIMAN-TAMALE RD.

CHAPTER EIGHTEEN

A Lot of Dancing, and Then Even More Dancing

On my way north, I stopped in Kumasi again, staying I don't know where.

MARCH 26

The strangest dream: A woman was being tailed by a suave sinister fellow. She was unaware but we (me and two unrecognizable others) tried to warn her. A woman approached us as we sat in a grim lush dining room, with a lost look in her eyes and a gun limp in her hand. I was the first to run, my usual dream about running, feeling I never can move, always slipping on the ground and going two steps slower for each one step ahead. The others joined me in escape but the woman drifted off, apparently uninterested in killing or stopping us. Then came the man, now dressed in something vaguely military (mostly the black boots and ugly green), an absolute threat, his long legs gaining on our frantic flight when suddenly I said to the others, "Why are the four of us running from one of him?" To which we all as if synchronized turned and grappled him to a slow successful strangulation. End of dream.

I have an Abidjan contact—Rah rah, cheap living!

I have my "why I won't marry" explanation down pat, but I wish to hell I could speak the whole truth—but there's no accounting for the rage and disgust and most importantly the miscomprehension it would provoke, and I don't feel it necessary to lay my private self on the line these days. For whom?

The scenery here in central Ghana gets quite dull after a few hours or days of it. Sure, the hills (scarps) are picturesque, the greenery pleasing, but on closer inspection it's all so tangled and dusty and repetitive. Perhaps I'm too much attuned to farmlands and open spaces . . . the sight of an organized productive farm near Lomé was a welcome relief—I'm sure they're somewhere but certainly not near the main roads. And as much as I enjoy in a different way (different than the pleasures I have from a European or American town/countryside) the African scenery, I am astonished by its total lack of grace. And I am more than ever convinced of my idea that the grace or pleasure comes from the visual pleasure I get from people rather than the landscape. For example, the meeting in Kumasi today of Ashanti "importants," all dressed stunningly in orange and black Adinkra cloth, the women's hair close-cropped with a black dye edging the hairline, all so spare and glowing, and again the calm of the colors and skin tone and lithe bodies.
I learned later that they were royalty (the hair style signified it) and the meeting continued the next day. Kumasi <u>is</u> their capital.

The conference of corporate executives at the Volta Hotel—the corpulent

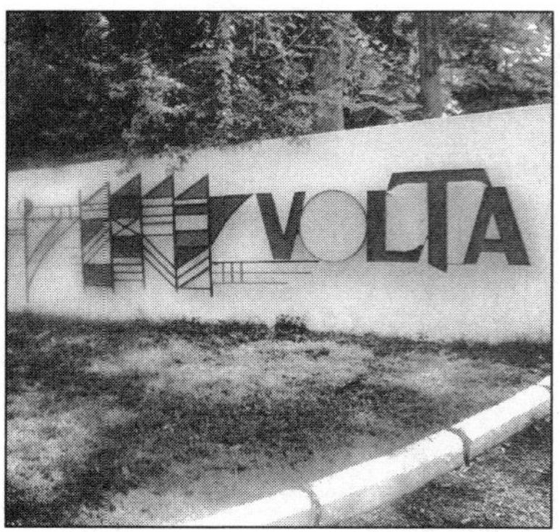

tight-shirted gold-chained pinky-ringed importer-exporter at dinner with his demands of wine and protestations of not wanting to be wealthy, and obviously enjoying the fact that he was. And that he decided against automation because "labor is cheap here" and more reasonably because of the dearth of electric power.

I don't think even the most presumptuous *oyibo* could act as condescendingly to the servant class here as Africans do, with their annoyed tone of, "Boy, bring it." etc.

I'm happy to be "back on the road again" and thinking of James Taylor's song Mexico that baby liked so much until she tired of it.

To see the general in the specific, the situation at large thru the individual, is to be not fooled. The salient points of contrast and similarity, e.g., between Saliha and Fatma, the life of Hamsatou or others as they represent women of their culture, is perhaps the nearest I can come to glimpsing the lives of women here, and wading thru a morass of complex sensations and information.

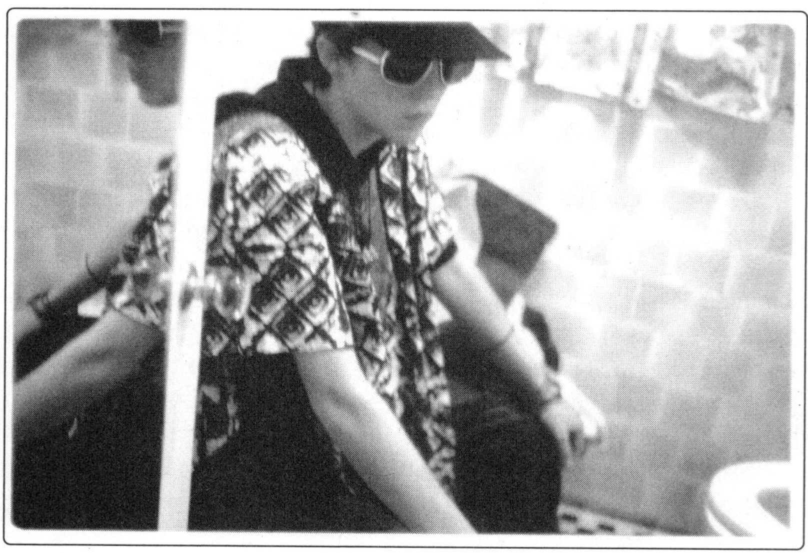

Had a dress made for Mimi, a soft gray cloth and hopefully a simple, elegant embroidery job. As much as I suspect she doesn't get turned on by an African flair in dressing, I think it will please her [1].

Finished the George Meredith novel [*The Egoist*]. Clara won, and the egoist was deceived and more importantly self-deceived in his indefatigable need to bolster his pride and his reputation for "independence" and power: He was an utter slave to duty and opinion. He thought himself the perpetrator of Clara and Vernon's romance and conqueror of Letty Dale, but as Meredith says: "But he had the lady with brains! He had and he has to learn the nature of that possession in the woman who is our wife."

A fitting comment on his delusions of grandeur, but unfortunately also on the sacrifices that women of character or insight have to make to their other senses, i.e., she had wisdom but could never find love, and had resigned herself to a union with a reprehensible but tolerable man, who at best might leave her in peace. A brilliant book on all counts but for the charming resolution, visible halfway thru the book, and not surprising as it is a 19th c. novel.

Perhaps the most priceless and hilarious passages were W.'s imaginings of supplicating Clara being a jelly mess to his masterful command. Of course none of the fantasies materialized, and it was good proof of the insane talent of men to insist on their rightness and control, no matter the circumstances.

George Meredith, I salute you with a slurp of Ghana's finest warm beer!

It was hoping too much to imagine Clara off on a solo discovery of the world, and one is only left to wonder how true the friendship is between C. and V.

Interesting: the strong part the fathers played, both of them demanding abject service and loyalty from their daughters, notably not for the women's sake but for their comfort in old age. So much for the thunderings and pleas of outraged parents, including mine with her warnings about me "not, I fear, ever being able to lead 'a normal life'."

No one has proved to me yet that the normal is desirable

Lovely last line about the Comic Muse compressing her lips to stifle an outburst of derisive and gleeful laughter. No sister could wish for more.

MARCH 27

I took the plunge again—paid a man named Ameru Mohammed to make Wing a dress, which I now alternate between fretting about and admiring.

The Kumasi Military Museum yielded a complete delight—discovering Nana Yaa Asantewaa. In the words of the army guide, no men were to be found to lead the Ashanti against the *second* debacle with the British in 1900 in their gross attempt to capture the Golden Stool. Guess what? A woman answered the call, and he rightfully referred to her as "our Joan of Arc." Thank you. A one-year battle, successful insofar as the British never got the stool (they got the fake one), and she lived to a sturdy old age. He epilogued with, "She's not a fine-looking woman but a great solider."

She was the Queen Mother of Ejisu.[110]

---

110 Ejisu was a former district, as well as the main town, that was located in the central part of the Ashanti Region of Ghana. For more on Asantewaa and the Asantahene royal house, see [2].

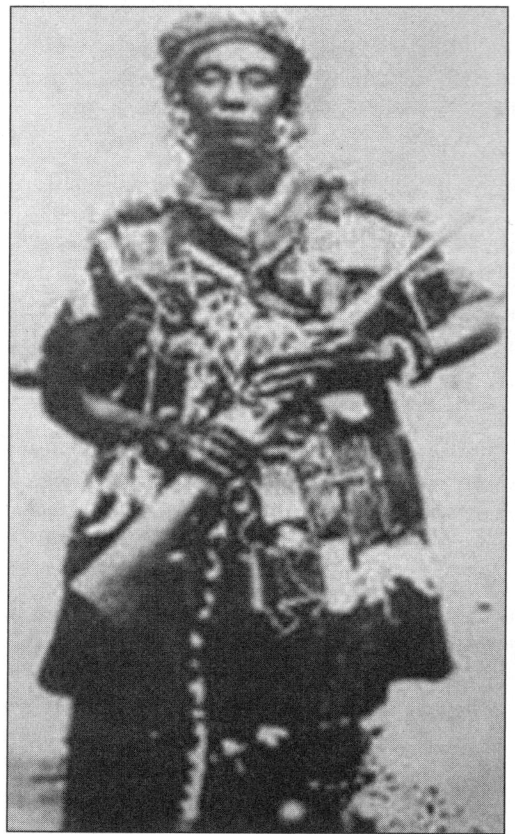

The original warrior queen

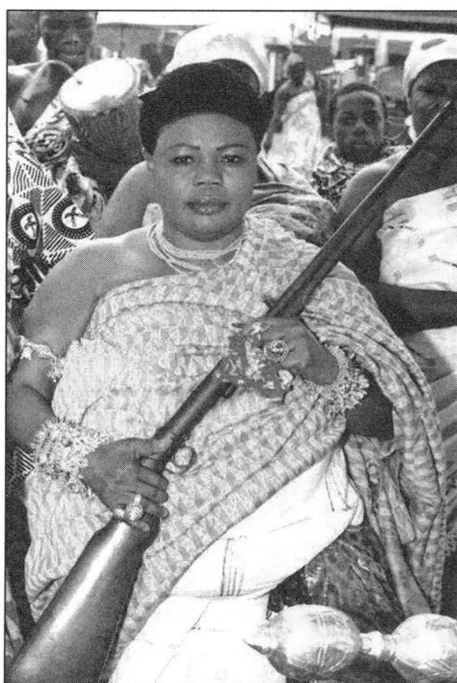

Her contemporary counterpart,
The Queen Mother of Ejisu,
Nana Yaa Asantewaa II

And I saw queen mothers today to melt me, to melt Strindberg. No words for the clarity in their eyes, the strong shoulders and proud bearing of cloth and jewels and power, the pure beauty in the profile photo of a princess of an Asantehene, the photo of the queen mother today, young and superior in form.
But admit it, they as well as the companion chiefs, are chiefs and gold-laden and treated to the obsequiousness of the masses as distastefully as any sheik or premier.
In his discourse on the brave "West Africa Frontier Brigade" to the Indian-Burma war, the guide answered my question, "But then you were fighting for the British Colonial power?" with a quiescent, "Yes, and for world peace."
Oh.
The mind permits leaps from her form of bravery to others much less admirable.
And the portraits of the British!
A sight for cynical eyes. I think he was perplexed by my outbursts of laughter at each one, but they have such sticks up their imperial asses.
I remembered Ayi Kwei Armah's words in the portrait of the present Asantehene, drowning in gold.

Carried a full bucket of water up two flights of stairs and was humbled at the remembrance of all the five-year-olds I've seen here, backs bowed beneath the same weight.

I have to be wary not to ask myself too often, "Well, why are you here if baby is 4,000 miles away?"
Time will tell.

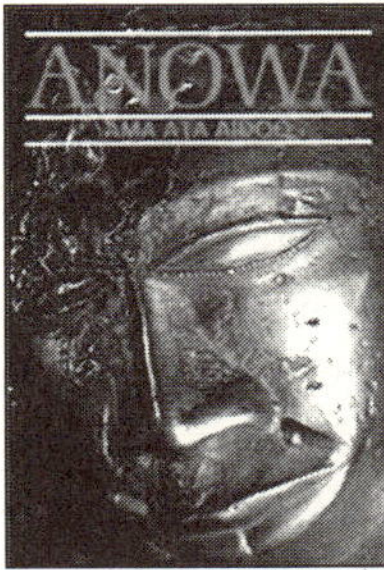

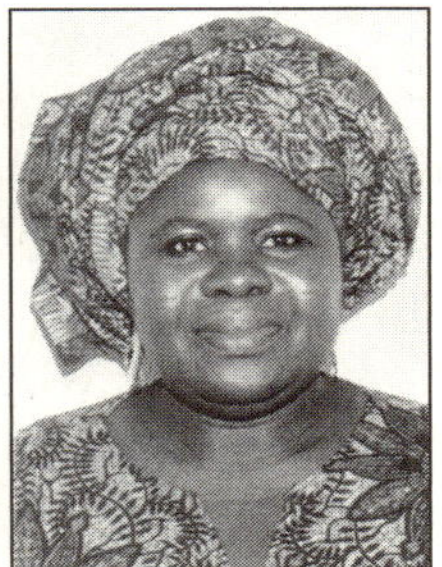

Going to Tamale tomorrow after a not-wasted day in Kumasi getting *Anowa* by Ama Ata Aidoo [3] and Emily Bronte's *Wuthering Heights* and then a good dinner and exercise and the glowing grey before a storm. Sometimes I keep myself pleasant company.
Better than the company I kept on any of those wretchedly undirected days in NY, rushing out of bed and up and down Fifth Avenue, away from her energy for fear of dampening it with my alternate obsession and paranoia. Not brave enough to admit my jealousy nor to admit the unfounded nature of it (because that would be to admit our mutual desire, a greater responsibility than the moody evasion of it).
Sometimes I write these words in the consolation that they are recorded and hence done with, but I suspect they are signposts to understanding. Also, if I am honest enough to dwell on them—but all I seem to dwell on is Mimi and how she looked at the train station that late October day and how I don't know at all what to say when I see in her the things that make me shake my head softly in delight [4].

I definitely need a soulful compromise between the aesthetic and politic. I am neither a Gandhi/Nader nor a Wilde/Weston. Perhaps a W. Eugene Smith[111] with my particular and necessary biases, but where is the <u>work</u>?

A grocery store here is something to be noticed and entered voraciously only to discover (I should suspect and be forewarned by now) nothing but rows of Milo [5] and sardines and biscuits. How to fathom that the simple American corner store holds more unknown delights than the best-stocked whites-only supermarket here?

How nice the days were with Kay, and even Mike, and the muttered "nice blouse" from Jean Pierre:[112] my crusty Ife "creation," shapeless and faded.
I have to keep up the semblance of journalist hunched over her work to fend off the guy pacing by.

---

111 Mahatma Gandhi and Ralph Nader, politicians and political activists. Oscar Wilde, writer. Edward Weston and W. Eugene Smith, photographers.

112 Mike and Jean-Pierre: more people, long-since forgotten, whom I met along the way.

The bottomless cruel stench of the charred cow's head and fish tails alley in the market, and the vultures crossing my path, was the ultimate revulsion for me so far. I cannot dismiss that as "Africana." It's gross.

It's so perplexing to be in an environment where you know the people are the same flesh and blood and century as you but are operating on such different impulses. The aspect that disturbs me the most is the feeling I get towards their modernity: that it's more a bright new dress shown off so proudly by a little girl, although it was bought three sizes too large in order for her to grow into it and it droops around her ankles; it's the unnatural quality of it, something almost entirely acquired, stamped on or squeezed into their former reality. And they don't jive so often. Not only that, but there are too many of the (what my education and mama has taught me) "vulgarities" of modern life, whether material, in some of the hideous clothes and car manias, or the smothering input of western sexual-labor values, the red-lipped, chauffeured women here, short skirted and smiling, so sweetly. And the pricks who confiscate the market women's power ("to protect the consumer" . . .) Ha! No one here is benevolent without a pressing ulterior motive. It's as if they're playing with something called new and better and hence desirable without considering the alternatives. And for damn sure the guy with a cold beer and woman with a new wig isn't going into fits of academic theorizing about Négritude [6] and the disintegration of traditional culture.

MARCH 28

Indeed, another well-placed stroke of what will come to be referred to as my Ghana luck: the Cynical Muse. Ten minutes outside of Kumasi I had a decided premonition, a conviction, that the bus would have a breakdown. Right on schedule. Climbing the slope to the ferry at Yeji the clutch snapped (or whatever clutches do). Bravissima! A perfect preview to the ferry ride later, surrounded by those lifeless faces, eyes that stare into nothing but his or her own cycle of scraping by in this tyrannical climate. I came back to the same bottomless realization of the bitchiness of life here, to put it gently. We all sat, each feeling more disconsolate than the next, in the penetrating heat of early afternoon, no cold drinks, almost no shade, no ferry, no mechanics, no towns. Every gesture here becomes a struggle; the peace of real comfort is rarely available, or even imaginable.

And the lake spoke eloquently for us. Cold steel ice blue, impenetrable, unsympathetic, a sheet of blue from water to sky, the horizon only approximately indicated by the bleached dead branches of trees submerged by the man-imposed lake. A stern mirror of our pathos.

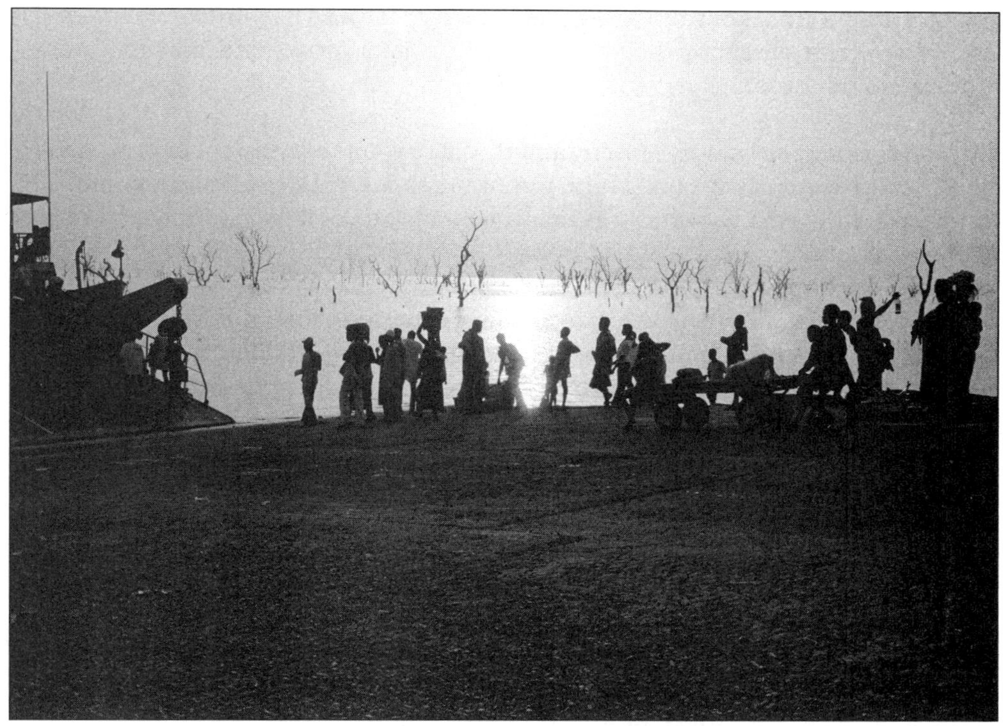

The ferry crossed Akosombo lake, created by flooding an area which thereby displaced 80,000 people and killed a lot of trees.

On a bus back to UST[113] in Kumasi, two older women sitting by me reached up and, chattering to me and each other in Ashanti, stroked my (soft, white) arm and gave me big admiring smiles which I suspect was to make me feel good—!? The rest of the people on the bus must die a quiet death at such exhibitions, not out of shame but out of sorrow [7].

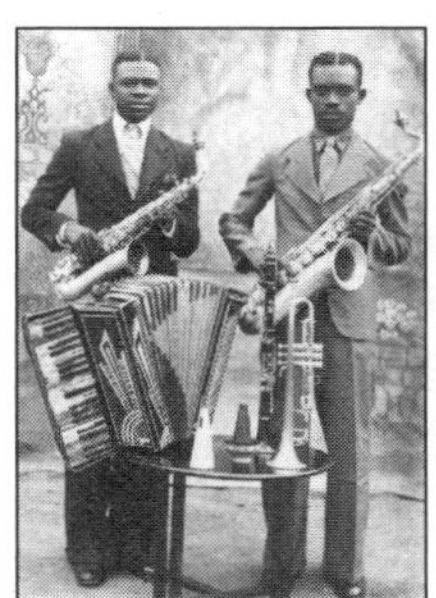

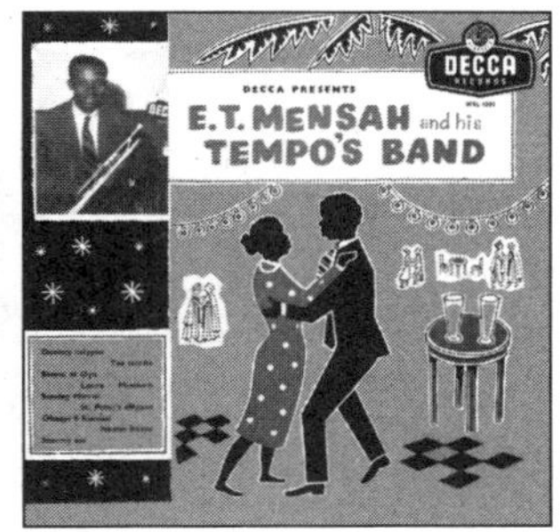

I feel quite contented now to arrive at a shabby hotel without running water, put on my mosquito coil, wrap myself in a *buba*, turn out the light and fall asleep to the Highlife music [8] and voices of babies.

E.T. Mensah, "The "King of Highlife" on right, with J.A. Mallet, 1937

113 The acronym for the Kwame Nkrumah University of Science and Technology.

If a restricted number of women around the world have been able to excel in their fields given the tremendous obstacles blocking their success, imagine what we could all do given a bit of encouragement!!

Learned a lesson with *kenkey*[114] today and the aftereffects of a dismal dinner: eating again late at night in my hotel room. Sure enough within three minutes of me tossing bones out the window, a goat sniffed it out. It remains one of the most unchewable chickens I've ever had to eat.
(I had to.)
One of those bleak nights in the company of paunchy aimless men and their mute women. How can I ever enjoy myself on such occasions with idle chatter and clever repartee when there's a sister in the room who reeks suffocates smolders in the boredom of perpetual exclusion? I can now say, "I won't marry" without flinching, laughing, or averting my eyes. Getting better all the time [9].

MARCH 29–30

Something strange and intangible screwed hell out of my original route north and now I have had two great things happen as a result: chancing upon Nana Yaa Asantewah by being back in Kumasi, and now, the Women's Talent Week in Tamale. [115]
In honor of Int'l Women's Year and every year to precede and succeed it, the northern region is sponsoring a week of festivities and lectures dedicated to admiring and teaching (praising and educating) women.

> **PART OF A LETTER TO MIMI:**
>
> A delightful surprise in Tamale. I didn't like the town & was planning to leave the following morning w/o bothering to extend my visa, but out of boredom or perverse discipline I decided to brave another bureaucratic hassle, and on the way discovered a ceremony of dance & speechifying to open the Women's Talent Week of northern Ghana. Better yet, it wasn't the apple pie & crocheting displays that we offer but hours of dancing every day & a conference on farming & birth control & market women & films, etc. Too much to stay the whole week but managed two days of it & lots of photographs . . .

So for three days I will be feasted with dancing and crowds of photographable women.[116]
At the opening ceremonies I appeared involuntarily in my filthy jean skirt and was politely but firmly, in a whisper, reprimanded by a certain official lady (Miss Fisata

114 A sourdough dumpling, usually served with stew.

115 I made no record of the location and have been unable to find anything online about the event. From the photographs, particularly those taken inside, it looks like a school rather than a municipal building.

116 A few of the photos from this day, more than others taken earlier, suffered the most damage in storage, but I've opted to include those anyway since there are no other available visual records of the event.

Kabache). We later talked together and she explained, "You see, I am a woman and you are a woman, and I didn't want to hear them talking about you like that." (Apparently the speaker's stand was raising its collective well-dressed eyebrows.) *Ça va, ça va . . .*

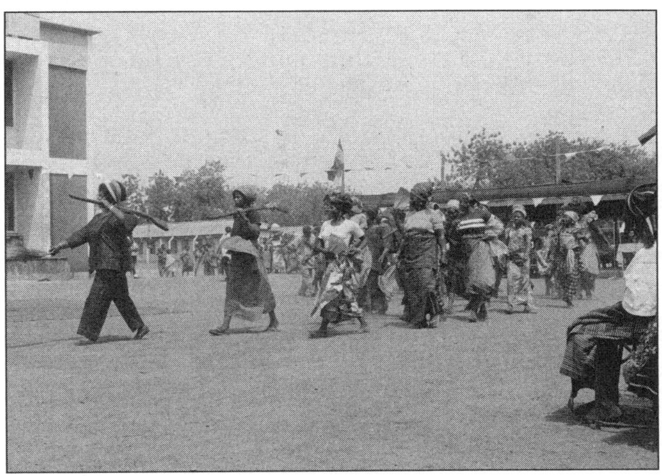

The Dagomba Women Warriors appeared first—the story goes that the Ashanti have held considerable influence over certain people in the north, and these groups have clans, of which these warriors are representative. They fired off wooden guns that exploded in gunshot, or puffed silently, outmoded perhaps even before WW I.

In regard to the Warriors, Madame Speaker[117] applauded them by saying, "This proves that when called to defend themselves, women can shoot as well as, if not better than, men." And the audience roared in agreement.

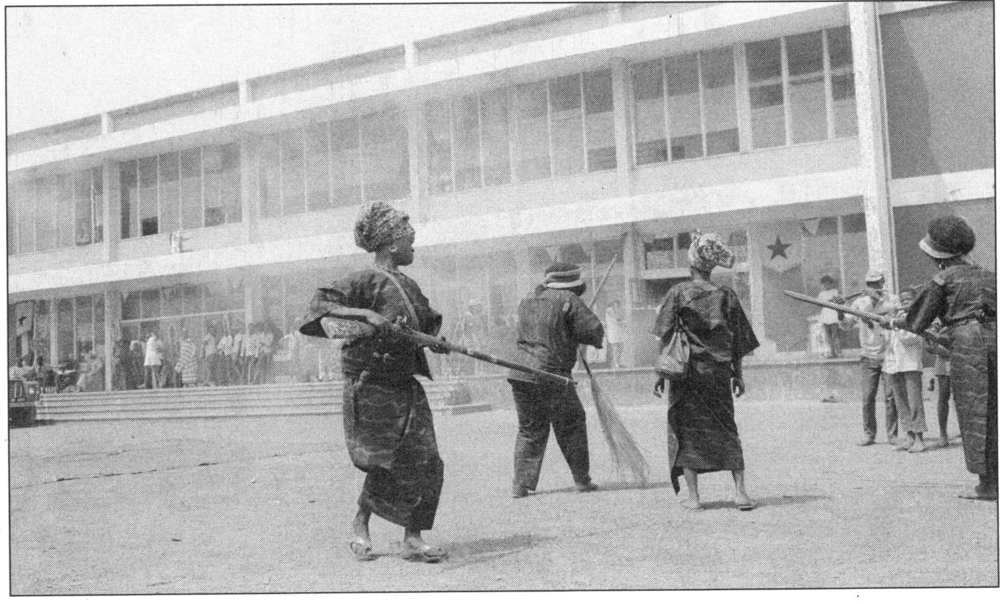

117 I have no record of the real name of "Madame Speaker."

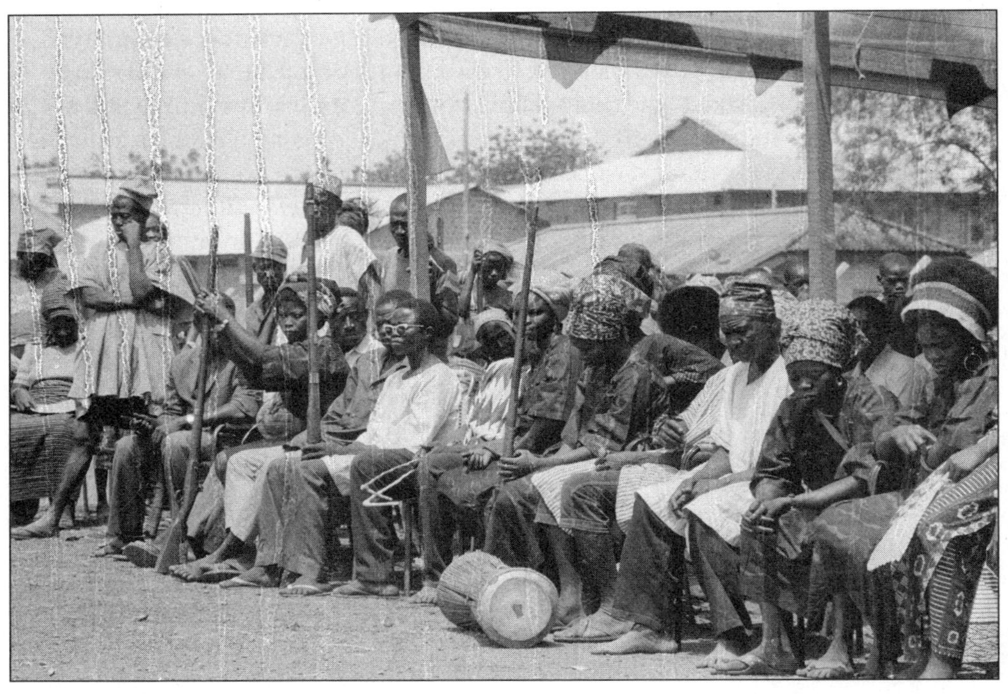

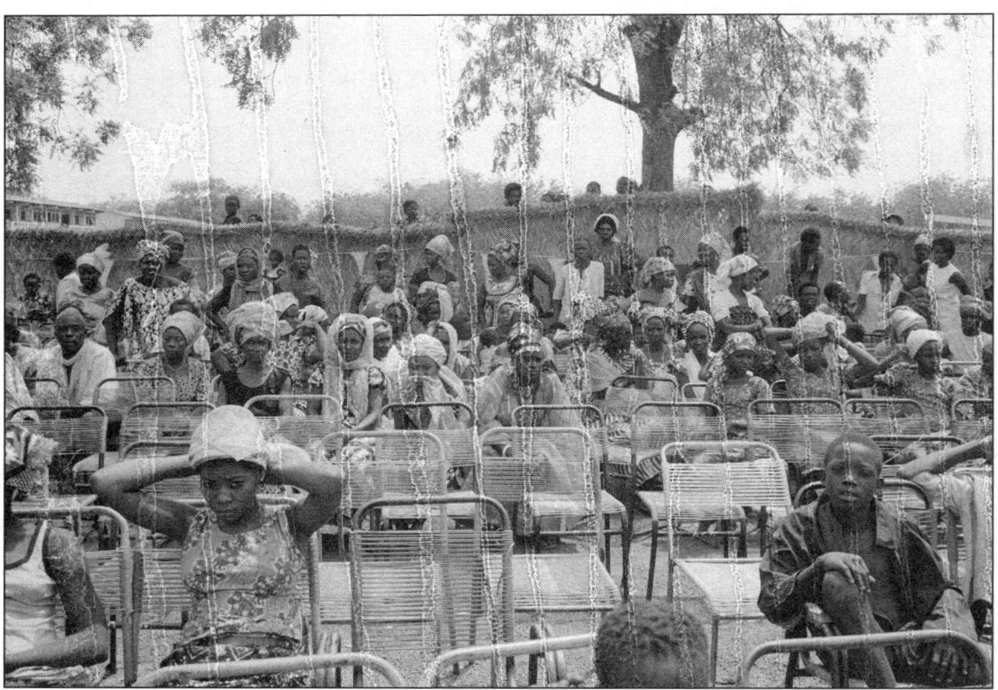

The Krobo women came with cowried calabashes and five serious meditative modest young girls with leaves between their always gently closed lips, the virgins of the village on display, it was their debutante ceremony, on the market for a husband. Beware the pubescent found de-virgined. Used goods, outcast from the village. It still persists. Madame Speaker insisted that it was even more preserved in the "uncivilized, pagan north" where they don't even have the sense to be Muslim, let alone Christian and advanced!

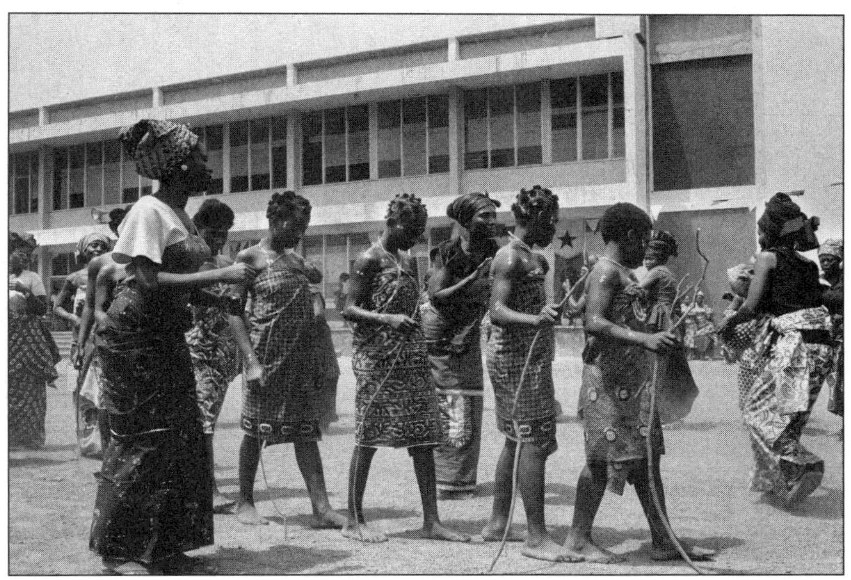

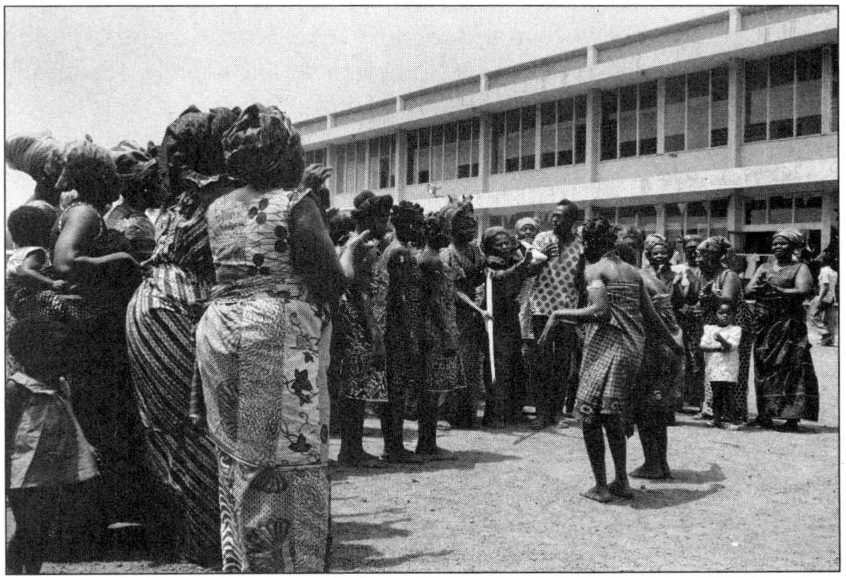

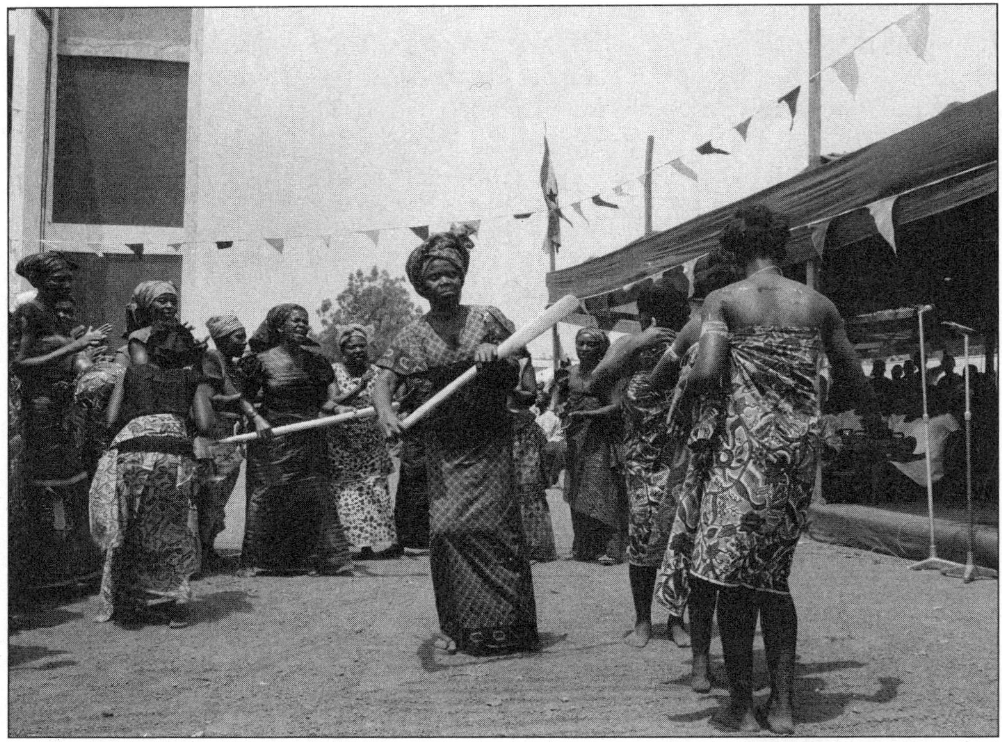

The dance of the Krobo women was "Dipo," performed again with the girls dressed in full regal attire, the younger bare-breasted, covered by multiple strands of heavy yellow and gold beads, arm and calf and ankle bead work, giraffe-print heaps of cloth around their waists, and the same remote expressions: head lowered, eyes averted, body immobile except for shuffling feet and slightly twitching arms. At moments a pair of them would face each other and communicate thru hand gestures, but the overall effect was one of meditation on the overpowering duties of life into which they were being initiated.
Fine for the place and time but when the older ones appeared swathed in pink, yellow, and green kente cloth and more beads and gold, they looked suspiciously like fatted calves on the market stage, vying for the best bid. The only consolation or comfort (not exactly that) is realizing that at least here the base motives and coercions for marriage are not masked by our sorts of perfumed abstractions. (I don't mean that marriages in Africa don't begin with love, but that the commodity is presented as such, and everyone is aware of the worth of her labor.)

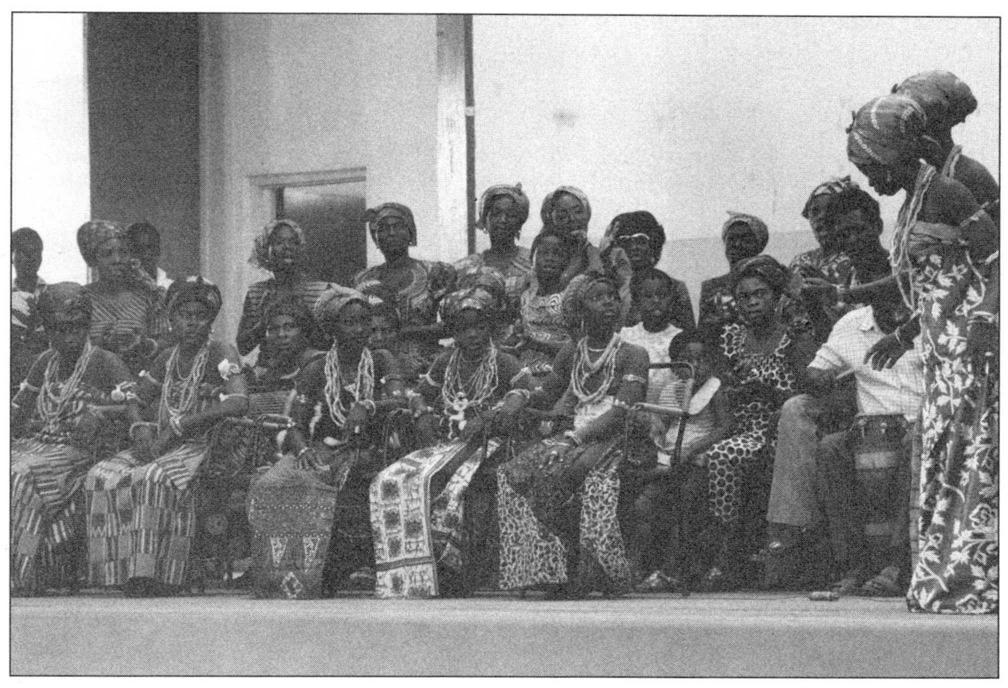

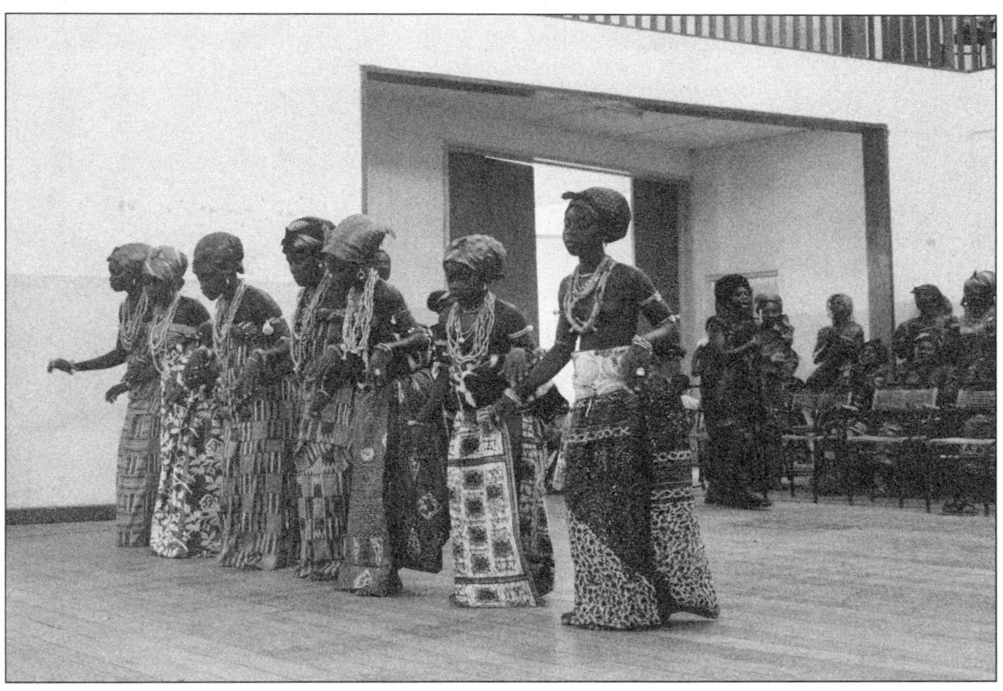

And then more and more dancing, on an unconducive stage but with an enraptured, cheering audience.

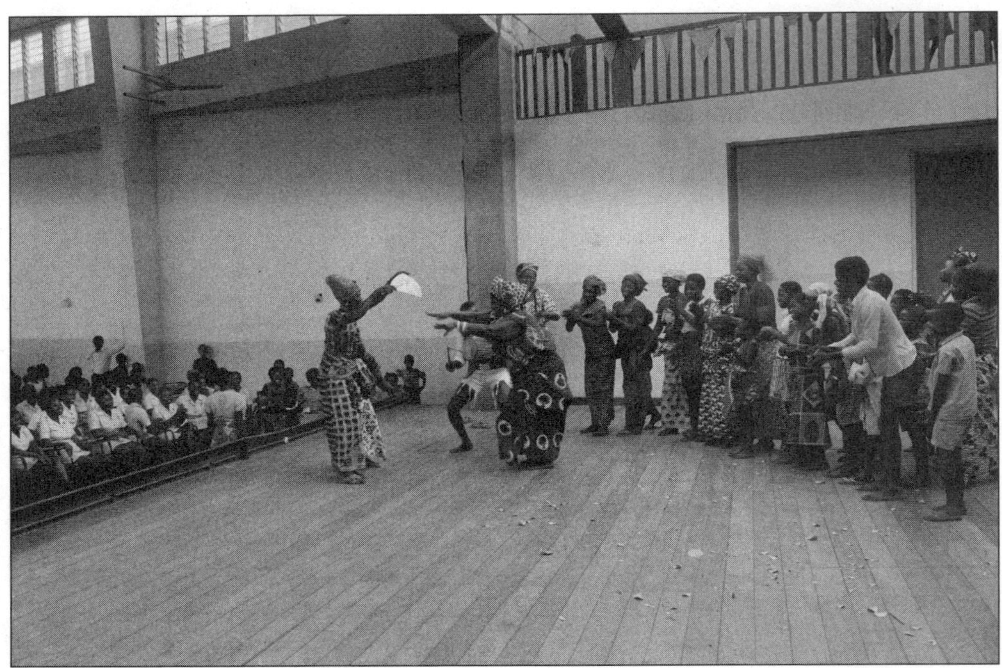

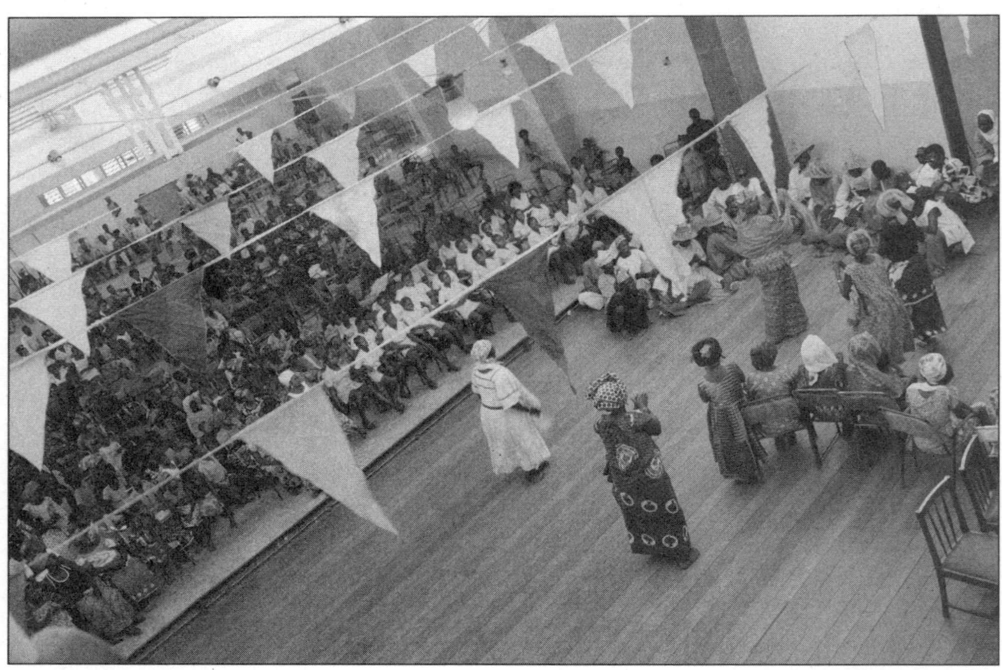

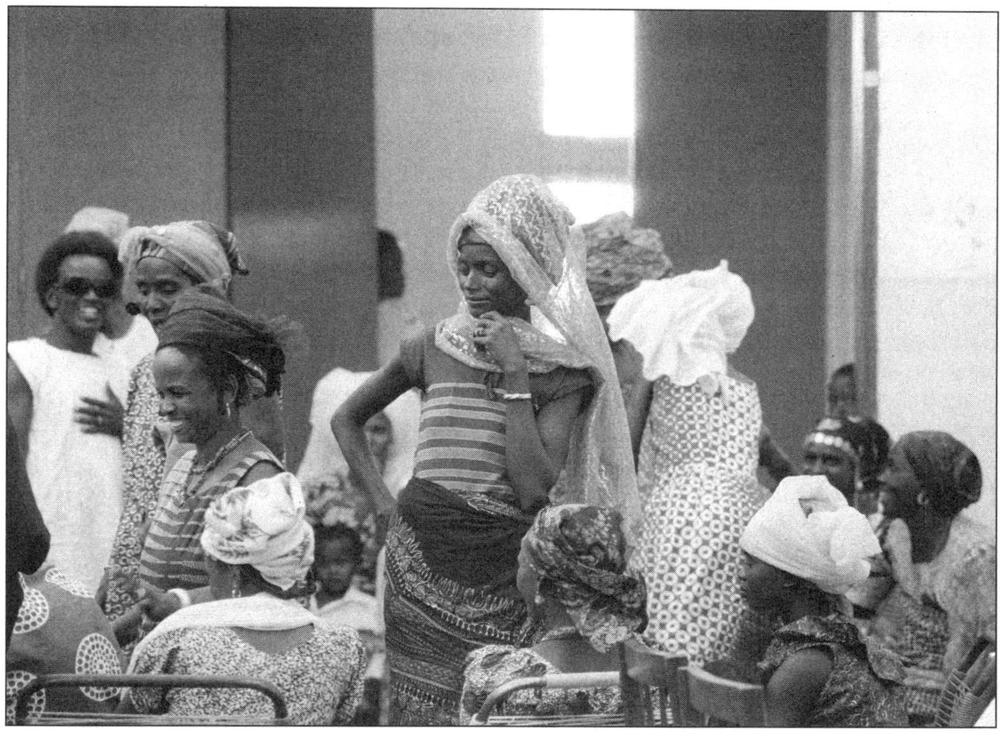

One woman was wearing a cloth that read, "*Si toutes les femmes du monde voulaient se donner la main*"[118] with a circle of international faces.

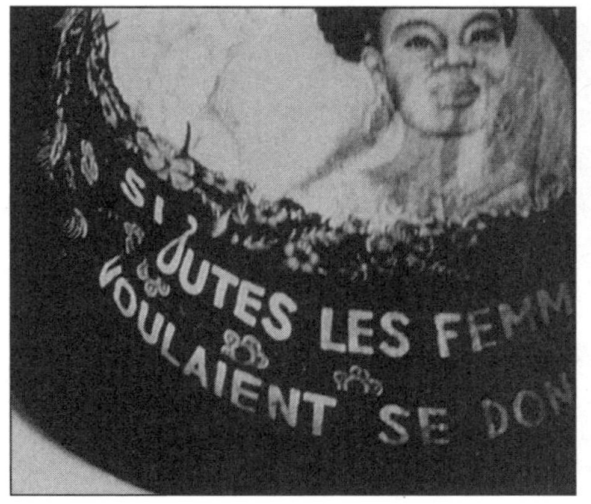

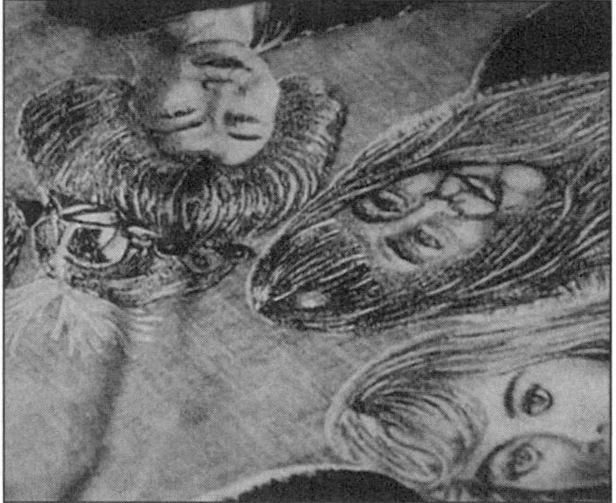

Frames from *But No One* (1982), a film I made in which a character was wrapped in this cloth.

118 "If all the women of the world would join hands"

There was a skit about role-playing; a nurse comes to a village where women only believe in native medicine; she takes a woman to the clinic where she's given birth control and nutrition info (the appearance of a woman doctor made the audience *cheer*).
And her "husband" was a woman dressed in smock and shades and cap who looked so much like a Chicago dyke that I couldn't take my eyes off her. I started getting undirected but strong erotic feelings just by seeing her and the associations it brought me . . . That to me she looked so normal and cool, and probably the cloth and jewel-laden women in the audience were somewhere between bemused and confused.

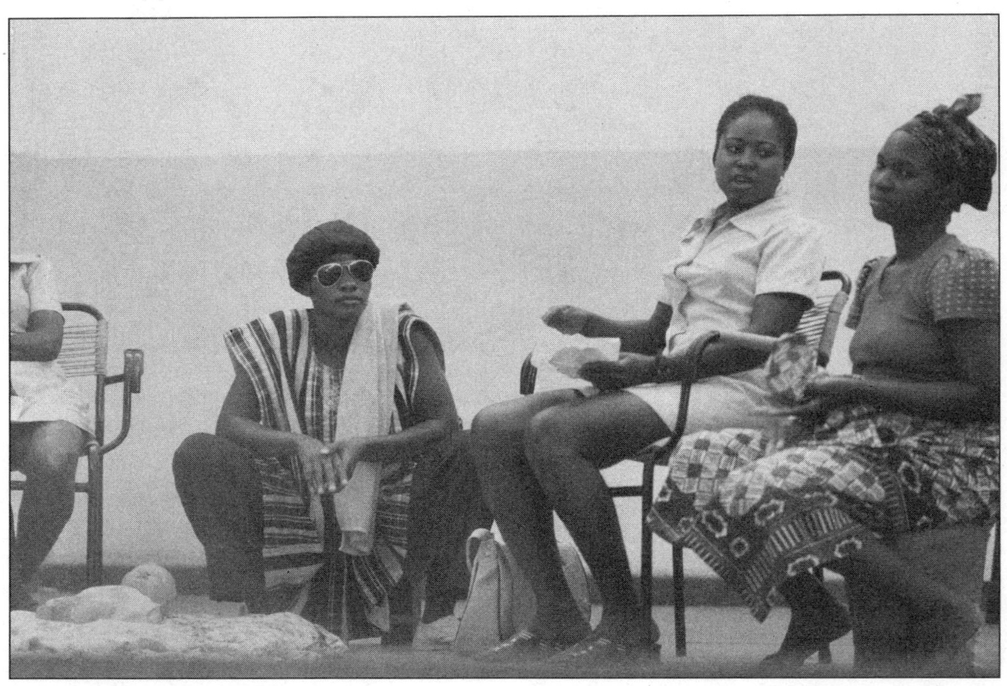

A marked feeling was that, compared to some cultural or social displays, for example by US women, this had no sense of apology or absurdity or modesty; they were absolutely together and fiercely proud, especially in the dancing, where the shared energy and communication was intense.
I can't convey the energy and ecstasy and pride of their dancing and the drumming and horn blowers.
And it felt so good having my camera even if I was the intrusive clambering photographer.

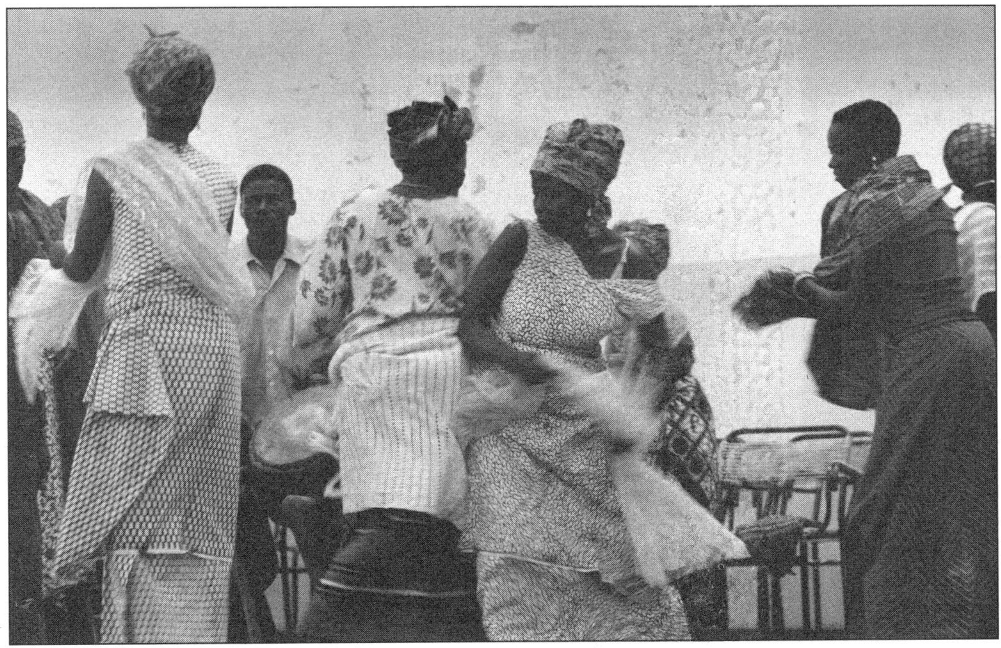

If art can be a reflection, prediction, and analysis of the political blood thru the social body, then I'm all for it and for me doing it.
And for all my inner fears that "this has all been done before and done better," NO. People yes have come to Africa with cameras to get scenic animal shots and sensuous bare-breasted shots but I'm after something a bit more <u>pertinent</u>, let's say—of events like this one.

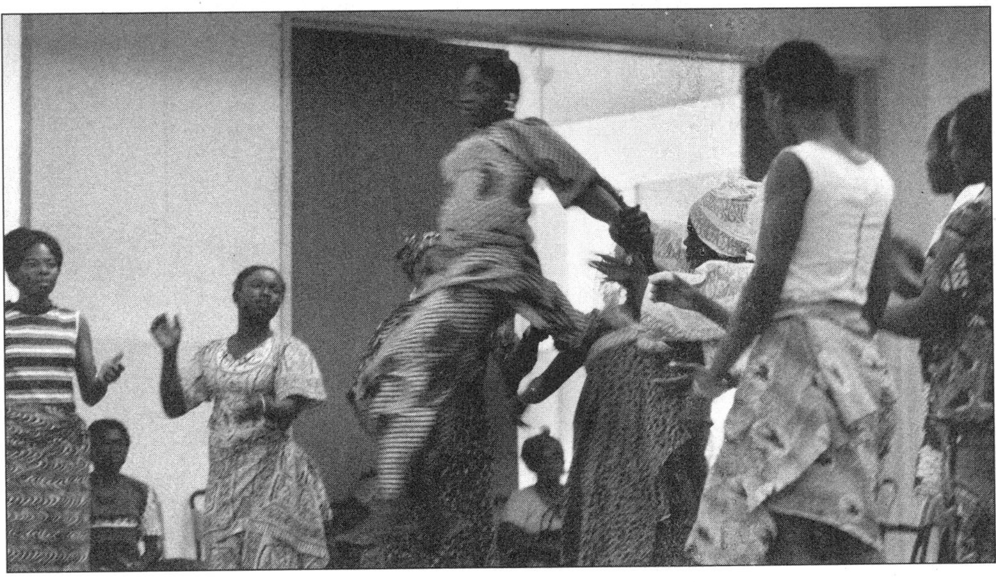

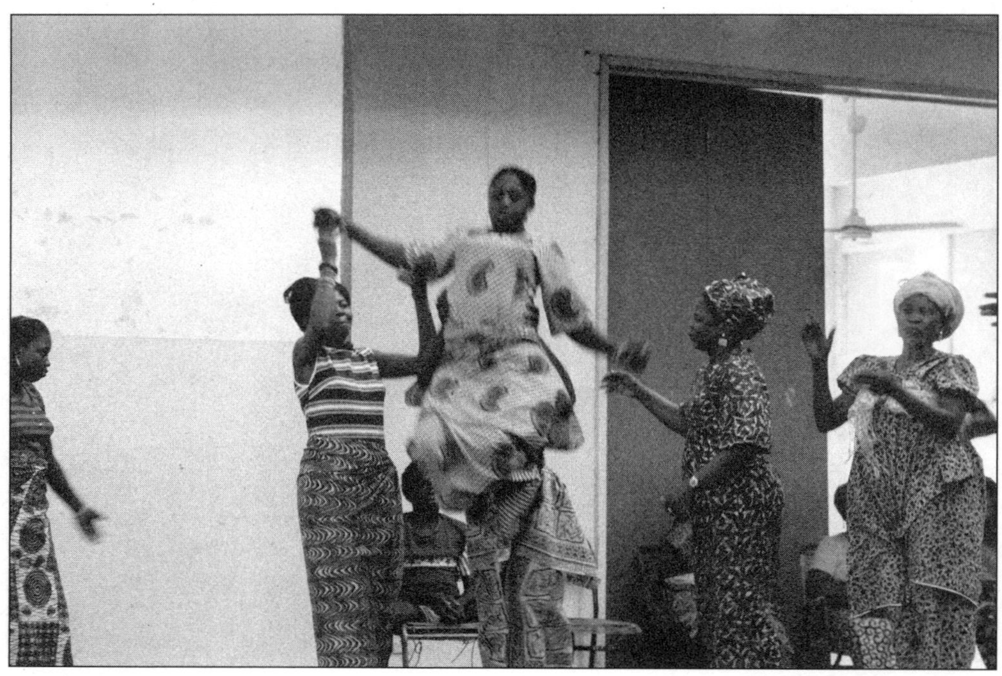

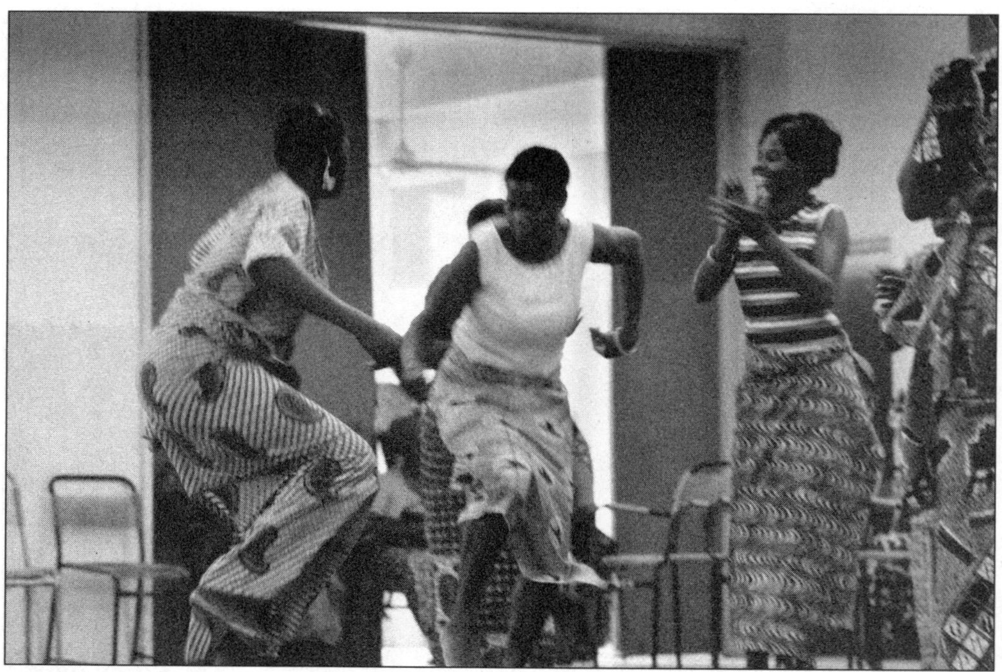

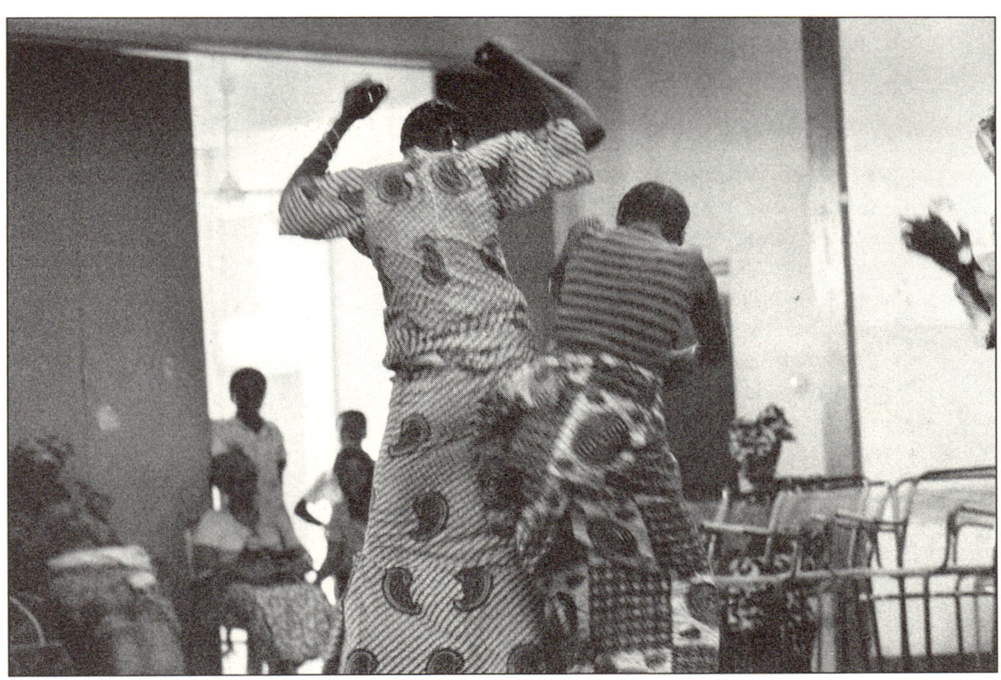

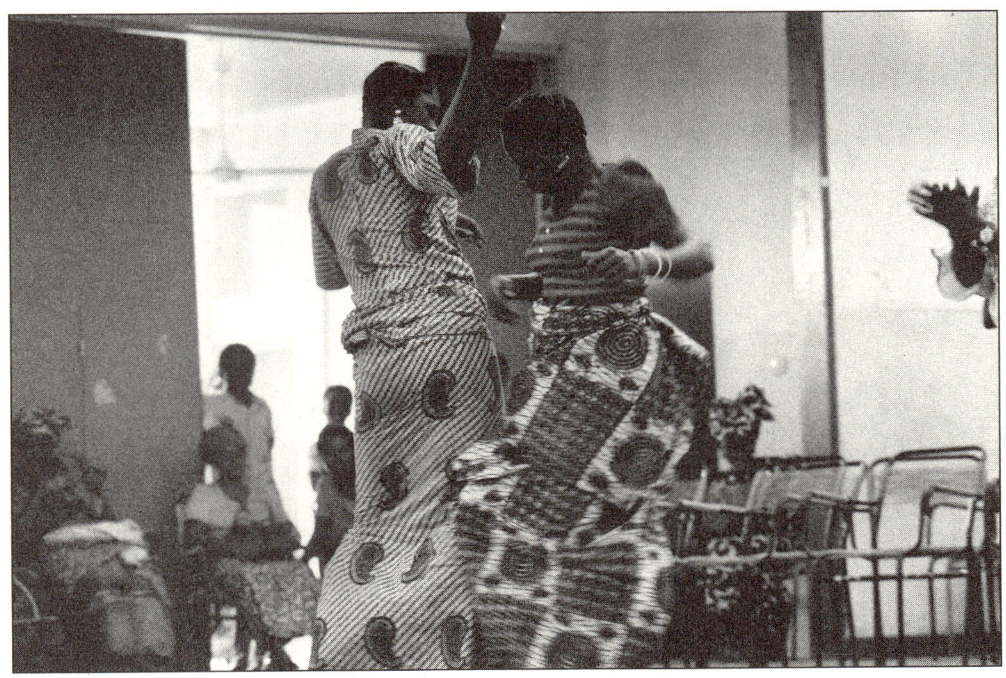

PART OF A LETTER TO MIMI:

[. . .] there was always a beautiful combination of very young, very old, and stately mature women, some of whom even danced w/ babies bouncing on their backs. There was never a sense of apology or moderation as I sometimes feel w/ other displays by women—they were unqualifiedly proud of their art & their sisterhood: It was a very woman-identified occasion. The major disappointment was the audience, largely consisting of kids & husbands of the women (they'd come from remote villages for the week). There should have been a word of commendation for all the women who couldn't come because they were at the market earning their daily beans & rice.

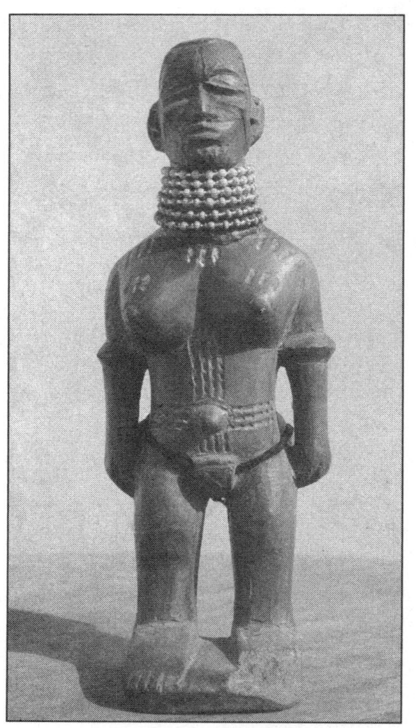

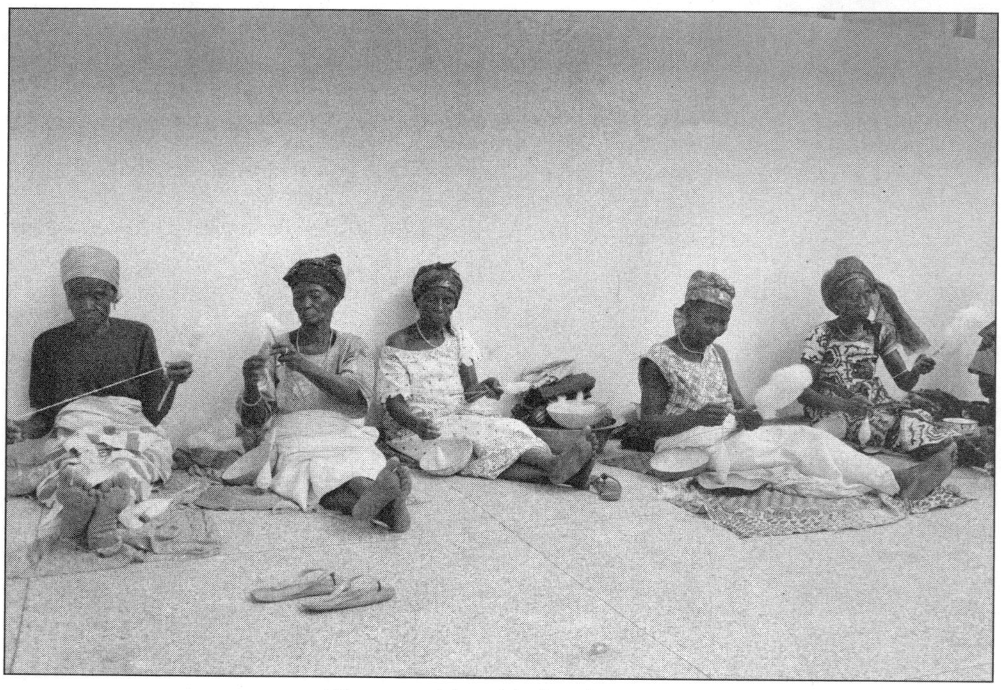

Women outdoors during the event

Reading *Anowa* by Ama Ata Aidoo, not brilliant or at the level of G.B. Shaw's writing, but it tells a painful, vivid truth about women, and is a very uncompromising presentation of it; her search in life for a husband companion but he ends up being after money and slaves and the glorious retirement in kente cloth and gold. She never changes, but gets wiser, and learns that (1) it will never be and (2) how alone she is in her dreams. Some beautiful passages of her defiance of parents and money and husband's offer of leisure. She insists on the life-giving value of hard work and self-respect/determination. They want to call her a witch, of course.

I keep seeing women here who are falling prey to our chains, the bewigged retiring young women with bare-chested gold-necklaced whiskered moneyed men, and they dance along to his plea of, "Do your best to imitate a frail white woman." I squirm and bleed and can't say anything to these women as a sister. They would put me in my place with a simple, "What would you do if all your youth was spent wishing for soft straight hair and a moment's peace from the grime and labor?" What would I do?
Perhaps the problems and issues of women in Africa have a different foundation than in the developed countries but as they begin to acquire what are wrongly considered "modern" ways they will be right where we were twenty or thirty years ago and for which we're still paying dearly. And the natural evolution from an economically strong African traditional woman to a technological one is not so clear: Witness the incredible struggles in socialistically-aimed African countries like Guinea-Bissau or Mozambique.

More on the opulence and godliness of the Ashanti (or all) chiefs—they showed a film as part of the event, *The Making of a King*, (the latest Asantehene) by Ghanafilms; was painful to see the writhing ecstasy of the people for the greatness of this latest royalty; believing in his divine ability to cement the people once again after the dissolution following the death of Prempeh II—a display of pomp, circumstance, slavishness, and dependence and how would they ever understand determination by all the people? Cabral [10] was right, as unsympathetic as he might have seemed in criticizing the chieftainship system.
And after all the dances & good feelings & strength, the series of films made in Ghana were all made by misters, and *Ghana Dances* had perhaps 8–10 examples & none were with women.

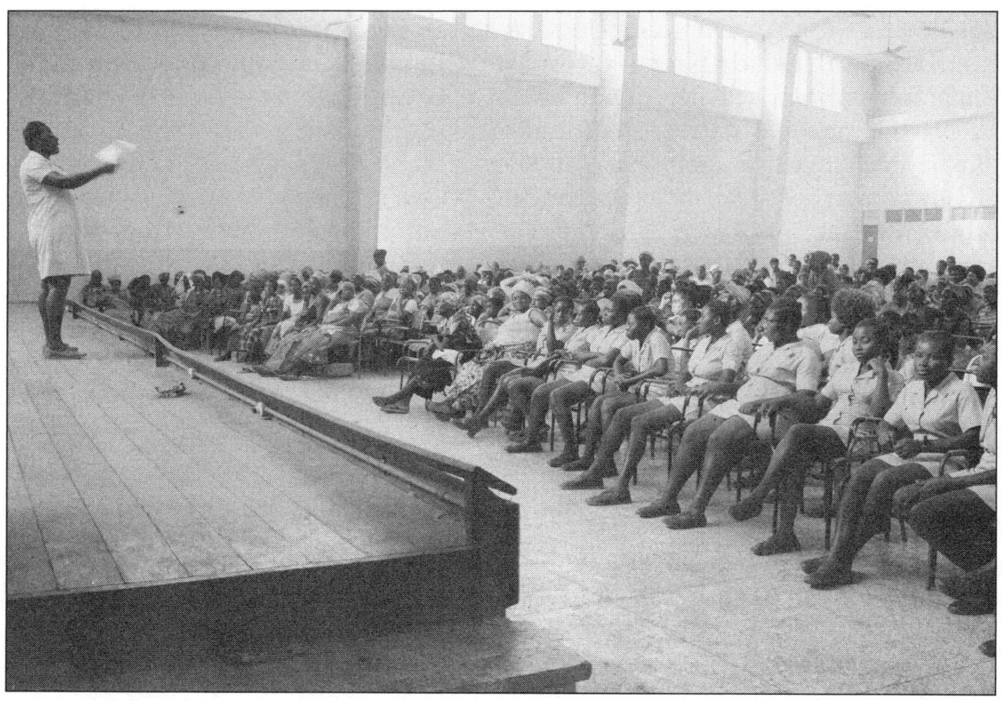

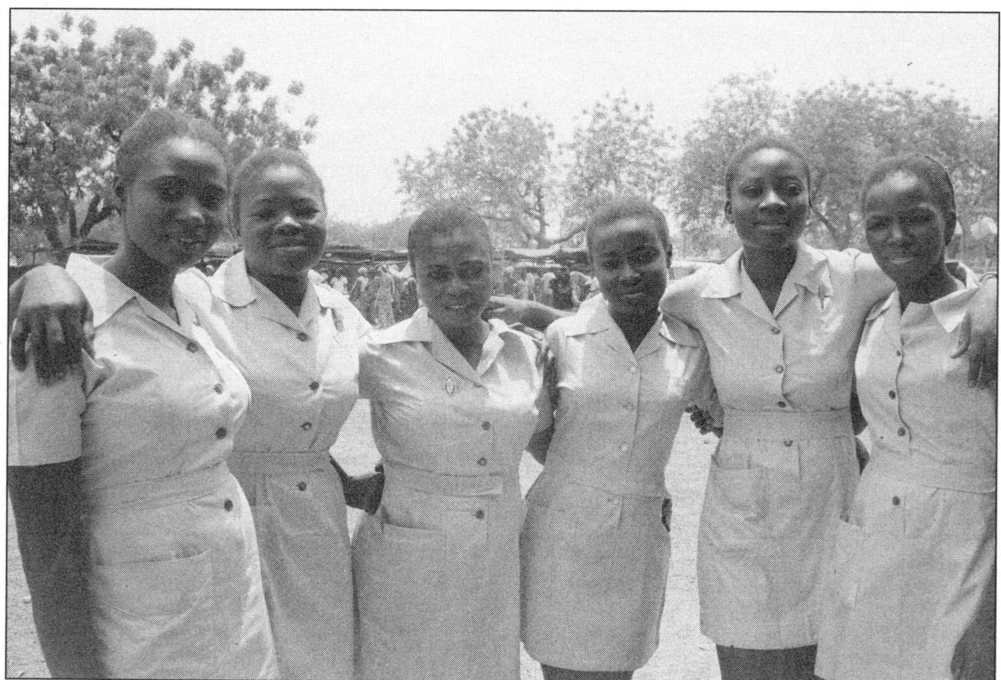

Millicent Ansah and other nurses from the Community Health Nurses School who were at the event.

I asked a question of the nurses with whom I'll travel tomorrow on their rounds of practicals in villages teaching health care to the women and babies . . . while my mind was urging my mouth to shut itself.
"Do you go to the hospitals there?"
"No, we usually gather beneath a tree."

It smells of the open sewage in this hotel room and across the way a shouting chanting voice is in full blast on a radio. A relaxing evening.

Did I once really have the naïveté to scoff at technological advancement? I'm certainly not prepared to "go back to nature" if it requires this amount of work.

This slowness is going to wipe me out soon if I'm not careful. And god how I crave vegetables. And magazines. I think I'm suffering the listlessness of *lousy* nutrition. Rice and beans and an occasional banana or orange. Well-balanced diet, hmm?

MARCH 31

Words will have to suffice for the unavailable visuals this morning. I had planned a trip to the village with the nurses. No chance. The three tutors, all in wigs and frigidly polite, told me that, "We're happy you're interested in our work, but we represent the Ministry of Health and there have been certain persons who . . . And please don't mention the name of our school in any of your articles."
And weren't we all the picture of deference and sweetness, the fragile air, the whispered smiles, and that was that.

This morning they were giving tests for pregnant women. They came streaming in the gates, sitting expectantly in the clinic, and to me it seemed such an impressive display, a solid improvement on the norm . . . and I looked on them as the few privileged of the many, only to realize again and again and again that the luxuries here are the givens at home.

I am totally without energy this morning; it disturbs me terribly.

My choice of transcribed conversations may seem sometimes satirical or patronizing but I think it's the honest outcome of the contact I've had. It hasn't been with Africa-conscious intellectuals nor often with extremely traditional people but those of the city who are aware of the outside world and walk a curious rope bridge between their past and a wild present and, obviously, groping is the result.

Today someone tried to sell me a US fifty cent piece for $1.50
"It's fine, madame, silver, madame."
Non merci.

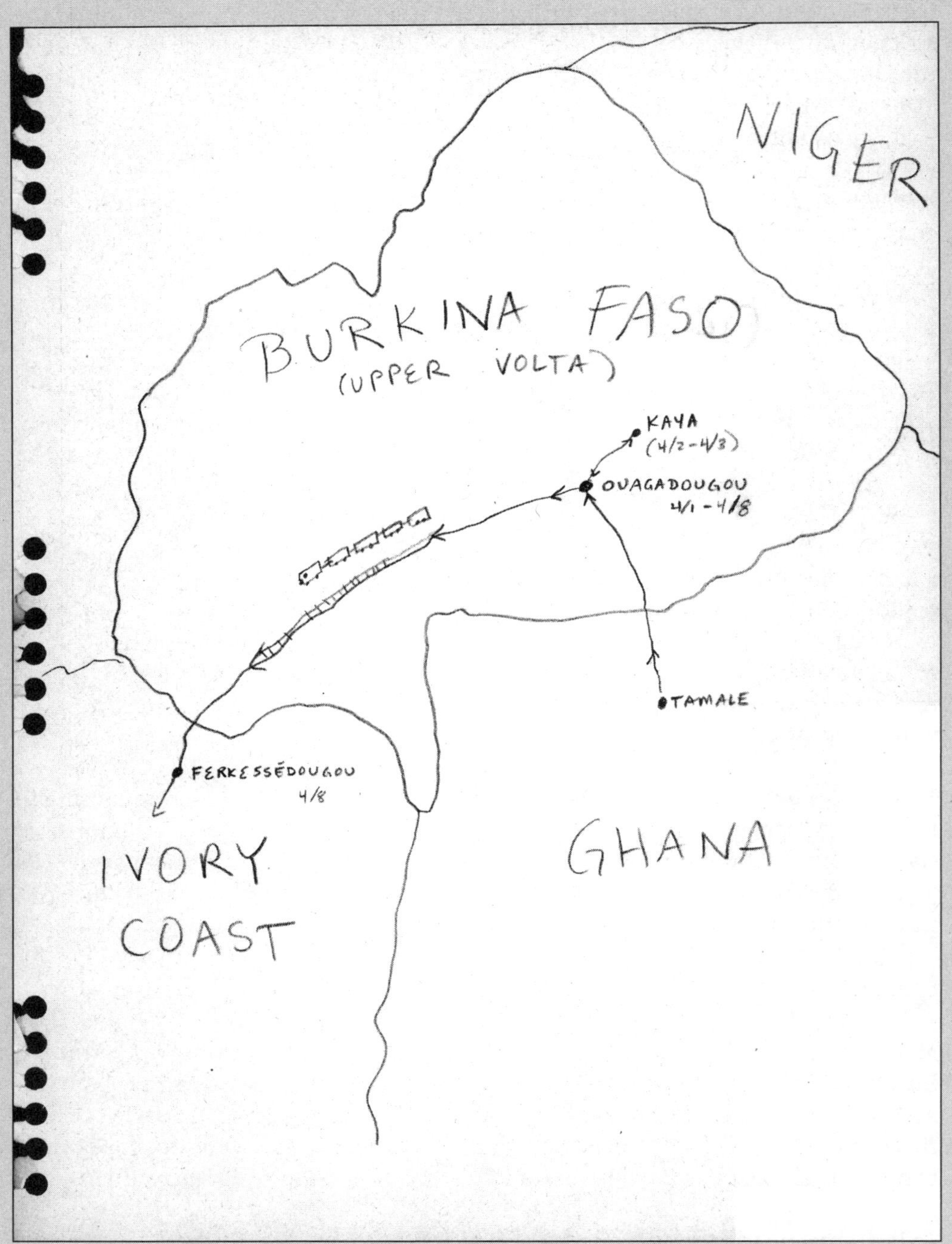
NIGER
BURKINA FASO
(UPPER VOLTA)
KAYA
(4/2-4/3)
OUAGADOUGOU
4/1 - 4/8
TAMALE
FERKESSÉDOUGOU
4/8
IVORY
COAST
GHANA

CHAPTER NINETEEN

IWY Versus FGM

I headed north to Ouagadougou, Upper Volta[119] on a bus which stopped overnight on the 31st in Navrongo, where I stayed at another Catholic missionary's place.

PART OF A LETTER TO MIMI:

Note on the front of the envelope pointing to the stamps:

This is the hairstyle of the women I mention in the letter, but much more elaborate than this pic.

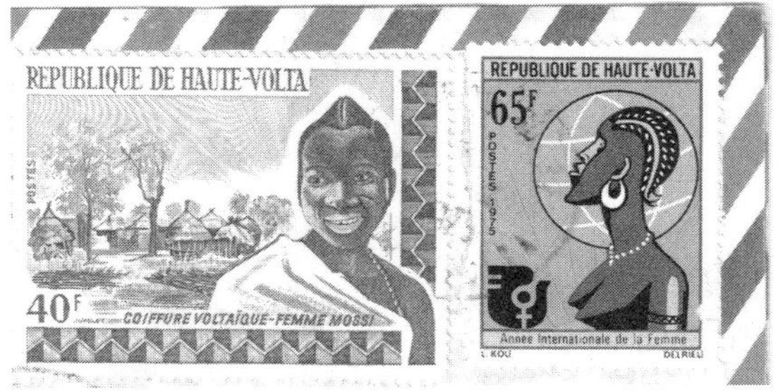

Dear Mimi,
I would be hard-pressed to shower mama nature with compliments & gratitude for her benevolence in this time & place. Probably 110° in the deepest shade, the ground looks like a polluted Chicago forest preserve in the most dessicated weeks of late fall. The market offers dispiriting quantities of tomatoes, rice, onions, & bread. Today's menu: water & a tomato & onion sandwich, of course. But I'm not unhappy, due to the availability of a shower, clean(est) room (in weeks) and a Catholic library which happens to have G.K. Chesterton (a true favorite since my time with my grandparents' Victorian chairs & Mozart & tea at midnite w/ only him as a companion) & 2 vols. of D. Richardson's *Pilgrimage* (that 20 volume novel which gave birth to "stream of consciousness" before old Jimmy Joyce; the D is Dorothy. Only now is she being recognized & reprinted).
And for these major amenities I have to thank the Catholic missionaries despite all my contrariness. And only a German Catholic could be so impeccable I suspect,[1] this strangely cheerful white woman in the uppermost town of Ghana, teaching atrocious Christian hymns to susceptible young Ghanaians (who can't carry a tune . . .)
[...]
But I was right in my feelings towards the desert & open spaces. I've only been here one day but already I feel calmer & happier, glad to be away from the enervating vivacity of the large towns. You can't imagine the racket I have to deal w/ in the towns, from

119 The country is now named Burkina Faso but I will retain the old name to be consistent with that time.

the shrieks of cocks & sheep & babies at 5 a.m. to the manic conversations over a 4th or 5th beer at midnite in the courtyards of the hotels. And when the lights go out, a starved dog or irate husband starts the nocturnal din—and I have very disturbing dreams all the time as a direct result, I think.

[. . .]

Ouagadougou. One of those place names rooted in my mind w/ a very particular Africa. And it is. But tonite I need dykedom, whatever that means, because I feel so good & so full of energy & clean

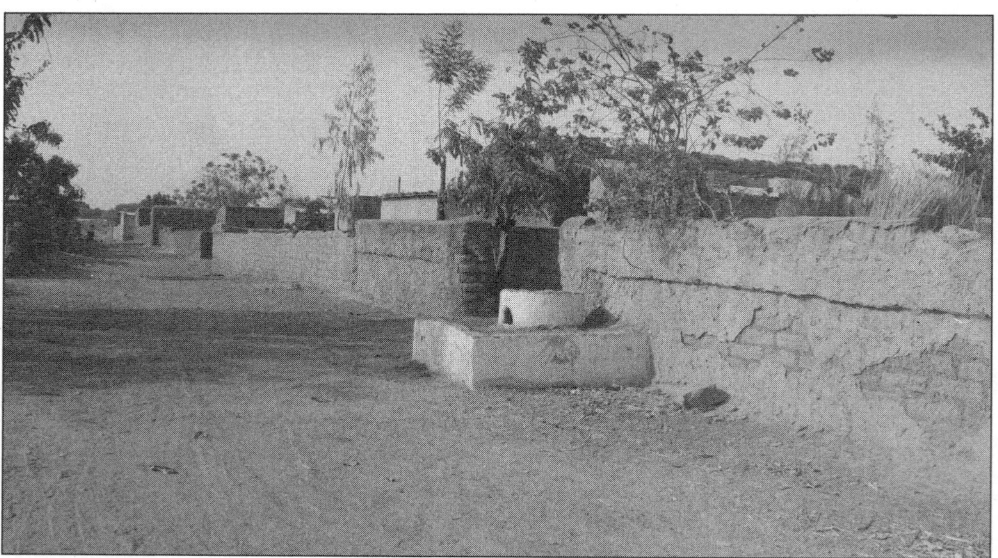

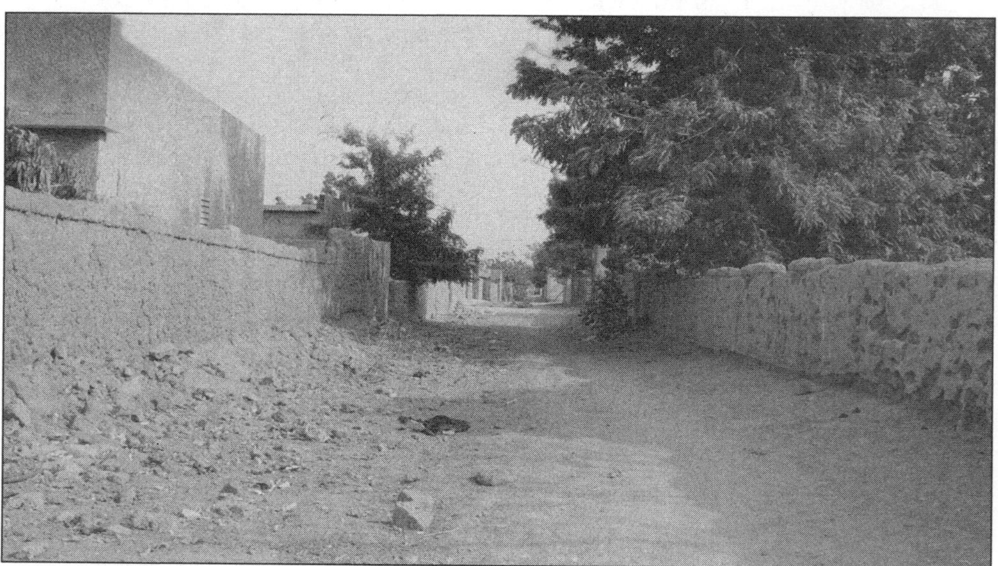

& ready to share it. And not surprisingly dykedom takes on wonderful proportions after these many months of pregnant women & svelte young African men.

The trip north from Navrongo yielded my 1st real Africana: a family of elephants munching trees by the roadside. It wasn't the Serengeti, but a thrill anyway. But no photos as they strolled away from our exclamations & door slammings.

The houses or communes of extended families in the bush are wonderful round mud huts attached with curved mud walls and perky straw roofs just like the Fulani hats, scattered across the austere, elegant plains, very forbidding but restful in a way that the tropical south can never be w/ its damnable excesses of green & confusion. Maybe I'll have to settle in New Mexico . . . Or live in a city & cherish the memory of these wild spaces which make me utter the terrible commonplace of "this is Africa as I want it to be" (& fuck the reality of poverty & despair, for a moment, please, while I romanticize). Ouaga, like any respectable French colony, has Dannon yogurt & covered sewers & is terribly expensive so I eat meat on sticks & local beer & do a lot of walking & parlering in terrible *français*.

PART OF A LETTER TO MY FATHER:

Written on the envelope:

Ouagadougou, Upper Volta, of all places

An adventure is only an inconvenience rightly considered, says old G.K. Chesterton. And I am proving his point at every turn. And (his home being Battersea): "I cannot see any Battersea here; I cannot see any London or England; I cannot see that door; I cannot see that chair: because a cloud of sleep & custom has long come across my eyes. The only way to get back to them is to go somewhere else; and that is the real object of travel and the real pleasure of holidays. Do you suppose that I go to France in order to see France? Do you think I go to Germany in order to see Germany? I shall enjoy them both, but it is not them that I am seeking. I am seeking Battersea. The whole object of travel is not to set foot on foreign land, it is at last to set foot on one's own country as foreign land."

I am at last in Ouagadougou, and it fulfills most of my fantasies, being an almost ethereal dusty wide-avenued desert town (discounting the hordes of thin-featured Parisian neocolonialists; this is the capital of U. Volta). I feel transformed in the desert. I think because of the endless open space and flood of light & the strange cleanliness that comes from sand instead of the ugly red clay in the south. I enjoyed the people in southern Ghana but not the climate (humid days drugged evenings) nor the terrain; there's something very disconcerting & unharmonious about the excess in the tropics, the confusion of green, the great walls of vegetation along the roads in proportion to which the sky becomes insignificant. The north has a subtle range of colors, verging on beige monochromatic but w/ just enough touch of yellow grass & sensuous grey baobabs (the color; the tree is not what I would consider "sensuous" but the cottonwood ranks as a sure favorite of mine) and darker brown clay huts to give the atmosphere a very natural consistency. Really, you & Mom did quite a job on me as an impressionable wide-eyed youngster: I am obsessed with substance, with measuring & worrying over the quality of each day, each experience, always being sure I'm doing "enough" & if not finding something to make it enough, weighing each event for its possible place in my hierarchy of substantive experiences etc. etc. etc. *ad fatigum.* (*sic*) It's not really at all such a bad thing, except for the (almost inescapable, oddly enough) times one is in a nowhere town with the barest essentials & a lot of time to kill (what an awful expression!). So I'm always plodding along filling time, and G.K. is a great companion for that, he can make a most notorious & hilarious thesis out of any imaginable trivia placed in his path. Have you ever read him, his essays ("On Turnpikes and Medievalism," "On Running After One's Hat," "The Advantages of Having One Leg" etc.)? He's a relentless foe of the idiocies of modern life (i.e., 1900–1930s) & makes some well-placed points. And along w/ Emily Brontë & George Meredith, a perfect writer w/ whom to sometimes escape the social realism of this sort of trip.

I may have mentioned this in my last letter, but my fixed mental association w/ talking to you is in Hutchins Dining Hall[120] —it almost becomes a point of meditation for me when I feel myself (easier every day) losing my grasp on Chicago. I've passed that point when traveling now becomes the norm the daily reality rather than the unfamiliar thing one is doing for a certain time. (Listen to me talk as if I've been on the road for years! But I pick up new sensations quickly & esp. I think because I changed abode & environment so much in the last few years.)

A pleasantly ironic sight throughout the Ouaga market: Women at their stalls in "*Année Internationale de la Femme*" cloth, whole rows of them breast-feeding babies & serving chop & sitting behind mounds of crimson & golden spices, all unconscious but very appropriate advertisements for consciousness.

Ah, they're so tough here but being so clearly & wrongly channeled into secretarial "positions" and, if lucky, acquiring houseboys to pound their *fufu* and give them leisure time to shop for trinkets & plait their hair. I'm being a bit harsh but what else should we expect if they (women & men) have been so overexposed to our values?

---

120 A dining hall at the University of Chicago, where he taught, and which I attended for my first year of college.

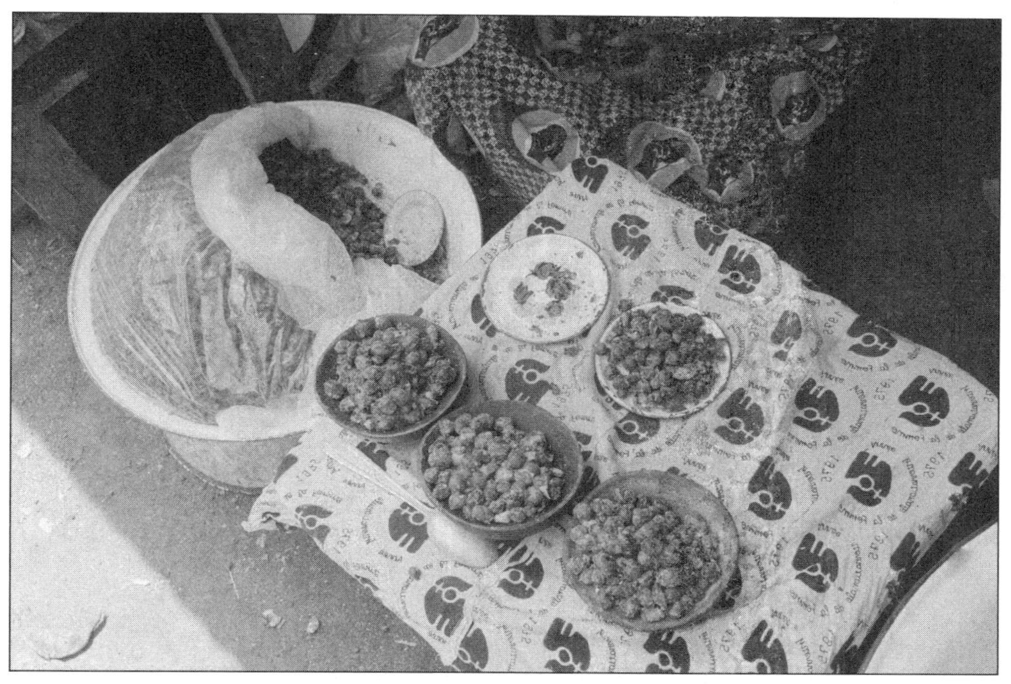

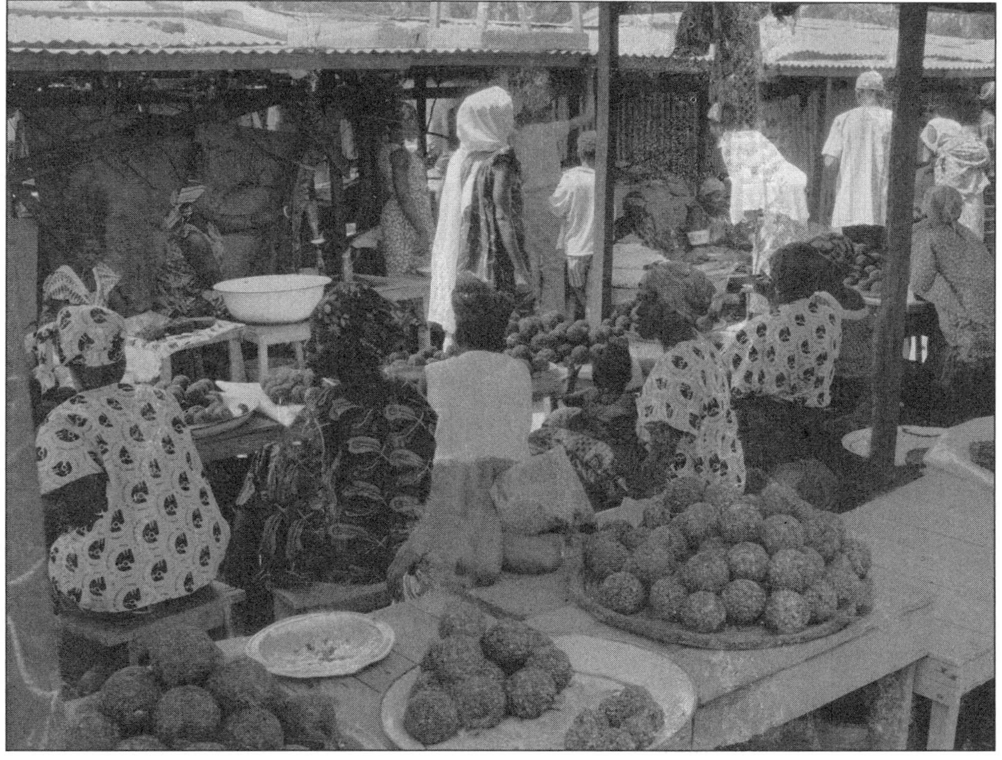

APRIL 2

More women today with IWY cloth, both the Upper Volta and the Togo style. Got a few photos only after a lot of plea-bargaining and grinning.

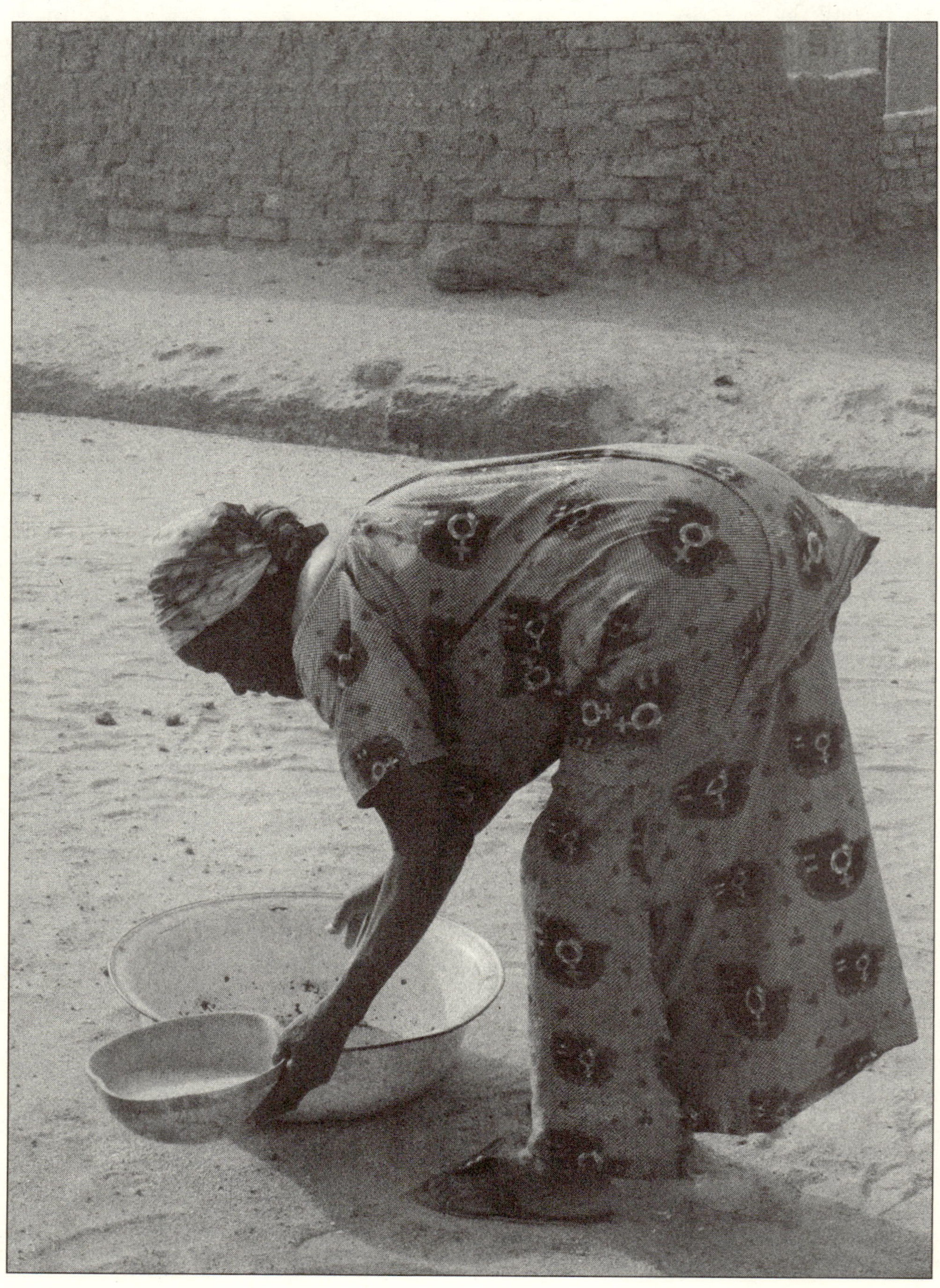

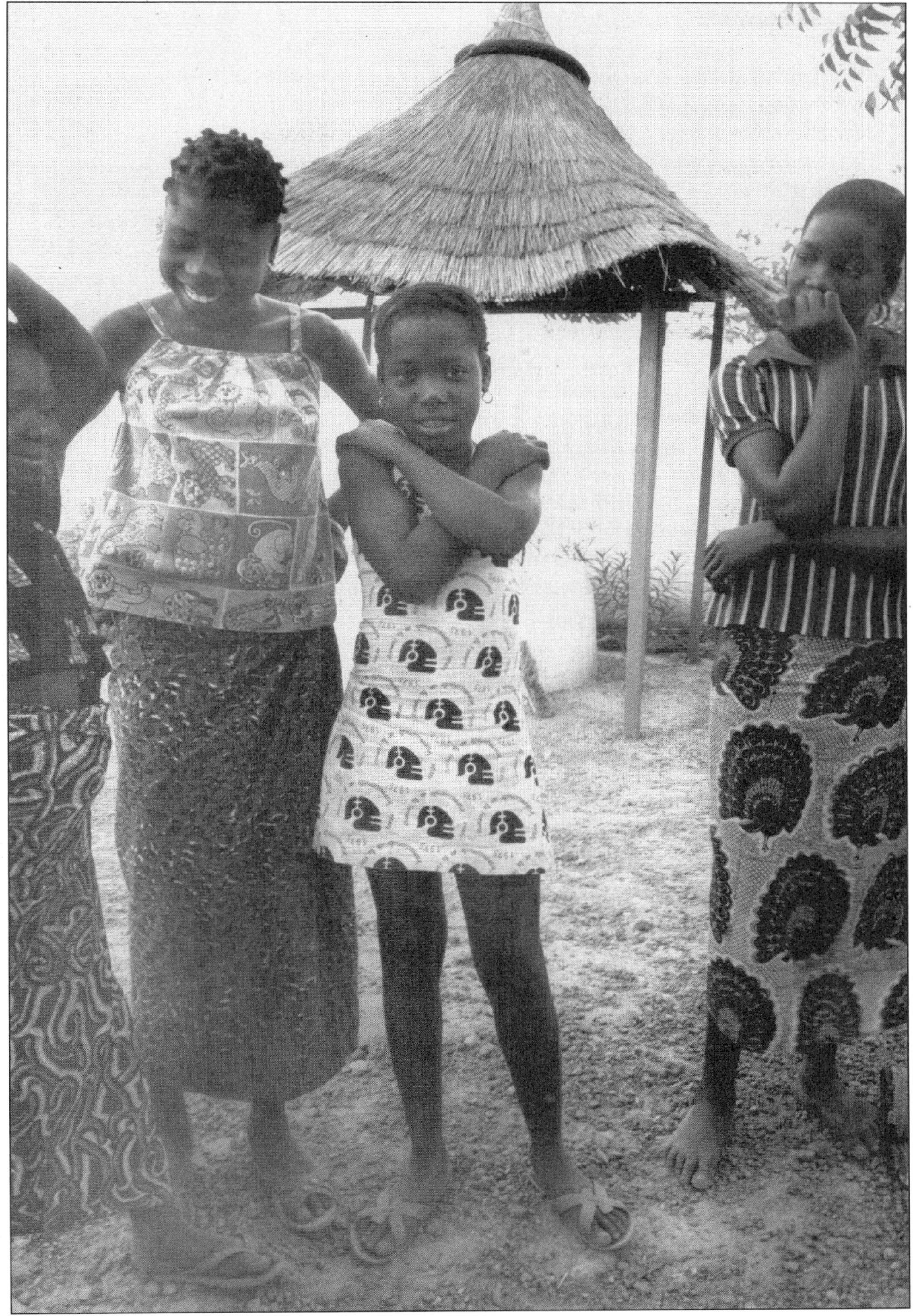

I must have met another PCV because I made a side trip to a village called Kaya and stayed there for two days. She might be the "Claudia" I refer to a few days later in the journal.

I am finding the breaking point at which I become a coward, or idealist, frantically trying to escape reality. My enthusiasm and concern in regard to the women here, their health problems etc. has been a central concern, but on a visit to Kaya, a usually poor town in this perpetually undernourished Upper Volta, I witnessed what I had mostly heard about: a weighing and nutrition-education session for mothers of malnourished babies, most of them ill with diarrhea. Most of them could have been cured or mitigated by "*l'eau de riz*," a liquid requiring one tbsp. of rice a day . . . and even this they couldn't afford. I was stunned to see so many babies at once in such deplorable condition, and the women didn't look much better off; one was even suckling two babies at once. They appeared to be genuinely concerned with the advice given to them by the PCV, but their stoicism in the face of daily hardship and trouble must override it, the realization that they can't afford even the most minor amounts of "medicine," let alone any real medicine that costs perhaps 1,000 CFA![121] (For example, for one baby with fungus in his mouth.) Another baby had a desperate, rasping breathing; each breath sounded like a thousand tiny bursting sticks from deep inside his distorted body; it had been like that for months. Didn't get photos because I became ill and had to go back to rest; my body is racked with pain and fatigue and diarrhea.

PART OF A LETTER TO MY FATHER:

> Spent two days in Kaya, a small town NE of Ouagadougou, witnessed a weighing-in session for malnourished babies & their depressed mothers.
> [. . .]
> A place like Upper Volta is so poor; to see the difference btwn here &, e.g., Nigeria is astonishing. There is something so obstinately perverse about this world in the uneven distribution of things; to me it becomes the ultimate rationale for the only workable solution: international cooperation on all levels.
> What a dream, but anything else will lead us deeper into despair than we are now.
> The French are so arrogant, such racists. I almost dislike traveling in "their" countries—I hope, if just for the sake of insulting their hell-bent pride in their language, that English becomes the language of West Africa. It's bad enough how they treat me as a foreigner in France, but on this soil they are in their prime, and a shameful one it is.
> It's getting a bit nerve-wracking now to be traveling; when I'm up north I'm in the hot dry season & the slamming heat of

121 In 1976, that was $1.88. In 2024, $1.88 = $10.67.

midday (i.e., from 10:00 - 4:00!) makes one's only impulse to sleep, and the rainy season of the south has me drifting around listlessly, unwilling to lay my thick sweaty body down but w/o enough energy to do much more. These climates aren't made for concentrated, energetic work except of the physical type (e.g., I think I would much more readily accept a well-digging job than research work here). You'd be amazed to see how slowly I'm learning to move; I never thought I'd succumb, but one has no choice in the end; I'm afraid I'll look like a somnambulist when I arrive in NY. Hello to Deborah.
Back by mid-June??
w/ love,
Susi
(why haven't I heard from you, eh?)

I'll never understand how men can scoff or sneer at women for their efforts when the motivation to rectify an unjustified wrong and to fight heroically for one's dignity and ideals has, since time immemorial, been the beloved (pre)occupation of most men, whether in theory or practice.
I suppose that they, being childish, just don't want to see anyone else doing as well in what they considered their domain: living on the basis of self-respect.

Last night, had a long, interesting discussion with an older San Francisco chap—been on the road for twenty months, going to India, been to the whole list of hot shit universities in the US and done translations and now his best friend and he are going into music—it was the first sensitive conversation I've had with a man about human relationships and hurt and parents in ages. I didn't feel any of the competitive quality, no impatience if I spoke *as* a woman, no imbalance in the respective amounts we talked about our feelings; he was just as ready to admit his hurts and most importantly he was genuinely interested. The most appalling trait in humans and particularly in men with women is to humor someone, to *concede* to listen to them. He spoke of a strong distaste for traveling with men because of that very same competition, struggle. And when I overheard a couple of these Americana PCV men conversing, I wonder that they don't drop to a timely death of boredom—they're so fucking superficial and well-protected, well-armored.

These courtyards full of wives with babies.

The trip to and from Kaya was fine, for the scenery, altho a strong breeze of perhaps 85 degrees blowing at one while sitting in the direct sunshine is an unpleasant but solid lesson learned of the pitiless land up here. Upper Volta I suspect will never get beyond the stage of mere survival; there are insignificant amounts of minerals (magnesium up north for which they're building a railroad but because of the cost of the railroad there won't be much final profit) and there really is nothing else in profusion except arid land, ill health, and mangoes.[122]

> **PART OF A LETTER TO LETTER TO MIMI:**
> Saw some (Mossi? Fulani?) women today w/ silver coins across the forehead & hair elaborately done in a sort of ridge back across their heads & heavy eyes lined in Kohl, lovely, and a pregnant woman w/ baby on back wrapped in cloth printed w/ "*année int'l de la femme*" w/ that ugly dove. Didn't have my camera, for the 1st time in months; maybe I'll see her again.
> Reading *Wuthering Heights* after somehow avoiding it for years & it's as reassuringly escapist as was *The Egoist*. I need depth & character after days of surface impressions & "one night stand" sort of conversations—some information & interest but never enough. And G.K. Chesterton has the most wonderful skill w/ language & irony & satire; look him up sometime, esp. his essays.
> It looks now as if I'll be back in mid-June, I'm going a bit quicker now (if that's ever possible here!). I feel healthy & lighter (but not ethereal, the climate isn't conducive, one is obsessed w/ base instincts like cold water & clean toilets). Wishing for a long conversation with you now.
> W/ all my love & good cheer,
> Susi

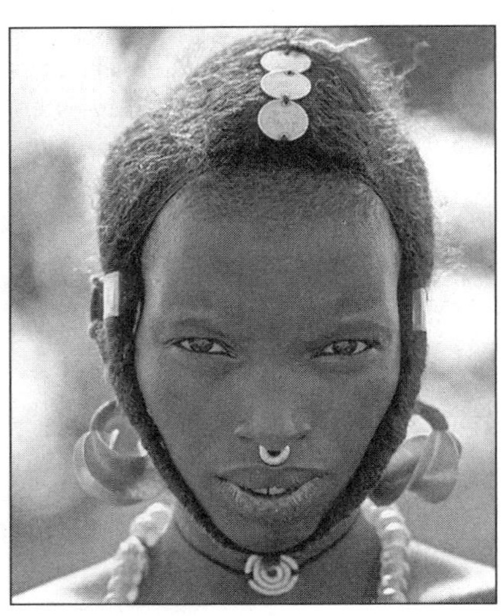

I'm not so intoxicated by these "exotic" women with silver coins and styled hair and amber beads and dark blue cloth and silent watchful eyes when I see them in this context. It all seems an exquisite apology for a miserable life; again, this ability to outweigh the physical hardship by getting succor from the psychic joys of life, like graceful carriage or skilled dancing. I don't criticize those arts but it's painful, coming from a physically comfortable environment, to see it within such a vicious physical cycle, an incessant and mostly unrewarding struggle for the minimum to keep the body alive.

I think that's why I can't take those "come to the mysterious and beautiful land of Africa" photographs, not even like Peter Beard's women [2], because that covers up a world of hard truths behind the sensual, exotic, and artful.

---

122 For a significant correction, see the first chapter note for Chapter 7.

APRIL 4–8

Spring is breaking thru on the city streets back home. Here, I'm listless in the pestering heat of midday and with the further annoyance of a belly heaving from the bloods. I wish I could stop them forever but the legal and financial complications are exhausting.

Nothing goes unsullied; I went to the corner tailor for hems in that old blue Greek dress and he tossed it almost contemptuously on the table and said, "*C'est à vous?*" [This is yours?]

The rest of our conversation was written in French but here it is en anglais . . . .

"This is yours?"
"Yes, yes, why do you ask?"
"No, it can't be yours."
"But why not?"
"You're white."
"Yes, and . . . ?"
"Yes, you're white."
"And?"
"But it's old. Whites never wear old things. You always wear new clothes."
I almost burst into a frenzy at him, but smothered it behind "Ah, no, that's just a dream."
He didn't even try to pretend to believe in that rejection of his concept.

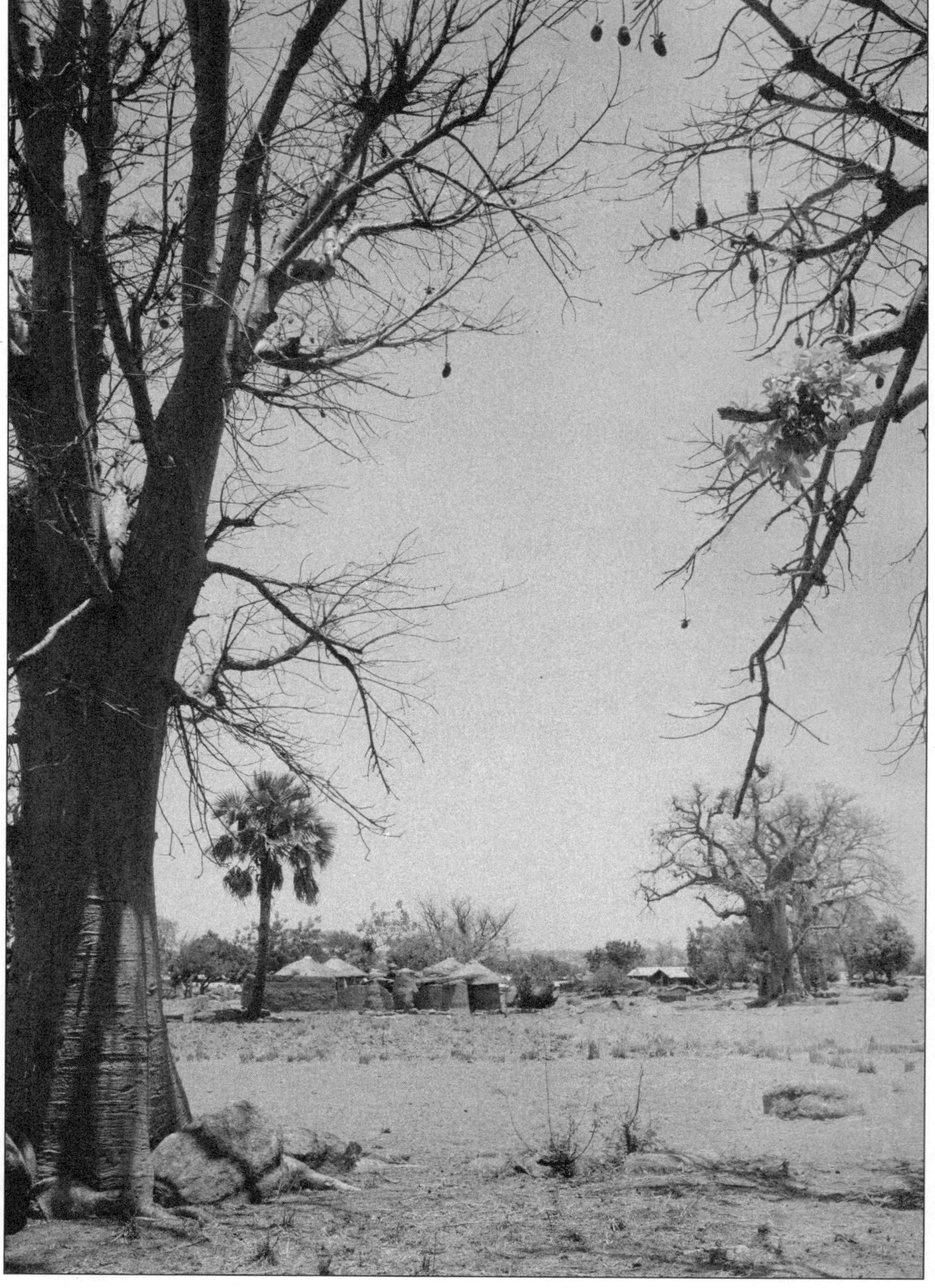

Took a ride to the bush looking for baobabs. Found them, and also a lot of clustered homes and yellow gray open space and soft noises, people moving quietly thru the fields, the day still cool with a faint breeze of night air, the dust paths traced with bicycle tracks carrying hay and chickens and yams to market, the deep peace of the countryside, the gentle isolation, the familial privacy.

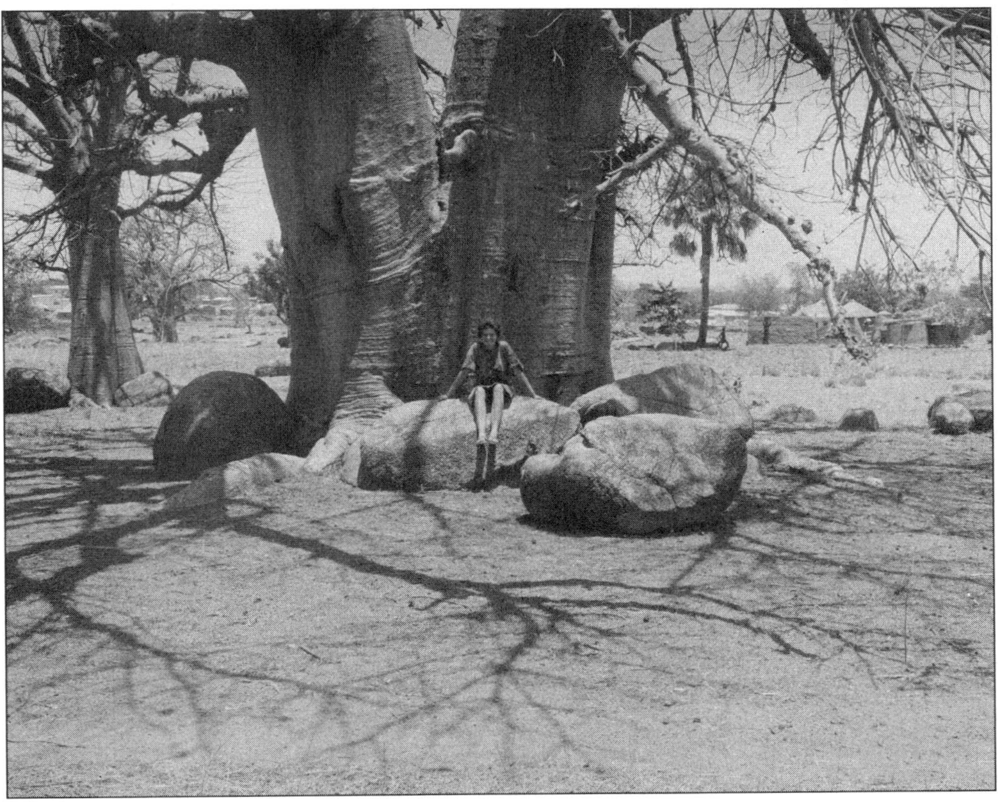

Apparently I should assume that any woman I see on the streets here (I don't know about Ouagadougou, but in the villages) has been excised when she was five or six years old. Some folks are trying now to re-educate the women to not do it to their daughters, but as one of them said to Claudia, "It's my husband's decision," and if one of these husbands (being Muslim) are grounded in the notion that sexual pleasure is not for women, they'll just keep it up as long as they can.
It's just impossible for me really to imagine that perhaps all the women here have had such a barbaric, inhumane thing perpetrated on them for whatever reason. I suspect if I saw it I would be terrified [3].

This map from 2021 shows its practice in the Middle East and Africa, but it's also practiced in other countries, most notably—because very extensively—in Indonesia. The second map indicates that (while not having current statistics).

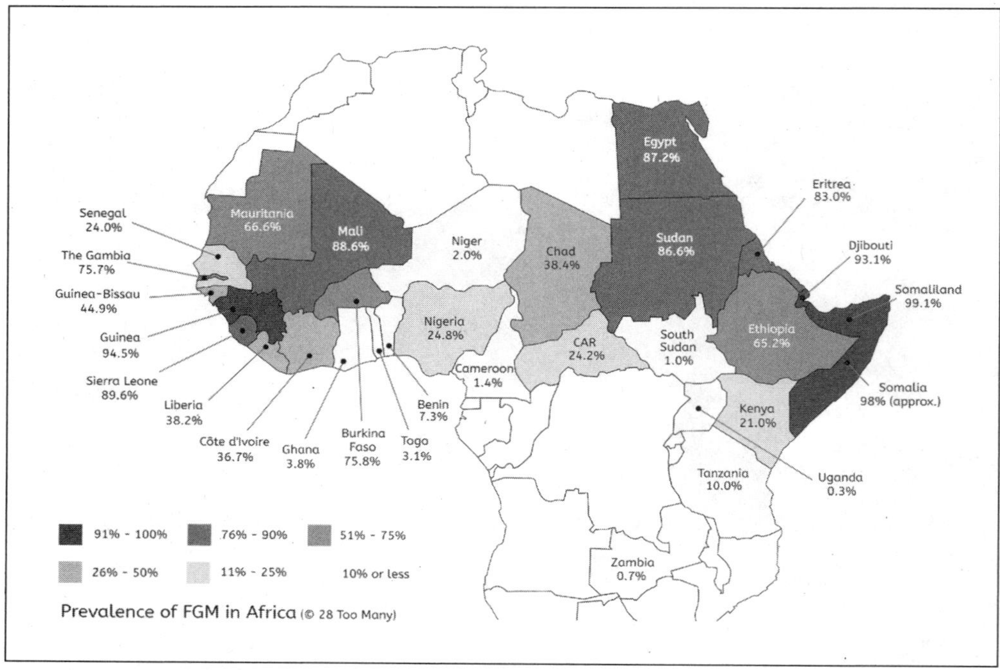

Prevalence of FGM in Africa (© 28 Too Many)

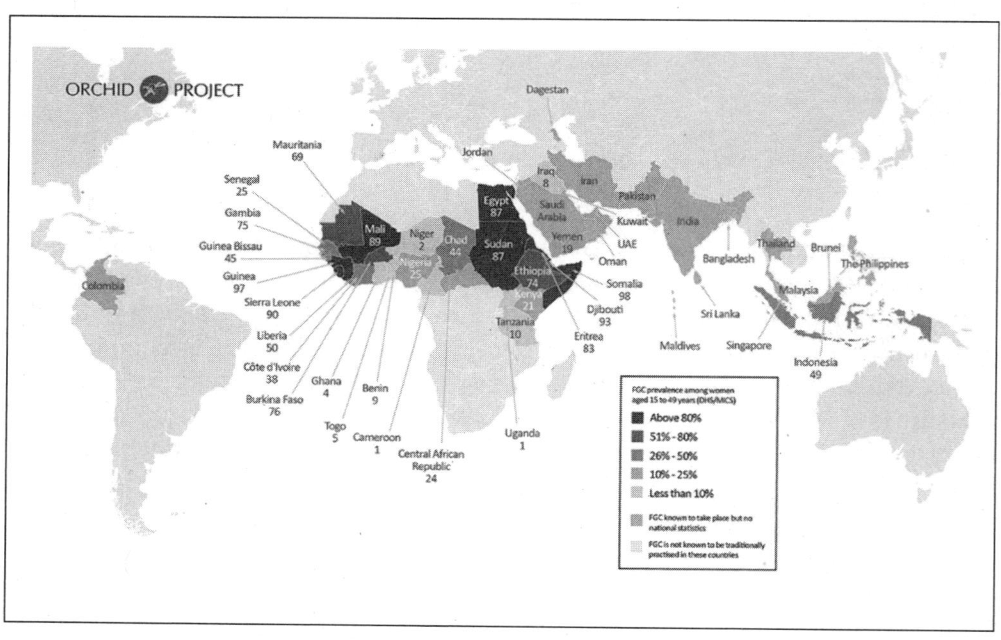

Even more disturbing is the fact that many countries in the first map, which represents millions of women, have made laws against the practice, but that hasn't done enough yet to stop the practice.

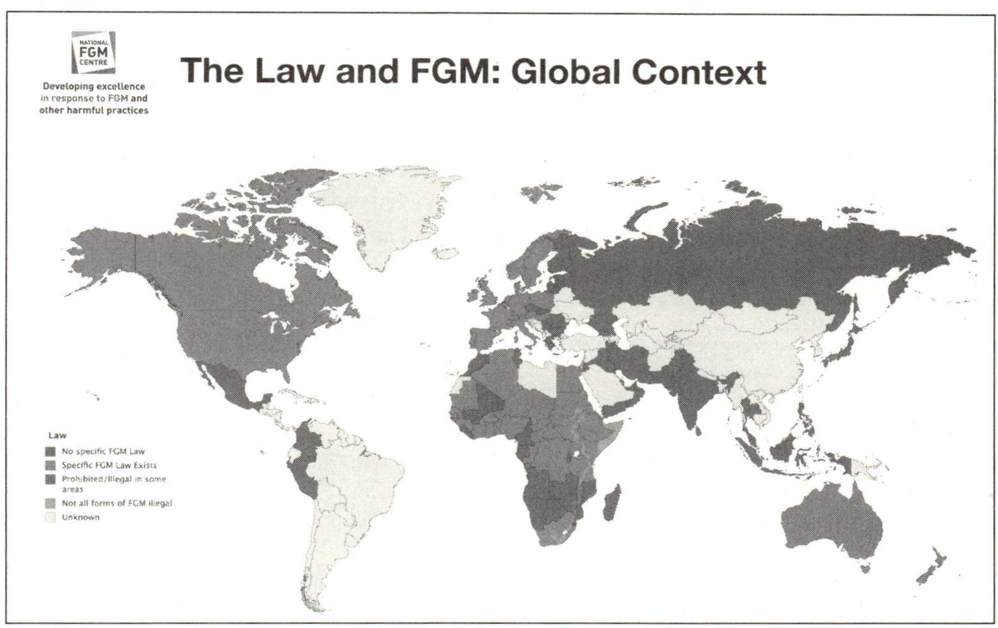

I am really going to give up on altruistic bureaucracies: The government of Haute Volta in honor of IWY initiated the "*animatrice rurale*" [rural leader/teacher]—an educational program on hygiene, health care, money-making schemes (sewing, small communal farms, crafts) i.e., to make the woman's proper place in the home more tolerable (or even initially tolerable).

Of course it's a flop.

Twelve PCV's working with their *Voltaïques* partners are in the villages, fumbling and conjuring and primarily disappointed.

One PCV woman's experience was that her local partner was less educated and skilled than she and hence expected her to be the authority figure. When the PCV refused that *petite functionaire* [lower-level functionary/administrator] privilege the local woman responded with indolence and irresponsibility. And regardless of those officiating or initiating problems, the program itself wound down to a scheme of teaching the women to hand-sew baby clothes.

While their place in the market and infant businesses and burgeoning governments and developing agriculture is being undermined by male-directed plans, they are being taught almost useless skills out of respect for IWY and international opinion. Oh yea [4].

And she, the PCV *animatrice*, said the same thing I've been dreading but seeing over and over: They'll eventually be in the advanced state that we were in the 1930s: happy housewives keeping a happy home together during a depression and supporting the boys at the front (the economic front).

And something else I heard about: That, as a form of birth control and tradition, women and men abstain from sex for nine months and two years after conception, i.e., after maybe one month of post-marital sex their intimacy is cut to the quick and repeatedly thereafter, since she's probably pregnant every nine months and two years after the last round has been run. From all evidence, however, that two years interim is not held to very seriously . . .

1984 finally read and digested and depressed and admitted. The doublethink I see time and again is America's blindness to how we introduce our "democracy" in places like Chile. Someone said it's not a question of making the world safe for democracy but making democracy safe for the world.

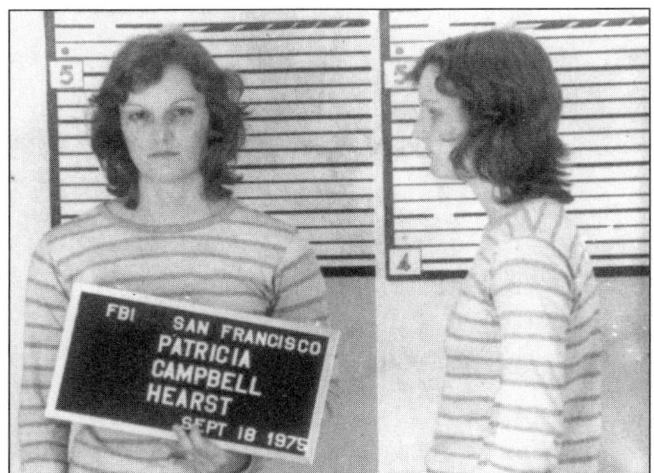

Patty Hearst was found guilty. The brainwashing, rape, closet, torture—all manufactured, and apparently the Harrises are rightfully furious with her for copping out on them, and Mrs. Hearst wept bitter golden tears at the verdict and Patty was stoical.

I feel so shitty right now, so restless so ill-contained so craving for the camaraderie of home; have had so little contact lately with Africans or with interesting whites and I'm tired of reading and so stumbling and ineffectual with my photography and too much heat and still the long trek to Abidjan, city of lights city of magic, and I wish to hell I could keep a coherent thought in my head for more than five seconds but today I decided that I want to continue my mannequin series when I get home—it speaks so clearly to me of the artifice that is our commercial reality, the starkness of it behind the comfort that comes with material splendor, the cloying message, the sleek perfection.

To show the humanity without hiding the inhumanity.

I'm so tired of the photo books on poverty whose text is full of technical notes and praise of the photographer.

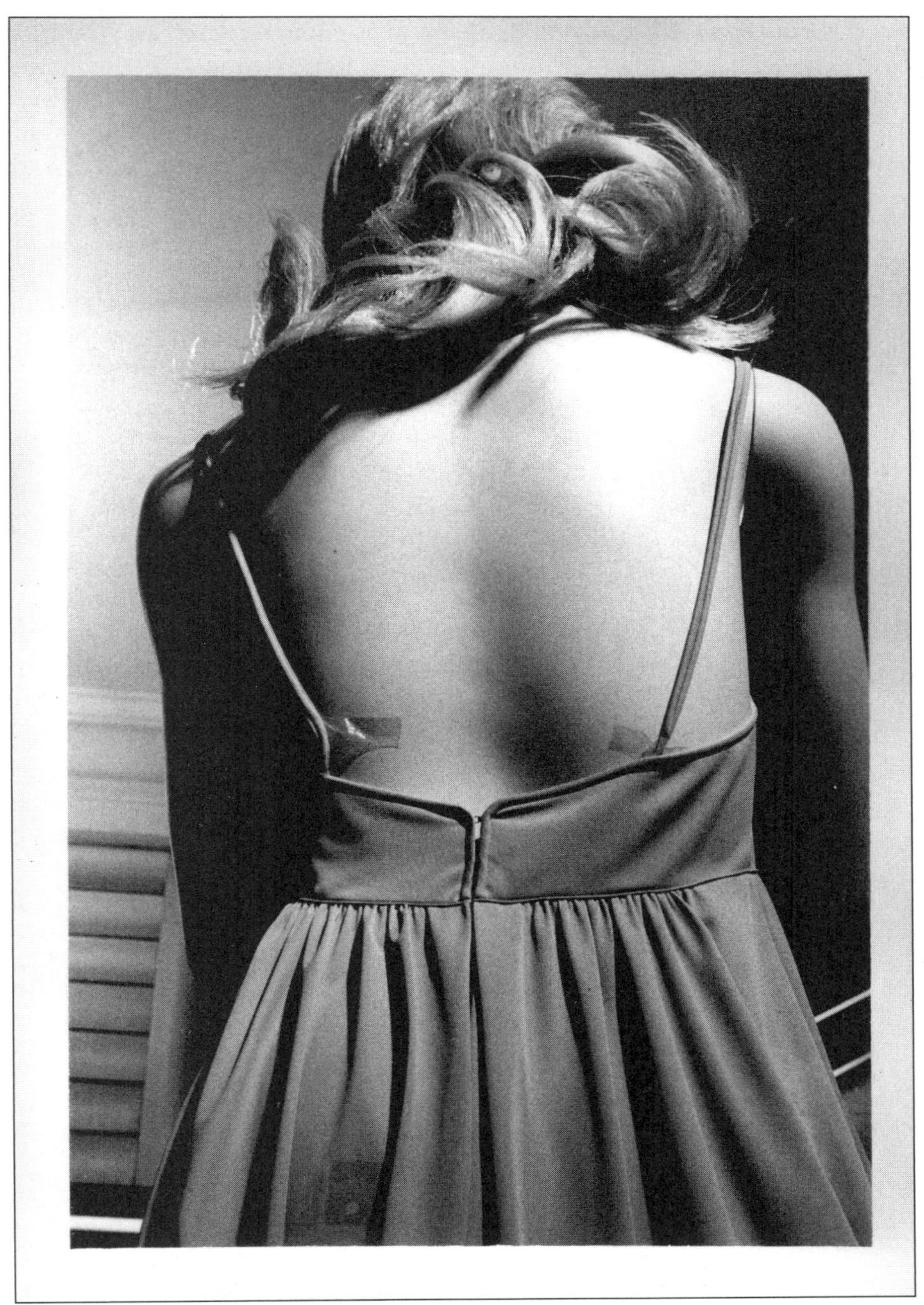

A photo from the mannequin series

Next adventure? The two-and-a-half-day trip by train from Ouagadougou down to Abidjan, the main city of the Ivory Coast (Côte d'Ivoire).

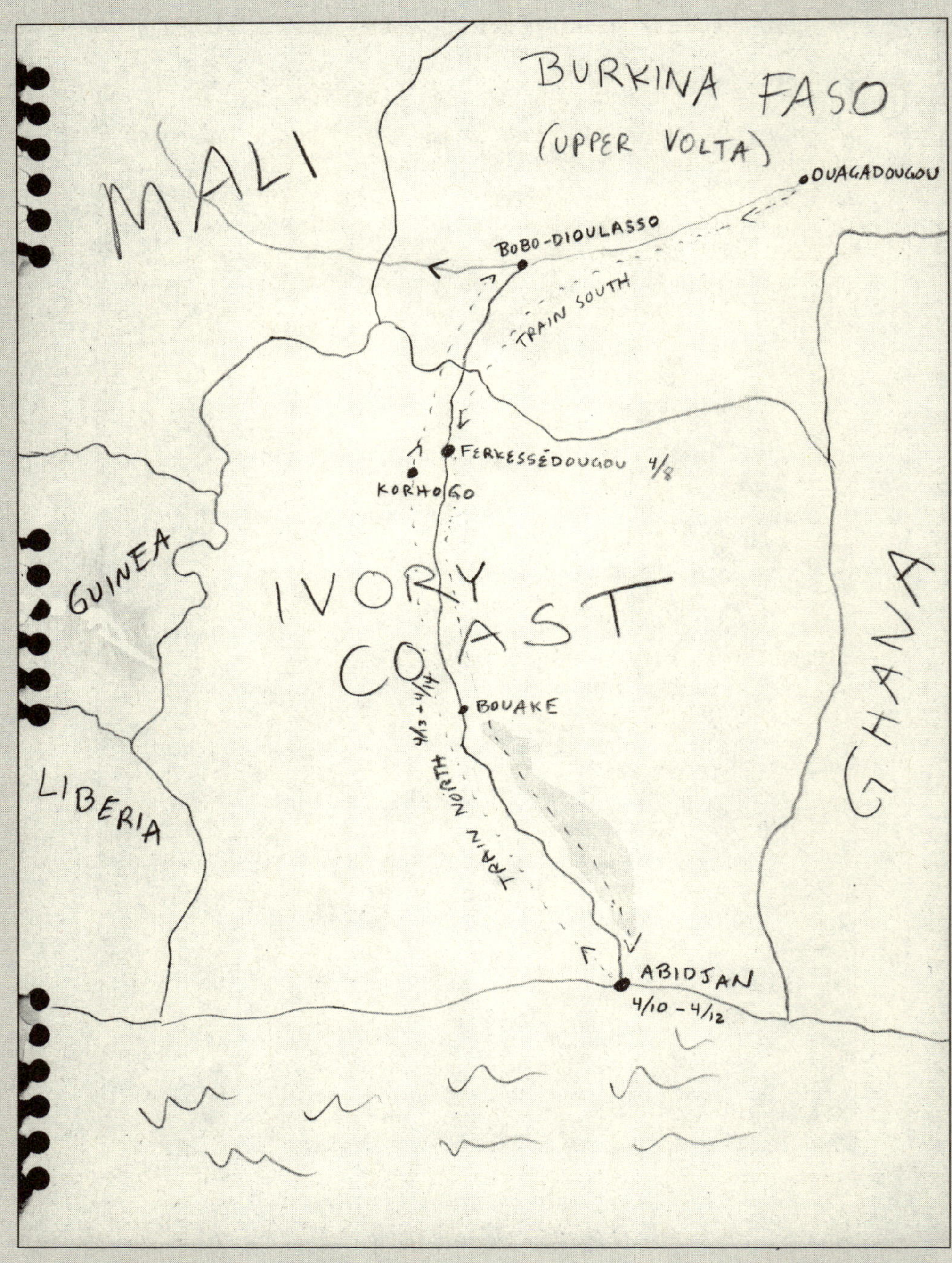

BURKINA FASO
(UPPER VOLTA)
MALI
OUAGADOUGOU
BOBO-DIOULASSO
TRAIN SOUTH
FERKESSÉDOUGOU 4/8
KORHOGO
GUINEA
IVORY COAST
GHANA
BOUAKE
4/13 + 4/14
TRAIN NORTH
LIBERIA
ABIDJAN
4/10 – 4/12

CHAPTER TWENTY

The Train, the Prince, and the Queen

PART OF A LETTER TO MIMI:

Well baby I fled the north & I'm going to flee the south (almost suicidal: more anon) & flee the north again & probably rid myself of Europe in a flash & sink into the bliss of an american speaking american eating american smoking city for a long while.
I headed north optimistically, and Ouagadougou (& the countryside) did have most of the desert charm that I had anticipated BUT, when I crossed the desert in January the days were 85°, the nites cold. April is an entirely different season, hot & dessicated, one can be no better than listless...which doesn't suit me for more than 5 minutes at a stretch. So I optimistically boarded the train, the famous train, for Abidjan, the famous Abidjan ("just like a European city"—and of course the adjective European is the highest compliment one can pay to anything here) [1].
Hell. 2éme classe. Just like in the most depressing African novels. Stifling air, chickens & plantains & hungry babies & the dead eyes of hungry exhausted Africans. A 3 hour breakdown in the peak heat of afternoon. A 5 hour wait sleeping on the platform at night. I didn't have a seat half the time but sat on the floor w/ my legs dangling out the door. A slight reprieve in 1ére classe because the conductor took pity on me—at first I refused saying, "C'est pas juste, il y a beaucoup de gens aussi fatigué que moi"[123] etc. but then my aching back & sore stomach & throbbing head & filthy overall feeling got the better of me . . . .but that was only 4 hours of a 2 ½ day trip.

The train stopped overnight in Ferkessédougou.

APRIL 8

The most appalling and fascinating sight yet in my annals of marriage and lovelessness: in Ferkéssedougou, I was invited home by "*le fils du prince de Ferké*" (?) [the son of the prince . . .]
Well, this prince was a decrepit old man with thickly-glazed, shivering, watery blue eyes, sagging lips and rotted teeth, a feeble 60ish year old body . . . and nothing else I could see to recommend him (not even, it seemed, much money). This grand patriarch, however, helpless as a baby in his chair with his prayer beads and a retinue of seven babies, all more or less the same age clambering around him, is the husband of ten wives and the father of probably thirty to fifty kids. Whenever I asked how many kids there actually were, they would roll their eyes, laugh, and say, "Ah, *beaucoup*!" [Oh, very many!]
Ha ha.

---

123 "It isn't right, there are many other people who are as tired as I am."

And to my dismay (but as the woman said yesterday, "After five months here nothing should surprise you.") I saw a quite beautiful and young woman with a small baby . . . another of his wives, this woman who has to fuck perhaps for the first time with a sodden, blind, but apparently potent old man . . . for what?
I cannot maintain "sacred respect of traditions" for these practices. They aren't justified to me in any way except economically, and as much as it might be a useless ideal I refuse to admit of lifetimes with one's most intimate partner based entirely on economics; I couldn't understand it even if she said she loved him . . . but perhaps she does? It's inconceivable.
They were Senufo and Muslim.

These are photos that the family gave me. I glued them onto paper pages of a photo album, so when I took them out to scan them, the paper was stuck to two of them and I couldn't see their names anymore.

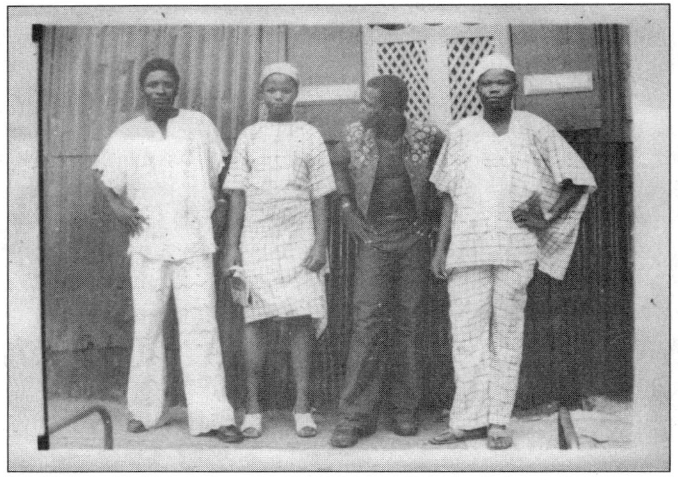

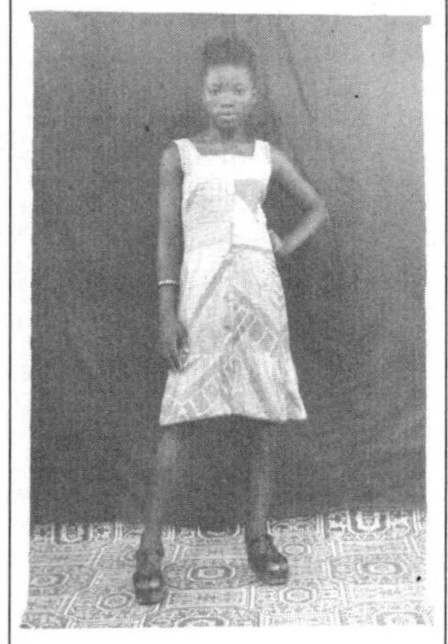

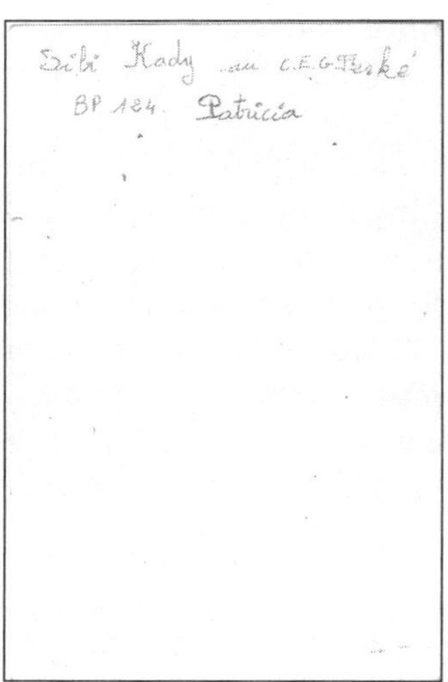

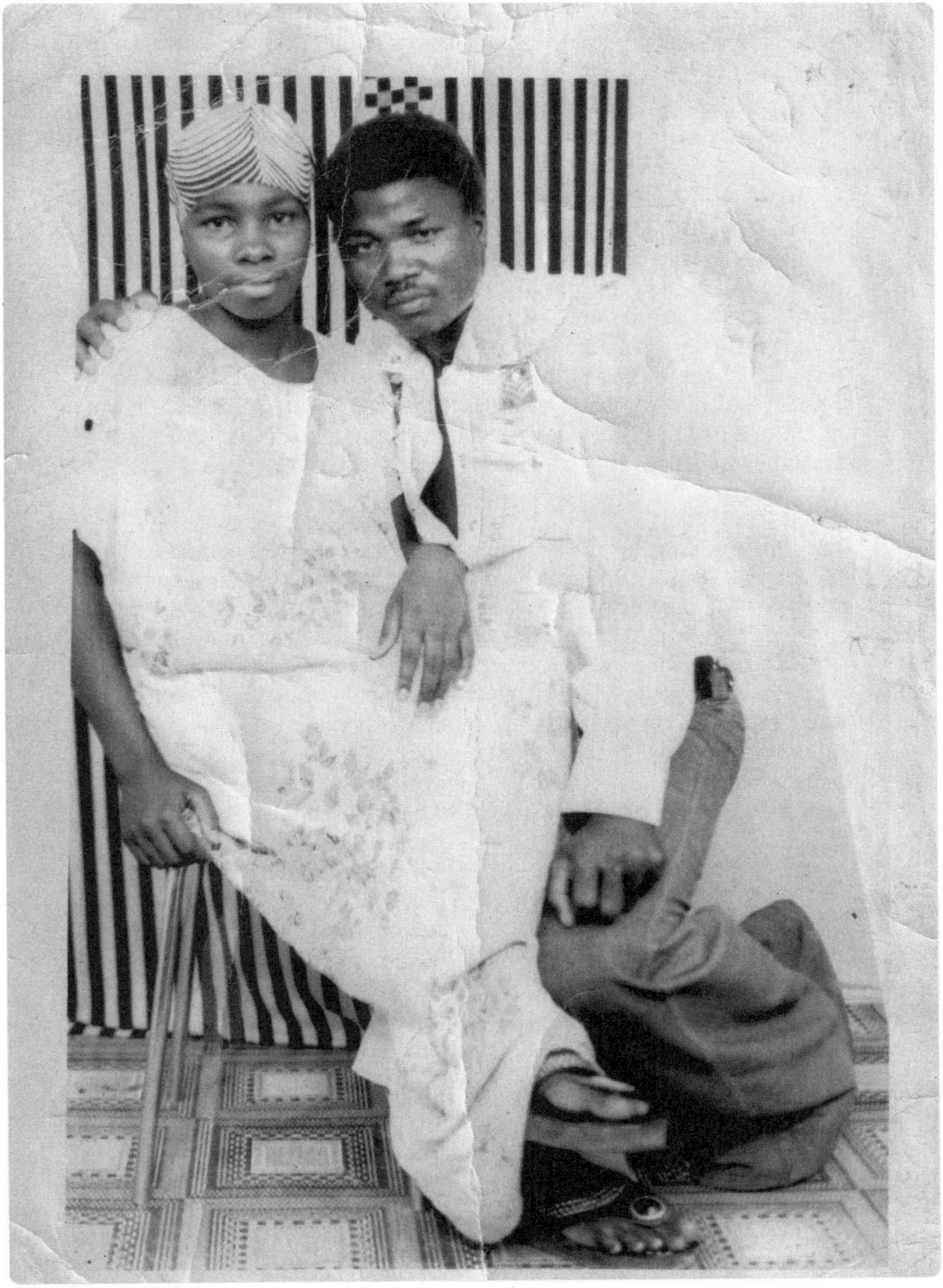

The area of Bobo Dioulasso and south was really beautiful, mostly open spaces of a fresh young green scattered with palm trees, small gardens, distant fogged blue hills, sugar cane fields.
And south, after Bouaké, I saw glimpses of New Hampshire in summer.
And wondered how Lein is doing.[124]

PART OF A LETTER TO MIMI:

I've been saying so cheerfully, "Ah, I haven't been sick yet" & everyone shakes their heads & says, "Just wait . . . " in an ominous tone. Rightfully so. For over a week now I've had different degrees & forms of diarrhea, but it all makes me feel weak & pissed off & on top of that my period & this train trip, which I have to repeat to get to Mali to fly north. So Abidjan is a welcome reprieve from the second round. When we drove in I felt exactly as if I was on the outskirts of Chicago in an airport bus—there are actually skyscrapers here, a skyline, highways . . . a rare sight in Africa.
[. . .]
I don't think now I would ever live-work here, nor travel much more in Africa. I only want to travel close to the source, i.e., eat & sleep & transport as the Africans do but it gets so depressing, I've never felt, even w/ all my years on the S. Side, such dismay at the lives of people, such compassion, & contempt for the conditions which I only have to tolerate but they have to live with day after day. There's no respite except in friends & good music & new cloth. Maybe tho if I lived here longer I could understand better how they psychologically handle the life they were given: but I'll bet they aren't such wizards at it. We don't like physical hardship & most people spend their lives & energy to earn a time of comfort & security & Africans are no different in that most human need. I used to decry their idea of "wanting to be like the whites" but no more. I can see now from where that desire comes.

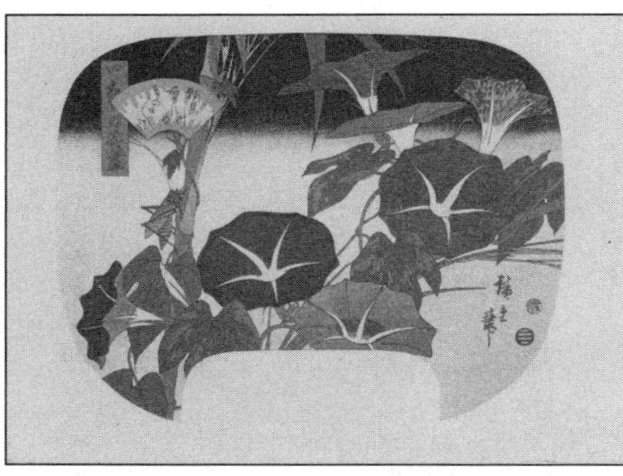

Isn't this card nice? I've saved it for months (got it last fall) & finally found the moment to use it—something cheerful to offset the blues, something exquisite to offset the "hand me down" quality of everything here, used & battered & poorly made.
But life goes on, somehow.

124 The nickname for my grandfather, Carl J. Friedrich, who had a summer house in New Hampshire. He'd been diagnosed with Alzheimer's in 1972.

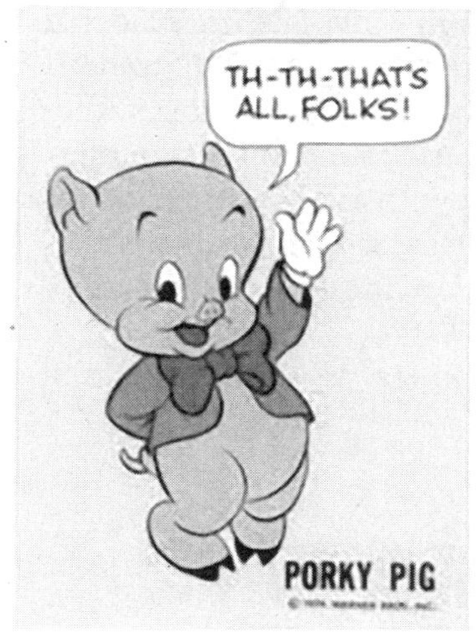

APRIL 10

Abidjan

Today I had one of my recurring (and I firmly believe inevitable) physical and nervous shatterings—roaming the streets, filthy dirty tears streaming down my sleepless face, having everyone snap their fingers, point to the sky and say "*la bas*" [over there] when I ask directions. After a 6 a.m.—9 p.m. train and a night with the family and a really sore back and then lorries to and from Korhogo, then hop on the noon train which broke down after an hour and remained thus for three and a half hours, then a five hour wait sleeping on the train platform for the next train and finally arrive to discover that my two leads for a sleep in Abidjan were dead ends. I was literally rescued by a nerve-wracked whirlwind of a French woman who rushed about and packed me off to a more sedate French couple who gave me *citron*[125] and cookies and coffee and eggs and cheese and jam and an apple and found me (oh my god, the theme music from a Porky Pig cartoon is blaring across the courtyard) lodgings with these clean *soeurs noirs*[126] at the *Maison des Jeunes Travailleuses*. Free for however many nights I wish (and I wish).

Driving here was a bittersweet scolding—I melted at the sight of the (Porky is bitching in distorted French) skyscrapers and highways and put myself in the airport bus coming into Chicago. And in the back of my mind was my scornful rejection of everyone's warning, "You'll love Abidjan, it's like being in a city back home." I humphed and said, "I've been in the bush for so long I don't relish the thought of a model city."—HA!

First of all, "all" that time in the bush was largely Lagos, Accra, Ouaga and other assorted capitals, and second of all, I do miss cities like hell. I do <u>not</u> usually enjoy arriving in a dusty tiny town, it doesn't fit my approach or needs at all, as it turns out.

And today after my sojourn with the Frenchies and clean walls and National Geographic, I almost shrank in dismay and disbelief when I went outside again and encountered the fact that yes, I'm still here, and for some while to come.

The thing that's making me so hostile and withdrawn and depressed recently is not contempt or hatred for Africans, but a body and soul revulsion of what this life <u>does</u> to them and doesn't do for them. I'm aware of my place and that I'm weighing the quality of life here by my criteria, but there must be certain absolutes of qualities with which to measure the tolerance level and pleasure level of life; when I feel myself de-energized and discouraged from fighting with the lorry system

125 A large citrus fruit similar to a lemon.

126 The order of the Black Sisters at the Home of Young Female Workers, a residence for young women domestic workers. See [2] for more info.

and eating the same food and feeling dirty and tired from walking, I imagine that Africans must have those same waves of, "Damnit, I'm fed up with this!" come crashing over them. But maybe I only permit myself the luxury of that annoyance because I know my words are more or less hollow, or at least fleeting: my circumstances can and do change, I'm not permanently stuck with any of these hardships. I'll never again scorn or pity the talk here of wanting the things a white man has—I want them, and anyone who covets some comfort and ease from burdens should want them [3].

To see the vacant eyes and closed lips as they watch the passengers entering first class . . . .

PART OF A LETTER TO MIMI:

If what I sampled tonite was *la cuisine française*, sentence me to 30 years of Hamburger King & African chop for my ingratitude & I will be a happy woman. The funny French lady who "saved" me yesterday in a motherly way felt that I was being neglected because they didn't serve meals where I'm staying. She came by this a.m. w/ promises of a dinner *chez elle*. She insisted it would be "*très simple*" & I said "*Oh, ça va, ça va*" thinking to myself Aha!

A good meal at last!

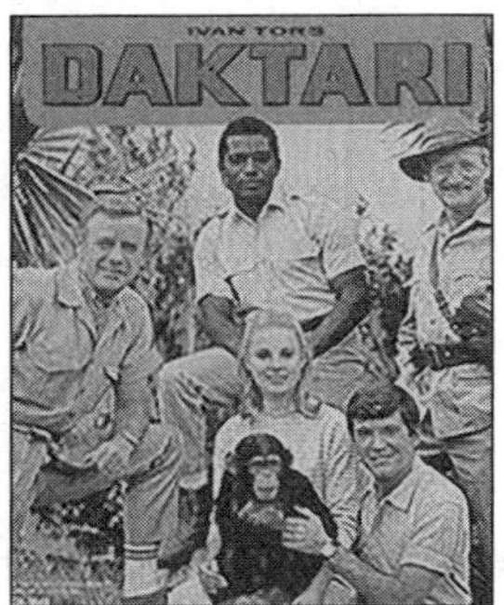

The 1st indication of discord was that everyone was glued to the TV watching *Daktari*—do you remember? That idiotic African adventure serial w/ the cross-eyed lion & Barbie blonde? The black actor kept calling everyone "patron" which here is a Stepin Fetchit [4] term, altho as I recall in the American version he was their colleague.

We had a tolerably good tomato soup, but it was just tomato soup, yes? & then in the typically French way we had hard-boiled eggs which became "*œufs au sauce blanche*" i.e., we used a bit of French bread to soak up the flavorless white muck that covered up the fact that they were just hard-boiled eggs. I thought, ah, now the main course. Vegetables à la something or other, *un peu de viande* [a bit of meat] delicately spiced. They brought out the cheese. Two tiny slices w/ more bread. A bit of good wine, just a bit. An orange. Then we settled back to watch a speech by the President of Côte d'Ivoire & a horrid wrestling match. And my stomach resigned itself to yet another disappointment. How I yearn for grubby unpretentious chop. When I *reviens chez toi*[127] I will expect a guided tour hand-in-hand to the finest deli New York has to offer for a true feast, yes? *D'accord.*

127 "When I return to you." And *d'accord* is Okay, agreed.

I'm tired of being in uncomfortable situations w/ people years older than me w/ whom I have nothing in common & no chance of getting into an interesting conversation because I'd constantly be (am) stepping on toes & faces. I think something in me really revived in being around the graphics group that I even lacked at Oberlin, where things were still a bit formal & strained (everyone "talking shop" & airing their well-educated opinions).
It was the 1st time I felt in the same age group, & that's important to me right now, to feel that I'm at a point where things are still new & fresh & undecided, rather than being around people (even if they're 24 or more) (w/ exception of the older WGC women) who are so comfortably entrenched in a certain limited reality. And I realize how much I dislike families, having to smile at kids & pet their family animal & listen to the husband ramble & the wife concede.

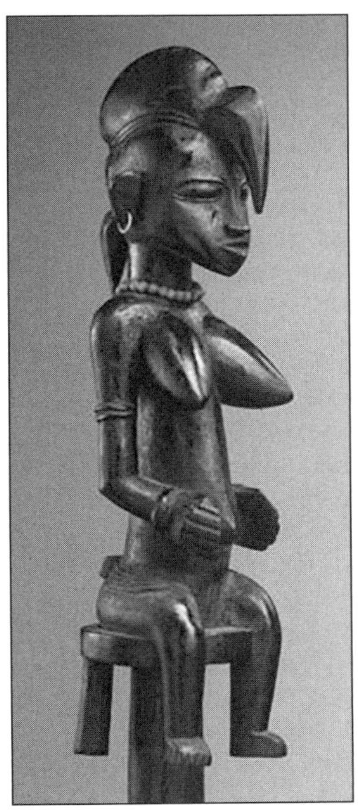

I saw a woman today who looked exactly like a Senufo [5] sculpture: her profile, the shape and size of her breasts and how she held her baby to suckle, the arch of her back . . . It was amazing, really.

I'm seeing more and more now how character types repeat themselves in human beings, e.g., the Frenchies yesterday, the various degrees of forthrightness, timidity and worrisomeness with which people deal with the world; the groping posture that one woman took in response to her husband's wellsprings of information (which of course he's developed over the years in response to her self-diminished one); the ill-channeled energy and self-assurance of the other turning her into a really neurotic mother dragging about her two girls and talking constantly to herself but knowing what she's doing—for example, in a situation like mine yesterday. And to listen to their Saturday afternoon sit-about-the-house-puttering conversation reminded me that often the only difference that separates African from French et. al. is the context of the drama; African women talk about neighbors and sewing and nasty cats and the price of things while sitting on a dirt floor with babies swarming about; these women did it in an air-conditioned very slick house with *citron* and cookies. And the most interesting of all: They spent, all told, four hours telephoning places to find me a roof while I was in Abidjan, never once mentioning that I might stay in their house; somehow the question was always hanging thickly in the air but treated as if a mirage.
It takes an African woman about four minutes to decide whether she'll take you in (and the answer of course is always yes).

In my opinion it's really a condemnation, rather than a commendation, of the French that they have the gall to praise Abidjan as the finest city in West Africa. What they're actually praising is the incredible skill of the French to impose their culture and lifestyle in such a twisted way on a country two thousand miles in head and heart away from France.
I predicted it: When I saw these bonny French ladies all decked out in Cacharels and Yves St.'s today rushing about to market I was never more impressed with the self-indulgence of it all; they're just showpieces and glorified mamas for the businessmen here, totally unproductive and over-consumptive [6].

A LETTER FROM MY MOTHER:

Dear Susie,
Maria called, read part of your letter. First notes since Lagos telegram. Where's my "night letter" (telegram) gone? Yes—mail to Niger (Niameh) might someday be coming back. At any rate just now got a p. card with a beautiful Fulani woman—anxious to hear all about the many different customs, what the facial customs denote—the wrapping of cloth etc.—Have you seen, photographed, bought (?) any pieces of sculpture? You were so close (or are) to the Bay of Benin. Swimming? Sharks?
I only hope that you wrote, wrote notebooks full.
There's an envy in me that you can travel, see, hear, and I wouldn't mind discomforts either, if I were younger. But it's an envy that does not diminish my love or admiration—'cause it's not a competitive situation. Ah, well you know all that.—
Mimi called last night—says she hasn't heard from you at all & can't understand it. Mentioned that your article had arrived. That she mailed a manila envelope to an Embassy (forgot where)—gave her the Accra info which I got from Wing yesterday—Today you say Abidjan & when this might get to you—where will you then be? It's almost a bit maddening, or like chasing a dog whose tail you caught and who swishes it right out of your hand zooming around a corner.
[. . .]
I've been reading Otto's new book *Going Crazy* and find some of his writing, ideas, wording rather banal. Also, using well-known people reminds me of the asininity of TV commercials using actors & actresses to tell one that our behind (or ass) should be wiped with multilayered soft tissue blah blah . . .
Maybe it'll get better as I go on. Got *The Best and the Brightest* and stood by twilight beside the kitchen sink (where I had unwrapped it) and started reading and went through the first several chapters. That guy <u>knows</u> how to write—or "paint" miniature portraits of men—But golly—it's 800 or more pgs.—when will I finish that? Chicago is, of course, what it always is—and the Election Blasts are what they always are: composite lies, accusations, barracuda attacks, snide remarks and above all

that [indecipherable] the halo of the Bicentennial. What a farce!
Where have all the true thinkers and uncorrupted politicians gone?
This must be off & I hope it reaches you somehow, somewhere.
With much love
From Pete & me
Mom

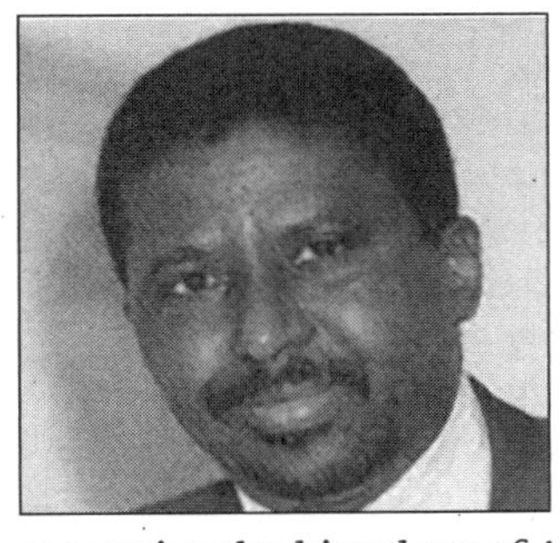

I just finished *Anne Zingha: Reine d'Angola, première resistante à l'invasion Portugaise* by Ibrahima Baba Kaké [7]—a true heroine, a true guerrilla fighter working from her teens until her old age to fight off the invasions by the Portuguese and Dutch. With "*centaines d'Amazones*," [hundreds of Amazons] whom she forbade to have sexual relations, and the loyalty of her people, she was a shrewd and uncompromising leader, succeeding in the late 1600s to draft a treaty with the Portuguese to recognize the kingdom of Angola as peers to the colonial peers. She became Christian in her youth to get in with the Portuguese, then renounced it as not befitting the ruler of a people who held traditional beliefs, then reclaimed it after the treaty so as to be under the law of the Pope, who could therefore force the Portuguese to hold to their treaty. She was wise but very ferocious; wise in the well-placed use of force in such a war as theirs.

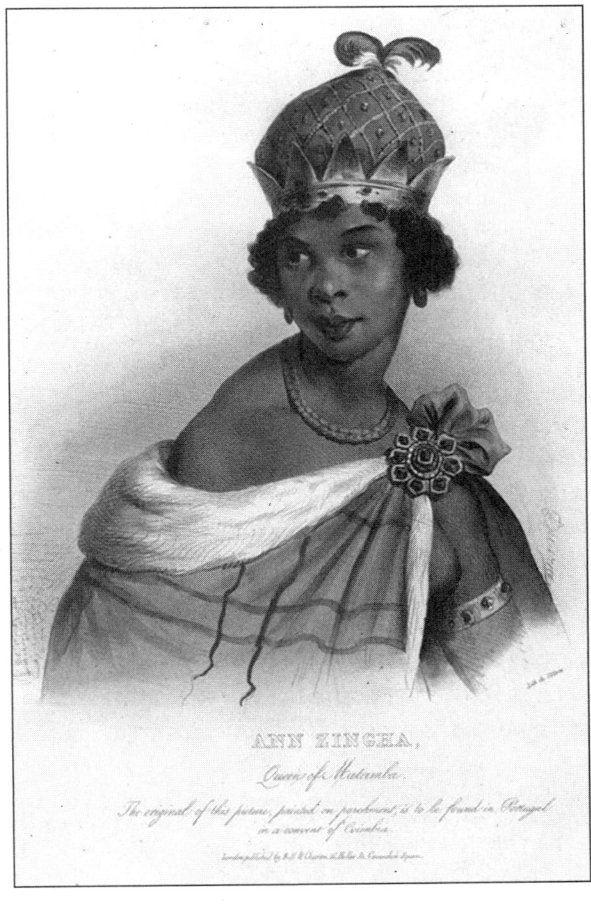

Ngola Mbandi Nzinga Bandi Kia Ngola *qui signifie «la reine dont la flèche trouve toujours le but»*
Her name means "the queen whose arrow always finds the goal."

Another loving letter from baby and quite interesting too, and a fantastic communiqué from BM [Barbara Morgan, a member of the Women's Graphics Collective] full of exciting plans about a San Francisco Graphics, a co-ed one, with of course lots of logistics, problems and promise.

PART OF A LETTER TO MIMI:

Baby I just got your 2nd letter, in Abidjan, & I'm so excited about everything even tho it's all confusion & a million different plans & projects.

Thanks for the note that CC got my article, I was a bit worried that it was lost. Keep up your cheer & your hard work & know that I love you too very much.

I feel quite ambivalent about the French at this point. I hate them for the racism that exudes from everything they say & do, but I am so grateful for Abidjan right now that I have to accept their fanaticism, which drives them to build an admirable model of a European city in the midst of Africa. I took a long stroll thru the Plateau, the rich *quartier*, full of perfume shops & cafés & skinny highheeled mascaraed French ladies with chubby children & *alimentations* selling quality yogurt & cheese & wine—and then crossed the bridge into Treichville, described in tourist books as "*le quartier le plus ancien d'Abidjan*" i.e., the African quarters, a *marché* swarming w/ tourists & sly merchants. I had a curious feeling of superiority, as if I'd seen so much more & this really was such a superficial or dandified version of the hard core sort of markets here (like the grand one in Kumasi) & all the tourists who'd arrived by plane in Abidjan & stay at the Hotel Ivoire & lug home a shitload of "African sculpture" & groovy tie-dyed clothes. I think even Yellowstone Park couldn't outdo these African cities in the type of tourists they attract.

Got a ride back w/ a Frenchie who insisted that Algeria was truly marvelous before the war. I mentioned that *au contraire* now they were really developing, & quite industrious, & he changed the subject . . . to how marvelous Abidjan is, the finest city in West Africa. I think the French have more of a stranglehold on Côte d'Ivoire than the British have for example in Ghana or Nigeria. [128]

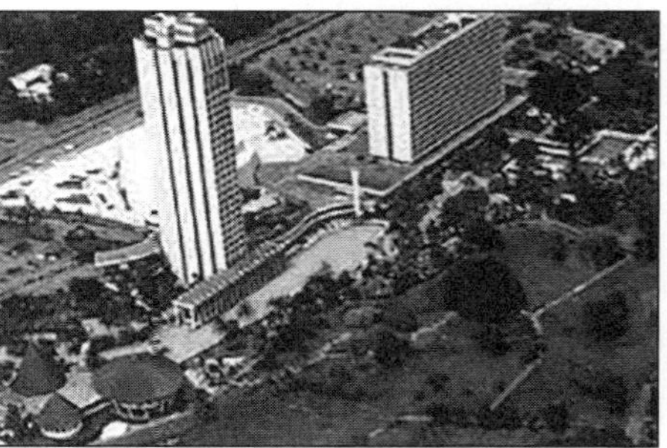

How strangely deserted Cocody [8] seemed, the houses quiet behind high fences, no families spilling into the streets. It says something about the state of things here that a hotel becomes a major tourist attraction, but that's exactly what the Hotel Ivoire is: the most luxurious, sumptuous, pristine, cushioned, delicate, sterile place I've perhaps ever been in. Everything is excessive. I got the sickening feeling that I was in the presence of the most concentrated # of pampered people I'd ever seen. It's

128 Formal French colonial rule was introduced in the 1880s following the scramble for Africa. In 1904, Ivory Coast became part of French West Africa until 1960 when the country regained independence from France—on paper. They didn't exactly leave.

inconceivable to me how soft their lives must be, continually cushioned by tasty tidbits and deep soft chairs and the finest of anything money can buy—it's the most spoiled existence imaginable. I would like, for one day, to put them thru the sort of traveling I do, or better yet the sort of usual day of an African. How can life be so debasing for so many and so sweet for the few?

I have traveled four times now with prisoners under curious circumstances. Once on a state transport with several policemen, all threateningly arranged across the back row of the bus. Another time, two just got on a lorry and someone instructed the driver re: their destination. There were a lot of sidelong glances at them and one of the man's hands had large chunks of flesh torn off, but nothing occurred except their frequent loud voices and laughter. This time, a small abashed man was helped onto the train accompanied by two unarmed men. His handcuffs were a few windings of white cloth, enough to render him incapable of sitting or standing unaided. These were typical to me of the general ambiance here, of all facets of society being out front, treated in a very straightforward, almost casual way. And the man today strolling aimlessly thru the market with nothing to cover his dusty nakedness but shreds of a brown coat. His big firm bare ass and matted reddened hair were somehow eloquent.

PART OF A LETTER TO MIMI:

I sat on the bridge surveying the traffic & every 5th or 6th car was not a white's, as in Lagos or Accra, but an African's. I suppose it's like the Brits in S. Africa. The French made it just fine for themselves here & aren't about to get out for anyone else's independence or development. But, e.g., I think in general the British were more or less content to evacuate Accra & Lagos, those being only remotely "livable" compared to Abidjan (but Accra & Lomé are still my favorite capital cities here).

My trip is coming to a quick end now not only from exhaustion & a sore ass but because I've gotten myself caught in the rainy season & for example can't really travel much by road because they get washed out & boggy, & up north it's the densest part of the dry season, unbearable.

[. . .]

Baby, I don't know what to do about myself, I feel like a lost cause. It's probably hard for you to imagine, because it seems that it's so easy for you to get into & maintain good conversations w/ no matter who, but I live in constant terror, it <u>is</u> a sort of terror, of not having anything to talk about when in company. Can you <u>fathom</u> it, that after 5 months of travel, seeing a million strange wonderful & dreadful things all new & complex, I wonder almost daily if I'll be able to talk about it when I get home. If everything will sound like drivel or textbook descriptions. It makes me so angry or worried that sometimes I can't even sleep thinking about it. I once told you that you have a funny talent for expanding on a topic and/or being able to talk at length & quite "authoritatively" about something w/ which you might actually only have had small acquaintance. (I don't mean that you're glib—it's a certain self-assurance that I mean to describe . . .)

I on the other hand tend to diminish all my knowledge, to make maybe a molehill out of a mountain, to always worry if I know "enough" about something before I "can" talk about it. Which is curious, because underneath or inside I get very direct opinions & sensations about things & am able to recall a lot of sources & arguments but somehow I balk when I have to bring it out. Damn it I get so angry about this. And now of course I fret constantly about my articles & my photos, every day reprimanding myself for not doing enough not making enough photos not asking more more more questions not being observant enough. I'd never need a slave-driving tutor, I think I have enough of one in myself; what I need is an encouraging one. I think the trouble is partly due to good old papa, whose opinion (despite all my contrary feelings about him) about my achievements I prize the most (or very much) & altho he oftentimes has told me he's "proud" of me etc., I still always think he considers me a bit lazy or superficial or whatever & I shrink from that.

And mama just lavished me w/ praise but of course that comes so often & in such unqualified doses that it doesn't mean much anymore, despite all her sincerity & good intentions. I wish to hell I had more of an "I don't give a shit about outside opinion" attitude but I do give one, & it weighs on me & my doings. And the worst thing about it is that the opinion the judgment always comes from a faceless intangible place, it's no one or no comment in particular, just the paranoia about "success" & *savoir faire*[129]. It seems to me it's a question of forging my way into a self-defined sort of life, doing the things that I value, reacting to things as is most honest to my nature & ideas, even to the extent of my clothes & diet & of course the most difficult: my work. I wonder constantly & w/o much headway what the hell I'm going to do all my life what kind of work can I be most proficient & satisfied in. I climb to the peak of optimism & courage & choose the most challenging thing, photographer or journalist or hot & heavy feminist & then quail & fall back on some silly alternative because of fear. It's awful, how contemptuous I can feel towards men who are so arrogant & self-assured & narrowly directed in their goals, & then realize almost how intrinsic that is to doing the thing one really wants to do, w/o the constant support or help that I've come to expect (& which usually isn't there as one begins such a task).

129 The ability to act or speak appropriately in social situations.

I want to be able to think more clearly & specifically on these things but the afraid part of my mind keeps getting in the way & diverting my concentration; it's like wanting to be totally involved in lovemaking & yet being uncomfortable w/ it & as a result thinking of a million triviata to cut me away from the experience.
And I almost feel that reading about "great women," instead of making me more determined, puts me in the same worrisome position as if I was reading yet another hero's tale; I always judge myself vis-à-vis them, & never quite meet the standards.
I wish I could dismiss this all as bullshit but it's too real for me right now.
It's very late now, the rain has been streaming down thick & loud all day & night & last night also, I'll try to get some sleep.
Susi

It was getting hotter and hotter as the rainy season approached, and I had a ticket to fly back from Bamako, Mali, so I had to get going.

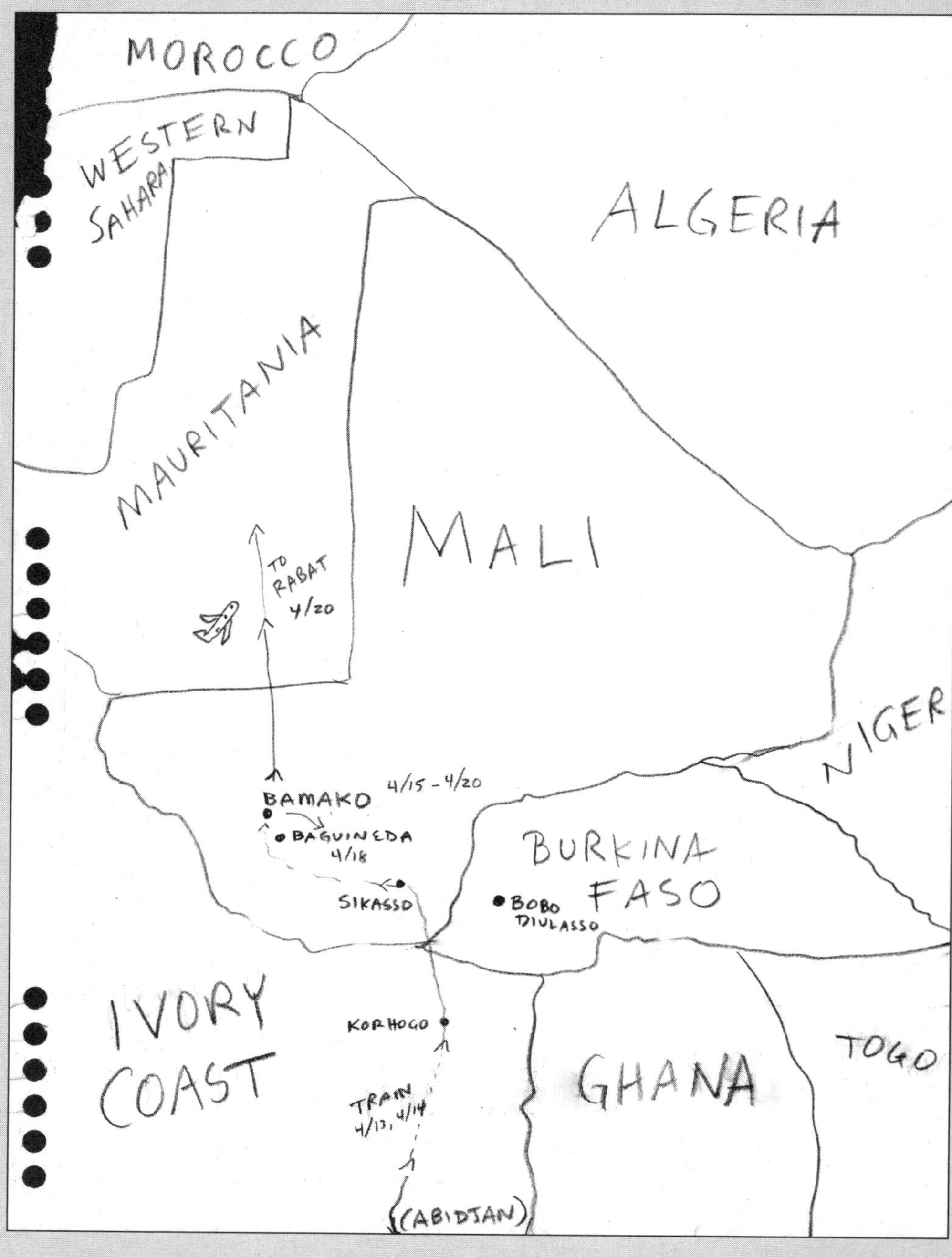
MOROCCO
WESTERN SAHARA
ALGERIA
MAURITANIA
MALI
TO RABAT 4/20
NIGER
BAMAKO
4/15 - 4/20
BAGUINEDA 4/18
BURKINA FASO
SIKASSO
BOBO DIULASSO
IVORY COAST
KORHOGO
GHANA
TOGO
TRAIN 4/13, 4/14
(ABIDJAN)

CHAPTER TWENTY-ONE

They Prefer Death over Shame

I headed north by train as far as Korhogo and then continued on lorries to Bamako where I would catch the flight to Casablanca.

APRIL 13–14

I think I finally reached and surpassed the tolerance maximum of travel here last night. I had spent two relatively relaxing days in clean Abidjan and felt myself steeled for the return train trip. I clambered on and got lucky—I could perch on the edge of a wooden, thinly padded, low-backed bench already occupied by two others. Everyone after me had to stand.

I was really trying to contain myself, to overcome my anger, and foresee pains philosophically, when an incoming train passed us. I caught a fleeting glimpse into the well-lit comfort and quiet of first class and a jolt of horror and sorrow went thru me . . . and of course the tears followed. It was such an unexpected, overwhelming, and perfectly juxtaposed lesson to me of the utter shit I/we have to put up with because of differential pocketbooks. It was the final slap after the Hotel Ivoire, and Africans have my undying empathy (as do the passengers on the bus at 63rd and Stony, etc.[130]) for all the time that it will take until we treat others with the same concern with which we pamper ourselves.

> **PART OF A LETTER TO MIMI:**
>
> I left Abidjan w/ a firm resolve to withstand my last leg of road transit in Africa: not a chance in hell. I clambered & shoved & fuck you'd my way onto the *2éme classe* train car & wrestled my way onto the edge of a low-backed wooden bench that already held two disgruntled folk. That was short-lived. I claimed one side of the hallway floor on the 1st class car & curled up, laid my head on the fiercely shaking filthy floor and fell asleep . . . Between stops, every twenty minutes of the 16-hour pleasure ride, someone opened the door, hard, onto my head. For a while I tried sitting up but then I'd nod forward in slumber, slam against the edge of the steel door.
>
> I was led numb and glazed-eyed off the train for coffee & a lorry to Sikasso . . . a short trip which managed to take 9 hours. Then a short 6 hour wait for the lorry for Bamako . . . .

Angela Davis spoke wisely when she learned her lesson in Cuba about romanticizing the working-class life; I've mentioned it before in referring to different situations, but today I found another instance, one which has gradually been more evident to me and which somehow deeply angers (and doesn't surprise) me: the profoundly false or

130 In a relatively poor neighborhood on the South Side of Chicago.

glorified or unrealistic portrait that we all (foreigners) have of Africa, Africans. Today, driving along the country road to Sikasso, we stopped for mangoes and to pick up more passengers at a village and there to my delight, for a moment, was a Peul woman, fully decked out in the large twisted gold earrings, dyed lips, nose plug, gold gold everywhere. And her companions were equally adorned. I stared at her and remembered the cover of Davidson's African book with the similar woman, and then I began to notice the surroundings, the limpid baby on her back, the lack of any produce except mangoes, and all that focused beauty and traditional African aesthetic was jammed right up against the context of daily life and all its routine and hardship. I've been thinking that photos have to show the humanity without hiding the inhumanity, as well as having to expose the beauty within its context.

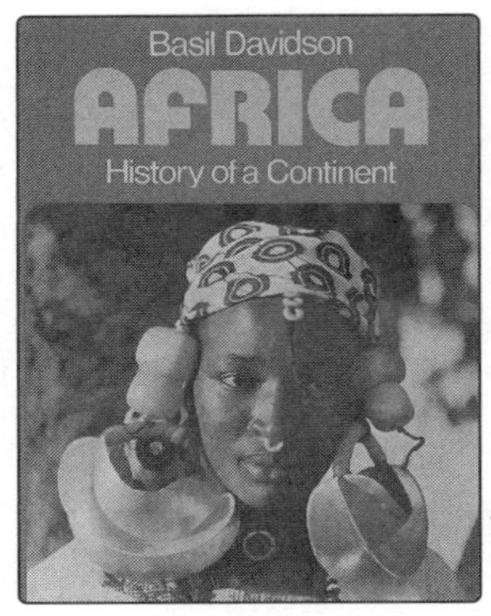

We are driving Sikasso-Bamako at night and I'm a bit nervous, but how could anything go wrong (please!!) on my last lousy ride in W. Africa?

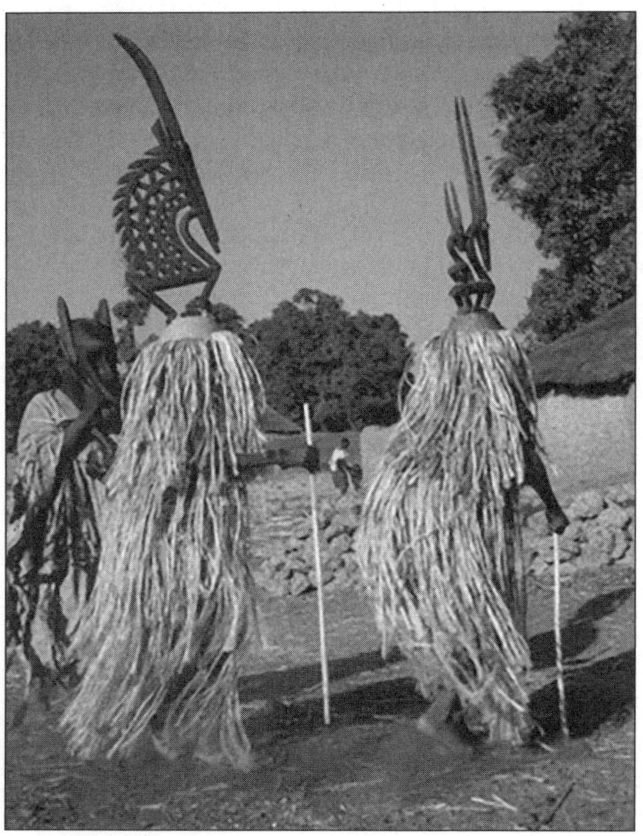

On the drive to Bamako at that aching point in the early morning I got into a talk with the driver and asked him what he could tell me that was special about the Bambara. He thought for a moment and said simply, "*Les Bambara préferent la mort que l'honte*."[131] And changed the subject.

Bambara men wear antelope masks to dance to Chiwara, Djenne, Mali, 1978.

131 "The Bambara prefer death over shame." See [1] for more information about the Bambara and the Chiwara dance.

PART OF A LETTER TO MIMI:

. . . the lorry to Bamako screeched in on a trail of glory & the stink of mangoes at 4 a.m.

I caught a few cozy hours of sleep on the unpadded bamboo rail cot at the police station before going into town to find all the hotels booked solid. 43 hours after my optimistic departure from the Paris of W. Africa I crawled into the P.C. hostel, didn't even bother to lie about my non PCV status & cried in the shower at relief from what felt like nothing more than 30 nonstop graphics budget meetings.

[. . .]

About remaining in New York: I feel confused. I'll be in a ridiculous schedule coming back: gonna be in Morocco late April, have to see it & get thru Europe & stay w/ you for a month all somehow before May 23, my sis's big day at Macalester [her college graduation] so something's gotta go. The best to do would be to arrive in NY May 24 & forever incur the wrath of Wing (well, I'd get to her wedding . . .). The other issue is $$, I used it, and feel very worried about the prospects of getting a job in the beginning of summer . . . anywhere. My spare funds should hold for a while but I REFUSE to fall into mama's "oh my big brave Susie" trip, "here's $500 for surviving your travels" charity. And I'm really going to have to do some wheeling & dealing to get all my photos printed! All this bitchy traveling will seem like kindergarten when I get home to those boring real problems. I suppose if I had some gripping idea of what I wanted to do I could see more clearly, but since I've given up on curing the world's schizophrenia, I'm a rebel w/o a cause . . . for a few weeks, at least.

I'm reading Alix Kate Shulman's *Memoirs of an Ex-Prom Queen*. I get a cold sweat on my palms when she digs back into those moments of being miles from nowhere trapped in a car admiring the view w/ a sweaty teenage boy, or getting abducted by the football team to an empty lot to get "pantsed" or god knows what other carefully forgotten tender childhood memory. But at this point she's 24 & still getting laid left & right as she tours Europe (& attempts to separate from hubby, whose parting gesture was a heroic rape) (an impassioned plea?). She obviously got through that.

I'd really like to read a *Leaves of Grass* about Africa; it seems the most perfect way of conveying the endless flow of people & sound & light here, the sense of time suspended & the inexhaustible sociability of people. Ah, Whitman is such a beloved of mine, he was my constant companion during a lonely Boston summer, along w/ Del Martin & Phyllis Lyon.

APRIL 15–18

I have less than one week left in black Africa and, of all things, it's Easter weekend. I really don't unwish any of this trip but I'm exhausted with it now and want a bed that smells of pine needles, and a Buñuel film, after a hard day's work.

PART OF A LETTER TO MIMI:

Yes baby it's a rough life here my Easter morning in Baguinéda, a pleasant town south of Bamako with a feast to bring tears to the nostalgic eyes of a DAR:[132] smoked bacon, hash browns, fried eggs, toast & Kool Aid. (Is she kidding?) That, my dear, is the frequent (but not <u>too</u>) life of the Peace Corps'ers, those altruistic roughshod self-sacrificing youth of the bush. We polished off the afternoon w/ 7-hand Monopoly (I closed 2nd to last, gracefully but quickly) and a long motorbike ride thru the state farm—an <u>immense</u> area of potentially rich land all lying naked & unloved beneath a parched sky; since the French left it's never gotten back to production. And then of course curried chicken & red wine for dinner under the Bamako night sky . . . whizzing w/ Niger River malaria mosquitos. And this apology for an exhausted traveler is accompanied by Phoebe Snow.

But believe, <u>only</u> by seeking out PCV's do I find a reprieve like this.

Mali, according to statistics, is the poorest country in the world per capita ($70 year).[133] When one has been in India and Niger, etc., poorer-than-thou figures become fairly useless; once you're this poor, a little less or more only matters to government officials. And walking back today from market at prayer time I saw the largest number of blind and handicapped beggars I've yet seen, and they were all tapping the momentarily benevolent and self-sacrificing hearts of the Muslims, who probably felt that if any time was good to give it must be now, while under the direct eye of Allah.

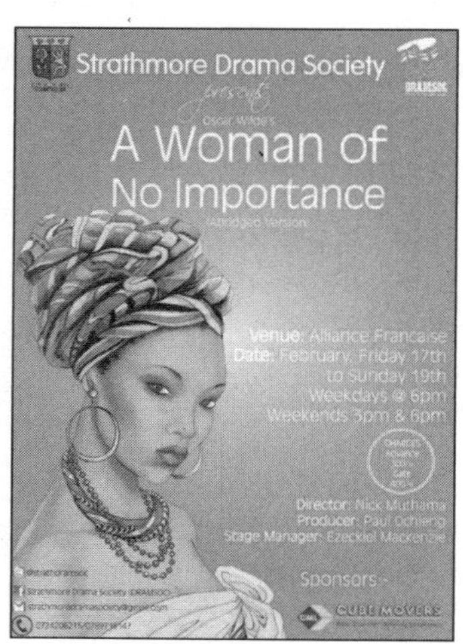

From *A Woman of No Importance* by Oscar Wilde, a comment made by Mrs. Allonby:

"Man, poor, awkward, reliable, necessary man belongs to a sex that has been rational for millions and millions of years. He can't help himself. It is in his race. The History of Woman is very different. We have always been picturesque protests against the mere existence of common sense. We saw its dangers from the first."

A production in Kenya in 2012

132 DAR: Daughters of the American Revolution, a sarcastic reference to someone devoted to all things American.

133 According to the World Bank website about per capita incomes, they say that it was $142, not $70, in 1976. By comparison, the per capita income in the USA in 1976 was $8,592. With the latest numbers available: In 2021 the per capita of Mali was $918, while in the USA it was $69,288. Burundi came in as the poorest in 2021, with a per capita of $272.

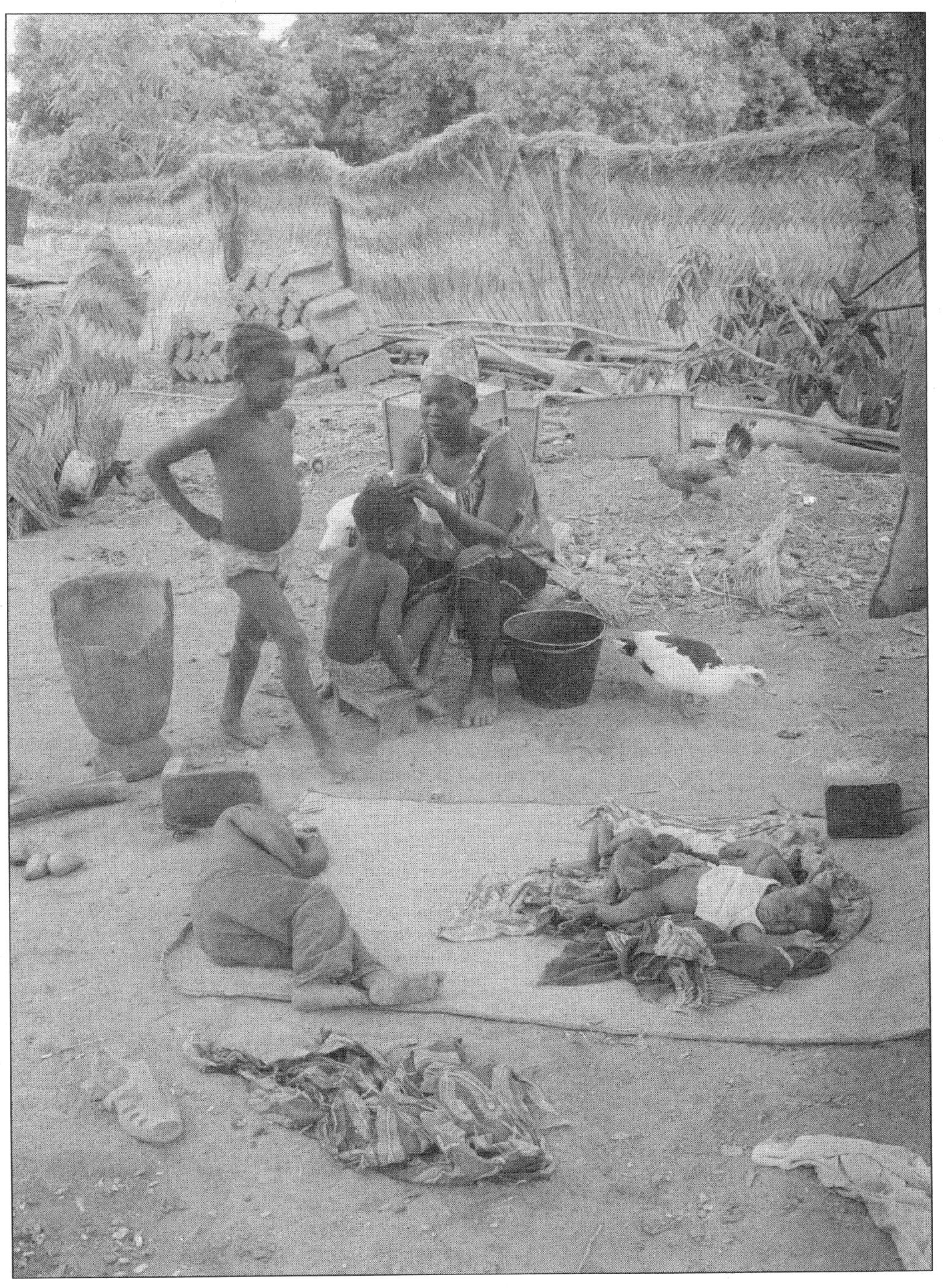

I am a bit concerned about the slamming feeling of guilt which might descend on me at home. Baby said something about "how status quo it all is" with us, and after seeing this end of life for a few months I might be quite horrified by that status quo; despite how much it means to me for energy and work it'll be a similar, but a more fierce version, of the feelings I've always had growing up between the South Side and my family and friends; the best and worst at once and unresolved, and it has always made me bitter and critical, and damn it, guilty because it's too big to do anything about and, as much as I conjecture and feel prepared, I never seem to make much headway doing anything constructive about it (but I do perhaps, gradually, by being informed) [2].

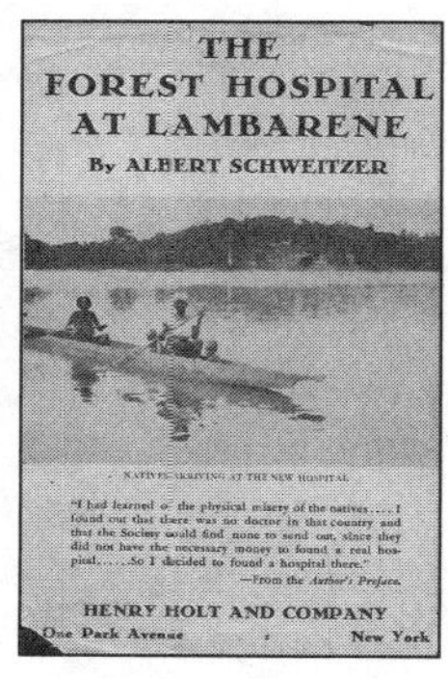

But even more here I have felt uncomfortable or uninterested in the glorified backbreaking selfless life of Albert Schweitzer [3] and the Peace Corps, etc. I've always admired those people (not the PCVs specifically, but as an example) and thought to follow in their footsteps, but there must be something in me that isn't so keen on that idea for my life's work, or I probably would've been heading in that direction already. Instead, I'm doing art photo projects and falling in love and trying to make the most of what little skills I have.
I don't think I'm hung up anymore with worry about the relative use of feminist work vs. other "more direct" help like what one does in the Peace Corps—that's all b.s.
Why is it that so many people seem to be able to do all their "non-altruistic" work (like artmaking) without any qualms??
Are my qualms only fabricated??
Sometimes yes, and that's another thing to clear up, SOON.

Reading Wm. O. Douglas, *Points of Rebellion* 1969:
"The greatest cause of alienation is that my generation has no one to turn to."
"Where there is a persistent sense of futility, there is violence; and that is where we are today."
Charles Adams: Our welfare state, "socialism for the rich, free enterprise for the poor."
For example, putting $600,000 into public housing subsidies and creating several million dollars in tax cuts to upper income housing; a $250 million subsidy for large scale farms and $7 for the welfare food program.
It's an excellent book, a general and highly critical overview of the myriad dangers we face, and the need for regenerative dissidence to make a dent in the military-industrial bureaucracy.
The increasing conformity due to a conditioned subservience to the comforts yielded by, and therefore dependent on, the machine era, and a weakening of the First Amendment. For example, it's not illegal to hold an ideology, but it is to act on it, etc.

He also really criticized the universities, with their Defense contracts and CIA tactics: What should be a forum for growth and criticism is the chicken hatchery of the Establishment.

APRIL 19

My last day was spent eating and slumming and reading and destroying my favorite silver bracelet . . . *triste* [sad] but inevitable.

> **PART OF A LETTER TO MIMI:**
>
> I feel almost uneasy today, my last day in Black Africa [4] for certainly a very long time to come. It's always hard to imagine when something like this is "over." An unlucky omen (oh bullshit on omens, it just happened to happen today): My most favorite prized purchase, from way back in Niger, was a "silver" bracelet. I went to get it cleaned; they boiled it in an acidic cleanser. It was only plated & the guts were aluminum, which proceeded to erupt & the whole thing fell into bits of a sad memory. I'm really unhappy about it, but no hope of recompense.
> Many kisses & a quiet cup of coffee with you,
> Susie

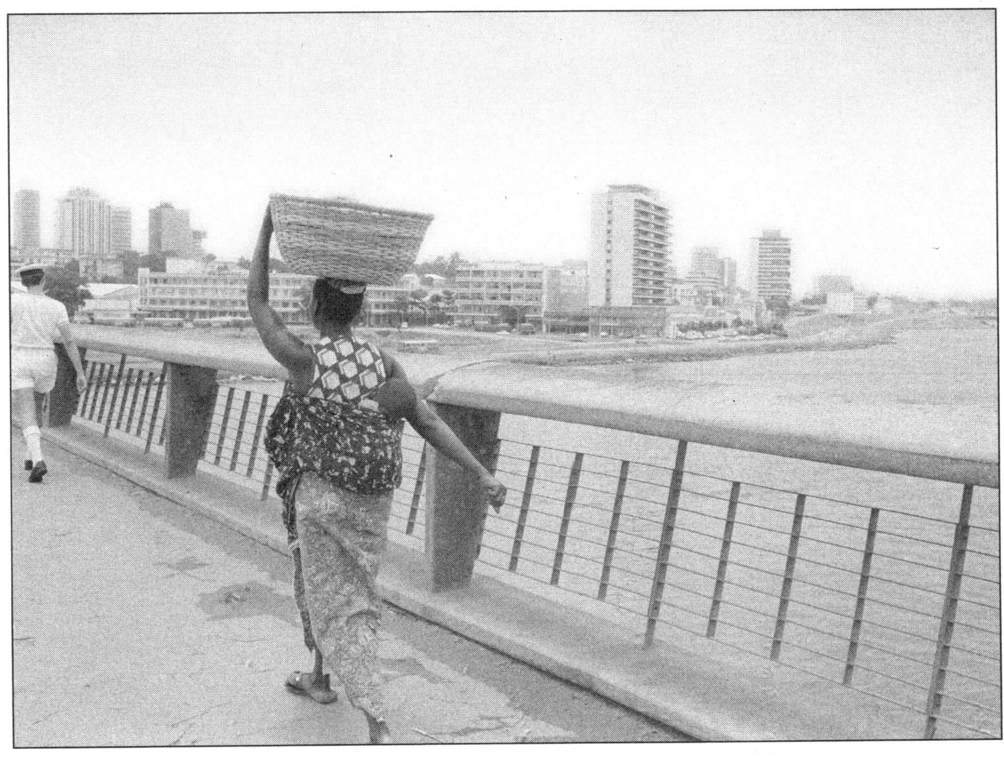

Bamako, April 19, 1976

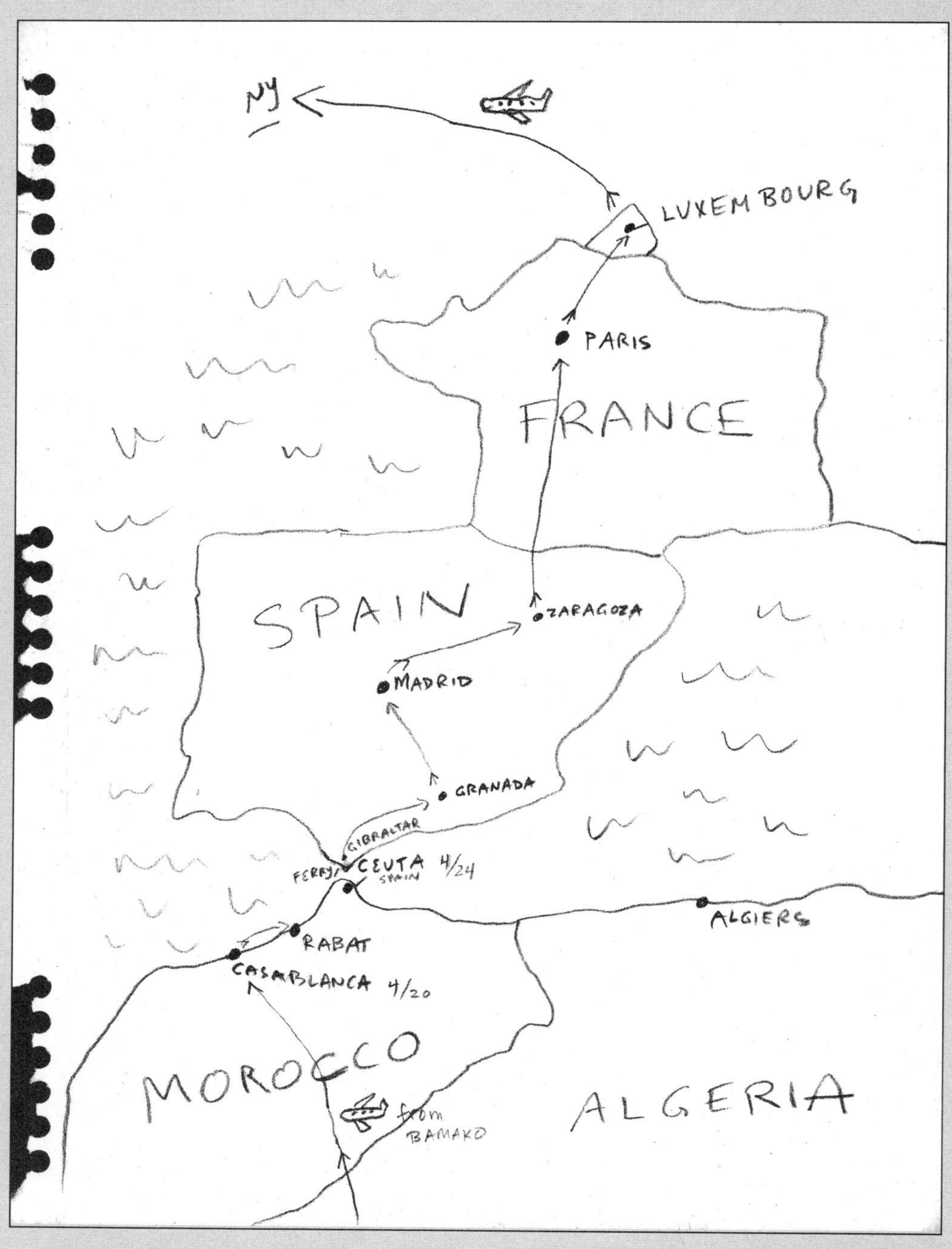
NY
LUXEMBOURG
PARIS
FRANCE
SPAIN
ZARAGOZA
MADRID
GRANADA
GIBRALTAR
FERRY
CEUTA
SPAIN
4/24
ALGIERS
RABAT
CASABLANCA
4/20
MOROCCO
ALGERIA
from
BAMAKO

CHAPTER TWENTY-TWO

Homeward Bound By Way of a Few More Countries

A PCV named Frank Rosica gave me a ride to the airport for my flight to Casablanca.

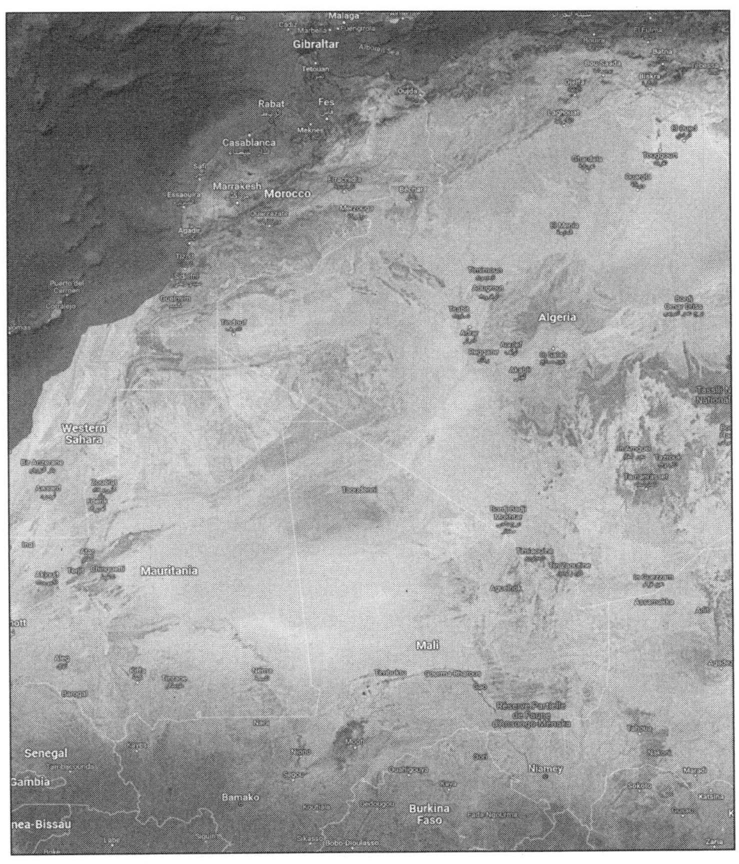

APRIL 20

So long, Africa.

I thought I'd engage the woman beside me in some small talk over our airline breakfast.

(This was originally written in French . . .)

"You're going to Paris?"
"Yes."
"To do what?"
"It's my husband."

(Why won't she look at me?)
"What does he do?"
(I know she heard me . . .)
"Is it the first time you're going to Paris?"
"Yes."
Suddenly the husband (I assume) leans forward and glares over at me. I resume my contemplation of the desert and hum *Homeward Bound* to myself.

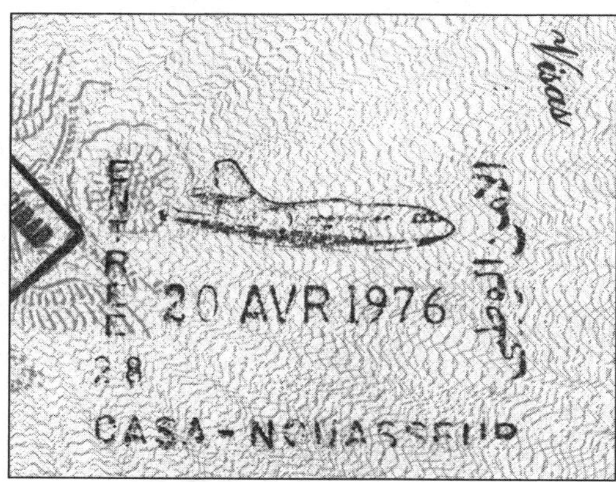

And I'm humming still. There's nothing in the world like landing in a country where poppies and buttercups and daisies fill the spring fields, and a cool, even wind blows.
The cobblestone streets, music, cleanliness of Rabat is so pleasant right now, the feeling of order, calm, and though it might be considered a poor country, the initial difference is staggering. I think I won't really know how little Africa has until I see again how much everyone else has.

PART OF A LETTER TO MIMI:

Well baby prepare yourself for some dirges & deep sighs when I get home, because I already miss Black Africa & this is my first day out of it!
The flight to Casablanca was really weird—3 hours in a propeller plane over nothing but sand & rock & clouds; it was absolutely beautiful tho, because the evaporated rivers & lakes have left an intricate pattern of arteries & veins & capillaries, like rich marble or an oak tree in winter. For hundreds of miles I could trace the course of a great river, the places which were probably rich farmlands, the main avenues of transport, etc.
But I kept reciting to myself the survival tactics for plane crashes in the desert that I'd read about in New York & wondered whether I'd've been prepared to walk the remaining 600 or so miles to Casablanca thru the scorpion- & snake-infested nights.
And it's SPRING here! We drove from the airport past fields lush with wildflowers, and I had the luxury of being cold in my cotton blouse & sandals, & yesterday I ordered a lovely beige wool jacket for the chillier Europe.
I'd been told that Morocco was a terribly poor country, but the initial impression is one of well-being, availability of any needed item, a delightful excess of clean restaurants & variety of food, & everyone seems to have enough clothing on. It really makes me

understand more clearly how much sub-Saharan Africa does not have & will not have for a long time to come.

But already I look around in vain for the laughter & muscles of the market women, & see only sly-eyed Arab men, & I miss all the skin & hustle & playfulness. I'm anticipating a real adventure trip down again thru the desert, over to Gao & the *pirogue* [canoe] ride down the Niger River to Timbuktu & Mopti . . . some day. It's supposed to be one of the classics here, but one can't do it in spring or summer. I really wish I could've gone back across the desert on the same route.

My money is diarrhea these days & the horror of unemployment looms larger than expected.

Someone's doing a Washington Square[134] outside, an old man w/ an Adidas bag is waxing wrathful at an unknown power & throwing pieces of an old stone in his general direction. Everyone is quite entertained & nonplussed.

I think I could spend my life in dingy hotel rooms. They have a certain timeless quality & leave me to do whatever I want undistracted.

Well I'm off for my 145th day of sightseeing and time-killing.

A big round of hugs to Cindy & Donna if they're w/ you now in NY.

Did you ever find your letters at your dorm?

Crazy love,

Su

APRIL 21–24

I took a bus directly from Casablanca to Rabat, about two hours distant.

The women here are less often veiled than they were in Algiers, and more young women are completely out of drag[135], and I almost don't feel paranoid here with the men—I think five months on the road has put enough dents in me to have fortified me well.

HA! That was written during the protective daylight. "A woman does not walk the streets alone at night in Arab countries . . . " they always chant, as a murderously true litany to men's evil ways.

I went to bed genuinely surprised last night: I was already missing the African air. I think no other country knows the same feeling, the relaxed and unpretentious quality, the gregariousness and playfulness of the people, and already here I see only market men, and my heights are slipping to remembered lows. I do feel a

134 A reference to Washington Square in downtown NYC where people often perform for the passing crowds, and where people also vent and carry on about whatever ails them.

135 "Drag" in the sense that the veiled garb was a form of costume that created an identity apart from who the women really are.

strong and welcome ease from being at least close to the skin color here—despite the fact that my walking about in crazy African dress sets me a wee bit off, I can somehow look at faces and see something remotely resembling me [1].
God but I miss the laughing shouting bitching bare-armed open-eyed sly tough black women. Here, they're all wrapped up in their caftans like stuffed sausage, always arm in arm or with a baby.
In my many hours alone, and with books like the one about Annie Zingha and the one by Aidoo, I tend to forget how perverse things are, and somehow I see African or Arab women as a distinct entity, until the other day when I met my second non-functional PCV wife, a thin-lipped sweet-mouthed American-style wife, and I was bitterly reminded how some women from all cultures just hand over their entire substance, identity, mobility, to their man.
I sit and stare and send telepathic overtures and grit my teeth and can't bear it. The more I dream of our freedom, the more like zombies those kinds of women become in my eyes.

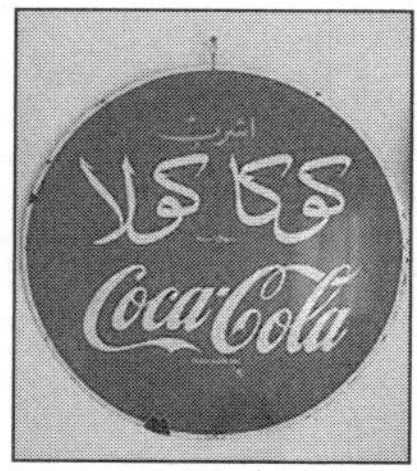

When Things Go Better With Coke, written in Arabic, can look as beautiful as a line of the Rubayat, I understand how exquisite form can hide a pedestrian substance.

This is the Google translation:
كوكلا محف عم لضفأ لكشب بهذت روملأا

A guy followed me for hours. I would sit in a café, he would sit nearby. I would go into a shop, he would follow me inside. I had told him repeatedly to leave me alone but he wouldn't stop . . .

I wish men hated themselves, somewhat; just a bit would be enough; if they only looked critically at themselves once in a while, they'd perhaps learn to see how vulgar they are, how insensitive, disrespectful, but mostly vulgar. But I had a good time. After the fact, I decided that the only good way to deal with anger is to let it OUT and turn the abuse around to him instead of remaining the victim. Twice I lashed out, LOUD, at men, and one time I had the guy against a wall with scared eyes and my fist shaking in his face. He fled, finally.

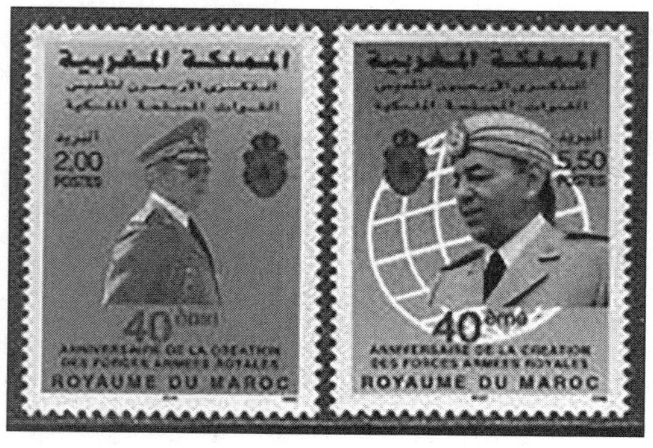

And then of course it's always apropos to embarrass hell out of them by shouting full strength, "If you don't leave me alone, I'll . . . " and the crowds gather, and he shrivels and fades.

King Hassan's fake smiles and arched brows gaze down patronizingly from every shop and restaurant wall, his books are prominently displayed in windows, his *Palais Royale* reeks of secret service and the people have been taught to think he's all right [2].

Women are functionally denied the greatest pleasure of sightseeing in Arab countries: entrance to the mosques. I was furious yesterday at the mausoleum of Mohammad V. The exquisite doorway of this mosque promised further delights but all I could do was speculate—my foul perverse dangerous body was prohibited entry.[136]

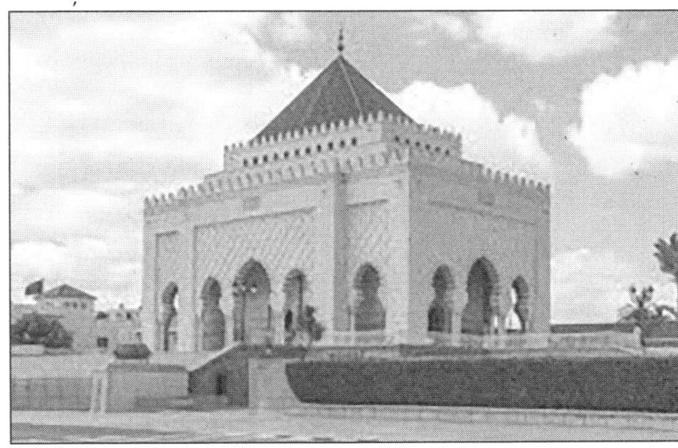

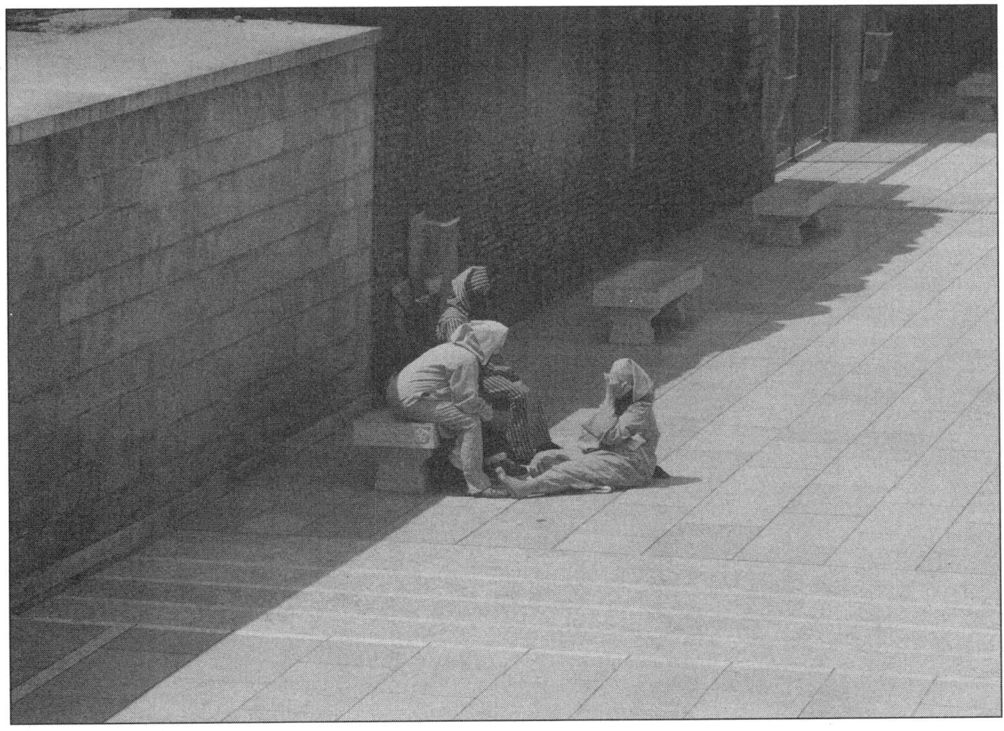

136 Judging from a recent picture online in which I can see some women, it seems that the rule has changed.

I got lucky today. Out of curiosity, I stopped in at the *Atelier Rahali Freres*. They wove beautiful carpets, and for an hour or two I was primarily in the company of the women weavers, away from the harassers.

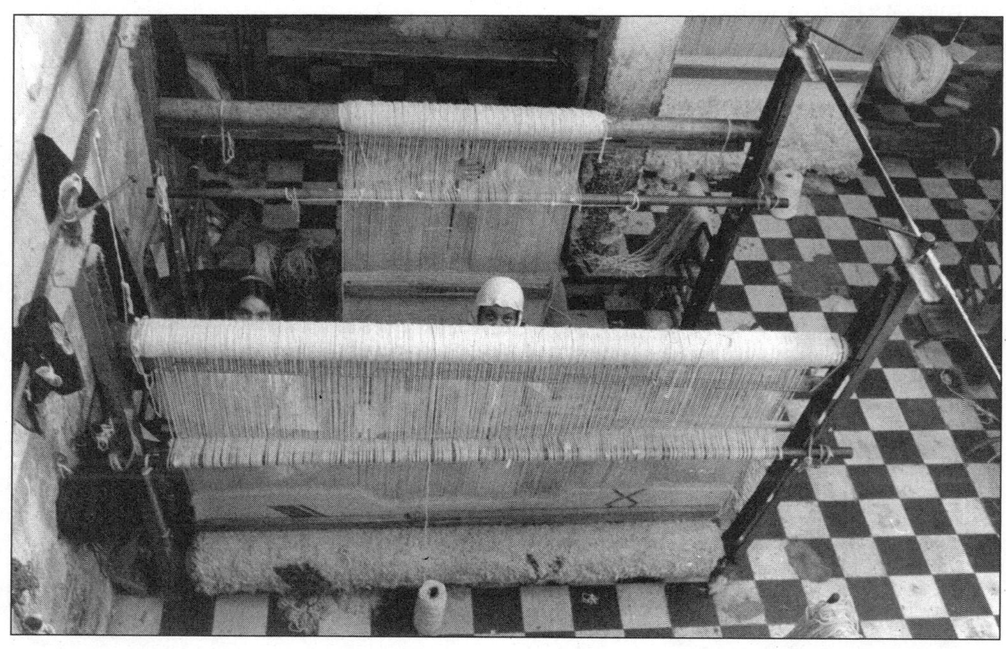

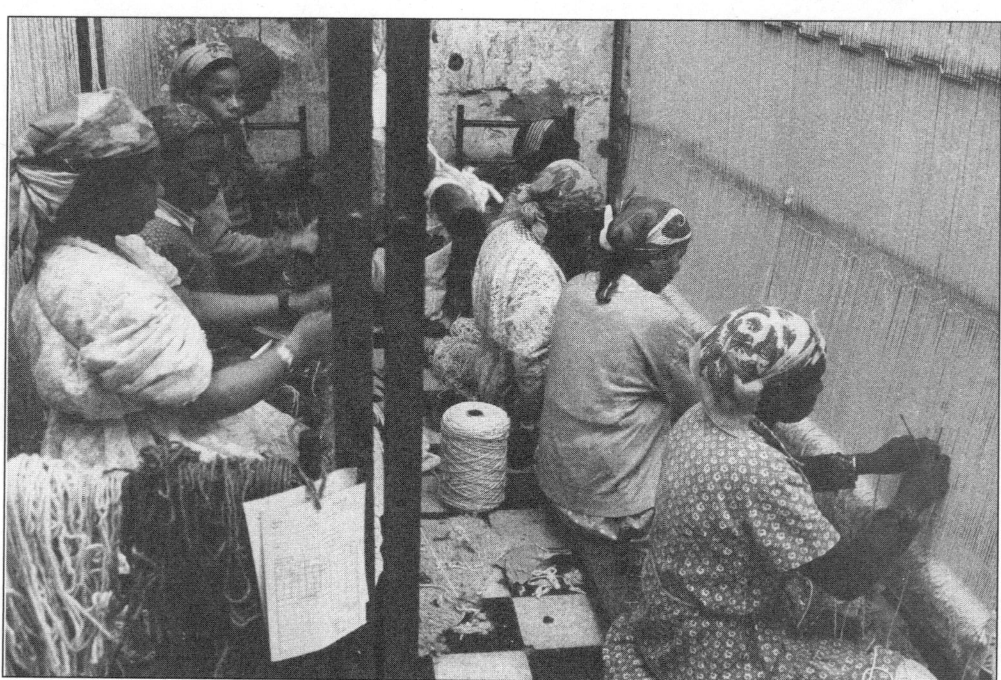

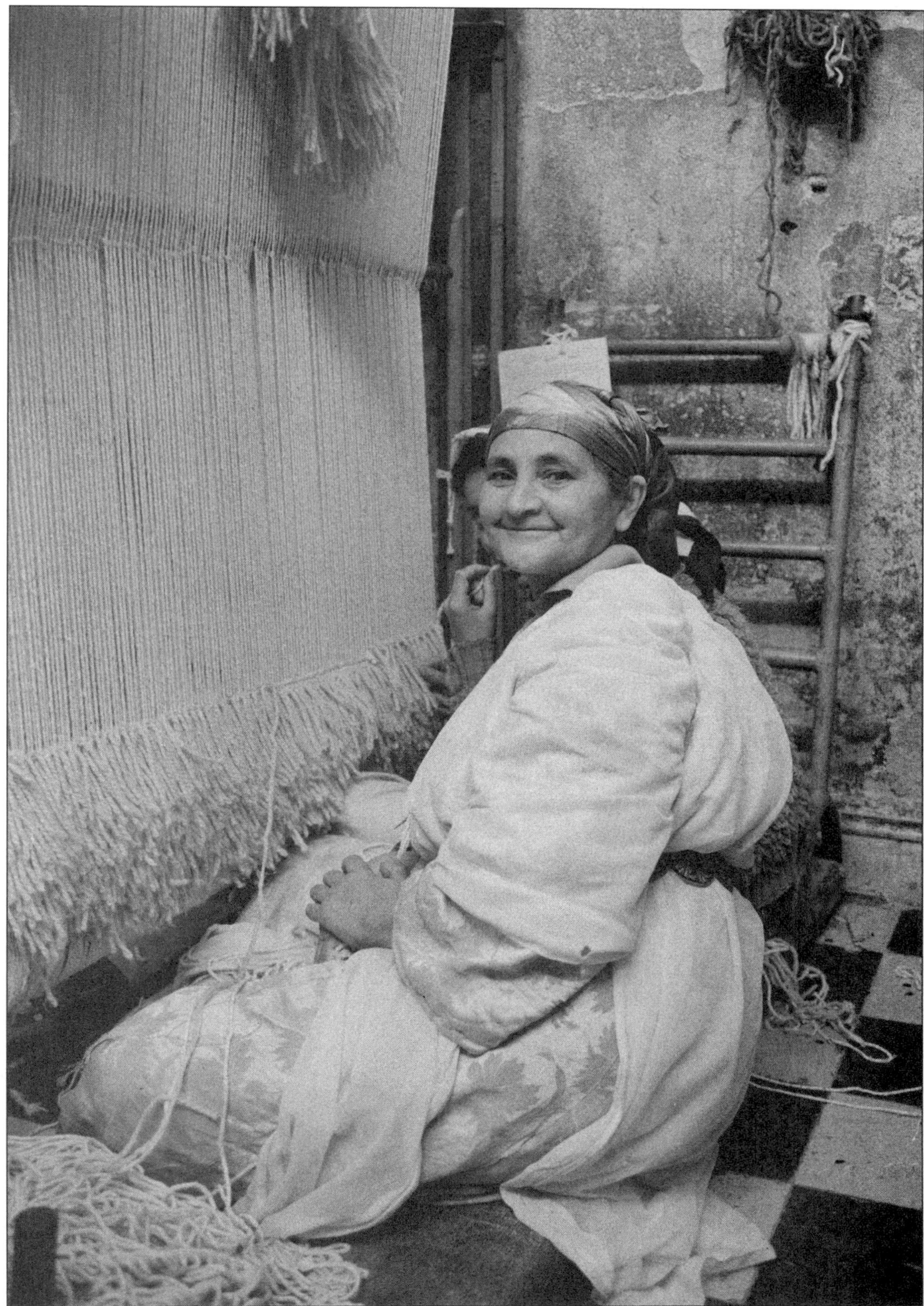

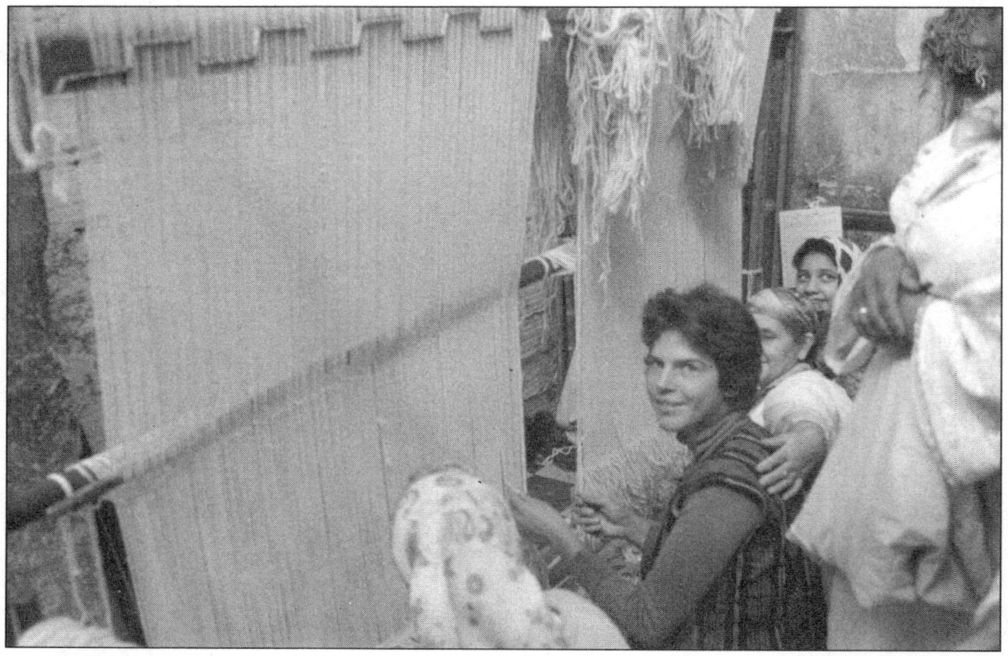

Wandered down to the water and found myself in a cemetery which had a lot of visitors. It appeared to be (from what little I know) a safe or allowable place where women could meet up outdoors and relax with each other apart from the presence of men. It was nice to see them hanging out together.

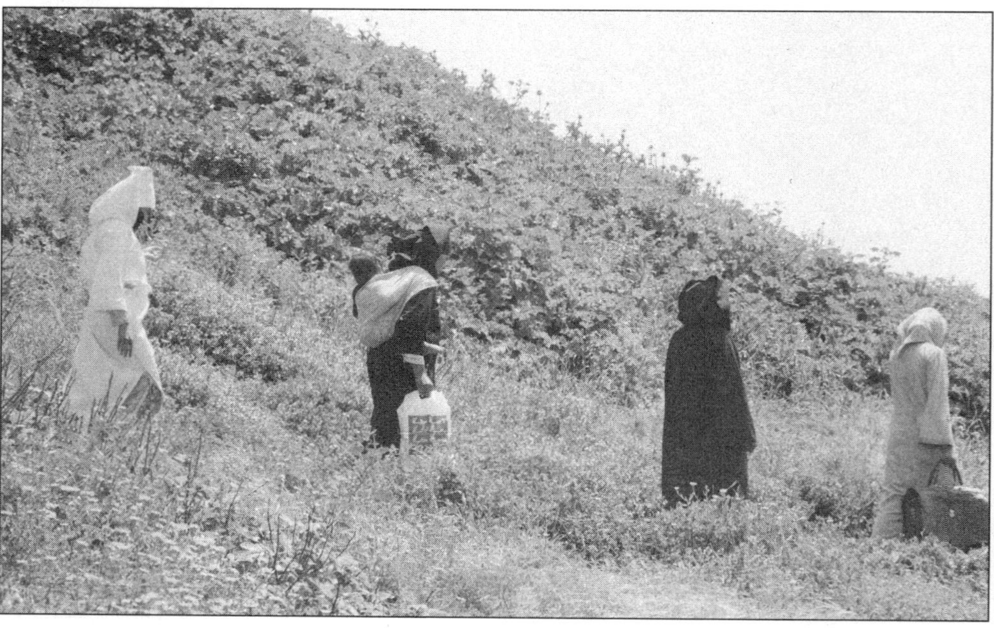

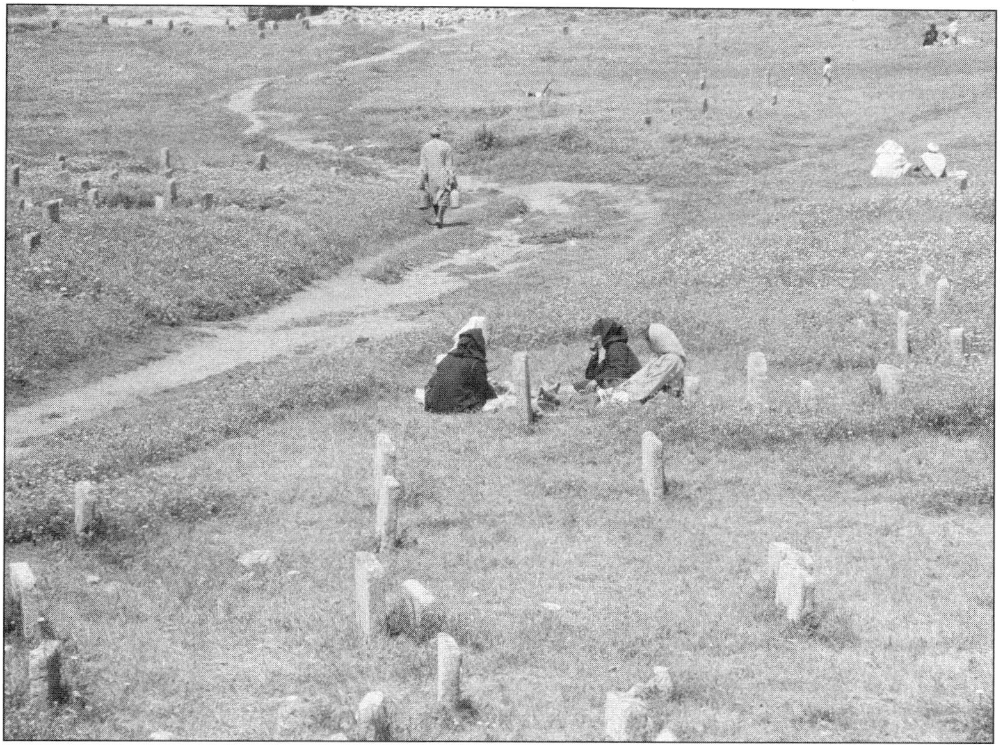

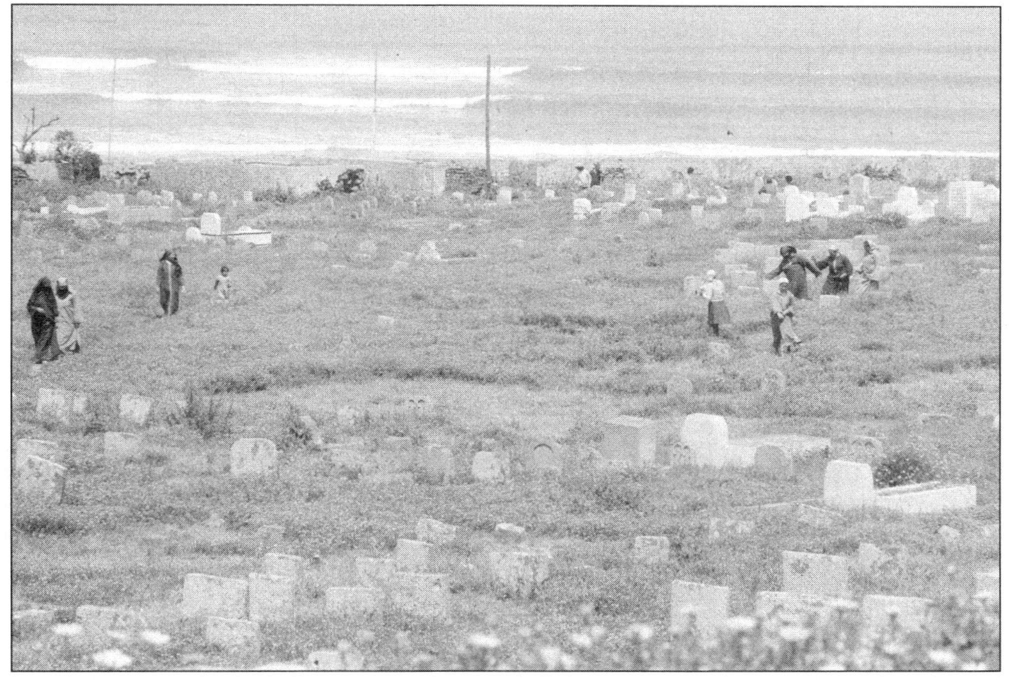

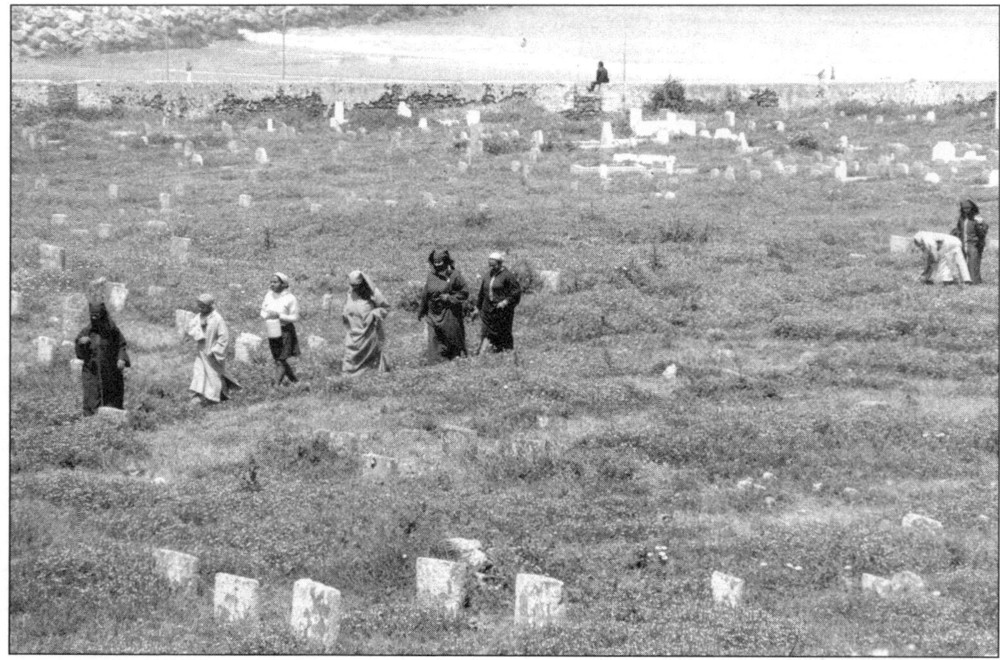

I saw a couple today, probably tourists, that I'd swear were true blue American dykes ca. 1970 and I almost followed them to absorb their being. It just set me tingling, the reminder and the promise.

Women are so cool.

I really like cloth, I realize. It's the art piece that I am first and foremost impressed by in any culture, it has more allure and possibility and substance to me than jewelry, it's not as aloof or unpliable, and one can mix and form and create with it. The possibilities are endless. I will one day have a house full of colors and detail, and six centuries and cultures all piled together in happy confusion, and I will dress big-boned and clear and richly hued [3].

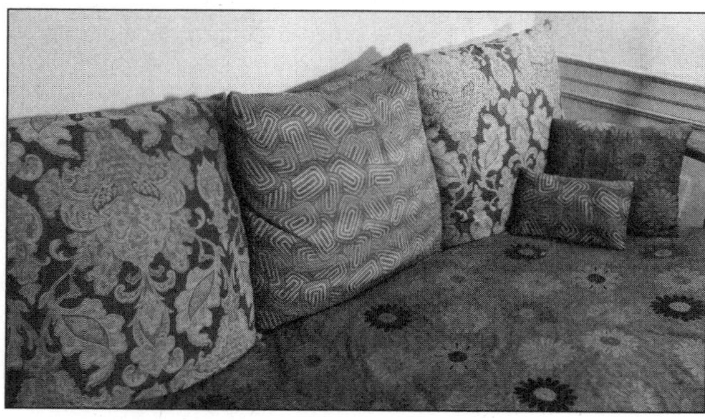

A few of the patterned things in our house now

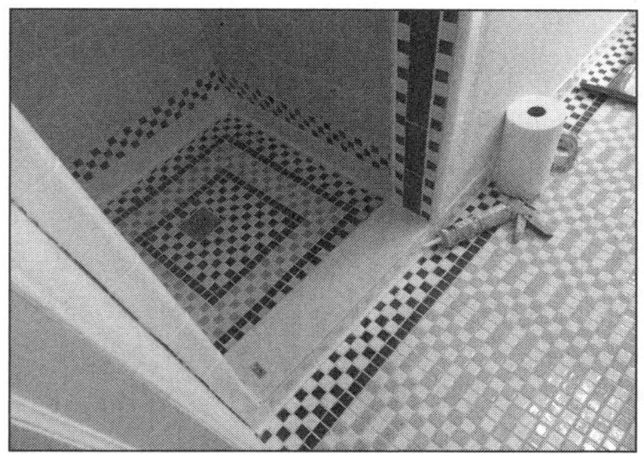

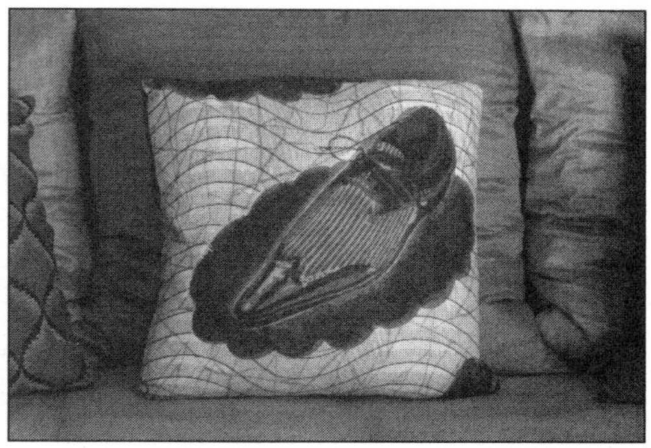

I think the fact that it's coming to light in rapidly growing numbers that most accomplished or cool women in history were dykes is a profound and eloquent tribute to the ghastly, intolerable quality of life with a man if one has any measure of dignity or self-preservation. I almost sometimes wish, for the sake of peace and moderation (neither of which though have much substance in this/my life) that it was less easy to condemn men, or that I could keep my mind more often on the exceptions, the Jon Witty's [a friend from college] and . . . . see, I can't think of any others . . . Oh yes, my brother Pete, but he's the coming generation. But in our society, the atmosphere and structures and daily experiences are mostly colored by official man rather than papa/brother/gentle-lover-if-ever man. And official, programmed, intrusive, abrasive man is intolerable. Sometimes for the sake of intellectual breadth and that divine artificial thing, "objectivity," I try to lay half the cause and effect on us women. It doesn't work. We may have our insidious, secretive inside manipulations, of which men like to accuse us as being truly artful in the application, but it's the old dead-end falsely reasoned criticism of, "How can I help but be strong, when she acts so weak and always wants me to make the decisions?" And if she did otherwise?? He would be outraged at the breach of her faith in the apparently divine (i.e., natural) system. And of course people groan and writhe and ask what the use is of leveling accusations and being so vitriolic and defamatory. First of all it gives me a real vengeful thrill (which they enjoy having but don't want anyone else to enjoy) and second and best of all, they deserve it.

I have again proved the affirmative to the query, "Is our experience really so substantially colored by our sex?"

I defy a man to travel and be able to put up with the conditions under which a woman has to travel. Men are just great (and immodest in admiring it) at physical endurance; they count the mosquito bites and ass bruises and parched days and sleepless nights of an "adventure" trip, and when we get together to swap stories I commiserate with them about the "hardships" which accrue from being a fellow: They're not as easily welcomed in homes, not given food or the front seat or a better bargain, as happens often with women travelers (and at the moment when they're offered to me, I savor the comfort or reprieve from daily bitches and backaches). But what of psychological/emotional/even intellectual comfort? That is, to me, a foremost requirement, and if one has that, one can ignore, if not enjoy, physical hardship, boredom, loneliness, or anything else irksome to be had in abundance in (African) travels. Those comforts, gestures of chivalry or pity or babying that we women receive are identical to the succors of the powerless, they only serve to alleviate our generally gloomy, threatening or restrictive situation momentarily. A kiss from hubby as he dashes off to a day out in the world is as fleeting and deceptive as that front seat in the lorry on an unpaved road; it calms the spirit until the familiar harassments and discomforts and disassociation from self (to save the self and offer an unpleasant and therefore hopefully undesirable self to the solicitor) sets in.

Dig it: A young man stuck in any Moroccan town for a day waiting for an evening bus can sit in the park and read, sit in a café and observe and meditate on the wonderful variety of unfamiliar folk going past, can roam endlessly thru the old new rich poor quarters of town, free to stare and laugh and chatter with the people.
A woman alone can go to the park until she's forced to flee the constant "*Ah, toute seule, mademoiselle?*" comments and go sit for a dizzy half hour in a café trying to ignore or curse into oblivion the quizzical, suggestive or hostile stares of the passing menfolk (and often the women, who simultaneously envy and suspect my breach of culture, my calculated gesture of indifference to the privilege and mobility of the chosen written in blood and gold) and my dearest wish is that all these gestures, these battles, these arduous hours day and night didn't have to be calculated, that I could move and pause and extend myself at will. But no chance of that, so then I hurriedly collect myself and wander on to the safety of a bookstore or bazaar or bank until I again have to plant myself, my tired ankles and aching eyes and the treadmill self-conscious corner of my brain, only temporarily, always alert for the last possible moment before I have to trudge on, away for a while from the derision and intrusion of men. They protest, they howl and groan and supplicate, they call it concern and attraction and cross-cultural study, they prostitute themselves as tourist guides and wizard linguists and aficionados of anything they can use to fill the minutes required to scrutinize my breasts and wonder about my hairy legs and calculate their chances. The truth that drones in my brain, taunts me, fascinates me, scares the shit out of me, is that they never seem to see themselves thru my hateful tired trapped eyes.
The question, of course, being: What are we going to do about this blissfully ignorant species?
I don't think I'm out to cure them, to lead them tenderly or brutally along the path to enlightenment; all I want is that they fucking leave me alone to my own discoveries. But the foremost discovery I'm crashing up against, being assaulted with and depressed by (remember, I qualify these feelings as the product of a single woman traveler, young, uppity, unconventional, and therefore throwing myself into places which I sometimes wish I'd stay away from—but if I did, it would keep me apart from those sides of life that men have been rightfully able to lay claim to, because we could never get ourselves into them to ascertain whether the men actually understood what they were pronouncing so grandly about) is that they're

going to be around, in all their selfish glory, until they wreak the final havoc they've been so busy inventing and consolidating.

[. . .]

Please don't throw the syrup of Christian love and Buddhist humanism in my pepper stew. That will come in a completely new form, devoid of one-sided chastity or self-sacrifice, moderation, that abhorrent home-is-where-the-heart-is (while the world is where energy is). We <u>don't</u> have any truly viable system to fall back on, because all those Christian and Muslim and Animist and Rationalist and Existentialist and Symbolist lovers and Tantric professors were out for a good fuck and then a quiet breakfast in bed, to contemplate the benevolence of their selfless selves.

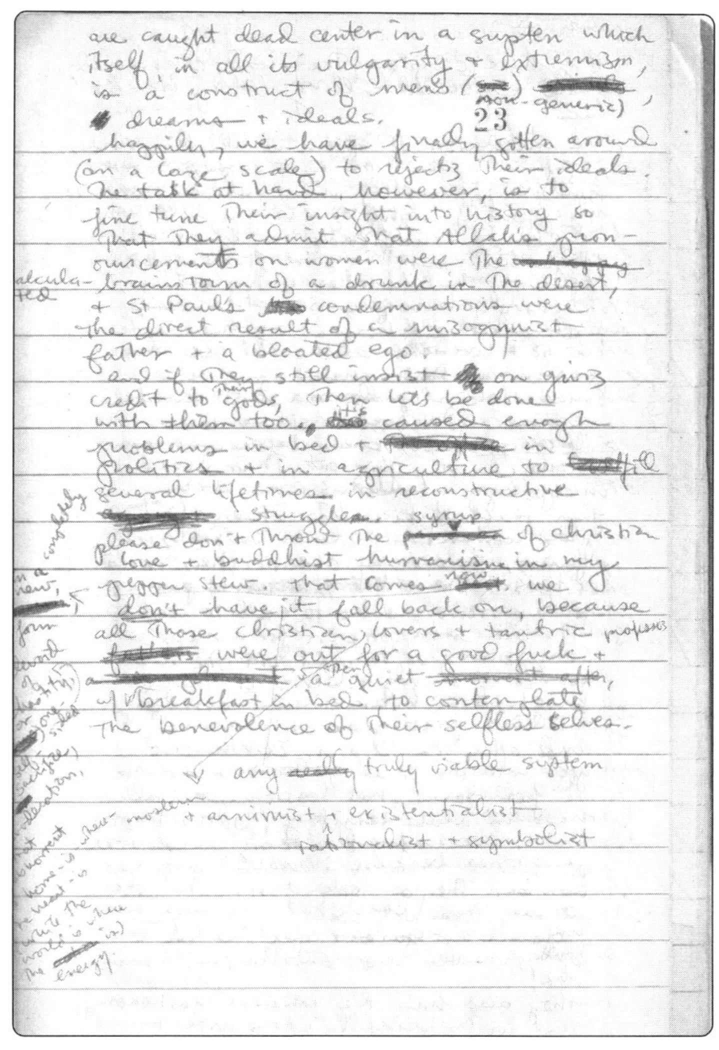

are caught dead center in a system which
itself, in all its vulgarity + extremism,
is a construct of men's (non-generic)
dreams + ideals.
23
happily, we have finally gotten around
(on a large scale) to rejecting their ideals.
The task at hand, however, is to
fine tune their insight into history so
that they admit that Allah's pron-
ouncements on women were the
brainstorm of a drunk in the desert,
+ St Paul's condemnations were
the direct result of a misogynist
father + a bloated ego.
and if they still insist on giving
credit to their gods, then let's be done
with them too, it's caused enough
problems in bed + in
politics + in agriculture to fill
several lifetimes in reconstructive
struggles.
please don't throw the syrup of christian
love + buddhist humanism in my
pepper stew. that comes new. we
don't have it fall back on, because
all those christian lovers + tantric profs
were out for a good fuck +
a quiet breakfast in bed, to contemplate
the benevolence of their selfless selves.
any truly viable system
+ animist + existentialist
rationalist + symbolist

And there's a lot more of this rant on the next few pages of the journal . . .

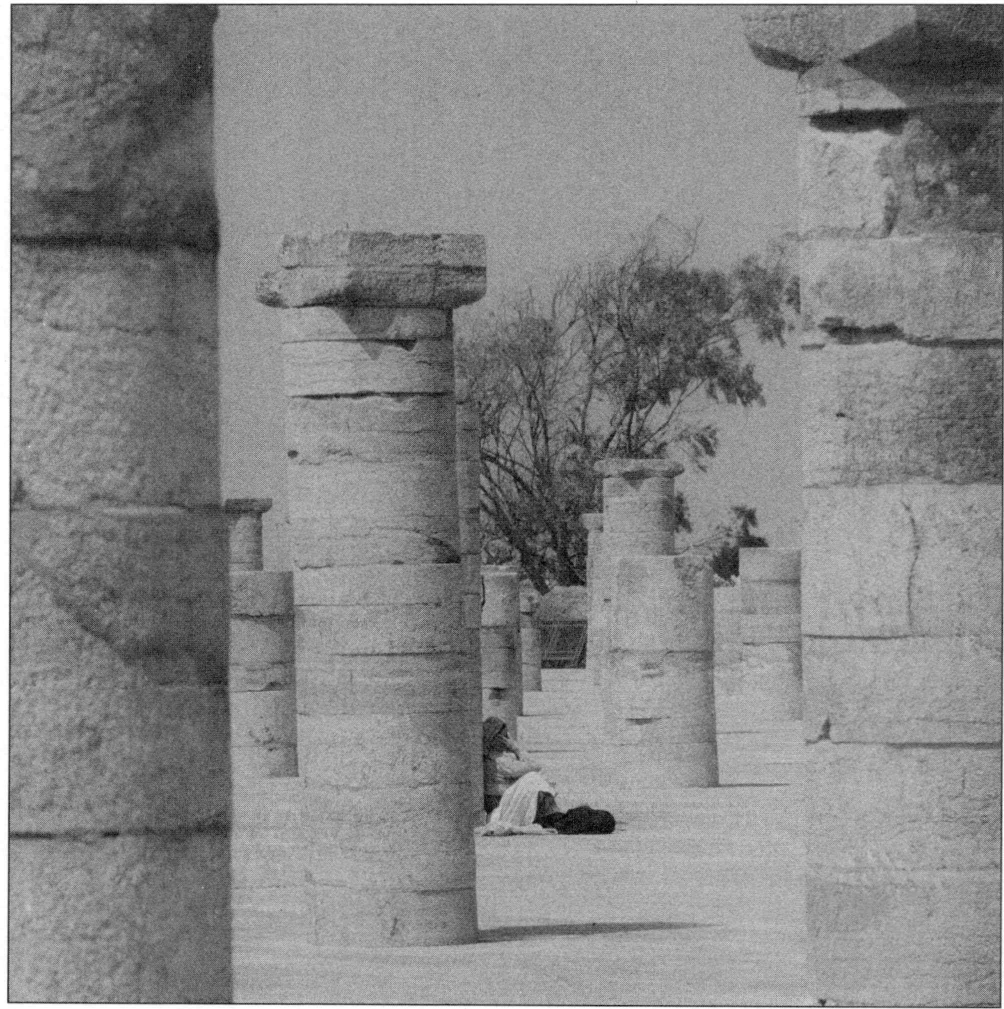

On April 24, I took a bus from Rabat to Ceuta and caught a ferry across the Strait of Gibraltar to Algeciras on the Spanish mainland. From there, I traveled up through Spain and France to catch my return flight in Luxembourg.

There's a lot in the third journal about my time in those countries, but they aren't germane to this project. Suffice it to say that a lot of the journal entries from Spain are me going ballistic because of the overwhelming Catholicism.

A POSTCARD TO MY FATHER:

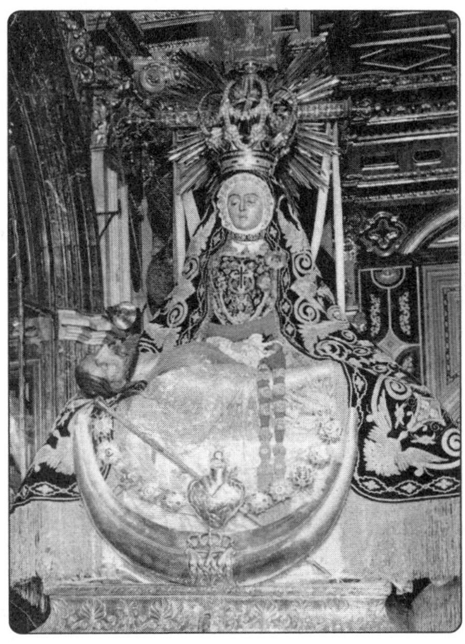

April 26
Dad—Spain is quite a jolt to my Africanized senses, & it's achingly clean & ordered & picturesque. I'm collecting photos of the morbid virgins that grace every church here, with their glass tears & red-rimmed eyes. If nothing else, Catholicism offers the cynic a lot of good laughs. I saw "The Trial of Oscar Wilde" tonight, of all the incongruous films to find in Granada. It must be the fresh air of liberalism which has entered the country (?). But it is a beautiful place, w/ the Sierra Nevada towering over the Moorish palaces & whitewashed homes. I'm still trying to readjust myself to clean restaurants & the European bourgeoisie, & I find that I already begin to miss the smells & sounds & anarchy of African towns. It was a great trip despite my aching bones & hostile intestines, and now I'm most anxious to get into a darkroom & not emerge for several weeks . . . lovely, lovely work after this half year of high intensity leisure. I heard from Mom that Lein is going into a steady decline; I hope he's still around, because I'd like to see him btwn. NY & Chicago (if I have the time, Wing is urging me to her graduation ceremony). I have a bad cold & must get up at 6 a.m. for the bus to Madrid (I refuse to hitch in Spain, altho it's putting a big dent in my purse—as long as I survived the Sahara and the 110° in Mali I'm not about to get knocked off in sunny Spain!)
Good nite.
Love & cheers,
Susi

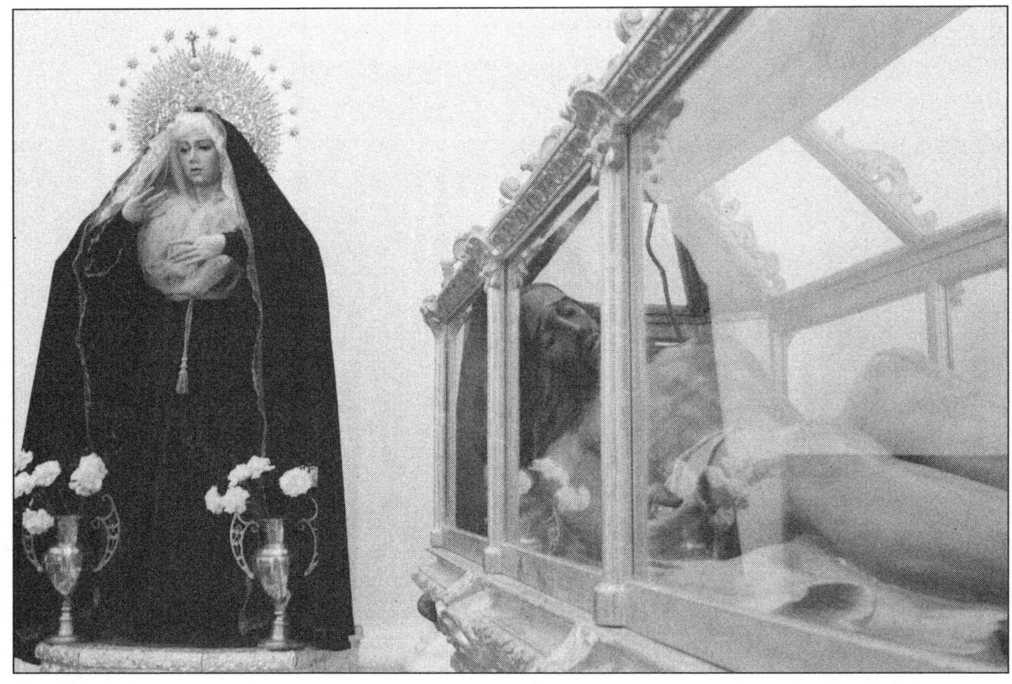

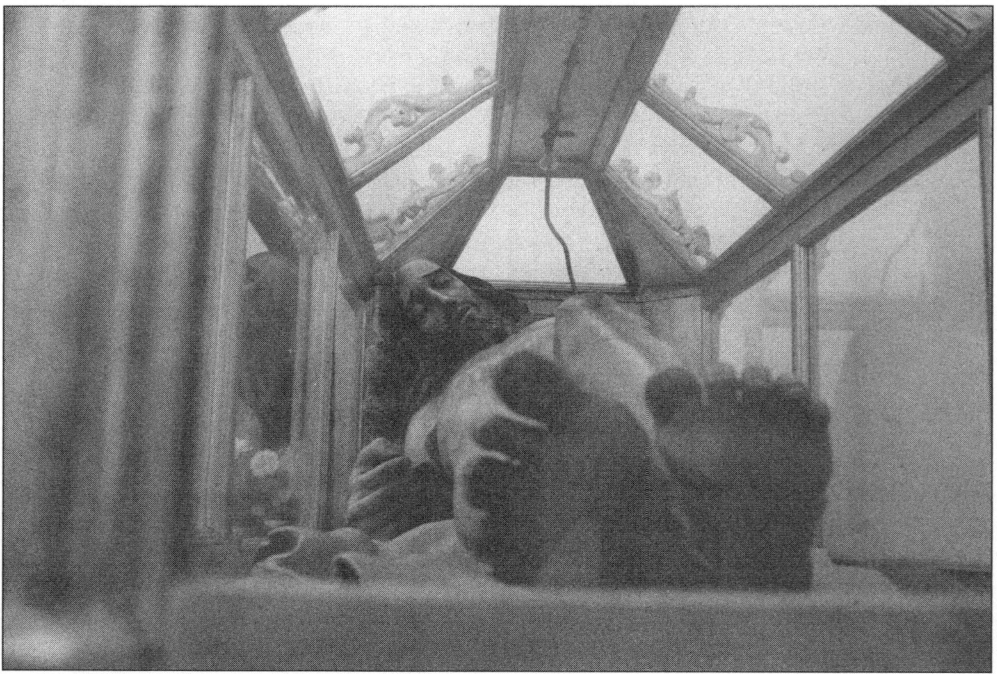

My photographs of this grim religion

Conversely, my time in Paris was heavenly because I was able to visit several lesbian "shrines": Shakespeare and Company, the bookstore started by Sylvia Beach and Adrienne Monnier and the house of Gertrude Stein and Alice B. Toklas [4].

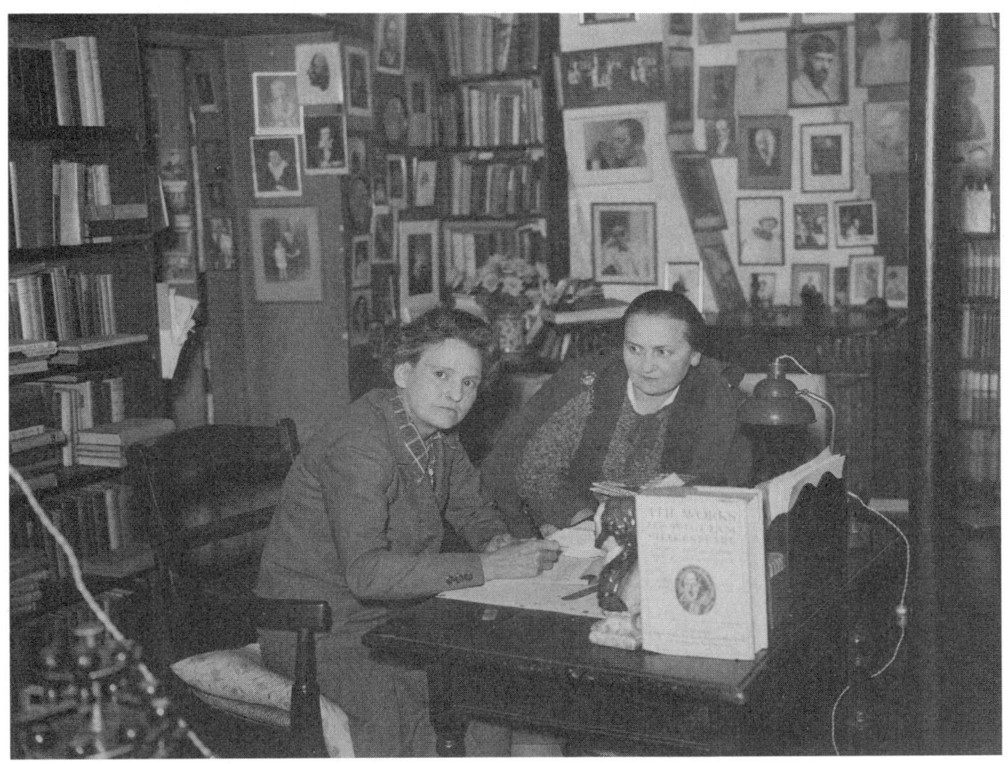

Sylvia Beach and Adrienne Monnier, photograph by Gisèle Freund.
The upright book in the foreground is James Joyce's *Ulysses*,
hidden beneath the slipcover for *The Works of William Shakespeare*.

On May 8, 1976, I arrived back in New York, and went to Chicago soon after to see my family.
When I think about my parents—and when one considers the ways in which twenty-first century American parenting restricts the movement of children and young adults—you might have some idea about how often I've been astonished that they "let me" go. Not that they could have stopped me: I was an adult, but I don't recall any huge effort on their part to try and prevent me from going.
And as I've made my way through this narrative, I've also been shocked every time I think about my mother and how she must have been feeling.
Perhaps my father also worried at times, but he was somewhat distant and fairly unrealistic: He would have tended to glamorize the "adventure" of it and block out any fears he had about what might happen to me.
In any case, two years after I started this project and some weeks after my mother passed away (on December 5, 2018), my brother sent me a package.
Among her books, he found a very old Rand McNally atlas. In the section with the maps of West Africa, there were many yellowed pages clipped from various newspapers that related to the regions through which I'd traveled, and there was this:

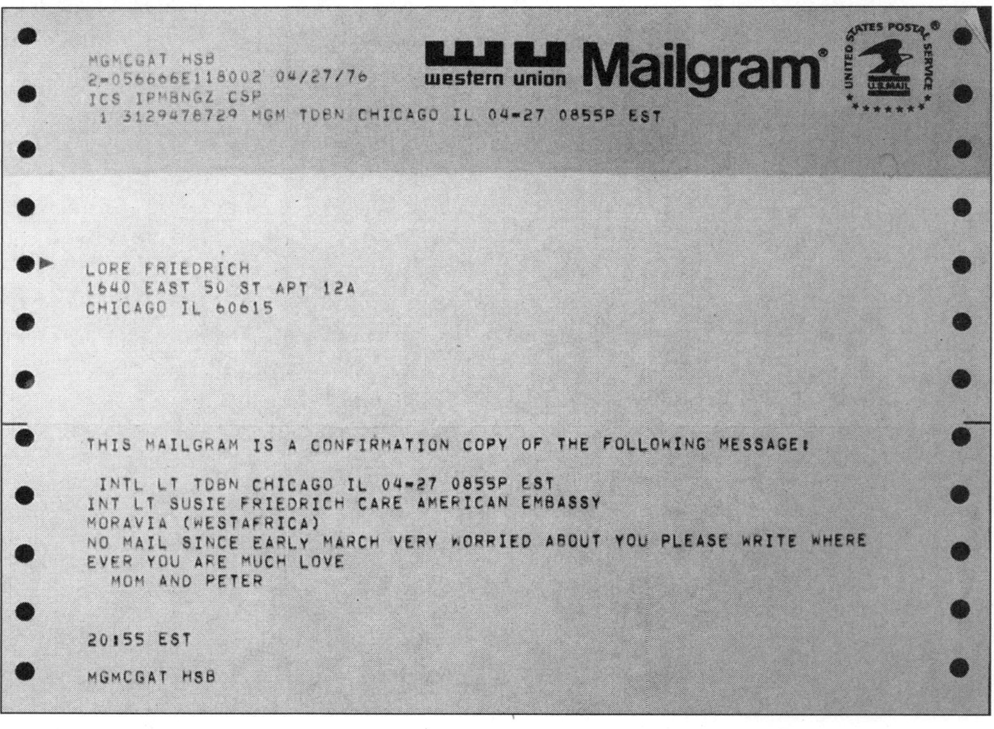

MGMCGAT HSB
2-056666E118002 04/27/76
ICS IPMBNGZ CSP
1 3129478729 MGM TDBN CHICAGO IL 04-27 0855P EST

western union Mailgram®

UNITED STATES POSTAL SERVICE
U.S. MAIL

LORE FRIEDRICH
1640 EAST 50 ST APT 12A
CHICAGO IL 60615

THIS MAILGRAM IS A CONFIRMATION COPY OF THE FOLLOWING MESSAGE:

INTL LT TDBN CHICAGO IL 04-27 0855P EST
INT LT SUSIE FRIEDRICH CARE AMERICAN EMBASSY
MORAVIA (WESTAFRICA)
NO MAIL SINCE EARLY MARCH VERY WORRIED ABOUT YOU PLEASE WRITE WHERE
EVER YOU ARE MUCH LOVE
MOM AND PETER

20:55 EST

MGMCGAT HSB

It raises a few questions:
How now, Moravia? It certainly isn't in West Africa. It's an area of the Czech Republic and also a small town in South Africa. Or maybe she meant it for Monrovia, the capital of Liberia? So how did the mailgram company accept this as an address?
She sent this on April 27. Why did she not have any mail from me since early March? I wrote her fairly often but it's true that in my collection of letters to friends and family, there are none to her after February!
In any case, I feel sorry, retroactively, for how much I must have terrified her.
I also know that the "wisdom," perspective or sympathy I express in saying that as a sixty-nine-year-old has no bearing on whether or not I would do it all over again as that twenty-one-year-old. Sign me up!

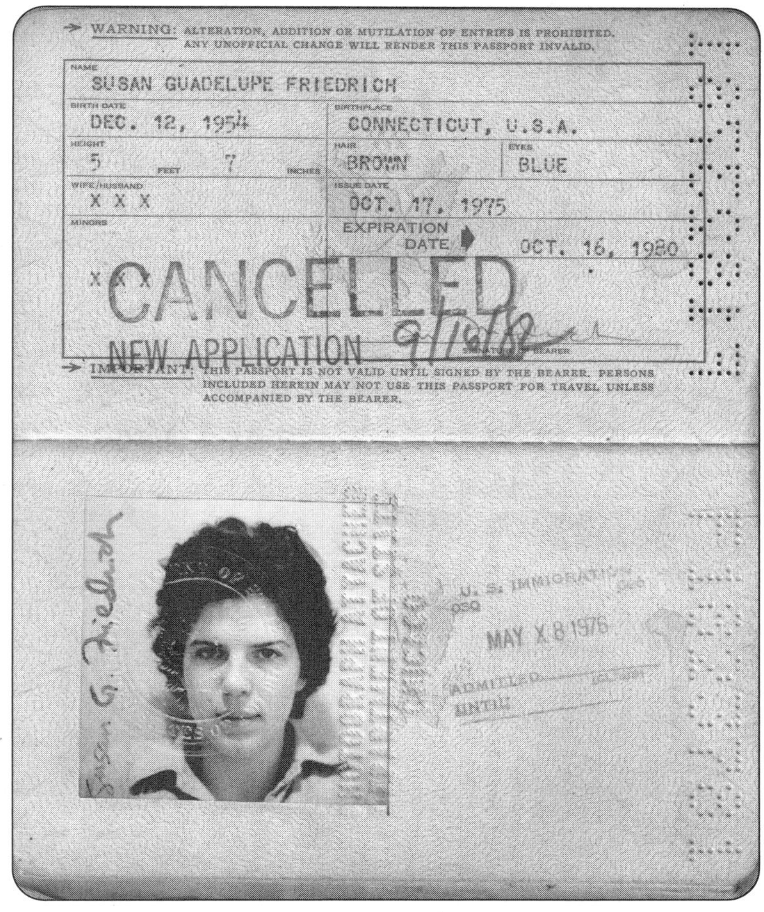
WARNING: ALTERATION, ADDITION OR MUTILATION OF ENTRIES IS PROHIBITED. ANY UNOFFICIAL CHANGE WILL RENDER THIS PASSPORT INVALID.

NAME: SUSAN GUADELUPE FRIEDRICH
BIRTH DATE: DEC. 12, 1954
BIRTHPLACE: CONNECTICUT, U.S.A.
HEIGHT: 5 FEET 7 INCHES
HAIR: BROWN
EYES: BLUE
WIFE/HUSBAND: X X X
ISSUE DATE: OCT. 17, 1975
MINORS: X X
EXPIRATION DATE: OCT. 16, 1980

CANCELLED
NEW APPLICATION

SIGNATURE OF BEARER

IMPORTANT: THIS PASSPORT IS NOT VALID UNTIL SIGNED BY THE BEARER. PERSONS INCLUDED HEREIN MAY NOT USE THIS PASSPORT FOR TRAVEL UNLESS ACCOMPANIED BY THE BEARER.

U. S. IMMIGRATION
030
MAY X 8 1976
ADMITTED
UNTIL

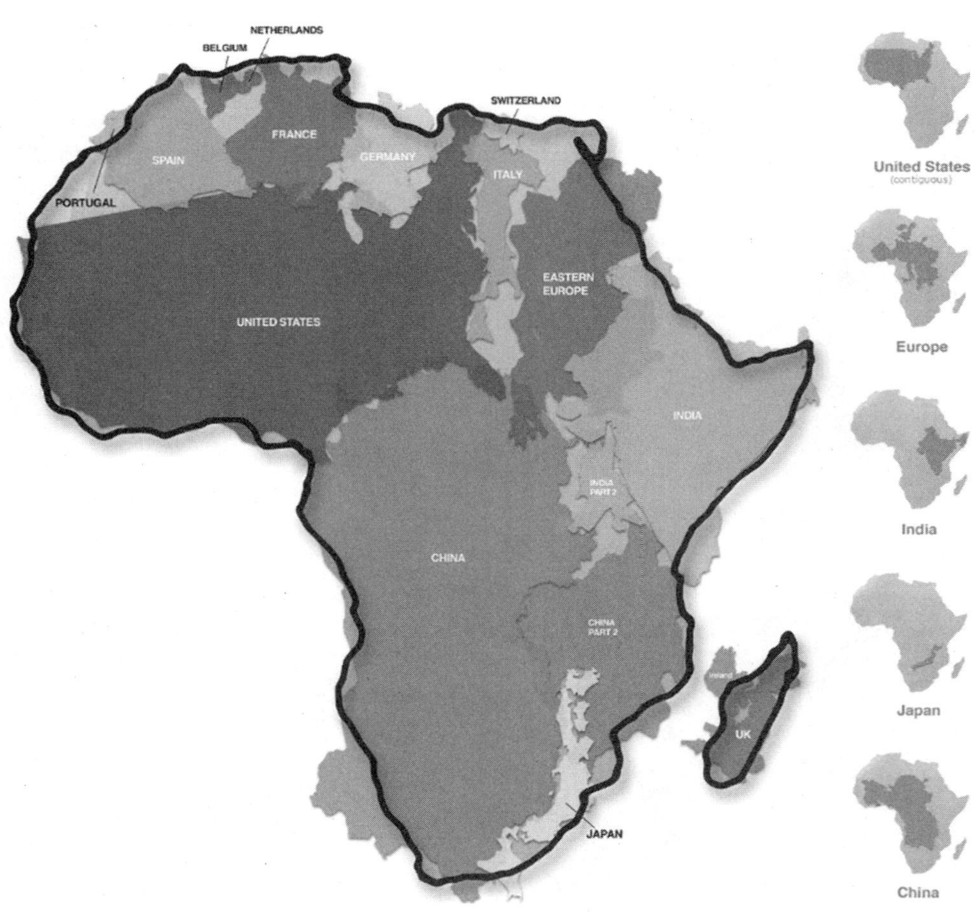
NETHERLANDS
BELGIUM
SWITZERLAND
FRANCE
SPAIN
GERMANY
ITALY
PORTUGAL
EASTERN EUROPE
UNITED STATES
INDIA
INDIA PART 2
CHINA
CHINA PART 2
UK
JAPAN
United States
(contiguous)
Europe
India
Japan
China

Chapter Notes

INTRODUCTION

Introduction, #1, page 4

Professor Yakubu Saaka (1945–2008) was a Ghanaian scholar with a PhD in Political Science from Case Western Reserve University whose expertise was in the government and politics of Africa. He is the author of several books, including *Local Government and Political Change in Northern Ghana*. Saaka began teaching at Oberlin College in 1972. During a leave of absence from 1979–1983, he was elected a member of Parliament in Ghana. Later appointed Deputy Foreign Minister, he became Ghana's Chief Delegate to the United Nations General Assembly and represented Ghana at the Organization of African Unity, where he was Vice-Chairman of the Liberation Committee in 1980. Oberlin College now offers an annual scholarship to a student from any African country through the Yakubu Saaka Memorial Fund.

Introduction, #2, page 5

While doing research for the book, I found a story about Professor Hekymara in *The Oberlin Review*. It confirmed my memories of his hostile behavior, and I learned that it wasn't reserved only for white students. (I wasn't aware of this action by the Black students because I'd left Oberlin after the fall semester to finish my senior year in Chicago.)

The story includes a quote from Ura Jones, the Afro-House Resident Coordinator, who was leading a campaign to get him fired: "He has used his position as an instructor as a political arena to belittle other blacks. He has made fun of black homosexuals, his colleagues, and others who aren't his kind of people."

(Pete Racher, "In spite of outcry, no word on Hekymara," *The Oberlin Review*, vol. 103, no. 50, May 9, 1975.)

CHAPTER 2

Chapter 2, #1, p. 22

The seventeen countries of West Africa are Benin, Burkina Faso, Cape Verde, The Gambia, Ghana, Guinea, Guinea-Bissau, Ivory Coast, Liberia, Mali, Mauritania, Niger, Nigeria, Senegal, Sierra Leone, and Togo, as well as the United Kingdom Overseas Territory of Saint Helena, Ascension and Tristan da Cunha.

CHAPTER 3

Chapter 3, #1, p. 28

Born in Oguta, southeastern Nigeria, **Florence (Flora) Nwanzuruahu Nkiru Nwapa** (1931–1993) was one of the first African woman novelists to be published in the English language in Britain. In 1966, at the age of thirty, she published her first book, *Efuru*, about the various struggles of an Igbo woman and the social fabric of a small village during the colonial period. *Efuru* became the first internationally published book by an African woman after Nwapa showed it to Chinua Achebe, a fellow Nigerian writer, and he sent it to Heinemann, his U.K publisher. Heinemann had created the African Writers Series in 1957 and Achebe was the series' first advisory editor. Back then, they were the go-to publisher for African literature, and from my research it appears that Heinemann was financially fair with their African writers.

Nwapa wrote several more novels, including *Idu* (1970) and *One Is Enough* (1981). In 1974, she founded Tana Press and, later in 1977, the Flora Nwapa Company, which published her own work as well as works by other writers.

Chapter 3, #2, p. 34

Stanlake John William Thompson Samkange (1922–1988) was a Zimbabwean historiographer, educator, journalist, and novelist born in Zvimba, Mashonaland, when it was still a colony administered by the British South Africa Company. Samkange was deeply involved in the liberal politics of Southern Rhodesia during the 1950s and 1960s but became disillusioned when he concluded that the white minority in Rhodesia would never accept any multiracial options for the country's government. He left the country for the United States in the '60s, where he earned his PhD, then worked as a journalist and taught African history at various universities in the US. In 1978, he returned to Rhodesia and became an advocate for nationalist policies. He held high offices in Joshua Nkomo's Zimbabwe African People's Union and Bishop Abel Muzorewa's United African National Council. Samkange is the author of several works of nonfiction, including *Origins of Rhodesia* (1968), and historical fiction, including *Year of the Uprising* (1978).

Chapter 3, #3, p. 34

Cecil Rhodes (1853–1902) died of a heart attack at the age of 49. He is said to have signed off with the words: 'So little done, so much to do." I'm glad that death stopped him from doing so much more damage.

Chapter 3, #4, p. 40

The Western Sahara War is an ongoing conflict between the Sahrawi Arab Democratic Republic/Polisario Front and the Kingdom of Morocco. The conflict originated with an insurgency by the Polisario Front against Spanish colonial forces (1973 to 1975), Mauritania (1975 to 1979), and Morocco (1975 and 1991). Today the conflict is dominated by unarmed civil campaigns of the Polisario Front and their self-proclaimed SADR state to gain independence for Western Sahara.

In Arabic, "Sahara" means "The Great Desert." In square miles, the Sahara is the same size as the continental United States. If you're going down it from north to south, it's the equivalent of driving from Maine to Miami or from Washington, DC to Denver—without a turnpike. In fact, mostly without any road at all.

Africa's total size is still vastly *underestimated* by most map viewers because the standard Mercator map projection leads to crucial misconceptions about the relative sizes of both countries and continents. The problem is not that Africa is sized incorrectly; it is in fact the most accurately sized continent on the Mercator map because it attempts to place the spherical shape of the world onto a flat surface, causing areas closest to the poles to be "stretched." Consequently, Africa barely changes in size while the countries further from the equator become quite inflated. This is how one usually sees the continents on a Mercator map:

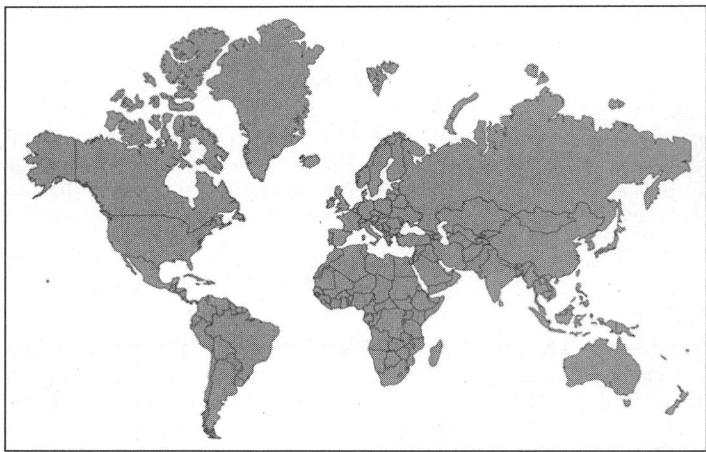

And this is their true size when adjusted, which reveals dramatic differences:

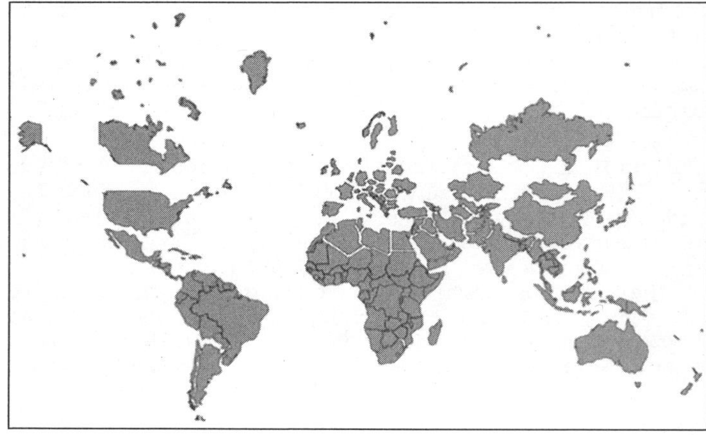

The next image shows the true size of Africa when correcting for the distortions caused by the Mercator. Nineteen countries fit within the African continent's shape. With a land area of 11.7 million square miles, it covers the same area as the USA, China, India, Japan, Mexico, and fourteen other countries combined.

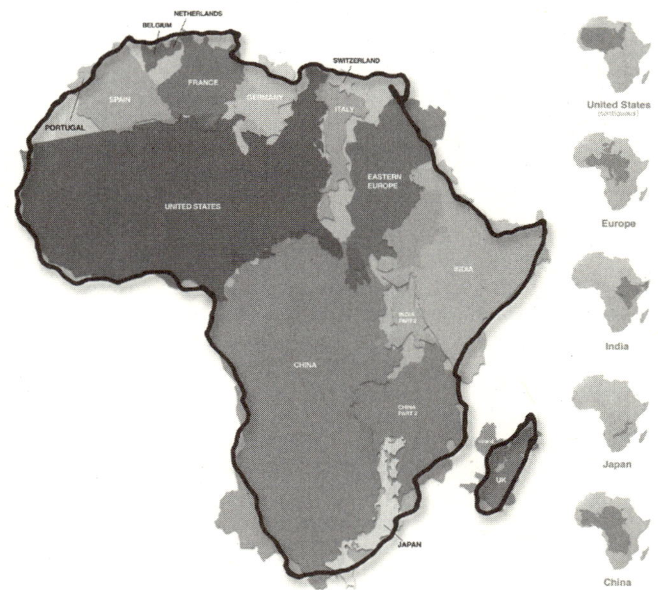

Chapter 3, #5, p. 43
My father was a linguist, so it probably made sense to him to give me *Winnie Ille Pu*. I had gotten the English version from him earlier, which I adored. The problem was that I didn't know Latin and had no interest in learning it.

Chapter 3, #6, p. 44
1975 was designated International Women's Year (IWY) by the United Nations because discrimination against women continued to be a persistent problem in much of the world. The UN also convened the first World Conference on Women in Mexico City that year. Since then, March 8th has been celebrated as International Women's Day.

The Conference, along with the United Nations Decade for Women (1976–1985, proclaimed by the General Assembly five months later at the urging of the Conference) launched a new era in global efforts to promote women's equality.

Chapter 3, #7, p. 45
The MPLA (Popular Movement for the Liberation of Angola) fought against the Portuguese army in the Angolan War of Independence (1961–74) and then defeated UNITA (the National Union for the Total Independence of Angola) and the FNLA (National Liberation Front of Angola), which were other anti-colonial movements, in the twenty-seven-year-long Angolan Civil War (1975–2002).

Chapter 3, #8, p. 46
Frantz Omar Fanon (1925–1961) was born on the island of Martinique under French colonial rule and was one of the most important writers of Pan-Africanism and Marxism during the years of the anti-colonial liberation struggle. His work drew on poetry, psychology, philosophy, and political theory, and his writings have had a profound influence across the global South. In his lifetime, Fanon published several key works: *Black Skin, White Masks* (1952), *The Wretched of the Earth* (1961) and a collection of essays, *A Dying Colonialism* (1959); two other collections of essays were published posthumously. Fanon was also a committed activist in the Algerian revolutionary struggle as a member of the Algeria National Liberation Front (FLN), ambassador to Ghana for the Algerian provisional government, and as a participant at conferences across Africa.

Chapter 3, #9, p. 48
In the early 1970s, Algeria began work on the Trans-Sahara Highway, slated to run 2,796 miles through three countries, starting in Algiers, crossing into Niger, and ending in Lagos, Nigeria. As of 2023, about 97% has been completed.

Back in January 1976, it only went as far as Ain Salah—about 781 miles. After that, the road was sand. Or piste, as it's called—a "road" of sand that's packed so hard it's like corrugated steel . . . . . BUMP! bump bump **BUMP** BUMP BUMP bump BUMP **BUMP!**. . . .for days on end.

The experienced drivers go off to the side because their trucks and cars ride high enough and because they won't get lost. Others, with no experience, also sometimes yield to temptation and go off-road. And get lost. And die.

CHAPTER 4

Chapter 4, #1, p. 51
The M'Zab Valley is a deep desert valley dotted with five walled cities from the eleventh century which sit within an oasis filled with palm and fruit trees. The architecture is of a Libyan-Berber style. Although each is independent, Ghardaïa is often used to refer to all five collectively. Each city sits on top of a rocky outcrop, with the surrounding sandstone houses leading up to a tall minaret that doubles as a watchtower.

Chapter 4, #2, p. 55
And that was certainly the case. Aside from small gifts, people also wanted copies of the photos I took of them. This was before you could attach a jpeg to an email: I had to make prints in my darkroom and then mail them to addresses that often seemed incomplete or which I could barely read. I did my best, and I had no idea what reached anyone except if I heard back, which rarely happened.

Chapter 4, #3, p. 55
Being in Ghardaïa was similar to how it had been in Algiers: women under lock and key, and men roaming about freely and being very vocal in their opinion of me. And in some moments, physical. So much for the romance of being in a magical oasis town in the desert. It's maddening when you can't just be in a place, can't immerse yourself in all the sights and sounds because a man is always dogging you.

And that was my reason for writing the rant, which is in fact shorter than what's in the journal. The #MeToo movement has had an impact, but we don't yet know if it will lead to lasting, major changes. Meanwhile, almost everything I experienced forty-seven years ago is still pretty much happening today. Regrettably.

And to the men reading this book: My brother said that the rant made him want to stop reading; he imagined that what I say in this chapter would recur later. (Of course, he understands why I'm ranting and he knows that I'm not throwing all men under the bus, just the deserving ones.)

We joked about me offering a "trigger warning" for any man who might be turned off, so here it is: If you're worried about a frequent recurrence of this kind of rant, have no fear. You won't encounter other lengthy rants later on and won't ever have the same kinds of experiences I had (lucky you!).

Chapter 4, #4, p. 60
Throughout my trip, the truck drivers usually took good care of me: they made sure I was fed and had water, and didn't threaten me sexually, nor did other male passengers on the trucks. But there were exceptions, like during this leg of the trip. Alan, the driver, pressed me constantly to marry him. The most absurd time came when we'd stopped by a magnificent outcropping of rocks sculpted by the ancient seas. I walked off to get some peace from him and take some pictures, but he followed and again begged me to marry him. When I said "No" for the nth time, he started crying. Crying! I could have slapped him. However, I was hundreds of miles in both directions from anyone and anywhere.

CHAPTER 5

Chapter 5, #1, p. 72
In 1890, the territory north of the Transvaal was chartered to the British South Africa Company, led by Cecil Rhodes, who acquired a huge block of territory which the company ruled for the next thirty-three years. In 1923, the company's charter was revoked and Southern Rhodesia attained self-government. Between 1953 and 1963, Southern Rhodesia was joined with Northern Rhodesia and Nyasaland in the Federation of Rhodesia and Nyasaland.

In October 1964, Northern Rhodesia became independent and was renamed Zambia. The Southern

Rhodesian colonial government felt that the continued use of "Southern" was now superfluous. The official name of the country, in the constitution adopted in 1965, became Rhodesia, but the British government refused to approve this because the country's name was defined by British legislation and couldn't be altered by the colonial government. As a result, Rhodesia was an unrecognized state in southern Africa from 1965 to 1979.

During this time, the British government continued referring to the country as Southern Rhodesia, but the shortened name was used by many people in the local government as well as in the House of Commons in the UK. In 1980, the country achieved independence and was renamed Zimbabwe.

Chapter 5, #2, p. 74

Unrelated to the contemporary OAS (the Organization of American States), this was the *Organisation armée secrète* [Secret Army Organization], a right-wing French dissident paramilitary organization operating during the Algerian War (1954–62). The OAS carried out terrorist attacks, including bombings and assassinations, in order to thwart Algeria's independence from colonial rule. Its motto was *L'Algérie est française et le restera*. ["Algeria is French and will remain so."]

Chapter 5, #3, p. 76

Võ Nguyên Giáp (1911–2013) is considered one of the greatest military strategists of the 20th century. He first grew to prominence during World War II as the military leader of the Viet Minh resistance against the Japanese occupation of Vietnam. Giap was a principal commander during the First Indochina War (1946–54) and the Vietnam War (1960–75). He was also a journalist, an interior minister in the Việt Minh government, the commander of the People's Army of Vietnam (PAVN), and defense minister. Giáp served as a member of the Politburo of the Vietnam Workers' Party, which in became the Communist Party of Vietnam in 1976.

CHAPTER 6

Chapter 6, #1, p. 79

Here I go again, noting that someone wasn't ashamed, as I did in Chapter 5 in relation to Miriam. Oy!

Maybe it's from having a German mother who worked overtime to keep everything spotless and give the appearance of being economically comfortable (which we weren't). She always seemed ashamed about how different her circumstances were in America compared to the fine home she had growing up in Germany. Moreover, my father came from a well-to-do American family and she often felt inadequate in their presence.

Living in Mexico and India didn't prepare me either; I was too young. This was my first time as an adult being in homes like Alan's or Miriam's. It was different than being in the home of a poor American, which is familiar; one knows how to gauge it; each person understands the cultural/economic background of the other, etc.

Anyway, I was painfully aware of the material differences between us—me coming from a relatively luxurious existence, them having so little—and I obviously projected my own feelings of embarrassment or discomfort onto them.

Chapter 6, #2, p. 83

Crossing into Niger produced a gradual change in the landscape. It was now the savannah, which I had seen in so many photos and movies about East Africa and which had dominated my imagination as a child, but I wondered if the term could be applied to that region of Niger.

Wikipedia enlightened me: A savanna or savannah is a mixed woodland grassland ecosystem characterized by the trees being sufficiently widely spaced so that the canopy does not close. The open canopy allows sufficient light to reach the ground to support an unbroken herbaceous layer consisting primarily of grasses.

So yes, it was still technically part of the Sahara, the desert, but it had somewhat more vegetation and I suppose could be considered a savannah. And because I was writing about crossing into this second African country, I looked up to see how many there are. Wow! Fifty-four! I could only name forty-two. If you feel like testing your knowledge, here they are:

Algeria, Angola, Benin, Botswana, Burkina Faso, Burundi, Cabo Verde, Cameroon, Central African Republic (CAR), Chad, Comoros, Democratic Republic of the Congo, Republic of the Congo, Cote d'Ivoire, Djibouti, Egypt, Equatorial Guinea, Eritrea, Ethiopia, Eswatini, Gabon, Gambia, Ghana, Guinea, Guinea-Bissau, Kenya, Lesotho, Liberia, Libya, Madagascar, Malawi, Mali, Mauritania, Mauritius, Morocco, Mozambique, Namibia, Niger, Nigeria, Rwanda, Sao Tome and Principe, Senegal, Seychelles, Sierra Leone, Somalia, South Africa, South Sudan, Sudan, Tanzania, Togo, Tunisia, Uganda, Zambia, and Zimbabwe.

Chapter 6, #3, p. 85
The Hausa people are based primarily in southeastern Niger and northern Nigeria. The Nigerian town of Daura is their spiritual home, and there is an especially large population around and in the town of Agadez. Over the course of the last five thousand years, significant numbers of Hausa have moved to parts of Cameroon, the Ivory Coast, Chad, Togo, Ghana, Sudan, Gabon and Senegal, as well as to parts of North Africa.

Chapter 6, #4, p. 85
I grew up on the south side of Chicago, where the sunrises and sunsets were intensely colored. We figured that it was due to all the steel dust in the air from the nearby steel mills. I don't know if that's true, but in the desert they didn't have the apocalyptic aspect which I had thought was normal.

Another surprising aspect of sunsets and sunrises in the Sahara is how quickly they happen. Is it due to the proximity to the equator? The sun seemed to fly up and down.

Chapter 6, #5, p. 85
The town of In-Gall (var. In Gall, I-n-Gall, In-Gal, Ingal, Ingall) had been a stop on the main roads between Niamey, the capital of Niger, and the mining town of Arlit or the provincial capital of Agadez. In the 1970s, the main road was repaved to transport uranium from the French-owned mines in Arlit, but the new road bypassed In-Gall, ending its use as a way station. Since then, its population has dropped from almost five thousand to less than five hundred. During the Tuareg insurgency of the 1990s, In-Gall was a prime fortification of the Niger armed forces; when peace was concluded in 2000 the old fort was reportedly abandoned.

Known for its oasis, In-Gall is the gathering point for the *Cure Salée* [Salt Cure festival], each September, when Tuareg and Wodaabe pastoralists celebrate the end of the rainy season. During the festival, In-Gall's population grows to several thousand celebrants, officials, and tourists.

Chapter 6, #6, p. 85
The boy tore off his green plastic shoes, put on the socks, put his shoes back on and ran off down the dusty road.

My grandmother knitted the socks for my father when he was a student at Harvard, so they had the Veritas emblem on them. I'd found them when visiting her and she gave them to me. As I watched the boy go, I was sure that my very patrician grandmother could never have imagined them on those feet and in that place.

Chapter 6, #7, p. 90
When the Tuaregs suddenly appeared the other night, after I'd been in such vast "empty spaces" for so many days, I couldn't fathom how it was that they were "out there." After all, my "distant" view at home was of a building across a busy street, not of the horizon many miles away.

So now, as we were plowing along through the savannah, a small figure appeared in the distance. It turned out to be a girl, maybe ten years old, standing with outstretched hands holding a small wickerwork platter with pieces of grilled goat cheese on it.

Where did she come from? And where were the goats?

CHAPTER 7

Chapter 7, #1, p. 94
Africa has the largest mineral reserves in the world. Europeans began mapping the interior of Africa in the nineteenth century, and when Henry Stanley revealed it to be full of raw materials needed to fuel the Industrial Revolution, the so-called Scramble for Africa began. In 1884, European countries and the USA met in Berlin to agree on the rules of African colonization, and from 1884–1914 the continent was in conflict as European countries took more and more territory from African states and peoples. Their natural resources were exploited throughout the colonial period, and the capitalist/postcolonial powers are now doing the same thing.

Niger is rich in uranium, which the French company Areva has been mining for several decades. Burkina Faso has gold, zinc, copper, manganese, phosphate, and limestone in substantial quantities as well as has reserves of diamonds, bauxite, nickel, and vanadium. Sub-Saharan Africa has the largest deposits in the world of cobalt, manganese and chromium. For three decades, China has secured mining deals with weak regulations and cheap labor; they are almost exclusively reliant on sub-Saharan Africa for its cobalt, and significantly reliant for manganese and chromium. Ghana is the continent's largest producer of gold, followed by South Africa and Mali. Ghana is also rich in aluminum, while countries like South Africa, Madagascar, Malawi, Kenya, Namibia, Mozambique, Tanzania, Zambia, and Burundi have significant quantities of neodymium, praseodymium, and dysprosium.

This is a book-length subject, so let it just be noted that Africa has been plundered, despoiled, and impoverished for centuries, and that the problem continues to this day, especially when it comes to the production of your smart phone.

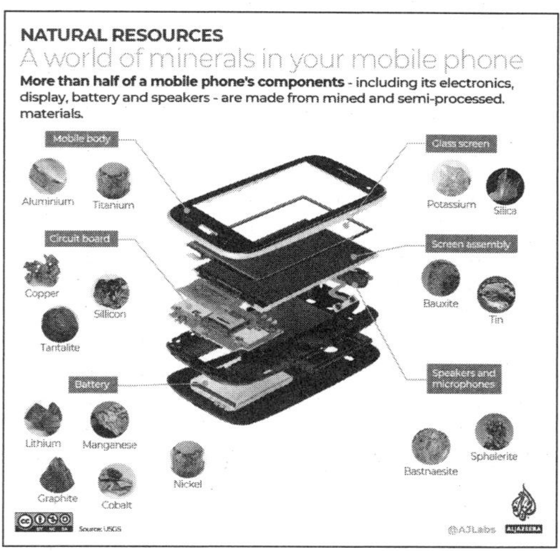

Chapter 7, #2, p. 96
That was my first time with the beverage, but later it was familiar and, in one instance, very special. On a walk one morning, I saw a man selling coffee from a small wooden table. I watched in amazement as he poured hot black tea into a cup, added a few heaping spoons of Nestlé instant coffee and then a few heaping spoons of sweetened condensed milk. Now THAT wakes you up!

Chapter 7, #3, p. 102
You'll hear more about this bracelet later, and when I discovered that it wasn't silver, I realized that I had paid a relatively high price for it. In 2024 dollars, \$40=\$226 and \$10=\$56, so the pride I took in bargaining was, in retrospect, pretty misplaced.

But I loved bargaining. I asked various people how it "worked" because I didn't want to cause offense, and I also didn't want to be a stupid tourist who paid through the nose. They all said, "Well, usually someone asks for maybe four times as much, and then you just see what you can do." So I would ask the price, make a counteroffer and then we'd go into a protracted and playful back and forth until I finally conceded. They would give me a big grin because they'd gotten their price, and we both knew it.

One time, in a market in Bolgatanga, the vendor and I were surrounded by a large group of onlookers laughing and cheering us on because the two of us inched . . . inched . . . inched our way down for such a long time. When I first got back to the states, I would sometimes offer a different price in a shop and then remember that we don't do that here. How boring.

Chapter 7, #4, p. 104
All world cuisines tend to include starch in every meal. Throughout West Africa, their starch dish is commonly prepared from corn, yam, millet or cassava. The women boil and then pound it to create something almost like bread dough and then shape into large balls for individual servings. The dish has a variety of names in the different countries: *paté*, *fufu*, *gari*, *tô*, *plakali*, *konkonte*, *attiéké*, *acheke*, etc.

There are many versions of this staple from country to country, but it was Ghana that invented it following the introduction of cassava (the root vegetable normally used there) by the Portuguese in the sixteenth century.

Like many traditional West African ingredients and dishes, *paté*, known as *fufu* in Ghana, has immense health benefits, which I just learned about. It's low in cholesterol and rich in fiber, potassium and resistant starch which feeds the beneficial bacteria in the gut and can reduce inflammation and promote digestive health. It also contains vitamin C, thiamine, riboflavin and niacin. In other words, *fufu* is a one-stop carb shop that does you a lot of good while filling your belly.

Chapter 7, #5, p. 115
The mythical spirit Mami Wata originated among the coastal southeastern Nigerians (the Efik, Ibibio and Annang people) but is now beloved in many areas of the Caribbean and West and Central Africa,

as well as among people in Louisiana who practice Voodoo. She's usually portrayed as a mermaid with a lot of hair and a snake, though there are many variations.

CHAPTER 8

Chapter 8, #1, p. 125

It's odd that I would mention computers in 1976 since I didn't get my first computer until an acquaintance built me a DOS-based one in 1992. Anyway, techies had been developing the machine for several decades and in 1977 three companies released the first commercially successful personal computers. Someone in the bush could never have afforded one, of course. Apple only sold one hundred of their Apple I's at a cost of $500 each ($2,827 in current dollars).

Chapter 8, #2, p. 126

Back then, citing the Tasaday was a common way to refer to people living outside of "civilization." I wondered how they'd fared in the intervening years and discovered that even in 1971 there were claims that the story was a hoax. And what a hoax! A detailed letter to the NYT written in 1988 by David Hyndman (a lecturer in anthropology at the University of Queensland) and Bernard Nietschmann (a professor of geography at the University of California) tells the true story.

In a nutshell: Manuel Elizalde Jr., the son of a rich Filipino family, was depicted as the savior of the Tasaday through his creation of Panamin (derived from "presidential assistant for national minorities"), a cabinet-level office to protect the Tasaday and other "minorities" from corrosive modern influences and environmentally destructive logging companies. In fact, he paid the neighboring T'boli people to take off their clothes and pose as a "Stone Age" tribe living in a cave.

Elizalde and Panamin exploited the T'boli (and other indigenous peoples) by allowing the logging of T'boli territory and using armed men to keep outsiders away. It was Mr. Elizalde who lived quietly, not the fictitious Tasaday, and certainly not the besieged T'boli. In 1983, Mr. Elizalde plundered $35 million from Panamin and fled to Costa Rica with many young indigenous women. The story goes on but suffice it to say that the fantasy of the Tasaday was totally manufactured (and for evil ends).

Chapter 8, #3, p. 128

It was shocking to see the wigs. In America, no surprise: Black women have had to contend forever with negative attitudes among white people toward their hair, so wigs were commonplace back then and still are to a fair degree. (It was a big deal when some Black women in the '60s started rebelling—notably Katleen Cleaver and Angela Davis—and I thought it was a welcome change.) But it was awful to see it here, where there was an incredible tradition of hairstyling, and where one would hope that prejudice against one's real hair wouldn't prevail. Alas, the tentacles of Western racism run wide and deep.

It wasn't as shocking to see the prostitutes, since women do this work on every continent, but they hadn't been visible to me when I was in more remote and underpopulated areas, so I was momentarily surprised to be reminded of this aspect of daily life. And by the way, I'm not implying that any woman in a short skirt is a sex worker. Even though some African women had adopted more Western fashions, a very short skirt usually wouldn't have been worn unless one was a sex worker. Moreover, one usually understands the difference between a woman lingering on a corner in a certain way and a woman who isn't working the trade but is just wearing a short skirt.

Chapter 8, #4, p. 129

It might seem odd that I was still hitching rides since I was now in areas where one could take lorries/mammy wagons. However, the lorries were always packed as full as possible with people and usually also with chickens or other animals and, if they said they were leaving soon-soon, you would sit for another two, three or more hours until it was sufficiently crammed for maximum fare income. So, a lot of times I just found it easier to catch a ride with someone in a car or truck.

Chapter 8, #5, p. 131

Wow, that must sound strange because there's a much more public face to life in African countries these days (though still not enough news coverage in the USA). But fifty years ago, aside from what was developing in books and movies by Black non-Africans who were traveling to, and engaging in, cross-cultural exchanges with Africans, there was mostly colonial narratives decorated by a backdrop of Africans in a dramatic African landscape, and novels by African writers which weren't that easy to come by or commonly promoted. Learning to populate Africa with Africans—learning to see it as their home entirely apart from all the awful overlays of colonialism—was quite a profound experience which taught me a lot about how deeply the colonial narratives had invaded our brains.

Chapter 8, #6, p. 132

While my brother was reading a draft of the book, he tried to find some of the people I hadn't been able to track down. He discovered Godfrey Chux Otiri and we're certain that it's him because he's listed as living in Denmark. Otiri writes poetry; Pete found one sample of his work from 2003 online. There was no further information about him.

Chapter 8, #7, p. 140
Playwright **Harold Athol Lanigan Fugard**, born in 1932 in Middleburg, South Africa, became internationally known for his incisive depictions of South African society during the apartheid regime. In 1963, his play *The Blood Knot*—a parable of two brothers who are affected differently by colorism—was produced in London and New York, becoming the first in a series he called *The Family Trilogy*. Fugard became more experimental in his later work, engaging in what critics have described as a more imagist approach to drama; these works include *Sizwe Banzi Is Dead*, *The Island*, and *Statements After an Arrest Under the Immorality Act*, all written in 1972. Fugard worked tirelessly throughout the 1970s and '80s to create and sustain theatre groups producing plays that defiantly indicted South Africa's apartheid policy. He died in March 2025.

CHAPTER 9

Chapter 9, #1, p. 144
I could simply have said that it sucked to be a dyke traveling alone in a place and at a time when my life was impossible to discuss or have accepted. I always had to hide and dissemble and that made me feel weird and shitty.

Chapter 9, #2, p. 146
This is what I sent to Cindy. It's hard to believe that I was working on something like this as I was traveling. It also makes me wonder about how much it affected my perceptions of things there, given that it was about the torture of women political prisoners. And it might seem incongruous for the article to be in an issue with this cover and containing various goofy items, but we understood how seemingly incongruous issues were often interconnected.

Chapter 9, #3, p. 146
Staff clubs were a longstanding tradition at some African universities, modeled after British gentlemen's clubs. In the past, they were mainly for the (primarily white) expats, with all the privilege and exclusivity that signifies. By the 1970s, they were no longer a "whites only" place (and of course there were also more students of color from many different countries), but they still seemed to reek of the original presumptions.

Chapter 9, #4, p. 147
Amos Tutuola (1920–1997) was a Nigerian writer, whose novel *The Palm-Wine Drinkard* (1952) became one of the first Nigerian novels to garner international acclaim and has since been translated into eleven languages. He was influenced by D. O. Fagunwa, a Nigerian author who had written similar folk fantasies in Yoruba, whereas Tutuola wrote in English. Throughout Tutuola's work, he blends Yoruba myths and cosmologies into surrealist prose narrative. He is the author of several other works of fiction, including *My Life in the Bush of Ghosts* (1954) and *The Village Witch Doctor and Other Stories* (1990).

As for my comment about somebody at the lecture alluding to Tutuola being ripped off by Faber and Faber: I cannot find any evidence of that now, so I won't insist that the information is correct, but I left it in my journal text because we know that sometimes publishers take advantage of authors.

Elechi Amadi (1934–2016) was a Nigerian novelist and playwright best known for his novel *The Concubine* (1966), which explores the tensions between tradition, religion, and the meaning of beauty in rural Nigeria. Amadi studied physics and mathematics at Government College, Umuahia, and the University of Ibadan, and later served in the Nigerian army. *Sunset in Biafra* (1973), his only work of nonfiction, recounts his experiences as a soldier and civilian during the civil war. He is the author of several novels, plays, and the science fiction book *When God Came* (2013).

Chapter 9, #5, p. 148
That's an understatement! I was stupefied by the heat and humidity. New York gets hot and humid, but this level was astonishing, and there was rarely any air-conditioning in the places I stayed. I would wander about during the day as best I could, waiting for the night to bring some slight relief. And I mean slight.

Moreover, being from a temperate climate means that you don't know how to cope with a tropical one: You still expect to do as much and do it as quickly as you did at home. I certainly observed people being slower, but was too stupid to learn from that and slow down.

Chapter 9, #6, p. 150
Professor Shamsudeen Onyilokwu Onche Amali (a.k.a. Samson O. O. Amali) was born in 1947 in Upu, Otukpo Local Government Area. He earned his B.A in English (with Honors) from the University

of Ibadan in 1970 and a PhD in Theatre and Drama from the University of Wisconsin, Madison in 1976.

Amali is a prominent bilingual playwright who writes in both Idoma and English. He is the first Nigerian to obtain a PhD in modern drama, first to become a professor of modern drama, and first professor of Theatre Arts to become a Vice-Chancellor of a university in Nigeria. In 2010 the Society of Nigeria Theater Artists (SONTA) presented him with a Lifetime Achievement Award.

Chapter 9, #7, p. 151

The Igbo (also referred to as Ibo in the past) are one of the largest groups in Nigeria, with their place of origin in southeastern Nigeria.

The name Igbo means "human community." In contrast to the Yoruba and Hausa, whose political systems are based on chiefs and kings, the Igbo were organized with semiautonomous communities; each village was ruled by an assembly of the common people. Archaeological finds in the area of Igboland trace back thousands of years; hundreds of bronze artifacts have been uncovered, some dating back to the ninth century AD, made with a much more complex casting technique than what was known and used in Europe at that time.

Chapter 9, #8, p. 152

In reference to this paragraph, my friend the writer commented, "You can't know this without going to Africa?"

To which I would reply, "Yes and no."

Yes: One should be able to see Africans as ordinary and equal members of the human community and I trust that has become normal in the twenty-first century, but back in the day, with so little good information and so much prejudice, the continent wasn't very clearly known by the majority of people living outside of it. Even with all the preparatory studying I'd done, Africa still had an aura of the unknown, of a place outside of the usual Western models.

No: It was being with them for so long that gave me a much deeper understanding of their place on our planet.

And even now I meet Africans who are bewildered, amused or angered when they encounter people who are surprised to learn that there are large, modern cities in Africa filled with people who use cell phones, drive cars, etc. Many people still think of it as a single, undeveloped country rather than a continent made up of fifty-four countries and a dizzyingly diverse population that uses modern conveniences and often lives in apartment buildings and houses "just like ours!"

Chapter 9, #9, p. 152

When I came home, I made a few pairs of summer pants out of African cloth and wore the blouse that was made for me in Nigeria until it wore out, but then I slipped back into my usual, western, ordinary way of dressing.

And also, sad to say, the vibrant colors in their fabrics perfectly complement Black skin tones but tend to make us white people look even more washed out and ridiculous. Maybe in my next life . . . .

Chapter 9, #10, p. 153

SWAPO (the South West African People's Organization) was an armed group in Namibia fighting for independence from colonial rule. They won independence from South Africa on February 9, 1990. ZANU (Zimbabwe African National Union), which split from ZAPU (the Zimbabwe African Political Union), was also an armed group fighting against colonial rule. They won independence from Britain on April 8, 1980.

CHAPTER 10

Chapter 10, #1, p. 157

Olokun is an *orisha*, a spirit sent to guide humans on how to live and succeed on earth; s/he is one of the most powerful yet dangerous of the *orishas* in Osha and Ifa. The name Olokun is a contraction of two words, "olo" meaning "owner" and "okun" meaning "ocean," which serves to describe a complex convergence of spiritual forces that are key elements in the Ifa concept of fertility.

Communities in West Africa and the African diaspora view Olokun variously as a female, male, or androgynous deity. S/he is believed to be the mother of Aje, the *orisha* of great wealth and of the bottom of the ocean. Olokun is revered as the ruler of all bodies of water and all other water deities and is highly praised for the ability to give great wealth, health, and prosperity to her/his followers.

The original bronze head from Ife, popularly known as the Olokun head, is in the Ife Museum. There had been much debate about whether it was the original, but the debate has now been settled: In 2010, a technical examination of it was carried out when it was brought to the British Museum for an exhibition. On its prior visit sixty years earlier, the Olokun head had been condemned as a sand-cast copy. The present study has definitively established that it is a hollow *cire perdue*, or lost wax casting, very similar in technique and composition to the other heads. This is the head unearthed at Ife in 1910.

Chapter 10, #2, p. 159

There are have already been a few places where I comment on dancers, on people's physiques, etc., and that might raise an eyebrow.

Here's the problem: For a few centuries, for all the wrong reasons and in all the wrong ways, mention has been made of Africans' physical attributes, their "natural rhythm," their "lascivious dancing," their body types, etc.—either as something ridiculous, like these from the twentieth-century Looney Tunes cartoon, *Jungle Jitters* . . .

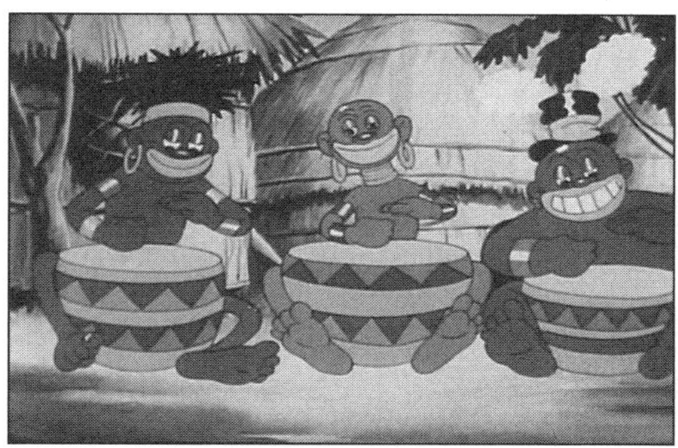

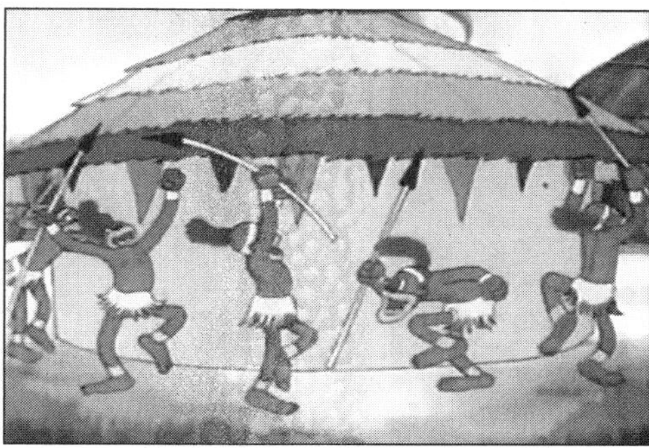

. . . or something to be misused, as in this Punch cartoon from the late nineteenth century.

Beyond being an exploitation of a singular woman, the "hymn" makes her a metaphor for the mineral riches of the continent and details the competition between the colonial powers to exploit those riches:

"The force, O Muse, and functions now unfold
Of Afric's Venus, graced with mines of gold;

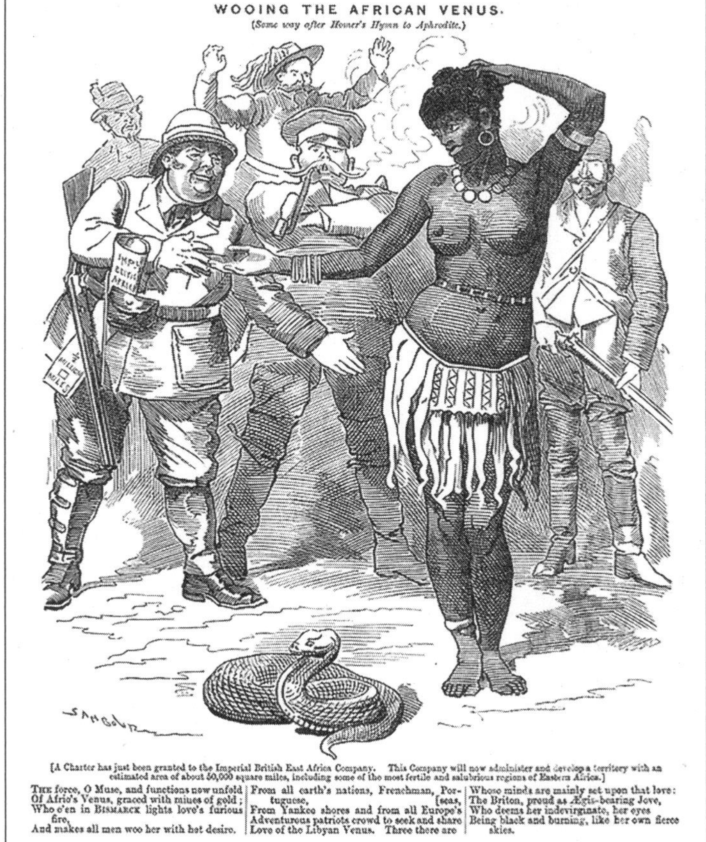

Here is the full text in *Punch, or The London Charivari*, page 131, September 22, 1888

WOOING THE AFRICAN VENUS

(Some way after Homer's *Hymn to Aphrodite*.)
A charter has just been granted to Imperial British East Africa Company. This Company will now administer and develop a territory with an estimated area of about 50,000 square miles, including some of the most fertile and salubrious regions of Eastern Africa.

The force, O Muse, and functions now unfold
Of Afric's Venus, graced with mines of gold;
Who e'en in BISMARCK lights love's furious fire,
And makes all men woo her with hot desire.
From all earth's nations, Frenchman, Portugese,
From Yankee shores and all Europe's seas,
Adventurous patriots crowd to seek and share
Love of the Libyan Venus. Three there are
Whose minds are mainly set upon that love:
The Briton, proud as Ægis-bearing Jove,
Who deems her indevirginate, her eyes
Being black and burning, like her own fierce skies.
He for her preference will do all he can,
Who never faltered in the face of man.
Shunning not strife, or Mars his warlike banes,
But much preferring Trade; his artizans
Taught all earth's countries all the Arts that are
Associate with things vehicular.
The Teuton next, a stalwart suitor he,
A trifle truculent, a mite too free,
Holding all things in war and wooing fair,
Hoping tomato cheeks and orange hair,
By force of contrast, may avail to win
The dusky Aphrodite—and her "tin."
Thirdly, the broad Batavian, scant of grace,
Who trusts a lucky "start" in the love-chase
Gives him such lead that they who run from scratch
The lumpy "limit-man" may fail to catch.
Others—the Frank, the Belgian—too there be,
But just as Paris had the choice of three,
So the Black Venus seems confronted now
By three chief suitors.
Swart yet stately brow
To which one wilt thou bend in coy selection?
O coal-black Charmer, all thy swart perfection
Of ebon-moulded limb and sable hair
To the hot winds of torrid Libya bare,
Witches the world as once, in style the same,
"The all-of-gold-made-laughter-loving-dame"
As CHAPMAN after HOMER calls her—did
At odorous Cyprus. Lifting languorous lid,
Late late in the world's history thou dost draw,
As did the Paphian when her form men saw,
Snow-white and rose-tinct from the waves arise.
Thou art not snow and rose-leaf to our eyes,
But "tawny-fronted," like the Egyptian Queen;
Yet what strange Cleopatra charms are seen
In thy most opulent blackness, that bewitch
All modern men who would be loved—and rich.
HOMER—and CHAPMAN—speak in diction bold
Of "Cyprian Venus, graced with mines of gold."
They write of one—but then 'twas not a man—
"Whom all the gold of Venus never can
Tempt to affect her pacts with god or man."
Well, that was not JOHN BULL, but priggish Pallas—
What man unto thy golden charm is callous,
O ebon-skin'd, yet aureate Aphrodite?
But stay! Poetic flights should not be flighty
That deal with themes like goddesses and gold.
Who is the new Anchises, kingly bold,
Whom rich-crown'd Afric Venus will approve
And dower with her profitable love?
Anchises with the Paphian had the pull,
Shall it be so today with brave JOHN BULL?
It looks a little like it. See him stand,
Love in his eyes, a Charter in his hand!
Such strenuous wooing is most apt to win
Women of mortal or immortal kin.
The swarthy Siren whom all men desire
Looks on him coyly, yet with eyes of fire,
Teuton, Batavian, Frank will Venus shunt?
Well, BULL is at least fairly to the front.

And here is a recent example of the same kind of racism:

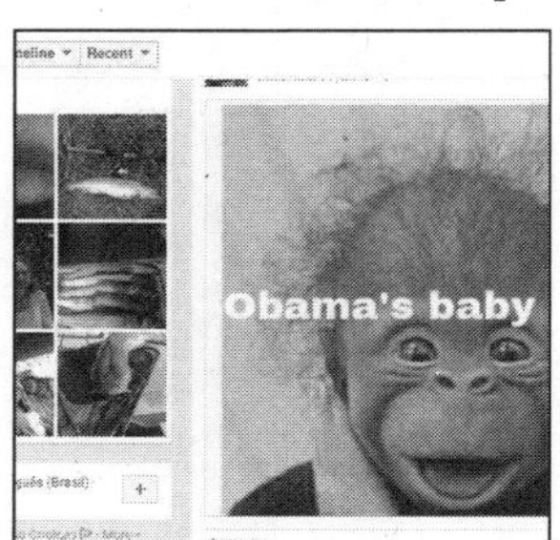

So it seems wrong to ever comment again on the physique, physical prowess, sensuality, etc. of Africans.

However, music and dance are central to most African cultures. They also have a history of making brilliant sculptural objects (figures and masks) and being great storytellers, but I would argue that music and dance are their most ubiquitous and known art forms. Moreover, the skill level of dance and music is astonishing. Have you ever taken an African dance class and tried to move to those complicated rhythms? It's very humbling. Western dance and music work on a different register; even American Black music isn't often doing the intensely complex rhythmic things that African music does.

And if that's the driving cultural force, then it leads to great physical agility and often superb physical form.

Every culture/country/ethnic group has its highest points, whether in the realm of art, food, gardening or something else related to the pleasures of life, and we tend to regard those accomplishments with awe and respect, but racism has often distorted that gaze when people talk about Africa in relation to its music, dance, or the physical prowess of many Africans.

Chapter 10, #3, p. 161

In 1976, that was $90 million and $567 million. Today? That would be $497 million and $3,134 billion. During college I didn't have a TV and didn't read the newspaper regularly, so I was often oblivious to major events. It was in Professor Saaka's class that I learned about the coup in Chile, which had just occurred (on 9/11/73) and was orchestrated primarily by Henry Kissinger. President Allende was assassinated, and tens of thousands of Chileans were killed or jailed.

I'd grown up on stories about WWII and been deeply opposed to US involvement in the Vietnam War, but this horrific event in which America was clearly implicated cemented my contempt for most of America's foreign policy. And then, only three years after the US-backed coup, America was giving six times as much money to the new dictatorial regime in Chile.

Chapter 10, #4, p. 161

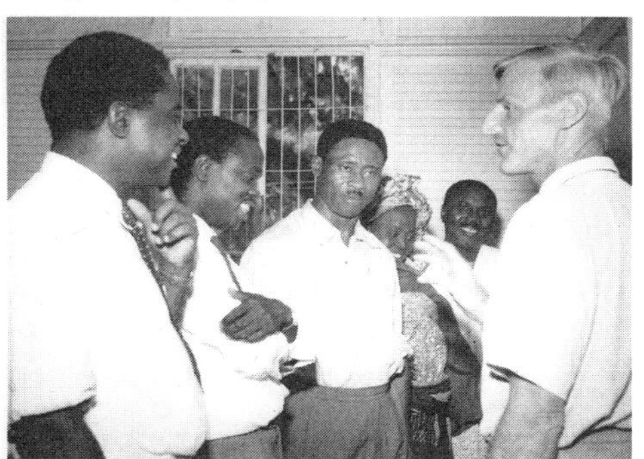

The museum was established in 1948 by **Kenneth Crosswaite Murray** (1903–1972), better known as K.C. Murray, and opened to the public in 1954 on land donated by the Oni of Ife, Oba Aderemi.

As an art teacher in the British Colonial Service, Murray was appointed to advise the Nigerian government on the effects of the colonial education system on local art. He arrived in Lagos in 1927 to teach. He took a leave in 1929 and then returned to Nigeria to teach arts at two Government Training Colleges. During this time, Murray advised the government about establishing museums and issuing relevant laws to prevent the illegal exportation of Nigerian artworks.

Prompted by the discovery of Nok Head artefacts on July 28, 1943, Murray was largely responsible for the creation of the Nigerian Antiquities Service in 1943 and became Nigeria's first surveyor of antiquities in the newly created service (which became the Nigerian National Commission for Museums and Monuments, or NNCMM, in 1979). Due to the Second World War, Murray's recommendations for the establishment of three museums could not be implemented, but he was permitted to continue purchasing antiquities pending the building of them. During his tenure as the director of the Department of Antiquities (DoA) he founded the Nigerian Museum in Lagos in 1957. He was succeeded as director by Bernard Fagg. He and Fagg worked tirelessly to claw back dozens of the finest Benin Bronzes from the UK and USA. Murray died on April 12, 1972 and was buried in Ikoyi Cemetery.

The prior DoA and the present NNCMM have established thirty-five national museums, located either in the state capitals or in historic places or towns and in many smaller communities; there are also local community museums, private galleries, and numerous historical/cultural monuments throughout the country.

Chapter 10 #5, p. 163

Akinwumi Isola (1939–2018) was the author of several plays and novels, which includes *Madame Tinubu* (1979), the translator of Wole Soyinka's *Death and the King's Horseman* (1975) into Yoruba, and created a production company that turned five of his plays into films directed by Tunde Kelani. He was born in Ibadan in 1939 and was a professor at Obafemi Awolowo University for several decades and a visiting professor at the University of Georgia. In 2000, Isola was awarded the National Merit Award and appointed a Fellow of the Nigerian Academy of Letters, and also received the Nigerian National Order of Merit.

Chapter 10 #6, p. 164

In the summer of 1973, between my sophomore and junior years of college, I biked alone for 710 miles from Wooster, Ohio to Boston, Massachusetts where I was going to take some classes.

Chapter 10 #7, p. 165

I had heard people refer to me as an *oyibo*. When I asked what it meant, it seemed to mean a white person, but in the sense of a "honky." In other words, it was slightly pejorative, slightly comical; not especially mean, but more than just a translation of "white person."

"Honky" was a commonly used term in America when I was young, so I became curious about its origins. Hello, Wikipedia:

> Honky was adopted as a pejorative in 1967 by Black Power militants within the Student Nonviolent Coordinating Committee (SNCC) seeking a rebuttal for the term "nigger." On June 24, 1967 H. Rap Brown, National Chairman of the SNCC, told an audience of Blacks in Cambridge, "You should burn that school down and then go take over the honky's school." Brown went on to say: "If America don't come 'round, we got to burn it down. You better get some guns, brother. The only thing the honky respects is a gun."
>
> Honky has occasionally (and ironically) even been used for whites supportive of Black Americans, as seen in the 1968 trial of Black Panther Party member Huey Newton, when fellow Panther Eldridge Cleaver created "Honkies for Huey" pins for Newton's white supporters.

Then I looked up *oyibo* to find out whether my prior understanding had any basis in reality. It's a Yoruba term, and it <u>is</u> slightly pejorative, but it's used to define or label expatriates in general; it can also be used to refer to a foreigner of color (including someone from another African country), so it seems to mean "other" or "stranger" rather than "white person." So honky isn't a good translation of *oyibo*, since it started out in America as a term that only designated white people. Anyway, this *oyibo*/honky is glad to have finally unraveled the mystery.

Chapter 10 #8, p. 173

Sunny Ade (born 1946) first toured America in 1982. He became known as King Sunny Ade, perhaps because he was born in Osogbo to a royal family from Ondo, thus making him an Omoba (prince) of the Yoruba people.

When talking about Nigerian music, one must also mention Fela Kuti (1938–1997), the pioneer of Afro-beat, whose birth name was Olufela Olusegun Oludotun Ransome-Kuti. His club in Lagos was called Afrika Shrine; he first toured America in 1969. Aside from being a brilliant musician, he was very active in his opposition to the Nigerian government.

I wasn't familiar with much contemporary African music before going. It was a time before CD's, and ordinary record stores weren't stocked up on African music. When I got back, I started going to an African record store in Harlem and got albums like Fela's *Zombie*, which he released in 1977.

CHAPTER 11

Chapter 11, #1, p. 179

The renowned shrine in Osogbo, designed and built by Susanne Wenger, is dedicated to Osun, the river goddess.

A complicating factor for me was that it represented two related yet significantly different "sources." The first and very impressive one is that Ife is the seat of the Yoruba kingdom and it is here, as well as in Benin, where all the greatest bronze and clay sculptures were—until so many were stolen by the British.

The second one was more problematic. It's where two white Europeans (the German writer Ulli Beier and the Austrian artist Suzanne Wenger) spent their lives interacting with Yoruba artistic traditions in their own work while also promoting contemporary Nigerian art and writing, and about whose work I already had some misgivings. Not really with Beier's work; my remarks in the journal were entirely based on my response to Wenger's shrines.

So here's some background, beginning with why I said that I should have been happy:

> The Mbari Mbayo Artists and Writers Club was established for African writers, artists, and musicians at Ibadan and Osogbo in Nigeria. *Mbari*, an Igbo (Ibo) word for "creation," refers to the traditional painted mud houses of the area...The name of the club was inadvertently altered when the Igbo word *mbari* was mistaken for the Yoruba phrase *mbari mbayo*, meaning "when we see it we shall be happy."

Ulli Beier (1922–2011) played a major role in advancing the cause of Nigerian art and literature by cocreating the first Mbari Club in 1961 with the performer Duro Ladipo. He was also a translator (from Yoruba to English) of major African writers, including Wole Soyinka, Chinua Achebe, and John Pepper Clark, and founded the magazine *Black Orpheus: An Anthology of New African and Afro-American Stories*. The journal quickly became the leading space for Nigerian authors to write and publish their works.

He and Wenger were married in 1949 but later divorced. At the time of his death, Professor Tunde Babawale described him as someone "who made passionate and indelible contributions to the development and popularization of Yoruba arts and culture . . . Beier provided an enduring platform for interaction between Yoruba indigenous ideas, beliefs and practices and the Yoruba cultural space, the legacy of which is the Iwalewa House at the University of Bayreuth, which continues to host scholars in different areas of African Studies."

Susanne Wenger (1915–2009), also known as Adunni Olorisha, was an Austrian artist who expatriated to Nigeria and later became a Yoruba priestess. She came to Nigeria while married to Ulli Beier and later married local drummer Lasisi Ayansola Onilu, by which time she was actively participating in the revival of the *orisha* religion. Wenger settled in Osogbo in 1961 and was commissioned by the Osogbo District Council to renovate the local shrines dedicated to orishas, particularly the Sacred Grove of Osun on the banks of the Osun River. She built an artist cooperative in Osogbo, founded the New Sacred Art Movement, and partnered with local artists to redevelop and redecorate the Sacred Grove with sculptures and carvings.

She was also a leading advocate for its preservation; it was made a national monument in 1965 and was later marked as a World Heritage site.

Participants in the Osun-Osogbo Festival in the groves had markedly dwindled prior to Wenger's revitalization of the shrines. In the decades since then, the it has become the largest and most important traditional festival in Yorubaland, if not in the whole of Nigeria.

Wenger was initiated into the cults of Obatala, Sopona, and Ogboni, and was later given the chieftaincy title of Adunni Olorisha.

Having updated my knowledge about Beier and Wenger, I am in awe of the fact that they dedicated their entire lives to Nigerian art, artists, and the religious traditions of the Yoruba, and I feel like an ass for writing such dismissive remarks about them back then.

On the other hand, part of travel is about finally seeing and analyzing what one only imagined back home, and when it came down to it, I thought the shrine was a bit goofy-looking; I was struggling with the mythical/religious aspect; and the glossy pictures I'd seen were quite different from the shabby reality. In other words, I was disillusioned. Alas. But that does happen sometimes.

Chapter 11, #2, p. 183

Adebisi Akanji (born 1935) worked with Susanne Wenger for over four decades. He introduced her to the technique of sculpting in cement and is the co-creator of most of the large cement sculptures in the Groves. Before meeting Wenger, he had widened his artistic interests to batiks and pen and ink drawings. Adebisi's work draws on his deep knowledge of Yoruba tradition and has been exhibited widely in Europe, the USA and Brazil. His commissions include The National Black Theatre in Harlem, NY, as well as houses and galleries in Lagos, Abeokuta and Osogbo.

Rabiu Abesu (born 1940) comes from a lineage of master Yoruba wood carvers. Quickly identified as an artist of exceptional talent by Wenger, she encouraged Rabiu to continue as a traditional but to create his own mode of expression. "I decided that I had to struggle to do my original carved work for posterity and the advancement of Yoruba culture and tradition. My inspiration comes to me from the Gift of God. The gift is my two inner eyes which always reveal to me what to carve from any wood."

Kasali Akangbe Ogun (born 1945), a master wood carver, comes from a long lineage of woodcarvers known as "Arelagbayi." The family profession, traditionally passed down from father to son, was interrupted for two generations due to the influences of colonialism. It was revived in the Akangbe Ogun family by Susanne Wenger in the 1960s. For the sculptures and decorative posts in the Sacred Grove, Kasali interpreted traditional Yoruba wood carvings of deities in a fresh and new way. Kasali has exhibited widely in Europe, the USA and in Lagos and he is now passing the art of Yoruba carving to his sons.

Chapter 11, #3,p. 186

It was such a battle back then. I had the same outbursts about the nascent lesbian feminist goddess worshippers at home. Some friends had become adherents, and I was trying to understand why human beings, anywhere on the planet, need and want a deity—whether male or female—who they can serve, who gives them a feeling of being protected, and to whom they can beg for help and forgiveness.

Given how hard life is, that does sound kind of sensible, but I've never been able to accept that. At least I'm fair about it: I sound hostile, rude, or racist speaking like this about an old tradition from another culture but, as an all-purpose atheist, I apply the same cynicism and doubt to every group of worshippers, regardless of country, color or creed.

CHAPTER 12

Chapter 12, #1, p. 189

Arthur Blessitt (born 1940) has a website. In 2023, at the age of 83, he was still doing it and by then he had over walked 43,340 miles in 324 countries, island groups & territories. He set the Guinness World Record for longest walk/pilgrimage. Crazy motherfucker.

Chapter 12, #2, p. 190
Oberlin was founded in 1833 by Reverend John J. Shipherd, a Presbyterian minister and Philo P. Stewart, a missionary. Disenchanted with what they saw as the lack of strong Christian principles among American settlers, they decided to establish a college and a colony based on their religious beliefs, "where they would train teachers and other Christian leaders for the boundless most desolate fields in the West.'' But I must have fabricated the Christian proselytizing that went on; when I attended, it was a very progressive school with an impressive history.

For example, Oberlin was the first college to accept women and Black Americans as students. In 1850, Lucy Sessions, an American abolitionist and feminist, was the first African American woman to complete a four-year course of a study at a college or university by completing a Ladies Literary Course, and in 1862, Mary Jane Patterson became the first African American woman in the United States to earn a BA.

Oberlin also played a very active role in the abolitionist movement and was a major stop on the Underground Railroad.

Chapter 12, #3, p. 198
I saw altercations like this several times, which were notably nonviolent. No one pulled out bats or guns, they just slapped at each other a bit and did a lot of yelling. From where I grew up, I always expected verbal fights to escalate to something much worse. I'm not saying there weren't Africans who committed violent crimes, but there was also this other way of dealing with conflict. And then there's the technique of public shaming, but I'll get to that later.

Chapter 12, #4, p. 205
Yes, it was in part the Yoruba. I was amused many years later when a Japanese friend talked about Koreans being so "aggressive." It seems that every group has some other group whom they diss. And I did get a very different vibe when I was in other places, like Ghana or the desert, and I would hear Ghanaians talk about how loud or money-grubbing the Nigerians are, etc . . .

CHAPTER 13

Chapter 13, #1, p. 209
I had no idea what it would mean to be in a major city during a coup, but I soon found out. I also learned a bit about the complicated political history of Nigeria and the equally complex reasons for the coup.

In July 1975, Yakubu Gowon (a Christian), who had been the head of state for nine years, was overthrown in a bloodless coup while he was away at a meeting of the OAU (Organization of African Unity). Murtala Ramat Muhammed (a Muslim) was installed as the new head of state. Muslim/Christian friction was a major element in the politics of Nigeria; there was always a jockeying for power, an effort to create (or upend) a balance between the groups.

Lieutenant Colonel Buka Suka Dimka (a Christian) plotted with a group to overthrow Muhammed and on February 13, 1976, Muhammed, his *aide-de-camp* and his driver were gunned down on the way to work. Dimka went on the radio and told the country that, "his government is now overthrown by the young revolutionaries." He was later caught, and during his testimony he implicated Gowon, who insisted that he had nothing to do with it. Gowon was living in exile in London; when he returned to Nigeria many years later, his name was cleared by the then president.

Soon after the coup, Olusegun Obasanjo (a Christian who had been Muhammed's chief of staff) was installed as head of state. He and three of his closest aides (Shehu Musa Yar'Adua, Theophilus Danjuma, and Allison Akene Ayida) also implied that Gowon was part of the coup; in 1980, Ayida said " . . . it was necessary for the surviving members of [Muhammed's] administration to find scapegoats quickly to avoid a backlash."

It's understandable that they would fear a backlash: In the sixteen years after Nigeria gained independence from Britain (on October 1, 1960), three of the five heads of state had come in via a coup. And then there were two more: In the sixty-four years since independence, fourteen men have held the office during sixteen time periods (two of them held office twice). Of those sixteen changes, seven were the result of either a coup (five) or an assassination (two).

Finally: There was intense anger and suspicion that the British and the Americans were involved in the plan, due in part to the general ways in which both powers had screwed over many African countries for a long time, but also due to the fact that Dimka met with the British high commissioner on the morning of the coup.

Chapter 13, #2, p. 211
Through the magic of the internet, I reconnected with Mary forty-two years later. She's a physician's assistant, still living and working in Madison. I mentioned the comment I made about "showing her colors" and explained that, back then, I was desperate to find anyone who was playing on our team. She laughed with understanding but said that she's happily married to a man.

Chapter 13, #3, p. 211
"What I Ate Where" is from Diane di Prima's wonderful 1961 collection entitled *Dinners and Nightmares*. Here are the first three paragraphs:

> i remember the winter the january i ate nothing but oreos. if you know what oreos are, they're those chocolate cookies two of them at a time stuck with sugar in the middle, and very addictive. i mean i really got hooked on them. there was this low armchair in my pad and I would sit in it and eat oreos and read and sometimes drink a little milk or water cause oreos in large numbers they tend to stick in your teeth.
>
> when i wanted company i would go upstairs and visit these two girls who were my neighbors. they were a little crazy. they liked oreos too but not as much as i did, i mean not three or four packages a day, but anyway they would sit there and eat them with me to keep me company, and they washed theirs down with ale. ale and oreos i didn't dig too much, together like that. but boy, to hear the wind blow and all that awful january rain and a bunch of windows looking out on old crumbling filthy brick walls, and to sit in the middle of all this eating oreos and reading was—well anyway it was a way to get through january. to get through january in manhattan is hard, to get through january and february the same year almost impossible.
>
> one of the best ways to get through i found was this of eating oreos. except that it makes you fat. really fat. even if you don't eat anything else and you think, shit, how can i get fat i haven't had breakfast or lunch or anything like that, but don't kid yourself. OREOS MAKE YOU FAT.

Chapter 13, #4, p. 215
Born in Kiagbodo, Nigeria, **John Pepper Clark** (1935–2020) earned his BA in English at the University of Ibadan, where he edited various magazines, including the *Beacon* and *The Horn*. After graduating in 1960, he worked as an information officer in the Ministry of Information, as features editor of the Daily Express, and as a research fellow at the Institute of African Studies at the University of Ibadan. For several years, Clark was a professor of English at the University of Lagos and co-editor of the literary magazine *Black Orpheus*. He retired in 1980 and in 1982, along with his wife Ebun Odutola (a professor and former director of the Centre for Cultural Studies at the University of Lagos), he founded the PEC Repertory Theatre in Lagos.

A widely travelled man, Clark held visiting professorial appointments at several universities in the United Sates. He was most noted for his collections of poetry, including *A Reed in the Tide* and *Casualties: Poems 1966–68* and plays like *The Raft*, *Ozidi*, and *The Boat*.

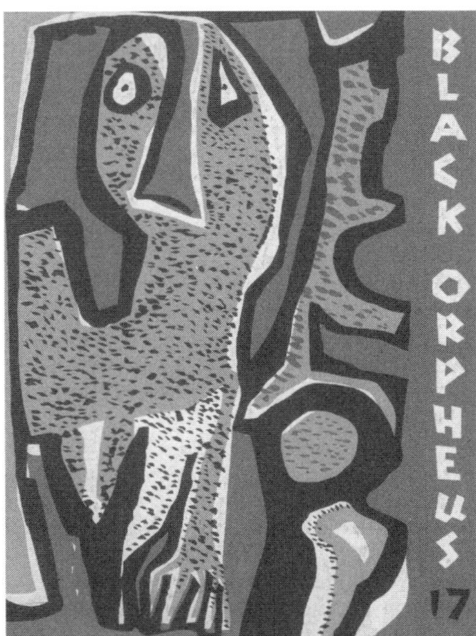

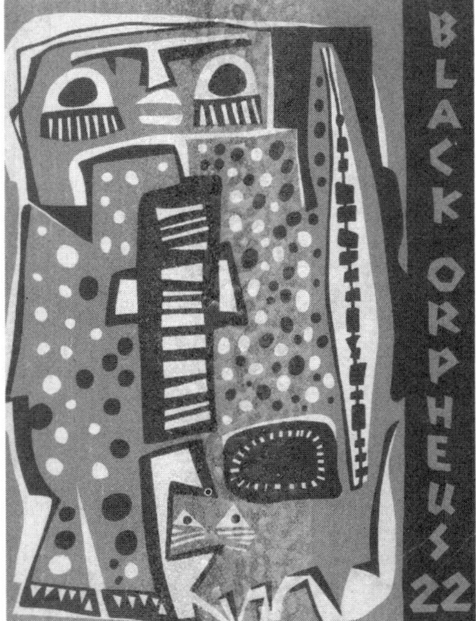

Two covers of *Black Orpheus* by Georgina Beier for issues 17 and 22.

Chapter 13, #5, p. 217
Nwazuluwa Onuekwuke "Zulu" Sofola (1935–1995) is considered one of the most distinguished women in Nigerian literature, being the first published female Nigerian playwright and the first female professor of Theater Arts in Africa. She taught for over two decades, first at the University of Ibadan and then the University of Ilorin and won a Fulbright Scholarship to SUNY Buffalo in 1988.

Sofola's plays use both traditional and modern African settings. Her most frequently performed plays are *Wedlock of the Gods* (1972) and *The Sweet Trap* (1977), which use tragedy and comedy to think about the longstanding tension between tradition, modernity and patriarchy.

Chapter 13, #6, p. 224
My friend the writer commented, "Were you just realizing this on this trip? I doubt it. Give this some thought and REWORK."

It's nice of her to think that I had overcome all the negative stereotyping that prevailed in America at that time, when Blacks were always the other, always set apart by segregation and racism. But in Africa, being Black was the norm. Skin color no longer signified a different status, as it almost always did in America, and almost always in the negative.

Not that color was without consequence: The privilege assigned to lighter-skinned Blacks often operated there as much as it did in America. Nevertheless, being in a part of the world inhabited almost entirely by Black-skinned people was a revelatory experience. From the wealthy man or woman passing by in a chauffeur-driven BMW to the destitute man or woman begging for food on the side of that same road, they were all Black.

And although I had been fortunate to mix socially with Blacks while growing up, and was attuned to the struggle for civil rights, the experience of traveling in Africa forced me to see more more clearly how much the racism in America had deliberately blinded white Americans—including me—to the daily lives of Black Americans.

So I didn't rework it. This is what I wrote back then, and I don't think much has changed since then.

Later, my friend the filmmaker commented on my other friend's comment: " 'they eat and bathe and . . . ' It's not naïve, as your writer friend suggests; that's a mantra which, in a racist culture, whites must remind themselves of repeatedly and not take such awareness for granted."

I agree with her. That work never stops.

Chapter 13, #7, p. 224
This is the more exact information that my student Titi, whose family is from Abeokuta, got from their mother and their aunt:

—Ige is the name for someone born with their legs first (which I wasn't).
—I wrote Bose-de but it would be Bosede (or Abosede) for someone born on Sunday.
—Aritetsoma means people who believe in logical thinking (not "anyone is a child").
—For that question, or the more specific one about "girls are okay too," her mother suggested three options: Omodara, which means a child is good (as in it's good to have the child, not that the child is well-behaved) or Omolabi, which means a child has been born.
—Titi also suggested Darasimi, which means God has been good to me.

So my name might be Bosede Omodara Abiodun Friedrich.

Meanwhile, I'm not sure anyone can tell that a newborn has the capacity for logical thinking, so I'll leave that one out, although it's nice for a parent to assign that skill to a newborn!

Chapter 13, #8, p. 225
Jùjú is a style of Nigerian popular music derived from traditional Yoruba percussion. The lead and predominant instrument is the *iya ilu*, the talking drum. The name comes from a Yoruba word *juju* or *jiju* meaning "throwing" or "something being thrown." Its name did <u>not</u> derive from the practice of juju (the use of magic objects common in West Africa, Haiti, Cuba, and some South American nations). Believed to have been created by Abdulrafiu Babatunde King, popularly known as Tunde King, it evolved during the 1920s in urban clubs across Nigeria. The first *jùjú* recordings were by Tunde King and Ojoge Daniel.

CHAPTER 14

Chapter 14, #1, p. 235
An interesting paradox here, labeling the white people's corpulence in this way, since in many parts of Africa being "fat" isn't regarded as we tend to see it (as unattractive, unhealthy, a sign of over-indulgence). Bigness, especially in women, is often valued and praised; being skinny is sometimes a cause for alarm. (African men would sometimes joke with me about white women being too thin: We didn't have anything for them to hang onto.)

But for me, the bigness of some white people there just seemed to indicate their wealth and access to rich foods and came across as something different than Africans who were the same size.

Chapter 14, #2, p. 241
I suppose that having "my own cabin" sounds nice, but this was a cargo ship with no cabins for passengers. I was in an almost bare room; the thin mattress was on a solid steel surface; unless the window was open, it was as hot as an oven; and all night long I was attacked by mosquitos. Nevertheless, at least I could suffer in private.

Chapter 14, #3, p. 241
I was wondering if I could find an image of this ship since I hadn't taken one myself, but on shipspotting.com people post pictures of ships they've seen, including funky rusty cargo ships like the Offin River, which I learned was built in Ghana in 1961. This picture was taken by Malcolm Cranfield in 1974, presumably when Larry was already on it (the second captain, who you'll hear more about later).

Chapter 14, #4, p. 246
It's worthwhile noting one of the many brutal consequences of the British colonial regime. It was remarkable that the museum had those pieces, considering that an estimated 3,000–10,000 objects were stolen when some 1,500 British soldiers destroyed Benin City, the Edo people's capital, during a deadly invasion now known as the "Punitive Expedition"(February 9–18, 1897). They razed the capital, killed civilians, exiled the Oba (king), and then built a golf course on the grounds of the former royal court.

The Kingdom of Benin was effectively destroyed and was made part of Nigeria, a country that was created when the European Powers divided up most of the continent into colonial states in 1864.

The so-called "Benin Bronzes" (in fact often cast in brass) are scattered throughout at least 161 museums around the world. There were numerous prior failed efforts made to have the work returned but in 2021, thanks in large part to the growing awareness that Black Lives Matter, some museums in the United States and Europe have begun to agree to repatriate the stolen goods. The Metropolitan Museum holds at least 160 items traced to the looting. So far, they have only made plans to return three works and otherwise will have a loan agreement with museums in Nigeria—which of course doesn't suffice. In 2021–22, Germany, Scotland and Ireland returned the works they own, which were intended to be displayed at the Museum of West African Art (MOWAA), which was built on the size of the razed Benin City and opened in fall 2024. As of October 2025, internal disputes between representatives from Edo State and the Oba of Benin have kept the works from public display (clay replicas are shown instead) and there are reports that a new museum, the Benin Royal Museum, will be built adjacent to the Oba's residence and will house the original bronzes.

This is a hugely complex situation with many moving parts, so time will tell how many more works are returned and in which museum they will be displayed.

Chapter 14, #5, p. 248
Queen Elizabeth's (and now King Charles's) Benin head of an Oba has an extraordinary story, having been looted twice.

In 1897 it was seized during the Punitive Expedition in Benin. Decades later, it came onto the London art market and was bought by the British colonial government for Nigeria's planned national museum, which opened in 1957.

It made its second journey to London in 1973 as a gift from the Nigerian president General Yakubu Gowon. Apparently, Gowon made a phone call to the home of Ekpo Eyo, the director of the Nigerian National Museum, and said that he wanted a gift for the Queen. The horrified museum director was instructed to allow Gowon to come and choose whatever he wanted. Diplomatic protocol required that the Queen should accept the gift, but that wouldn't have been possible if it were known to be an antiquity seized from Nigeria's leading museum and exported without the required antiquities license. It was deemed to be a "modern replica" and put on a shelf in the Royal Library at Windsor Castle along with such curios as a fragment of the Berlin Wall. And it stayed there, despite the fact that Malcolm McLeod, the British Museum's keeper of ethnography, warned the government that Nigerian politicians were plundering their own collection and said, "General Gowon gave the Queen one of their Benin bronzes last year, an item which was well known to the [British] Museum."

In 2002 it was included in an exhibition at Buckingham Palace of gifts for the Queen. An analysis by John Picton, a West African specialist, proved it to be an original, dating from around 1600. After the Royal Collection Trust (RCT) was told that it was authentic, they moved it from the library in Windsor Castle to the grand vestibule.

I emailed the RCT in 2024 to ask if they planned to offer it to the Museum of West African Art in Nigeria. They wrote back saying, "In response to your query about whether the object would be returned: The Royal Collection is held in trust by the Sovereign for his successors and the nation and is not owned by The King as a private individual. As such, the King would take advice from the RCT, who would consult a range of internal and external stakeholders."

I'm not sure why they have to consult anyone, since it's obvious that it's been stolen at least once, and seemingly twice.

Chapter 14, #6, p. 251

From the ship, I could witness the catastrophic phenomenon: As far as the eye could see—and further—there were an estimated 350 to 450 cargo ships loaded with cement, anchored and idle. How did this happen? Two reasons are given.

1) The port of Lagos was too small to handle increasing traffic, so a lot of cement was ordered for a massive expansion of the docks.
2) There was a pressing need for a lot of new housing which would be built from cement.

   To meet these needs, ministers from five different areas of the government all placed huge orders. HUGE. And then, realizing their error, they refused to honor the payment, so the ships could neither dock and unload nor return to home base with their cargo. As they sat idling for many months, the heat and damp made all the cement turn into . . . *cement*.

Moreover, some of the cement which was unloaded had "gone bad." When people mixed that with good cement, it caused some constructions to collapse—for example, a building at the University of Ife, killing one person and injuring eighteen others.

Needless to say, most of the sailors eventually abandoned their ships. When the problem was finally addressed, nothing could be done to salvage the ships, so many of them were sunk. Others washed up on beaches, creating all sorts of hazards. Over the years, attempts have been made to clear them away, but imagine what it takes to deconstruct a massive tanker.

Chapter 14, #7, p. 252

Larry Dzameh was the second captain of the Offin River. He had arranged my passage and was a gentleman during the voyage, doing what he could to make me comfortable in that old rust bucket.

But he also claimed to have fallen in love with me, and one evening there was a very awkward moment when he started to kiss me and I hurriedly withdrew. I wasn't scared; I just felt bad about disappointing him. And I wasn't surprised when he proposed marriage, having already been proposed to so many times during my trip.

I didn't see him again in Ghana, but we had an ongoing correspondence, and I agreed to meet him when his ship docked in New York a year later. I felt nervous because of lying to him about my "boyfriend" (this was 1977, after all) but we spent a nice day and then he wrote one final letter telling me that although it made him sad, he understood why he should back off since I had a boyfriend. Always the gentleman.

I haven't been able to find him through social media or the shipping line. Maybe in these more enlightened times I could explain the dilemma I had been in and why I couldn't come out to him. Mostly I would love to know that he had gotten married and was happy.

CHAPTER 15

Chapter 15, #1, p. 255

I have no idea where I stayed in Accra; probably in a cheap hotel since I refer to it as a dingy room. And from the reference to Friday, this must have been my first night in town. God only knows how I ended up at the party I describe, but I was saying yes to any possibility of socializing!

Chapter 15, #2, p. 255

Being alone, I would often strike up a conversation wherever I came across some seeming-American; at other times, they would approach me. In Ghana, I also started encountering Peace Corps Volunteers. (PCVs were also active then in Niger and Togo, but I didn't meet any in those countries.)

President John F. Kennedy announced the formation of the Peace Corps on March 1, 1961. Of the countries I visited, the Peace Corp still operates in Ghana, Burkina Faso, and Togo. Due to safety concerns, it suspended operations in Niger in 2011 and Mali in 2015. It was never in Nigeria or the Ivory Coast.

I'd never met a PCV before, but I had toyed with the idea of joining up. The trip gave me an interesting glimpse into their world and made a persuasive case against ever joining!

Chapter 15, #3, p. 255

Akua'ba are wooden ritual fertility dolls from Ghana and nearby areas. The best known *akua'ba* are those of the Ashanti people which have large, disc-like heads. Other tribes in the region have their own distinctive styles. Traditionally, these dolls are carried on the back of a woman either hoping to conceive a child or to ensure the attractiveness of the child being carried. When not in active use, the *akua'ba* is ritually washed and cared for.

Chapter 15, #4, p. 256

On January 13, 1972, **General Ignatius Kutu Acheampong** (1931 – 1979) led a coup d'état to overthrow the democratically elected government of the Progress Party and its leader, Dr. Kofi Busia. Acheampong ruled Ghana until July 5, 1978, when he was deposed in a palace coup. On June 26, 1979, he was executed by firing squad, together with two other former Heads of State and five other senior military officers following the 4th of June revolution that brought Flight Lieutenant Jerry Rawlings and the AFRC (Armed Forces Revolutionary Council) to power.

Chapter 15, #5, p. 260

Gail and I were getting ready to leave Accra, so I bade farewell to Sam. I didn't see him when I came back to Accra, but he wrote me five long letters. He was a remarkable guy, so ambitious, an aspiring entrepreneur, and his letters detailed how we were going to go into business together. They also told me about the several times he was robbed, most grievously at a hotel in Monrovia where all his money was stolen—amounting in current dollars to almost $2,000 —as well as his seaman's papers.

Back home, I imagined for a few moments that we could create our transcontinental import-export business, but I was a poor twenty-one-year-old with no clue about how to do such a thing, so our plans just died on the vine. While writing the book, I tried to track him down, but I didn't have any luck finding him—or his sister, who had been living in NY.

CHAPTER 16

Chapter 16, #1, p. 267

Unfortunately, the transatlantic trade of enslaved Africans—about which Americans probably know the most—was not the only one, although it was the largest in volume and intensity. As Elikia M'Bokolo wrote in *Le Monde diplomatique*: "The African continent was bled of its human resources via all possible routes. Across the Sahara, through the Red Sea, from the Indian Ocean ports and across the Atlantic. There were at least ten centuries of slavery for the benefit of the Muslim countries: from the ninth to the nineteenth century, four million enslaved people were exported via the Red Sea, another four million through the Swahili ports of the Indian Ocean, perhaps as many as nine million along the trans-Saharan caravan route, and eleven to twenty million (depending on the author) across the Atlantic Ocean."

The transatlantic trade of enslaved people began in 1526 with the first Portuguese voyage to sell enslaved people to Brazil, and it continued for three hundred years. By the peak of the trade in human beings and gold in the 1800s, there were more than fifty forts along the coast of Ghana (referred to as the Gold Coast when it was a British colony). This was the last stop for enslaved Africans being shipped to the Americas, who had often been sold and resold as slaves within Africa before meeting this even more brutal and permanent extraction from their homes and families.

On March 25, 1807, the Abolition of the Slave Trade Act entered the statute books in the UK, making the slave trade illegal throughout the British colonies, but trafficking between the Caribbean islands continued until 1811—and another source says that the trade of African people to Brazil and Cuba continued until the 1860s. In the United States, with over four million enslaved people in the South, some Southern congressmen joined with the North in voting for abolition. The 1807 Act became effective on January 1, 1808, which stopped the legal flow of new Africans into this country, but the practice of slavery continued in much of the United States until 1865; enslaved people continued to be bought and sold within the Southern states, and illegal smuggling also continued throughout those years.

The slave fort in Dixcove was named Fort Metal Cross. A *New York Times* story from 1990 mentions that it has "a guesthouse for low-budget travelers only," which I was glad to find as a fact because I was incredulous about my journal reference to that aspect of it. About twenty-five remain. Some have been maintained as historical sites where tourists can learn about the slave trade, while others have been retrofitted to serve as post offices and other functional offices. One of them, Osu Castle (a.k.a. Christiansborg Castle or Fort Christiansborg) is the seat of government in Ghana.

Chapter 16, #2, p. 270

Bad news: I was hoping that the situation would be much improved four decades later, but globally, women continue to trail men in education, economic opportunity and political leadership. According to the 2021 Global Gender Gap Index, Ghana ranks 117th out of 156 countries—the twenty-third in sub-Saharan Africa—and women's income in Ghana is just 29.2 percent of men's, second worst on the continent after Mali (28.1 percent).

Ghana's 2021 census found that while women outnumber men in the service sector, they are underrepresented at management levels. More females than males have never attended school and lack literacy, and they still lag behind in ownership of key assets and financial autonomy. Among parliamentarians in Ghana, only 14.6 percent are women, and among assembly members, only 3.6 percent are women.

Ghana's constitution prohibits gender discrimination and mandates "reasonable regional and gender balance in recruitment and appointment to public offices" and its long-awaited Affirmative Action Act, which calls for women to achieve parity in the public sphere by 2030, was finally passed in September 2024. Strong majorities of citizens express support for women's right to equality in hiring, land ownership, and political leadership, but sizeable minorities also consider it likely that female candidates for elective office might suffer criticism, harassment, or family problems.

It isn't much better in Nigeria. Women have remained largely underrepresented in the realm of political power throughout Nigerian history. Since the beginning of electoral democracy in 1999, public campaigns, proposed legislative reforms, and internal measures within political parties have attempted to address the gaping gender imbalance, yet in Nigeria's most recent general elections women's representation in office had not only failed to increase, but appears to be in decline. A 2019 report by the Centre for the Development of Democracy and Human Rights revealed that women won less than 5 percent of all contested seats and were restricted to only 17 percent of all ministerial appointments. Current statistics show a paltry 11.2 percent female membership in both chambers of the Ninth National Assembly. Of the thirty-six states of Nigeria, five states did not field a woman candidate for the Senate, while one State did not field any woman for the House of Representatives.

Chapter 16, #3, p. 275

I had already seen instances of public shaming (like everyone surrounding a thief in the market) and I was impressed by this way of bringing the person into line without causing any physical harm. It was now amazing to find myself in that position. Having my breasts slapped . . . Hmm . . . Not to be forgotten, and the only response was to scurry away.

Chapter 16, #4, p. 275

Ayi Kwei Armah was born in Takoradi, Ghana in 1939, when the country was still a British colony. (On March 6, 1957, Ghana became the first colonial African country to win the struggle for sovereignty.) He was educated in local mission schools before leaving for the United States in 1959 to complete his secondary education at Groton School and, later, his BA at Harvard University. Armah is the author of seven novels, including *The Beautyful Ones Are Not Yet Born* (1968), and numerous short stories. His work often grapples with the age of colonialism, the tensions between tradition and modernity, and the crises of moral and spiritual faith in Ghana.

Chapter 16, #5, p. 276

From 1824–1900 there were several wars fought by the Ashanti against the British, who were trying to control—i.e., steal—their territory because of its gold deposits.

My first thought on reading that journal comment was, "How weird!!" Did the wall texts in the museum describe the British as "courageous"? I would only describe them as rapacious.

Second weirdness is the adjectives I use to describe the Ghanaians who fought on the side of the British. Perhaps I call them slaves because the wall text said they were enslaved people who were forced to fight with the British? And one might call them traitorous if one thought that they were fighting against their own people, but I did some googling and learned that the African troops/"slaves" were mainly from other tribes in the region (like the Fante) who were sometimes attacked by the Ashanti and therefore wanted to join the British forces to put a stop to those raids.

Finally, calling them Ghanaians is getting ahead of things. That area was called the Gold Coast when it was a British Crown Colony and was only named Ghana after independence.

A few weeks later at another museum I learned more about who was doing the fighting; see Chapter 18, note #2.

CHAPTER 17

Chapter 17, #1, p. 279

Efua Theodora Sutherland (1924–1996), born in Cape Coast, was a Ghanaian playwright, director, dramatist, children's author, poet, educationalist, researcher, and cultural activist. She founded the Ghana Drama Studio, the Ghana Society of Writers, the Ghana Experimental Theatre, and a community project called the Kodzidan (Story House). She also spearheaded an African publishing house, establishing the company Afram Publications in the 1970s. Sutherland's works include the plays *Foriwa* (1962), *Edufa* (1967), and *The Marriage of Anansewa* (1975), along with a 1960 photo essay *Playtime in Africa*, co-authored with Willis E. Bell, which made an argument for the necessity of play in children's development. In 1980, Sutherland proposed a pan-African theater festival to be held in Ghana. This became the biennial Pan-African Historical Festival known as PANAFEST, first held in 1992 and continuing to this day.

Chapter 17, #2, p. 281

Gnassingbé Eyadéma (born Étienne Gnassingbé) (1935–2005) was the President of Togo from 1967 until his death in 2005. He participated in two successful military coups, in January 1963 and January 1967, and became President on April 14, 1967. As President, he created a political party, the Rally of the Togolese People (RPT), and headed an anti-communist single-party regime until the early 1990s. Reforms lead to multiparty elections, but he consolidated power and won elections in 1993, 1998, and 2003. The opposition boycotted the 1993 election and denounced the 1998 and 2003 election results as fraudulent. At the time of his death, Eyadéma was the longest-serving ruler in Africa. Thirty-eight years.

Eyadéma had an extensive personality cult including, but not limited to, an entourage of one thousand women who sang and danced in praise of him; portraits which adorned most stores; $20 wristwatches with his portrait, which disappeared and re-appeared every fifteen seconds; and the comic book depicting him as a superhero with powers of invulnerability and super strength.

As for the comic book: Serge Saint-Michel did other editions about African leaders, all published by the Afrique Biblio-Club, including ones about Mobutu Sese Seko, Leopold Senghor and Felix Houphouet-Boigny. I cannot find any credit for who did the artwork.

Chapter 17, #3, p. 289

The reference to my "funny body" was about me being "fat" in an odd way: the left side of my belly, ribs and breast stuck out noticeably from the right. When I came home, they discovered a thirteen-pound cyst on my spleen which had been growing for many years, which I had just ascribed to being "built funny." The surgeon who removed it said that it could have hemorrhaged at any time, leading to certain death if that had occurred while I was in any of the remote places on my trip.

Chapter 17, #4, p. 291

The Gambaga Scarp is a line of cliffs which form the elevated northern boundary of the Volta River basin and the eastern section of the granite plateaus of Wa and Mamprusi. To the south is another narrow plateau, followed by a gradual descent to the surrounding land. Because of the elevation (1,000–1,500 feet), the climate is relatively cool and moist.

Chapter 17, #5, p. 294

Shirley Temple (Black) appeared in forty-three films between the ages of three and twenty-one. She retired from film in 1950 at the age of twenty-two. Temple played alongside many leading men, but her favorite costar was the great Black American tap dancer Bill "Bojangles" Robinson, with whom she appeared in four films.

In 1969, when Temple was forty-one years old, President Richard Nixon appointed her as a US delegate to the United Nations. During her twenty-three-year diplomatic career, Temple became the first woman to serve as US ambassador to Ghana, the first woman chief of protocol at the State Department and the first woman US ambassador to what was then Czechoslovakia, where she witnessed the country's 1989 Velvet Revolution and the fall of the Communist regime.

In June 1972, she took on one of the biggest roles of her life: United States delegate to the annual United Nations Conference on the Human Environment, held for the first time that year in Stockholm. Less well known is her pioneering involvement in planning and executing the conference: Temple took over as leader when the US delegation's chairman left the conference's second preparatory meeting early. While other American leaders sought out traditional European allies, Temple forged connections with representatives from developing countries "from Afghanistan to Zambia," as she notes in her memoir.

One of Stockholm's most prescient undertakings was a petition initiated by Margaret Mead and Barbara Ward and championed by Temple which called for a "radical change" in the number of women involved in environmental policymaking decisions. The document noted that among the 113 nations in attendance, only eleven delegations included even one woman. Temple took that gender imbalance and made it international news: "Shirley Temple Black Backs Woman Power," the Associated Press reported when the petition circulated.

CHAPTER 18

Chapter 18, #1, p. 300
Oh lordy, lordy: the memory of bringing home these dresses and blouses for my various people! They tried to be nice, but none of them would ever wear something that were so outside the norm of how white American women dressed. I meant well and was enthusiastic about the items after having admired all the types of dresses and blouses, but yeah . . . I ended up wearing what they politely admitted they simply couldn't.

Chapter 18, #2, p. 301
I'm surprised that she wasn't mentioned at the Accra National Museum in their account of the wars against the British. Or maybe I missed it?

There were several Anglo-Ashanti Wars between 1824 and 1900. In the final one, which began on March 28, 1900, **Yaa Asantewaa**—who was then sixty years old—led a rebellion called the War of the Golden Stool, also known as the Yaa Asantewaa War. More than 2,000 Ashanti and 1,000 British and Allied troops were killed. (Both totals were higher than from all previous Anglo-Ashanti wars combined.) The war ended, however, after six months. Yaa Asantewaa was captured by the British in 1901 and quickly exiled to the Seychelles, where she died in 1921 at age eighty-one—but the British never captured the Golden Stool.

Wilhelmina J. Donkoh once wrote; "The world has been blessed with numerous women of great courage. These include Queen Idia of Benin, Queen Amina of Zaria, Queen Ndeta Yalla of Senegal, Nongqawuse of the Republic of South Africa, Queen of the Ndongo of Angola, Kimpa Vita of Kongo, Rosa Luxemburg of Poland, Martha Schad of Augsburg, Queen Elisabeth of Great Britain and a host of other brave women leaders. Nana Yaa Asantewaa was the most prominent of the lot, in the African context. Her courage to fight the British occupation in West Africa in spite of an initially unmotivated front put up by the Ghanaian men puts her at the top of Africa's greatest female leaders."

The Asantehene (King of all Asante) is the absolute monarch of the historical Kingdom of Asante and Asanteman, which comprises the Ashanti region in southern Ghana, the homeland of the Asante people. He is also the titular ruler of Kumasi, capital of Asante. Between the seventeeth and twentieth centuries, the Asante Empire and Confederacy comprised part of present-day Asanteman and portions of present-day eastern Côte d'Ivoire.

The Asante royal house traces its line to the Oyoko (an *abusua*, or "clan") Abohyen Dynasty of Nana Twum and the Bretuo Dynasty of Osei Tutu Opemsoo, who formed the Empire of Asante in 1701 and was crowned Asantehene.

The Asantehene is traditionally enthroned on a golden stool known as the *Sika 'dwa*, and the office is sometimes referred to by this name. The current Asantehene is Otumfuo Nana Osei Tutu II, born Nana Kwaku Dua, who ascended as the sixteenth Asante king in April 1999.

Chapter 18, #3, p. 303
Ama Ata Aidoo (1942–2023) was a Ghanaian author, poet, playwright, politician, and academic who has been hailed as one of Africa's leading literary lights as well as one of its most influential feminists. In 2000, she established the Mbaasem Foundation in Accra to promote the work of African women writers. Throughout her career, Aidoo sought to illuminate the paradoxes faced by modern African women still burdened by the legacies of colonialism. She is most known for her novel, *Our Sister Killjoy, or Reflections From a Black-Eyed Squint* (1977), which explores such themes as diaspora and postcolonialism, and her play *The Dilemma of a Ghost*, which takes cultural dislocation as a prominent theme. In 1992, she won the Commonwealth Writers' Prize for her novel Changes.

Aidoo was a major Pan-Africanist voice who spoke passionately about the centuries of exploitation of the continent's natural resources and people. "Since we met you people five hundred years ago, now look at us," she said in an interview with a French journalist in 1987, later sampled in the 2020 song "Monsters You Made" by the Nigerian Afrobeats star Burna Boy. "We've given everything, you are still taking. I mean where will the whole Western world be without us Africans? Our cocoa, timber, gold, diamond, platinum. Everything you have is us," she continued. "I am not saying it. It's a fact. And in return for all these, what have we got? Nothing."

Chapter 18, #4, p. 303
My friend the writer said I should delete the previous mention of Mimi because it's "a whole other story." She's partly right: In a book about my travels through West Africa, musings about my faraway girlfriend don't advance the narrative. But the musing was done by a very young woman who had come out less than a year before. Everything about being a dyke was fresh (and scary), and being in a place where it couldn't be talked about made the experience more vivid and intensified

my thoughts of home.

So yes: During the trip, part of me was that crazy young woman who put herself in a lot of unexpected situations and recorded those in the journal. But I was also lonesome and lovesick Su, who didn't understand why she'd left her first chance at love (and sex!) behind, and that belonged as much to my experience, and the journal, as when I hitched a ride from point A to point B.

Chapter 18, #5, p. 303

Milo, the "Tonic Food Drink" is still being sold by Nestlé. They say: "Milo contains Vitamin B2, B3, B6, B12, Vitamin C and iron which contribute to the reduction of tiredness and fatigue. A nutritious breakfast coupled with an active and healthy lifestyle can help your child stay active and focused." Others say: "Because Milo powder does contain useful nutrients, it may be a better choice than other sweetened or diet drinks when made mainly with water but remember that a glass of Milo made per the instructions has nearly two teaspoons of sugar."

Chapter 18, #6, p. 304

Négritude is a framework of critique and literary theory developed mainly by francophone intellectuals, writers, and politicians of the African diaspora during the 1930s. Its initiators included the poet Aimé Césaire from Martinique, Léopold Sédar Senghor (the first President of Senegal), and Léon Damas of French Guiana. Négritude intellectuals disavowed colonialism and argued for the importance of a Pan-African racial identity among people of African descent worldwide. Négritude intellectuals employed Marxist political philosophy in the Black radical tradition.

Chapter 18, #7, p. 305

My friend the writer asked me how I could know they were feeling sorrow. Good question. I suppose that my time there led me to think that they would be sorrowful about such displays. Or maybe I was just projecting because a scene like that would certainly make me sorrowful.

Chapter 18, #8, p. 305

Highlife originated in Ghana early in the twentieth century. It uses the melodic and main rhythmic structures of traditional Akan music but is played with Western instruments. In the 1920s, Ghanaian musicians combined foreign influences like the foxtrot and calypso with Ghanaian rhythms like *osibisaba* (Fante). Highlife was associated with the local African aristocracy during the colonial period, and was played by numerous bands including the Jazz Kings, Cape Coast Sugar Babies, and The Accra Orchestra. E. T. (Emmanuel Tettey) Mensah (1919–1996), considered "the King of Highlife," was active from the 1930s through the 1980s. His fame skyrocketed after he appeared with Louis Armstrong in Accra in 1956.

Chapter 18, #9, p. 306

Yes, until I got married in 2013 to the woman I met in 1979. We never planned to get married, but the passage of the Marriage Equality Act in New Jersey in 2013 invalidated domestic partnership for the insurance policy I had via my job in that state. But I still call her my partner. After a lifetime of not picturing myself married, "wife" will always sound foreign to me.

Chapter 18, #10, p. 319

Amílcar Lopes da Costa Cabral (1924 –1973) was a Bissau-Guinean and Cape Verdean agricultural engineer, Pan-Africanist, intellectual, poet, diplomat and one of Africa's foremost anti-colonial leaders. He was assassinated on January 20, 1973, about eight months before Guinea-Bissau's unilateral declaration of independence.

CHAPTER 19

Chapter 19, #1, p. 323

My mother and my paternal grandfather were both born in Germany (though both spent most of their lives in America) and both of them embodied to a fair degree what I just described. My background and upbringing made me a sensitive towards all things German, including my very mixed feelings about their seeming obsession with order and cleanliness. But as we know, national stereotypes are just generalizations, about which there are many exceptions. Some Germans are slobs, and some non-Germans are very "German."

Chapter 19, #2, p. 332

Peter Hill Beard (1938–2020) was an American artist, photographer, diarist, and writer who lived and worked in New York City; Montauk, NY; and Kenya. His photographs of Africa, African animals, and the journals that often integrated his photographs have been widely shown and published since the 1960s.

The irony of me writing about him like that in the journal is that when I was back in NY, I had a version of this photograph by him on my studio wall for many years (seen here in 1980). So, although I objected to some of the ways in which he represented African women, I was very attached to this image; she was so beautiful and looked so strong and happy.

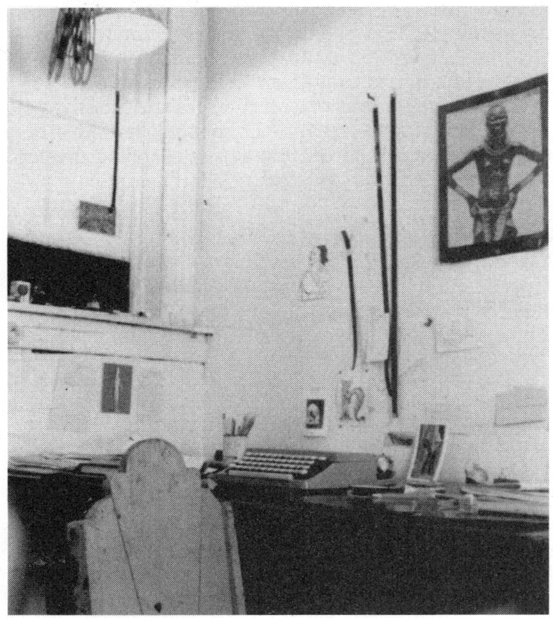

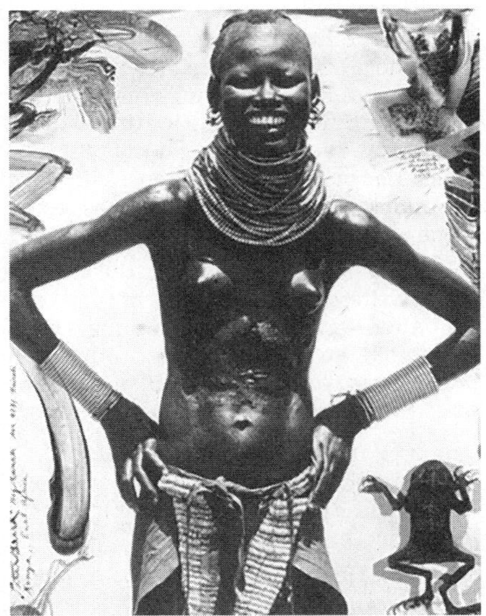

Chapter 19, #3, p. 335
For any of you lucky enough to not know yet what excision is, I'm sorry to be the bearer of such bad news. It's the practice of cutting out the clitoris. There are varying degrees of awfulness. Some groups, in addition to performing a clitoridectomy, also do "infibulation," in which the labia are sewn shut so that the man often has to use a knife before (or for) penetrating the woman.

This has been done to millions of women and is still being done in 2024.

It used to be referred to as "female circumcision"—a dishonest false equivalency. Male circumcision involves removing the foreskin, not the penis. A man would have to have his penis cut off for this term to be equivalent to what is done to women. And circumcised men still have orgasms.

With more activism about the issue, the term "female genital mutilation" (FGM) was coined and is now used most of the time, although not by people who still would make a case for this being a normal "cultural practice." For anyone who still thinks this is acceptable, I recommend reading Nawal El Sadawi's 1977 book, *The Hidden Face of Eve: Women in the Arab World*. It describes the experience in gruesome detail because it was inflicted on her at age six.

FGM is one of the great crimes against humanity. According to a recent World Health Organization report, "More than 200 million girls and women alive today have been cut in thirty countries in Africa, the Middle East and Asia where FGM is concentrated." Yes. More than 200 million women are currently living out their lives without experiencing some basic/essential things: sex without extreme pain, and sex which leads to orgasm.

FGM is a feminist issue. It is an alleged "cultural practice" used to control women, and the excuse of "we've always done it" is no reason to continue doing it. In the USA, we've had our own misogynistic "cultural practices" to overturn; it wasn't that long ago that women couldn't vote, own property, open a credit card account, or hold any number of high-powered jobs. But excision goes far beyond any of these.

A few years after my trip, I went to the U.N. Commission for Women and got a three-hundred-page report full of first-person accounts by women who had been excised and infibulated and also full of justifications by women and men for continuing the practice. It was harrowing to read and made me understand much more about what the price was for women, both physically and psychologically.

There are laws against torture, yet there are doctors in the USA (and Europe) who still perform this in a surgical setting "so that it's safer and more hygienic." Some countries, responding to public pressure, have outlawed it. Some still haven't. The great Senegalese filmmaker Ousmane Sembène very courageously made a film about it, *Moolaadé*, in 2004.

Chapter 19, #4, p. 337

I recall reading some years after my trip about this problem, and how absurd it was that the foreign aid groups and corporations helping Africans start businesses were only training the men, when everyone there knows that it has always been the women who handle the money, who run the markets, who usually are the businesswomen.

That awareness has slowly started to have an impact. Funding for women-led businesses throughout the continent, and particularly women-led startups, it isn't yet at all on par with the funding for men, but the numbers are improving. The Biden administration reported that the US International Development Finance Corporation (DFC) announced $358 million of new investments, including projects under DFC's 2X Women's Initiative, which has catalyzed billions of dollars of projects owned by women, led by women, or empowering women.

But the specifics from country to country are too complex to fit into a chapter note.

CHAPTER 20

Chapter 20, #1, p. 341

My friend the writer wondered whose opinion that was: Africans? Others?

I would say that it was held by many foreigners who consider a comparison to Europe to be a compliment, but I also heard it at times from Africans. They may or may not have been able to make the comparison from direct experience, but they would surely be aware of it as a commonly held prejudice. If they wanted to compliment a city to a foreigner, they could employ this comparison as a sure-fire way to make the person like the place.

Chapter 20, #2, p. 345

The "Black Sisters" name is unrelated to being Black. Their congregation originates from a late Middle Ages movement called "Cellites" which originated in the Rhineland, spread rapidly through the Low Countries and was devoted to the ideal of poverty. They took the name "Black Sisters" because the Black Plague was rampant in Europe and they were dedicated to treating people in need.

Chapter 20, #3, p. 346

It's difficult to separate a worthy impulse—honoring all cultures and recognizing how many cultures have been oppressed by various outsiders—from an indefensible one—romanticizing and even lionizing all aspects of daily life for people from those cultures. The latter can blind them to people's hardships and make them turn those hardships into something "authentic," untouchable, beyond question or critique.

There was a fascinating story in *The New York Times* a few years ago which I now cannot find, despite endless searching. It described the experiences of a people (in the Amazon, I think) who had only just emerged from the forest—perhaps because of logging or some other encroachment—and who had been entirely unknown to others before they emerged.

One remark from a woman in the group made a lasting impression on me. They were nomadic hunter-gatherers, and she described the pain she suffered from walking barefoot for many hours a day. She said that she liked not having to always be on the move now, that she could rest and that her feet didn't hurt anymore.

As for my experiences in Africa, both during this trip and when I was working in Kenya in 2013: It was quite common to meet people who only ate two meals a day—which often had far fewer calories or protein than one needs—and also to meet people who only ate one meal a day. While doing hard work. Or attending school.

So? "Do unto others as you would have them do unto you," and wish for others all the things that you have and that you take for granted. That way you won't think that living in harsh conditions without enough food for your family is "authentic." It's deprivation, and no one deserves to live with that.

Chapter 20, #4, p. 346

Lincoln Theodore Monroe Andrew Perry (1902–1985) was of Jamaican and Bahamian descent. By the age of 20 he was a vaudeville performer and the manager of a traveling carnival show. He and his partner decided to adopt the names "Step" and "Fetchit" for their vaudeville act from a racehorse named "Step and Fetch It." When Perry became a solo act, he combined the names to create his professional name, Stepin Fetchit.

Perry parlayed the persona into a successful film career, becoming the first Black actor to earn $1 million and the first one to receive featured screen credit in a film. He signed a five-year studio contract in 1927. His highest profile was during the 1930s in films and on stage, when his persona of

Stepin Fetchit was billed as the "Laziest Man in the World." Perry had a concurrent career writing for *The Chicago Defender*, one of the earliest and most influential Black newspapers in America.

His film career slowed after 1939 and nearly stopped after 1953 because Black Americans considered his persona to be an embarrassing and harmful anachronism. However, the Stepin Fetchit character has undergone a re-evaluation by some scholars in recent times, who view him as an embodiment of the trickster archetype.

Chapter 20, #5, p. 347

The Senufo live primarily in the areas of northern Ivory Coast, southeastern Mali and western Burkina Faso.

As a combined art history & studio art major at Oberlin, I did an independent study course in African art. No one in the art history department specialized in any African art except Egyptian—the one African culture that was studied by the Euro-and Asia-centric art historians back then.

They agreed that I could be advised by Professor Saaka, the Ghanaian political scientist with whom I'd taken courses. I guess they figured, "What the hell, he's from Africa, he's bound to know something about it . . . "

1 + 1 = nonsense.

He laughed and said he knew nothing about African art—or any other art—but kindly agreed to be my advisor. I wrote a fifty-page paper about Senufo masks and sculptures. He said it was interesting, but we both knew how preposterous the situation was.

As for being amazed at seeing a contemporary woman who looked like a classic Senufo sculpture: the same thing happened to me once when I emerged from the National Gallery in Berlin and recognized that the faces of contemporary Germans were so reminiscent of their portraits from hundreds of years ago. Art often holds up a wonderful mirror to humanity.

Chapter 20, #6, p. 348

Some reason for my attitude towards these women has to do with how my mother lived as an expat wife whose husband's work took her into two hardship environments. She didn't do recreational shopping and wear Cacharel when we were in Mexico and India because my father insisted that we live as the locals do, and I think in some ways my mother preferred that. She probably would have disliked and felt intimidated by the fancy wives at the local expat clubs, and she was contending with a workload that didn't leave room for afternoon teas or cocktail parties. As a little kid, I'm sure I picked up on their disdain for, or distance from, that classic expat lifestyle and all that it implied.

And her experience as an immigrant probably contributed to her being such a solid correspondent, even if a letter she wrote only got to me a month or two later.

Chapter 20, #7, p. 349

Born in Kankan, Guinea, **Ibrahima Baba Kake** (1938–1994) studied at the University of Dakar and then traveled to Paris in the mid-60s, where he was the producer of the show *Mémoire d'un continent* on RFI and the director of collections at Nouvelles Editions Africaines. Kake was a major historian of African history and culture, writing several volumes of nonfiction including including *Afrique, berceau de l'humanité: préhistoire*, the 4 volume *Journal de l'Afrique*; and *Sékou Touré, le héros et le tyran*.

Chapter 20, #8, p. 350

Cocody is one of the ten urban communes of Abidjan. It is upmarket, with an abundance of mansions where most of the wealthy businesspeople, ambassadors, and other affluent people live. The district is home to the embassy of France, the Université Félix Houphouët-Boigny, the Hotel Ivoire (which for a long time was the only African hotel to have a skating rink) and, since 2009, the largest US embassy in West Africa.

Treichville is one of the other urban communes, which Wikipedia describes as "lively." When I was there, it was a dirt-poor area, crammed with people living in mostly squalid conditions, but with a huge market and certainly not with the eerie, deserted character of the wealthy neighborhoods. In all the cities I visited, there were the gated, upscale neighborhoods and then the rest, which weren't.

CHAPTER 21

Chapter 21, #1, p. 356

The Bambara are a Mandinka people native to much of West Africa, primarily southern Mali, Guinea, Burkina Faso and Senegal and are associated with the historic Bambara Empire. Today they make up the largest Mandinka group in Mali, with 80 percent of the population speaking the Bambara language, regardless of ethnicity.

Chiwara (also spelled Chi Wara or Tyiwara) is the antelope spirit that taught humans how to cultivate the land. According to Bambara legend, Chiwara used his antlers to dig into the earth and his hoofs to cover the seeds. Bambara farms became so bountiful that they had too much corn for their own use, so they wasted it, thinking it was so easy to cultivate. Chiwara grew disappointed and buried himself in the earth. The elders regretted losing him and ordered that a mask be made to honor him. Since then, many elaborate masks have been created; these are reserved for the best and fastest workers of the land. It is a great honor to wear the mask and dance the ceremonial dance, which represents both genders and carries with it moral lessons and religious symbolism.

Chapter 21, #2, p. 360

I blur a crucial distinction in referring to the South Side as the place where I grew up. Technically, the South Side encompassed much more than my one area of it, called South Shore. Parts of it were primarily white ("my family and friends" refers to the white people I knew, many of them Irish Catholic families). Other areas were largely Black middle- and working class. For example, Michelle Obama grew up about twenty blocks from our apartment building. On the South Side, you only had to travel a short distance to enter a neighborhood with a different community.

In my experience, it was a valuable environment in which to be raised. At that time, the two communities didn't have a lot of crossover, but especially during high school I had an alternative to the all-white enclave because the student body was much more diverse, and increasingly so as white flight sped up.

Meanwhile, there was a landmark Supreme Court case that bears directly on this situation. After racially restrictive covenants were declared unconstitutional by *Shelley v. Kraemer* (1948), Black families began to move out of overcrowded Black neighborhoods into South Shore. The South Shore Commission initiated a program they called "managed integration" to check the physical decline of the community and achieve racial balance. The initiative was largely unsuccessful in achieving the latter goal, and some white residents resisted this change through violence against Blacks who moved into the neighborhood. In 1960, the population was 90 percent white and 10 percent Black. By 1970, the population was 69 percent Black and 28 percent white, and by 1980, the population was 94 percent Black. By the late 1990s South Shore had developed into a middle-class Black community. Developers built a shopping plaza at Seventy-First and Jeffery Boulevard, and the cultural life of the area was enhanced when the Park District purchased the waning South Shore Country Club in 1972 and converted it into a cultural center. The South Shore Current Magazine was launched with a mission to share the "Good News from Chicago's Cultural Soul Coast."

Chapter 21, #3, p. 360

"Not all was sunny with Schweitzer's social commentary. In recent years, many have taken him to task for decidedly paternalistic and racist descriptions of his African patients that would offend many a 21st century observer. For example, he once said, 'The African is indeed my brother, but my junior brother.' On other occasions, he opined, 'I let the Africans pick all the fruit they want. You see, the Good Lord has protected the trees. He made the Africans too lazy to pick them bare.' The list, alas, goes on and his prejudices are difficult, if not impossible, to ignore." (From "Dr. Albert Schweitzer, a renowned medical missionary with a complicated history" by Dr. Howard Markel on the *PBS Newshour* website.

Chapter 21, #4, p. 361

I'm saying Black Africa (a commonly used term) to distinguish the area of the continent below the Sahara from that in the north, which is more consistently Arabic in ethnicity, therefore not as populated by Blacks as is sub-Saharan Africa. Obviously, this is a simple verbal convenience for referring to the complex, multi-faceted population throughout the vast continent.

CHAPTER 22

Chapter 22, #1, p. 366

I knew something about American racism before I left home, and something about the devastating effects of colonialism in so many African countries. I learned much more about the latter during my time on the continent. As for the former, I certainly learned something about what it means to be a minority.

As a white person in America, one can try one's best to understand how it is for Blacks to be so often in the minority—the only two in a class, the only one at a party, the only three in an office—but it isn't possible to really <u>know</u> that until you're the only one in the room.

Which I often was: the only white on a bus, on a truck, in a house, in a shop. When that happens, you know that you're being seen as someone apart from the rest—because you are. But it's ridiculous to say that one can "really know that" because—at least from my experience in America—how one is seen as a white person in a majority Black crowd is never the same as how a Black person is seen when they're in a majority all-white crowd, given the legacy of white supremacy and white privilege.

But, without minimizing that disparity, it's fair to say it's difficult for a person of any race or ethnicity to not be at least somewhat/sometimes in the presence of those who look like them. One can't help feeling apart, somewhat alone and out on a limb. So, after many months spent almost entirely in the company of Black Africans, it makes sense that I would find some respite in being around others who looked even a little like me, even though our cultural & ethnic differences meant that it was foolish of me to imagine some actual resemblance or shared viewpoints and experiences.

Chapter 22, #2, p. 367

Hassan II (1929–1999) was King of Morocco from 1961 until his death in 1999. A member of the Alaouite dynasty, he was the eldest son of Mohammed V, Sultan, then King of Morocco. Hassan was one of the most severe rulers of Morocco, an autocrat who was widely accused of authoritarian practices, particularly during the Years of Lead (from the 1960s–1980s), which were marked by state violence and repression against political dissidents and pro-democracy activists.

Chapter 22, #3, p. 372

Well, I'm not sitting here "richly hued," but at least the couch in my studio lives up to that promise, yes? I had so much fun choosing the combination of fabrics to work with.

That couch is in a house that my partner and I bought when I was fifty-six. I had always fantasized about having a "Moroccan room" and now I thought I could finally create one. We went to a store that sells genuine Moroccan tiles, and I started crying when I learned that a single border above the tub would cost $700. Instead, I got the cheapest American tile and fashioned a new pattern by cutting apart rows to offset the checkerboard. It's not Moroccan, but at least it's visually playful and emulates, very modestly, their inventive way with pattern. And of course, there's no end to wonderful African wax-print fabric, like this one I found at a store in my neighborhood, out of which I made a pillow.

Chapter 22, #4, p. 379

The Shakespeare and Company bookstore was founded in 1919 by Sylvia Beach and her life partner, Adrienne Monnier, and it's still open for business today. It was famous among lesbians for being a dyke-centric environment in which writers like Djuna Barnes would congregate. To the non-lesbian world, it was famous because all the major male writers of the time gathered there. But perhaps most famously it was Sylvia Beach, among all the publishers in Paris or anywhere else, who had the balls to publish Joyce's *Ulysses*—and to first edit it with him. Put that in your, "Wow, what women have done . . . " pipe and smoke it.

Thanks and Acknowledgments

There are many phases of work in putting together a book like this, and numerous people helped over the past nine years. I'm very grateful to all of them. But I first had to go on the journey, and I couldn't have done it without the support and encouragement of my mother Lore, my father Paul, and Professor Yakubu Saaka.

Meanwhile, the journey would have been entirely different if it weren't for the generosity of all the people who took me into their homes, fed me, gave me a bed, provided company during times that were often quite lonely, and gave me all sorts of useful information about the town I was in and how to get to the next one. I'm still in awe of how kind and helpful they were.

My first step was to transcribe the journals, and Ariel Hahn began that work. Alas, my handwriting is almost illegible, so we soon agreed that I should do the rest, but her first efforts allowed me to see what was possible.

The photographs I took required high-resolution scans, which I was able to do for free at the Digital Learning Lab in the McGraw Center for Teaching and Learning at Princeton University with the expert help of Sorat Tungkasiri and Daniel Claro. When those scans revealed the drastic damage that had occurred to a fair number of images, it was Karen Cattan, Alyse Delaney and Brent Ridge who applied their Photoshop skills to repair them as best as possible. I also want to thank Nick Sharpe and Alyse Delaney for printing all the photographs which I mounted in a show I did at the CoLab space in the Visual Arts Center at Princeton in the spring of 2022.

I'm a filmmaker, not a writer, so it was C. Carr who did a line edit of the first draft and, being an astute reader, vigorously applied her red pencil to point out what wasn't yet working and made very good notes about various changes I could make. She continued to help me with many small and big changes until my book was finally done.

A year or two after the first draft, when I had what I hoped was closer to a final version, Peggy Ahwesh, Yvonne Rainer, my brother Pete, and my sister Maria read it through and pointed out how it could still be improved. All of them were also great in a more general way through the years by fielding phone calls from me when I needed a morale boost or had a question about how to take the next steps.

Other people helped in smaller but nevertheless significant ways. Adam Black helped me correctly convert all those foreign currencies to USD both in 1976 and today. Malcolm Cranfield led me to the source of the photos of the Offin River and the "Cement Armada." Barbara Epler and Christopher Wait at New Directions Press gave me good advice about potential publishers and photo researchers, as did Matthew Sharpe. Valie Export was very generous in allowing me to use her photos without payment. Simone Gikandi provided me with valuable information about various Nigerian writers' relationships with their publishers. Jun Kuromiya translated the two Japanese letters. Dale Pelletier sent me some of our old classroom photos from grade school. Peter Sipe owned a copy of the Eyadema comic book—long out of print—and he was kind enough to send it to me so that I could make scans from it. Titilayo Sodimu gave me accurate information about the meaning of some Nigerian names. Denise Williams, a friend from high school, helped me clarify what I was writing about that time with our friends. Charles Wolfe translated two letters from the French. And finally, numerous friends gave me suggestions about potential publishers, including Zoe Beloff, Cynthia Madansky, Louis Massiah, Lynne Sachs, Matthew Sharpe, César Ustarozz, and Linda Villarosa.

And then there are the people who kept me going in the most fundamental ways.

The main person is Cathy Quinlan, my partner for life and a great thinker and critic. She gave me many good suggestions and had the forbearance to listen to my gripes and worries and then my despair about ever finding a publisher, for which I am inexpressibly grateful.

The other is Janice Juwayriah Hassan, my therapist. I had been seeing her before I started the book and continued during the first four years of the work (i.e., until Covid hit). It was invaluable for me to talk openly and often with her about the many questions and concerns I was having about the project. Her wise and encouraging words really kept me going.

Last, but not least, this book wouldn't exist without Dan Simon, the founder and publisher of Seven Stories Press. When he saw the manuscript, he made a major suggestion which I agreed to implement, and it really improved the flow of the story. He then did a great job as my editor.

I'm also very grateful for the fine work done by others at Seven Stories Press: to Katherine Seger, for her excellent copyediting work; to Rasheeda Saka, who reviewed the copyedited manuscript with me and helped in various other ways to marshal the work to the printer; to Ruth Weiner, for fielding numerous worried phone calls and emails from me and helping to smooth the way; to Serina Solin for her final proofreading; and of course to the designer, Stewart Cauley, who did such a great job of wrestling with a book that has more than four hundred photos and so many small blocks of text. I'd say he won the wrestling match.

Credits and Permissions

CHAPTER 2

P. 13

Poster by the Women's Graphics Collective courtesy of Julie Zolot.

P. 14

Poster by the Women's Graphics Collective (from a design by the Chicago Women's Liberation Union).

CHAPTER 3

P. 26

Iskov, Sonja, *Gallery Wall of Posters*, December 1975, photograph, as printed in the book *Det skete på Kvindeudstillingen Charlottenborg 1975* by Birgit Pontoppidan. Birgit Pontoppidan Forlag, 2017. Used by permission of the photographer and the author.

P. 27

Wolfschwenger, Gertraud, *Valie Export – Body Sign Action*, 1970, photograph, © VALIE EXPORT, Bildrecht Wien, 2024.

P. 27

Lesser, Kurt, *Valie Export – Brechbare Regeln einer Kraft - Poetischer Flugversuch, 1975 – Aktion Performance*, December 1975, photograph, © VALIE EXPORT, Bildrecht Wien, 2024.

P. 27

Lesser, Kurt, *Valie Export – Brechbare Regeln einer Kraft - Poetischer Flugversuch, 1975 – Aktion Performance*, December 1975, photograph, © VALIE EXPORT, Bildrecht Wien, 2024.

CHAPTER 5

P. 76

L., Daniele, *Tuareg woman.*, 2010, photograph, https://www.club-des-voyages.com/niger/albums/galerie-photos-de-daniele-l-u5872-g1/index8.html.

CHAPTER 6

P. 84

Backer, Albert, *The Sign to Arlit*, December 1991, photograph, Wikimedia Commons, https://en.wikipedia.org/wiki/Trans-Sahara_Highway#/media/File:Hoggarpiste1991a.jpg.

P. 93

Lundberg, Dan, *View of Agadez*, 1997, photograph, Wikipedia, http://en.wikipedia.org/wiki/Adadez#/media/File: 1997_227-16A_Agadez_hotel.jpg.

CHAPTER 7

P. 115

Jean-Paul Nsimba Mika, *Mami Wata*, 2012, painting, © 2024 Artists Rights Society (ARS), New York / ADAGP, Paris.

CHAPTER 9

P. 143

Dugdale, Brian, *Ibadan University*, ca. 1962–1971, photograph, Yoruba History—by NNP, @YorubaHistory, https://threadreaderapp.com/thread/1207937682149646336.html.

P. 151

Jones, G.I., *Agbogho Mmuo, Igbo maiden spirit maskers near Akwa, north-central Igbo area, Nigeria*, 1935, photograph, Ukpuru, https://ukpuru.tumblr.com/post/150406874087/agbogho-mmuo-igbo-maiden-spirit-maskers-near.

CHAPTER 11

P. 183

Berger, Julius, *Susanne Wenger, Adebisi Akanji and Rabiu Abesu*, ca. 1970s, photograph (from a pamphlet from this event: The Osun Osogbo Grove, Nigeria's UNESCO World Heritage Site, Campaign Launch & Art Exhibition 2015).

P. 187

Stencilled adire cloth (textile), Nigerian maker (c. 1900–1924), courtesy Withworth Art Gallery, University of Manchester/Bridgeman Images.

CHAPTER 13

P. 225

Durojaye-Prüfer, Cecilia, *The Ifesowapo dùndún ensemble performing in Igbo Ora, southwest*, January 16, 2016, photograph, used with the permission of the photographer.

CHAPTER 14

P. 241

Cranfield, Malcolm, *Ghana Black Star Line's 1961 Flushing built OFFIN RIVER arriving at Avonmouth on 2nd March 1974*, 1974, photograph, used with the permission of the photographer.

P. 247

Granville, Reginald, *Interior of Oba's Compound Burnt During Seige of Benin City (present day Nigeria), with Bronze Plaques in the Foreground and Three British Soldiers of the Benin Punitive Expedition 9-18 February 1897*. 1897, photograph.

P. 250

Cranfield, Malcolm, *PERAMATARIS anchored off Lagos on 4.1.76 with MAGNA SPES and ARCADYRA*, 1976, photograph, used with the permission of the photographer.

P. 250

Alamba, Sunday, *The rusting hulk of an abandoned petroleum ship*, Thursday, March 15, 2012, photograph, San Diego Union Tribune, posted Sept 3, 2016, https://www.sandiegouniontribune.com/sdut-abandoned-ships-a-rusting-hazard-in-nigeria-waters-2012may01-story.html.

CHAPTER 16

P. 266

Ventura, Carol, *Anthony Boakye prints an adinkra cloth with a calabash stamp in Ntonso, Ghana*, 2008, photograph, Creative Commons CC BY-SA 3.0.

CHAPTER 17

Pages 282, 283

IL ÉTAIT UNE FOIS. . . EYADEMA, published by Afrique Biblio Club, © 1976, story by Serge Saint-Michel, drawings by Dominique Fages, images courtesy of Peter Sipe.

P. 296

Photographer unknown, *Shirley Temple with First Lady Pat Nixon and Chief Nana Osae Djan II in Ghana*, 1972, photograph, courtesy of the U.S. National Archives and Records Administration.

CHAPTER 18

P. 305

Photographer unknown, *Two members of the Accra Rhythmic Orchestra, J.A. Mallet (left) and a young Emmanuel Tetteh "E.T." Mensah (right)*, 1937.

CHAPTER 21

P. 356

Lenars, Charles & Josette, *Bambara men wear antelope masks to dance to Tyi-Wara, the mythological half man, half antelope, who is believed to bring good luck to farmers*, ca. January 1978, photograph, Djenne, Mali.

CHAPTER 22

P. 379

Freund, Gisèle, *Sylvia Beach and Adrienne Monnier*, photograph, 1938, used by permission of the Department of Rare Books and Special Collections, Princeton University.

CHAPTER NOTES

P. 400

Cover of *Black Orpheus* issue 17 (June 1965) by Georgina Beier.

Before the Internet

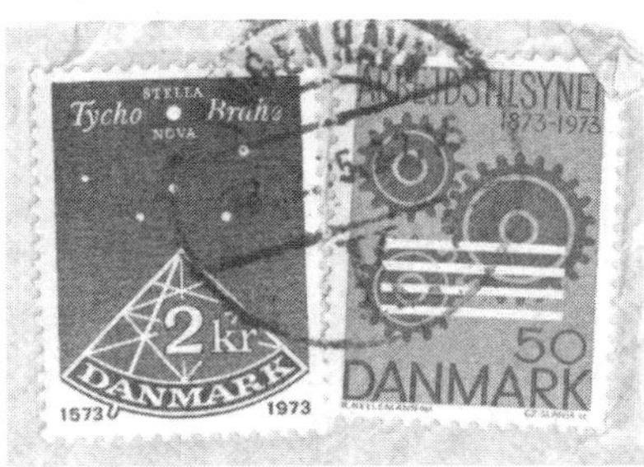

From a letter to Mimi from Denmark, December 13, 1975

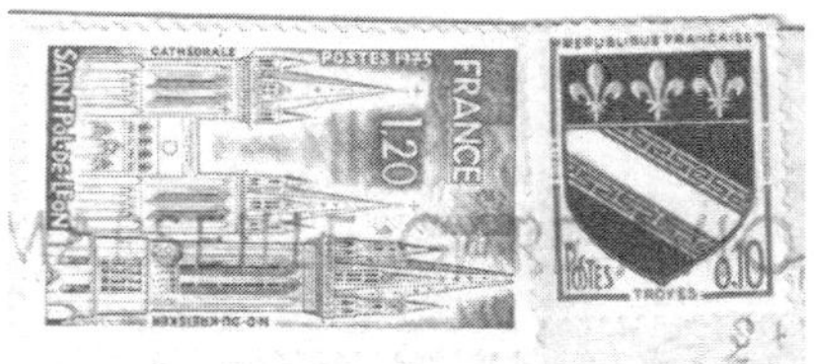

From a postcard to my mother and brother from France, December 25, 1975

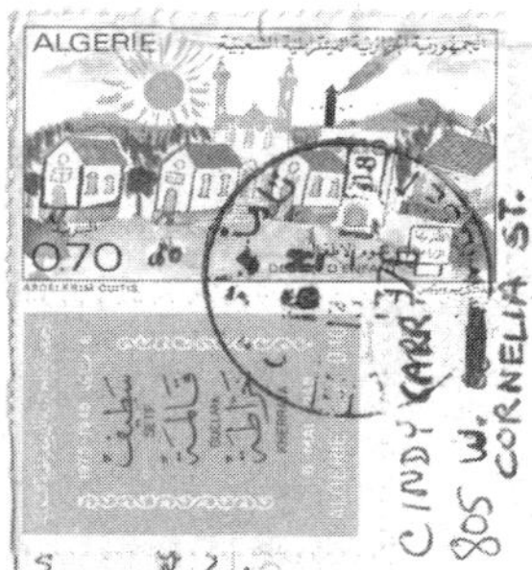

From a letter to Cindy from Algeria, January 9, 1976

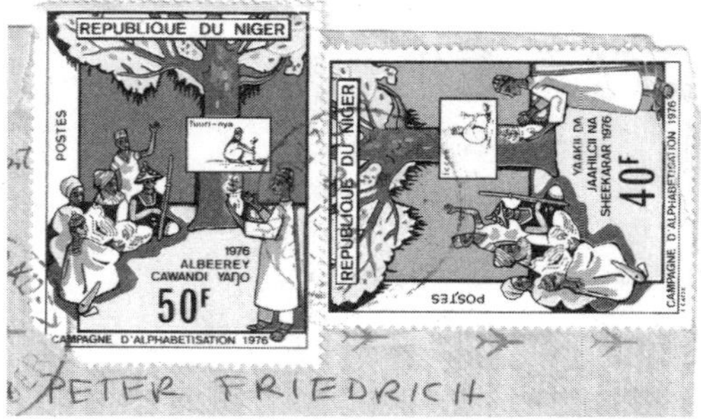

From a letter to my mother and brother from Niger, January 16, 1976

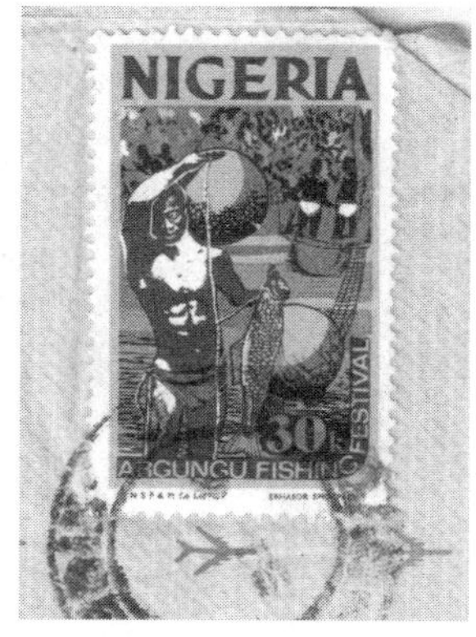

From a letter to Mimi from Nigeria, January 22, 1976

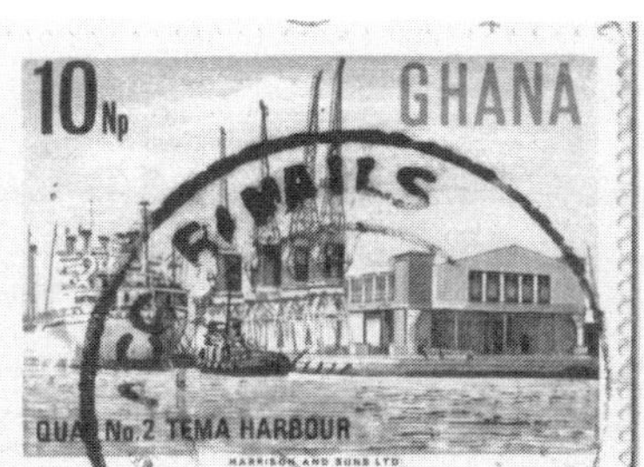

From a letter to Mimi from Ghana, March 16, 1976

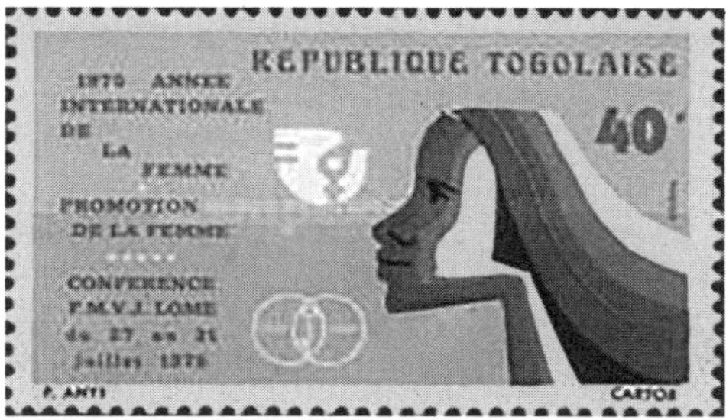

I didn't send any letters from Togo, but I found this cool stamp online

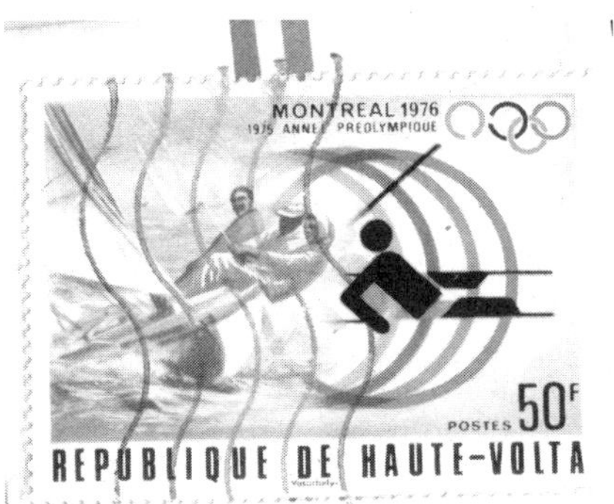

From a letter to my father from Upper Volta (Burkina Faso), April 6, 1976

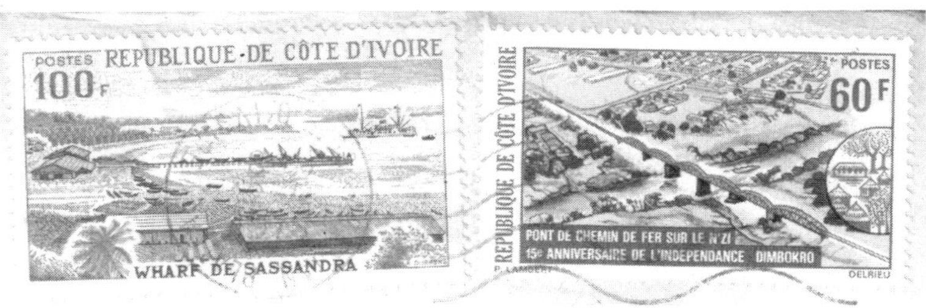

From a letter to Mimi from Ivory Coast, April 10, 1976

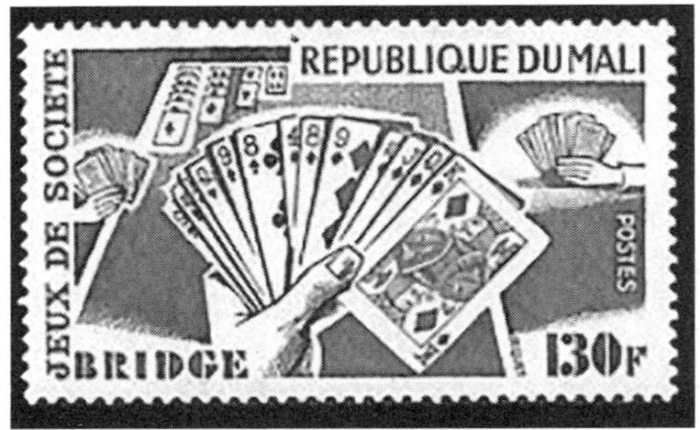

I didn't send any letters from Mali, but I found this cool stamp online

From a letter to Mimi from Morocco, April 21, 1976

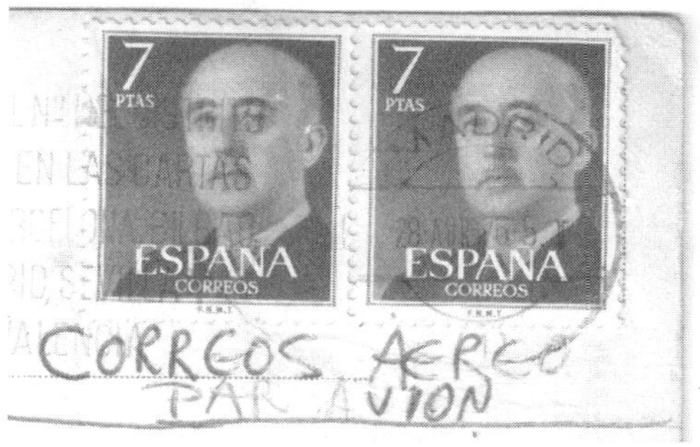

From a postcard to my father from Spain, April 26, 1976